THE LAST LINOTYPE

THE LAST LINOTYPE

The Story of Georgia and Its Newspapers Since World War II

Millard B. Grimes
Chief Editor and Writer

CONTRIBUTING EDITORS
Calvin Cox
W. H. Champion
Tom Sellers
Waldo (Bo) M^c^Leod
Richard Hyatt

Published by
MERCER UNIVERSITY PRESS
and the
GEORGIA PRESS ASSOCIATION

MERCER
MUP

ISBN 0-86554-190-6

The Last Linotype

Mercer University Press, Macon GA 31207

Printed in the United States of America

All books published by Mercer University Press
are printed on acid-free paper that exceeds
the minimum standards set by the
National Historical Publications and Records Commission.

Contents

Dedication

Dedicated to all those who have experienced the painful but exhilarating tension of "getting out the paper."

Newspaper

A newspaper can drop the same thought into a thousand minds at the same moment. A newspaper is an adviser that does not require to be sought, but comes to you without distracting your private affairs. Newspapers therefore become more necessary in proportion as men become more equal individuals, and more to be feared. To suppose that they only serve to protect freedom is to diminish their importance; they maintain civilization.

De Tocqueville

Introduction

On May 16, 1975, the History of Georgia Journalism Committee of the Georgia Press Association met in Atlanta and adopted a recommendation to the GPA summer convention.

The recommendation said, in part: "The committee will be authorized to get a working journalist to write the history of Georgia newspapers from 1950 to 1975, with the objective of having the manuscript in hand by next July (1976). Every newspaper in Georgia would be asked to submit its own brief history. Size of book to be approximately 400 pages and similar in quality of production to *Georgia Journalism, 1763-1950*, which was published in 1951. — Tom Burson, chairman."

That recommendation began the process which has finally resulted in the publication of a new history of Georgia newspapers, mainly covering the years since World War II, and limited for the most part to newspapers which were members of the Press Association.

Obviously, the 1975 committee's goal of "having the manuscript in hand by July 1976" was not achieved, but the delay did make it possible to get nine more years of Georgia newspaper history in this volume, and they were nine very eventful and exciting years.

Georgia Journalism, 1763-1950, written and compiled primarily by John Talmadge and Louis Griffith, both then on the faculty of the Henry Grady School of Journalism at the University of Georgia, was a unique account of a state's newspapers, and this current volume continues that tradition, providing more information on Georgia's newspapers and the people who owned, published and wrote for them than is available on any other state's papers.

As stated in the 1975 recommendations, an updated history "should be similar in quality of production to *Georgia Journalism*." That has been the goal of those who have worked on this current volume, and fortunately we had advantages that the writers of the first history did not have. First, of course, the period covered is much shorter — about 40 years compared to 187 — and the people and records were much more accessible. In addition, the greater use of photographs and the improvements in printing processes have made it possible to include many more illustrations in this volume, including a number of historic front pages.

This volume is different in several other ways. It devotes separate chapters to various newspapers or types of newspapers. It also has a section on the Georgia Press Association, which goes all the way back to its founding in 1887. Included in the GPA section are a list of all presidents since 1887; a list of all chairmen of the Georgia Press Institute since its founding in 1928; a brief biography and picture of all GPA presidents since 1945; a list of all Better Newspaper Contest winners in the four top categories since 1960; and a list of all GPA convention sites since 1950.

The book is about Georgia, as well as about Georgia newspapers. One chart which should be of interest to all readers shows the population from 1920 to 1980 of each Georgia county. Population trends have had an enormous impact on the newspaper business as well as on other aspects of Georgia's development. It is a far different state than it was at the end of World War II.

And, of course, the newspapers of Georgia are different than they were then. They are different in how they are produced; different in how they are owned; different in the kind of news and opinions they carry; different in the makeup of their personnel.

This book is an attempt to tell how and why these changes occurred, and while the information is primarily about Georgia and its newspapers, it is relevant for newspapers throughout the nation.

As with the earlier history project, the biggest stumbling block was finding someone who had the time, incentive and willingness to oversee the project and do most of the research, writing and compiling. There were also the problems of compensating an editor-author and of financing the book. Even though the Georgia Press Association was promoting and supporting the idea, the method of financing had not been resolved.

After four years as chairman of the history committee, and with little progress made toward the book, I sat down one day and wrote an outline of what I thought a new history of Georgia newspapers should include. I tentatively named it, "The Last Linotype," a reference, of course, to the change from hot type composition which mainly relied on linotypes, to cold type composition which is a photographic process. I looked over the outline and decided I would just try and do it myself, despite a lack of experience in this kind of writing.

With the cooperation and support of the Georgia Press Association board and the office staff in Atlanta, questionnaires were sent, material was collected, and over a period of about two years this book evolved. In many ways it is like the Sunday edition of a large metropolitan paper, with special sections for every taste. Whether the reader's interest be in larger-city dailies, smaller-city dailies, non-metro weeklies, the suburban press, the mechanical revolution, the news revolution, the Georgia Press Association, or simply in Georgia and its history of the past 35-40 years, there should be something of value in this book. There also is editorial comment, which any good newspaper should include.

Many editors, publishers and reporters contributed to the information, either through questionnaires, special articles, personal interviews or through shared research. In most cases they were asked to tell their stories in the third person so that the book would have more unity and because people usually tell their own stories more openly and fully in third person than in first. I also followed that policy in writing of the newspapers and events with which I was involved, feeling that I could convey the information more effectively in third person.

As work progressed, I realized that virtually every newspaper in Georgia has a great story to tell, and many of their stories would fill a book by themselves. I hope this volume will encourage individual newspapers to publish editions or books telling their own story. More than 250 newspapers have been published in the state during the period covered and an attempt has been made to relate as much as possible about many of them. Some of them get more space than others, of course, partly because of available information, partly because those papers were more involved in the major changes the book seeks to explain and emphasize.

Atlanta and its newspapers were a special case, of course, and Calvin Cox, who in a 37-year career at *The Journal* and *Constitution* held almost every newsroom job, has provided an informative and entertaining look inside the state's largest newspapers. Richard Hyatt, who was on the staff of the short-lived *Atlanta Times,* contributes his recollection of that newspaper's rise and fall.

For the chief editor and writer, Columbus and the Columbus newspapers were also a special case. Their story is told in much more detail than others because I used them to illustrate the atmosphere, the changes and the personalities which were common to most newspapers since World War II.

Having spent more than 20 years as a full-time employee, and seven more years as a contributing editor to the Columbus newspapers, as well as living in Columbus for 30 years, I obviously had more firsthand knowledge and a wider store of information, memos, and other research items about them.

The Columbus chapter delves more deeply into the lives of the people who passed that way during almost 40 years, and into the way newspaper companies operate.

This book concentrates on people, and on the challenges which newspapers faced as businesses and information media. There is less emphasis on their daily performance or the positions they took.

But in words and pictures there is in this volume an enormous amount of information, some trivial, some important, but all helpful in an understanding of what happened to Georgia and its newspapers since World War II.

I believe this book needed to be written and published, and I hope that it will be updated at regular intervals in the future. It is a fascinating story of what I believe was the Golden Age of newspapers, both in Georgia and the United States. As mentioned, many people contributed to the book, but I would like to especially thank Kathy Chaffin, executive manager of the Georgia Press Association, and her office staff, for the invaluable service they provided; and also, W. H. Champion of Dublin, who collected the information on GPA presidents since World War II. Other contributors are mentioned in the bibliography at the back of the book.

Like any edition of a good newspaper, this book may contain a few errors, but what it tries mightily to do is tell the truth, which is more important sometimes than simply having all the facts straight. Georgia newspapers have not been well served by most of the articles about them which have appeared in various magazines through the years, principally because it was hard to recognize the newspapers or the people involved through the articles' prejudices or premises.

I hope every person and every newspaper in *The Last Linotype* is recognizable, and that the truth emerges along with all the facts, which is the best that any good journalist can expect.

Millard B. Grimes,
Spring, 1985

Chapter I

The Great Newspaper Era: View From the Mountaintop

A Time of Fear and Trembling

In 1732, Benjamin Franklin was closing out an edition of his newspaper, *The Pennsylvania Gazette*, when a friend came into the office after returning from a trip west of the Allegheny Mountains. The friend related to Franklin that he had seen Indians building fires on high hills and then with the help of a blanket they would send messages in smoke to Indians on the other side of the valley.

"What were they telling each other?" Franklin wanted to know.

"They were telling each other the news with smoke signals," the friend replied.

A look of anguish came over Publisher Franklin's face. "Smoke signals to send news!" he exclaimed. "This is going to mean the end of newspapers."

That story, oft-told, and credited most recently to J. Montgomery Curtis, longtime director of the American Press Institute, illustrates the venerable and durable nature of the uncertainties which beset newspaper publishers. Beginning with Franklin they have always feared that obsolescence was just around the corner.

Never were they so certain of that fate as in the year 1950. Rare indeed was the newspaper executive who perceived in that dawn of a new communications age that it would be a Golden Age for newspapers, and that they would not only survive but would on the whole prosper to a degree never before imagined by print media proprietors. In 1950 TV news still consisted mainly of a line of type running across a still scene displaying the station's call letters. The single line usually told of the weather, and occasionally offered a news bulletin. At night a few hours of entertainment were shown. Local newscasts and national newscasts were yet to come on a regular basis.

But newspaper executives could see the threat. Some of them still hadn't come to grips with radio which had been carrying news reports for 25 years. They feared that the combination of words and pictures on television, right in the living room (which was where most sets were located in pre-den America), meant the end of the newspaper's role as the chief carrier of information, advertising and pictures.

It didn't seem fair. Newspapers were just beginning to enjoy a measure of prosperity after a decade of economic depression followed by newsprint and personnel shortages during World War II. Finally, things were improving in several ways.

The GI bill had put millions of former soldiers into college and a lot of them were studying journalism, providing newspapers for the first time with college-educated employees in the newsrooms and the advertising departments. To many old-time editors it was a mixed blessing. To some publishers it meant that journalists were going to expect higher pay than in the past.

Now the new threat loomed on the horizon — television. Even in those fledgling days of the new medium, its potential was apparent, although few could imagine how sophisticated, how total and how encompassing television's news coverage would become in the next 30 years.

It was enough in 1950 to fear the strip of words running across a stationary screen.

All of the older media — newspapers, magazines, movies, radio — knew that at best they faced a challenge to their usual ways of doing things. At worst their survival was at stake. Radio eventually would change the most, although in its new incarnation it would find an audience larger and more intense than it ever enjoyed in pre-TV years. Magazines have multiplied in number but only a handful of titles that were popular in 1950 survive in 1984. The movies, perhaps most directly challenged by TV, have gone through three decades of turmoil and transition, but in the 1980s they remain an important force, economically and culturally. As with magazines, the great and powerful movie studios and movie makers of 1950 did not survive.

By contrast, the leading newspapers in the United States in 1984 are about the same as they were in 1950. Even more remarkably a typical copy of *The New York Times* in 1984 does not look very different than a copy from 1950. The same is true of *The Wall Street Journal*, a specialized daily newspaper which has the largest paid circulation in the nation.

The Atlanta Journal and *Constitution*, Georgia's two leading newspapers, have changed in appearance more than *The Times* or *Wall Street Journal*, but the change is mainly in style and emphasis rather than basic shape, content or role.

What a reader from 1950 would mainly notice is how many more pages are in each edition of these papers. He might also notice that the pages are obviously narrower, but not shorter.

But the fact is that newspapers have survived and prospered in the television era without altering the basic appeal and appearance they had in 1950.

What has changed considerably, however, is the way the newspaper is prepared; the scope of its content; and in most cases, its financial status — all for the better. There have also been vast changes in who works at newspapers and who owns them.

In 1950, the linotype machine was still the latest invention in most newspaper composing rooms, and it had been patented in 1886. Many newspapers had presses that were manufactured in the 19th century.

A pencil, a pad and a manual typewriter were the only tools of the reporter and the copy editors. Men with ink-stained muscles put metal type into page forms and passed them on to other muscled men called stereotypers who made heavy lead plates of the pages which were then placed on the press by more muscled men.

Most of this would change in the next 20 years, and newspapers would be better for the changes. But in the first flickering light emanating from TV sets, a lot of publishers were wondering if anyone would even look at newspapers when they could get news on the box in the living room. Even more important, would advertisers spend money to buy newspaper space once TV got its act together and could send out an advertiser's message in sound and living color?

In Georgia and other southern states the fears were perhaps more widespread than in other parts of the nation. The simple fact was that a lot of southerners couldn't read well, and the South's comparatively low per capita income and narrow retail base did not offer the level of advertising support available in other sections of the country.

Of the potential readership probably less than 25% had completed high school, and although newspapers are allegedly written for people with a sixth grade education, readership tends to increase in a more educated populace. In addition, Georgia's paid dailies and weeklies virtually ignored the one-third of the population that was black. Sports and other activities at black schools were seldom, if ever, covered; weddings and engagements of blacks weren't carried. About the only black activity that found its way into the newspapers was crime. Blacks had less reason to buy a newspaper and they were also generally poor readers. They were a ready-made market for television. Newspaper coverage of black activities would change too, of course, but only as the society in general and the schools changed.

Another big difference in the Georgia dailies of 1950 was that all but the two Atlanta newspapers were owned and operated by people who lived and worked in the cities they served. The large newspaper groups which would dominate the industry within the next 30 years were still in the formative stage.

Atlanta, however, had attracted two pioneers of chain publishing. The first was the most famous U.S. publisher in the first half of the century, William Randolph Hearst, who acquired *The Atlanta Georgian* in February, 1912. Hearst had a reputation for sensationalizing the news and filling his newspapers with such non-journalistic items as comic strips and crossword puzzles, and, in fact, Hearst's 27-year tenure in Georgia accelerated the movement of other newspapers toward the kind of features, columnists and specialized sections which have enlivened newspapers and made them a better package of information and entertainment. *The Atlanta Journal*, for instance, added a picture supplement in 1919, printed on the first rotogravure press purchased by a Georgia newspaper.

But Hearst's extravagant habits — both on his newspapers, and in his personal life — forced him to sell off some of his properties in the 1930s, including *The Georgian*. James M. Cox, a former governor of Ohio, and the Democratic presidential candidate in 1920, bought both *The Georgian* and *The Journal* in 1939, and immediately closed down *The Georgian*, leaving *The Journal* as the only Atlanta afternoon daily and making it clearly the dominant newspaper in the state.

Cox was nearly 70 when he came on the Georgia newspaper scene, and the Atlanta purchase would prove to be the most important step in building the communications empire which has become Cox Enterprises.

His candidacy for president 20 years earlier had ended disappointingly when Republican Warren G. Harding, another Ohio newspaper publisher, defeated him by the widest popular margin in a presidential election to that time. Cox turned out to be the luckier candidate, however. Harding died in disgrace three years later while Cox devoted himself to building his newspaper and radio holdings. His vice presidential running mate of 1920, 39-year-old Franklin D. Roosevelt, stayed in politics, and also found a second home in Georgia, at Warm Springs.

Indirectly, Cox became a significant factor in Georgia politics. A generation of the state's political candidates campaigned against Cox as the "Yankee owner of them lying Atlanta newspapers."

In 1950, when he was 80, Cox bought *The Atlanta Constitution* thus bringing Atlanta's afternoon and morning dailies under the same ownership. Such monopolies already existed in the state's other major cities, except for Augusta, where the morning and afternoon papers did not come under common ownership until 1955.

The total circulation of Georgia's 29 daily newspapers in 1950 was about 750,000, of which *The Journal* (245,000) and *The Constitution* (187,000) had 432,000 or 58 percent. On Sunday, *The Journal and Constitution* (after they were merged) ranged up to 500,000, which was more than 70% of the total Sunday newspaper circulation in the state.

Cox promised that the news staffs and editorial staffs would remain separate and that the two newspapers would still compete for news and take independent editorial positions. Many old *Constitution* hands feared they would be overshadowed and dominated by *The Journal* executives since *The Journal* was Cox's first newspaper in Georgia.

But for more than 30 years there was indeed strong competition between the news staffs of the two newspapers. Not until 1982 was the old fear realized and the staffs merged, following a national trend. The editorial pages remained separate and they still take contrary positions on issues and candidates. Ironically, *The Constitution* has become the more widely circulated newspaper, and its executives have been the most influential during the years of common ownership. Jack Tarver, a *Constitution* associate editor when Cox bought the newspaper, soon became general manager of both newspapers, and then was chief executive for many years. Ralph McGill, the *Constitution* editor, and later Eugene Patterson, who succeeded him, had nationwide reputations exceeding any of the *Journal* editors of that period.

Cox died at the age of 88 and the *Journal* and *Constitution* became the flagships of his empire. For many years the reputation of being "Yankee-owned" and "too liberal" clung to the papers, although it never seemed to hinder their success. Georgians swore at them and by them, but no well-informed resident of the state would have been without one or the other. Whatever else they might have been, the Atlanta newspapers always had excellent sports coverage, popular local columnists, lots of comic strips, pages and pages of advertising from the South's retail trade center, and one of the nation's best Sunday magazine supplements.

They eventually encountered the problems which have afflicted most large-city newspapers during the past 15 years. The unprecedented increases in the price of fuel and newsprint were especially damaging to large and widely-circulated newspapers. When those items were relatively cheap it could make sense to ship the afternoon *Journal* all over Georgia and the Southeast. In the 1970s, the cost became excessive. At the same time traffic congestion in the central city was making it more difficult to distribute an afternoon newspaper there. Atlanta's metropolitan area was one of the most dynamic in the nation, but its core city was declining and the population was becoming increasingly poor and black, neither of which had ever been the best customers for newspapers.

Competition for print advertising also kept multiplying. The suburbs were getting their own home-based daily newspapers, and a large chain of free-distribution weekly newspapers sprang up around the central city, covering most of the counties in the metropolitan area.

But Atlanta's two dailies had the resources to fend off the various challenges, and actually reversed their circulation decline in the 1980s, while maintaining both morning and afternoon publications at a time some large cities were being left with only one newspaper.

One of the most interesting challenges to the Atlanta hegemony came in 1964 when a direct afternoon competitor called *The Atlanta Times* was launched, with the support of thousands of Georgians who bought nearly

$5 million worth of stock in the newspaper venture.

The *Times*, with former congressman James Davis as publisher, was unabashedly conservative in its editorial positions, offering itself as an alternative to the "liberal" *Journal* and *Constitution*, and proudly labeling itself as "home-owned" and "home-operated." Its board of directors included an impressive array of state business leaders, and it managed to attract a number of competent professional journalists and ad executives to the staff.

June, 1964, the month *The Times* started, seemed to be a propitious time for a more conservative newspaper in Georgia's largest city. A few weeks after *The Times'* debut, the Republican party chose Barry Goldwater, leader of the party's conservative wing, as its presidential nominee, and in November Goldwater, staunchly supported by *The Times*, became the first Republican ever to win Georgia's electoral votes. *The Journal* and *Constitution* both supported the Democratic candidate, Lyndon Johnson.

But for *The Times* the dollar count was not as favorable as the vote count. Its reservoir of good will and money ran out swiftly in the wake of a series of unwise moves by its directors and management. *The Times* lasted only 14 months. Its instigators had a vision of the future but they used both the tools and the rationale of the past, buying thousands of dollars of hot type and letter press equipment when cold type and offset were already the obvious wave of the future, and basing their challenge to the Atlanta newspapers on a philosophical basis rather than a business and news basis.

Georgia's Other Dailies

Outside of the Atlanta metro area the daily newspaper scene in Georgia has changed very little since 1950. There were 29 daily newspapers in the state that year and there are 34 in 1984. Only one daily published in 1950 — *The Macon News* — is no longer published in 1984. No other single fact so dramatically demonstrates the stability of daily newspapers in Georgia during the past 34 years. When considering the changes that occurred in radio stations and magazines, the survival of every daily but one through this period of transition is truly remarkable. Almost without exception Georgia's dailies also enjoyed the greatest advertising and circulation growth of their existence during those years.

But something did change. It was ownership. As mentioned, only the Atlanta newspapers were owned by a chain or group in 1950. By 1984 chains of one type or another owned 27 of the state's 34 dailies. Nearly all of the nation's large newspaper companies are represented in Georgia, including Knight-Ridder, Gannett, Harte-Hanks, Thomson, Roy Park, Walls and Multimedia. In addition, there are several Georgia-based groups, the largest being Cox Enterprises, which has moved its headquarters from Dayton, Ohio, to Atlanta. The largest group which actually began and is also headquartered in Georgia is Morris Communications of Augusta, owner of the Augusta, Savannah and Athens dailies.

Thomson, which owns more separate newspapers (80 and rising) than any other group, has come on strong in Georgia in recent years and now has seven of the state's dailies, its highest total in any state except Ohio. Based in Toronto, Canada, Thomson's second newspaper acquisition in the United States was *The Dalton Citizen-News*, purchased in 1962 shortly after *The Citizen-News* became a daily.

In terms of paid circulation, the Cox group, with the two Atlanta dailies, is far ahead in Georgia with a 1984 total of 411,000 of the state's total daily circulation of 992,000.

Next in circulation are the six Morris dailies, which include *The Savannah Morning News* and *Augusta Chronicle*. Knight-Ridder has four dailies in Georgia, including newspapers in the other two metropolitan areas, Macon and Columbus.

The Georgia dailies still under local and non-chain management are *The Albany Herald, The Marietta Daily Journal, The Gwinnet Daily News, The Rome News-Tribune, The Dublin Courier-Herald, The Waycross Journal-Herald,* and *The Brunswick News*.

The only 1950 Georgia daily that has reduced its frequency since then is *The Cedartown Standard*, which reverted to twice-weekly in 1961. Another 1950 Georgia daily, *The Valley Times-News* of West Point, moved its plant a few blocks away, but across the state line into Lanett, Alabama, and in effect has become an Alabama-based newspaper.

Cities served by weeklies in 1950 that now have dailies include: Dalton, 1962; Lawrenceville (Gwinnett), 1966; Warner Robins, 1969; Statesboro, 1970; Jonesboro (Clayton), 1971; Conyers (Rockdale), 1978; Carrollton, 1980; and Milledgeville, 1982. In addition a morning daily was started in Athens in 1965.

While Georgia's metropolitan newspapers (Atlanta, Savannah, Columbus, Macon and Augusta) have increased very little in paid circulation since 1950, or even dropped in the case of Atlanta, the state's smaller dailies have all increased, some of them dramatically. In 1950, 16 of the state's 29 dailies had less than 8,000 circulation, including the dailies in

Athens, Gainesville, Valdosta, LaGrange and Marietta, all of whose paid newspaper circulation has at least doubled in the years since. In the same period, of course, single copy prices and subscription rates increased by 400 to 500%.

Georgia's Weekly Newspapers

Looking at the weekly newspaper field in Georgia, one sees vastly more change since 1950 than in the daily field, and as with the dailies it has mainly been change for the better. Paid circulation and advertising have climbed dramatically despite more competition and shifting populations.

There were about 200 paid weeklies listed in the 1950 Georgia Newspaper Directory. The number was down to 150 in the 1984 directory, but the survivors are much stronger and more informative than their 1950 predecessors. As noted, several weeklies converted to daily or were merged to form dailies. In the Atlanta metro area, a number of weeklies were absorbed into the free-distribution *Neighbor* or *News/Sun* chains, which are not listed in the GPA directory. Then in several cases competitive weeklies went out of business or were bought by a competitor. But only a few communities which had a weekly in 1950 do not have one in 1984.

The most important changes are in the total paid circulation of the remaining weeklies and in their increased number of pages and variety of content as compared to 34 years ago. Only eight Georgia weeklies in the 1950 directory listed more than 2,000 circulation, and about a third had less than 1,000. By 1984, 40 weeklies listed more than 4,000 circulation and only 10 had less than 1,000.

But cold figures do not tell the whole story. Although it is a fashionable myth that the weekly press was courageous and influential in the dim and distant past the facts are quite different. Before World War II, with a few brilliant exceptions, the weekly publisher in Georgia usually made his living as a commercial printer while the newspaper was a hobby, filled mainly with community social notes on teas and weekend visits. Weekly newspapers carried few, if any, pictures, and precious few ads. There was little separation of news into departments such as sports, social items or regular news. Weekly newspapers were mainly written about the few, for the few and read by few.

In 1985 most of Georgia's weeklies are more complete than the small dailies of 1950, and some of them are better than the larger dailies of that period. They carry pictures; they cover the news; they departmentalize the news; their owners and managers are primarily in the newspaper business; they are better printed, better made up, and better written. A lot of them can even meet the payroll and take care of the monthly bills.

What made the difference? Many things, of course, but two things mainly. First, the new technology had much more impact on weekly newspapers than on dailies. It shifted emphasis from the back shop to the front office. Secondly, the counties which weeklies served were changing. They became more urbanized, less agriculture-oriented, which meant there were more retail stores, more shopping for groceries, more people living in "town."

The composing and printing of newspapers shifted from metal to film. Film processors and the camera became the key components in transferring words to paper. That made production cheaper and allowed a reallocation of financial resources to the news and advertising departments. But because of the new printing technology, newspaper publishers found it difficult to compete for commercial printing with larger plants and thus most of the publishers had to find a way to make a living on revenue from the newspaper. Central plants became practical where a number of weeklies could be printed on the same press and by the same pressmen, thus sparing many publishers from having to own a press and hire the people to run it.

Women increasingly moved into more positions on newspapers. In 1950 women were seldom seen in a composing room. By 1984 men are almost as rare as women were then. Women have also become reporters, ad managers, editors and publishers. They had been the bookkeepers for years, and still are.

In summary, the past three decades have been a Golden Age for newspapers, particularly in Georgia, which did not have especially prosperous newspapers before World War II. After competing with television for 35 years, and radio for 65 years, newspapers in the 1980s still take in more advertising dollars than TV and radio combined. The number of daily newspapers in the nation is slightly more than 1,700, which is substantially the same total as in 1950. A few dailies in large cities have gone out of business but for each one of those lost a new daily started, usually in a growing suburban county.

Surveys indicate that nine of every 10 Americans read a newspaper every week, and seven of 10 read one every day. That number looks even better to advertisers because the readers tend to be the people with the most education and the most income, and thus the most money to spend.

Paid circulation nationwide has increased despite the rising price of newspapers, and the shutdown of some very large circulation papers. In Georgia, paid circulation is much higher than in 1950. Advertising and readership have continued to climb in the face of free-distribution and shopper publications; easier and cheaper ways to send pre-print advertising through the mail; cable television; and fewer traditional family units which are the backbone of most newspaper readership.

Editor and Publisher magazine declared in 1983: "The newspaper business has never been healthier," and the facts seem to support the claim.

One of the most encouraging signs of the print media's vitality has been the circulation success of *USA Today*, a daily national newspaper published by the Gannett Corp. Despite evidence that people had all they wanted to read, especially in the way of daily newspapers, *USA Today* climbed to more than 1,300,000 paid sales a day in just two years, and most of these were sales off news racks. It had shown that there is still an audience for even more daily printed news, which surprised most publishers.

The Uncertain Future

But in 1985, as in 1950, there is a lot of fear and trembling in newspaper offices. Golden ages have a way of tarnishing, and the road ahead still looks uncertain for newspapers.

Publishers wonder if enough people still like to read; they wonder if a computer will replace the newspaper; they worry about the delivery system and the rising cost of that system.

They are encouraged only by the impressive resiliency newspapers have shown to every challenge, including most recently low-power TV, videotext and other technological means of avoiding the printed word on a newspaper sheet. None of these have yet prospered.

Looking ahead from 1950, few could have foreseen the bright future or the technological changes that have overtaken the industry, and few would venture a guess as to what newspapers will be like in 2020—or even if they will still exist.

It may be, however, that the gravest threat to newspapers is not from without but from within.

In 1985, much more than in 1950, the bottom line is discussed far more frequently than the banner line at most newspaper offices. Although more publishers than ever are now coming from the news ranks, there is a growing impression that newspapers are looked on first as "properties" that produce income, rather than as a primary means of informing the public about what's going on.

Financial strength is essential, of course, if the press is to be free and independent, but several factors in the 1980s are pressuring newspaper companies to strive for ever higher profit margins, often at the expense of the news and information function, which is, after all, the purpose for which they were created and granted federal constitutional protection.

Among these factors are the high prices paid by buyers for newspapers in recent years, which pushed the debt service of the purchasing company to levels requiring huge cash outflows; the fast-changing technology which demands more capital investment in order to keep up with each new development; the decision of the larger newspaper companies to offer stock to the public and thus enter the competition on stock exchanges, which tends to reward the most recent balance sheet and to penalize costs that look beyond the next dividend payment.

This last factor has the most dangerous potential. Few newspaper companies were on the stock market until the 1960s, and thus their operation was beholden only to an individual or to a small group of stockholders, not to thousands as is the case when a company goes "public." Now, newspaper executives have to consider the effect of their actions on the price of their company's stock as well as the effect on the operation and future of the newspaper or newspapers under their management. In some cases they also could eventually face the takeover threats by minority stockholders which have resulted in costly battles for some corporations.

Newspapers, much more than other businesses, must be independent not only of government control but also of public pressure, and broad stock ownership contains at least the threat of such pressure.

The more obvious challenges which are so threatening to newspapers are also still out there. Newspapers have won important battles but the war goes on . . . for the reader's attention and time, for the advertiser's dollar, for the public's confidence and respect. Despite the prosperity most newspapers have enjoyed since 1950, and the improved technology, there has been a down side. No one disputes that television has preempted many roles once reserved only for newspapers. No editor is as well known to the public as the 6 p.m. anchor person on the local newscast. The concept of what news for newspapers actually is has been changed by television's incessant eye on events as they happen. In 1950 readers sought out newspapers to find out what happened. Now, in most cases, they know what happened because they actually saw it happen on TV. Newspapers must offer something more.

What newspapers are offering in greater degree is news of their specific community and area. Newspapers are still the main source of such essential information as who died, who got engaged and who married. Newspapers are still "specialized" publications for the area they serve, which no other medium quite duplicates.

Newspapers are better today than they were in 1950, and fortunately so. They must be better in 1990 than they are in 1985, and that will require more than just investment in new equipment. It will require investment in a total quality product, compiled by better — and better-paid — editors and reporters.

From the summit of The Great Newspaper Era, the view ahead is hazy and uncertain and fraught with dangers from within and without. Georgia broadcast mogul Ted Turner has called newspapers "the dinosaurs" of today's media, implying they will be extinct in the not too distant future. No publisher surveying the graveyard of once great newspapers or magazines such as *The Washington Star, The New York World, The Philadelphia Bulletin, The Saturday Evening Post, Look, Collier's* and others, can comfortably challenge that view.

Fortunately, Georgia has few significant newspaper tombstones. Its Great Newspaper Era was even better than the nation's, and whatever the future holds that period (1950-85) is one deserving closer inspection and a full measure of nostalgia.

Newspapers have been called "literature in a hurry." That may be why there are not more histories of the industry and of individual newspapers. Nobody takes time to stop and write them. But fortunately some people did stop long enough to compile a history of Georgia newspapers from 1763 to 1950. This book is the story of the years since 1950 — The Great Newspaper Era — the likes of which are unlikely to ever occur again.

There is an Island . . .

This is also a book about Georgia, its communities, its politics, its scenic wonders, its growth and progress.

How do you begin describing Georgia, with its unique diversity of geography and people, its storied history of tragedy and triumph, its potential for present and future greatness, its reluctance to abandon past inglories?

Well, you could begin on the easternmost outskirts of the area that has become Georgia, the fabled Golden Isles, where facts and legends are difficult to distinguish.

One of the islands is called Jekyll after Sir Joseph Jekyll, a friend of General James Oglethorpe. He was the largest financial contributor to Oglethorpe's voyage to the New World.

There is a stretch of beach on Jekyll where the ocean, the sand, the rocks and Jekyll's wind-twisted trees converge within a space of a few yards. Jekyll does not have what could be called a pretty beach but it does have one of the more interesting beach fronts to be found anywhere. The rocks, large and rough and new-looking by comparison with their surroundings, were put there by men and machines, as a barrier against the pounding surf which each day engulfs the narrow stretch of sand between the wooded dunes and the low-tide line.

The rocks were placed by men but only God and centuries of ocean-driven winds could make trees such as the ones which line Jekyll's shore, bent into grotesque shapes but still stubbornly standing against their ancient tormentors.

Florida's broad, white sandy beaches are more familiar to most Georgians and other sun-seekers than the dingy sand of the Golden Isles, but Florida's beaches have no trees, and few rocks. Their tides are more subdued than the waves which daily try to surmount the barriers along the Jekyll beach. Nor do they have the history which lends Jekyll and the other Golden Isles an added grandeur.

At night, looking across the finger of the Atlantic separating Jekyll from St. Simons, one can easily see the St. Simons lighthouse, made famous by Eugenia Price's popular novels about life on the Golden Isles in the 1800s.

St. Simons doesn't have to depend on fiction for a colorful past, however. The Battle of Bloody Marsh, fought on St. Simons in 1742, determined whether the English or the Spanish would control and settle the area which became the nation's southeastern states. General James Oglethorpe's troops defeated the Spanish, who had come up by sea from St. Augustine and other Florida settlements.

John Wesley, founder of the Methodist church, preached on St. Simons in the 1730s, at the Christ Church, which remains today at the same site, close by the tree under which Wesley gave some of his early sermons, copies of which are still available in the church vestibule.

Christ Church gained even greater fame than the lighthouse because of the Eugenia Price novels, whose real-life characters are buried in the old graveyard adjacent to the church. A favorite tourist pastime is looking for the gravestones of Anson Dodge, his wives and children, and the other men and women from the trilogy which tells of the people who restored the church and rebuilt the lighthouse in the years after the Civil War. The books, in order of their publication, were "The Beloved Invader," "New Moon Rising," and "The Lighthouse." The author eventually came to St. Simons to live, writing several non-fiction books about the Golden Isles, plus other novels about the southeast coast, including "Savannah," a story of that Georgia city in pre-Civil War days.

But the tourist walking along the Jekyll beach, looking across the inlet at St. Simons and its lighthouse, is already on historic ground. Georgians might be accused of provincialism for claiming that Jekyll has special charms, and that its blend of deep woods, beach, gnarled oaks, ocean and marshes make it an island unique among all the islands of the world. But Jekyll has objective proof of its qualities, attested to by no less than a group of doctors commissioned by the richest American families of their time to select the perfect island paradise on which these millionaires could find comfortable respite during the harsh winters that disturbed their peace in such places as New York City, Newport, Rhode Island and Saratoga Springs, New York.

The scouts were sent out in 1885 by these families, which included the Rockefellers, the Pulitzers, the Morgans, the Pullmans and the Goulds. They visited the French Riviera and other places near and far, and then finally recommended as the most desirable island paradise, little Jekyll off the coast of Georgia. It was in the same latitude as the Riviera, Cairo and San Diego, but had the advantage of being only a 24-hour train trip from New York City, or a leisurely cruise down the intercoastal waterway, a method of travel especially favored by newspaper tycoon Joseph Pulitzer, who made Jekyll one of his favorite retreats. Pulitzer was on his way to Jekyll by ship when he died in 1911.

Jekyll fulfilled the requirements for climate, beauty, good water and accessibility. The millionaires formed a club which then bought Jekyll from the French family DuBignon, who had owned it for nearly 100 years, after moving there in flight from the French Revolution. The price, in 1886, was $125,000. Cleveland Amory, the chronicler of the Gilded Age millionaires, wrote: "Jekyll was not only the greatest of the country's social islands, but one so legendary in prestige that in its heyday its winter residents reportedly controlled one sixth of the entire world's wealth."

The Jekyll Island Clubhouse and Hotel opened in 1888, the first of the grandiose structures built on the island by the millionaires. It would accommodate 100 guests and was used as a hotel for the next 80 years. This hotel was the center of Jekyll activities and had the only kitchen and dining facilities on the island. Since there were never more than 12 privately-owned cottages on Jekyll at any one time during the 56 years of the Millionaires' era, many Jekyll Club members and their guests stayed at the hotel, or at the nearby San Souci Apartments, which were completed in 1897. They are believed to be the nation's first condominiums since each of the apartments was privately-owned.

Two especially historic events occurred on Jekyll Island. The first was in 1858 while the DuBignons still owned it, and a ship named The Wanderer landed on Jekyll with the last load of slaves ever brought to the United States. This landing was 50 years after the slave trade (although not slavery itself, of course) had been outlawed by the U.S. government. The Wanderer's crew had reportedly lured 350 Africans on board before setting sail for the U.S. About 300 survived the voyage and were unloaded at Jekyll where they were sold to South Carolina and Georgia plantations, just two years before the outbreak of the Civil War. They thus were the last Africans brought to this country as slaves, and they were freed four years later by the Emancipation Proclamation and the invading federal troops.

But the most important event in Jekyll's history, as far as influencing the future of the country and the world, occurred in the autumn of 1910 when five of the leading financial experts in the nation met secretly at Jekyll during its "off season" to draw a proposal for revision of the U.S. financial system.

Headed by U.S. Senator Nelson Aldrich of Rhode Island, grandfather of future U.S. Vice President Nelson Rockefeller, this group spent 10 days working in what is now the lounge of the Jekyll Island Club and Hotel, writing a report which would become the Federal Reserve Act and would create the Federal Reserve Bank and Board which controls the money supply and supervises banks in the U.S. to this day. The Republican-dominated Congress and President William Howard Taft rejected the federal reserve plan but in 1914 President Woodrow Wilson and the new Democrat-controlled Congress adopted it, changing the course of American financial history.

Particularly in the 1980s the role of the Federal Reserve Board has come to the public's notice because of its effect on interest rates and the money supply, and the prominence of Paul Volcker, who is probably the best known of all Federal Reserve chairmen.

The same Congress which passed the Federal Reserve Act, composed in the opulence of Jekyll's Millionaires' Club, also adopted another financial measure which was to do much toward ending the Gilded Age of unlimited riches for a select number of American families. That measure was the first federal income tax law.

Fourteen years later the great stock market crash of 1929 further decimated the number of millionaires. Other factors were working against social resorts such as Jekyll and Newport and Saratoga. The younger generation of the families which bought Jekyll did not care as much for the island's isolation, or the small-scale hunting which had been the favorite pastime of Jekyll's original millionaires.

In April, 1942, a few months after the U.S. became involved in World War II, a German submarine torpedoed a tanker in St. Simons Sound, causing the U.S. government to order the evacuation of Jekyll for fear that its wealthy residents would attract an enemy attack. The evacuation was conducted under the leadership of General George Patton. The club register, now in the Jekyll Hotel library, shows General Patton and his wife as the last names signed in the official guest book. The millionaires' era had ended.

In 1947 the Jekyll Island Club sold the island to the state of Georgia for $675,000, complete with the elegant clubhouse and the several "cottages" still standing. Governor M. E. Thompson, Georgia's first lieutenant governor, who became governor when Eugene Talmadge died before taking office, arranged the sale, which turned out to be one of the great transactions in the state's history.

A causeway from the mainland to Jekyll, across the famed marshes of Glynn, was completed in 1954, and the Aquarama convention center was opened in 1962. Lots for private homes are leased to residents by the state, and commercial development on the island has been carefully supervised and restrained.

Jekyll, St. Simons, Sea Island, Midway, King's Bay, Savannah — with the largest officially designated historic district in the nation — they are Coastal Georgia, the state's oldest and most historic section.

But there are other Georgias.

There is a Mountain . . .

There is the Georgia of brooding mountains, and winding roads, and rushing streams, where people live and farm and in some places play. And there is one particular mountain, called Brasstown Bald, which rises up to 4,784 feet, the highest elevation in the state. Its strangely barren peak has an observation tower from which you can see into three other states. You can see neighboring Blood Mountain, nearly as tall at 4,458 feet, and a site of legends. You can see the towns of Blairsville and Young Harris, appearing like cardboard villages placed on a huge canvas. On a clear day you really think you can see forever.

Georgia's mountains are not tall in comparison with those further north in Tennessee or North Carolina, but there is a haunting quality that gives them a special magic. They are low enough to be climbed, they are undeveloped enough so that the roads still wind through them rather than over them. Farms and homes dot Georgia's mountains. They are not just scenery, they are still where people live and work.

The view from the peak of Brasstown Bald provides the most striking contrast to the view from Jekyll Island's beach, and emphasizes Georgia's remarkable geographic diversity.

The northern part of the state contains many roads that take a traveler on a trip through the mountain and meadow scenery. Probably the road with the sharpest hair-pin turns and stunning views is a 40-mile stretch of U.S. 76 from Hiawassee to Clayton.

From Brasstown Bald it is a short, but mountainous journey to the Alpine Village of Helen, which has become the most popular tourist spot in North Georgia. Helen was a small, declining town when its residents decided to recreate it as a Bavarian village, complete with the architecture of that area, the shops, the foods, and eventually many other attractions.

Helen, located near the headwaters of the Chattahoochee River, began its ascent to prominence in 1969 and became a major tourist attraction within two years. It has continued to expand, with more motels and promotions, including its popular Octoberfests.

There Is a City . . .

Georgia has several important cities, but it has only one Atlanta, which is not only Georgia's major city but is the major city in the southeast quadrant of the nation.

Atlanta, with over two million population in its metropolitan area, has the nation's busiest airport; is third among U.S. cities in number of conventions and conventioneers; and is the business and commercial headquarters for the southern states.

It has major league teams in baseball, football and basketball, and its skyline is a match for any U.S. city in quality if not in quantity. The view of that central city skyline is impressive coming in from almost any direction, but the most spectacular may be the view from I-20 West, which is more horizontal and over a flatter terrain.

In downtown Atlanta itself the top floor of the 72-story Peachtree Plaza Hotel ranks with Brasstown Bald and the beach at Jekyll as an observation point not to be missed. Each of those points is so vastly different in perspective, so far removed in style, and so illustrative of Georgia and its variety.

The best closeup panoramic view of downtown Atlanta is probably from the 17th floor lounge of the Downtown Sheraton, near the Georgia Tech campus, looking south toward the major hotel and commercial area.

There is another view in Downtown Atlanta that deserves mention, not so much for its beauty or its haunting qualities, but for its significance. That view is the lobby of the Hyatt Regency Hotel, looking up the atrium for 21 floors of hotel hallways opening onto a single first floor lobby.

This was Atlanta Architect John Portman's great breakthrough in hotel design when The Hyatt opened in 1967 and it also proved to be symbolic of a great breakthrough for Atlanta.

As recently as 1950 Atlanta was just one of several major southern cities, not as well known as New Orleans or Miami, not as industrial as Birmingham, not as celebrated in song and story as Memphis or Nashville or Richmond.

Its metropolitan population that year was about the same as Birmingham's, and Birmingham was gaining. The same was true for the states of Georgia and Alabama. Georgia's population (3,444,000) was less than 300,000 ahead of Alabama's 3,061,000.

Atlanta did have a relatively tall skyline left over from a building boom in the 1920s but there hadn't been a skyscraper built in 20 years, nor had the city added a truly impressive hotel since World War II. The tragic Winecoff Hotel fire of 1946 which took 119 lives may have had a dampening effect on high rise buildings.

But the future was stirring in the 1950s even though it would be the

1960s before Atlanta truly gained prominence and became one of the dynamic urban areas in the nation. The 1950 stirrings were primarily the four-lane ribbons of concrete being laid throughout the city and nearby counties, and the growing importance of air travel, and of Atlanta's airport as a transfer station for most flights in the South.

If you had to pinpoint one event and one year that signalled the beginning of modern Atlanta — and modern Georgia — it would have to be 1964 and the decision to build Atlanta-Fulton County Stadium for major league baseball and football teams.

Atlanta became big-league in a variety of ways in the mid-60s, a period which coincided with Carl Sanders' term as governor and Ivan Allen Jr.'s term as mayor.

The stadium paved the way for the South's first major league athletic teams, and Atlanta got them, which even non-sports fans must realize was a crucial victory, stamping Atlanta as the South's "major league" city, and providing a reason for millions of Americans to take notice of Atlanta who had never heard of it before.

In 1966 the Downtown Marriott Hotel opened, providing an elegance that was new to Atlanta and the South. A year later came the Hyatt Regency, which was not only elegant but had the breath-taking atrium which changed hotel design throughout the nation.

The interstate highways, begun in the 1950s, were now extending into the nearby counties, and growth followed in their paths. Atlanta's growth after the Civil War was a result of its importance as a railroad transportation center. In the 1960s its airport was the fulcrum. The airport itself brought many jobs, but more important it provided the reason for national companies to locate their regional offices in the Atlanta area. In the 1970s and 1980s the airport would also be a major reason for Atlanta's phenomenal emergence as a national convention site.

The Atlanta metro area soon left its old southern competitors far behind in population. Its growth also sparked a surge in the statewide total. As noted, Georgia and Alabama were within less than 300,000 of each other's population in 1950. Thirty years later, Georgia's population was 5,464,265 to Alabama's 3,890,000 — a difference of nearly 1.5 million. Georgia's most impressive gain came in the 1970s when it added one million people.

Metro Atlanta made the difference. More than half of Georgia's population gain in the past 30 years has been in the 10 counties bordering on Fulton.

There Is a Garden . . .

Then there is a unique garden in Georgia, a series of gardens really, spread over many miles of Harris County in middle west Georgia, near the Alabama border.

Callaway Gardens may be better known and more highly regarded in national circles than in much of Georgia. *Money Magazine* calls the Gardens one of the "Ten Fabulous Family Resorts" in the United States. *Changing Times* ranks it among the six best U.S. resorts catering to families.

The gardens were the dream and development of Cason Callaway, a textile executive who left his job as president of the Callaway Mills in LaGrange in 1938 to work on transforming a large area of West Georgia woodlands into gardens of native flora in which people could ride, walk or bike for miles, viewing the kind of natural beauty that usually lies hidden beyond the highway traveler's eye. Changing the woods to a garden took Callaway nearly 20 years, but one horticulturist said the transformation would have taken nature two centuries.

Callaway eventually developed much more: a vegetable garden that has helped farmers discover better methods of production; 13 lakes with a beach front 200 miles from the nearest ocean; five golf courses, including a championship course which is one of the most beautiful and challenging in the South; an amusement area which includes annual circus performances and musical presentations; and a convention center, which attracts conventions and seminars from throughout the nation and world.

While Callaway was developing the area, a frequent visitor to his Blue Springs farm near Hamilton was a neighboring farmer named Franklin D. Roosevelt, who came over from Warm Springs, 20 miles away. Roosevelt first came to Warm Springs in 1924 for rehabilitation from the polio attack which left him permanently crippled. He found that the waters of Warm Springs allowed him to swim, float, and even kick his withered legs. Overjoyed by the new feeling in his legs, and also by the friendliness of the Georgia people, Roosevelt established a resort home at Warm Springs before he was elected president in 1932, and then during his 12 years as president it became his "Little White House."

Roosevelt loved the view of the Georgia pine forests from atop Pine Mountain. So he bought some 2,200 acres, about 150 acres of which were pasture and crop land. A gentleman farmer in his native New York,

President Roosevelt was more of a real farmer in Georgia, and his farmland produced cattle, hogs and poultry as well as fruits and vegetables. These products supplied much of the food for the Warm Springs Foundation during the rationing period of World War II.

It was Roosevelt's interest in farming that led to his friendship with his Georgia neighbor, Cason Callaway, although the Democratic president and the retired textile executive disagreed "fundamentally on all the fundamentals," as Callaway explained it. He considered Roosevelt an indispensable leader but one who harbored dangerous economic theories.

Roosevelt died at his Warm Springs home early in his fourth term as president on April 12, 1945, just three weeks before the death of his great enemy, Adolf Hitler, who had become dictator of Germany in the same year Roosevelt became president.

So Georgia has islands and intriguing seashores, and brooding mountains where people still live, and a garden that covers half a county, and a great city. But Georgia has even more that is different.

It has a swamp, for instance, with 400,000 acres of waterways, swamp prairies and floating islands. Located in Ware County, near the Florida border, the Okefenokee is the nation's second best-known swamp, next only to Florida's Everglades, but while Florida has a bigger swamp and more beaches it doesn't have any mountains, in fact not even a good-sized hill, and trees are hard to find except for palms.

Elliott Brack, general manager of *The Gwinnett Daily News,* summed up Georgia's natural wonders in a column on Nov. 30, 1983 which listed his choices as the Seven Wonders of Georgia.

Brack's wonders: 1. The Okefenokee Swamp; 2. Stone Mountain; 3. The Marshes of Glynn; 4. Providence Canyon, or "Little Grand Canyon," near Lumpkin; 5. Brasstown Bald mountain; 6. Tallulah Gorge and Falls; 7. Cumberland Island.

Few states can match those natural wonders for diversity.

Carter and the Georgia Press

About 100 miles due south of Warm Springs and Roosevelt's Little White House is the home of another U.S. president, James Earl Carter, known as Jimmy both on and off the ballot. Carter, elected in 1976, is the only native Georgian ever to hold the presidency and was the first resident of a true southern state to be elected president since the Civil War.

Oddly, Carter, the kind of New South liberal who usually enjoyed strong support from southern newspapers, did not have broad or enthusiastic support among Georgia publishers and editors, neither when he ran for governor (in 1966 and 1970) or for president in 1976 and 1980.

Only two dailies — *The Athens Daily News* and *The Cartersville Tribune-News* — supported Carter in his first bid for governor in 1966. He ran third that year in the Democratic primary, behind Ellis Arnall and Lester Maddox. Maddox won the runoff and went on to an unusual victory over Republican Howard (Bo) Callaway, son of Cason Callaway, when write-in votes for Arnall prevented either Maddox or Callaway from securing a majority of the popular votes in the November general election. Callaway had a small plurality but under an 1827 Georgia law the final selection went to the State House of Representatives, which elected Maddox when it met in January.

Carter, who made no public endorsement in either the runoff or the general election, went back to his peanut warehouse at Plains and began planning for the 1970 gubernatorial election. His chief opponent in that race was former Governor Carl Sanders, whom many Georgians credited with having the most progressive administration since Arnall's in the mid-40s. Whether by coincidence or design, Sanders was governor when a lot of good things began happening for Georgia.

As in 1966, few daily newspapers endorsed Carter, although he did get support from *The Columbus Enquirer,* which split with its afternoon counterpart, *The Ledger*.

Carter did not enhance his standing with editors and publishers when he used his time at a candidates' forum during the 1970 Georgia Press Association convention to read a letter he'd written to *Atlanta Constitution* Editor Reg Murphy, which he claimed Murphy would not print. Murphy was a strong supporter of Sanders.

But as has often happened in Georgia, the candidate with the fewest newspapers behind him got the most votes. Carter won easily over Sanders and then defeated the Republican candidate, TV newscaster Hal Suit, in the General Election.

Carter's relations with the press did not improve noticeably during his term as governor, except that his most powerful critic, Murphy, left *The Constitution* to be replaced by Hal Gulliver, a Carter partisan.

Georgia's editors were little more impressed than editors in other states when Carter announced in December, 1974 that he was running for the Democratic presidential nomination. Several headlines exclaimed: "Jimmy Carter's Running for What???"

But it was Georgians — and the money of Georgians, including Anne

Cox Chambers, daughter of James Cox, and the chief stockholder in the Atlanta newspapers — who provided Carter with the base for his stunning primary victories in 1976, and his eventual ascent to the presidency.

Carter was actually less popular with southerners than Governor George Wallace of Alabama, who was also a presidential candidate in 1976, as he had been in 1964, 1968 and 1972. But Wallace, crippled in 1972 by a would-be assassin's bullet, and shadowed by the segregationist stands that made him a national figure, was obviously not a candidate who could win the final nomination. Southerners, sensing a chance for one of their own in the White House for the first time in more than 100 years, gave Carter decisive victories over Wallace in the Florida and North Carolina primaries, and in the process made him a viable candidate in all states. The little-known, one-term governor from Georgia won the nomination over a large field of better-known Democratic leaders, and then defeated the incumbent Republican president, Gerald Ford, in November.

Ford was not without newspaper endorsements in Georgia, however, especially from the William S. Morris group, which included Augusta, Savannah and Athens. Morris, appointed to the Board of Regents by Governor Sanders, had not been reappointed by Governor Carter.

Another powerful journalistic and political opponent was Albany Publisher and Mayor James Gray, who ran fourth behind Carter in the 1966 governor's race. The Atlanta, Columbus and Macon dailies all endorsed Carter, however.

Many small dailies and weeklies made no endorsement at all, which was a statement in itself, indicating a lack of enthusiasm for their state's favorite son candidate.

Carter's presidency presented the state's newspapers a unique opportunity for news coverage at the national level and for access to government officials since many of Carter's appointees were Georgians. Carter also made frequent visits to the state. His term should have been a peak time of national coverage for Georgia dailies, and it did seem to spark additional activity at the Atlanta dailies. For the most part, however, the state's other dailies continued to rely on wire service reports. The Washington bureau for the Macon-Columbus dailies actually closed during the Carter years.

In 1980, Georgia newspaper support of Carter was even less enthusiastic than in 1976, reflecting the national consensus which was building against him. He carried Georgia in the General Election against Republican Ronald Reagan, but his margin was 10 percentage points lower than 1976. Georgia was one of only six states that Carter did carry in 1980.

Carter and his family returned to Georgia to live after his presidential term, with homes in Plains, Atlanta and Gilmer County. He is also on the faculty at Emory University and is working toward construction of a presidential library in the Atlanta area.

But for a relatively young former president, Carter's influence and visibility in his home state have not been impressive.

In 1982, he did produce one of the better presidential memoirs in U.S. history, "Keeping Faith," and it enjoyed good sales around the country. In fact, his administration has proven to be remarkably successful from a literary standpoint. Rosalyn Carter's "First Lady From Plains," is the largest selling book ever written by a president's wife; Press Secretary Jody Powell's "Other Side of the Story," has also sold well, while making some significant points about the media and its influence in the nation; Ham Jordan, Carter's chief of staff, is the author of "Crisis," a book dealing mainly with the Iranian hostage crisis, and it too has sold well. Adding in Lewis Grizzard, the *Constitution* humor columnist, and Dr. Ferrol Sams of Fayetteville, whose book on life in rural Georgia, "Run with the Horseman," also became a best-seller, Georgians have been as prominent on the literary scene in the early 1980s, as they were on the political scene in the late 1970s.

Other Georgia politicians who successfully took up their pens (or word-processors) in this period were Lieutenant Governor Zell Miller, with "Great Georgians," a book about outstanding leaders of the state; and 6th District Congressman Newt Gingrich, whose book, "The Opportunity Society," is regarded as the blueprint for future Republican policies.

But Georgia political reporters have not been part of the literary revival sparked by the Carter presidency. Books about Carter, before, during and after his presidency were mainly written by reporters from outside the state.

Other Political Powers

Carter's career was like a shooting star, both at the state and national level, appearing suddenly and brilliantly and then fading almost as swiftly. He took the oath as governor in January, 1971, and gave up the presidency in January, 1981, and that decade encased his time of prominence.

Other Georgia political figures of the time had longer periods in the spotlight and greater influence in some respects. The most dominant

Georgia political figure since World War II would have to be Herman Talmadge, who served as governor from 1948 to 1955, and then as U.S. senator from 1957 to 1981. While the state's dailies were divided about Carter, they were virtually unanimous in their opposition to Talmadge, especially in his younger days. It was a family tradition. They also had opposed his father, Eugene Talmadge, in the elder Talmadge's campaigns for governor and senator.

The elder Talmadge died in December, 1946, after winning a fourth term as governor a month earlier. Several hundred Talmadge supporters, who apparently knew Gene was in poor health, had written Herman's name in on the governor's ballot in the General Election, and when Gene died they claimed that the state legislature should choose a governor from the two leading vote-getters. Herman, with his few hundred write-ins, came in second since there were no other candidates on the ballot in the general election.

Incumbent Governor Ellis Arnall would not surrender the office to Herman, however, even after the legislature elected him, thus precipitating Georgia's famous "two-governor" battle. Arnall felt that Lieutenant Governor M. E. Thompson was the legal successor, and the courts eventually upheld that position. Thompson was sworn in to serve until the next election in 1948. Herman, then only 32, stepped aside and began gearing up to run for the office on his own.

For nearly 20 years Georgia had been basically divided along pro-Talmadge and anti-Talmadge lines, and Herman carried that tradition into a second generation. He scored a narrow victory over Thompson in 1948, but then defeated him easily in the 1950 governor's race. With his second victory, Talmadge established a dominance in state politics that his father never enjoyed. For nearly 30 years Talmadge himself was unassailable at the polls and the two governors who followed him, Marvin Griffin and Ernest Vandiver, were Talmadge proteges.

Like his father, Talmadge found it popular to attack "them lyin' Atlanta newspapers," and most of the other newspapers in the state. But his rhetoric mellowed after he went to the Senate, and by the time he sat as a member of the Watergate investigative committee in 1973 he was regarded as another in the line of Georgia's "statesman" senators, such as Walter George—whom Talmadge replaced—and Richard B. Russell, who had died in 1971. Both George and Russell had defeated Eugene Talmadge in the 1930s when he sought to move from governor to senator.

Talmadge encountered both personal and political problems in the late 1970s. He was censured by the Senate for questionable financial dealings, was divorced, and underwent treatment for alcoholism. Earlier, one of his two sons had drowned in a boating accident.

In 1980, Talmadge found himself facing the first real political race he'd had to make since 1950 — 30 years earlier. He led a field of four in the first Democratic primary and then defeated Lieutenant Governor Zell Miller in the runoff.

But a little-known Republican, Mack Mattingly, who had never held public office, defeated the once-invincible Talmadge in the November General Election. Mattingly was the first Republican to win a statewide race in Georgia in 110 years.

Miller, in the primaries, and Mattingly in the General Election, got most of the newspaper endorsements.

Although Talmadge personally had lost no elections until 1980, he did lose two crucial constitutional amendment elections while he was governor, when he sought to extend the county unit system of voting to general elections. In both 1950 and 1952 his amendments were defeated, and in 1962 a federal court threw out the county unit system altogether on the rather obvious grounds that it discriminated against voters in larger counties. The state's dailies had strongly opposed the Talmadge amendments and had long editorialized against the county unit system.

As mentioned, most newspapers opposed Talmadge in his early races. They were also solidly against Marvin Griffin when he ran for governor in 1954. In fact, Griffin may have suffered more than any governor of the period at the hands of the press, which is ironic considering that he is the only bona fide newspaperman to serve as governor in this century.

Vandiver, the winner in 1958, was overwhelmingly favored by the newspapers, but he had only token opposition. Carl Sanders, in 1962, was virtually hoisted into the race by newspaper encouragement, when the only other choices seemed to be Griffin or Lieutenant Governor Garland Byrd. Sanders defeated Griffin with near-unanimous support from the daily press. The end of the county unit system made no difference as Sanders won in both the popular and unit count.

In the 1966 primary Ellis Arnall had most of the newspaper endorsements but lost the runoff to Lester Maddox, who had none. Bo Callaway was heavily endorsed in the general election but failed to gain a majority of the popular votes, with Maddox being elected by the legislature.

Sanders was again a newspaper favorite in 1970 but lost to Carter.

Four years later George Busbee won the first of his two terms as governor with only minimum newspaper backing in the first primary. Even his hometown paper, *The Albany Herald,* backed Maddox, who was running for a second term. Bert Lance and Harry Jackson, the other major candidates, got several big newspaper endorsements. Busbee won the runoff against Maddox, and went on to a second consecutive term when the state constitution was amended to let governors succeed themselves.

Perhaps the most interesting governor's race of recent years from the standpoint of endorsements was in 1982 when newspapers showed a remarkable lack of unanimity on who should be elected.

All six major candidates in the Democratic primary got some daily newspaper endorsements. The Atlanta dailies split, with *The Journal* backing Joe Frank Harris and *The Constitution* going with Bo Ginn. Norman Underwood, Jack Watson and Buck Melton all had at least one big-city newspaper endorsement, and Billy Lovett got the endorsement of his hometown *Dublin Courier-Herald,* which happened to be owned by his family.

In the runoff between Ginn and Harris, *The Journal* stayed with Harris while most other large dailies went with Ginn. Ginn, the first primary leader, was also endorsed by all four of the losing candidates in the first primary. Harris' subsequent victory showed that politicians don't have any more influence than newspapers.

But whatever they might say on the stump, political candidates seek and cherish newspaper support, and they do this more openly and aggressively in the 1980s than back in the years when newspapers presumably had more influence. The wooing of newspapers has become more deliberate and sophisticated and few serious statewide candidates openly attack newspapers today as the Talmadges did in years past.

The contradiction is that in the 1980s politicians spend most of their advertising money on television, radio and billboards. Newspapers rank somewhere behind telephone pole posters and airplane banners when it comes to allocating the ad money.

At both the daily and weekly levels newspapers were probably less "political" during the Great Newspaper Era than they were before World War II. The volume of information that is turned out is so much greater than in the past that all sides and many views get an airing. The extreme partisan is rare among publishers or editors in the 1980s, and Georgians as a whole appear less sharply divided than in the Talmadge era or earlier.

Two-party politics, which seemed to be on the verge of a breakthrough in the 1960s, fell back in the 1970s but is on the rise again in the 1980s with President Ronald Reagan energizing Southern Republicans. The majority of Georgia dailies have been nominally Republican at the national level since the Eisenhower campaigns. Now even the Atlanta newspapers, long regarded as "liberal," and certainly Democratic, have become more conservative, as have the Macon and Gainesville newspapers, which were once regarded as "liberal."

But the real story of Georgia newspapers since World War II is that they have more news, more pictures, more information, more ads, and for the most part more readers, who despite TV and other distractions are better readers than they were in 1950.

Hal Steed, a Georgia newspaperman of the pre-WWII period, wrote a book in 1941 which he called, "Georgia: Unfinished State." The title has stayed in the public memory longer than the book, which was mainly a travelogue through depression-era Georgia.

In the 1930s, Steed found a state still backward by most modern standards; still with a road system that supposedly triggered Gen. Sherman's famous observation that "war is Hell"; still controlled by politicians beholden to the county unit system and all of its implications; still the southern state most wedded in many respects to the Old South, but with the greatest potential for becoming the hub of a New South, which, in fact by 1984 Georgia has become.

It did not happen easily and there are still stubborn pockets of resistance to the 20th century throughout Georgia. But since Steed's travels in the 1930s — nearly 50 years ago — Georgia has moved a considerable way toward being "finished." Georgians live in the largest, most diverse state east of the Mississippi . . . a unique area of coastline, mountains, forests, swamps and one of the nation's great cities.

Next to Florida, it was the fastest growing southern state from 1960 to 1980. By the year 2000 Georgia should be one of the nation's 10 most populous states.

But like its newspapers, Georgia may be at the apex of its growth and its greatness, with the loftiest plateaus already in the past.

Some of the most significant breakthroughs of the past 20 years will not be available in the next 20 years. The major cities, especially Atlanta, face the problems common to most U.S. cities, a declining white and higher-income population, a growing poor and minority population, living squalidly in the shadows of the skyscraping office buildings and convention hotels.

Savannah, the nation's great model of restoration, must keep on restoring or its buildings will lapse back into the past from which they were rescued.

The textile mills which nurtured many Georgia communities will never again employ the large numbers of people they once did.

People will always have to eat, but food and livestock can now be produced by fewer workers, and that has probably made the biggest difference in what Georgians do for a living.

Fewer people live in the half of Georgia south of Macon in 1985 than did in 1920. The population stabilized during the 1970s, mainly because fewer black families moved out, but except in scattered enclaves such as Albany and the coastal area little growth is expected in the near future.

A population projection for Georgia compiled by the State Office of Planning and Budget in 1983 estimates that the statewide population will reach 6,462,000 by 1990, and 7,442,000 by 2000, a gain of nearly 2 million over the 1980 census. The growth is projected to be mainly in the northern counties, especially the suburban counties of Atlanta.

But projections have a way of going astray. In 1960 DeKalb County was projected to be larger than Fulton by 1980. In the new projection, it is still second to Fulton in the year 2000, while Gwinnett, a latecomer in the growth cycle, is expected to be third, moving ahead of Cobb, Chatham and Richmond.

What Georgia will become as it is further "finished," is uncertain, but the old certainties appear secure.

On the beach at Jekyll the waves will still battle against the rocks while the trees stubbornly resist the wind. On Brasstown Bald, on a clear day you'll still be able to see . . . forever. The dogwoods and azaleas in Mr. Callaway's gardens will bloom in the spring, bursting brilliantly but briefly, in nature's age-old ritual.

In Atlanta, buildings will rise and fall. A new John Portman will think of another way to shape hotels. Some innovative cook will come up with a new fast food. Traffic congestion in Atlanta should actually decline as more office parks and more businesses move to the perimeter of the city.

And the newspaper will come out . . . because somehow newspapers always come out, no matter how unlikely it seems at times to those caught up in the task of compiling them.

This book is mainly about the way Georgia newspapers have come out since 1950, and about the people who own, edit and write them, and put them "to bed" every day or every week.

It tells of a technological revolution, which was mainly aimed at speeding up the way newspapers are composed and printed. But perhaps the most revealing fact about the newspaper business is that despite all the changes and improvements in production capability and speed during the past 35 years, most newspapers have just as much trouble making deadlines and getting out by the assigned time today as they did with typewriters, linotypes and letter presses.

The deadline has withstood all of the miraculous machines designed to tame it, and remains the unchallenged dictator of the newspaper business, as intimidating to young reporters on terminals as it was to old Homer Garrett of Doerun, Ga., who kept setting type by hand until the late 1970s.

The skyline of Atlanta has become one of the state's most impressive scenic wonders . . . Atlanta-Fulton County Stadium is in foreground.

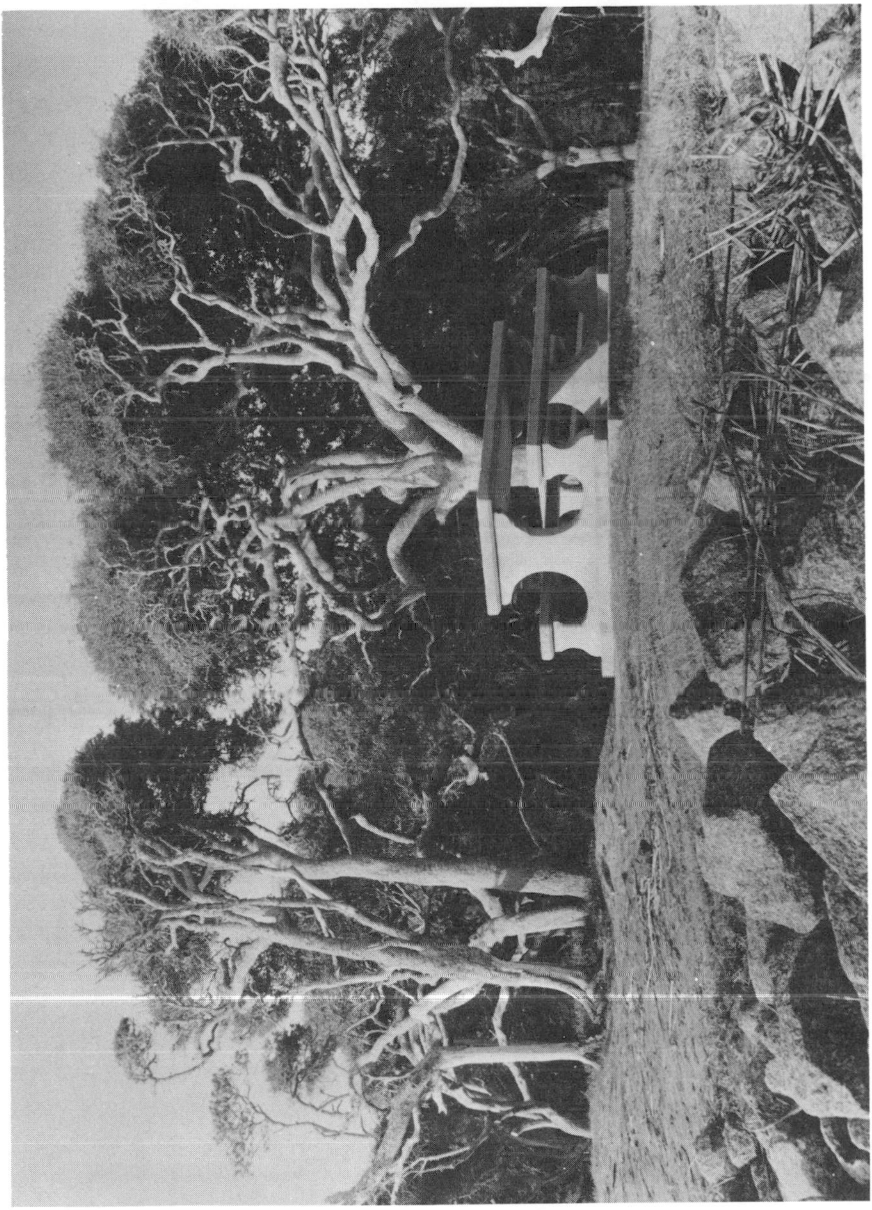

The twisted trees and rock-bound coast of Jekyll Island, where the country's richest families once played, and Georgia's journalists have convened for a quarter century.

Chapter II

The Last Linotype: An Easier Way To Do It

Mergenthaler's Miracle

One day in the mid-1950s, an ink-stained veteran of hot-type composition glared into the sparkling-clean enclosure where his newspaper company was experimenting with composition of ads by the "cold type" method. By later standards the machines were primitive, but in the 1950s they were miraculous in comparison with the cumbersome linotypes and ludlows on which newspapers were then composed.

The sweating, grimy makeup man, hands indelibly marked with the ink from thousands of galleys, observed with a sigh: "Out here we're still printing like Ben Franklin, and in there they're printing like Buck Rogers."

And, in fact, newspapers in the late 1950s were not very far removed in their composition methods from Ben Franklin, who would have been comfortable with the flatbed presses and the handset headline and ad type still used in 1950s newspaper plants. The linotype would have surprised and delighted him, since he had to compose body type by hand. But by the 1950s, the linotype had been in general use for some 70 years and it was still the most modern machine in many newspaper plants.

A linotype machine was at once a formidable, complex and delicate monster, requiring the attention of skilled and patient operators who spent years learning its intricacies, and entire careers becoming its master. In hot-type days, the linotype operator was one of the most skilled positions on a newspaper and was usually paid more than any of the news personnel, and sometimes more than the editor. In fact, the editors and publishers of many weeklies got their start as linotype operators.

Because the machine's durability was as legendary as its contrariness, a publisher figured he could invest the time and money to train an operator since a linotype was the only foreseeable means of composing the newspaper. Obsolescence seemed no danger.

But actually there were a number of better and easier ways to compose type, and they had been around for many years. They were used in commercial printing, magazines and in various other types of publications. They were not unknown to newspapers, and some small newspapers had used other printing methods; however, most publishers seemed to think they had too much of an investment in hot type machinery to consider a shift to other ways of printing and composition. Employees themselves, especially those in unions, naturally were reluctant to see new methods introduced which might make not only their machines obsolete, but also their skills.

To those entering the newspaper business after 1960, the use of linotypes and hot metal for so long by newspapers must seem shortsighted and irresponsible, and conclusive evidence that newspapers have always resisted change in every aspect of their operations. But the linotype and its hot metal compatriots definitely had their good points. In fact, there are still newspaper people who believe the linotype provided a sharper, easier-to-read text than any cold type composer yet developed, and that metal type assured a neater, more professional makeup because the lines were almost invariably straight, the spacing even and consistent, the hyphenations less erratic.

Linotype's body or text type has been the most difficult part of printing for cold type to duplicate, and even the Mergenthaler Company, which manufactured linotypes, was unable to provide the same precise spacing or escapements between letters in cold type machines as it had in hot type.

The keyboard on a linotype had 90 keys, and skilled fingers were needed to make sure that each key performed its function. When the operator touched a key, a mold or matrix would be released from a metal case, or magazine, at the top of the linotype. A moving belt carried the matrix to its proper place in the line, with spaces between words formed by wedge-shaped slugs released by other keys. The line of matrixes was then transferred to the metal-casting mechanism on the machine where they were automatically spaced; next, molten metal was forced into the faces of the matrixes, forming the lines of metal letters. These lines then moved into a tray, called a galley, which usually held enough lines of type to fill a regular newspaper column. The linotype machines would automatically return the matrixes to the magazine so they could be used again and again.

Ottmar Mergenthaler patented the linotype machine in 1884 and it was first used successfully in 1886. Until Mergenthaler's invention, all type was set by hand, much in the way Gutenberg had done some 400 years earlier.

Mergenthaler, a native of Germany, was only 32 on the day his typesetting machine was tried in the plant of *The New York Tribune*. That was July 3, 1886. He sat down at the keyboard of the strange contraption of tubes, levers, gears, and molds, and tapped a key. The machine whirred and clicked with the sounds that would become so familiar in the composing rooms of the world during the next 75 years and spit out a thin metal slug, its face shaped in eight words of shining type.

Whitelaw Reid, *The Tribune's* publisher, smiled broadly as he gingerly picked up the warm metal. "Ottmar, you have done it," he said, "a line o' type."

According to Mergenthaler Company's official history, that was the casual christening of the new machine as a "linotype," which revolutionized the printing industry and gave newspapers the means to become a far more important force in mass communications.

Mergenthaler's success came after years of failure by other inventors and many experiments by Mergenthaler himself. Mark Twain, the popular author, had lost much of his fortune investing in composing inventions. The newspaper publishers of New York City had once offered $500,000 in prize money to anyone who could perfect a machine to replace hand composition of newspaper type.

Mergenthaler had immigrated to the United States from Germany in 1872, and soon found work as a printer. In 1883, he began devoting all of his time to developing an automatic composing machine. On July 26, 1884, he demonstrated his first machine to a small group, but two more years were needed before the machine actually produced type for a newspaper and became the linotype machine. The main reason for the long delay was finding a metal that was versatile enough to use for the letters in the linotype machine. The essential part of Mergenthaler's invention was the small brass matrix which replaced founder's type, and a method had to be developed for mass production of these matrixes.

Newspaper publishers provided the funds for Mergenthaler's experiments, as well as the costs of starting his manufacturing company. Without this support from the newspaper industry his work — and his invention — would have been long delayed, if, indeed, he would have found the right components in his relatively short lifetime. Mergenthaler died in 1899 at the age of 45.

Because the linotype created its own type, then remelted the type for further use, it not only cut costs of composition by an enormous amount, but also meant that long aisles of type cases and tons of worn type could be thrown out. With the linotype, approximately 80 pages could be composed and made up in the floor space previously needed to make up eight pages — a 10-time jump in production space, not to mention the greater speed and labor-savings.

A good linotype operator could set about 150 letters a minute, or 24-30 words, but because of the machine's cumbersome operation at translating the letters into type, the average words per minute was somewhat less. In addition, there was much "down" time on linotype machines when they would not operate properly for various reasons. Operators usually had to be mechanics as well, and larger newspapers kept several full-time repairmen on hand. The linotype machine dictated the rest of the newspaper's production operation for the 80 years of its dominance.

The metal type it produced had to be placed in page forms "upside down" so that when the letters were pressed against a mat for casting into a page plate the image would be reversed into readable form. Pages were made up in metal frames mounted on heavy metal carts. Physical strength was an important asset for the printer in hot type days, which was one reason that hot type composing rooms were almost exclusively a male domain. Only in the last years of hot type did a few women come in as linotype operators.

On most newspapers the composing room had the highest payroll of any department, both in total amount and also per person, since the skilled positions of linotype operator and makeup man were numerous and commanded higher salaries than the so-called white collar jobs on the newspaper.

The impact of the linotype machine and its hot type requirements thus affected the entire newspaper operation in several far-reaching ways: composition employees were virtually all men; the composition department took the largest percentage of the total newspaper payroll; and all work on actual composition and makeup of the newspaper had to be done by composing room personnel, usually highly skilled and of long tenure, with news personnel having limited control and involvement in composition and makeup.

But a sweeping change was bearing down on the printing and newspaper business. It would not only alter the way newspapers were composed, but also would alter who composed them and how the newspaper's financial resources were distributed. From Gutenberg in 1440 to Mergenthaler in 1884, printing equipment changed very little; then, from 1884 to 1955, there was another period of stability. But, in the past 30 years, the changes have been so fast and frequent that the "miracle machines" purchased one year would sometimes be obsolete by the following year.

The process that would make these changes possible began taking shape almost 125 years earlier when Joseph Niepce, a French physicist, produced the world's first photograph in 1826. Niepce's achievement paved the way for the modern printing industry, not to speak of photography in general, which put the world in pictures rather than in words and paintings.

In 1852 W. H. Fox Talbot of England patented photoengraving, a process for making halftones, another vital step. But it was another French man who laid the groundwork for offset printing. He was Alphonse Poitevin, who invented photolithography in 1855. By the late 1800s, early offset presses were being used to transfer type to labels for cans and boxes.

This, however, was not the offset printing known today. An American, Ira Rubel, accidentally discovered the offset method for printing on paper. While operating his press, Rubel, a paper maker and printer, unintentionally transferred the inked images onto the rubber-covered impression cylinder instead of onto the paper. Then, when he ran the paper through the press, the impression cylinder offset the images onto the paper. Rubel noticed that the offset images were unusually sharp. His accidental discovery of offset printing in 1906 soon was in general use for commercial printing; but it would still be almost 60 years before a rotary offset press for newspapers was developed.

The pieces were in place, however: photoengraving, halftones, cold type, offset printing. All of them stemmed from photographic processes, and publishers quickly made use of them to improve their newspapers with pictures and rotogravure sections, but few seemed to recognize the potential for overall printing which existed in the photo process.

One of the first and most popular rotogravure sections was in *The Atlanta Journal's* Sunday edition starting in the 1920s.

Georgia's First Cold Type Newspaper

The spark that started the shift to offset printing in Georgia may have been a speech at a Georgia Press Institute in the early 1950s by Johnathan Daniels of *The Raleigh, North Carolina, News and Observer*.

In that speech Daniels said that the best printed newspaper in North Carolina was still produced on a press that had been built in the 19th century. It was his opinion that the press manufacturers hadn't come up with anything better in the 20th century. He also complained about the lack of improvements in composition equipment. "A few spiral gears have replaced tooth gears but otherwise there has been no basic change in the hot metal method of setting type in this century," Daniels stated.

Daniels also mentioned the slow pace of the linotype or intertype machines, which could produce only one to one-and-a-half galleys per hour, or 22 to 33 inches. In most newspaper shops, he said, anything over 18 point type was still being set letter by letter on Ludlow and Monotype machines.

"Several men have to be employed to do nothing but make spacing material to fill in the blank space in advertisements so the form can be locked up," he pointed out. He cited the other drawbacks of the long-time printing methods used by newspapers, such as use of mats which had to be heated, then cast into metal, sawed out and mounted, with the same process necessary for the completed pages — all a slow, laborious, time-consuming operation.

Daniel's conclusion was that there should be an easier, faster, and more economical way of producing newspapers than with hot metal.

One of the Georgia publishers who heard that speech was Charles Lambdin Hardy Sr., editor and publisher of the weekly *Gainesville News*.

Hardy agreed wholeheartedly with Daniels' assessment of the production handicaps which newspapers, large and small, faced in the 1950s.

Hardy had as modern a weekly newspaper plant as was available in that period, with two straight-matter composing machines (linotypes); a Ludlow for display type; a new Elrod space-making machine; a modern casting box and an AB Duplex printing press. But even with this equipment he found it difficult to get out two weekly newspapers, *The News* of Gainesville, and *The Northeast Georgian* in Cornelia.

"Overtime was eating up our profits," Hardy recalls. "We needed a cheaper, faster method of printing." Hardy also faced another problem. The other newspaper in Gainesville had converted to a daily schedule in 1947, and for *The News* to compete he felt it had to carry more local pictures and have a superior print job.

The limitations on use of photographs, illustrations and other artwork was another reason publishers were looking for some other means of printing. Most small dailies and weeklies could not justify their own engraving department, which meant they had to send photographs and non-mat illustrations to engraving shops in nearby cities to have them engraved and mounted. This was very expensive as well as being inconvenient and slow, virtually eliminating the chance to have timely photos. Because of the expense and logistics, most small newspapers in hot-type days carried very few local photographs and illustrations.

Larger newspapers, which had their own engraving departments, paid a high price for the use of illustrative matter. A journeyman engraver was even more valuable, in skill and in payroll cost, than a linotype operator.

In 1955-56, the years when cold type first made an appearance in the newspaper business, these were the national average pay scales for some of the production positions on newspapers:

Photo Engraver	$3.29 an hour
Typographer (linotype operator, etc.)	3.12 an hour
Pressman and stereotyper	3.02 an hour
Mail room (circulation)	2.59 an hour

Pay scales in smaller cities — and in Georgia — were lower , of course, including Atlanta, which ran about .06 an hour behind the national average.

As can be seen, the photo engraver was the highest paid position on the production side of the newspaper. Few newsroom personnel were paid by the hour, but the 1955-56 average would have been about $2.40 an hour for reporters and copy desk personnel, based on a 40-hour week, although most news personnel worked more than 40 hours without additional pay.

Hardy, a weekly editor, who had grown up in the newspaper business and the hot-type process, was the first publisher in Georgia to try and do something about the cost and inconvenience of hot type production.

He seemed an unlikely candidate for that distinction, having been bred and schooled in traditional methods. He was born into a newspaper family, the son of Albert Sidney Hardy Sr., who was an editor and publisher for 50 years and served as president of the Georgia Press Association in 1909 and 1910. Charles' brother, Albert Hardy Jr., who was then publisher of *The Commerce News*, served as GPA president in 1949-50.

The elder Hardy bought *The Gainesville News* in 1897 and was its publisher for more than half a century. In addition to being GPA president, he was also the first Georgian to be elected president of the National Editorial Association (1943) which later became the National Newspaper Association. It was during Hardy's term as president that the NEA established an advertising department to solicit advertising for its members throughout the nation.

When Charles took over *The News* from his father he was well steeped in traditional journalism and the ways of weekly newspapers. He graduated from the Henry Grady School of Journalism at Georgia in 1930 and worked for two years at *The Griffin Daily News* under Quimby Melton Sr. In 1932 he returned to Gainesville to assist his father on *The Gainesville News*, with the idea of eventually converting *The News* into a daily newspaper. Hall County, in the 1930 census, had reached 30,313 in population, making it the tenth most populous county in the state. But unlike several Georgia counties of less population, it did not have a daily newspaper.

The Hardys' plan for a daily was stymied by many factors, among them being the Great Depression, when mere survival was difficult. Then came World War II and the shortage of newsprint and other materials, which prevented expansion.

Shortly after the war ended, the competing *Gainesville Eagle* was sold to a local radio station owner, Charles Smithgall, who immediately changed it into a daily (See Chapter VII) thus getting a jump on the Hardys.

By 1954, the competition of a daily in the same city and the increasing cost of hot-type composition had convinced Charles Hardy that the survival of *The News* depended on taking a bold, new direction, a direction that not only his fellow Georgia publishers, but publishers throughout the nation, had been reluctant to take.

Hardy wanted to convert to offset printing, and there was only one other newspaper in the country being printed by the offset method at that time, the Opelousas, Louisiana, *Times*.

Hardy, writing some years later, recalled his visit to Opelousas and his impressions of the earliest cold type newspaper operations:

> My brother, J. Milton Hardy; my future editor, Paul Rilling; my production manager, Cedric Heath and I went to Opelousas and studied that newspaper's production for a week. They were using a dual composition method by having a linotype machine set some of the type, then pulling proofs for paste-up, and secondly, they were using a newly-developed Just-O-Writer for the rest of the straight matter composition. The Just-O-Writer punched a perforated tape which was then run through a reproducer which justified the lines to the desired column width.
>
> For headlines and ad type, they had a Headliner machine which anyone could operate by turning a dial to the letter wanted and punching a button to make an impression on photographic tape. The size and type letter was determined by the type disc placed in the machine.
>
> After all the headlines, display advertising and body type were trimmed to the desired width and length with scissors, they were pasted onto a sheet of paper the size of a newspaper page, with blue lines for column rules. The blue lines, and other marks in blue pencil, did not photograph. The composition and paste-up was a simple, speedy operation not requiring any elaborate skills or costly salaries. The only special skill personnel were the camera man who photographed the finished, pasted-up pages and developed the plates, and the pressman.
>
> The Opelousas process was perfect for the kind of pictorial newspaper which we were planning, eliminating the high cost of photo engraving, since photos could be taken and the negative or a copy used right on the pasted-up page instead of having to have a cut or engraving made.
>
> In 1954, as far as we could determine, there were only two web-fed offset presses on the market, a Webendorfer marketed by American Type Founders, and another one which was only

one plate wide with pages being aligned by means of a strobe light. While in New York seeking a suitable press I learned of a new composing system being developed in Boston by a brother of Winston Garth, the superintendent of Gainesville Cotton Mill. The brother, Bill, was working with the American Newspaper Publishers Association in developing a photographic composer which could produce all sizes of type needed in newspaper production. I signed a contract to buy the 13th machine, with delivery scheduled within a year.

While I was in Boston, Mr. Garth told me of a Hess and Barker Press Manufacturing company, in Philadelphia, Pennsylvania, which had built an offset press that the American Newspaper Publishers Association was experimenting with in Easton, Pennsylvania. The Hess and Barker two-unit press proved to be what we were looking for. It could produce eight full size pages, or 16 tabloid, at a speed of up to 25,000 per hour. Additional units could be added as needed. It proved to be a good press, and Mr. Barker and his son were most cooperative.

Thus the wheels were in motion for Georgia's first offset, cold-type newspaper. At the same time, Hardy and his associates were planning to convert a long-time weekly newspaper into a daily which would be in competition with another daily in the same city. Gainesville, in 1955, was still a relatively small city, with about 15,000 population, but Hall County had grown to more than 40,000 and was the trade center for Northeast Georgia.

It took almost a year to get the equipment in place and the plans completed for the hot-type, letter-press weekly *Gainesville News* to become the cold-type, offset daily *Gainesville Morning News*.

"We made *The Gainesville News* a morning newspaper in order to be first with most of the news which broke in the afternoon and at night," Hardy explained. "Also at that time statistics showed that morning newspapers had a wider trade area and more of a chance at rural subscribers. And, of course, we thought it would be best not to butt heads with the established afternoon paper. We knew it would be difficult for two afternoon papers to exist in Gainesville."

Since the press capacity was limited, it was decided to start *The Morning News* as a tabloid-size newspaper so that more pages could be run each day, giving an impression of a larger newspaper.

The Gainesville Morning News published its first daily edition on November 22, 1955, becoming the first offset newspaper in Georgia and only the third in the United States, being preceded by one day by the Middletown, New York, *Herald*. Later in the same week, a new daily was started in Albertville, Alabama, using equipment similar to that at the Gainesville operation.

In addition to Hardy, the publisher, the department heads included Paul Rilling, editor; Ted Lippman, news editor; Johnny Vardeman, sports editor; Mrs. Walter Stancil, woman's editor; Bill Reed, state editor; Arne Nielson, advertising manager; Reggie Mitchell, advertising sales; Hollis Cooper, circulation manager; Cedric Heath, production manager, and James Addington, head pressman.

In his column for the first issue of *The Morning News*, Hardy wrote:

> As far as we can determine right now there is nothing we cannot do with this photographic method of production . . . . We all have a lot to learn about the new machines, the new process of paste-up, plate making and printing with the offset press. We will try many things, some will be good and some bad, but we can be given credit for the will to try and we will eventually settle down to a new type daily newspaper especially adapted and suited to this section of North Georgia . . . .
>
> "I have dreamed and planned a daily newspaper in Gainesville for some 23 years and now this is the first issue . . . . a dream come true. The reason I am able to specifically state 23 years is because 23 years ago I returned to Gainesville after working two years on *The Griffin Daily News*, a paper edited at that time by the most capable newspaperman I have ever known, Quimby Melton, Sr. I was fresh out of college and Mr. Melton hired me at the handsome salary of $35 a week which was tops in those days. When I think back, it is astonishing how little I knew about the newspaper business although I am the son of a newspaper man. But it did not take Mr. Melton long to straighten me out, and his sound advice has been of benefit ever since. I came back to Gainesville in 1932 to assist with the weekly *News* but always keeping in mind that someday I would make a daily newspaper of it . . . ."

Hardy hoped that more and better local photos would give *The*

Morning News an advantage over its afternoon competitor. "We supplied every editorial employee with a camera and used as many pictures as possible," he recalled. "The 100, 115 and 133 line screens we used in our halftones provided magazine-like clarity and won wide praise from everyone who saw them."

But like other cold type pioneers, Hardy and his associates were too far in front of the tide, and the established competition had too many advantages.

The Morning News lasted for just over eight months, with the final edition printed on July 31, 1956. Hardy blamed its demise on "inadequate financing," writing that it would take another "$50,000 to $100,000 to make this paper go."

In his final column, Hardy proved a prophet of remarkable accuracy. "This pioneering in a new field of printing," he wrote, "has been most fascinating and it holds tremendous potentialities two to five years from now. [He was right on the button, since 1960 — five years later — offset really began taking off.] I am still of the opinion that most weekly and small daily newspapers under 25,000 circulation will be published by this method 15 to 25 years from now [right again, but too cautious since many larger dailies were also offset 25 years later]. The only thing holding it back is the lack of research within the industry or a combination of research by manufacturers of offset equipment and supplies. I am firmly convinced that some day newspapers will be printed on offset presses using paper plates that cost only a few cents apiece [that still hasn't come about] and that all composition matter in a newspaper will be on film that will be pasted in place and then transferred to a paper plate."

Editor Paul Rilling wrote in that final edition: "We have proven we believe, along with a handful of other papers, that the offset process is practical. It is less expensive and it provides new horizons for picture coverage and flexibility of operation. As it becomes perfected technically it will prove the answer for more and more small newspapers throughout the nation.

"We have attempted to emphasize the average citizen of the area. We have featured pictures of his churches, his club activities, his children in class and group projects . . . ."

That was the exact formula many small dailies and weeklies were to use in the following 30 years, a formula not common then because photos were so costly to produce in a newspaper.

Years later, Hardy wrote:

> Although I deeply regretted that *The Morning News* was not a financial success, I am delighted that the offset method of newspaper production opened the eyes and minds of the newspaper business and dealt a death blow to the slow, cumbersome 'hot metal' method which for years had done nothing to improve and speed up production methods.
>
> Until 1955 the weekly and small newspaper publishers were at the mercy of used printing machinery dealers. Few small newspapers could afford the high prices of new composing machines, presses and plate-making equipment, and as a result they were equipped with used and rebuilt machines which were usually unreliable. Printing equipment manufacturers geared their sales to the big dailies, and the smaller papers survived on hand-me-downs.
>
> Although *The Gainesville News* was only in production a short time, it proved that the cold type method of newspaper production was faster, cleaner, cheaper, more versatile and feasible. *The News* was 10 to 15 years ahead of its time, but the eventual dominance of cold type production could be seen in the 1950s.

Hardy was a far-sighted pioneer who recognized the advantages to which the new methods of composition and printing could be put. Five more years passed after he launched *The Morning News* before cold type and offset really gained a foothold in Georgia newspaper production, and almost 10 years passed before other newspapers used the process to its fullest potential by running more photos and providing more imaginative ad layouts.

Unfortunately Hardy's own newspaper career was virtually over at the age of 47. He sold his offset press to Louisiana State University where it was used to produce the student newspaper for a number of years. He then continued to operate a commercial printing shop in Gainesville for many years, and in the 1960s was involved briefly in the ownership of *The Gainesville Tribune*, a weekly launched in 1959 (See Chapter VII).

His son, Charles Jr. (Buzzy), has carried on the family newspaper tradition. Hardy Jr., was a young carrier for his father's fledgling cold-type effort in 1955-56. In 1962 he went to work on *The Commerce News*, while he was a junior at the University of Georgia. He succeeded his uncle, Albert, as publisher of *The News* in 1968 and became the sole owner in 1978.

The First Offset Weeklies

By virtue of being owned and printed by *The Gainesville News* when *The News* converted to offset, *The Northeast Georgian* of Cornelia was the first Georgia weekly to be set in cold type and printed on an offset press.

When *The News* folded in July 1956, the *Georgian* continued to be printed in *The News'* commercial shop for several months, and the ownership passed to several Cornelia businessmen interested in keeping the newspaper alive.

But by the summer of 1957 the future looked as bleak for Georgia's first offset weekly as it had been for the first offset daily. Publication of *The Georgian* was suspended for about three months while the owners looked for a professional newspaperman who would come in and revive it.

The man who came was a logical choice. Robert A. Yates, a native of Missouri, had worked on *The Northeast Georgian* from 1938 to 1948, filling every job on the paper at one time or another. It had been owned during that period by S. C. Heindel, whose main interest was job printing. Yates, who came to Cornelia after seeing a classified ad for a newspaper apprentice on *The Georgian*, married a Cornelia girl, Inez Hardy (no kin to the newspaper Hardys of Gainesville). The Yateses left when he was unable to make a deal with Heindel to buy *The Georgian* in 1948. Heindel later sold it to Charles Hardy Sr., but the opportunity came again for Yates in 1957.

By this time Yates was a linotype operator on the Wichita, Kansas, *Eagle*, after working on a number of newspapers in both the news and production departments in Missouri, Texas and Kansas. A relative of Mrs. Yates wrote them about *The Georgian's* suspension and suggested they get in touch with the owners. So nearly 10 years after leaving, and 20 years after first arriving in Cornelia, Robert Yates returned and took over ownership and management of *The Northeast Georgian*.

For about 13 weeks he continued to compose on cold type equipment, and had the newspaper printed on an offset press in an Easley, South Carolina, print shop. He recalls that in 1957 there just weren't enough of the devices which were developed later to simplify cold type composition and makeup.

"There were no waxing machines, for instance," Yates said. "Everything had to be put down with rubber cement, and once it was down you didn't move it. There was no tape for borders and rules. The only machines for setting headlines and ad type were extremely slow. I had been in hot type all my life, of course, and so I bought an old linotype machine for about $2,000, got a sheet-fed letter press and went back to hot-type, letterpress production."

The Georgian continued to print by the old method until 1968 when Yates changed again to cold type, installing a one-unit web offset press. It was the first web offset press in North Georgia since Hardy's attempt at offset newspaper printing 13 years earlier.

Yates built a new building the year he changed to offset and became the printer for several weekly newspapers in the area. In 1974 he sold *The Georgian* to Jerue Babb's Community Newspapers, which also include *The White County News*, Cleveland; *The Dahlonega Nugget*, Dahlonega; *The Tri-County Advertiser*, Clarkesville; and *The Clayton Tribune*. (See Chapter IX.)

Yates retired from the newspaper business in 1981 and his son-in-law, Bobby E. Williams, and daughter, Mary Ellyn Williams, took over management of *The Georgian* and its related publications. Yates was honored for his 50 years as a journalist at the 1983 Georgia Press Institute.

"I was lucky that I could make the switch from hot to cold type," Yates says. "A lot of printers in my generation never adjusted." Despite the many advantages of cold type, Yates says that there are considerably fewer job opportunities in printing today for young men who once could look to printing as a lucrative field.

"I also still get upset by the peculiar hyphenation you see in computer composition today," he said. "And, of course, the spacing of letters, lines and headlines is not as precise as it was in hot type."

In writing of Georgia's cold type pioneers, the emphasis has been placed on established, paid-circulation newspapers. *The Gainesville Morning News* descended from a long-established and respected weekly, and *The Northeast Georgian* had been published since 1892.

But there were other cold-type, offset publications in Georgia, including free-circulation newspapers and some early-day shoppers. One such publication was *LaGrange Life*, a weekly "picture newspaper" printed on thicker, glossy newsprint, which was published briefly in the late 1940s in LaGrange. It used magazine techniques and probably experienced some magazine-like costs. It soon vanished into that large graveyard of aspiring newspapers whose founders thought that a brighter print, more pictures and color would be enough to lure readers away from their established reading habits.

The first Georgia newspaper to use cold type and an offset press which is still being published and has used the process continuously since installing it is *The Darien News* of Darien, down in McIntosh County on the coast between Savannah and Brunswick.

Darien is one of Georgia's oldest communities, having been established in 1736 by some of the settlers who came over with James Oglethorpe three years earlier.

But *The Darien News* is a relatively young newspaper. It was started in June 1951 by W. P. Lunceford, who was 70 years old at the time. He had spent most of his life as an educator and was a former superintendent of schools for McIntosh County. At the time Darien and McIntosh were without a home-based newspaper, although a number of newspapers had started and stopped during the previous 100 years. With a 1950 population of just over 6,000, McIntosh was not particularly small as Georgia counties go, but it was one of the only ones without its own newspaper.

The other Georgia counties in the early 1950s which did not have a home-based, paid-circulation newspaper were Baker, Chattahoochee, Echols, Quitman and Webster. GPA records indicate that Baker, Echols and Quitman have not had a home-county newspaper since World War II, and probably longer. Chattahoochee had a small weekly for a few years in the 1970s, and Webster shares the name of *The Stewart-Webster Journal*, which is based in Stewart County. (See Chapter IX.)

Lunceford gave Darien and McIntosh a newspaper again, and in December 1953 he sold it to Charles and Maude Williamson. The sale included no equipment, since *The News* was composed and printed entirely at a plant in Jesup.

Charles and Maude were coming back to their hometown to operate the newspaper. They were both graduates of Darien High, Class of 1943. Charles went on to the University of Georgia after serving in World War II and was one of Dean John Drewry's student assistants until his graduation in 1950. He went to work for Sanders Camp at *The Walton Tribune* and learned something about both hot and cold type in the shop which the Camps had in Monroe.

Charles then returned to the Georgia east coast to work for Union Camp. He kept his job with Union Camp for several years after acquiring *The Darien News*, which had a circulation of less than 500 and a doubtful future.

But in January 1957, the Williamsons took the step which put them in a stronger financial position as publishers and printers and also made *The Darien News* the second offset weekly in Georgia and the first one that has continued to be printed offset without interruption.

Williamson discovered that he could get equipment for a cold-type operation much cheaper than he could for hot type, and since he was starting from nothing he decided that would be the way to go. The way at that time was difficult for a small operator. The press he bought was a Long-Drum Multi-Lith, sheet fed, with a 16 x 21 printing image, which meant he could only run two tabloid pages at a time. A 10-page tabloid required five separate runs, with folding and inserting.

In addition Williamson decided to use regular newsprint although only slick-finish, thicker stock was then recommended for that type of press. But the newsprint worked, he found, and so McIntosh County got an offset newspaper, composed by cold type.

The type was set on IBM executive typewriters which justified the type into columns, but the printed result still looked like typewriter copy. Headlines were composed by taking letters off sticks of impressions, one at a time, and gluing them to the page.

The Williamsons soon improved their equipment, obtaining a comp-set varityper, and also expanded their job printing operations.

About 14 years later another dramatic change came for *The Darien News*. On the Sunday morning of November 14, 1971, at 3:45, a rare five-alarm fire occurred in Darien — and the fire was at *The Darien News* building. It raged out of control and totally destroyed the building, the equipment and all of the newspaper's files.

The exact cause of the fire was never determined, but the fire marshall said there was evidence of arson. Williamson understood why arson was a possibility. Although *The News* could not be described as a crusading newspaper it had dutifully reported on the criminal activity which was then prevalent along U.S. 17, the main highway from the northern United States into Florida during those years.

"There were slot machines, clip joints and prostitution in McIntosh County in the 50s and 60s," Williamson says, "and we always tried to be diligent in reporting news of arrests and closings of certain establishments. Just a few weeks before the fire we reported in a lead story that three establishments had lost their liquor licenses because of sales on Sunday. Just putting their names in the paper made a lot of those folks mad. They thought we shouldn't even print anything about what was going on." The citizens of Darien offered a reward for information on the fire and its cause, but no one was ever arrested.

In any case, Williamson faced an uncertain future on that Sunday morning, without equipment, without a building, without his files, and without much insurance. He recalls that he got a call on Monday from Elliott Brack, then the publisher of *The Wayne County Press* in Jesup, who told him to bring his news and ads down to his plant and he'd help get the newspaper out for him.

"We had it printed at the Piggly Wiggly plant in Vidalia for several months after," Williamson said, "while we bought new equipment and built a new building." He went back to his first employer, Sanders Camp, and purchased a Heidelberg press as the centerpiece of the new plant. In March 1972, only four months after the fire, *The Darien News* was operating in its own plant again, and within five years, Williamson had paid off all the debts incurred from the fire and the rebuilding.

The Darien News has been and remains a family enterprise. At the time of the fire Charles M. Williamson III was 14 years old and already an apprentice at the shop. "I was 45," the elder Williamson recalls, "and I wasn't sure I wanted to try and rebuild at that age, so I asked my son if he would like to have *The News* and printing business some day. He said he would but asked that Mrs. Williamson and I stay on until we are 65. So we went ahead and rebuilt."

In 1983 *The Darien News* masthead listed Charles M. Williamson Jr., as editor and publisher; Mrs. Charles M. Williamson Jr., as managing editor; Charles M. Williamson III as associate editor; and Kathleen Williamson (their daughter) as associate editor.

Because of its many years as a tabloid, *The News* still presents a tabloid appearance on its front page, but the paper then opens up into a broadsheet for the rest of its pages.

Cedartown and West Point

After Darien got into cold type in its small way in January 1957, nearly a year-and-a-half passed before the next step was taken toward full conversion of a newspaper to cold type and offset in Georgia. This time the newspaper was more established than a brand new daily, such as *The Gainesville News*, nor was it a struggling small weekly such as *The Northeast Georgian* and *Darien News*.

But it would be fair to say that *The Cedartown Standard* was definitely a struggling daily, and indeed would be a semi-weekly before many years passed.

Cedartown had less than 10,000 population in the 1950s, and Polk County had less than 30,000 with the population divided between Cedartown and Rockmart, which had a strong weekly newspaper.

A few years earlier *The Standard* was the first newspaper to be bought by Carmage Walls when he went out on his own from General Newspapers. Walls was intrigued by the possibilities which cold type and offset held for the growing number of small dailies and various-sized weekly newspapers which he and his companies were obtaining at a rapid rate. Walls is perhaps the most outstanding example of entrepreneurship in the American newspaper business, although his name is little-known among many working newspaper people. He once said he had made millionaires of 24 people, but that figure is probably low. For certain, he made it possible for more newspaper employees to own newspapers than did anyone else in the United States.

It was appropriate that Walls would be the inspiration and innovator who would bring the first full offset, cold-type operation to Georgia because he was always looking for better ways to achieve economy and expansion.

In the early autumn of 1958 a web offset press was installed at Cedartown. It was a Vanguard, later to be known as Cottrell and Harris, driven by chains. It was only Vanguard's thirteenth press to be specifically designed for newspapers. It had no blankets as such, and its cylinders were solid metal. At the time, Goss and Fairchild King had yet to produce their first web offset press.

Cedartown also got the justowriters, varityper headliners and other cold type paraphernalia then available. It was Walls' testing ground for the new printing processes, and he sent two of his favorite young proteges, Jim Boone and Ben Smith, to Cedartown to learn all they could about how to produce newspapers without metal type and ink in the composing room and without the heavy lead plates in the press room.

Walls owned another daily newspaper in Georgia, *The Valley Times-News* at West Point, and his second cold type operation was installed there in the spring of 1959, a few months after Cedartown's conversion. There was a significant difference at West Point, however, in that only the composing room was converted to cold type. The printing of the newspaper continued to be done on a letterpress. The pasted-up cold type page was photographed, and the negative was used to make a lead plate instead of the thin zinc plate used on offset presses.

As employees on *The Valley Times-News* were wont to say, "We had the worst of both systems." At the time, cold type composition was still uncertain and often unpretty, and the continued use of a letterpress deprived

The Times-News of the sharper, brighter reproduction of photographs which offset allows.

In fact, the first few weeks after the conversion in West Point were an unparalleled disaster. *The Times-News* had been a five-day daily for only eight years. It was formed from three weeklies in 1950, and it served a unique market, which actually was more compatible for three weeklies than one daily.

West Point, of course, is hard on the western border of Georgia. The Chattahoochee River, which forms the Georgia-Alabama border to that point, actually cuts through the downtown area of West Point, with part of the town being on the west side of the river, including the part where *The Times-News* plant was then located. But the Alabama line is a couple of blocks west of the river, where West Point and Lanett, Alabama join in one of those state border situations that produce such odd arrangements as a church in which the pulpit is in Alabama and the pews are in Georgia.

The "Valley," which was the community served by *The Times-News*, was comprised of two incorporated cities — West Point, Georgia, and Lanett, Alabama — and five unincorporated communities, which adjoined each other in Alabama.

The news staff was small, of course, consisting usually of no more than three full-time employees plus some county correspondents, and yet the staff had to try and cover governmental, police, social and sports activity in two states, eight towns (counting nearby LaFayette, Alabama) and three counties, Chambers in Alabama and Troup and Harris in Georgia. West Point, in addition to its other peculiarities, had one residential area which protruded from Troup County into neighboring Harris County.

A phone call to any of the three county seats (LaGrange, LaFayette and Hamilton) was long distance, but that was the only method of getting news of the sheriff's activities and other county business. The immediate Valley area contained three high schools, all very intent on maximum coverage and jealous of any excess words or photos about the other two.

The Valley's only industry of consequence was the West Point Manufacturing Company, one of the largest textile operations in the nation, and textiles were in a slump during the late 1950s.

Walls bought *The Times-News* from J. C. Henderson of Alexander City, Alabama, in late 1955 and brought in Davis Haines as publisher. Haines was a youthful, urbane New Yorker, well-connected in Charles Marsh's old General Newspaper group which had nurtured Walls and given him his start toward being the man who probably owned all or part of more newspapers than anyone else in the United States.

Haines had to supervise the installation of the cold type operation in the winter and early spring of 1959, on top of the various other handicaps under which *The Valley Times-News* operated. Justowriters were still fragile machines almost four years after Charles Hardy had used them in Gainesville, and their "down" time rivaled that of linotype machines. They produced type much faster than linotypes, but the type was not as readable, well-spaced or eye-appealing, something which many readers noticed.

Much worse, however, was the result obtained from using cold-type pages, with stripped-in veloxes, on a letter-press. For the first few weeks the pictures and many ads came out black or very dark in the final printed product. The pictures gradually improved, but they continued to have a grey overtone, reminiscent of old scan-o-graver photos, and they were more of a detriment than an asset, even though the process made it possible to use many more local pictures.

The ragged type, crooked headlines and ad type were also detriments, and in the first six weeks of the cold type operation *The Times-News* lost 20 percent of its paid circulation.

Walls visited the plant during this time to find out how the experiment was going. He got little encouragement. Haines and most of his staff frankly doubted that cold type was there to stay. In a memo to Walls, Haines wrote that it was a good process for composing advertisements but he felt it was not practical for body type.

At that time, as noted earlier, cold type compositors were still without such conveniences as a waxer or competent headline machines. Rubber cement on brushes was used to affix items to a page, and copy was very difficult to get straight or move once put down.

But on a day-to-day basis the worst problem was the unreliable justowriters. *The Times-News* had three of them to compose all of its local, wire and advertising body type. The breakdown of just one of them made it difficult to meet deadlines. But on several occasions all three would go down, which was when the news staff discovered the real value of cold type. The editor would clip AP stories from the out-of-town morning newspapers (which *The Times-News* had authority to run) and glue them on pages to fill up when he couldn't get enough type set. Surprisingly the stories clipped from other papers often came out better on the final page than the justowriter type.

Circulation began to increase, and by autumn *The Times-News'* appearance had improved, although it was still printed on the letterpress, as it would be for two more years until the installation of a three-unit Goss in the fall of 1961.

The Valley Times-News had about 4,800 subscribers when it changed to cold type, and the number fell below 4,000 during the spring of 1959, when the pictures (and some ads) were black and the type was hard to read. "What saved us from worse losses were our young carrier boys who begged their customers to stay on for awhile," Haines said. "A lot of the subscribers stayed with us to help the carriers even though they couldn't read the paper."

The emerging pattern of cold type employment was evident early in *The Times-News'* experience. As a relatively small daily, it did not have a large composing room staff in its hot-type days, but changes were still made as several young women, mostly typists, were hired to operate the justowriters, displacing the former linotype operators. The men from the old composing room still did some page makeup, but mainly they moved into the camera room and plate-making, and a couple of them started learning to be pressmen.

This was to be an important result of the changes wrought by cold type and offset. The new technology did not fit the old employees, and that was a major reason why changes came slowly in the newspaper business even after the new technology proved itself. Men whose fingers were adroit and whose strength was helpful for putting pieces of metal into place for an advertisement or a page often were clumsy and ill-at-ease working with scissors and razors, cutting out "paper dolls," as some termed it, or handling flimsy, elusive slivers of paper rather than the firm slugs of type, that went in straight and did not need a delicate touch to assure even lines.

Many who had been printers for 20 and 30 years suddenly faced the challenge of learning the difficult new trade of cameraman or pressman, for in the world of cold type and offset those were the male jobs, at least on medium and small newspapers.

Women moved in to take over the typesetting, the makeup of ads and pages, and in many cases newsroom personnel assumed a large part of these duties which previously had been performed only by production employees.

In the fall of 1961 a three-unit Goss web offset press was installed at West Point, completing the conversion begun almost three years earlier by adding the important ingredient of offset printing to cold type composition.

Photos, of course, became much clearer on *The Times-News*, although the justowriter type faces remained a drawback to readership for virtually the entire decade of the 1960s.

Meanwhile at Walls' other Georgia cold type operation in Cedartown, a different direction had been taken. Cedartown, as noted, had an offset press in 1958 when it switched to cold type, so it avoided many of the problems suffered by its sister newspaper 100 miles south.

Cedartown had other problems, however. It was at best a marginal daily operation, never having more than 4,000 paid subscribers, faced with a weekly competitor for several years in the 1950s, and then in the early 1960s having to deal with a market in the throes of a serious economic depression due to the shutdown of a mill.

With the most advanced cold type operation on a Georgia newspaper at the time and one of the best early web presses, Cedartown's management felt compelled to move more and more into commercial printing in an effort to support its lagging newspaper revenues.

In August 1961 *The Cedartown Standard* dropped from five times a week publication to twice a week. Wallace L. White, who had been the publisher of *The Standard*, became president of Southern Publications, which was the printing company, and William L. Wadkins became publisher of *The Standard*.

White, along with Walls and Syd Gould, who was the Walls Company management advisor for the Cedartown operation, felt that a better press was needed to handle the volume of commercial work that was available. The big press companies were finally making web offset presses for newspapers, and Goss, a long time leader in letterpress, had come out with its first offset newspaper press.

Walls ordered a four-unit Goss for Cedartown with a folder in the middle of the unit so that two separate 8-page sections could be printed. The press was installed and went into operation in December 1961. Its speed was 12,000 an hour (with luck, according to pressmen of that period). Compared to the former press at Cedartown and to other presses which had been or were then used in newspaper production in Georgia, it was the fastest and most advanced.

The Standard carried a special section on December 20, 1961, announcing the new press, with photos of all the employees and an explanation of what their function was in the cold type and offset operation.

Both White, president of Southern Publications, and Wadkins, publisher of *The Standard*, had come to Cedartown from Paragould, Arkansas. White had been editor and general manager of the daily newspaper in Paragould when the Walls group purchased it. He came to Cedartown in

1958 to be publisher and oversee the conversion to offset.

Wadkins, a native of Mississippi, had worked for White in Paragould and then joined him in Cedartown in 1959. Wadkins, only 30 when he became publisher of *The Standard*, has continued to work on Georgia newspapers, moving to Cartersville in 1965 as assistant to the publisher of *The Cartersville Tribune-News;* then to Jonesboro in 1969 where he was associate publisher and then publisher of *Clayton News/Daily*.

Others on that 1961 Cedartown staff who went on to distinguished careers included Ben Smith, listed as the assistant manager and superintendent of composition, who became publisher of the Fort Payne, Alabama, newspaper and then formed his own group of newspapers in the 1970s; Shelton Prince, a young press apprentice who would become head of Southern Publications while still in his 20s, a prominent Alabama publisher (*Jasper Mountain Eagle, Selma Times-Journal*), and president of the Alabama Press Association (1980); Grady Bynum, an engraver from Columbus, who pioneered many camera procedures for offset; and Cecil Dill, who would be the head pressman on *The Athens Daily News* in 1965-67, and has been press foreman at the Galveston, Texas, newspapers for many years.

The amount of commercial (or job) work being done at Cedartown can be gauged by the number of personnel in the press-camera and composing rooms. There were 15 full or part-time men in the press-camera room and 14 women in composition. Many dailies the size of *The Cedartown Standard* had only two or three employees in press and camera and five in composition after converting to offset.

But Cedartown had become one of the largest printing operations in the state of Georgia. Pre-prints, or inserts, were not nearly as numerous then. They were usually called "circulars" and often consisted of no more than one sheet. But the advent of web offset presses, with their more attractive use of color, illustrative matter and larger number of pages, greatly accelerated the number of advertising pre-prints.

Cedartown's Southern Publications was the first of the big web-offset printers in Georgia, and it handled millions of pre-prints for Sears, Big Apple and other national advertisers, keeping the press running virtually around the clock at its 10-12,000 pace. Soon a fifth unit and a second folder were added, providing 20 full-page capacity, or 40 tab pages.

In the meantime Walls had become involved in the largest newspaper transaction of his career. As a rule, Walls and his associates preferred to buy small and medium-sized newspapers. But in 1963 Walls had the opportunity to acquire the Montgomery, Alabama, *Advertiser-Journal*, which at the time had a total paid circulation of about 90,000 and was considered the state's most influential newspaper.

Walls bought the Montgomery newspapers and became their publisher, moving his headquarters to Montgomery from Guntersville, Alabama. He soon faced the threat of a strike by the pressmen on the Montgomery newspaper, and partly as a precautionary measure he had an offset press installed in a separate building in Montgomery and began doing commercial printing as a subsidiary of Southern Publications in Cedartown.

By 1964, the commercial market was changing in Georgia as more web presses were installed in the Atlanta area. Cedartown was still getting lots of work, but its prices weren't keeping up with costs, and its press was not as fast as the newer ones with which it had to compete.

A decision was thus made to close down the printing operation in Cedartown, move the press to other Walls properties, and do all commercial work at the Montgomery plant. Wally White, Sheldon Prince, and others from Cedartown moved to Montgomery with Southern Publications. White later left and opened a printing company of his own in West Memphis, Arkansas. Prince, who had begun working in the Cedartown plant in his early teens, and had become a production manager before he was 20, eventually became the top man at Southern Publications. In 1970, at the age of 28, he became president and publisher of the Jasper, Alabama, *Mountain Eagle* and later moved to Selma, Alabama, to be publisher of the daily *Times-Journal*.

The press units from Cedartown were scattered among several plants, and *The Cedartown Standard* had to be printed on a new offset press which had been installed at nearby Cartersville.

Bill Wadkins remained in Cedartown as publisher after the printing operation moved, but in 1965 he also left, going to Cartersville as assistant to the publisher.

Doug Pearson succeeded Wadkins as publisher, and some 15 years later Pearson would succeed Prince as publisher in Jasper, Alabama, when Prince moved to Selma.

Cedartown, in its six years as an offset pioneer, was the training ground for several men who went on to own and operate large groups of newspapers (Jim Boone, Ben Smith, Prince), for several publishers and dozens of press and cameramen.

Decade of the Big Switch

In 1960 the Georgia Press Association directory listed only two weeklies and one daily as offset publications. The weeklies were *The Darien News* (discussed earlier) and *The Weekly Tribune News* of Cartersville. Since *The Tribune-News* was not listed as an offset newspaper again until 1964, its 1960 listing was obviously in error, which means the only paid offset weekly that year was Darien. Cedartown was the only daily newspaper listed as offset because *The Valley Times-News* was still printed on a letterpress.

But the big switch was close at hand. Newspaper people on large and small operations were seeing the advantages of cold type. The larger newspapers were making the change from hot to cold type in ad composition, which was where the advantages were most obvious and the results most rewarding, both in flexibility and appearance, and in cost control.

For Georgia weeklies, the change started slowly, with only seven weeklies listed as offset in 1961, four years after Darien became the first. Three of the seven were Atlanta suburban newspapers, *The Weekly Star* of West End; *The Tucker Tribune*; and *The Fayetteville News*. Cedartown, now listed as a weekly, was the largest, and the other three were small South Georgia papers in Darien, Hahira and Kingsland. The *Warner Robins Sun* was also offset at that time, but was not designated as such in the GPA directory.

The first big increase appeared in 1962 when 13 weeklies changed to offset. Then there was a lull in conversions during 1963 (seven changes) and 1964 (five changes). The pivotal year seems to have been 1965 when 18 Georgia weeklies made the switch. By then the pioneers had worked out many of the problems, and equipment makers were catching up, particularly with presses.

Another landmark was reached in 1968 when there were 14 weekly conversions, and for the first time there were more offset weeklies (100 of 188) in Georgia than hot-type, letterpress. The years of 1970 and 1971 saw a total of 43 weeklies make the change: 25 in 1970, the single-year high for conversions, and 18 more in 1971. That brought the total of offset weeklies in the state to 152 of the 186 being published.

By 1977 the total number of weeklies listed in the GPA directory had dropped to 161 due to mergers, changes to non-paid circulations, and a few discontinued publications. The 1977 directory listed 159 of those 161 as offset publications, the only exceptions being *The Sparta Ishmaelite* and *The Omega News*.

The Omega News later ceased publication and *The Ishmaelite* was still using hot type when its linotype operator died in 1978. The small weekly's printing was then moved to Alva Haywood's Warrenton plant, and Haywood later bought *The Ishmaelite*.

It was the last hot-type weekly in Georgia and the last newspaper, weekly or daily, to still be printed entirely by the old process of hot lead and letterpress. (*The Doerun Courier* was still being handset at the time but was not listed in the GPA directory. See Chapter IX.)

Pioneers Without Honor

Thus the conversion of hot to cold type covered a period of about 20 years in Georgia, with most of the conversions taking place in the seven years from 1965 to 1971.

Ironically, none of Georgia's early cold type newspapers, headed by farsighted and progressive publishers who saw the future and reached for it when others were hesitant, were fully successful, nor have those publishers received much credit for trailblazing the path which every newspaper in the state eventually followed.

Charles Hardy Sr., the most innovative of publishers in the 1950s, had to fold his *Gainesville Morning News* after less than nine months of publication. The *Northeast Georgian* of Cornelia was suspended for several months and later reverted to hot type production.

The Darien News, with less than 1,000 subscribers when it changed to cold type, has grown in its relatively small market, but in 1983 its subscribers totaled only 2,600. It averages 10 pages a week.

The Cedartown Standard retrogressed from daily (Monday-Friday) to semi-weekly, then lost its press, and has never again been the printing center it was in the late 1950s and early 1960s.

The Weekly Star of West End, *The Tucker Tribune* and *the Hahira Gold Leaf* are no longer published; *The Fayetteville News* was sold in a bankruptcy sale in 1963; and *The Southeast Georgian* of Kingsland has gone through several ownerships.

While it is true that newspapers in the 1980s are still "cold type" as compared to the "hot type" of a couple of decades ago, the methods by which most of them are composed are as different in the 1980s from the 1960s as the 1960s were from the 1890s. Cold type itself has moved through several stages in the past 30 years.

During the 1950s and 1960s the basic cold type text machine was the

Singer Company's Friden justowriter, a strike-on machine which produced a mediocre type face that was not as pleasing to the eye or as readable as the linotype's letters. None of Georgia's large daily newspapers changed to cold type during the "strike-on" period. Virtually all of the weeklies and smaller dailies which switched went through several years with the justowriters and the "strike-on" method of typesetting. Some papers, notably *The Newnan Times-Herald*, continued to set type on linotype machines and pull proofs for their pages rather than change to the "strike-on" type faces. "Strike-on" meant that the keys directly hit the paper which would be pasted on the page.

Then, in the late 1960s, Compugraphic Corporation introduced a series of machines which revolutionized the way type was set for the cold type process. Instead of "strike-on," a tape could be fed into a photocomposition machine which would imprint type from a film strip onto ectamatic paper.

The first Compugraphic photocomposition machines were the 7200 for headlines and ad copy and the 2900 series for text type. The 2900 would also set lines much faster from tape than the Singer system.

Although other companies were to bring out their own photocomposition equipment, Compugraphic quickly became the dominant provider of cold type machines for medium and small newspapers and for commercial shops. By the middle 1970s, 80 percent of the cold type equipment in non-metropolitan newspaper plants came from Compugraphic. Each year seemed to bring a new breakthrough, as the machines were improved and in many instances actually dropped in price from the previous year.

In 1971 Compugraphic introduced its Compuwriter series which eliminated the need for tape. Compuwriters were direct-input machines which produced columns of type as fast as the operator could type. This eliminated the punching of the tape and the running of the tape through a second machine. The Compuwriter was, in effect, an input and output machine within itself. For small newspapers, the most attractive part of Compugraphic was that its machines were economical and usually easy to repair.

The two men primarily responsible for developing Compugraphic Corporation and its vital role in cold type composition were William Garth, whom Charles Hardy had met in 1954 when looking for cold type ideas in Boston, and Ellis Hanson, an engineer who perfected many of the concepts that improved cold type.

Garth died in 1977 and Hanson has retired. Compugraphic itself hit a slump in its momentum during the late 1970s when its basic market was saturated, and it was slow coming up with a front-end system for the newest "revolution" in typesetting, which was the shift to Video Display Terminals, on which reporters and editors typed their own stories onto discs, thus virtually preempting the compositor's role.

By the early 1970s the justowriter was more extinct than the linotype machine, and strike-on was as obsolete as metal slugs. This sudden turn of events caught one giant company, none other than IBM (International Business Machines), in one of the rare times when it has been too late with too little. About 1968 IBM developed a strike-on system, using the IBM type ball, which was a great improvement in clarity and flexibility over the justowriter and similar machines. For one thing, the IBM system allowed the use of boldface letters, which the justowriter never perfected. It was also faster. A number of newspapers seized on the IBM system as an alternative to the older strike-on methods which had clearly outworn their welcome, not to mention that the machines themselves were just about worn out after a few years of pounding.

IBM's strike-on machines could only be leased, not bought, and the newly-emerging photocomposition machines were much cheaper to buy than IBM's were to rent — or later to buy when that option was offered. One cost advantage that IBM and other strike-on processes did have was that they used regular grade paper, while the photocomposition systems required the much costlier ectomatic paper, or film.

But photocomposition was clearly the wave of the future — at least for five or six years. That's how fast the future was changing in composition systems. The OCR (Optical Character Reader) enjoyed a brief popularity, mainly on larger newspapers. But the video terminals quickly became the most widely used input machines as newspapers entered the 1980s, and they may represent the limits of typesetting efficiency for this decade.

Systems are now being perfected for an entire page to be made up on a video screen by the editor, which does not bode well for today's composition workers.

Of course, many smaller newspapers are still using machines bought in the 1970s and find them adequate for their needs. The main problem they face is continued service and parts for machines that may be five to 10 years old. Compugraphic, in order to strengthen its financial depth, sold its controlling stock to Agfa-Gaevert, a Dutch company, in 1982. Service and parts are no longer guaranteed for the 7200 and 2900 series, nor for most of the Compuwriter machines, which were the three series that gave Compugraphic its dominance in the field a few years ago.

This development is pressuring more and more newspapers to adopt newer systems even while their present ones are satisfactory, and thus the revolution continues. Soon the Compuwriter, introduced in 1971, may be as extinct as the linotype or justowriter.

The old "romance of printing" has been irrevocably changed in the past three decades, and probably none too soon. Metal type and ink and arid smoke have disappeared from composing rooms, to be replaced by wax and film and the odor of chemicals. As it is in motion pictures and television, the camera in various forms has become the most important instrument in the production of a newspaper.

In newspapers below metro size women have replaced men in virtually all composition positions, and the revolution also has made it possible to reduce the number of composing positions significantly. As an example, on one large Georgia daily, the composing room now has 20 positions compared to 80 positions 10 years ago. Yet more pages are being produced now than then.

This chart shows the comparison in typesetting speeds as the different methods have been developed:

Year	**Newspaper Lines Set/Minute**	**Innovation**
1454	1.0	Movable type
1886	4.9	Linotype
1932	5.6	Punch-paper tape driven Linotype
1960	14.0	Computer-hyphenated and justified paper-tape-driving Linotype
1964	80.0	Photocomposition
1978	5,000.0	Photocomposition machines

Plants are cleaner today, of course. The use of photographs and of color has jumped enormously, particularly on smaller dailies and weeklies where local pictures were few and far between before cold type and offset.

As a percentage of operating costs, production has declined dramatically, mainly from the elimination of positions, but also from the lower salaries paid to composition employees in cold type compared to hot type.

However, ectomatic paper, chemicals and other cold type items are more expensive than lead, which was the main material needed in hot type production.

The material that has increased in cost the most for newspapers is the most indispensable one — newsprint. At the beginning of the cold type revolution newsprint cost about $130 a ton. By 1983 the price for a ton was $450, and only a glut on the market has prevented it from soaring well past $500.

If newspapers still had the same percentage of costs for production in the 1980s that they did in the 1950s, plus the tripling of newsprint prices which has occurred, very few — large or small — would have survived.

That may be the most enduring significance of the technological revolution — and the most valuable contribution of the men and women who had the foresight and made the sacrifices to assure its success.

The Switch To Offset in Georgia, Year by Year

YEAR	CHANGED TO OFFSET DURING YEAR	TOTAL NUMBER OFFSET	NUMBER WEEKLY NEWSPAPERS
1960	2	2	192
1961	5	7	194
1962	13	20	198
1963	7	27	197
1964	5	32	196
1965	18	50	189
1966	14	64	189
1967	22	86	189
1968	14	100	186
1969	9	109	184
1970	25	134	185
1971	18	152	186
1972*	11	145	168
1973	6	151	165
1974	6	157	166
1975	2	159	165
1976	1	158	163
1977	0	159	161

*The 1972 directory does not list any of the "Neighbor" newspapers; consequently, the notable decrease in number of weeklies and total circulation from 1971 to 1972 is explained primarily by the absence of these eight weeklies and those other, older suburban newspapers which had merged with them.

Information for this chart was obtained from a study of Georgia Newspaper Directories by Dan Kitchens, a member of the University of Georgia faculty, for his Masters of Arts thesis, "A Profile of Georgia Weekly Newspapers," which was completed in 1981.

Linotypes all in a row; many were needed on larger dailies.

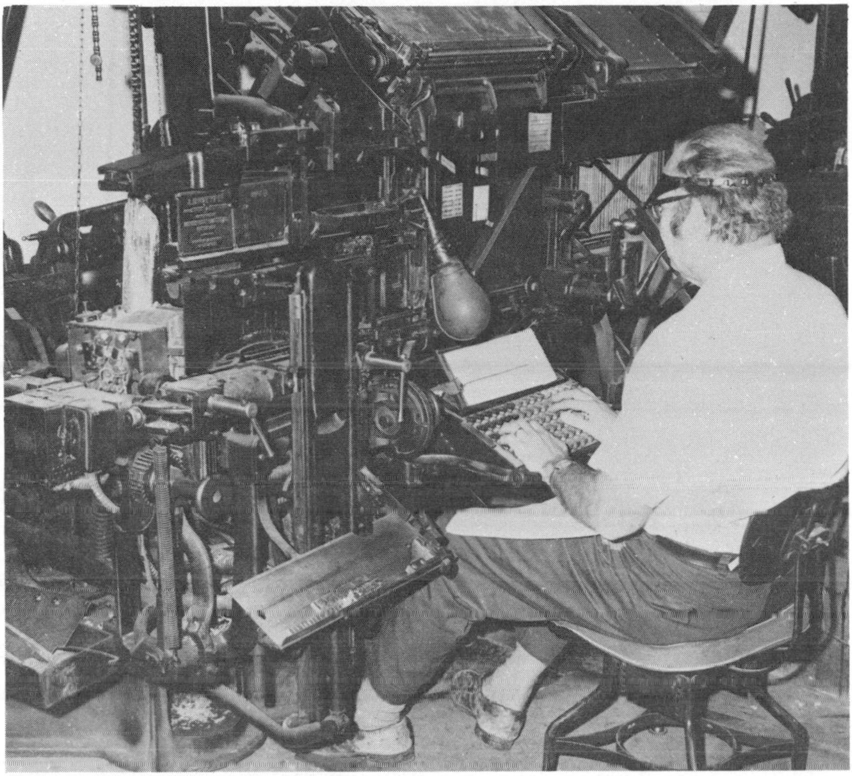

Operator at Linotype machine . . .

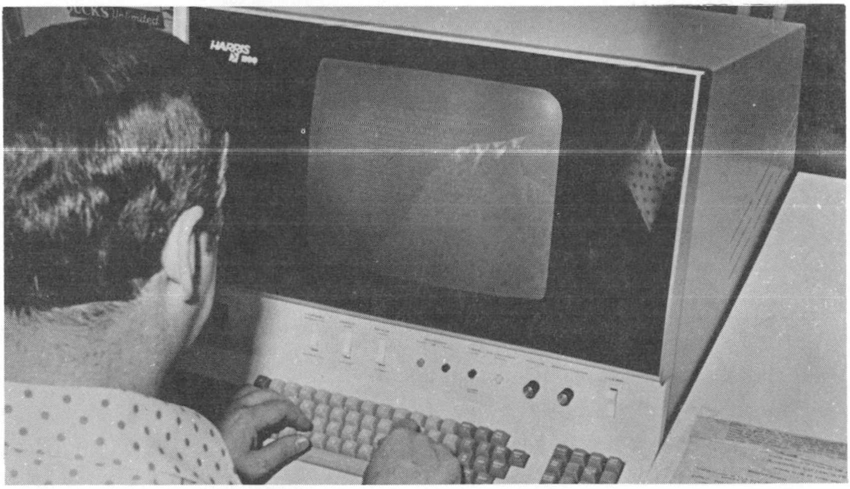

. . . He gets a different view on terminal.

Hands that once locked metal type into place . . .

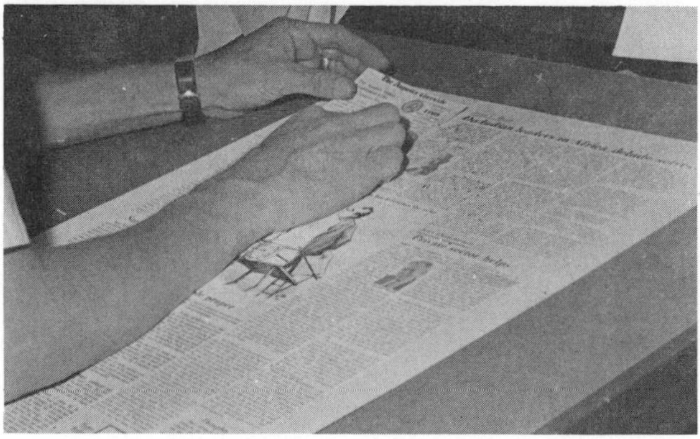

. . . now delicately adjust slivers of paper.

Hands of hot-type printers got a lot dirtier.

Charles Hardy Sr., Georgia's first cold-type newspaper publisher.

Roberts Yates . . . He revived Northeast Georgian *after its early cold type demise.*

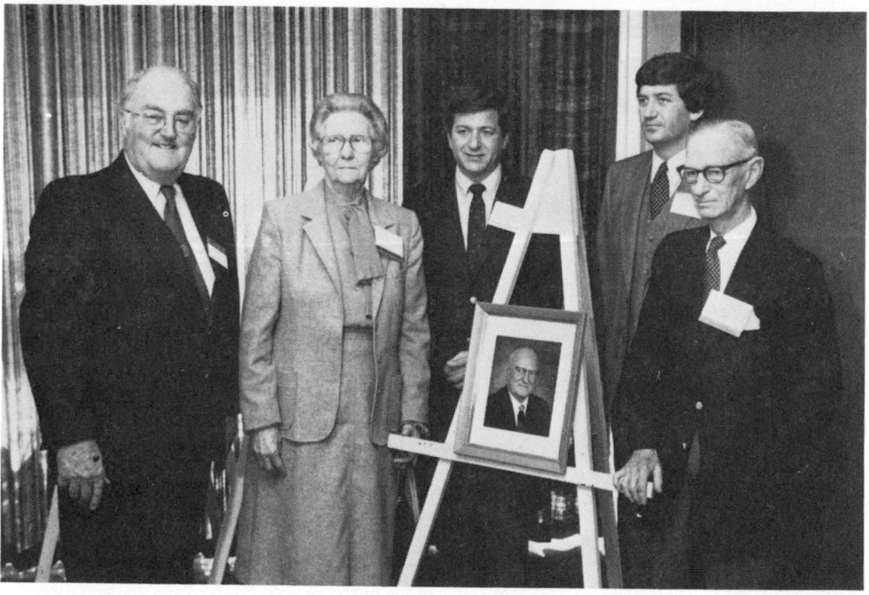

Charles Hardy Sr., at right, on occasion of his father's induction into Georgia Newspaper Hall of Fame in 1982. Portrait is of Albert S. Hardy Sr. L to R, Scott Cutlip, Journalism School dean; Mrs. Charles Hardy; Charles (Buzzy) Hardy Jr.; W.H. (Dink) NeSmith, GPA president.

1971 fire destroyed building and press of Georgia's first offset weekly. Young Charles Williamson and friend view charred machinery.

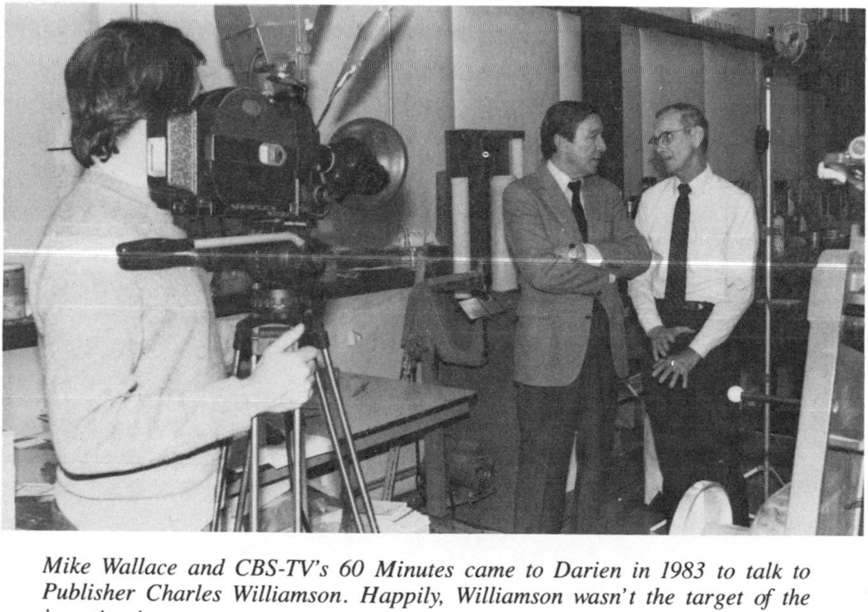

Mike Wallace and CBS-TV's 60 Minutes came to Darien in 1983 to talk to Publisher Charles Williamson. Happily, Williamson wasn't the target of the investigation.

Chapter III

The Heavyweights: Atlanta and Its Newspapers

Prophets Without Honor

Time magazine, in its 1984 decennial listing of the nation's ten best daily newspapers, failed to include either *The Atlanta Constitution* or *The Atlanta Journal*, Georgia's two largest and inescapable newspapers. Not only were they left off the Top 10 list, they were not even included among the newspapers deemed worthy of honorable mention.

Actually the omission says more about *Time*'s selection method than it does about *The Constitution* or *The Journal*, which most Georgians and many southerners know instinctively are the preeminent newspapers of this region. Actually, in years past, *The Constitution* was usually included in the listings of "best newspapers," rising as high as sixth in the rankings during the 1960s. *The Constitution* is obviously a better all-around product in 1984 than it was 20 years ago, and several of the newspapers which have replaced it in the Top 10 haven't really improved all that much, so what happened? Why did *The Constitution* fall from favor?

Well, mainly the newspaper profession is much too award-conscious, although awards are often based on capricious factors. For certain the very human judges who determine awards are swayed as much by their prejudices and enthusiasms as by well-constructed stories or proper attention to reader interests.

Time's selectors were obviously influenced most of all by how many Pulitzer Prizes a newspaper had won, and in that respect the Atlanta newspapers have indeed lagged. But in so many other ways *The Atlanta Journal* and *Constitution* have improved in recent years, even from the very lofty standards they have always set. Georgians who travel around the country and sample the metropolitan newspapers in other cities will soon yearn to get back to the overall competence of the Atlanta newspapers, no matter how much they might complain about them. Actually, the complaints are heard less in 1985 than in the past.

By almost any measure, the Atlanta newspapers are the outstanding conveyors of information, analysis and entertainment south of Washington and east of Chicago. Florida's major dailies, *The Miami Herald* and *St. Petersburg Times* (both on *Time*'s Top 10 list) are provincial by comparison. In sports, business and entertainment coverage, the Atlanta newspapers are clearly superior. Their excellence in sports coverage is a tradition going back many decades. The Sunday magazine has been recognized as a pacesetter among newspaper magazines for 60 years. No other newspaper outside the major media capitals has produced in recent years a columnist with the popularity of a Lewis Grizzard, or the enduring appeal of a Celestine Sibley. None have enjoyed the services for 30 years of two such capable sports columnists as Furman Bisher, long recognized for his brilliance, and Jesse Outlar, whose informative readability may have even more fans than Bisher.

Many other talents have been nurtured or have come to full flower on the Atlanta newspapers, including book and movie reviewers such as Eleanor Ringel and Michelle Ross; TV columnists such as John Carman, and the ultimate man-about-town, Ron Hudspeth.

But the decline of the Atlanta newspapers in national esteem — including their failure to win Pulitzers, which is also political in large measure — is not surprising. It has been fashionable among media critics for some years to belittle the Atlanta dailies. This tendency apparently dates back to the 1960s with the resignation of *Constitution* Editor Eugene Patterson; the departure of Jack Nelson, a Pulitzer Prize reporter, and the death of Ralph McGill, whose reputation as a southern liberal assured *The Constitution* a place among top-rated newspapers.

In *Time* magazine's special edition on the South at the time of Jimmy Carter's election as president, the section on the South's Best Newspapers didn't mention *The Journal* or *Constitution*, foreshadowing their absence from the nation's top newspapers in the 1984 listing.

Ironically, while the Atlanta newspapers have been criticized by most Georgians through the years for being "too liberal," their critics in the newspaper profession and among media analysts condemn them for being too conservative, both in personnel policies, and in news presentation. One such critic charged in 1973 that "the city of Atlanta far outstrips the quality of its two papers. Since the 1960s *The Constitution* and *The Journal* have been getting no better, and certainly worse on the editorial pages, while the city is growing and becoming more important all the time."

Novelist Pat Conroy, author of *The Lords of Discipline*, was quoted in a 1977 article in *Brown's Guide* magazine as saying: "The *Journal-Constitution* has come to represent too much to me: the diminishment of the English language, the debasement of the city of Atlanta. There are no excuses. It is a shame and a crime, and I am sorry that we will live and die under the yoke of such banality."

So, from both left and right, the Atlanta newspapers have gotten an ample share of abuse, their consolation being that they have continued to enjoy a rare dominance in their own state, and are still the best known and read newspapers in the Southeast.

It is true that since the departure of Patterson and the death of McGill they have lacked the standout editorial page performer who is often the catalyst for national recognition. Jim Minter, who in 1985 is editor of both newspapers, has not held that post long enough to gain a national reputation. Reg Murphy, who followed Patterson as editor of *The Constitution*, apparently had the ingredients of a management superstar as he has gone on to be publisher of *The San Francisco Examiner* and later *The Baltimore Sun*. The Atlanta newspapers deserve some credit for his development, as they do for Patterson's.

Hal Gulliver, *Constitution* editor during the Carter administration, probably had the closest ties to Carter of any editor in the nation, which should have given the Atlanta newspapers an advantage during the years when Carter and other Georgians dominated the national news. But it didn't help Gulliver, who left both *The Constitution* and the newspaper business in 1982.

Perhaps the best known editorial columnist on the Atlanta newspapers in 1985 is Bill Shipp, on the staff for 30 years, who is associate editor of *The Constitution*. He is an especially keen observer of the Georgia political scene.

Minter, whose administrative duties limit his writing output, has the touch and toughness to become a powerful editorial voice on the Atlanta papers, but his relatively conservative leanings probably preclude any wide acceptance among critics at the national level.

There have been problems for the Atlanta newspapers, of course, just as there have been problems for all large metropolitan papers in the U.S. They have gotten better in the past few years to some extent because they had to reverse a circulation decline. Like other large cities, Atlanta has lost the middle-class families who were the most reliable subscribers and core of circulation for many years. The suburbs are harder to reach, particularly for an afternoon paper. Television is more of a competitor in the central cities because that's where local TV news coverage is strongest.

The Atlanta Journal and *Constitution* probably reached their peak in paid daily circulation dominance on the Georgia newspaper scene in the middle 1950s, a few years after they both became members of the Cox Newspaper chain.

In 1958 their combined daily circulation was 454,000, with *The Journal* far out front with 257,000, while *The Constitution* had 196,000. Total circulation of all dailies in the state at that time was only 881,000, which meant that the two Atlanta dailies had 52 percent of the total.

Then somewhat ironically, as the percentage of Georgia's total population became increasingly concentrated in the 10 counties immediately around Atlanta, the Atlanta newspapers' percentage of coverage declined. By 1976, the combined total was down to 445,000, as *The Journal* dropped to 235,000, while *The Constitution* was rising slowly to 211,000.

There were a number of reasons for the circulation decline. In the middle and later 1970s, newsprint prices and gasoline prices both almost quadrupled after a long period of relative stability. The cost of these items affect large metropolitan dailies to a far greater extent than smaller dailies or weeklies. A newspaper such as *The Journal,* for instance, was still selling in the early 1970s for 10 cents even though it might have had 100 pages, while a small daily or weekly with 10 pages also sold for 10 cents. That meant 90 sheets of additional newsprint and when prices dramatically jumped newspapers finally had to begin pushing up their own prices, both for single copy sales and home delivery.

At the same time the accelerating fuel prices caused *The Journal,* in particular, to pull back from the further reaches of the state, and from areas of neighboring states where *The Journal* had for many years been available by both carrier and single copy sale.

The pre-date *Journal,* which was actually the previous day's paper with a current dateline, was discontinued. It had been *The Journal*'s way of reaching the rural areas of South and Middle Georgia, and thousands of Georgians had accepted a day-old paper in order to get *The Journal.*

By 1982-83, the combined circulation of *The Journal* and *Constitution* was down to 392,000, and *The Constitution* had passed *The Journal* in circulation for the first time in this century. *The Constitution* had 209,000 to *The Journal*'s 183,000, a slide for *The Journal* since 1972 of 72,000 daily subscribers, which raised some doubts as to whether an afternoon newspaper would continue to be feasible.

The news staffs also were combined about that time, prompting further questions. But actually a corner had been turned. In the six-month ABC audit for mid-1983 the combined circulation had gained 10,000 over the mid-1982 figure, rising to 403,452 and the increase was continuing in the mid-80s.

Throughout the past three decades, *The Sunday Journal-Constitution* consistently stayed above 500,000.

The combined circulation of all dailies in the state was 995,000 in 1982-83, giving the Atlanta newspapers 40 percent of the total, down from the 52 percent that was common until the 1960s but still impressive.

Each of the Atlanta dailies could easily be the subject of an entire book, and only the highlights of their story can be covered in this volume. They were pacesetters before World War II and have been pacesetters in the years since. A definitive treatment of these newspapers and of the many fascinating people who worked on them, who in a significant way molded modern Georgia, is a task that deserves the attention of future historians.

For this volume, Calvin Cox, who spent 37 years on the Atlanta newspapers, has skillfully gathered up the many threads of their story and woven a tightly-told and remarkably illuminating account. Cox has managed to give attention to the highlights of those years while still including many interesting anecdotes and personal glimpses of the people whose names and works are familiar to so many Georgians. He has lifted the veil on one of the largest business operations in the state, which is a mystery even to others in the newspaper field. His account also touches on the points raised in this introduction. Cox, who retired in 1982, at one time or another did almost everything an editor can do in a newsroom. He was copy editor, city editor, news editor, associate editor, Sunday editor and assistant managing editor.

A native of Greenwood, Mississippi, he learned to operate a linotype machine while still in high school, which led him into newspaper work. After service in the Army during World War II he was on his way home to Greenwood in 1945 when the train stopped in Atlanta. He had an hour's layover so he walked down to the old Constitution building at Alabama and Forsyth streets and applied for a job. He was put to work on the copy desk and the train left without him.

As an observer of the newspaper scene in Atlanta for so long, Cox was uniquely prepared to tell the story of those years.

The Journal and *Constitution*

BY CALVIN COX

Atlanta, in 1950

Atlanta and Georgia—and newspapering—were significantly different in 1950.

Items:

— The city still had 94 passenger train arrivals and departures daily from its two major railway stations in 1950. Today, the stations are gone, and the Southern Crescent stops at Brookwood Station once in the morning and once in the evening.

— The Atlanta airport handled 768,922 passengers in 1950. In 1983, two terminals later, the volume was 37,919,812.

— Atlanta had one enclosed shopping mall in 1950, the Arcade, between Peachtree and Broad streets downtown. The Arcade had fancy grill stairways and railings, three floors of small shops and offices, several restaurants and a large goldfish pond. By the end of 1983, the Atlanta area counted 15 large regional malls.

— Atlanta in 1950 hadn't seen a new skyscraper since 1930 (the William Oliver Building on Peachtree). The next one wouldn't appear until 1955 (Fulton National). During the years that followed, they sprang up practically every day.

The big newspaper story of 1950 in Atlanta was the purchase of the morning *Atlanta Constitution*, established in 1868, by the afternoon

Atlanta Journal, established in 1883.

A page one announcement, set two columns and headed "A Statement," declared, "Rumors persist that the two Atlanta newspapers are going to be merged. We think the people are entitled to know the facts."

The statement said that only the Sunday papers would be combined and that separate papers would continue during the week. Editorial policies would remain independent.

"We are fully aware of the greater responsibility which is thrust upon our shoulders in the merger of these two great newspapers," the statement said. "Economic reasons have played a large part in dictating this move on our part.

"It is our desire," the statement continued, "to build greater newspapers on the firm foundations of *The Journal* and *The Constitution*; to give our readers better newspapers and greater service, to be constructive forces for good in Atlanta, Georgia, the South, and the United States . . ."

The announcement was made by Clark Howell, president and publisher of the Constitution Publishing Company, and James M. Cox, chairman of the board, The Atlanta Journal Company. The date was March 19, 1950.

Former Governor Cox of Ohio acquired a formidable and historic newspaper property in *The Constitution*. The Howell family had come into an ownership position in 1876 when Capt. Evan P. Howell became president and editor-in-chief.

One of Howell's first acts was to hire Henry W. Grady as political editor. By 1880, Grady, 30, had obtained a loan and bought one-fourth interest in *The Constitution* for $20,000. His new title was managing editor. A famed orator, Grady became renowned as spokesman for a "New South."

Other notable writers on the early *Constitution* were Joel Chandler Harris of "Uncle Remus" fame and the poet Frank L. Stanton.

The two papers at the time of the merger were engaged in spirited campaigns to buy young elephants for the Atlanta zoo to replace one named Coca, who had died. *The Journal's* pachyderm was being paid for by donations from school children, giving the tykes a personal stake in the new animal. The *Constitution's* elephant was backed financially by more general donations and a major gift from Asa Candler Jr., donor of the first Coca to the zoo.

The Journal won a close elephant race, although there were only scant hours difference in the arrival times. *Constitution* reporter Jack Nelson and *Journal* reporter John Pennington almost came to blows late in the night when Nelson was found snooping about the zoo in an effort to scoop *The Journal* on its own elephant.

Constitution political editor M. L. St. John explained the newspaper merger by saying, "We're putting all our elephants in one basket."

The Constitution, a little over two years before the merger, had moved into a spanking new newspaper building at the corner of Forsyth and Alabama streets, catty-corner from the ancient red brick pile where Grady, Joel Chandler Harris and Ralph McGill had worked.

McGill came to *The Constitution* from *The Nashville Banner* in the spring of 1929 as assistant sports editor. He was made executive editor of *The Constitution* in 1938 and editor in 1942. The next year he hired Jack Tarver as associate editor. Each on his own path was to become a major force in newspapering.

Tarver spent most of 1949 in South America on a Reid Fellowship. Before he got back, change was in the wind.

After the merger was announced, Tarver said, he received a call from the publisher of the *Arkansas Gazette* in Little Rock and was asked "if I would consider the job of editor. I said, 'Yes, sir, I would like to come talk to you about it.'"

Before that trip came about, George C. Biggers, president of the new corporation, Atlanta Newspapers, phoned to say "The governor (James M. Cox) wants to talk with you and Ralph."

Tarver said he and McGill went to the top floor of the Miami News Tower on Biscayne Bay. "And here was the governor sitting there, nine o'clock in the morning. And he said, 'I know how you boys feel; you feel like you've been sold out.' And he said, 'I won't lie to you; you have been, but just remember I bought you because I wanted you' . . . buttering us up."

That night, after the lights were out, Tarver said, "McGill called across the room, 'Well, Mr. Tarver,' he said, 'all of our old problems are over with, and we've got a whole set of new ones.'"

By the first week in June 1950, *The Constitution* and *The Journal* daily papers were being printed in *The Journal's* new plant at 10 Forsyth Street, a long stone's throw from the two-and-one-half-year-old *Constitution* building. The combined Sunday paper, making its first appearance on June 4, 1950, with a combined press run of 475,000 copies, was printed in both buildings.

In appearances July 11, 1950, before the Atlanta Kiwanis Club, Editor Wright Bryan of *The Journal* said the economic merger of the papers would result in financial savings that would allow both papers to give greater coverage and community service, and Editor McGill of *The Constitution* reported that Governor Cox believed that well-known newspaper chains had made a mistake in trying to impose overall news and editorial policies. The governor, said McGill, thought such practice was contrary to the public good and is also bad business.

This was the straight stuff, for after the merger the papers continued to be unrelenting foes six days out of the week and part-time on Sunday. Operating in separate newsrooms, the staffs gave each other no quarter and scant "hellos" for more than 30 years. There was no exchange of information between the newsrooms and no trading of information. *The Journal* city desk, for instance, would never call *The Constitution* city desk to see if it was covering any specific event. Assignments were made individually by each paper.

The public, of course, did not believe this. A person handing over a news release would add, "How about getting this in *The Constitution* (or *Journal*), too." Told that a separate item would have to be given to the other paper, the visitor inevitably would respond, "It's all one paper."

Putting out a joint Sunday paper wasn't a bouquet of sweet picas either. Certainly there was cooperation, with advance planning meetings and all that, but the Sunday editor often felt like a guy shooting rapids with feet in two separate canoes.

The papers had similar news and editorial imperatives, of course, both situated in Atlanta and viewing a Georgia government that was overwhelmingly stacked against large urban areas.

A county unit system of apportioning legislative representation and counting votes in statewide elections made the offices almost voiceless. First a party scheme, then put into law in 1917, the unit system assigned each county no fewer than two unit votes, but no more than six. The eight largest counties had six votes each, the next 30 had four, and the remaining 121 had two each. The candidate with the most popular votes in a county would receive that county's unit votes. This meant that small Echols County, for instance, had 100 times greater voting power than did Fulton County, the state's most populous.

An excerpt from a McGill column of February 12, 1950, is a sample of the papers' concern about the unit system:

"At the base of our trouble is our system — the county unit system. No governor, Gov. Talmadge (Eugene's son, Herman, in this instance) or any other man, can really speak for and stand for what is best in Georgia as long as they must be slave to the county unit system . . . No other state has it, and all our Southern states do as well as we do and some do better. It is an iniquitous device which holds us down to the level of the worst and the most corrupt and greedy among us."

Fighting the county unit system and other aberrations of the political structure was just part of the concerns of *The Journal* and *Constitution*.

In the fall of 1950, a gifted woman reporter, Margaret Shannon, did a series for *The Journal* entitled, "The 15 Worst Schools in Georgia." Shannon and photographers showed in superb word-photo packages how physically backward many of Georgia's rural schools were.

William I. (Bill) Ray, who became managing editor of *The Journal* in April 1950 and later rose to president of Atlanta Newspapers, recalls the project.

"That was a magnificent series. It led to the Minimum Foundation Program for Education in Georgia. It was one of the first times anybody had combined photographic and reading materials to win a major prize, the Sigma Delta Chi national award. . . . Pat LaHatte at that time was picture editor, and LaHatte and Shannon worked wide by side, getting the right pictures to illustrate the points Shannon was making in her stories."

George C. Biggers, who was president of *The Journal* at the time of the merger, was named president of the new Atlanta Newspapers and Tarver was made general manager in 1952.

Jack Spalding, native Atlantan, reporter and editorial writer, at different times, for both papers, and long-time (1956-78) editor of *The Journal*, summed up Biggers as "a very upright man, a very smart man, a very straight man, but a very stern man and a man with a low boiling point. He was always worried about McGill. They lived in two different worlds."

Spalding was writing editorials on *The Journal* under Wright Bryan in the early '50s when Biggers asked him to move over to *The Constitution* editorial department. "You've got one job," Biggers told Spalding. "Keep McGill from writing his column and the lead editorial on the same day."

"Mr. Biggers was afraid of Ralph because he was too liberal, and it was bad for the paper's image in the community. So I was supposed to act as a modifying influence," Spalding recalls.

If Biggers was afraid of McGill, the feeling was thoroughly reciprocated. "Ralph was as scared of George Biggers as I would be in a cage of rattlesnakes," Jack Tarver said. "They never understood each other, and I, unfortunately, came to be kind of an intermediary."

Tarver related how McGill on one occasion wrote a two-page memorandum to Biggers about a proposed trip and at the end said, "I would like to have your thoughts on this."

The memorandum came back, Tarver said, with Biggers' green-ink response at the bottom: "Whatever you wish. GCB." McGill brought the paper to him, Tarver said, and asked, "Wonder what he means by this?"

"I said, 'Damn, McGill, if you can understand English, whatever you wish.' 'Ah,' he said, 'there's more to it than that.'"

"But that was typical of their relationship."

The closest to a crisis the two came, Tarver said, was when Dwight Eisenhower was running for the presidency. "McGill traveled with and got very much impressed with Ike, who was a Republican. Cox and Biggers were devout Democrats.

"The governor (Cox) used to call me and say, 'Tarver, what do you think McGill is going to do?' And I would say, 'Governor, I don't know,' and he would say, 'I don't want to influence him, but . . .'

"George Biggers finally asked McGill what he intended to do, which offended McGill greatly, that anyone would think that he was not going to support the Democratic party. He called me that night, 'Mr. Tarver, you probably are going to be editor of *The Constitution* tomorrow.' And I said, 'Why?' He said, 'Damn it, I've just had enough, I'm going to quit.' I told Ralph don't do anything silly. 'You need to talk to George tomorrow.' Later that night he sat down and wrote me a long letter about it, how he loved me and how he appreciated my acting as a buffer, and so forth, but professing that while he admired Ike greatly he couldn't visualize a military man in the presidency at that time. That was the nearest thing to a crisis the two of them had."

Spalding remembers McGill "as a preacher. He was an evangelist. He was a passionate and emotional man. I often wondered how far he would have gone as a churchman. He died an Episcopalian, but it seems to me he would have done better as a Church of God member."

Awards and Crusades

The Journal and *Constitution* of that period had many excellent investigative reporters, just as they do today. Jack Nelson of *The Constitution*, now Washington bureau chief of *The Los Angeles Times* and one of the nation's top reporters, won a Pulitzer Prize during his 12 years with *The Constitution*. He came to Atlanta in 1952 from Biloxi, Mississippi. John Pennington, Margaret Shannon, Pat Watters and Charlie Pou filled investigative roles at *The Journal*, as did Bill Shipp, Bruce Galphin, and Marion Gaines at *The Constitution*.

Pennington set the tone for a decade of penal investigations and reform when he found on a concrete and steel solitary confinement wall at the Buford Rock Quarry Prison for Incorrigibles the scrawled message, "Thay is no God."

That this was so in the prison system appears to be borne out by other news stories in the 1950s and the 1960s.

Pat Watters of *The Journal* was among reporters covering the infamous leg-smashing incident at the Rock Quarry Prison on July 30, 1956. Thirty-six convicts smashed bones in their legs with sledgehammers. Prison officials said there was "nothing wrong" with the way the prison was being run. The warden was quoted as saying the leg smashing was in protest of work loads. Gov. Marvin Griffin declared he would insist that discipline at the camp be "fair, just, but strict." He admitted that "incidents of this kind appear to set the prison system back a little."

Jack Nelson reported in October 1962 that a warden's "house boy" resisted when he was ordered into the "hole" (solitary confinement) at the Baldwin County Public Works Camp. The prisoner, it was reported, said he would "die and go to hell before I'd go in the hole for doing nothing." A guard, acting on the warden's orders, shot and killed the prisoner, according to statements by officials and prisoners. A coroner's jury said the slaying was "justifiable."

Bill Shipp wrote that "teen-agers and adults, felony convicts and misdemeanor prisoners, sane and insane, expectant mothers, homosexuals and drug addicts" were crammed together in three wooden dormitories at the Georgia State Prison for Women in Milledgeville.

* * *

In the darkness of early Sunday morning, October 13, 1958, dynamiters blasted the Jewish Temple at 1589 Peachtree St. NE. Damage was estimated at $200,000. *Constitution* and *Journal* editors ran page after page of coverage.

Harold Martin in his book, "Ralph McGill, Reporter," tells how McGill first got the word on Sunday afternoon upon returning from a speaking trip to the Georgia mountains. "Soon after, in his office," Martin wrote, "in twenty minutes of furious, uninterrupted writing, he produced three typewritten pages that smoked with anger and with shame." The front-page column, entitled "A Church, A School," said, in part:

"Dynamite in great quantity ripped a beautiful temple of worship in Atlanta. It followed hard on the heels of a like destruction of a handsome high school in Clinton, Tennessee.

"The same rabid, mad-dog minds were, without question, behind both. They are also the source of previous bombings in Florida, Alabama, and South Carolina. The schoolhouses and the church were the targets of diseased, hate-filled minds.

"Let us face the facts. This is a harvest. It is the crop of things sown.

"It is the harvest of defiance of courts and the encouragement of citizens to defy law on the part of many Southern politicians. It will be the acme of irony . . . if any one of four or five Southern governors deplore this bombing. It will be grimly humorous if certain state attorneys general issue statements of regrets. And it will be quite a job for some editors, columnists, and commentators, who have been saying that our courts have no jurisdiction and that the people should refuse to accept their authority, now to deplore.

"It is not possible to preach lawlessness and restrict it . . .

"You do not preach and encourage hatred for the Negro and hope to restrict it to that field. It is an old, old story. It is one repeated over and over again in history. When the wolves of hate are loosed on one people, then no one is safe."

The Journal had a front-page editorial with a moving head: "A Desecrated Temple Cries Out to Heaven."

In 1959, McGill was awarded a Pulitzer Prize for editorial writing, based primarily on the column, "A Church, A School."

The next year *Constitution* reporter Jack Nelson received a Pulitzer for his investigation into conditions at the Milledgeville State Hospital for the Insane.

Nelson found that:

— A nurse had performed major surgery;

— A fourth of the doctors at the hospital had alcoholic or drug addiction backgrounds;

— A doctor had used experimental, unapproved drugs on patients under a research program funded by drug firms.

The Georgia Press Association nominated Nelson for the Pulitzer, with supporting nominations from the Medical Association of Georgia and the Schaefer Committee, a group named by Gov. Ernest Vandiver to investigate conditions at the state hospital.

* * *

Following the twisted skeins of the Marvin Griffin administration (1955-59) was a time-consuming job for reporters.

A summary story by Jack Nelson, one of the chief investigators, declared the administration had been scarred by scandals in four major departments: highway, revenue, purchasing and corrections. At one point State Corrections Department Director Jack Forrester ordered the warden of the Wayne Prison Branch to go pick up a road scraper "lost" for a year. A reporter found the machine at a rural roads project being constructed by a private contractor. There were news stories of kickbacks and misuse of state equipment and cash. Griffin in later years pointed out, "I'm about the only governor I know of who got a clean sheet after investigation." (He appeared before the Fulton County grand jury.) This was not true of everyone in his administration.

Nelson in summarizing the Griffin years pointed out the good. Schoolteachers got four raises, the state bought Stone Mountain, a rural roads program was done, the University of Georgia got a $25,500,000 science center, Tech received funds for a nuclear pile.

Years after leaving office, Griffin joined newsmen at a lounge after the annual Cracker Crumble affair. Eyeing Nelson, the governor said, "You know what I'd be thinking about Monday morning?" (Griffin held a press conference each Monday.) "No, governor," said Nelson, "What would you be thinking?" Griffin put on a grim look, "I'd be thinking, what has that little SOB got on me today?"

Although it was possible to joke later, Griffin said and did some things during his Capitol years to indicate he didn't exactly love *The Journal* and *Constitution*. It was Griffin who had his revenue commissioner, T. V. (Red) Williams, put out a regulation that there could be no more liquor advertising in newspapers with more than a third of their circulation in dry counties. The May 14, 1958, order affected only three papers in Georgia: *The Journal, The Constitution* and *The Macon Telegraph*.

Jack Tarver, who the previous December had been named president of Atlanta Newspapers after George Biggers suffered a stroke, declared the papers would not be intimidated "by puny pressures brought by those who would have us forget our public obligations, even as they have apparently."

Dixon Oxford, Gov. Ernest Vandiver's revenue commissioner, threw out the advertising ban in February of the next year. The ruling cost the

Atlanta papers an estimated $350,000 in revenue. Oxford said he was rescinding the order and also another one saying all liquor advertising must be approved by the revenue commissioner for two reasons: "(1) They were an effort to punish certain newspapers for exposing graft and corruption in state government, and (2) The order interfered with freedom of the press."

Tarver said recently, "I never had any real enemies. The last time I saw Marvin Griffin (who died in 1982) he and I had a great evening reminiscing and so forth." Tarver recalled that he has a tape of a Griffin speech in which the ex-governor said, "The cold-nosed bloodhounds of Tarver and McGill have been down in my home county, just because they paved the road by my farm. I told those fellows, 'Put that machinery on the other side of the road.' "

William B. Hartsfield, mayor of Atlanta for almost a quarter of a century, kept a keen eye on the newspapers. It was the mayor's habit to secure the first edition of each paper and peruse it carefully in the off-chance an error had crept into the pages.

On one occasion, at least, he convinced *Constitution* managing editor William H. (Bill) Fields that a factual error had been made. Fields, recalling the instance, finally agreed to take the story out of the paper, with the admonition to Hartsfield that if indeed the story was correct he would put it back in the next day's run at the exact point he took it out. The story was right, and Fields did.

* * *

Tarver recalled that shortly after *The Journal* and *Constitution* merger, James M. Cox told him and McGill that he would never come upon the newsroom floor of *The Constitution*, because he didn't want to be an influence on *The Constitution*. In the memory of veteran employees, he kept that promise. Consequently, when the Governor died July 15, 1957, at the age of 87, many employees had never seen him, but the long obituary told them what kind of man they had missed.

Born on an Ohio farm, Cox served as the Middletown, Ohio, correspondent for the *Cincinnati Enquirer*. Later, he worked full-time as a reporter for the paper. He managed to get together the financing to buy his own newspaper, *The Dayton Evening News*, at age 28.

Cox served two terms in Congress and was three times elected governor of Ohio. In 1920, he was the Democratic Party's presidential candidate, with Franklin D. Roosevelt his running mate. Another Ohio publisher, Warren G. Harding, led Republicans to a sweeping victory, using a front porch campaign and calling for a "return to normalcy." Cox and Roosevelt stood strongly for Woodrow Wilson's advocacy of a League of Nations.

As a newspaperman, Cox believed in strong, unencumbered papers. Standing upon and dedicating a new bank of presses in *The Journal's* mechanical building shortly before the merger with *The Constitution*, Governor Cox said, "I would want this press to be a courageous one, because in my conception of things, a cowardly press might be more harmful than a corrupt press."

A statement by Governor Cox published after he bought *The Journal* in 1939 said a newspaper "should tell the truth as intellectual honesty can discern the truth. To try by vague and pointless preachments and evasion to please everyone is bad faith. Persisted in, it pleases none and exposes a lack of character which people will soon appraise."

Reflecting on his own career at the Atlanta newspapers, Bill Ray said, "The important thing is that we published a fearless operation. We were fortunate to have Governor Cox as the owner and to have people in charge of the operation who were news-oriented. We published the kind of newspaper that newspaper people should have appreciated; maybe the community leaders didn't necessarily appreciate it.

"Don't misunderstand me, we supported all the community things that would make Atlanta progressive. We were not anti-business or anti-community. We just didn't let anybody influence us on printing the news as the news should be printed."

On July 31, 1958, James M. Cox Jr. was elected chairman of the board of Atlanta Newspapers to succeed his father.

The Civil Rights Struggles

The Supreme Court in the 1950s and the early 1960s had handed down decisions which would make profound changes in the lives of Georgians, politically and racially.

McGill, in a column written April 9, 1953, entitled "One Day It Will Be Monday," said, "Days come and days go, and Monday is among them, and one of these Mondays the Supreme Court of the United States is going to hand down a ruling which may, although it is considered by some unlikely, outlaw the South's dual school system, wholly or in part.

"It is a subject which, because of its emotional content, usually is put aside with the remark, 'Let's don't talk about it. If people wouldn't talk about these things, they would solve themselves.'

"It is an old reaction, best illustrated by *Gone With the Wind*'s Miss Scarlett O'Hara who, when confronted with a distasteful decision, pushed it away with the remark, 'We'll think about that tomorrow.'

"But 'tomorrow' has an ugly habit of coming around."

McGill discussed existing court suits, the possibilities before the Supreme Court and called for calmness, "whatever the decision."

Monday came May 17, 1954, when the Supreme Court ruled "separate but equal" unconstitutional in Brown v. Board of Education. In 1955, the court said public schools in Southern and border states must desegregate "with all deliberate speed."

By spring 1960, the tops were coming off the stools in downtown Atlanta short-order eateries: the sit-in had arrived. Drugstore and variety counters were the original targets, followed by government cafeterias and department store restaurants.

An estimated 75 blacks sought service in eight downtown Atlanta stores on Wednesday, October 19, 1960. *The Journal* sent 11 reporters out to cover the story. Martin Luther King Jr., who had come to Atlanta from Montgomery, Alabama, early in 1960 to be co-pastor with his father of the Ebenezer Baptist Church, was among those arrested. Dr. King was in a group arrested at Rich's Magnolia Room.

Margaret Shannon of *The Journal* recalls the scene. "Bruce Galphin (of *The Constitution*) and I were there, and we sat in those rocking chairs they had there, and when King showed up they wouldn't let him in. He was arrested and they took him away."

Although Georgia faced many more sit-ins, civil rights demonstrations and the desegregation of its schools, forces were coming to bear in 1960 that would have significant impact on race relations.

The Sunday *Journal* and *Constitution* on January 17, 1960, published a private letter Georgia School Board Chairman James S. Peters of Manchester, a long-time stalwart in the Talmadge political organization, had written to Roy Harris of Augusta. The letter by the influential Manchester banker said integration is "inevitable" in Georgia. The only question in doubt, Peters said, was whether the schools would be integrated by the integrationists or by the segregationists. Almost exactly a year later, *The* Sunday *Journal* and *Constitution* published another letter by Peters, this one to his Congressman, John J. Flynt. In it, Peters said the majority of Georgians favored the program of newly elected President John F.

Kennedy, including federal aid to education.

During the eventful year of 1960, a number of changes were taking place at *The Journal* and *Constitution*. Ralph McGill moved from editor of *The Constitution* to publisher. He would continue his front-page column, but the new title would free him from mandatory retirement at 65. Eugene Patterson, executive editor of the two papers, was named to succeed McGill as editor. Patterson, a native of Adel, Georgia, had come to *The Journal* in 1956 as editorial writer. Bill Ray, managing editor at *The Journal* for 10 years, was made executive editor. Pat Kelly succeeded Ray at *The Journal*.

Georgia ran into its first school integration crisis, appropriately enough, at the oldest institution of higher education, the University of Georgia at Athens.

Charlayne Hunter, 18, and Hamilton Holmes, 19, both of Atlanta, integrated the University of Georgia on Wednesday morning, January 11, 1961. The state had appealed fruitlessly to the Supreme Court in an effort to stop a lower court order for the admission of the two students.

That night, a crowd of students and townspeople estimated variously at 2,000 and 500 persons converged on Center Myers dormitory, where Miss Hunter was assigned. Reporters Bruce Galphin and Barbara Milz were covering the late-breaking story for *The Constitution*.

"Rocks were thrown through dormitory windows and hurled at police, university officials and newsmen. Police and youngsters battled openly . . .

"At one point a group of cars pulled up and occupants tossed copies of the Ku Klux Klan newspaper, *The Rebel*, into the crowd.

"Police arrested at least one paddy-wagon full of young men. A man in the crowd offered 'to go bond' for all arrested."

Galphin and Milz reported the march on Center Myers began after Georgia lost to Tech in an overtime basketball game. "About 200 young men converged on Miss Hunter's dormitory and began shouting, 'Nigger, go home.' Others in the rapidly growing crowd took up the chant."

Athens police used tear gas to quell the rioting.

The next fall the Atlanta schools admitted their first black students, with only minor incidents. The integration — including entertainment of hordes of visiting newsmen — was adroitly handled by Mayor William Hartsfield, Police Chief Herbert Jenkins, and school officials.

There were more hard civil rights stories ahead, but the staffs of *The Journal* and *The Constitution* had two major ones behind them, at Athens and in Atlanta.

* * *

A major publishing project somewhat removed from the tensions of 1960 was begun March 4, 1960: *The Atlanta Century. The Century*'s run consisted of 272 weekly pages made up in the style of 100 years ago and published each Sunday in *The Journal* and *Constitution* starting with the period 13 months before the War Between the States began and running right on through to the end. Norman Shavin of *The Journal-Constitution* staff was editor of the epochal publication, which was published in full-page book form after the weekly project came to an end.

* * *

June 3, 1962.

"It was a beautiful morning," Ralph McGill wrote in his column. "Some of the humid heat had fled before scattered showers in the night and a breeze which blew in the first hours of dawn. The sky was new-washed blue."

Many persons were just going to church when the news came. A loaded Air Force Boeing 707 jetliner had crashed on takeoff at Paris' Orly Field. One hundred and two Atlantans and 13 other Georgians were among the 130 persons who perished in the crash, the worst, at that time, in aviation history. The charter craft was headed back to Atlanta after an art tour of Europe, and among the passengers was a major portion of the civic and cultural leadership of the city.

"This was my generation . . . my friends," said Atlanta Mayor Ivan Allen Jr. Mayor Emeritus William Hartsfield called the crash "The greatest tragedy to hit Atlanta since the Civil War."

Constitution Editor Eugene Patterson wrote, "It is doubtful any American city has ever lost, at a single stroke, so many of its finest."

Staffs of both newspapers came in from a quiet Sunday to a frenzied effort to record the horror of a fiery moment. *The Journal* assembled 113 obituaries and many photographs for a "Special Extra" that hit the streets late in the afternoon. Six members of one family died in the crash. *The Journal*'s club editor, Margaret Turner, also was among the victims.

Hundreds of Atlantans came downtown, many waiting in front of *The Journal-Constitution* building on Forsyth Street for the first papers. *The Journal*'s Extra provided page after page of coverage.

The Constitution, with much later deadlines for its regular editions, supplemented and completed the column after column of individual obits. The paper's stories also attempted to portray the great sense of loss in the community. Persons walking on Forsyth Street searched for words. "Atlanta's going to be affected socially and culturally. I have never seen a city hit so hard" . . . "My doctor and his wife were killed." . . . "I am a member of the Atlanta Art Association. This means we all have to pull together. It will take time, a lot of time, to recover from this loss." . . . "I knew a lot of them on board. You couldn't hurt Atlanta worse than this." The last paragraph of Frank Veale's story said, "Rarely has so much sadness been crammed into one Atlanta street. It was a night of sorrow."

The next afternoon, McGill sent a note to the city desk. "I sat for an hour this morning at breakfast reading *The Constitution*, and I came to the studied conclusion that in some 40 years of newspaper work for me, the job the staff did on the Monday morning edition is the best over-all newspaper accomplishment I have ever seen . . ."

* * *

Newspaper people are an introspective bunch. When they aren't attending conventions or talking about their businesses, they often write about it. Sometimes they combine the two. Here's Ernest Rogers, a favorite columnist on *The Journal*:

"No doubt about it, there have been some changes made. I mean in the newspaper business. This has been verified in conversations with some of the more seasoned newspaper people attending the current (1960) session of the Georgia Press Institute.

"For example, take women. There are many here who can recall the days when the thought of having a woman on his staff would cause even the hardiest city editor to have a nervous breakdown. It was all right for them to work in the society department but as for hustling spot news — never . . .

"Now, however, it is agreed that many of the best all-around reporters in the business are women, and experience has taught that they can tackle any kind of story with every expectation of doing as good a job as their masculine counterparts.

" 'They are especially good,' one veteran remarked, 'on stories demanding persistence. There is something in their makeup that won't let them give up until they get what they want. Any husband knows that.' "

* * *

The Constitution's Bill Shipp and reporter Fred Powledge of *The Journal* were on the Ole Miss campus at Oxford the night of September 30, 1962, a Sunday, when James Meredith arrived accompanied by federal marshals to become the university's first black student. Before the rioting ended Sunday night, two persons were killed and scores had been injured.

"That night," says Shipp, "was one of the few times covering the news that I actually felt my life really was in danger. People were firing weapons, throwing bricks and bottles, and anybody who was a stranger — black or white — was in serious difficulty — very dangerous. I got trapped outside the Lyceum on the quadrangle, couldn't get in. I took off my tie, and I took off my shoes and wedding band, and just tried to mingle in with the mob."

McGill, appalled by the violence, wrote: "The national integrity certainly must come first in all our hearts. Next in importance is education. The South, despite its sacrifice and efforts, still has less education for its children than do other regions. The future is going to belong to the best prepared. That the South in bitterness and anger would defy the national authority for the sake of slogans and traditions long without validity is one of the great ironies of the last half of the 20th Century."

* * *

The Sixties were years of spectacular change in Atlanta. Ivan Allen Jr. became mayor in 1962 and would continue for eight more years the sort of visionary leadership William Hartsfield had provided for nearly a quarter of a century. The downtown connector was finally put together in 1964 with the completion of a huge interchange at the Capitol, tall buildings were rising on the skyline, and a breath-taking hotel opened in 1967.

It became a favorite weekend pastime for Atlantans to take unsuspecting visitors to the Hyatt Regency, steer them through a routine entranceway — then tell them to look up. That's when the exclamations spilled out — even "good-gosh-a-mighties" — for soaring upward was a huge 21-floor atrium with glass-enclosed elevators speeding up and down one side. Atlantan John Portman's design of the Hyatt-Regency changed the appearance of hotels all around the world.

The 1960s also were big for sports in Atlanta. The city and Georgia always had been avid followers of Bobby Dodd's Tech Engineers, Wally Butts' and Vince Dooley's Bulldogs, and the Cracker baseball team.

Suddenly, there was a vast new dimension. Major-league baseball came in 1966 with the Braves, big-time football the same year with the Falcons. And the Hawks hit the hardwoods in 1968.

The Journal and *The Constitution* always had been strong on sports coverage, sending flocks of scribes to the fall gridiron games when other Southern papers were providing much lesser coverage.

George Biggers, president of Atlanta Newspapers upon completion of the 1950 merger, was an ex-sportswriter, and he kept a watchful eye.

Jack Tarver and Bill Ray agree that Biggers was insistent that the combined Sunday paper have thorough coverage in its sports pages of "every Podunk game." Ed Danforth, legendary *Journal* sports editor, out of earshot referred to Biggers as "the executive sports editor." The staff took unusual measures to see that he was satisfied. It was Biggers' custom to take green pen and mark up the good and bad of each Sunday section.

Guy Tiller, an assistant editor, was in charge of the Saturday night production. He made a replate as late as he could possibly wait to get the last scores in. And then, said Tarver and Ray, he would go by Biggers' house in the early morn and substitute a replate for the edition that had been delivered. That kept the static down some.

Furman Bisher came to *The Constitution* as sports editor in 1950 and moved to *The Journal* in the same capacity when Ed Danforth retired in early 1957. Jesse Outlar, a sports writer at *The Constitution* since 1947, moved to the top spot on the morning paper. Together, Bisher and Outlar have spoken to the sports public for nearly 70 years.

Danforth, known as Colonel, was a hard man to follow.

Sportswriters always seem more likely than not to a have brilliant way of putting words together. The Colonel was a master. His story of the 1953 Kentucky Derby won Danforth the opening pages in the publication "Best Sports Stories of 1953," and Sport Magazine named the story among the 10 best of the decade.

Danforth's lead:

"Native Dancer had a date to see a fellow in the garden in front of the pagoda at Churchill Downs about some roses but by the length of a handsome head, he was late."

Danforth's last column appeared in *The Journal* of February 3, 1957, the end of a 40-year career in sports in Atlanta. His staff members "contrived to look the other way," Ed Miles wrote, "when for the last time Saturday afternoon he shot the carrier bolt of his typewriter to center position and replaced the machine's plastic cover with fingers that fumbled a little."

One of the delightful additions to first *The Constitution* and then *The Journal* for a stretch of 22 years was sports columnist Harry Mehre, the former Georgia (59-34-6) and Ole Miss (39-26-1) football coach. He had an oft-told joke about his days at Athens. "I had a lifetime contract at Georgia, but in 1937 the almuni declared me legally dead."

Mehre played football at Notre Dame while studying to be a journalist, or vice versa. "Rockne may not have been as great a coach as people thought," Mehre often said. "Otherwise why would he have switched a great fullback like me to center?"

It was Mehre who first said of Alabama's fabled Coach Bear Bryant: "If Bear can't walk on water, he knows where all the stumps are hidden."

The old coach retired from writing in 1972 after suffering a stroke. In September 1978 at age 77, Mehre died. "I hope," Bisher wrote, "that somewhere in Heaven there's an old press box he can go to on a Saturday afternoon and some of the old gang will be there."

The Inevitable Horrors

A researcher unwinding the newspaper reels of the 1960s finds his hand turning slower and slower, as though the subconscious is trying its mightiest to prevent the unveiling of the inevitable horrors.

Such a day is November 22, 1963, when Lee Harvey Oswald killed President John F. Kennedy in Dallas, Texas. The shooting happened at 1:30 p.m. Atlanta time. United Press International moved the first flash at 1:34 p.m. The President was pronounced dead at 2 p.m.

It was one of the shattering days of history. *The Journal* was readying its first Blue Streak edition. The paper was held and made over for a series of Extras. *The Constitution* made more space available for its Saturday editions but held to its regular 8 p.m. Friday first-edition time.

Many Americans can look back today and describe that one frozen moment when they first heard. *The Constitution* had an exchange journalist visiting the newsroom for several weeks at the time of the assassination. A wrenching experience for one of *The Constitution* editors was coming into the office early on Sunday morning to find the Egyptian the only person in the newsroom. He was seated in front of a small television set weeping silently.

* * *

Bill Fields, after 17 years with *The Constitution*, 13 of them as managing editor, was moved in the fall of 1964 to *The Journal* as managing editor, succeeding Pat Kelly, who took a job in North Carolina. Tom McRae, who first came with the paper in 1937, succeeded Fields on *The Constitution*. McRae served during World War II as combat correspondent and managing editor for the Mediterranean edition of Stars and Stripes. Very quiet and modest, McRae used his photo hobby to assist reporter Jack Nelson in recording cash exchanging hands in a police gambling scandal in the 1950s.

The Vietnam War, abroad and at home, along with the civil rights struggle, continued as heavy news events on through the 1960s.

Both papers very early in the civil rights struggle appointed reporters specializing in civil rights coverage: Bruce Galphin on *The Constitution* and Margaret Shannon on *The Journal*. *Journal* and *Constitution* reporters were at Little Rock, New Orleans, and at Tuscaloosa, where Gov. George Wallace made a symbolic stand in the schoolhouse door. (Reporter Bill Shipp recalls, "I happened to be standing very close to Wallace and Assistant U.S. Attorney Nicholas Katzenbach, and I looked down at Katzenbach's pants legs around his knees, and they were just quivering.") Wallace, at Katzenbach's order, stepped aside.

Atlanta during the troubled racial times was spared riots such as Los Angeles, Detroit and other cities experienced, but on a Tuesday afternoon and night, September 6, 1966, it came to the edge of major trouble. Seventy-three persons were jailed and 16 were hospitalized after a rock-and-bottle melee. A Molotov cocktail was blamed for a fire at a tire warehouse. The uproar happened in a six-block area near Atlanta Stadium, set off apparently when a white policeman shot and wounded a black fleeing arrest. After the rioting was over, black leaders and Police Chief Herbert Jenkins blamed Stokely Carmichael and other members of the Student Non-violent Coordinating Committee for causing the trouble.

Mayor Ivan Allen was at a meeting at City Hall when the rioting started. He went immediately to the scene and walked through the crowds in an attempt to quiet the passions. One of the unforgettable scenes was the mayor atop a police car, bullhorn in hand, pleading for calmness from a shouting, fist-waving mob.

After the tumultuous day was over, *The Journal* said editorially, "Magnificent work on the part of the police, the personal courage and leadership of Mayor Ivan Allen and the cooperation of responsible Negro political and religious leaders kept Atlanta out of murderous trouble Tuesday evening."

Scores of reporters covered the scene, including veteran City Hall writer Raleigh Bryans of *The Journal*. Satellite disturbances occurred elsewhere in the city, but the stadium melee was the main event. Reporters during subsequent coverage went out equipped with riot helmets, a disturbing sight for editors accustomed to handing out more tranquil assignments.

* * *

An incident during the 1960s while *The Journal* and *The Constitution* were in the 10 Forsyth St. building illustrates a mischievous side of the complex Ralph McGill character.

Across the street was a building which housed a number of human rights organizations, so many, in fact, that the address was known quite facetiously, of course, to the across-the-street reporters as "the Bomb Throwers' Building." Among the tenants was the American Civil Liberties Union, run then by Chuck Morgan, who left Birmingham after publicly questioning the efficacy of Bull Connor's police-dog, water-hose law enforcement methods.

McGill looked late one afternoon from his office over to Morgan's and saw that the ACLU chief was pouring a round of drinks for company assembled in his office. McGill picked up the phone and said in his most sepulchral tones, "Chuck Morgan, this is God. I see what you're doing."

Tarver recounts the occasion a North Georgia superior court judge found McGill, *Constitution* managing editor Fields, and police reporter Keeler McCartney in contempt after publication of documents the judge had expressly denied the paper. "You know, they can put you in jail for contempt of court," Tarver reminded McGill. "Well, I'll serve," McGill replied, "but it will be an honest debt." The convictions were overturned on appeal.

Eugene Patterson, who during his years as *Constitution* editor had visited the Vietnam front and fought racial injustice in editorials and as a member of the U.S. Civil Rights Commission, in May 1967 joined colleagues Ralph McGill and Jack Nelson as a winner of the Pulitzer Prize. Patterson was cited for his editorials, with particular mention of his defense of Julian Bond's right to be seated by the Georgia House, though Patterson was not in agreement with the anti-war views that caused Bond to be voted down.

* * *

April 4, 1968, was another fateful day of the 1960s.

The Reverend Martin Luther King Jr., civil rights leader, 1964 winner of the Nobel Peace Prize, was assassinated outside his motel room in Memphis, Tennessee.

Ralph McGill wrote in the next morning's *Constitution*:

"White slaves killed Dr. Martin Luther King in Memphis. At the moment the trigger man fired, Martin Luther King was a free man. The white killer (or killers) was a slave to fear, a slave to his own sense of inferiority, a slave to hatred, a slave to all the bloody instincts that surge in a brain when a human being decides to become a beast.

"In the wake of this disaster in Memphis, a great many such slaves must consider if they wish to continue serving their masters of fear, hate, inferiority, and beastliness. It is something of an irony that Dr. King was free and hated by so many slaves. It is perhaps too much to hope, but much of the violent reaction to this bloody murder could be blunted if in every city and town there would not be a resolve to remove what remains of injustice and racial prejudices from schools, from training and job opportunities, from housing and community life in general."

Celestine Sibley, *Constitution* reporter and columnist, remembers hearing the news on her car radio while sitting out a rainstorm in a truck stop while driving from Atlanta to Shreveport, Louisiana. A grandson was asleep on the backseat. She thought then, she said, of the time "My child Mary had gone to Montgomery to be in some bus demonstration. And I called Martin Luther King and said, 'My child isn't even 16 years old and she ought to be passing history at school instead of making it.' He laughed and said, 'Well, let me see if I can find her.' He did find her, and he sent her home by airplane with an aide to escort her. Of course, she was mad as hell at me. But I thought about it that night, sitting at the truck stop, that I didn't even thank him, that good man, I didn't even thank him for sending my wild young'un home."

An assemblage estimated at 200,000 gathered in Atlanta for services beginning Tuesday morning, April 9, for the 39-year-old departed leader. From his church and his father's church, Ebenezer Baptist Church on Auburn Avenue, a mule-drawn wagon slowly made its way through the streets 4.3 miles to the Morehouse College campus where outdoor services were held. Among the vast throng of mourners were Sen. and Mrs. Robert Kennedy, Vice-President Hubert Humphrey, former Vice-President

Richard Nixon, Gov. Nelson Rockefeller, Eartha Kitt, Sammy Davis, Floyd Patterson, Sen. Edward Kennedy, Jacqueline Kennedy — the names go on and on. Outside Ebenezer, *Constitution* political editor Remer Tyson reported, there were screams of "Bobby, Bobby" when the senator from New York and his wife emerged. A few short months later he, too, would fall before an assassin's bullet.

Changing of the Guard

On September 11, 1968, Eugene Patterson resigned as editor of *The Constitution*. The parting came because a young editorial-page protégée, B. J. Phillips, wrote a column critical of a proposal by the Georgia Power Company to pass on to consumers a 10 percent federal surtax. Miss Phillips' editorial column, representing a voice for the younger generation, had first appeared in *The Constitution* while she was an undergraduate at the University of Georgia.

Jack Tarver, as usual, got a first edition at home the night the Georgia Power column appeared. Harold Martin's book, *Ralph McGill, Reporter*, relates what happened in these words:

"He called Patterson and suggested, with considerable asperity, that Miss Phillips should confine herself to matters within her field of competence. Patterson responded that he had no intention of telling his columnists what they should or should not write, so long as they stayed within the boundaries of the libel laws and the canons of good taste."

Editor Patterson wrote out his resignation that night, Martin relates.

Speaking of the episode years later, Tarver said the president of Georgia Power had called and "wanted to come down and bring his graphs and charts" to explain why it was necessary to request a rate increase of 10 percent. Tarver said he checked with the editors of the two papers about attending such a meeting and that they indicated they had no plans to make an issue of the rate plan. He said he called the Georgia Power president back and told him he saw no need for a meeting.

"I get the first edition," Tarver said, "and here is B. J. taking out after the power company . . . It really put us in an embarrassing situation."

Tarver explained that he intended to announce soon a 20 percent increase in the price of the Sunday paper, from 20 cents to 25 cents, and increases in the home delivery price of the daily *Journal* and *Constitution*. However, Tarver continued, he did not make these plans known to editors while discussing Georgia Power's proposal to pass along the 10 percent federal surtax.

The departure of Patterson, effective October 1, was a hard blow for McGill, who wrote a warm column of farewell headed "An Essay On Separation."

Martin's book says Patterson's resignation caused no rift between McGill and Tarver.

It was McGill who hired Tarver as associate editor of *The Constitution* in 1943, and it was Tarver who, after being called to the management side of the paper, "steadied the soapbox" for McGill, who came under fire from many quarters for his editorial stances on sensitive issues, especially during the turbulent sixties.

Tarver began his newspaper career on the weekly Vidalia, Georgia, *Advance* shortly after graduating from Mercer University in 1938. Then he started his own weekly, *The Toombs County Democrat*, in Lyons, Georgia. From there he went to *The Macon Evening News* as associate editor and became editor in 1941.

When he joined *The Constitution* in 1943, he wrote a daily column, mostly satirical in nature, that was widely popular. In the late 1940s, during a period when *The Constitution* was losing money, Major Howell called him to the business side to turn the paper around, which he did within a year.

After the merger, Tarver was named assistant to the president. Two years later, he became general manager, 1952-69; then vice-president in 1956; president, 1957-75; president of Cox Enterprises in 1969; and vice chairman of Cox Enterprises in 1976. He retired in 1984.

During his leadership, the newspapers continued to grow in circulation and revenues.

In his book, Martin described Tarver as "one of those rare newspapermen whose journalistic genius lay as much on the business side as the editorial." While he kept a relatively low profile to the general public, Tarver was a mover and shaker in Atlanta and in the newspaper and other industries. He served on the board of several major corporations and was chairman of the board of the Federal Reserve Bank of Atlanta from 1961 to 1967. He also was active and had leadership roles in many state, regional and national newspaper organizations. He was chairman of the Associated Press from 1977 to 1983.

While almost three-fourths of Tarver's career was in management, he was always closely involved in the news and editorial operations of the newspapers. He was quick to find fault and quick to praise. A gifted writer,

Tarver resumed his columns in the Sunday *Journal* and *Constitution* in 1975. They were titled "Our Town (one guy's opinion)" and contained much of the same biting satire that had peppered his earlier daily columns when he first joined *The Constitution*.

Reg Murphy, who had been *The Constitution*'s political editor from 1961 until November 1965, when he left to join a management consultant firm, was named editor to succeed Patterson.

* * *

The sorrows of the 1960s were not over even as the decade came to its final year.

Ralph Emerson McGill of Soddy, Tennessee, who dreamed of and fought courageously for a better South, died of a heart attack two days before his 71st birthday. He and his wife, Mary Lynn, were dinner guests of friends and had gone to the living room to talk when a heart attack came. The date was February 3, 1969.

A friend of the mighty and the humble, recipient of awards and degrees in numbers almost beyond numbering, McGill's greatest legacy was in the land around him: it had become more tolerant and more understanding, closer to brotherhood, because he had been there.

Tributes came from across the nation and from around the world. The Alaska state legislature passed a resolution as an expression of grief. It said, "His words became the prickly conscience of the white man, the clarion call of freedom and pride to the black man, and the voice of civil rights and liberty to all men."

More than 10 years after his death, Atlanta novelist Paul Darcy Boles wrote this of McGill in a review of "The Best of Ralph McGill," a compilation of his columns:

"There was red clay in the style, and there was also extreme sophistication. Sophistication in the sense of knowing where the nub of a problem lay, and pointing straight to it like a setter at quail. The underbrush of controversy and confusion around it didn't matter a whit to him. He went to the heart of it in about five sentences. It was always plain as sun on a mountain lake where he stood — plain, too, that he hated not the haters, but hate itself. Not the self-deluded, but the blindness that deluded them."

A street is named in Atlanta today for Ralph McGill, and a school, and scholarships sponsored by *The Constitution* and *Journal* reach out to young Southern journalists. He lives yet in his land, in measured ways no one can define.

* * *

The Constitution and *Journal* have always been prodigious producers of special editions and of investigative series. Special editions are generally run as part of the Sunday paper, taking advantage of the large combined circulation. Series often start there, for the same reason.

The "Face of Georgia" edition was published October 26, 1958. Made up of 120 pages in six sections, the edition reviewed the past, examined the present, and predicted the future. When the regular news, feature, and magazine sections were added in, the total pages that Sunday were 300.

A year later another paper of that same size was published to commemorate the millionth citizen in the five-county metropolitan area.

A July 26, 1964, edition commemorated the 100th anniversary of the Battle of Atlanta. Called "Plus 100," the regular and special pages of the edition added to a total of 260.

The "Amazing Atlanta" edition of January 18, 1970, featured section-front articles by Reg Murphy, Jack Spalding, Margaret Shannon, and others. It reviewed the decade of the 1960s.

A *Constitution* series in 1961 entitled "The Fading Counties" brought cries of outrage from the counties so designated.

When Durwood McAlister became managing editor of *The Journal* in 1968, he found a belief among reporters that management thought it was all right to cover racial news, but that feature series were frowned on. McAlister put six reporters to work on "The Two Atlantas," a report following up the work of the National Advisory Commission on Civil Disorders (the Kerner Commission). The series won a major national award.

* * *

One of America's most amazing accomplishments, the attainment of a goal set by a young president, came on Sunday, July 20, 1969.

Constitution staff writer Jeff Nesmith said it this way in a story datelined "SPACE CENTER, Houston:"

"Man landed on the moon Sunday at 4:17 p.m. Atlanta time.

"And within seven hours, astronauts Neil Armstrong and Edwin

Aldrin were seen via television throughout the world as they first timidly, then almost playfully, walked about the strange new world for more than two hours. Armstrong stepped upon the surface at 10:56 p.m."

For the Street Sales edition, *The Constitution* set the headline "Men Walk On Moon" in 144-point type and printed it in red. An ear carried a moon graphic and the words "Souvenir Edition."

* * *

All the years *The Constitution* and *The Journal* were operating out of separate newsrooms, they had the services of a joint photographic department (which in 1984 had 28 employees).

Photographers, as part of the news team, went into tense situations even more conspicuously than did notepad-toters because of their equipment. Their courage and daring is the stuff of folklore among reporters. Marion Johnson, Bill Wilson, Ryan Sanders, Kenneth Rogers, Hugh Stovall, Edna Weston, Buddy Colley, Charlie Pugh, Charlie Jackson, Guy Hayes, Floyd Jillson.

In the editorial departments, strong right hands holding pens propped up numerous editors — Cliff Baldowski on *The Constitution*, Lou Erickson on *The Journal*, and in recent years, Sam Rawls and Gene Bassett. Baldy's cartoon of a falling-down town, victim of its own stand against civil rights, won a national Sigma Delta Chi award.

* * *

The Journal and *Constitution* buildings have been picketed through the years by representatives of practically every shade of political and social thought: Ku Kluxers, civil rights activitists, fascists, a labor leader in the company of a donkey with editor Reg Murphy's name on it, and Iranian students. Name a cause, it has probably been there. On June 4, 1970, Gov. Lester Maddox joined the list.

Provoked by an editorial opinion opposing a call for a special session of the General Assembly, Gov. Lester Maddox on May 29 banned *Journal* and *Constitution* boxes from the Capitol grounds. He had the boxes hauled away by state trucks.

The governor, accompanied by family members, picketed the newspaper building for an hour, ignoring a pseudo-throne management had put out for his use. Picket signs accused the "leftist" newspapers of using "news columns, editorials and cartoons for lies, half truths, rumors and voices that are misleading and harmful to Georgia and all Georgians."

A *Journal* story reported that the governor autographed several copies of *The Journal* extended by bystanders but turned away the request of "a young hippie-type girl who asked him to autograph a peace sign. 'I'm not signing any more. You go take a bath and I'll sign it for you,' " the governor was quoted.

As the Maddox governorship was coming to an end, Bruce Galphin, then an editorial associate on *The Constitution*, wrote a book entitled, *The Riddle of Lester Maddox*. Nothing better illustrates the aptness of the title than does the governor's behavior in the case of the banned newspaper boxes.

In an emotional interview June 26 at the Governor's Mansion, Maddox told *Constitution* political editor Bill Shipp that the 25 vending machines hauled away from the Capitol area could be returned, because both papers "treated my controversy about the boxes just about as fair as anything I've ever seen."

The governor also sounded a fervent call for freedom of the press.

"The only way I know this country can stay free is if the people know the truth. And the only thing I know they've got left to give them the truth is the newspapers. If the newspapers don't do it, this country can't go on. The survival of *The Constitution* and *The Journal* is needed in this country."

Maddox couldn't run for a second term, so he settled for the lieutenant governor's race in 1970. And won it.

That was the year Jimmy Carter and former Gov. Carl Sanders came down to a runoff. Tarver cites that race as an example of how the Cox family didn't let their own personal desires result in pressure on the papers. "Anne Cox Chambers (daughter of the governor) had signs that big" — holding out his hands — "on both sides of her Mercedes for Jimmy Carter, and Murphy and Spalding were supporting Sanders." (The editorial pages gave Sanders' previous administration high marks.) Carter won with 59.42 percent of the vote.

Later, in the 1972 presidential race, there was a case of direction from on high. Jim Cox Jr. sent out a memorandum to the Cox papers saying, according to Tarver, "If he were editor, this is what he would do," and recommended support for Richard Nixon over Democrat George McGovern. Tarver said he didn't think the suggestion had any effect in Atlanta, "because I don't think anybody was going to support McGovern anyhow."

* * *

Beginning in 1968, *The Journal* and *The Constitution* set forth on a three-phase building program that by June 1972 would have the entire operation in new buildings. The papers were in new production facilities by 1970, complete with 52 units and six folders of Goss Mark II presses with automatic pasters and an automated newsprint roll-handling system. A computerized newspaper bundle conveyor and truck-loading procedures were also part of the new mechanical building, which fronted on Spring Street.

Just around the corner from the old home at 10 Forsyth Street, the new office building at 72 Marietta St. was bounded on the east by Fairlie Street and on the west by the Sixth District Federal Reserve Bank.

The floors of the new building were thick with carpeting, a first for the newsrooms of *The Constitution* and *The Journal*.

* * *

That one of the most bizarre, and chilling, events in the annals of any newspaper was under way became known about 9.15 p.m. on February 20, 1974, when *Constitution* managing editor Jim Minter picked up his ringing telephone. The caller said, "This is Reg Murphy. I've been kidnapped by the American Revolutionary Army." Minter made a joking response. Then a strange voice was on the phone: "We'll be in touch with you in another way."

This indeed was very serious business.

The beginning of the kidnapping was a telephone call the afternoon before to Murphy at his office. A man who said he was owner of a construction company declared he had 300,000 gallons of fuel oil to give away in order to secure a tax break.

Murphy made a few inquiries and "found that it was possible — though somewhat improbable — that he could get a tax break." The editor agreed to meet the caller at Murphy's home near Emory University Wednesday night.

They went out to the stranger's car, Murphy related, and after about 30 minutes of riding, there was an announcement.

"Mr. Murphy, you have been kidnapped," the driver said. "We're going to straighten out this damn country. We're going to stop these lying, leftist, liberal news media." (The quotes are from Murphy's long narrative of the 49-hour kidnapping.)

The first night was spent at what Murphy deduced to be a private residence. Two tapes of Murphy speaking were made there. The second night was spent in a motel (somewhere in South Carolina, Murphy thought). In between, the editor was kept bound, gagged and blindfolded in the trunk of the automobile.

Utilizing the Murphy tapes, arrangements with randomly selected third-party intermediaries contacted via phone and a final, cinching call in which Murphy was to prove he was still alive, the kidnapper — who referred to himself as "the Colonel" — worked out details for a payoff and the release of his victim.

Jim Minter, dressed as directed in a short-sleeve sports shirt, slacks and tennis shoes and driving an open Jeep, was to put the $700,000 ransom at the edge of a southbound sign on Georgia 400 near Alpharetta. Minutes afterward, Minter called the FBI to report he had seen the money picked up.

Less than an hour later, the kidnapper phoned to announce he had the money and that Murphy would be released "around 9 o'clock somewhere in Atlanta."

Still blindfolded, Murphy was turned loose in the parking lot of a motel at I-85 and Shallowford Road in north DeKalb County.

A joyous reunion with family and colleagues followed.

That same night, William A. H. Williams and his wife, Betty Ruth, were arrested in their Lilburn home and the ransom money was recovered.

Found guilty on three charges, Williams received a 40-year sentence. His wife pleaded guilty to charges of concealing a felony and received a three-year suspended sentence.

Two years later, on appeal, a three-judge federal court granted Williams a new trial, saying it had found prejudicial errors by the government and that pre-trial publicity made it impossible for Williams to get a fair trial in Georgia. The second trial was shifted to Key West, Florida, where Williams received, once more, a 40-year sentence. After serving nearly nine years, Williams was released to a halfway house in El Paso, Texas, with parole authorized for February 22, 1984. Williams, who was 34 years old when he was first convicted, earned a high school equivalency diploma and several college degrees, including one from Mercer University, where Murphy had graduated.

The Constitution staff won high praise for its dual role of news people and negotiators, especially executive editor Bill Fields, who ran a news center at the paper for visiting journalists and also participated in discussions with the "Colonel."

Several days after it was all over, Murphy sent a typewritten note to the Sunday editor suggesting a travel article for the Sunday paper, but was rebuffed by a reply that said: "We have a firm policy against buying travel articles from persons who travel in the trunks of automobiles."

* * *

James M. Cox Jr., chairman of the board of Cox Enterprises, parent firm of the family-owned newspapers, died in Miami October 27, 1974, at age 71. Although much of the emphasis in his business life had been directed toward the Cox radio and television interests, then Cox Broadcasting, Jim Cox Jr. was regarded by newspaper associates as an accomplished and caring leader in the publishing field.

Tarver had a call from Jim Cox during the Reg Murphy kidnap episode, and during the call, Tarver, who then was president of Cox Enterprises as well as president of Atlanta Newspapers, remarked, " 'It has just occurred to me that it was your $700,000 I sent out there in those two suitcases.' He said, 'Well, there wasn't anything else to do.' "

Cox's hobbies included flying and yachting. In 1942, at age 39, he joined the Naval Air Corps as a lieutenant and served until 1945, when he left the corps as a lieutenant commander. A graduate of Yale, Cox maintained a lifelong interest in higher education and was a member of the board of trustees of a number of colleges. The family made sizable donations to the University of Miami. A science center there was named for the younger Cox. His death left two surviving sisters, Anne Cox Chambers of Atlanta and Barbara Cox Anthony of Honolulu, as the dominant owners of Cox Enterprises, Inc., a privately held corporation. Cox Communications, successor to Cox Broadcasting, is a publicly held corporation with its shares traded on the New York Stock Exchange.

The Changing Technology

Far-reaching technological changes were beginning to emerge in the newspaper publishing field by the 1960s and 1970s. After the merger of *The Constitution* and *Journal* in 1950, the papers were produced by 43 typesetting machines, 23 of them used for news type, four for headlines, and 16 for ad composition. A good Linotype operator could put out eight to eight-and-a-half lines a minute. Later, tape punched in the production department and tape versions of wire-service stories were fed into "reading" units attached to Linotype keyboards. Tape-driven Linotype could produce as many as 15 lines per minute.

Not far down the road, and coming on fast, were "cold type" and the computer age, where stories keyed into a terminal at the Winter Olympics in Yugoslavia, for instance, could be bounced by satellite in a trice to newsrooms in America. During the New Hampshire presidential primary in February 1984, *Constitution* editorial page columnist Bill Shipp routinely updated his column at night via portable computer from his home in Cobb County.

First, there were stories read into the computer by an optical character reader, then makeup of advance section and classified pages via cold type. By February 1970, *The Journal* and *The Constitution* were entirely cold-type productions, and by March of the next year the newspaper newsrooms had a total of 50 Talstar T-4000 computer terminals.

The Etaoin Shrdlu era of newspapering was over. (Etaoin Shrdlu was an occasional typographical monstrosity appearing in print during the hot type days. Linotype operators filling out a junk line would run an index finger down the first two rows of the keyboard, giving the world Etaoin Shrdlu.)

Mayo Morris, one of four women Linotype operators at *The Journal* and *Constitution*, reached retirement age before the Big Change. A story in a 1971 edition of the *Headliner*, *The Journal* and *Constitution* company newspaper, reported: "I just couldn't say good-bye to friends I had been so closely associated with for 38 years. I asked my foreman Bill Weir to let me leave December 30 instead of the next day, when I was scheduled to retire. I said please not to tell anybody I wouldn't be back."

The production department changes, vast as they were, went smoothly, said Minor J. "Buddy" Ward, now president of the Atlanta Newspapers. Ward, who started as an apprentice in 1953, said, "It was such a gradual, evolutionary sort of change-over. Not a crash program kind of thing that required extensive training efforts. Basically, we were doing the same type of jobs with slightly different materials."

And in the future?

"The next thing I anticipate happening is the implementation of a pagination system where all the pages are composed on a screen and transmitted to a typesetting device as one unit, possibly with ads being pasted in after the fact and possibly with ads set in position just like news."

And after that?

"There may be a direct computer-to-plate system where instead of dumping a paginated page to a typesetter device, we'll just dump it to a plate making device."

* * *

Content and makeup of the papers also were changing during these years.

One of the earliest areas to undergo alteration was the society pages. In February of 1975 announcement was made that "because of space limitations," the papers would discontinue accepting pictures for engagement and wedding announcements.

The new feature sections had much broader horizons. Television pages were placed there, and specialists in areas from the visual arts to rock music reviewed the big shows. More movie, and dance, and serious music news was run. Feature articles were included to appeal to the young, to men, and maybe even to women. The young professionals, the singles, the homemakers, the people about town, all were targeted. One assistant managing editor referred to the new sections as the "dessert section" of the paper.

Yolande Gwin has written about Atlanta society for 50 years. She started at *The Constitution* as a society writer and in the 1960s moved to *The Journal* as society editor.

Now she does a society column for the Sunday paper. Musing about the changes, she said in an interview, "Now we don't use any pictures at all, and the marriage announcement is limited to 75 words. I notice in the paper that they have gone over the limit many times, which I suppose couldn't be helped. It is awfully hard to keep within a limitation of 75 words. Then they stopped using society features and things like that; and it just became more of a, just a . . . no more society."

Miss Gwin acknowledges Atlanta is different now, although the exclusive clubs and debutante balls are still big parts of society.

"Everybody used to love to read about the brides and what they wore, and all that, you know, and they don't do that anymore. It might be the city of Atlanta has grown so we can't do it for every one so we can't do it for one. That's the way I look at it . . ."

Yolande in her 1983 book, *Yolande's Atlanta*, relates that she broke the first story of *Gone With The Wind*. Here, in her own exuberant words from a 1984 interview, is how it happened:

"One day I was sitting there looking at a blank sheet of paper; I didn't have any news. And that's when I happened to remember kidding Peggy (Margaret Mitchell) about writing the "Great American Novel," so I called her up and said, 'How about that Great American Novel, have you ever finished it? I need some news.' She said, 'You won't believe it, but Macmillan has taken it.' And I said, 'Goody, goody. Grand.' And I put a piece in the column (written under the name Sally Forth) about it, never expecting it to be what it was, you know." The date was February 9, 1936.

* * *

In 1971, James G. Minter Jr., executive sports editor of *The Journal* since 1962, was named managing editor of *The Constitution*. Reg Murphy left the paper in 1975 to become editor and publisher of *The San Francisco Examiner*. He was succeeded as editor by associate editor Hal Gulliver, who first came to *The Constitution* in 1962 as a reporter.

Bill Ray was named president of Atlanta Newspapers in 1975 and was replaced as general manager and executive vice-president by Thomas H. Wood. At the end of 1976, Ray retired, and Wood became president. James Cox Kennedy, grandson of Governor Cox, became executive vice-president and general manager.

Cox Enterprises, Inc., moved its offices to the ninth floor of the new *Journal* and *Constitution* news building in 1974. Garner Anthony was named chairman to succeed James M. Cox, Jr., Anne Cox Chambers was named chairman of Atlanta Newspapers, and Barbara Cox Anthony was named chairman of Dayton Newspapers.

* * *

In 1976, Tarver was named vice chairman of Cox Enterprises, Inc. Succeeding him as president of CEI was Charles E. Glover, president of Dayton Newspapers, publishers of the Dayton *Journal Herald* and *Dayton Daily News*. Tarver continued as publisher of *The Journal* and *Constitution*.

Jimmy Carter, elected president in 1976, appointed Mrs. Chambers, a longtime supporter, as U.S. ambassador to Belgium. During her service there, Belgium's King Badouin presented her with the nation's second highest decoration, the Order of the Crown.

Early in 1984 in Atlanta, Mrs. Chambers was honored with the

Human Relations Award at the annual banquet of the Institute of Human Relations of the American Jewish Committee. The presentation was made by former President Carter.

Responding, Mrs. Chambers pledged to continue the tradition of "forthright speech" represented by her father, James M. Cox, and by Ralph McGill.

* * *

The Saturday editions of *The Journal* and *Constitution* were combined September 18, 1976, into *Weekend*, a traditional newspaper with expanded attention to leisure time, including a large tabloid section with entertainment features, restaurant reviews, suggested weekend trips, and extensive listings of every imaginable activity.

* * *

There are some who think that newspaper people are fairly normal people, and, in a way, they are right. Reporters and editors have wives, children, mortgages, dreams — and occasionally a streak of zaniness.

Lee Fuhrman, a dapper rewrite man for *The Constitution* who at times wore spats, was known to yell "Stop the presses" into the phone and "Get me the President" while schoolchildren were visiting the city room.

Paul Jones, a gifted writer for more than 40 years on *The Constitution*, knew many of Hollywood's biggest stars. Covering the making in Georgia of "The Great Locomotive Chase," Jones was recruited for a role. He said, "They went that-a-way."

Hugh Merrill was summoned to *The Journal* city desk early one morning for an assignment by city editor Bob Johnson. "I can't do it," said Merrill.

Johnson regarded him icily. "What do you mean, you can't do it?"

"Because," said Merrill, ripping open his shirt to display a colorful T-shirt, "this is a job for Superman!"

News editor Allen Hauck gazed upon a page-one proof of *The Constitution* one night to read with some astonishment "Giant Buzzard Batters Northeast." He grabbed the phone for the composing room. Of course, the page had gone in reading, "Blizzard." Just a little joke on Hauck.

Another time *The Journal* suspected the night *Constitution* crew of getting news tips off *The Los Angeles Times* wire, a service subscribed to by *The Journal*. So, right after Jimmy Carter was elected president, electronic geniuses associated with *The Journal* put a phony news item on the L.A. wire saying Jack Tarver of Atlanta Newspapers was expected to be named secretary of the treasury (after all, he had been chairman of the Atlanta Federal Reserve Board). The story went by the computer screen unnoticed in a routine clearing of the *L.A. Times* wire. The patient plotters put the story in the system again. This time it was seen.

The news desk called managing editor Eddie Sears at home. He called Tarver late at night. Mr. T. told Sears it was a gag.

If any of this foolishness ever gets in the paper, newspaper histories are going to be considerably livelier than they are now.

The public, or part of it, may be to blame for bizarre behavior in newsrooms. Newspapers get incredible telephone calls (Do alligators run faster than horses?) and incredible visitors.

Journal reporter Bill Montgomery was sitting in for Julia Battle, answering the city desk phone while she was at lunch. Here is his report:

"A black man dressed in a white suit, white shirt, and white tie came to the city desk and said solemnly to Bob Johnson: 'I'm God.' Johnson looked up, went back to whatever he was doing, and said, 'God, I'm afraid I don't have a minute for you.' The guy stood there kind of blank and turned around and left."

On another occasion a young man accosted Hank Ezell at *The Journal* city desk, ranted and raved for a while and finally left. A couple of days later Ezell came upon him emptying a pistol into the sky at Five Points. Luckily, no one was injured.

* * *

One of the biggest sports stories ever came with the swing of a bat in Atlanta/Fulton County Stadium at 9:07 p.m., April 8, 1974: Hank Aaron of the Atlanta Braves broke Babe Ruth's home run record total of 714, which had stood since 1935.

The Constitution had the break on the story. Here is Wayne Minshew's page one lead:

"Hank Aaron cut off a huge slice of baseball history for himself Monday night. He did the impossible. He broke the unbreakable record, the one even Babe Ruth himself thought might stand forever.

"King Henry hit the 715th home run of his career."

The Constitution used two eight-column lines of 84-point type and a color shot of the historic swing.

Inside, a half-page picture diagrammed the 385-foot swat over the left field fence. Sports editor Jesse Outlar noted that more than 50,000 persons were on hand and that millions more were looking on TV. "News is history shot on the wing, and they saw the Hammer establish the greatest record in sports."

* * *

The Journal and *Constitution* had for years maintained one- or two-person Washington bureaus, mainly to report on the activities of the Georgia delegation and on legislation particularly applicable to the state and/or the South. Occasionally, the Washington people would cover a national story.

In early 1974, Cox Enterprises, the parent firm of a growing chain of Cox newspapers, established a bureau in Washington. David Kraslow, who had been with *The L.A. Times* and with *The Washington Star-News*, was named bureau chief. He hired three national reporters and two people for the office staff. *The Journal* and *Constitution* Washington correspondents and those representing other Cox papers were to coordinate their work with the new bureau, which moved in June of its first year to the National Press Building at 1901 Pennsylvania Ave.

National bureau reporters were a tremendous help in augmenting the coverage of Jimmy Carter's presidential campaign, particularly by providing in-depth reviews for the Sunday paper. With Carter's election, two more reporters were added to the bureau staff.

In August 1977, Kraslow went to the Cox-owned *Miami News* as publisher. Andrew Glass, one of the first reporters in the bureau at its start, was named Kraslow's successor. In 1979, the Washington bureau began an arrangement with *The New York Times* whereby stories from the Cox wire would be provided for *The New York Times* News Service. Jim Bentley, former *Constitution* city editor, was named news editor at the bureau.

By 1984, the Washington bureau had expanded internationally, with correspondents reporting from Toronto, Mexico City, Buenos Aires, Tokyo, Rome and Miami (for the Caribbean and Central America).

The bureau has five regional correspondents in the United States and also moves on its wire stories supplied by Cox newspapers.

The Washington bureau provides specialized coverage and investigative series, as well as reporting from the Washington beat. Joseph Albright won a national Sigma Delta Chi award in 1981 for his series of stories on defects in America's nuclear command and control network. The next year, Albright and Cheryl Arvidson won the Raymond J. Clapper Memorial Award for their series "The Snub-Nosed Killers: Handguns in America."

In addition to the reporting of the Washington bureau from foreign lands, foreign editor Randal Ashley of *The Journal* and *Constitution* can call on his own network of 16 stringers in 14 countries.

* * *

On Monday, February 6, 1978, *The Constitution* and *The Journal* emerged with new looks, based on open section fronts throughout the papers. Previously, long-standing advertising contracts had prevented such a change. The Sunday paper also was redesigned.

There were other changes at the papers early in 1978. Jack Spalding retired as editor of *The Journal*. *Journal* managing editor Durwood McAlister succeeded him. Jim Minter, managing editor at *The Constitution*, moved to the same spot on *The Journal*. Assistant managing editor Edward M. (Eddie) Sears became the new *Constitution* newsroom boss.

(Persons at high editorial and newsroom levels frequently were moved from paper to paper through the years, but reporters and sub-editors practically never made such switches.)

The venerable Atlanta *Journal-Constitution* magazine also was changing through the years. During the 1979-80 editorship of Nancy F. Smith, who came from *Texas Monthly*, the magazine's format was modified and a new name, *Atlanta Weekly*, adopted.

The magazine, a crucial part of Georgia journalism since its beginnings as a supplement of *The Journal*, was 72 years old February 11, 1984. For 44 of those years, the magazine was directed by its original editor, Angus Perkerson, who in 1940 won the National Headliners' Award for "general excellence in editing a locally produced Sunday newspaper magazine."

Margaret Mitchell was one of his staff members, and among those who contributed articles were Will Rogers, the humorist, Harold Ross, a *Journal* reporter who later started *New Yorker* magazine, and famed golfer Bobby Jones.

George Hatcher, who had been in newspapering in Atlanta since 1929, was named editor of the magazine in 1957. He was succeeded in 1971 by Andrew Sparks. Lee Walburn became editor-in-chief in the fall of 1980. He directs a magazine that has shorter articles than in the past, a greater varicty of subjects covered weekly under departmental headings, a column by the editor, and stories of the arts, the fad, the concerns, the challenges, the heritage of contemporary Georgia.

Atlanta Weekly, second oldest newspaper magazine in the country (to that of *The New York Times*), fills a vibrant role on Sunday and is recognized as a leader by numerous awards.

* * *

In the late summer of 1978, Patricia LaHatte, promotion director for Atlanta Newspapers, wrote a story for Editor and Publisher that began as follows:

"When the South's major newspapers, *The Atlanta Constitution* (morning) and *The Atlanta Journal* (evening), are in the dark about something — anything — THAT'S news . . ."

At 11:39 a.m. Wednesday, August 16, a pile driver working at the site of the Metropolitan Atlanta Rapid Transit system Omni station went through major electric connectors supplying power to a six-block area.

The Journal had just finished printing two editions when the lights went out — and stayed out until 12:14 p.m. Thursday. While the power was gone, *Constitution* managing editor Sears and approximately 25 staffers moved out to the plant of the Decatur News Publishing Company and put out a four-page combined *Journal* and *Constitution* for delivery Thursday morning. *The Constitution* was back on its regular production run by Friday morning and *The Journal* by that afternoon.

The Atlanta papers had a happier story involving MARTA to report less than a year later. With all kinds of dignitaries and plain people on hand, the rapid-rail system began regular services between the Avondale and Georgia State University stations Saturday, June 30, 1979. Sharon Bailey, who had covered MARTA for five years for *The Constitution*, wrote the story for the Sunday *Atlanta Journal and Constitution*.

Also in 1979, *Journal* assistant city editor Chet Fuller accepted the coveted "Green Eyeshade Award," the major honor accorded Southeastern journalists yearly by Sigma Delta Chi, for "A Black Man's Diary," a 10-part series based on three months of travel about the region in the role of an unemployed black man looking for work.

Many series require considerable composure on the part of the writer or writers. An instance in 1974 comes to mind. Reporter Jeff Nesmith and assistant managing editor Jim Rankin of *The Constitution* were investigating anti-poverty expenditures in rural Hancock County, where John McCown, a dynamic black leader and chairman of the county commission, had attracted millions in federal and foundation funds.

Nesmith and Rankin were in the clerk of court's office when his phone rang. The conversation at that end was very brief, consisting of, "Uh huh . . . two of them."

Investigative series and articles, and stories that simply portray a cause for action continue to be primary concerns of *The Journal* and *The Constitution*, along with regular coverage of breaking news.

Here, briefly listed is a sampling of regional and national attention focused on *The Journal* and *Constitution* as a result of news coverage in the recent past:

— Media Appreciation Award from the United Negro College Fund (1978), to *The Constitution* and reporters Alexis Scott Reeves, Jerry Schwartz and Steven Holmes;

— The top Robert F. Kennedy Award (1980) to *The Constitution* for a series of articles, "The Underpaid and Under-protected," focusing on exploitation of the working poor in Georgia, by Paul Lieberman and Chester Goolrick, with the assistance of reporters Lee May, Charlene P. Smith-Williams, and Steve Johnson;

— Media Award for Economic Understanding (1980), to *The Constitution* for a series of articles on energy prepared by a team of 28 writers;

— American Bar Association Gavel Awards (1980), to *The Constitution* for a series entitled "Voting: A Right Still Denied," by Paul Lieberman, Ken Willis and Chester Goolrick, and to *Atlanta Weeky* for an article, "Women Lawyers: Is There Equality Under the Law?", by Faye Goolrick;

— Sidney Hillman Foundation Award (1981) to *The Constitution*, for a 10-part series, "Black and Poor in Atlanta," by 20 reporters, photographers and editors;

— National Headliner Club Award (1981) to *The Constitution*, for coverage of the case of Atlanta's missing and slain children;

— Associated Press Sports Editors Association Awards (1983), to *The Journal*, for having the best daily sports section in the nation and to the Sunday *Journal* and *Constitution*, for having the second best Sunday sports section in the nation;

— George Polk Award (1984) to *Journal-Constitution* reporters Paul Lieberman and Celia Dugger, for their series, "Kaolin: Georgia's Lost

Inheritance." The series revealed that only a small portion of the wealth of the white clay goes to the families who own the land and that the kaolin industry has escaped taxation of its raw material.

As always, *The Journal* and *Constitution* kept affairs at the Capitol under close observation, writing stories in 1983-84 on Capitol renovation and on pension abuses that resulted in grand jury indictments on the one hand and legislative reform on the other.

The Journal and *The Constitution* in the fall of 1979 began publication of four editions called "Extra." Directed to community news, the tabloid papers were made a part of the regular *Constitution* and *Journal* papers on Thursdays. The four new editions covered DeKalb, Cobb, North Fulton and In-town (Atlanta). In 1983, three more Extra editions were added, with offices in Gwinnett, South Fulton and Clayton.

* * *

The Constitution staff suffered a staggering loss in January of 1980: Leroy (Flash) Noles died. He started at *The Constitution* in 1937 as a copyboy, and he remained a copyboy, having at the end a somewhat nebulous title of "head copy boy."

"It's the end of an era at *The Constitution*," publisher Jack Tarver said.

"He was our secret weapon," *Constitution* managing editor Eddie Sears declared. "He was the guy who held it all together. We all loved him very much, and we'll miss him."

Executive editor Bill Fields said, "Leroy was the pillar of *The Constitution*. He was an old-fashioned copy boy who looked after everything, knew where it was, and knew how to get it."

Three columnists and an editorial also paid tribute.

John Schaffner, who came to *The Constitution* in August 1977 and served as executive news editor and assistant managing editor, was named managing editor February 11, 1980, succeeding Eddie Sears, who moved to *The Journal* as managing editor. Sears replaced Jim Minter, who succeeded the retiring vice-president and executive editor Bill Fields.

* * *

A story that began in July 1979 with the discovery of the decomposed bodies of two black teen-agers grew into one of Atlanta's and the nation's most frightening series of murders. Before the story ended in a Fulton County courtroom on Saturday, February 27, 1982, the bodies of 27 slain black teen-agers and young adults would be found. As the story grew, *The Journal* and *The Constitution* each had several reporters assigned full-time, and their work was augmented constantly by the reporting of others.

Media people from all across the country and from many foreign lands came to Atlanta. The pressures and complexities and racially sensitive nature of the case of the missing and murdered children was a part of the newsrooms for many months, officially ending only when Wayne Williams, 23, a black, was given two sentences of life for the slaying of two of the victims.

"The coverage of the missing and murdered children tested the professionalism of both newsrooms daily," Jim Minter said. "It was a treacherous story, complicated by nuts and cranks, media invasion, and the potential explosion of the community. At the beginning, we made a decision that we would not exploit the story for the purpose of selling newspapers. We did not . . . Journalistically, it was our finest hour."

* * *

The Constitution and *Journal* have always had columnists — editorial and newspage — with wide appeal: McGill, Patterson, Spalding, Murphy, McAlister, Gulliver, Shipp, Tarver. The list goes on and on.

Doris Lockerman, named an associate editor by *The Constitution* in 1948, wrote a column at various times for both the news and editorial pages. Ralph McGill announced her appointment in a page-one story. "The new associate editor and her staff will not patronize women, but will recognize them for what they are, intelligent, interested, influential persons."

The Journal's Morgan Blake and Ernest Rogers were great favorites. Rogers, writing a few months before his retirement in the fall of 1962, recalled a speaking appearance before the Georgia Press Institute.

"I pointed out that during the 18 years and three months I have been at it some 5,400 columns have been written with a total output of approximately 4 million words . . . If all those words had been arranged in the proper sequence, they might have amounted to something."

Hugh Park's "Around Town" newspage column in *The Journal* chronicled, in the words of an associate, "the complex moods of a growing city through the simple deeds of its rare and common people." Before becoming a columnist, Park was a top-line reporter.

Harold Martin's basic job was writing for *The Saturday Evening Post*, but he also had a wide following as an editorial-page columnist for *The Constitution*. Generally, he wrote everyday things, of children and animals and uncomplicated joys. But he could also plumb the deepest emotions.

And there is the incomparable Celestine Sibley, who for more than 30 years has covered the great stories and also written a column that reaches out and enfolds a vast audience. She can fix broken dreams and tell the recesses of life's mysteries. As long ago as 1951, her column — of a child, 8, sitting by herself because the family couldn't sit together in a crowded restaurant, yelling down the counter, "Mommy, don't people ask the blessing in this place?", and the counterman answering, "We do, sister. You say it." — won for Celestine the national Christophers award. And as recently as 1982, Celestine was presented the first Jim Townsend Award for her book, *Children, My Children*.

Lewis Grizzard came out of the University of Georgia to a sports-writing job on *The Journal* in 1968 and in 1971 succeeded Jim Minter as executive sports editor when Minter went to *The Constitution*. Later, he had two news jobs with *The Journal* and *The Constitution*, didn't like either job, and finally emerged as executive sports editor of *The Chicago Sun-Times*. From there, he came home to Georgia to write a sports column for *The Constitution* and less than a year later to a newspage column in early 1978. Syndicated now, Grizzard is in more than 130 newspapers, more by far than any other Atlanta-based columnist ever attained.

* * *

Finally, the Staff Merger

On May 8, 1982, the unthinkable was announced: the news staffs of *The Journal* and *The Constitution* would be combined by mid-summer. President Tom Wood made the announcement in a news story published in "Weekend," the joint Saturday paper. Editorial departments would remain distinct, and each paper would retain its own identity. The move was being made, Wood explained, to do away with duplicate assignments and to provide wider coverage.

This was tough news, combining separate newsrooms where the mightiest of both papers had trod. But it was a challenge.

There were other changes.

Wood, president of Atlanta Newspapers since 1977, announced his resignation in a story published May 28, 1982. Charles Glover, president of Cox Enterprises, Inc., announced Wood would be succeeded by David E. Easterly, vice-president of operations for the Cox newspaper group, a newsman with 19 years of experience.

Wood in his resignation paid tribute to *The Atlanta Journal* and *The Atlanta Constitution* and their staffs. He said, however, "there comes a time when there is a question of direction and priorities. Mr. Glover and I have decided it is time for a change. I wish them well, and I am sure they wish me well."

Easterly announced on May 30 that Jim Minter had been named editor of *The Atlanta Journal* and *The Atlanta Constitution*. Minor J. "Buddy" Ward was named executive vice-president and general manager at the same time.

In March 1984, Ward was made president, in charge of non-editorial operations, and Easterly became publisher. Minter continued in charge of editorial and news operations.

Hal Gulliver, editorial page editor of *The Constitution*, left the paper on June 18, 1982, to enter another field. He had been editor nearly seven years.

Gulliver was succeeded by Tom Teepen, who came from the *Dayton Daily News*, where he had been editorial-page editor since 1968. He began as a reporter there in 1959.

Eddie Sears, managing editor of *The Journal*, was named managing editor also of *The Constitution*, the person in overall charge of the combined news operation. John Schaffner, managing editor of *The Constitution*, left the paper and the profession, staying in Atlanta in public relations/advertising.

Sears, reflecting on the newsroom merger after two years, said, "This is the only 'offensive' merger I've ever heard of — no paper failed, nobody was laid off, no 24-hour newspaper."

The news and editorial departments, plus reference and photo, now total 385 persons.

Bureaus have been established for the Carolinas, Tennessee, Mississippi and Florida. And a roving staffman also has been provided for the region. In Georgia, bureaus have been established in Athens, Macon, Savannah and Columbus.

At the time of the newsroom merger, each paper had seven or eight persons in its business news reporting departments, and *The Constitution* had made business a section front.

The combined business news staff now totals 26 persons, including editors and reporters.

Nick Poulos, business editor, said, "I think the primary responsibility of our business staff is to give our readers as much news as possible in the area they live in — in other words, local business news . . . We also have to offer them a balance of local, national, and international news. So we have to be very good at making tough judgments."

Poulos said that with regional banking looming, the papers will have to pay increased attention to activities in other key business areas in the South.

Sports pages in Atlanta have an enviable position. There are big-league professional sports and strong college football and basketball teams across the Southern region. And fanatical followers by the stadiums full.

Furman Bisher recalls he had eight staff members in 1950 in *The Constitution* sports department. Today, there are 44 persons on the combined *Journal* and *Constitution* staffs.

* * *

How do you measure papers over a 35-year period?

Such an appraisal, as McGill often said about politics, is not an exact science.

The first combined Sunday paper published after the merger came out June 4, 1950. It had a total of 240 pages. On page one, the lead story said Atlanta Mayor Hartsfield had called the leader of striking transit operators "an arrogant labor dictator." The big wire story was a $400,000 flood in Galveston, Texas. A two-column box above the fold said the paper was the largest Sunday newspaper ever published in Atlanta. The print order, said the announcement, was 475,000 copies.

The Sunday *Atlanta Journal* and *Atlanta Constitution* of February 26, 1984, had 544 pages, counting zoned advertising inserts. The lead story, by Joseph Albright of Cox News Service, was datelined BEIRUT, Lebanon, and told of U.S. peacekeeping Marines pulling out of that anguished country. The first of a two-part series, on page one, had a headline saying, "How dirty cash turns into clean profit." The articles, by Cheryl Arvidson of Cox News Service, were investigating the illegal money-laundry industry, "which annually handles billions of dollars from criminals and tax evaders." There was a story by staff writer Bill Montgomery reporting how the changing of charges in drunk-driving cases was allowing thousands of drivers to hold on to their licenses. A story out of New Hampshire, by Andrew Mollison of the Washington Bureau, was setting the scene for the upcoming Democratic primary.

Audit figures for the fall of 1983 placed the circulation of the Sunday paper at 539,835. The dailies in the same audit were at 218,298 for *The Constitution* and 182,283 for *The Journal*. The afternoon paper, after a circulation drop extending over a number of years, has shown gains on into 1984.

Today's Sunday paper, of course, is much more diversified than that of the 1950s. A free-standing Travel section certainly is appropriate for a city with the second busiest airport in the United States. Home section, the arts, book review pages, analysis section, business, a local news section, fashions, *Atlanta Weeky*, *TV Week* (a television booklet added in 1980), international, national sections. And advertising.

The Atlanta Journal and *The Atlanta Constitution* in 1950 had a combined classified ad count of 577,032. The 1983 ad count for the two papers, including Sunday, was 2,804,104. And other types of advertising are up by large margins.

Comparing physical properties is not too difficult, but putting the spirit of a city, state or region, the opportunities and freedoms of a people into a computer is beyond capabilities.

When Jim Minter was named editor of *The Journal* and *Constitution*, he said in a column:

"Mainly, newspapers are here to tell the truth, report the news fairly and without fear, and offer leadership where they can.

"*The Atlanta Journal* and *The Atlanta Constitution* historically have done that. We are and have been committed to helping make this city and its environs work for all people, rich or poor, black or white, newcomer or pioneer family."

* * *

The Journal and *Constitution* have 4,172 employees, and when one looks back through the eventful years, there is a sadness that more persons cannot by name be made a part of this history — the composing-room foremen, the printers who have saved many an edition, the stereotype crews, the pressmen, the advertising people, circulation, mail room, reference, business office, secretaries, clerks, artists, all the skills and talents that put out newspapers 365 days a year.

This is their story, too.

The Atlanta Times: A Forbidden Dream

BY RICHARD HYATT

On the day *The Atlanta Times* died, Billy Dilworth, its most popular columnist, went to church and the preacher called on him to offer a prayer. The congregation had just finished singing, "Rescue the Perishing."

But until Dr. Roy McClain, Atlanta First Baptist, called his name, Dilworth wasn't hearing much of anything. Years later he remembered feeling "lower than a snail." His knuckles turned white as he gripped the pew in front of him and he wondered if he should just try and run for the door. But he didn't run and he still recalls the short prayer he finally managed to mumble.

"Our father, we thank you for a good day . . . a good church . . . a good pastor. Amen."

It had been anything but a good day for Dilworth whose amen was uttered so softly that Dr. McClain had to repeat it for the congregation to know Dilworth had finished talking with the Lord. Dilworth asked McClain after the service why he had called on him to pray that night.

"Because you needed it," McClain replied.

A dream of many Georgians had died that day. There were several hundred like Dilworth who had put muscle and mind into making *The Atlanta Times* a dream that worked, but there were thousands of others who had contributed various amounts of money and their hopes and — yes, their real and imagined grievances against what they considered a monolithic newspaper empire in Atlanta. Dr. McClain sensed that for people like Dilworth in particular that the closing of a newspaper was akin to the death of a close human friend.

On Wednesday, August 31, 1965, *The Times* made its obituary its final banner story.

"*Times* Suspends Publication," the headline read that afternoon. Three words telling readers that the owners had discovered their dream had turned into a financial nightmare.

The atmosphere was so different from just 14 months earlier, June 12, 1964, when the front page brassily told Atlanta "Hello, We're Here." That day's paper heralded a new voice for Atlanta. People jostled each other to grab a copy from the paper's green racks downtown and backed traffic up Forest Road in front of the plant, braving a thunderstorm for a copy of that historic first edition.

It was an excitement Atlanta hadn't felt in decades. Not since *The Atlanta Georgian* was founded in 1903 had Atlanta welcomed a new daily paper. And in 1939, it had said goodbye to *The Georgian*. Now those citizens who had believed generations of suspender-popping politicians who railed about those "Lyin' Atlanta newspapers" had that new voice. A conservative voice, nurtured by a fear of changes that were taking place in the South where voters had suddenly discovered there was a political party other than the Democrats, and supported by 10,000 stockholders — many of whom were more at home in the super market than the stock market.

The Times hit the streets that June, but the idea had been born years before. The organization was chartered June 9, 1961 with a board of directors composed of Guy W. Rutland Sr., E. E. Andrews, Douglas N. McCurdy Sr., Walter T. Austin, George M. Bazemore, James C. Davis, J. W. Hughes, A. V. Kennedy, Warren P. Sewell and Allen M. Woodall Sr. Original shares sold for $2 each and by the end of that year 252,350 shares of first issue stock had been sold.

As the needed capital was raised, the organization began to take shape. Judge James C. Davis — who had lost his Congressional seat to fellow Democrat Charles Weltner — became chairman of the board and later publisher. Davis was a silver haired former judge from DeKalb County who felt he had a debt to settle against *The Constitution* and *Journal* which had supported his more liberal opponent. Davis' first move as publisher was to name Luke Greene as editor. Greene had been associate editor of *The Journal* seven years and a working Georgia journalist for nearly 25 years.

As summer approached, Davis and Greene began recruiting a news staff. One of their first recruits was Luther Thigpen who joined the paper as managing editor — the same position he had held on *The Augusta Chronicle*. Thigpen remembers that assembling a news organization wasn't hard.

"Word got around and we had no shortage of applications from good, sound news people," said Thigpen, now publisher of *The Leaf-Chronicle* in Clarkesville, Tennessee. "It was the challenge that attracted people, the challenge of starting up a new paper in a city like Atlanta and competing with newspapers like *The Journal* and *Constitution*.

"I don't think too many of us thought about the politics. In fact, I thought we could function in spite of politics," Thigpen said. "The politics affected some management decisions, but I don't think we let it affect the news columns. I just did what I thought was right."

Thigpen's original staff included city editor William C. Surber, formerly managing editor of *The Nashville Banner*, news editor Ron Gibson, formerly of *The Birmingham Post-Herald*, sports editor George Short, formerly of *The Chattanooga Times* and Sunday editor Loyall Solomon, formerly of *The Savannah Morning News*. Their first assignment was to put together that first edition in a city so new to them that they didn't know how to find Peachtree Street.

When a reader picks up his paper every day he takes it for granted that it'll have a comic page, that he'll be able to get advice from Abby or Ann, that he can read his horoscope and that there'll be an editorial page with columns to get his blood flowing. But assembling those features takes time and that was what Thigpen and other early staff members spent the months before publication doing.

Finally, it was time to get the presses — which once had turned out *The New York Herald-Tribune* — rolling full speed. That first day *The Times* press run topped 180,000 papers, with 95 of the 128 pages being advertising. Davis claimed the paper began with 144,000 paid subscribers, making it the third largest in Georgia.

In a front page editorial, Davis promised readers that *The Times* would "print the news factually, objectively, unslanted" and that it believed "that a primary objective of a newspaper is always to be fair."

The paper's lead editorial that day depicted the paper as "a new voice on the journalistic sound track of this city." The writer compared the paper's cause to Thomas Paine who once said, "It was the cause of America that made me an author."

Greene's first column chronicled the days leading up to that first edition. He remembered the hours of preparation and the meticulous tasks that had to be undertaken.

"And if real dedication means anything in this business — and I am one who believes that it does — then a big part of the battle already has been won," Greene wrote. "But as with politics, the people are the final judges. I only hope they like us enough to match our own enthusiasm."

In the beginning, reader enthusiasm did match the staff's. The first Sunday paper was a strong package, matching the first edition. However, by Monday the number of typographical errors had grown and the over-taxed circulation department also was having problems. But optimism still ruled and within a few months, Davis told stockholders that not one penny had been borrowed and promised a dividend was forthcoming. It was an exciting time, though the excitement soon turned to apprehension.

But whatever was ahead did not affect the staff. The news people were a collection of fresh-faced young people just out of college looking forward to a future and grizzled old newsmen looking backward at an often forgettable past. They had come aboard as strangers, seen the paper become a reality, then later clung together for survival as paychecks bounced like a beach ball and the front door became a revolving door for employees.

For the reporters, it was a romantic adventure.

"In October, I was covering a high school football game between Sale Creek and Tyner around Chattanooga and in January I was covering the Georgia Legislature, competing against journalists like Reg Murphy and Jack Nelson," remembers Frank Stansberry who became political editor of *The Times* and is now in public relations for Coca-Cola at Disney World in Orlando.

"It was exhilarating but frustrating," Stansberry said, recalling the excitement of Atlanta in the 1960s. "Hotels were being built and the interstates were cutting through the middle of town. The Civil Rights movement was just getting under way. Martin Luther King Jr. was an Atlanta minister. In the South, it was a grist mill of change, a time of life rivalling the Civil War. And we were part of it."

Dilworth, who was metro editor of *The Times*, is now state editor of *The Athens Banner-Herald* and a legendary country music DJ in northeast Georgia. He looks back on his peers in Atlanta as family.

"You had people from the country, sophisticated city people, young people working on their first newspaper job and a sprinkling of old timers who gave the newsroom so much flavor. To me, Atlanta was like going to Paris, the beginning of a real dream, working on a paper in a vibrant city. It was a country boy's dream," Dilworth said.

This was near the end of that era when newsrooms echoed the pounding of upright Royal typewriters and composing rooms smelled of sizzling lead. The news staff was caught up in that traditional atmosphere, going head-to-head with *The Journal-Constitution* and in unguarded moments even bragging about beating them to a story. But at the other end of the sprawling plant there was the reality of the bottom line.

From the beginning there were questionable decisions. New furnishings were bought when rented and used ones would have worked just as well. Then there were desks that were too big for the offices for which they were planned, a fleet of green trucks that were bought instead of leased and the purchase of a new Goss press that put the company in debt from which it couldn't escape.

The odds against *The Times* were long under the best of circumstances, but for most of its short life it operated under managerial and decision-making procedures which would have tested the stability of *The Journal* and *Constitution* in their best years.

Davis was 68 when he became publisher of *The Times* and his main qualification for the job was an intense dislike of the existing Atlanta dailies. He had no concept of what a newspaper operation really was but he did give *The Times* an image and a symbolic leadership that was beneficial. Not so the board of directors and corporate officers, who shared with Davis a lack of knowledge about the business and a resentment against the other Atlanta papers, but who lent no leadership to *The Times*, only bad decisions.

A power struggle which developed on the board caused Davis to walk out in November. He later returned and continued to have the title of publisher but he never again wielded authority.

Actually, the strong man in *The Times*' early management was I. M. (Mel) Orner, a veteran newspaper official who had most recently worked with *The St. Petersburg*, Florida *Independent*. Orner had put together the staff and plant, and had exerted as strong a hand as the board would allow him. He was overruled on some critical decisions, such as distribution of *The Times* on a statewide basis, which the board wanted and Orner opposed, and which totally overloaded its capabilities at a crucial time. In November, *The Times*' president, A. P. Jackson, a concrete company executive in Hapeville, demanded that the circulation manager and the advertising manager be fired. Jackson apparently had become angered by many complaints passed on to him by subscribers who couldn't get the paper, or the inevitable errors that torment a new operation. This led to Davis' walkout.

Orner had been planning a 10-day vacation cruise for late November and he decided that nothing should interfere with that, even Davis' resignation. Orner told a meeting of the board that he was running the newspaper, even though the board was now divided over retaining him. He left the office on November 27, and issued a memo to department heads telling them to follow his directions and policies until he returned on December 10.

But shortly after Orner left a memo was posted announcing that the board had appointed one of its members, Thomas Callaway, as "Acting Director, in charge of all operations of *The Atlanta Times*." It was also about this time that employees learned that cash was short. They had previously been assured that plenty of money was available, mainly from stock sales, which were continuing.

The department heads and other employees didn't know what to think or who was really in charge. Several department heads went to Davis' house to urge him to return and take charge, but he felt he couldn't do anything against the board's opposition.

Then in an incredible turn of events word came that Orner had died while on the Caribbean cruise and had been buried at sea. Thus, by default and a tragic death, the board members in revolt against the original *Times* management had prevailed. What was most unusual was that during this period the officers and directors owned less than five percent of *The Times'* total stock. They had the power with very little investment of money.

The Times in some respects was an elaborate stock sale plan from the start, playing on Georgians' fabled animosity against *The Journal* and *Constitution* to promote sales.

By August 1964, a total of $4,199,170 in stock had been sold in *The Times*, with the average purchase being $350, which meant that thousands of Georgians had indeed backed up their resentments with their money. About 80 percent of the stock was sold in the metropolitan Atlanta area, and about $604,000 was paid in commissions to stock salesmen through the summer of 1964. When *The Times* company declared bankruptcy in September 1965, more than $4.5 million in stock had been sold, and apparently had been expended during its months of operation.

Money had already become a problem when Orner died and Davis was relieved of authority. The board then began going through a series of management officials. One of them was Phil Turner, who had been circulation manager of *The Clarkesville*, Mississippi *Gazette*, a paper of 5,500 circulation. Turner came in January, and during his brief time he wielded a sharp axe.

"This new general manager had come on board and his first act was to tell me to cut the news department staff in half — from 36 to 18," Thigpen said. "It fell my lot to do it. These were good people — people I had hand-picked. They had done a great job. But I had to make the choice. I looked at the people and tried to predict what would happen to them if they were let go. I finally realized that whatever 18 we let go, it could just as easily have been the other 18. But all of that was forgotten when I sat across the desk from them. I remember one man just sitting there, his eyes saying 'Why me?' I couldn't answer him. People took it hard. Nobody wanted to give up the battle."

For the last six months, chaos was the order of the day. There were more cutbacks and the few replacements who were added were not the same quality as the original staffers. There were Friday mornings when employees were asked to wait until after 2 p.m. for their checks. There were Fridays when they were asked to wait until Monday. There was a Friday when they were asked to accept three-fourths of their pay in cash with an open promise on when they'd get the rest. There were many Fridays when an *Atlanta Times* check was suitable only for framing.

Stansberry remembers a staff trick.

"If you deposited your check in your checking account and it bounced, then all of the checks you wrote on your account wouldn't be any good. So we would go to Fulton National Bank, get in one line and cash our checks, then get in another one and deposit the money in our account," he recalled.

The newspaper was falling apart, but the staff was pulling together. There were wakes that were more like parties which in reality were ways to feed some of the people who were finding it difficult to pay their grocery tab. There were jokes so they could laugh at things that should have made them cry. And there was still the challenge of putting out a paper every afternoon.

The challenge was met. The group that remained still competed for stories, still met its deadlines and still hoped that someone would march in with a pocket full of money instead of the pocket full of dreams with which the founders had arrived. There was talk of H. L. Hunt investing Texas money and talk of Lammont DuPont Copeland pouring in new capital. Copeland, a scion of the DuPont industrial empire, considered investing one million dollars, but withdrew his offer when debts were higher than he anticipated.

"I got involved with that," remembered Loyall Solomon, who had succeeded Thigpen as managing editor. "I had worked with the board, especially this one fellow. Later, after the paper had closed, I read where he killed himself right there in *The Times* old building. He came in one day with a list of people that this old Tennessee boy couldn't believe. He had been calling them, trying to attract investors."

Why did that day arrive? The theories are as long as *The Times*' list of creditors. They had over-spent and been under-financed. They had never been able to consistently sell advertising to Atlanta's major retail stores. They had tried to become a statewide paper too soon. There had been too much bickering among board members. There had been poor management. There had been still unexplained problems in production and circulation. There had been too many decisions based on ideology instead of sound journalism or good business. Whatever the reason, by late August *The Times* was doomed.

The deadline the board set was August 31. Efforts continued the week before and into that weekend, trying to find someone who would pump new life into the paper. Rumors flowed freely that something would happen, but that's just what they were — rumors.

Work that morning began as usual. Copy clerks tore stories from the wire machines and carefully wrapped the tapes for the linotype machines. Reporters were on the phone. Ray Rogers, a political reporter, was trying to confirm whether axe handle-toting cafeteria owner Lester Maddox was going to run for governor of Georgia. The sports department was doing a wrap-up on the first pro football game played at Atlanta Stadium the previous Saturday. The copy desk was trying to squeeze as many words as they could into 30 point headlines. The first edition looked like any other day's newspaper, but there was something different in the air that Tuesday morning.

As people finished their first edition work, they hung close to their desks. Reporters from the courthouse and other spots wandered into the office along with people who weren't scheduled to work that day. There was something about the clock and something about the closed door to the board room that made everyone in the building know that the deadline approaching was more than an every day final edition.

"Around 11 a.m., we set a deadline of noon," said Solomon, now the owner of Holston Coal Company in Kingsport, Tennessee. "We had two front pages in type and ready — one a regular news front, the other one announcing we were folding. I sat in Judge Davis' office waiting, but nothing happened. Finally, we had waited as long as we could. Roscoe Pickett (who had emerged as the paper's major share-holder) told Luke to do it. Luke told me to go back to the composing room."

The board room was at the front of the building and between there and the composing room was a long hall, passing through retail advertising, the library and finally the newsroom. Both sides of the hall were shoulder-to-shoulder with staff members. The silence shouted. Not a typewriter key or a ringing phone was heard.

"I walked straight on back. I didn't say anything to anybody. I couldn't," Solomon said. "Sid Richards was the shop foreman. I told him which page to roll. Then I stood there and cried."

No one had to announce what had happened. In seconds a room that had bristled with anticipation and excitement 14 months before had been turned into a room full of goodbyes. The owner of the grill down the street called and said cold beer was on the house and many people adjourned to a plastic-seated booth. It wasn't long before the lights of TV crews were glowing and somber broadcasters were standing in front of abandoned typewriters and clattering presses doing an obituary on a newspaper. The phones were busy with other newspapers calling to offer leads on jobs.

Years have passed. The green newspaper tubes along Georgia roadsides have turned to rust or are bringing a good price at flea markets. James C. Davis and Luke Greene are dead. Other members of the news family have scattered around the country — some still working for newspapers. In nostalgic moments, they still wonder what could have been. To them, *The Times* is more than rolls of microfilm in a library reference room.

"We were part of journalism in Georgia," Thigpen said. "It was history. I don't regret a thing."

"We were working with and competing against landmark journalists," Stansberry said. "Ralph McGill was there at *The Constitution*. So was Gene Patterson. There was Reg Murphy, Jack Nelson and we had people like Paul Hemphill. It was a chance at the big leagues."

"The fact that we didn't make it and almost made it adds to the glamor," Dilworth said. "I still miss the smell of hot-type in a composing room. I guess for a long time a lot of us waited for a reunion that never came."

In his parting editorial, Davis said, "There are times when, whatever the cost, we must try. In this battle we have lost, but we lost trying."

The old *Times* building is now a warehouse, but the best evidence that times have changed is the street from which its green trucks, decorated with the wings of a phoenix, once rode to deliver the news. Two decades ago it was named for a Confederate hero — Nathan Bedford Forrest. Now, it is named for a hero of liberal journalism — Ralph McGill.

After Bankruptcy

Robert Carney, who was advertising manager of *The Times* during its short, turbulent life, and later worked with *Family Weekly* in the southeast, wrote the most interesting book on *The Times*. He called it, *What Happened at The Atlanta Times*, and it should be required reading for anyone contemplating the start of a new newspaper. Carney was witness to much of the inside squabbling on the board which helped bring a speedier demise. He also included in his book many memos and stock reports which traced the efforts to first raise money and then to keep *The Times* afloat.

In addition Carney related what happened after *The Times* folded and declared bankruptcy, and how its fate continued for years to affect thousands of Georgians who invested their money and/or efforts.

When bankruptcy was declared one of *The Times'* main assets was $742,000 in money still outstanding on stock purchases. Many who bought stock made a down payment with the remainder due on terms in years to come. When *The Times* folded, those buyers probably thought their obligation was ended. But not so. In October 1968, a suit was filed against all stockholders who still owed more than $300 on their *Times* stock. The total number of defendants was 2,082, the most ever served by one suit in Georgia history. The trustee estimated that it would cost $26,000 just to issue subpoenas to that many defendants. But the suit went on, despite many complaints from stockholders that they had canceled their stock subscriptions, or had been told they would have no obligation if the newspaper folded. Many finally settled, according to Carney's book, with sums ranging from $600 to $46. The cases and the bankruptcy proceeding were still going on when Carney wrote his book in late 1969.

A person mentioned only briefly in the account above, but who played a crucial role in *The Times*, was Roscoe Pickett, an Atlanta lawyer and a former legislator from Pickens County (Jasper). Pickett owned more stock than any of the other directors, which still wasn't much as a percent of the total shares. His participation in *The Times* was limited during 1964 because he ran for the U.S. Congress as a Republican against Democrat Jim McKey in the 4th District, which was primarily DeKalb County. Sen. Barry Goldwater, the Republican candidate for president that year, easily carried the district against President Lyndon Johnson but Pickett lost to McKey, 39,000 to 24,000. Pickett had no doubt expected an endorsement from *The Times*, but it never came, although *The Times* strongly supported Goldwater, who was the first Republican candidate for president ever to carry Georgia.

In March 1965, Pickett was named president of *The Times* company and the board gave him a virtual free hand in making decisions from then until the shutdown. His name was listed on the masthead, and he had more authority for a longer period at *The Times* than any other executive. Mainly, Pickett didn't have to answer to the board, whose members had by now either lost interest in the newspaper or realized that it not only wasn't going to make them any money but would probably cost them money.

The death rattle was already evident when Pickett took over. The paid circulation had dropped to 40,000 in May, and was probably no more than 15,000 on the final publication day. Classified ads which had been strong in the early months had declined. Merchants, sensing the end and observing the many shifts in management, became even less supportive. Features, Sunday comics, pages had all been slashed. The *Sunday TV* book was dropped.

By July Pickett asked employees to "loan" the company their week's salary. In effect the company couldn't meet the payroll. The employees, who worked so hard and strived so mightily to make *The Times* work, often in the face of serious obstacles thrown up by the management, were the biggest losers in many ways. When the paper folded they were left without jobs or severance pay and many of them hadn't been paid in full for several weeks. Money that was put in escrow for several years' salary to attract some of the key department heads had been spent or was not available to pay them off.

The Times was the most ambitious of the many new newspapers started in Georgia since World War II. The next most ambitious was *Thursday*, a weekly in Columbus which was launched in 1973 and lasted only sixteen weeks (see Chapter V). Both of these newspapers, *The Times* and *Thursday*, were more carefully planned, more heavily financed, and had stronger personnel than new papers that have prospered and grown. For example, in 1965, the year *The Times* folded, *The Gwinnett Daily News* was started in Lawrenceville and is now one of the best dailies in the state. In that same year *The Athens Daily News* was started against the existing *Banner-Herald* in Athens and it was sold for a profit 30 months later. It is still being published.

Clayton News/Daily and *The Rockdale Citizen* are other new dailies which have been successful in the Atlanta metro market. Nearby Carrollton now has a daily newspaper, started in 1981. The Neighbor chain of 27 community weeklies and the Sun/News group have prospered as print competition in the Atlanta metro area indicating that there was an advertising market for a medium such as *The Times*. The stories of the new dailies and metro Atlanta groups are told in later chapters of this book. In the chapter on weeklies, there are several examples of new weeklies which have started and not only have survived but have supplanted the older weeklies in their communities.

The examples of these successful new papers provide a useful comparison with *The Times* to see where it went wrong despite the time, effort and relatively large amount of money ($4.5 million from stock sales) which was poured into it.

First, it should be noted that direct — as opposed to indirect — competition with a large metropolitan daily is virtually non-existent in the U.S. in 1984, and was extremely rare in 1964. *The Times* would have been better served to have started out as a DeKalb County newspaper, aiming at that very large market, instead of as an "Atlanta" newspaper. At the time, DeKalb had more than 300,000 population and a daily with *The Times*' resources could probably have dominated it. In fact, it always had more paid subscribers in DeKalb than in Fulton. But the *Times*' board members were not content to look for the less confrontational way. Their real intent was to twit the noses of the *Journal* and *Constitution*.

Secondly, *The Times* started nine years after Charles Hardy introduced offset, cold type printing to Georgia newspapers, and a large number of papers had already switched to offset when *The Times* made a huge investment in hot-type equipment and letter presses, which were obsolete the day they were installed.

Thirdly, most of the new ventures which have succeeded in Georgia were the idea and responsibility of one strong newspaper-oriented publisher, who did not have to answer to a committee of decision-makers.

Nevertheless, *The Times* was an intriguing and dramatic chapter in Georgia newspaper history in the past 40 years. Its newspaper objectives have been accomplished by other publishers, because there are now many more newspapers, daily and weekly, in the Atlanta metro area. Many of its political goals were also realized. Goldwater carried Georgia. Lester Maddox, one of its most loyal advertisers, became governor in 1967. Ben Blackburn succeeded where Pickett had failed by defeating McKey for the 4th District congressional seat in 1966. Pickett, who was also the Republican chairman for Georgia, was a supporter of California Gov. Ronald Reagan for the party's presidential nomination in 1968. Most Georgia Republicans backed Richard Nixon but Pickett's choice eventually made it, ushering in the conservative era which *The Times* had heralded nearly 20 years earlier.

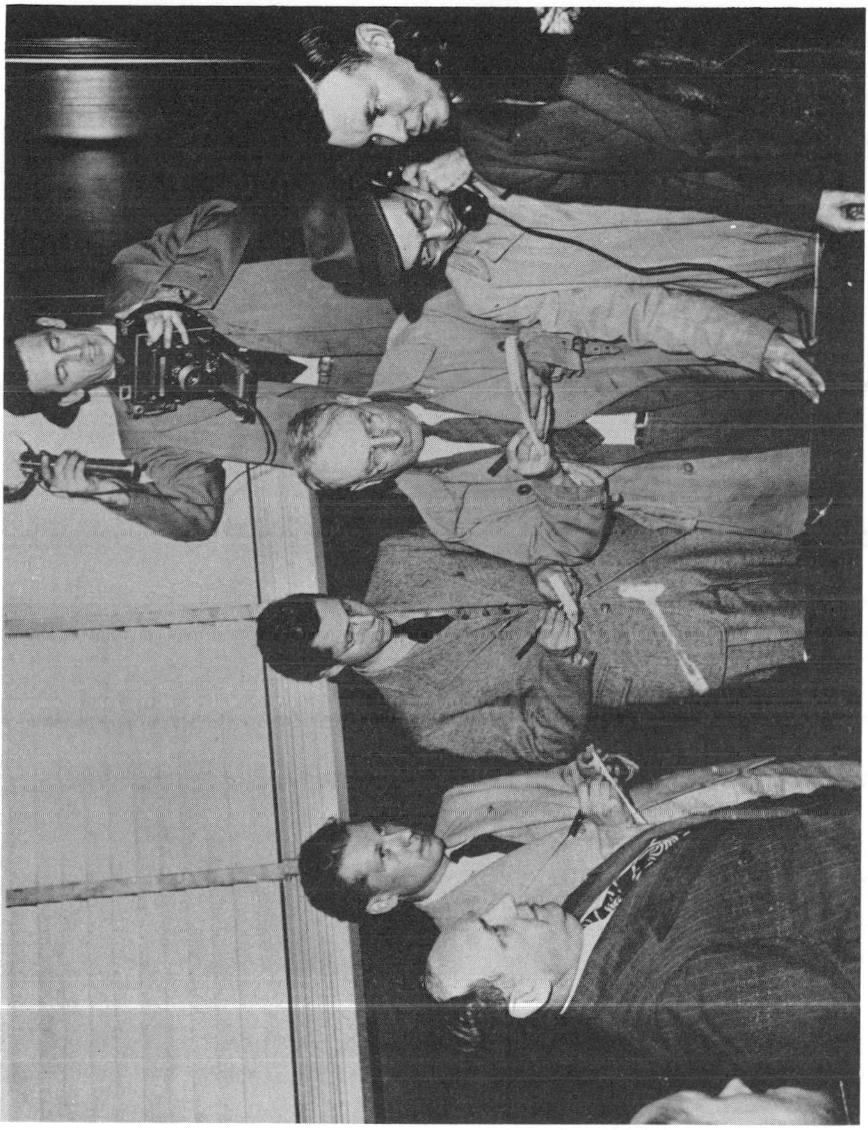

A historic scene in Georgia politics was this face-off between Ellis Arnall (left) and Herman Talmadge (right) in January, 1947, when they both claimed to be legally serving as governor. Man on telephone is Jack Tarver, an editorial writer for The Constitution *who would later rise in the organization.*

A tradition started by Henry Grady in 1884 has been continued by Constitution *editors. When a Democrat is elected to replace a Republican as president a small cannon is fired to mark the event. In photo above, Hal Gulliver,* Constitution *editor in November 1976, prepares to light the charge after Jimmy Carter was elected over Gerald Ford. Grady's monument stands at right. Among the spectators are Jasper Dorsey, Southern Bell official; Jack Tarver,* Journal-Constitution *publisher; Bert Lance, Atlanta banker, and James Roosevelt, son of President Franklin Roosevelt.*

Jack Tarver was the dominant figure on the Atlanta newspapers for 20 years and a key employee for nearly 40 years, serving as associate editor, general manager, president and publisher. He was the rare combination of an outstanding writer and astute executive.

Reg Murphy, Constitutión *editor from 1968 to 1975, became nationally-known when he was kidnapped. He later was publisher of* The San Francisco Examiner *and* The Baltimore Sun *papers. At right is rolltop desk used for years by Ralph McGill and Eugene Patterson, and allegedly used originally by Henry Grady.*

Clark Howell, whose grandfather bought The Constitution *in 1875, was* Constitution *publisher when the newspaper was sold to Cox Newspapers in 1950. He continued in that post until retiring in 1960. He died in 1966.*

George Biggers became president of the combined Atlanta operation in 1950 and held the post until 1958. He constantly worried about "what McGill would do," but wanted a strong sports section, and closely monitored the sports staff.

Jim Bellows, at podium, is a former Atlanta and Columbus newsman who later was editor of The New York Herald-Tribune, Miami News *and* Los Angeles Herald-Examiner. *At right is a pensive Ralph McGill, who introduced Bellows for his speech.*

Anne Cox Chambers, board chairman of Atlanta Newspapers, was U.S. ambassador to Belgium during Carter Administration. She is generally listed as the richest individual in Atlanta and probably Georgia.

Ralph McGill, editor, then publisher of The Atlanta Constitution, *became one of South's best-known newspapermen. Won Pulitzer Prize for editorials in 1958.*

William I. Ray was Journal *managing editor, then executive editor, and eventually general manager and president of Atlanta Newspapers.*

Tom Wood came up through accounting department to become president and publisher in 1976. He resigned in 1982 and moved to Florida where he operates weekly newspapers.

David Easterly, a former city editor from Ohio, came to Atlanta as ANI president in May 1982; he assumed title of publisher in 1984.

Minor J. (Buddy) Ward, began as apprentice in composing room in 1953; was named ANI president in 1984.

James G. (Jim) Minter was one of state's top sports writers before becoming Constitution *managing editor in 1971. In 1982 he was named editor-in-chief of both* The Journal *and* Constitution, *the first person to hold that position.*

Eugene Patterson was Constitution *editor from 1960 to 1968; he won the Pulitzer Prize for editorial writing, 1967. Later he was managing editor of* The Washington Post, *then president and publisher of* The St. Petersburg *(Florida)* Times.

Jack Spalding was a steady if not spectacular editor of The Journal *for 22 years (1956-1978), an unusually long tenure for J-C editors.*

Durwood McAlister, a veteran J-C newsman, succeeded Spalding as Journal *editor. Became editor of editorial page under revised arrangement in 1982.*

Hal Gulliver, Constitution *editor from 1975 to 1982, was early and enduring supporter of Jimmy Carter's campaign and presidency.*

Tom Teepen came from the Dayton, Ohio papers to become editorial page editor of Constitution *in 1982, succeeding Gulliver.*

William M. (Bill) Fields was managing editor of Constitution *13 years, and of* Journal *for four years. He was executive editor of both papers until his retirement in 1981.*

Edward W. (Eddie) Sears succeeded Minter as Constitution *managing editor in 1978, then as* Journal *managing editor in 1981. He became managing editor of both newspapers when staffs were merged in 1982.*

Furman Bisher, one of nation's most colorful sports writers, has been an Atlanta sports editor for 34 years, on Constitution *(1950-57) and on* Journal *since 1957.*

Jesse Outlar is a 40-year Atlanta Constitution *veteran and has been its sports editor since 1957. He and Bisher have given Atlanta a stretch of experienced and able sports commentary unmatched for longevity on any other U.S. metropolitan newspapers.*

Leo Aikman was one of Constitution's *most popular columnists in 1960s and 1970s. His knowledge of Georgia and homespun anecdotes also made him a favorite on the speakers' circuit. He died in 1977.*

Celestine Sibley has been a Constitution *columnist and reporter for 40 years, and is also the author of several books, the most recent,* Children, My Children, *having won the first Jim Townsend Award.*

Bill Shipp has been on Constitution *staff since early 1950s. An associate editor since 1976, he is best-known for his columns on state government. He covered the riots at Ole Miss in 1962.*

Jack Nelson won a Pulitzer Prize for investigative reporting during his years on Journal-Constitution. *He left in the 1960s and later became Washington bureau chief for* The Los Angeles Times.

Lewis Grizzard in a relatively short span of time has become the most spectacular star among the many produced by the Atlanta newspapers, excelling as a columnist, a best-selling author of books, and an after-dinner entertainer in demand throughout the nation.

Leroy "Flash" Noles was The Constitution*'s legendary "copy boy" for 43 years, from 1937 until his death in 1980. He never held any other position, but executives called him the "pillar" of the newspaper.*

The Atlanta Times

Georgia Owned — Georgia Operated

METRO FINAL

Weather: Partly cloudy, warm

VOL. 2, NO. 80 — 522-0220 — ATLANTA, GA., TUESDAY, AUGUST 31, 1965 — ★ ★ ★ — 18 Pages, 2 Sections — Price 5c

Times suspends publication

Publisher's statement

We announce with deep regret that this is the final issue of THE ATLANTA TIMES.

Promised and expected financial support was withdrawn in March, and our revenue has not yet been sufficient to bring us to a break-even point.

I have been glad to work for the better part of three years without compensation, and in addition, to contribute financially to the extent of my limited means toward the publication of the paper. I am grateful indeed to all who have joined in this effort.

Since the beginning of time battles have been fought. Some are won. Some are lost. All the Minutemen did not survive at Concord and Lexington, but their principles did.

We have not survived in this battle. More than 27 million at the ballot box last year supported the philosophy we support, but that battle was lost.

There are times when, whatever the cost, we must try. In this battle we have lost, but we lost trying.

Notwithstanding the outcome of this battle, it is my hope and prayer that down the road which lies ahead the war may be won.

JAMES C. DAVIS, Publisher

(Times staff photo by Julian Cornett)

Burglary ring broken by DeKalb police

DeKalb County Detectives W. J. Rayner and L. R. Butler stand amidst merchandise confiscated that had been taken from approximately 100 homes in a four-county area. Four youths have been arrested in connection with the burglaries, which ran into the thousands of dollars in loot.

Financial woes cited

It is with deep regret that The Atlanta Times, after more than 14 months of publication, is forced to suspend publication effective with this edition.

On June 12, 1964, The Times made its initial bow in Atlanta and Georgia to meet what was considered a real need for another newspaper in this community.

Through these months a dedicated corps of workers has endeavored to give the people of this city and state a factual newspaper whose editorial voice proclaimed a philosophy of responsible conservatism and an unflagging devotion to the principles of constitutional government.

This mission, we feel, has been carried out in a spirit that evidenced our desire to be of service to a growing metropolitan community and a state that is on the march economically.

★

From the beginning we were quite aware of the many thorny problems involved in launching a major metropolitan newspaper in a competitive market.

In many respects our reception has been most gratifying, and we still believe there is a hunger on the part of countless Georgians for this type of newspaper.

But as almost anyone associated with modern-day publishing knows, the success of any daily newspaper operation is dependent on advertising to keep it economically healthy. This advertising must be in sufficient volume to cover the many heavy expenses that burden a daily publication of this size and scope.

★

Unfortunately, the response from major advertisers has been disappointing, despite persistent efforts to increase it, and The Times has found it impossible to continue without this very necessary support on which it must rely for its principal source of revenue.

Our difficulties and heartaches have been many, but we have battled the odds with an unflinching faith that, given enough time, our efforts would be rewarded.

It was only after all avenues for survival had been exhausted that a decision was made to cease operations, and we take that step with extreme reluctance.

In so doing, we wish to thank those advertisers, stockholders and thousands of readers who have remained loyal and supplied the encouragement that brought us this far.

It is with this feeling of gratitude, mixed with understandable sorrow, that we say, "Good-by."

Step up seen in bombings

SAIGON (UPI)—U.S. Strategic Air Force B52 bombers from Guam struck Viet Cong targets tonight in twin raids in South Viet Nam for the first time, a U.S. military spokesman reported.

It was disclosed only Monday the raids by the big eight engine jet bombers have had such a devastating effect on the Viet Cong they could be expected almost daily.

Th double barreled raid today against Viet Cong concentrations came shortly after a Communist force overran the Vietnamese outpost of An Hoa in apparent revenge for the big American victory near Chu Lai, inflicting "moderate" casualties on the defenders. Government troops retook the village a few hours later without a fight.

Today's double raids took place in widely separated parts of South Viet Nam.

The first flight of an unspecified number of the gigantic bombers struck a Viet Cong area in Quang Tinh Province, 320 miles northeast of Saigon early this evening.

The second flight was carried out "shortly thereafter" against another suspected Viet Cong area barely 30 miles north of the capital—the notorious Communist Zone D stronghold hit often before.

★

Only Monday the Air Force spokesman disclosed B52s had hit targets in the same two areas over the weekend. Today's double strike brought to 16 the number of such attacks since June 18 when the big bombers were first used against Zone D.

The early B52 raids were criticized in some quarters because there was no immediate proof of their effectiveness. Land forays into bombed out areas failed to find the vast quantities of Viet Cong dead evidently expected.

But later evaluation indicated the bomber, the biggest in the Air Force arsenal, had disrupted Viet Cong life seriously and it was decided to step up the pace.

Giant firm to locate in Lavonia

LAVONIA — A giant weaving operation — Pacolet Industries Inc. — will locate in this northeast Georgia city, officials announced Tuesday morning.

The firm, a subsidiary of Deering-Millikin, will construct its third plant in Georgia—a 500-loom weaving mill and first reports say between 500-600 persons will be employed.

Construction on the Spartanburg, S.C.-based industry will begin "at an early date." Drilling for water was started Monday.

The sprawling industry — Lavonia's newest in several years —will be located near the old airport site a short distance from the city.

Officials did not announce a date for completion, although sources close to the situation said the work should be finished in a matter "of a few months", depending on weather this fall and winter.

INDEX

Maddox candidacy said definite

By RAY ROGERS
Times Staff Writer

Lester Maddox, who will open his new Pickrick Furniture Company in Atlanta early in September, is a definite candidate for governor of Georgia in 1966, reliable sources said Tuesday.

Maddox, colorful states' rights advocate who closed his Pickrick Restaurant here rather than follow a federal dictate to integrate it, has said that an announcement will be made in the near future concerning his candidacy.

"The present administration and those that have announced for the race so far are out of step with and out of touch with the people of Georgia," Maddox charged.

"They have tried to mislead the people of Georgia, and they now recognize their failure and in an attempt to further mislead and confuse the people, they are trying to identify themselves as conservatives," he added.

"The people of Georgia won't buy this," Maddox said, "it is too little too late."

★

The Atlantan has just returned here from Washington, D.C., where he was refused an audience with President Lyndon Johnson.

Maddox sent a telegram to the President before leaving the capital city saying that "your refusal to reply to my many wires and your refusal to grant me a short interview during my visit to Washington gives further evidence to the hate, prejudice and discrimination that seems to have become a part of your being.

"Either from causes cited, or because of shame, you refused to give me an audience to express my views which are representative of millions of Americans. Your signing of the Civil Rights Act of 1964 and the Voter Rights Bill into law is action contrary to the laws of God and the commandments of thou shalt not steal, kill, covet or commit adultery.

"It is also contrary to the U.S. Constitution and your very life, teachings and voting record through the year of 1960. In so doing you participate in the stealing and destruction of the liberty, property rights and financial worth of many Americans.

"You have stated, and you said you were sincere, that such legislation was 'a farce and a sham, an effort to set up a police state in the guise of liberty,' a greater truth was never spoken, Mr. President. The police state is here and you, sir, are responsible for this tragedy.

"This program of yours, that you predicted would produce a police state, continues to breed death, violence, property destruction, hate, discord, riots an strife throughout America — rather than life, peace, progress, love and unity.

"The first responsibility of government is to protect the lives and properties of its citizens. In this responsibility you have failed completely. In the name of God and what is Constitutional, you should take immediate steps to restore this country as 'one nation under God' and restore and preserve the U.S. Constitution.

★

"Failing to do as suggested, then you should immediately resign from office, along with your vice president, for failing to uphold your oath of office and the U.S. Constitution. It would be best for all Americans to lose their President and Vice President than to lose their liberty."

In his race for governor of Georgia, Maddox will be opposing such candidates as former governors Ellis Arnall and Ernest Vandiver.

Police press search for missing corpse

The director of the Donehoo Funeral Home in Hapeville has been in the mortician's field for 19 years but all he could say after someone apparently stole a body from his funeral home was, "this never happened before."

"I thought the employes were kidding when they said Mr. Lowe's body was stolen," said Fred Burns, owner. "I hope we can get it back."

The employes, Walter Peppers and Melvin Hiers, awoke Monday morning to find the body of Charles Samuel Lowe, 39, of East Point missing from its casket. Also missing was the registry book of relatives and friends who had come by the home to view the body.

Lowe was shot and killed at the home of Mrs. Elizabeth Boleman in Austell. Police are holding her estranged husband Milan O. Boleman in connection with the shooting.

The body was snatched sometime between 11 p.m. Sunday and 7:40 a.m. Monday, according to Burns. Employes discovered a cut screen on the side of a nearby porch.

Police said the body apparently was moved out a side door onto the driveway at the far side of the funeral home.

It had been examined by a medical examiner and then embalmed, Burns said.

Police said the upper part of the caske was left open, as is customary.

Sage Sam says:

Dear Mr. Editor:

Today, the schooling the children are getting is so good that the parents are having troubles just keeping up with them. It is a familiar sight now to see me and my wife huddled together over our daughter's new math book. So far we have been able to solve all the problems. The trouble has been that she sees how much trouble we're having and she's only in the sixth grade.

I see that some places are having special schools for the parents so they can learn the new math. I keep tellin' myself that I'm as smart as the next fella, but what would I do if I took the special course and flunked?

With everybody worried about political plots, I'd like to suggest there is a plot that is going to degrade us parents in the eyes of our children.

Sagely yours,
Sam

Just like a woman

Betsy tries to make up her mind

MIAMI (UPI) — Hurricane Betsy was at a standstill today in the tropical Atlantic, an ideal target for possible attempts to "seed" the 80 mile an hour storm with strength-sapping silver iodide crystals.

Directors of the joint Navy-U. S. Weather Bureau "Project Stormfury" flew into the storm early today and were expected to announce whether it can be seeded without danger.

The second tropical twister of the 1965 hurricane season came to a halt Monday night about 300 miles north of San Juan, P. R., near latitude 22.8 north, longitude 65.8 west.

Forecaster Raymond Kraft said Betsy was expected to remain nearly stationary until mid-afternoon, then begin drifting slowly toward the northwest.

Kraft said Betsy "poses no threat to any land area for the next day or two," a factor which will weigh heavily in the decision whether or not to seed the storm.

★

Warm trend on the way

The forecast for Atlanta and vicinity calls for partly cloudy and slightly warmer weather today, tonight and Wednesday. Temperatures are expected to range from a high of 85 to a low of 65. Wednesday's high will be 86.

Thundershowers covering about 20 per cent of the extreme north portion of the state are predicted.

The high pressure ridge and cool air over the Atlantic and southern states continues to move eastward. A low pressure system is expected to move in, raising temperatures over the Mississippi valley and Great Lakes area.

Truce gained in GOP rift

WASHINGTON (UPI) — Gov. William W. Scranton of Pennsylvania predicted today that GOP splinter groups whose members are "truly interested" in the Republican party will wither away.

He included Barry M. Goldwater's free Society Association in his forecast of the disappearance of independent GOP organizations which have sprung up since the 1964 election defeat.

Scranton made his observations at a news conference after he addressed a closed breakfast session of House Republicans.

He said GOP National Chairman Ray C. Bliss was trying to bring all elements of the party together and wanted to make the regular party organization so strong that there would be no need for splinter groups.

★

Bliss reported today he had reached a truce with Goldwater to harness the party's resources to elect Republican candidates. He met privately Monday with the 1964 GOP presidential nominee.

Bliss' report on his private conference with the 1964 presidential nominee came after a GOP Coordinating Committee meeting debate on splinter groups, including Goldwater's conservatively flavored Free Society Association.

The committee met to go over task force reports on civil rights and the balance of payments problems, but it made so many changes that it decided to release the reports later. Although Goldwater was no longer present, it then began discussing the many independent Republican groups formed since the 1964 election defeat.

Bliss, who was one of the first to deplore formation of the Free Society Association, already had arranged a private session later with Goldwater.

Since the task force reports were withheld, four major party spokesmen were sent empty-handed to a heavily attended news conference.

DeKalb grand jury chastises officials

The DeKalb County grand jury presentments released Tuesday severely criticize all parties involved in the commission and school board controversies, in effect telling accusers to "put up or shut up" because "the people of DeKalb County deserve better service from their employes."

In other action the grand jury, June term, endorsed the school bond issue, said it sees no need for an outside audit of the school system's books, criticized both former County Commission Chairman C. O. Emmerich and current chairman Brince Manning for failure to construct two underpasses approved in 1962 and to be built out of bond issue funds, and agreed with a former grand jury that "all possible speed" is necessary in constructing railroad crossing safeguards.

The presentments were signed Monday by foreman, C. E. Gunthorpe and secretary, Earl H. Dukes.

After noting the multiple charges and counter charges flying both on the county commission and the county school board the grand jury said, "If there is an individual, or a group, who have first-hand knowledge of any wrong-doing by an employe of the county, it is the duty of that individual or group to bring charges against that employe before the proper body. Failure to do that, it would appear, indicates that such criticisms; charges or counter charges, from the accused or the accusers, are insincere and intended only for personal or political gain. The people of DeKalb County deserve better service from their employes."

The Grand Jury went on to plea — "public officials should stop debating their differences through the news media. This practice is detrimental to the morale of county employes; citizens; the business community;

See DEKALB, Page 2A

Regime offers resignation

SANTO DOMINGO (UPI) — Brig. Gen. Antonio Imbert Barrera's junta regime offered its resignation under apparent pressure Monday night, probably clearing the way for installation of a provisional government in the crisis-torn Dominican Republic.

The Organization of American States (OAS) is expected to press ahead with plans for the installation as provisional president of 44-year-old former Foreign Minister Hector Garcia Godoy, although it is not certain whether he will be able to count on the support of the generals who backed Imbert.

The junta chief announced his offer to resign in a surprise telecast Monday night. He announced, however, that the junta will refuse to sign the draft agreements associated with the interim Garcia government.

Col. Francisco Caamano Deno's rebels agreed last week to sign the proposed agreements, which had been revised to meet rebel demands.

Imbert said his regime, which exercises effective control of all but one square mile of Dominican territory, will remain in office until a provisional government is installed.

A junta spokesman said this means the Imbert regime means to go on with "business as usual" for the time being. He said it may take some time to form a provisional government.

The final front page of The Atlanta Times.

METRO MEDLEY

The road ends

A little of each of us at The Atlanta Times will die today.

A corpuscle or tiny cell, perhaps. But enough so that all will know that a part of human life will expire simultaneously with this newspaper.

Death will come the very moment those huge, iron and steel presses finish printing Volume 2, No. 80—the last copy of a newspaper that lived and breathed as part of a city and state for almost 15 months.

The road began on a warm June 12. A Friday, the calendar says. It's seemed so long and so many bridges have been crossed that nobody can remember much except it was such a good day.

The noise of typewriters, excited voices of inspired reporters gathering the news. A great era seemed just ahead and journalism was embarking on probably its most exciting voyage in many a decade.

The end comes on a hot August 31—and the men who will write about our demise may say it was inevitable and that we really never had a chance. We won't have the opportunity to answer and that makes this column doubly difficult to write.

2 a.m.

How does a newspaper die?

You wonder—even at 2 a.m. on the last day—a time when most of the city is sleeping and quiet.

The telephone is mostly silent. An occasional caller wants to know what time it is and he's told the hour is late and it is.

The teletype in the wire services room bats out a sad story—more American soldiers are dead on a far-away battlefield in Viet Nam.

Even the fluorescent lights seem darker but the Elektron machines and stock market tickers appear to be making more noise than usual even in idle gear.

It's a strange feeling sitting behind a typewriter in a spot that has been so active, so alive, so real for more than a year.

Why?

Why does a newspaper die?

You grasp for the answer as you search for the proper words.

Then you remember talking with others in the newsroom who experienced newspaper deaths before. They didn't know why.

This is the second for Dan McElleney, the photographer who came to Atlanta to shoot pictures of wrecks, luncheons, and all sorts of affairs. The first paper death for him was the New York Mirror.

But this one in Atlanta is different, Dan said, because of the many long hours of wondering and hoping. In New York, he got the sad news one night on television after he'd been home from work only a few hours.

George Short, the copy desk chief, counts this his second newspaper death. The first was in Chattanooga and he was just a young man, but, even then, it seemed so unreal.

Strange breed

Newspaper people are a strange breed.

This is their nature. They have to be different to adjust to the world about them and its rapid changes.

The Times family is no different from any other journalistic tribe. Except, perhaps, ours has been the most loyal in the history of the Fourth Estate.

Maybe this has been the reason the paper was able to endure the many hardships and pressures. The staff—from the president, publisher, editor, managing editors, on down—has been one swell bunch of troupers.

It's been a happy family—and that's.. what makes breaking up and dividing and leaving so difficult.

We'll cry

Yes. All of us will cry.

The women, the men. The whole bunch.

Ours will not be tears of regret. Not at all. Rather, a tribute and reminder of the gallant, strong battle we've all waged. Many even before the first issue rolled off the press.

But we won't surrender or give up. No, never!

Our aims, our purposes will be the same. Maybe they will just be in another locale before a different audience and, all the while, we will be carrying the message of truth and free enterprise and patriotism and God's Goodness to His people.

So, The Atlanta Times goes out in a blaze of glory. We fought a good battle—the best we knew how.

But apparently even the best was not

(Times photo by George Cornett)

A good way to start the day

Phil Campbell, Georgia commissioner of agriculture, left, and Rep. Howard (Bo) Callaway, seated right, agree with John Johnson, director of mass communications department, Georgia Farm Bureau Federation, that a "better breakfast makes a better day." The trio met at the Dinkler Motor Hotel Monday to help launch a month-long Better Breakfast promotion aimed primarily at school children. The campaign is being conducted by the Georgia Egg, Milk and Pork Industries. Callaway was guest speaker at the morning breakfast session.

The Atlanta Times — Georgia Owned — Georgia Operated

Tues., Aug. 31, 1965 1-B **Metro Page**

Clayton bond vote tomorrow

The Clayton County Grand Jury has come out in favor of a $2 million bond referendum set for a vote Wednesday, Sept. 1.

In a special resolution passed during the August term the Grand Jury recommended to all registered citizens that the bond issue, which would provide necessary matching funds for a modern, 150-bed hospital, be passed.

"The providing of such a modern health care facility will serve as an additional attraction to our county by industries seeking new locations in their expansion programs," the resolution stated.

The resolution said that in all likelihood the increase in bonded indebtedness could be absorbed in whole or in considerable part by the steady increases in the county's tax digest.

The resolution was submitted by Grand Jury foreman Deryk P. Spiker and acting secretary Robert McMullen.

If approved, money from the bond issue for the hospital would be matched by funds from the federal and state governments bringing total to $4 million. Of this, the federal government would contribute $1.5 million and the state, $.5 million.

Total bond indebtedness of Clayton County is now approximately $1.5 million.

Two Georgians die in Viet Nam

WASHINGTON (UPI) — The Pentagon has listed two Georgia soldiers as killed in action in Viet Nam.

The names of the two Army men, both from Columbus, Ga., were released here Monday.

The victims are identified as Pfc. Kenneth D. Johnston, husband of Mrs. Carol F. Johnston, who now lives in Columbus. And Sgt. Leverne W. McKinley, husband of Mrs. Christa McKinley, also living in Columbus.

In police murders

Setting is complete for Gwinnett trial

By FRAN SMITH
Times Staff Writer

On Oct. 4, 1965, the quiet town of Lawrenceville will once again become the center of attention and will be besieged with reporters, photographers, and spectators from all over Georgia and the surrounding area.

On that date, approximately 17 months after three Gwinnett County policemen were found handcuffed together and shot to death with their own service revolvers, three men—one a former Gwinnett chief of deputies—will face the jury on charges of murder.

Lawrenceville has been brought to the public's attention two other times during the long, tense 17 months—once when the brutal murder was discovered and the other time when the three men were brought before the Grand Jury for indictments in connection with the murder.

★

April 17, 1964 patrolmen Jerry R. Everett, 28, and Ralph K. Davis, 49, were on their way to take officer Jesse Marvin Gravitt, 52, to his home. Gravitt had become ill on the job.

On their way, they made a detour to check a suspicious car call on Arc Road just off Beaver Ruin Road in a secluded part of the county.

The next morning, the abandoned police car was found pulled off the road. About 100 yards from the car, the three bodies of the policemen were found handcuffed together in heavy underbrush. The policemen had been shot 14 times with their own guns.

After an extensive search through those 17 months following the slaying, three men were brought before the Grand Jury July 1 and indicted. True bills were returned against Alex S. Evans, former chief deputy of the Gwinnett Sheriff's office; Wade Truitt and Vincent Williams. Oct. 4 these men will go to trial.

★

According to the Sol. Gen. Reid Merritt and the trial judge, Superior Court Judge Charles Pittard, there is expected to be an overflow of spectators wanting to see the trial other than family, friends, and newspaper people.

Judge Pittard has said that no arrangements are being made to seat the overflow at the court room.

"We have room for about 300 people in the courtroom," he said, "and that's how many people we will allow in there."

★

"There will be no standing in the aisles," he added emphatically. "I think we've got to remember that this is a trial for these three men and not a show for the public."

The judge stated further that they expect no real problems from the excess of people wanting in the court room or from those in the courtroom. "I think this will be an orderly trial," he said.

According to Sol. Gen. Merritt this trial will attract more attention than most murder trials. "You don't get as much interest in murder trials as you did years ago," he stated, "but I think you will in this one."

Negroes apply at school then change their minds

By United Press International

NASHVILLE, Ga. — Thirty-two Negro students who had filed applications for transfer to white schools, have decided not to change schools, Berrien County School Supt. Lossie L. Gaskins said Monday.

None of the 32 Negro students who sought transfer to four white schools in this south Georgia county showed up for classes Monday. Instead, they enrolled and attended opening day classes at the all - Negro Nashville ... sideration by the superintendent's office. Later, he added, the parents of the children came to his office and withdrew the applications.

★

He quoted the parents as saying that their names had been "forged" on the applications.

The superintendent said there was no truth to one report that the applications were withdrawn because of economic pressure by the white community.

Crime ... ready:

By SHARON BROWN
Times Staff Writer

Mayor Ivan Allen Jr. sai[d] Monday night the city is pr[e]pared to confront organize[d] crime should a gambling synd[i]cate try to move into Atlan[ta] with the coming of major leag[ue] sports.

He listed four factors whic[h] he said would prevent it: (1[.]) The city is fully alerted. (2.) O[r]ganization to set up a comple[te] line of communications in t[he] metro area is underway; (3[.]) The Atlanta Crime Commissi[on] is studying the problem, a[nd] (4.) The recent establishment [of] a security force within the p[o]lice department.

His remarks came in reply [to] a battery of seven newsmen w[ho] fired questions at the thr[ee] mayorality candidates in [a] "meet the press" type progra[m] sponsored by the Northside J[ay]cees.

"The size of the city tends [to] attract crime elements," [the] mayor said. "Crime does ex[ist] and you have to confront it."

M. M. (Muggsy) Smith, [one] of his opponents, attacked [the] new Internal Security Divisi[on] saying it has "destroyed [the] morale of the police depa[rt]ment."

"I'm not in favor of an [in]ternal security force," Sm[ith] said. "How would you l[ike] someone looking over y[our] shoulder all the time?"

He said because of the n[ew] division, Atlanta policemen w[ere] "afraid to go into a lottery pl[ace] to make n arrest" beca[use] somebody might think they w[ere] in the lottery business.

Reuben Taylor, the third c[an]didate, protested the low sala[ries]

Parade open[s] DeKalb fair this year

DeKalb County Fair ope[ned] Monday for a six-day run [fol]lowing a parade along Can[dler] Road and an opening addres[s by] County Commission Chair[man] Brince Manning.

Pointing to several impr[ove]ments which have been m[ade] at the fairgrounds by the c[oun]ty and the DeKalb County [Jay]cees, sponsors of the Fair, M[an]ning said:

"This annual fair is a [tra]dition of long standing in [the] county which has been enj[oyed] and encouraged through [the] years by all citizens intere[sted] in the development and prog[ress] of our community.

"The county commissio[n] join with me in officially [open]ing this 1965 fair. We know [that] thousands will take adva[ntage] of the many fine forms of [en]tertainment offered here t[his] year."

A program of improveme[nt at] the fairgrounds is under wa[y by] the county and the Jaycees.

Improvements accompl[ished] this year include removal o[f] buildings from the ground[s, re]placed by a new building, [con]structed to provide 4,000 sq[uare] feet of exhibit space. The [elec]trical service underwent [reno]vation, offering better [light]ing on the midway and [other] parts of the fair grounds[;] the wiring is now undergr[ound]. Ample parking space is [avail]able.

The fair runs through S[atur]day night, opening each d[ay at] 1 p.m., except Saturday [when] the gates will open at 9[.] The James Drew Shows, [with] 20 major rides, is a featu[re of] the midway. In addition, [there] are numerous other exhibit[s and] displays.

Display of the Georgia-Alabam[a ...]

The California Community Services Display of the Georgia-Alabama Moose Association was rebuilt ... master, West Point; R. W. Howard, past

Final second (local) front page of The Atlanta Times.

Chapter IV

The Light Heavyweights: Augusta, Savannah, Macon and Columbus

Four Similar Cities

There is only one Atlanta and only one statewide newspaper combination in Georgia. But at the next level — what might be called the light heavyweight division of Georgia cities — there are four communities which are strikingly similar in metropolitan population, retail sales and newspapers.

A casual glance at the population figures does not truly reveal how closely they resemble each other, so some explanation is necessary.

In the 1980 census the home counties of these four cities reported the following populations:

Chatham (Savannah)	202,226
Richmond (Augusta)	181,629
Muscogee (Columbus)	170,108
Bibb (Macon)	151,085

Bibb has fallen slightly behind the in-county population pace of its Georgia rivals, but its location in the geographic center of the state and close proximity to Houston County, the state's fastest growing suburban county outside of the Atlanta area, put Bibb on equal footing with the others.

Populations of the respective cities in the 1980 census were:

Columbus	170,108
Savannah	141,389
Macon	116,400
Augusta	47,532

These city populations obviously do not reflect the importance or size of each city's metro area since the total for Columbus includes all of Muscogee County due to consolidation (see Chapter V), and Augusta obviously has not been aggressive in extending its city limits during the past 30 years. Richmond (as seen) actually has passed Muscogee in county-wide population.

Since 1920, Chatham and Bibb have approximately doubled in population while Richmond tripled and Muscogee quadrupled. When the surrounding metropolitan areas are added, the four areas are virtually identical in population, despite the 50,000 difference from Bibb to Chatham in county-only populations.

Annual retail sales for these four counties in the 1980s also underline their similarity. For 1983 total sales were $1.1 billion in Chatham; $963 million in Richmond; $874 million in Muscogee; and $851 million in Bibb.

Except for the larger Atlanta metro counties, the next Georgia county after these four in retail sales volume is Dougherty (Albany) with $499 million, providing a clear dividing point from the "light heavyweights" to the next level of Georgia counties.

What also sets Augusta, Savannah, Macon and Columbus apart is that for most of this century they were the only cities in the state except Atlanta that had both a morning and evening newspaper. Athens joined the select group in 1965 and still had both a morning and evening newspaper in 1985, despite being a considerably smaller market. (See Chapter VIII for explanation.) In September 1983, Macon consolidated its morning and evening newspapers and now has only a morning paper. The following 1983

ABC circulation totals for the eight newspapers then serving these four metro areas provide an idea of why the consolidation seemed feasible:

Savannah Morning News	56,251
Savannah Evening Press	20,345
Total	76,596
Augusta Chronicle (m)	58,639
Augusta Herald (e)	18,369
Total	77,008
Macon Telegraph (m)	52,063
Macon News (e)	17,986
Total	70,049
Columbus Enquirer (m)	34,060
Columbus Ledger (e)	26,500
Total	60,560

As can be seen, except in Columbus, the morning newspapers are considerably ahead of the evening papers in circulation, and the evening circulations have been steadily declining. In addition, the opportunity for growth is much better on the morning papers because they can be more easily transported to outlying counties and in city news racks during non-rush traffic hours.

Of course, the afternoon newspapers in all of these cities still have circulations higher than most of the afternoon papers in smaller communities, but the trend in the nation's larger cities is toward the single morning or all-day newspaper, to which the resources and talents of the entire news staff can be directed, and in which all of the best features, columns and comics can be carried.

The 1983 circulation totals of the four morning-evening combinations also show the Columbus newspapers somewhat further behind the totals for the other three than might be expected since the populations of the four areas are similar. The lag is on the morning Columbus paper *(The Enquirer)* since *The Ledger* has a larger circulation than the other afternoon "light-heavyweights."

There are several reasons for the lag, none owing to lack of determination, effort or product. The main one is simply geography. To the immediate west of Columbus lies Alabama, where several Alabama dailies fiercely contend for circulation in the only really populous counties around Columbus. Potential subscribers to the north are about as close to Atlanta as Columbus, and thus the Atlanta dailies are formidable competition. To the east and south lie Georgia's poorest, most thinly-populated counties, which have been losing residents during the past 30 years. As one Columbus circulation manager remarked: "You can't sell newspapers to pine trees."

The following circulation totals from 1952 show the beginning of the trends evident in the 1983 totals:

	Morn.	Eve.	Total
Savannah	48,267	24,499	72,766
Macon	36,519	16,812	53,331
Augusta	43,344	28,430	71,774
Columbus	21,688	26,481	48,169

About midway through this period, in 1966, this is how the circulation figures looked:

	Morn.	Eve.	Total
Savannah	56,576	24,950	81,526
Augusta	46,785	21,224	68,110
Macon	48,769	24,009	72,778
Columbus	34,700	33,016	68,716

By 1982, the totals for the four morning-evening combinations had changed again, and these were the figures:

	Morn.	Eve.	Total
Savannah	56,318	20,313	76,631
Macon	51,313	19,334	70,667
Augusta	57,308	18,559	75,867
Columbus	31,134	26,776	57,900

A comparison of these circulation figures over a 30-year period shows that combined circulation in 1982 was higher for all four combinations than it had been in 1952, but was lower in three (Savannah, Macon and Columbus) than it had been in 1966. Augusta not only showed an increase over 1966, but its combined newspaper circulation had moved to virtual parity with Savannah's, and the 1983 report put Augusta slightly ahead of Savannah.

Afternoon circulation had declined in Savannah and Augusta from the 1953 and 1966 figures, while Macon's afternoon total had risen over 1953 but was down sharply from the peak reached in 1966. The same was true for Columbus. The afternoon *Ledger* had lost its circulation lead over the morning *Enquirer* in 1964 but the two papers' total had stayed about the same until both declined during a changeover from independent carriers to company carriers in 1980-81 (See Chapter V).

Circulation is related to many factors, of course, and a first look at the above figures would seem to indicate that over three decades circulations did not keep pace with population.

The fact is, however, that population growth in Chatham, Muscogee and Bibb counties has been relatively small since 1960. (See population tables, Appendix I.) After adding a total of 83,000 to its population in the 20 years from 1940 to 1960 (75,000 to 158,000), Muscogee added only 12,000 in the following 20 years. During that same period, the other two counties in its metro area, Chattahoochee in Georgia and Russell in Alabama, actually lost population.

Chatham (from 188,000 in 1960 to 202,000 in 1980) also grew slowly, as did Bibb, from 141,000 to 151,000 in 20 years. Only Richmond had a big population jump in those years, from 135,000 to 181,000, with a 20,000 increase in the decade of the 1970s, which no doubt accounts for its newspaper circulation comeback from the low point of 1966.

Macon's newspapers were helped by the high growth rate in neighboring Houston County, where the combined circulation of the *Telegraph* and *News* was 6,800 in 1983. Augusta's papers benefited greatly from the growth of neighboring Aiken, South Carolina, where they have 15,000, and of Columbia County, Georgia, where they have 8,082 circulation.

The only county in the Savannah trade area with comparable growth has been Liberty County (Hinesville) where *The News-Press* circulation is 2,300.

Columbus' only sizable circulation outside its home county is in Russell County, Alabama, (Phenix City), which is just across the river, with 7,400. That total has been virtually the same for 30 years.

So basically the growth in the cities themselves came mostly in the 1950s, with little growth since then, and there have been losses in some surrounding counties.

Another factor in circulation performance over the past three decades is the subscription rate and news stand price. A daily newspaper was five cents and the Sunday edition was ten cents in 1953. Home delivery was about $2 a month.

Those prices were still in use in 1966 when circulations were higher than in 1983. But home delivery is $6 a month or more in 1985, a 300 percent rise over the 1966 price, and single copy prices are 25 cents daily and 50 cents or more on Sunday, which are 500 percent increases.

Newspapers were under-priced for many years, of course, and the increases are justified. They also coincided with the rapid rise in the cost of newsprint, from $140 a ton in 1968 to $450 a ton in 1983.

Even at 25 cents a newspaper is a bargain for the reader. A pound of newsprint, blank with nothing on it and in a big, cumbersome roll, costs 23 cents in 1984. That pound of newsprint, transformed into an easy-to-read product with thousands of words and many photos collected from throughout the world is then sold to the reader for 25 cents. On many days the Augusta, Savannah, Macon and Columbus papers will weigh more than a pound, and the Atlanta papers weigh more than a pound several times a week.

Nevertheless, the rise in price has undoubtedly affected newspaper circulation. Faced with the proliferation of other print media, not to mention the various other forms of communication, newspapers are in an unprecedented battle for both the attention, time and money of the audience, and Georgia's light heavyweights have done well to increase their circulation totals over 1953. Atlanta's, as noted in Chapter III, has declined.

Another interesting statistic is the percentage of homes each of these newspaper combinations cover in their home counties.

Based on the 1983 ABC report, those percentages are:

Augusta (Richmond) 60%
Columbus (Muscogcc) 61%
Macon (Bibb) 70%
Savannah (Chatham) 69%

Both Columbus and Augusta newspapers were at the 70 percent mark until about 1981. That was when Columbus changed its carrier system. The Augusta papers had an overall increase during the 1980-1983 period because of the rapid growth in neighboring counties, but they were losing circulation in Richmond County.

To sum up, Savannah and Augusta's newspapers, which have been owned by the same company (Morris Communications) since 1960, have historically been very close in circulation, as they are today. The morning papers have been dominant, and that dominance is wider now than previously.

Macon and Columbus have been owned by the same company (Knight-Ridder) since 1973. In Macon, the pattern of Savannah and Augusta was followed, with a dominant morning newspaper, which expanded its circulation lead in recent years and now is the only daily paper in the market.

Columbus, by contrast, had the second largest afternoon newspaper circulation in Georgia (after *The Atlanta Journal*) for many years, and its afternoon paper led its morning counterpart until the middle 1960s. Its morning and evening circulations are still closer than the others, although the morning paper moved clearly ahead during the 1970s. Total circulation for Columbus has traditionally trailed the three comparable operations, but the margin narrowed in the 1960s.

What is perhaps most remarkable in comparing circulation totals for these four newspaper combinations from 1953-1983 is the similarity in the totals despite 30 years of enormous changes in style, content, personnel, circulation efforts, price and all the other factors that presumably would make a difference.

Methods of counting should also be added to that list, although all the totals used are from ABC reports. Counting was more precise and careful in 1983 than in 1953, and that factor may have considerable influence on the totals.

Augusta: The Morris Dynasty

An interesting point about the morning newspapers in this chapter is that they are all much older than the Atlanta newspapers. *The Augusta Chronicle* traces its lineage to 1785 and thus lays claim to being the oldest newspaper in Georgia that is still being published. Next in longevity is *The Macon Telegraph*, established in 1826, and third is *The Columbus Enquirer*, established in 1828.

Although Savannah has the honor of being the first Georgia city to have a newspaper, (*The Georgia Gazette*, founded by James Johnston in 1763), *The Morning News* was not started until 1850.

The afternoon newspapers in these cities all began in a seven-year period of unusual newspaper activity in the state, 1884-1891. *The Macon News* dated back to 1884; *The Columbus Ledger* to 1886; *The Augusta Herald* to 1890 and *The Savannah Evening News* to 1891.

Only *The Milledgeville Union-Recorder*, which traces its ancestry to a newspaper started in 1820 (when Milledgeville was the state capital), and *The Athens Banner-Herald*, founded in 1832, compare in age with the morning newspapers in the light heavyweight cities.

While *The Augusta Chronicle* is the oldest of Georgia's current newspapers, it was the last of the larger city newspapers to gain full control of its competition. It was not until 1955 that *The Chronicle*, under the leadership of William S. Morris Jr., bought the competing afternoon *Herald* and gave Augusta a morning-evening combination similar to those in Atlanta, Savannah, Macon and Columbus. Columbus and Savannah have had one ownership since 1930; Macon since 1940; and Atlanta since 1950.

Morris rose from a bookkeeper's job at *The Chronicle* to become the founder of the largest newspaper empire developed by Georgians. Morris and his heirs eventually owned the Augusta, Savannah and Athens newspapers in Georgia, the Jacksonville, Florida papers, plus others from Juneau, Alaska, to Key West, Florida, as well as television, radio and commercial printing facilities.

The founding father of this media dynasty was born in 1903 in Augusta and lived there all of his life. He was a bookkeeper for a bank when he was offered a similar position at *The Chronicle*. During the depression of the 1930s, *The Chronicle* fell on bad financial times and came under the control of the International Paper and Power Company. Morris had moved up to business manager and then publisher. He led *The Chronicle* back to economic health, and then in 1945, with the help of the Auto Finance Company, Morris bought out the IPP company and became controlling partner on *The Chronicle*.

Morris' far-ranging interests and energy were not restricted to the newspaper field. He was a vigorous participant in Augusta politics, serving one term in the state legislature and two terms on the University Board of Regents. His term in the legislature was notable because he defeated Roy V. Harris, the incumbent House Speaker and reputed king-maker of several governors. Morris won his term in 1946, and according to the excellent history of *The Augusta Chronicle* written in 1958 by Kenneth Crabbe and Earl Bell, Morris and Harris "were acutely allergic to each other" after their election battle.

"They would frown and all but growl when passing each other on the street," the book related. "Finally their feud flared into a physical battle in an open courtroom, and the encounter remained the talk of the town for days to come. A full account of the incident was carried as a top right story on page one of *The Chronicle*." Crabbe's and Bell's version of this incident, as it appeared in their book, follows:

> Arguments were being heard in Judge Grover C. Anderson's division of Richmond Superior Court over the disputed leadership of the state Democratic Party. Morris was chairman of the Democratic Executive Committee supporting Gov. M. E. Thompson. Harris was counsel for a faction adhering to Herman Talmadge and was in court to plead the suit of James S. Peters of the Talmadge-aligned group which was challenging Morris'

claim to party chairmanship. At this time, Talmadge forces were also questioning Thompson's right to the governor's chair.

The fight between Morris and Harris exploded shortly before Judge Anderson mounted the bench. Walking up to Harris, Morris asked, 'Roy, do you publish *The Augusta Courier*?' (The reference, explained *The Chronicle* story, was to a political weekly devoted mostly 'to caustic criticism of Governor M. E. Thompson and which had frequently called Morris derogatory names').

Harris' answer was, 'Yes, Bill, I do.'

'Well,' said Morris, 'anyone who publishes that is a . . .'

Harris instantly lunged at Morris, striking him in the face.

'Morris grabbed him,' *The Chronicle* account continued, 'and the two men sprawled on the floor of the jury box, where they scuffled for some moments before onlookers intervened and separated them.'

Harris then shouted, 'I don't let anybody call me a . . . to which Morris retorted, 'I called you one!' and the scuffle was renewed. While the two men were grappling on the floor, C. Nolan Bowden, a political firebrand who published an occasional broadside called *Talking Turkey*, waved his cane and shouted 'Let's settle this thing right now!'

Shortly after the fight was broken off, the two antagonists settled their differences. Morris, who had immediately taken his place beside his attorneys after the fight, took the opportunity during an intermission about an hour later to send word to Harris that he would like to apologize. Then the two approached each other and Morris said 'I'm sorry, Roy, for what happened. I guess I got a little mad.' 'I'm sorry, too, Bill,' Harris replied, and the two shook hands.

Later in the day there was betting on the streets that *The Chronicle* would either ignore the sensational incident or, at the most, give it only a few lines inside. Morris soon squashed any such idea. That afternoon, while the town was all abuzz, Managing Editor Louis C. Harris happened to meet his boss in front of the Chronicle Building.

'Want to see me, Louis?' Morris asked.

'Well — not particularly,' Harris replied.

'I thought you might want to know how to play that story.'

'I think I know,' said the managing editor. 'Front and top right.'

'Do you think it worth that?' Morris asked. Harris nodded assent.

'Just use your own news judgment then,' Morris said, and concluded the conversation. What he did not know at the time was that both Harris and General Manager Pat H. Rice Jr., had decided to resign if the story was suppressed.

The fact that *The Chronicle* carried what amounted to a blow-by-blow account of the fracas was an indication of the paper's firm policy of printing the news objectively and according to worth, without any special consideration of persons. This policy, veteran staff members firmly believe, had much to do with the paper's subsequent expansion.

As an aftermath of the scuffle, Judge Anderson on November 22 cited Roy Harris, Morris and Bowden in contempt of court; but later, upon the apologies of all concerned, let them off with a lecture. Shortly thereafter, on December 5, he overruled Morris' demurrer in the quo warranto proceedings brought by Peters. The suit later went to the Georgia Supreme Court where Peters won. Morris and Harris meanwhile had buried the hatchet.

Prior to his 1947-48 tenure in the legislature, Morris already had gained statewide recognition as a member of the Board of Regents of the University System of Georgia when Gov. Eugene Talmadge declared war on the University of Georgia. Morris was one of a minority of five who bitterly criticized Talmadge for what they termed his political interference with the University and with the Georgia School of Technology radio station WGST. Shortly before Talmadge was defeated for re-election Morris resigned from the Board, but was reappointed by Gov. Ellis Arnall for a term which expired in 1952.

The Chronicle and *Herald* merged their mechanical, circulation, and business departments on January 1, 1949, under a newly-created agency, Newspaper Printing Corporation. The move, which was financially helpful to both papers, did not affect the separate news and editorial policies of the two papers. *The Chronicle* moved its offices and equipment from the old Coca-Cola Building in the 100 block of Seventh Street, where it had located after a disastrous fire in 1921, to the Herald Building on Broad Street. The Sunday edition of *The Herald* was discontinued December 26, 1948, with Herald subscribers receiving instead the Sunday *Chronicle*.

On February 18, 1955, the Chronicle's main headline announced: CHRONICLE BUYS HERALD AND DOWNTOWN BUILDING. The story quoted Morris, co-owner of *The Chronicle* with his wife, Mrs. Florence H. Morris, as saying that the final consummation of the transaction was expected within a few weeks with both papers operating under Southeastern Newspapers, Inc., a subsidiary of the newly-founded Augusta Newspapers, Inc., both of which Morris headed as president. Sale price of the 65-year-old *Herald* and the Herald Building, which was renamed the News Building, was announced as $1,517,000. The new owners announced that part of the stock would be offered to the public. Morris became editor as well as publisher of *The Herald*.

In the fall of 1956, shortly after Morris' interests had expanded even further with acquisition of radio station WRDW and WRDW-TV, the publisher was stricken with a serious illness which forced his withdrawal from *The Chronicle-Herald* presidency for more than a year. At this point, James W. West, who had an extensive journalistic background including executive positions with *The Knoxville Dispatch, Nashville Banner* and *Raleigh Times*, was lifted from his position of general manager for Newspaper Printing Corporation, agent of *The Chronicle* and *Herald*, to the presidency of the corporation. At the same time, Morris' son, young William (Billy) S. Morris III, was named assistant to the president. By 1958, Morris had resumed the presidency; West moved on to another newspaper post in Jackson, Mississippi, and Pat H. Rice Jr., assumed a large portion of the executive duties of the corporation, together with young William III, who remained as assistant to his father.

Morris achieved another significant career milestone in 1960 with the acquisition of the Savannah newspapers from Mills B. Lane and Alvah Chapman Jr. In 1965, his sons, William and Charles, bought *The Athens Banner-Herald* from the estate of Bowdre Phinizy, who had been the editor and publisher of *The Augusta Herald* for nearly 40 years until his death in 1931.

Morris received many honors during his career, including selection by the Association of County Commissioners as the Outstanding Citizen of Georgia in 1960. The commissioners' citation said of Morris: "He is a man who will not lose his individuality in a crowd, a man who is not afraid to say No though all the world says Yes."

He died on April 11, 1967, and was succeeded as head of the company by his son William Morris III.

A Battle Between Brothers

Billy Morris took over a successful and expanding media empire, but he was to carry it to even greater heights than his father probably had imagined. And he had to do it after surviving an emotionally and financially draining battle for control of the company against his brother, mother and sister.

That Morris III would do well in his chosen profession was uniquely forecast in a "special" edition of *The Augusta Chronicle*, published on

October 4, 1934, the day of his birth. This edition was so special, in fact, that only one copy was printed and delivered, that being to the William S. Morris home on Augusta's Lake Forest Drive.

The following account is given in Crabbe and Bell's history of *The Chronicle*:

> Dominating the front page was a "streamer" that fairly screamed. Large and lurid, big and bold, it announced, heralded, and otherwise proclaimed:
>
> "HEIR IS BORN TO EMPEROR WILLIAM II"
>
> The story was to the effect that the "Crown Prince," born the day before, was to be named for his proud pater; that the mother, "Empress Florence," was doing well, and that the father also was expected to survive, although as to the latter the doctor had at first been dubious.
>
> And there were "spot pictures" all over: of "loyal subjects" hailing the baby's birth, of "royal couples" wiring felicitations from abroad, of the doctor who had delivered the heir to the House of Morris. And, as a crowning wonder, "a note written by the infant just after birth" was reproduced in "its own handwriting." The story was signed by "Dr. John Stork."
>
> It was all in fine fun, of course — a facetious, secret "extra" with fabricated photographs gotten out by *The Chronicle* crowd as a congratulation and a surprise to their employer, William S. Morris, then the paper's general manager, and his wife, the former Florence Alden Hill of Aiken — and as a warm welcome, also, to the eight-pound baby, who in due course was christened William Shivers Morris III. Very soon, however, everybody was calling him "Billy."

On October 2, 1956, the eve of his 22nd birthday, Billy Morris was named assistant to the president of Southeastern Newspapers, Inc., thus becoming probably the youngest journalist ever to hold so high an executive position with papers as large as *The Chronicle* and *Herald*. He at once began active participation in all phases of the operations.

In a public statement, his father, Publisher-President William S. Morris, said: "The appointment of my son to this newly created position follows a course that was charted for him and toward which he has worked for several years.

"He has been interested all his life in the newspaper profession and is extremely well grounded on the basis of schooling and experience. I feel that he will be of great help to me personally and to our organization."

Three months later, January 2, 1957, when his father was elevated to the chairmanship of the board of directors in addition to his post of publisher and James W. West was promoted to president and treasurer, young Morris became West's assistant and also was added to the directing board, thus being enabled further to lighten his father's load. He continued in this same position with his father when the elder Morris resumed the presidency a year later.

Following early in paternal footsteps, Billy Morris' first job was a *Chronicle* route, whereas his father had been a *Herald* carrier back in the days just before the 1916 fire. And it was in the role of *Chronicle* carrier, incidentally, that young Billy made front page news by forgetting one morning to pitch a paper at a certain home where a certain citizen was waiting to read it before coming to work downtown. Perhaps it wouldn't have mattered so much if it hadn't been Billy's own home — and the slighted and slightly irked customer his own father, the paper's publisher.

Most of young Morris' training was designed to fit him ultimately for the newspaper field. He completed his early education at William Robinson School and Richmond Academy in Augusta. Then, in 1952, he was graduated from the Darlington School at Rome. Subsequently he entered the University of Georgia and in 1956 obtained a degree from its School of Journalism. While a student there he served successively as reporter, assistant news editor, news editor, managing editor, and editor of *The Red and Black*, the university's student publication.

After his father's death, Billy became president of the company and publisher of the Augusta newspapers. His younger brother, Charles, was vice-president and became publisher of the Savannah newspapers.

Then about two years after the death of the elder Morris, a law suit seeking $19 million was filed against Billy Morris in Richmond County Superior Court by his brother, Charles, his mother, Florence Hill Rickenbacker (she had remarried), and his sister, Florence Alden Morris.

According to an article in *Editor and Publisher* on May 3, 1969, the majority of voting stock in Southeastern had been held by Jefferson Standard Insurance Company in the form of debentures and stock options granted in exchange for loans. Neither Billy, Charles, their mother or sister owned a controlling portion of the voting stock.

The suit charged that Billy Morris arranged to acquire the debentures and options held by Jefferson Standard, thus giving him a total of 61 percent of the voting stock and clear control of the company. This acquisition, the suit charged, diluted the equity of the plaintiffs, who previously held voting stock comparable to Billy's, giving them relatively equal voices in corporate matters.

The suit asserted that the late William S. Morris intended that the ownership of his three children in Southeastern Newspapers should be equal. It further stated that differences between Billy Morris and Charles Morris regarding managerial authority and policy were being worked out when Billy Morris made arrangements with Jefferson Standard to acquire all of the debentures and stock options in his name.

Had other stockholders known of the negotiations, the complaint stated, the corporation itself would have acquired the debentures and options, leaving the relative stock holdings of the principals the same as they were while Jefferson Standard held the controlling stock.

Billy Morris reacted by filing a countersuit charging that his brother, Charles, "has been devoting his time and energy to efforts adverse to the interest of the company (Southeastern Newspapers)."

The counterclaim alleged that Charles Morris purchased properties "in his own name for his own individual interest in direct competition with Southeastern Newspapers Corp . . . and used assets of Southeastern to carry on negotiations to purchase various newspapers for his personal benefit."

During 1968, the counterclaim alleged, Charles Morris "did secretly negotiate to acquire newspapers in Thomasville, Georgia, Murfreesboro, Tennessee, Portsmouth, New Hampshire, and Bay City, Texas."

In effect, Billy Morris' countersuit charged Charles Morris with negotiating to buy other newspapers for his personal ownership which could have been bought by Southeastern, and that he used his position with Southeastern to locate potential acquisition properties.

In regard to the suit filed against him by Charles, his mother and sister, Billy Morris denied that their equity in Southeastern had been affected by his purchase of controlling stock from Jefferson Standard. He said the only difference was that he (rather than Jefferson Standard) now had control of the company. Of course, to the other stockholders that was the difference that mattered.

He admitted that he had purchased the securities from Jefferson Standard and that the purchase was "privately and confidentially negotiated." He denied, however, that "such acquisition was adverse to the interest of the plaintiffs of the corporation."

At a court hearing, it was brought out that Billy Morris paid $3.6 million to Jefferson Standard for the debentures it held, giving him 61 percent of the corporation stock. The money was borrowed from Georgia Railroad Bank and Trust Company at an annual interest of $275,250.

In December 1969, a Superior Court judge ruled in favor of Billy Morris, dismissing the suit brought by his brother, mother and sister. The ruling, in effect, said that "there is no genuine issue as to any material fact, and that William S. Morris III is entitled to a judgment as a matter of law."

The struggle for control of Southeastern Newspapers had a considerable effect on several Georgia newspapers, as well as on the several other newspapers throughout the nation which Billy or Charles Morris would buy and operate.

With control of Southeastern and its resources from the Augusta, Savannah and Athens newspapers, Billy Morris bought out the remaining stock owned by the family members who had sued him, and formed a new corporation which would become Morris Communications.

Charles resigned as publisher of the Savannah newspapers, but continued to make his home and headquarters in Savannah using the money he got from the buy-out to establish his own publishing company. He eventually bought newspapers, printing companies and TV stations from New York to California, and from Statesboro (his only Georgia newspaper) to Key West, Florida, (which was later sold to the Thomson Newspaper Group).

In 1972 Billy Morris made two more large purchases, the Lubbock and Amarillo, Texas, newspapers, and then retrenched for several years before his acquisition masterpiece in Jacksonville, Florida.

In 1968 Paul S. Simon, former vice-president of the John P. King Manufacturing Company, one of the Augusta area's largest textile firms, joined Southeastern as vice-president, treasurer and comptroller.

Simon no sooner assumed his new position than he was assigned to work on the purchases of the Juneau, Alaska Empire and *The Athens Daily News*, which were completed in 1969.

Following Billy's successful bid for control of the company, Simon assisted him in acquiring *The Lubbock Avalanche Journal* and *The Amarillo Globe-Times*, forming a new subsidiary, Southwestern Newspapers Corporation. These were followed by purchase of *The Neighbor*, a Tampa, Florida free distribution weekly, and in the late 1970s of weeklies in Elberton, Hartwell, and Royston, Georgia, plus Southwestern Publications in Amarillo, a printing operation.

In 1981 the bi-monthly *Quarter Horse News* in Fort Worth, Texas, was added to the properties owned by Morris Communications.

Then on November 18, 1982, came an announcement that rocked the newspaper business. Morris Communications Corporation had outbid such giants as Cox Enterprises, Capital Cities and The Gannett Corporation to purchase the Florida Publishing Company, owner of *The Florida Times-Union*, *The Jacksonville Journal, St. Augustine Record* and Crescent City, Florida *Courier-Journal*. The reported price of $200 million was the highest ever paid in a single newspaper transaction.

The Jacksonville Coup

Morris' interest in the Jacksonville papers went back to 1960 when the purchase of the Savannah papers was completed. He recalls that his father looked at the Jacksonville situation about that time and overtures were made to the Atlantic Coastline, which owned the papers, but the railroad was not interested in selling.

Morris and his father kept in touch with the Jacksonville situation through the years, and ironically, Billy Morris had an appointment with Tom Rice, president of the railroad, to discuss the possible purchase of the papers on the morning his father died.

But it was not until 15 years later, December 31, 1982, that the dream of father and son was realized with the purchase of the Jacksonville papers from CSX Corporation of Richmond, Virginia, the parent company.

How did a small, privately-owned company snatch such a prize from the giants in the business?

"It was simple," Billy Morris commented. "We got it because we outbid them."

It took more than just outbidding the big three. Billy Morris readily admits that once he has made up his mind, he is quite determined.

"It was a dream of my father's to own the Jacksonville papers. Jacksonville is a growing, splendid community, and we wanted to be a part of it. I have a real feeling I have finished something my father started," he said.

Morris is quick to admit there are several people who have been essential in the success of his company, and in particular he singles out Paul Simon.

"Paul Simon has been an invaluable asset to this company because of his financial acumen, attention to detail, and his loyalty to me and my family," he has said.

With the Jacksonville purchase behind him, Morris announced on January 4, 1983, that Simon had been elected president of Morris Communications. In the same announcement he said that he would continue as chairman of the board and chief executive officer of the corporation.

The purchase of the Jacksonville properties, and how Morris justified the price he paid, was the subject of a 1982 article in *Forbes* magazine. The article also goes into the intricacies of high finance and newspaper operations which have made possible many similar purchases of smaller properties for remarkably high prices. With permission of *Forbes*, the article is reprinted here:

A LESSON IN EMPIRE BUILDING

Something happened in Jacksonville, Fla., last month that set the newspaper world on its ear. Tiny $100 million (estimated sales) Morris Communications Corp., a privately held firm based in Augusta, Ga., outbid such giants as Cox Enterprises, Capital Cities and Gannett to buy $57 million (sales) Florida Publishing from railroad holding company CSX for an estimated $200 million, or 30 times earnings. That's the most money ever paid for newspapers. With a 203,000 combined circulation for the two main properties bought — *The Florida Times-Union* and *Jacksonville Journal* — that works out to around $1,000 per reader.

A deal like this proves a private company with guts can triumph over larger public corporations because it doesn't have to answer to shareholders and so can better leverage cash flow to shelter future earnings. Because it doesn't have to worry about the effect on current earnings, a company like Morris can take full advantage of stepped up depreciation and the borrowing power of its cash flow.

The late S. I. Newhouse stayed private and built his family's $1.4 billion newspaper empire. So if there's any lesson to be learned from William S. (Billy) Morris III, it is that there are empires still left to build.

Who is Billy Morris? At 48, he's the eldest son of a bookkeeper who rose from being business manager of *The Augusta Chronicle* in 1931 to sole owner by 1955. That same year he bought the town's afternoon paper as well, and its CBS television affiliate followed in 1956. Four years later the station was sold to fund the purchase of Savannah's two dailies. By then, Billy, a journalism graduate of the University of Georgia, had taken over the family business, his father having suffered a stroke.

Billy finally became CEO in 1966 (a year before his father died), and there has been nothing but expansion ever since. Besides the Augusta and Savannah properties, Morris Communications now own dailies in Juneau, Alaska; Lubbock and Amarillo, Texas; two in Athens, Ga.; plus three weeklies; a free-distribution shopper in Tampa; four printing companies and the *Quarter Horse News*. Along the way Morris also managed to buy out his brother, mother and sister, who disagreed on how he was running things. Today, brother Charles separately operates his own $50 million (sales) Morris Newspaper Corp., a chain of 23 dailies and weeklies from Mount Kisco, N.Y., to Statesboro, Ga.

Morris pooh-poohs his own success. "I'm just a good old Southern boy trying to make a living," he says. Aw shucks, Billy. The Jacksonville acquisition is hardly moseying down to the general store.

Here's what happened. Last summer $5.4 billion (sales) CSX hired Lehman Brothers Kuhn Loeb to auction off Florida Publishing. Besides Jacksonville, this includes the St. Augustine daily and a small weekly. It was streamlining operations and no longer saw the need to hold on to the papers. Stephen Schwarzman, the Lehman partner who managed the transaction, shrewdly let the market set the price. After all, earlier in the year Gannett coughed up an estimated $110 million for two Jackson, Miss., papers and another in nearby Hattiesburg.

To the industry's surprise, and to Morris' he won. "We didn't have any idea we could outbid those guys," he says. "My money was on Gannett. But they whipped us in Jackson, and I ended up with this one; so I guess that's fair play."

The winning bid was a blockbuster. In the end the issue was decided because a public company like Gannett typically wants new properties to become net contributors to income after three or four years, allowing for interest and goodwill writeoffs. At 30 times earnings there was no way that Florida Publishing could do that. How then can much smaller Morris Communications come out above the water?

"It doesn't make a bit of difference to me whether or not I wipe out my earnings on the bottom line," says Morris. "This is a cash flow exercise. My earnings will come back when my interest drops and the principal is paid off. And they will come back very nicely, indeed."

Details of the deal are sketchy. But it is possible to make a rough estimate of how it will work. Chances are Morris borrowed almost all of the acquisition price from a group of banks led by Chase Manhattan. Assume a rate somewhere near prime, recently at 11½ percent. That would put interest charges, at least initially, at around $20 million. Jacksonville's current cash flow isn't enough to cover that. Last year, for instance, pre tax operating income was some $13 million. Even when you add back depreciation of $4 million or so, that's still just $17 million.

But Morris can swing it. Here's how. First, combine the pre tax operating income of Jacksonville and his old company — together, some $38 million. Next, subtract depreciation.

Ordinarily, that would be about $12 million. However, he now can write up the Florida assets to current market value. He also can turn some goodwill — like editorial staff, subscription list and library — into hard assets. All this could provide an extra $4 million in depreciation.

So what would be left after depreciation is $22 million or so. That's just enough to service his debt and still show a small profit, on which taxes must be paid. Then, by adding back the $16 million in depreciation — it's cash, after all — Morris still would have $17 million in cash flow to run the company and pay down the principal of his loan. Some observers also expect him to cut expenses, which could raise Jacksonville's operating margins from 20 percent to 30 percent.

As long as no unexpected capital expenditures come up, Morris should have little difficulty paying off the banks in several years. Of course, this will drastically shrink income. But that's a small price to pay for becoming 60 percent larger and getting into a growth market like Jacksonville, which is up 2 percent to 3 percent a year.

After a few years, Morris undoubtedly will try to repeat this shrewd leveraging of cash flow. While Billy Morris may not end up another S. I. Newhouse, he certainly has shown he belongs in the major leagues.

Louis C. Harris, Editor

Many outstanding journalists have been associated with the Augusta newspapers during the past 35 years. The one who played the longest and most important role on the newspapers and in state journalism was Louis C. (Lou) Harris.

Harris' background is covered in the following excerpt from *A History of The Augusta Chronicle:*

THE LOUIS HARRIS STORY

On March 1, 1959, eleven days after the unexpected death of *Chronicle* Editor R. L. M. Parks, Publisher William S. Morris announced his choice of a successor to the paper's editorial chair — and once again he turned to the higher echelon of his news staff to make the choice. His selection as successor to Parks was Louis C. Harris, executive news editor for both the *Chronicle* and the *Herald*.

Harris was indeed well qualified. In his more than a quarter century of newspaper work, his imagination and unfailing news sense had brought him wide recognition. On more than one occasion his reportage had brought added honors to the already honor-laden *Chronicle*. And in at least one instance, he had literally "scooped" the world by breaking in *The Chronicle*, as a copyrighted exclusive, a story of the utmost international significance.

The story "broke" on the morning of May 9, 1956, and carried the news that Georgia's aging senior senator, Walter F. George, had decided not to run for reelection to the seat he had held for thirty-four years. As the ranking congressional expert on foreign affairs, George was invaluable to the administration, then at loggerheads with the Russians. His loss to the administration and to his colleagues in the Senate would be felt beyond Washington and the nation itself. It would resound through every chancellory in Europe and Asia, and might even alter the shaping of American foreign policy. Yet of this important development there was no single word in any newspaper throughout the world, other than *The Chronicle*.

In his story, Harris said he had been advised of a possibility that Sen. George would withdraw, and he was sent by Publisher William S. Morris to the senator's home in Vienna to discuss the report.

"The information . . . was from such a highly placed individual and given in such a confidential manner that not even Sen. George was told by this writer of its source," the story stated.

"Because it was not possible to violate the confidence and report the rumor at that time — unless George had confirmed it — no story was published.

"Today, no longer obligated by the original source and fully aware of the senator's plans for an announcement, *The Chronicle* is able to say that he will not seek to retain his Senate seat."

Harris' exclusive story did not go without acclaim. When the Georgia Press Association met later in the month at Savannah, it departed from its regular business agenda to adopt unanimously a resolution praising *The Chronicle* for its "enterprise in the field of political reporting" on the basis of Harris' story.

Louis Carl Harris was born in Montgomery, Alabama, February 20, 1912. Starting work at the age of ten, he completed high school, then obtained his first newspaper job at the age of 19 as a carrier for *The Montgomery Advertiser*. A year later he came to *The Chronicle* as assistant circulation manager, and 18 months later was named circulation manager of the Athens (Georgia) *Daily Times*. He remained there only three months. "It was the only job from which I was ever fired," Harris once commented. "But for me it was a blessing in disguise because I then left the circulation field and began editorial department work."

This work was at *The Chronicle*, to which he returned early in

> 1934. He served first as a cub reporter, helped out on the sports desk, was then made state editor and, when he left in October of 1938, was telegraph editor. In the meantime he had also doubled as staff photographer, gaining some fame in 1938 with a picture of a gun battle between police and two safe crackers. The picture was published not only in the United States but throughout the world.
>
> Harris left *The Chronicle* to become police reporter on the Pontiac (Michigan) *Daily Press*. He remained in Michigan — where his civic activities gained him election as a director of the Michigan Junior Chamber of Commerce — until November 1940, when he volunteered for military service.
>
> Harris' active duty overseas carried him through the invasion of North Africa, then Sicily, and into the landings at Salerno, in Southern Italy. In 1946, after his release from the Air Corps, Harris went back to Pontiac to become telegraph editor of *The Daily Press*, returning to Georgia a year later to accept the position of executive editor of *The Columbus Ledger*. His stay in Columbus was a brief two months. Offered the managing editorship of *The Chronicle*, he returned once again to Augusta, which he had left nine years earlier.
>
> Himself at times a controversial figure because of stands taken on various political subjects, both in articles and in speeches he has made throughout Georgia and South Carolina, Harris frequently decried the absence of the rough and tumble journalism of the thirties. "Newspapering today — and it's right that it should be — is a much more polite business than it used to be," he once observed. "But I think it was more fun in my early days. It is even rare now when someone threatens my life."

During his lengthy tenure with the Augusta newspapers, Harris accumulated numerous journalistic honors, including president of the Georgia Press Association in 1968.

In 1978 the House and Senate of the Georgia General Assembly passed resolutions praising Harris for his contributions to Georgia journalism, and fellow citizens honored him with a dinner in Augusta attended by some 500 friends, dignitaries, colleagues, and government officials.

Harris died of cancer June 22, 1978.

A number of other long-time executives have left their mark on the Augusta newspapers.

Edward B. Skinner, general manager of *The Augusta Chronicle* and *Augusta Herald*, began his career with the newspapers in 1942 as a district manager in the Circulation Department. He was transferred to the composing room in 1944, became night foreman in 1964, news foreman in 1965, general production foreman of both newspapers in 1969 and production manager in 1970. He was named business manager in 1972 and became general manager in 1973, a post he still held in 1984.

Skinner, a native of Augusta, is a past president of the Greater Augusta Chamber of Commerce and the Georgia Associated Press Association.

W. Howard Eanes came to *The Augusta Chronicle* as managing editor in 1974 from Washington and Lee University, Lexington, Virginia, where he taught reporting and editing for five years. A native of Petersburg, Virginia, he was a reporter and editor on a number of Virginia newspapers before coming to Augusta.

Eanes served two terms as treasurer of the Associated Press Managing Editors Association (1982-1984), after serving two three-year terms on the association's Board of Directors and chairing committees for five years.

David L. Playford, managing editor of *The Augusta Herald*, began his career with *The Augusta Chronicle* in 1951, became telegraph editor in 1957 and news editor in 1963. He was named managing editor of *The Herald* in 1967.

Born in Honolulu, Playford has been in Augusta since 1942. He is a member of the Board of Directors of the Associated Press Managing Editors Association and has been a member of committees of that association and the Georgia Press Association.

The Chronicle and *Herald* have not only continued to win honors for their news and editorial content but were leaders among daily newspapers in adopting the latest printing techniques.

Harris-Intertype has said that both Southeastern and the Gannett Company made major contributions to the concept and specifications of its video terminal and electronic newsroom.

In 1974, a Goss offset press was installed, making Augusta the first of Georgia's larger newspaper companies to totally convert to cold type and offset.

The Chronicle, the South's oldest newspaper in continuous publication, celebrated its bicentennial in 1985.

As a part of that celebration, the newspaper is publishing a Bicentennial Edition covering the growth of the newspaper and the Augusta area. The edition will be printed in six issues over a six-month period beginning in May 1985.

The history of the newspaper, *The Augusta Chronicle, Indomitable Voice of Dixie, 1785-1960*, also will be updated as a part of the anniversary observance. The second volume will cover the last 25 years.

The first 175 years of history, written by Earl Bell and Kenneth Crabbe, will be reprinted and the two volumes offered as a package. The first volume was published in 1960 as a part of the newspaper's 175th anniversary.

The new volume will be written by Augusta native Edward J. Cashin, chairman of the Augusta College Department of History, Political Science and Philosophy. Cashin is author of "The Story of Augusta," published in 1980.

Savannah, A City That Was Rescued

Savannah was the first English settlement in Georgia, its first capital, and for nearly 150 years was the state's largest and most important city.

The Georgia colony, established by James Oglethorpe in 1733, quickly proved its value to the British empire by serving as a barrier to further northward movement by Spain's New World colonists. Georgia, in fact, probably determined that the area which would be the southern United States is English-speaking and of English heritage rather than of Spanish or French heritage. At the time Oglethorpe claimed Georgia for Great Britain, the Spanish had already been in Florida for 175 years, and the French had a stronghold in New Orleans and Mobile. The territory Oglethorpe called Georgia included most of present-day Alabama and Mississippi, and the Spanish and French moved no further north after Georgia was established.

Two hundred and fifty years later there are many legacies from Oglethorpe's far-sighted policies, and one of them is the unique plan which he designed for Savannah. Oglethorpe laid the settlement out in squares, with ample space between lots to guard against the spread of fire. Five-acre garden lots were provided for each family dwelling house.

Oglethorpe's squares have survived, but his original plan for the area was abandoned as early as 1750. The Trustees Garden, started by Oglethorpe and the earliest settlers, contained such exotic items as silk and wine grapes, which were desired by the British Empire, and which some of Oglethorpe's financial supporters hoped could be produced in the new colony.

But Savannah's future was determined by its proximity to the Atlantic Ocean and its fine harbor. It had become an important port by the time of the Revolutionary War, although it lost its political dominance when the capital was moved to Augusta in 1786. President George Washington visited Savannah in 1791 and is reported to have been more impressed by the beauty of the city's women than of the city itself.

Savannah's fame as a port was enhanced in 1819 when the Steamship *Savannah*, financed and owned by Savannahians, left Savannah on May 22, to make the first trans-ocean voyage mainly propelled by steam. It docked in Liverpool, England, on June 20. Another president, James Monroe, visited Savannah during this period and inspected the steamship before its historic voyage.

Unfortunately, the *Savannah* was ahead of its time. Steam navigation on the Atlantic proved too expensive, and the *Savannah* was stripped of its engines and became simply another sailing ship. Ill fortune continued to follow the *Savannah*, however, and it foundered on a sand bar off Long Island, New York, in 1821 and sank to the bottom of the ocean.

The city's luck seemed to take a downturn along with its namesake ship. In January 1820, a raging fire wiped out the old section between Broughton and Bay streets, destroying some 460 buildings. Just a few months later a yellow fever epidemic struck, causing most of the city's 7,500 residents to leave the area for a time. Nearly 700 deaths were attributed to the fever. It was from those tragic disasters that the Savannah of today began to rise. By 1825 Savannah had rebuilt to the point that it could give a gala welcome to the French general, Marquis de LaFayette, a hero of the American Revolution who was touring the country some 50 years after he came as a young general to assist military operations against the British.

Savannah was unquestionably the cultural center of Georgia during the nineteenth century, and as noted earlier, the first Georgia newspaper had been founded there in 1763 by the Scotsman, James Johnston. Johnston's *Georgia Gazette* had a turbulent history, although it was the only newspaper in Georgia for more than 20 years. Its final edition appeared in 1802, following the death of Johnston's son, Nicholas, who had operated it after his father retired. Johnston wrote his newspaper's obituary stating that his poor state of health "rendered him unable to continue the publication of this paper."

By then another newspaper, *The Columbian Museum and Savannah Advertiser*, was available, and *The Savannah Republican* was founded the year *The Gazette* folded. Later there was *The Georgian*, founded in 1818, and then *The Morning News* in 1850, the only present-day survivor of Savannah's early newspapers.

The Columbian Museum was Georgia's first daily newspaper in 1817, but it went out of business in 1822, a victim no doubt of the fire, the fever, and perhaps most importantly, the new *Georgian*, which was also a daily.

By the time of the Civil War Savannah had a population of 15,000, was a major port for shipment of cotton, and had become in the words of one English visitor, "a showy little city." It had benefited from the attentions at one time or another of several outstanding nineteenth century architects. William Jay of England had been brought to Savannah in 1817 by the cotton merchants. His work can still be seen in the Owens-Thomas House and the Telfair Museum. Isaiah Davenport was more of a builder than an architect, but the brilliance of his design is obvious in the Davenport House, which has been beautifully restored. Charles Cluskey of Ireland and John S. Norris of New York were other noted architects who came to Savannah before the Civil War. The Custom House was built in 1852 under Norris' direction.

Thus it was that a city of infinitely more impressive and valuable buildings than Atlanta awaited the arrival in December 1864 of Gen. William T. Sherman and his maurauding Union armies, which had burned Atlanta and laid waste to much of the Georgia countryside on its historic March to the Sea. Savannah was the destination when the armies left Atlanta, and General Sherman telegraphed President Lincoln that he would present him Savannah as a "Christmas gift."

But Sherman, perhaps charmed by Oglethorpe's squares and the variety of architecture to be found in Savannah, spared the city from destruction. He made his headquarters in the Green-Maeldrim House, which is presently the parish house of St. John's church.

In fairness to Sherman (who has never gotten much fairness from Southerners) it should be mentioned that he spared many homes and structures that were of historical or architectural significance during the length of the March, most notably in Madison.

During Reconstruction the cotton trade thrived again in Savannah. There was constant activity on Factor's Walk, and in 1886 Savannah was called the world's major trading center for cotton. It gained another important distinction in 1912 when one of its well-known citizens, Juliette Gordon Low, formed the first Girl Scout troop in Savannah. The national headquarters of the Girl Scouts is still located in Savannah, and Juliette Low's home is one of the most popular tourist attractions among the city's historic homes.

But what Sherman had spared in 1864, the ravages of time and neglect were slowly destroying by the middle of the 20th century. Isaiah Davenport's exquisitely-wrought home was a shabby tenement, divided into many apartments. So were many of the other outstanding homes built in the early 19th century. River Street and Factor's Walk were largely deserted and their buildings abandoned.

In 1955 the Davenport House was marked for demolition to clear the way for a parking lot. Its precious old bricks were also considered more valuable for use in new home construction than to remain where they had been placed 160 years earlier.

But in that same year a group of Savannah citizens, who were upset by the razing of the old city market, had organized the Historic Savannah Foundation, with the aim of saving some of the city's outstanding architecture by buying the old structures and restoring them. The first house bought and saved was Isaiah Davenport's. From that beginning Historic Savannah's achievements were unprecedented. The movement transformed Savannah from a fading "old lady" to one of the nation's most interesting cities in the 1980s.

Twenty-five years after the first restoration Savannah had the largest Historic Landmark district of any American city, 3.3 square miles. More than 1,000 buildings in that area have been restored. River Street's abandoned warehouses are now shops, restaurants, lounges and museums which make it a competitor to New Orleans' Bourbon Street, only without Bourbon Street's sordidness. Several large hotels, especially the Hyatt, which overlooks River Street, have helped make Savannah a popular spot for conventions and tour groups. Its most unique accommodations, however, are in the restored homes and old inns. These inns are reminiscent of similar ones in New England, which may be older but are no more picturesque. No other city in Georgia — or in the South — provides such historic and charming lodging.

The Savannah Newspapers

There is a certain parallel between the city of Savannah and its daily newspapers. By the 1950s they showed signs of needing restoration, and they received a restoration about the same time Historic Savannah Inc. began salvaging the city's old houses.

This description of the Savannah dailies which appeared in the book *Georgia Journalism*, aptly sums up their position in the 1950s: "*The Savannah Morning News*, now 100 years old, is as conservative, sedate and independent as the day she was founded, Jan. 15, 1850 . . . Financially she is as solid as the Rock of Gibralter, and her editorial page is widely quoted. Admittedly a bit old-fashioned in her type dress and makeup, there is nothing of the sensational to be found in her pages. The appearance of *The Morning News* is not as out of place as it would at first seem. Southeast

Georgia, in and around Savannah, is the cradle of the state. Nowhere else is to be found the old world atmosphere, the long-lived traditions and the respect for that which is old . . ."

One of the Savannah dailies' idiosyncracies was a policy of carrying local stories and photos on the back page of the first section. These stories were continued "backward" into the paper if they had to be jumped. The front page was devoted solely to stories from the wire services and wire photos. Occasionally a local story or photo would appear on the front page, but according to old time employees it had to be "a hell of a story." This policy of running nearly all local stories on the back page was continued into the 1970s when Jim Whyte, during his time as general manager, agreed with the editors that it was time for a change.

But change of a dramatic fashion had already come to the Savannah papers, sparked by one of Savannah's leading citizens, Mills B. Lane Jr., president of Citizens and Southern Bank, and Alvah Chapman Jr., who would later become the chief executive officer of one of the nation's largest newspaper empires.

On August 21, 1957, Herschel V. Jenkins, 86 years old, and publisher of the Savannah newspapers since 1926, sold the papers to a company (Savannah News-Press Inc.) headed by Lane, with Chapman as president and publisher. Jenkins had been head of a company called The Morning News Inc., which had acquired the Press in 1930.

Chapman came from St. Petersburg, Florida, where he was vice-president and general manager of *The Times*. At 36, he was a third-generation newspaperman, grandson of the founder of the Page Corporation, which in 1888 had bought *The Columbus Ledger*.

Chapman immediately set about revitalizing and enlarging the entire Savannah operation, with particular attention to the news and editorial staff. He installed the papers' first engraving department; strengthened the circulation department's delivery system with a larger fleet of trucks, set up a bureau in the state capitol in Atlanta, bought a second-hand but faster and larger press, acquired a battery of six automatic typesetters with accompanying TTS tape-punching keyboards, and formed promotion and art departments. Then he went out to find and hire new talent for all departments, keeping the on-board talent he deemed compatible with his fast changes, and firing those who were not compatible.

The Chapman-decreed changes most noticeable to the public were found in the newspapers' deeper commitment to community involvement. He declared war on gambling, vice and machine politics. He came down hard on the side of public school and highway improvements, and the historic preservation movement. As private groups moved to save and restore the old houses and other landmarks, which in later years would make Savannah world-renowned, Lane and Chapman gave full encouragement, with publicity, editorial support and financial support.

The Lane-Chapman years in Savannah would be short in number, however. In early 1960, a philosophical rift began to develop between the two partners. Long-time Savannahians speculated that Chapman had bolted out of the starting gate too fast and, once on the track, had run even faster. Lane, who headed the vast Citizens & Southern National Bank System, later would say he found newspapers and banking incompatible.

The sale of the Savannah properties to Southeastern Newspapers Corporation was announced on July 13, 1960, less than three years after the Lane-Chapman purchase. William S. Morris, publisher of *The Chronicle* and *Herald* in Augusta, was head of Southeastern. His sons, William S. Morris III and Charles Hill Morris, were associated with him in the expanding Augusta operation. Billy Morris says that the Savannah purchase was perhaps the easiest of the many he would later be involved in. "They wanted to sell and we wanted to buy," he recalls.

Charles, the younger of the brothers, became publisher of the Savannah papers in April 1966. The Chapman goal of providing newspaper leadership for a better Savannah was continued by the Morrises. Charles Morris guided the papers through a period of growth and community leadership in which they supported better roads, law and order, historic preservation and restoration, improved schools, governmental reform and development of Savannah's historic riverfront as a special attraction with unique tourism appeal. With the exception of complete governmental reform — specifically, the consolidation of city and county governments which special political interests still resist — all of these have come to pass.

Charles Morris left the Savannah papers in November 1970 after a dispute with his brother over management policies. William S. Morris III had become head of Southeastern after their father's death in 1967. Charles continued to live in Savannah, and established headquarters there for his Morris Newspaper Corporation, which runs a group of small dailies and weeklies throughout the United States. *(The Statesboro Herald* is his nearest newspaper). His company offices are in the restored Oliver Sturges House on Reynolds Square.

The Savannah papers continue as influential forces in the 27-county Coastal Empire, with bureaus in Brunswick, Jesup, Statesboro, Hinesville,

Vidalia-Lyons and in Beaufort and Hilton Head Island, South Carolina. They also publish *The Hilton Head News*, a weekly printed in the Savannah plant.

The papers now occupy the entire block of property on West Bay Street between Whitaker and Barnard Streets, utilizing in that complex the small corner building at Bay and Whitaker which was built in 1819 by Col. James Johnston, nephew of Georgia's first newspaper publisher. That building has been restored externally to conform to Savannah's historic preservation standards and houses the classified and accounting departments.

In July 1975, the Savannah papers installed a $2-million Goss-Metro offset press, following the lead of their sister papers in Augusta as large dailies going offset. In 1982, the papers completed the addition of two units and a color deck to the Goss-Metro, creating a press capacity for 112 pages. The addition and its attending construction and building modifications cost another $2 million.

The business operation also is computerized. The circulation department has a data bank that includes names and addresses of all subscribers, plus 172,000 addresses in an eight-county area. The data bank is in the process of expansion into an additional eight counties.

Following are brief biographical sketches of persons who have played significant roles on the Savannah dailies during recent years:

DONALD E. HARWOOD — General manager since April 1973, Harwood came to Savannah from *The Memphis Commercial Appeal* and *Press-Scimitar* where he was advertising director. He earlier was with *The Chicago Tribune*, both in Chicago and in its New York Eastern advertising office. He is a graduate of the University of Minnesota and an Air Force veteran of the Korean conflict. He is a native of Rochester, Minnesota. In Savannah, he has been president of the Chamber of Commerce, served on the Airport Commission, and on the board of numerous civic and benevolent organizations.

WALLACE M. DAVIS JR. — Executive editor since 1969, Davis began his career with the Savannah papers before graduation from Savannah High School in 1947, working part-time on the sports desk of *The News*. He continued as a summer intern while earning his journalism degree at the University of Georgia, and left the Savannah papers only once — to serve with the Marine Corps during the Korean conflict. He has been a reporter and assistant city editor of *The News* and city editor and managing editor of *The Press*. As executive editor he supervised the consolidation of the news staffs of the two dailies.

THOMAS F. COFFEY JR. — Coffey's association with the Savannah papers began in 1935 as a carrier for *The Evening Press*. He became *Press* copy boy upon graduation from Savannah High School in 1940, and in subsequent years held every job in the newsroom. He is the only person to have been managing editor of both *The Evening Press* (1964-67) and *The Morning News* (1967-69). He left the papers three times — in 1942 for World War II Army service, in 1956 for television news, and in 1969 for the public sector as assistant city manager of Savannah. He returned in 1974 as associate editor in charge of *The News*' editorial pages. He also writes a daily column.

WILLIAM J. ROBERTSON — Joining *The News* as editorial writer in May 1944, Robertson had worked on papers in Roanoke and Richmond, Virginia, and in Delaware and Pennsylvania, and for the Associated Press in Washington, Atlanta, Birmingham and New Orleans. He became editor of *The News* in 1948 and executive editor in 1953. Robertson guided the staff of *The News* until his death in July 1955.

JOSEPH E. LAMBRIGHT — Joining *The News*' staff as a reporter before World War II, Lambright returned from Navy service to work on *The Brunswick News* before rejoining *The News*' staff. He became managing editor in 1950 and was the chief editorial writer before leaving to enter politics in 1958.

FRANK P. ROSSITER — Creator of the popular local column, "City Beat," Rossiter was a member of *The News*' staff from 1932 to 1966, with time out for Navy service in World War II. Rossiter served as city editor and managing editor. He left the newspaper to enter the shipping business, and later ventured into politics. He was elected city alderman four times, and was Savannah's mayor pro tempore (13 years) longer than anyone else. He died in January 1983.

JOHN L. SUTLIVE — A second-generation editor of *The Evening Press*, Sutlive succeeded his late father, W. G. Sutlive, in that post in the summer of 1940 and held it until his retirement in June 1964. Sutlive's career on *The Press* spanned 44 years and he and his staffs earned many journalistic honors. He served Savannah in several roles of civic responsibility, including the presidency of the Board of Education. He died on Georgia Day, February 12, 1979.

JACK J. COOK — As long-time city editor of *The Evening Press*, Cook had a reputation as a tenacious newsman. He joined the staff in 1916 as a reporter and served as telegraph editor and sports editor before becoming city editor in 1940, a post he held until ill health forced him to transfer to the job as chief librarian in 1959. He retired in 1970. Cook also was a civic leader, heading the Board of Education and the Savannah Port Society, and assuming roles of leadership in the Methodist Church. He also is a lawyer.

A Pulitzer Prize Weekly

Savannah also has an urban weekly newspaper, and a most unusual one. It actually started in 1978 but took the name of *The Georgia Gazette*, which had been dormant for 176 years, since James Johnston, the state's first newspaperman, folded his *Georgia Gazette* in 1802. Also revived was *The Gazette*'s original masthead and Johnston's motto: "I have endeavored to conduct myself in the publication of my paper, as impartially as I could."

Founders of this modern *Gazette* were Albert Scardino and his wife, Marjorie. Albert is listed as editor, and Marjorie, who also has a full time law practice, is the publisher. Controversy, financial adversity and respect in the profession have been abundant for *The Gazette*. Like most urban weeklies aligned against a large daily morning and afternoon combination, it has struggled to establish a niche.

But a victory of unusual proportions occurred in April 1984, when Editor Scardino was named national winner of the Pulitzer Prize for editorial writing. He was the first weekly editor since 1963 to receive the honor, and the first Georgia editor so recognized since Eugene Patterson in 1967.

Scardino's Pulitzer was based on 10 editorials he submitted, on subjects ranging from regulation of hydrogen sulfide pollution to corruption in state government (specifically the case of Labor Commissioner Sam Caldwell) to discrimination against women in county government.

Scardino, only 34 when he wrote the Pulitzer-winning editorials, had earlier won the Golden Quill editorial award from the International Society of Weekly Newspaper Editors.

The Gazette and Scardino did not arrive at their honors easily. Survival has always been the first priority, and Scardino welcomed the $1,000 award money that goes with the Pulitzer almost as much as the honor. In 1982 *The Gazette* had fallen off to about 10 pages per issue, and the overall staff had to be cut from 26 to 12, with the news staff reduced from six to two. *The Gazette*, like many other non-urban weeklies, has a commercial printing business which helps pay the bills.

By 1984 the number of pages was up to 20 a week and circulation was

2,500, which compares to a combined total of nearly 80,000 on the two Savannah dailies. Scardino says *The Gazette* caters to a professional, "upscale" audience and tries to be like the "Week in Review" section of a good Sunday newspaper. Although it gets its share of news breaks, analysis is *The Gazette*'s forte, and Scardino's editorials are the cutting edge. Scardino has definite opinions on many subjects, including the role of newspaper editorial pages. "I don't think the founding fathers thought of free speech as including a spectrum of views in one publication," he says. "Instead the spectrum of opinion should be covered by many publications, espousing a diversity of strong, biased viewpoints."

Scardino is obviously making a case for urban weeklies such as *The Gazette* to provide strong contrary views to the editorial pages of the traditional dailies. It was this theory that spawned many of the so-called "alternative" newspapers in the 1960s and 1970s. Few of them survived — or even started — in Georgia, *The Gazette* and *The Athens Observer* being the most notable, although *The Observer* has become more of a community weekly. Albany has *The Journal*, which has survived for more than 30 years with a somewhat sensational approach to the news.

"We see ourselves clearly as advocates," Scardino said. One of his campaigns that was cited by the Pulitzer committee was opposing the use of tax-exempt bonds for private construction in Savannah, a method many cities have used to attract industry, shopping centers or malls, and hotels-motels, and which had been helpful for Savannah's increasing role as a tourist center. But Scardino feels the bonds are "welfare for the rich."

He considers his recognition by the Pulitzer committee as an honor for other editors of urban weeklies, most of which are members of The International Society of Weekly Newspaper Editors. "I think there's a revival of the independent weekly and this should encourage the trend," he says. "Most of the editors are about my age (mid-30s) and they have in common a much stronger watchdog approach to community news and opinion. They have also had impact on the dailies in their community and their performance. *The News* and *Press* have pulled themselves out of the cellar in the last five years and started to do a lot of things we started first — and doing them better than we did."

But Scardino still feels the Savannah dailies have weak editorial pages. Their last firm stand, he contends, was a forthright opposition "to the drought affecting the coastal area."

Scardino, whose father is a prominent Savannah urologist, attended Columbia University in 1966, when it was a hotbed of anti-Vietnam activisim. He went on strike with students his sophomore year when one group seized and held the administration building. He worked for several newspapers during this time, including *The Savannah News-Press* and *The Atlanta Constitution*. His interest in Indian history led him to retrace the "trail of tears" in the summer of 1972, and the following year he spent six weeks at Wounded Knee, South Dakota, covering an Indian uprising for the Savannah newspapers.

After marriage to the former Marjorie Morris of Texarkana, Texas, he became interested in film-making, but then he and Marjorie decided to return to Savannah and start *The Gazette*. They and their children live in one of the restored homes of Savannah's Victorian district.

The road to the Pulitzer was harrowing and uncertain. Scardino admits that *The Gazette* has almost folded on several occasions, but has been rescued by some of its 57 stockholders and his mother, Kay Scardino.

"By the time we turned a profit in the last quarter of 1983, the paper had lost $520,000," Scardino told a reporter for *The Atlanta Constitution*.

Scardino broke the first report of an FBI investigation of State Labor Commissioner Sam Caldwell in 1982, and it was the stories of that investigation which he felt had the best chance to win a Pulitzer. They were entered in the Community Service category. He almost didn't enter the editorial category because he had to justify the $20 entry fee.

The Scardinos are proud of the honor, but in the summer of their Pulitzer they still don't know what the future holds for *The Gazette*. The hours are long, the money is scarce and the audience is small, which most weekly newspaper publishers understand. But not many win Pulitzer prizes. Sometimes the price of a Pulitzer is discouragingly high. Julian Harris of *The Columbus Enquirer* had to sell his paper two years after his Pulitzer in 1926. Eugene Patterson, another Georgia winner of an editorial-writing Pulitzer, left his post on *The Constitution* two years later. (See Chapter III.)

The Scardinos, in the final analysis, are seeking to prove there is a role for a hard-hitting urban "alternative" weekly. The jury is still out.

(Editor's note: The jury came in with a verdict in February 1985 when Scardino announced that *The Gazette* would cease publication because it had lost the county's legal advertising. Scardino said he was taking a job with *The New York Times*.)

Macon: Death in the Afternoon

Except for *The Atlanta Journal* and *Atlanta Constitution*, the daily newspaper read by more Georgians than any other in this century has been *The Macon Telegraph*, a tradition in many Middle Georgia homes for decades.

The Telegraph often fell behind *The Augusta Chronicle* and *Savannah Morning News* in actual numbers, but virtually all of its subscribers were Georgians, due to Macon's central location, while a portion of the *Chronicle* and *News* readers were South Carolinians.

But if there was any question as to which newspaper ranked third behind the Atlanta dailies in Georgia readership, it was settled on September 6, 1983, when *The Telegraph* merged with its afternoon counterpart, *The News*, and became *The Telegraph and News*, a single newspaper for Macon and its circulation area.

Because *News* subscribers were automatically converted to *Telegraph* subscribers, the immediate effect was to give *The Telegraph and News* a circulation of nearly 70,000. By the end of 1983 this figure had settled down to about 67,000 due to the loss of afternoon street sales and some duplication in the carrier-delivered subscribers. Management also estimated that it lost a small number of subscribers who simply did not want a morning paper, but they were pleasantly surprised at how small the loss turned out to be. Another encouraging sign was that the circulation of *The Sunday Telegraph* and *News* averaged 90,234 during December, a record high that offered a goal for the daily editions. By 1985 the daily circulation had surpassed the pre-merger total.

The merger of the morning and afternoon newspapers in Macon was the first of its kind in Georgia but was in keeping with a trend that seems to be gaining momentum in the nation. Later in 1983 the Memphis, Tennessee, newspapers announced a morning-afternoon merger. Earlier, cities such as Minneapolis, Lexington, Portland, Orlando and Buffalo had become one-newspaper cities. The reason for the sudden rash of "deaths in the afternoon" are outlined in excerpts from the following column by *Telegraph-News* publisher Edmund Olson on September 4, 1983:

There has been a trend in Middle Georgia to a single newspaper per household. This is not unique to our area, but is nationwide. The number of households subscribing to both of our newspapers has declined from 7,500 in 1978, to 1,894 at present. Since people want a single newspaper, we think our resources would be more wisely invested in a combined paper looking toward the future needs of our readers and advertisers. If we were in financial trouble or had a single objective of increased profits, we would have folded one of our newspapers, dismissed the staff and continued to publish the other newspaper without any change. Instead, we are merging the professional staffs of our two newsrooms, increasing the size of our morning paper by an average of three pages, combining the features of both newspapers, adding more commentary and expanding our coverage in Middle Georgia. This would not have been possible with the duplication of effort inherent in a two-newspaper operation. Therefore, our combined paper will be bigger and more complete than either *The Telegraph* or *The News*."

Olson estimated that about 97 percent of the households receiving either *The Telegraph* or *The News* would take the new *Telegraph* and *News*, and at the end of 1983 his forecast was holding up.

A more detailed analysis of why the merger came about was included in a history of *The News*, carried in its final edition, Friday, September 2, 1983.

> The existence of *The News* was tenuous because, like many afternoon papers in a nation whose evenings were absorbed by television, and whose work schedules and lifestyles had changed, it lost circulation slowly but steadily. More than 22,000 subscribers bought it in 1969; as it ceases publication today, the number is down to barely 16,000.
>
> Various strategies were attempted. In 1975 CASHWORD, a puzzle game with a payoff for the winners, was instituted. It has lasted for eight years.
>
> About the same time the paper went after street sales with large headlines over sensational front-page stories. Often, once the reader got into them, they were concerned with matters remote from Middle Georgia and decidedly lacking in larger significance. One headline trumpeted the approach of the dreaded killer bees. Another screamed about a deadly tornado — in Texas. That sort of thing ended after a couple of years.
>
> To make the readers feel close to the paper, consumer and religious news were increased. Reader participation contests like the Yukky Sandwich, Ugly Dog and First Day of School writing contest developed.
>
> *The News* went out of its way to provide something different, something personal, in covering the world's affairs.
>
> When Elvis Presley died, *The News* put out a special 'Elvis Edition' Aug. 17, 1977, with a full-page poster-type photo covering Page 1A with the headline, 'The King is Dead.'
>
> *The News* suffered its own shock Dec. 20, 1980, when Editor Joe Parham, 'Mr. Macon News' to people across the state after 31 years at the helm, unexpectedly died. Early the following year Ed Corson assumed the editorship and Barbara Stinson became managing editor.

On Jan. 20, 1981, as President Reagan was being sworn in, the long-anticipated release of the U. S. Iranian hostages finally took place. The final edition of *The News* that day had a huge headline, letters three inches tall, reading 'Hostages Freed.' It had been typeset in the largest letters available, then blown up even further photographically, days in advance.

On March 30, 1981, one of the rare extras appeared: 'Reagan Shot, Injured.'

In a final effort to increase its quality and stem the circulation decline, the paper underwent a thorough overhaul. The 'new *News*' appeared May 11, 1981. Bolder, blacker headlines (in which only the first word and proper names were capitalized) were obvious features of the design change.

Less obvious but more important were more local news, more prominently displayed; a news summary on front; the regular appearance of local 'Middle Georgia columnists' on the editorial page; distinctive feature and sports sections; new comics — and a motto: Our beat is the heart of Georgia.

But still readership fell off.

So *The Telegraph* and *News* are merging into one paper.

It is a process that actually began in 1930, more than 50 years ago. At that time the Sunday editions of the *News* and *Telegraph* were combined into the familiar Sunday paper. Years later, in 1974, the Saturday editions were combined. There was little demand anymore for a Saturday afternoon paper.

Then, with hard economic times demanding efficiencies, the "women's page" staffs of the two papers were combined in February 1980; so were the sports staffs. Since then a single merged staff has produced the feature and sports sections for each paper. (Only the news and editorial staffs remain separate.) At first the sections were almost identical. "Clones," some readers protested. In May 1981 the decision was made for the merged staffs to produce completely different sections for each paper, as they have through today.

So what happens Tuesday is really the final step in a process that began 53 years ago."

Since World War II, a number of daily newspapers have been started in Georgia, but very few old ones have folded, and the demise of *The Macon News* was certainly the most significant in terms of longevity (founded in 1884) and importance. The only other daily newspapers to disappear completely in that period were *The Gainesville Morning News*, Georgia's first offset newspaper, which published for about nine months as a daily, and *The Atlanta Times*, which was published for 14 months.

Randal Savage, a staff writer for *The Telegraph and News*, provided a poignant account of how the employees feel when they know they are putting together the last edition of a newspaper. His story, which appeared in the Sunday, September 4 edition of *The Telegraph and News*, is reprinted here:

> They were like junior high school students who'd bruised and torn their bodies in a vicious game of tug-of-war — too tough to cry, yet too hurt to keep the pain from reflecting in their eyes.
>
> So they came to work just like every other day — arriving early, plotting strategy, making assignments, chatting, joking, writing stories, writing headlines, laying out pages — doing all the things necessary to put out a paper.
>
> It was Friday, Sept. 2, 1983, the last day *The Macon News* was published. *The News* and *The Macon Telegraph* have been merged into a new paper called *The Macon Telegraph and News*. The merged paper begins publication Tuesday.
>
> Friday was a sad day for the editors and reporters of *The News*, a 99-year-old newspaper with the slogan "Our Beat Is the Heart of Georgia".
>
> But they hid their sadness in nostalgic smiles and kept it hidden by staying busy putting the final package together.
>
> "I'm not going to cry," said Managing Editor Barbara Stinson. "I'm going to put out this newspaper, and I'm not going to cry."
>
> And she didn't cry for the most part.
>
> She didn't cry when a red, white and brown newspaper cake with *The News'* slogan on top was presented to the editors and reporters about 10:30 a.m.
>
> She didn't cry when Publisher Ed Olson, General Manager Billy Watson, Executive Editor Richard Thomas, Editor Ed Corson, City Editor Roger Bull and other editors and reporters gathered in the library for a farewell snack.
>
> She didn't cry when George Doss, a dean of Middle Georgia news-gatherers with 34 years experience in political reporting, submitted his final political story for review.
>
> She didn't cry when the last copy of the newspaper dropped from the presses.
>
> But she did cry a few minutes later when she returned to her desk to look over business pages for a weekend paper, a task she undertook every Friday after her paper had been printed.
>
> "I realized that was the last time I'd do it," she said. "Can you imagine? Crying over a business page."
>
> Earlier in the day, the reporters busied themselves with their normal assignments, John Gaines, City Hall reporter, "made my usual rounds, a run through City Hall."
>
> Doss, the seasoned veteran, sat before his video display terminal with his ever-present bonded lead pencil hanging from

his mouth as he put the finishing touches on his final *News* story.

Cheryl Fincher, health writer, like Stinson, wore black to commemorate the occasion. Bo Sammons, court reporter, did his routine work and interviewed the Ca$hword winner for a story.

Steve Bills, business editor, busied himself by laying out six pages, writing a business story and doing a question-and-answer profile.

Cynthia George, the last journalism student to take intern training at *The News*, was happy because she "had the only (local) front-page story" in the final edition.

"It means a lot to me today because in the short time I've been here I've become really attached to the paper and the people. We have such a camaraderie," she said.

They all expressed sadness over the demise of *The News*. But they also said they're excited over the challenge of being part of the new paper.

"I feel sad in a way," Doss said. "I'm sort of opposed to change in general. But I've seen a lot of it, and it's always worked all right. I'll look back. But I'll be looking forward to the future."

The final edition of *The News* was on Friday, September 2, 1983, and it carried a large box across the top of the front page with each year of its existence listed (1884-1973) and the words, "Final Edition," in all caps. It turned out to be a big news day, with stories on President Reagan's response to the shooting down of a Korean airliner by a Soviet MIG, and the death of U. S. Sen. Harry Jackson. The only local story was an interview with Frank Wrye, a Macon resident who had been reading *The News* for 66 years, and who said he was sorry *The News* was folding. "It's another marker we're throwing on the side of the road," he was quoted. "They're looking at it from a standpoint of making money, not what the readers want."

Gallantly, *The News* reporter, Cynthia George, recorded the disgruntled reader's words, right alongside a column headlined, "To Our Readers," which sought again to explain the transition and assure readers that they would be getting a better product.

Rick Thomas, executive editor, wrote in a message to readers: "This means the beginning of a new, bigger and better newspaper for Middle Georgia. The new *Macon News and Telegraph*, quite simply, will be a better newspaper than either of its predecessors, good though they may have been through the years. Readers will lose few, if any, of their favorite features from either paper. The same number of reporters and editors will be working on one newspaper instead of splitting their efforts between two.

An average of three full pages of space per day will be added, allowing us to provide more features, more commentary, more sports coverage.

"It's a good move, and we're excited about it."

The logic of the argument is irrefutable, and it will not be lost on the management of other morning-afternoon newspaper combinations, both in Georgia and the rest of the nation. The combined Sunday, Saturday and holiday editions which have become commonplace for most of these publications demonstrate what can be achieved by pooling the staff, resources and features. A couple of years earlier, the Atlanta newspapers began carrying its popular local columnists, Lewis Grizzard and Ron Hudspeth, in both *The Constitution* and *Journal*, on the theory that readers who bought *The Journal* shouldn't miss seeing Grizzard, and *Constitution* readers should not be deprived of Hudspeth. That logic can be extended to the sports, editorial and feature columnists, and to the comics and Dear Abby and Ann Landers.

A number of *Macon News* readers joined 66-year reader Wrye in complaining about the loss of *The News*, and their letters were printed in the final edition. Among the comments were: "*The News* has become one of my daily habits and I shall miss this particular enjoyment and enlightenment each afternoon. My routine is overturned . . . . There has been some degree of competition between the two papers and I regret that we have become a one-newspaper town . . . ."

Ronnie Thompson, the well-known former mayor of Macon who had been opposed by the newspapers, but later became a columnist for *The News*, took a more complimentary vein in his letter for the final edition:

"Merging *The Macon News* with *The Macon Telegraph* is a journalistic landmark in our state. The most permanent thing known to mankind is change. Hopefully, it will be a change for the better. I wish the effort well and I am personally proud to have been associated, both good and bad, with *The Macon News*."

The first public announcement of the merger was made in stories in *The Telegraph and News* on Monday, July 25. It had already been a summer of significant changes at the two papers. A few weeks earlier Edmund Olson had been named publisher, with Billy Watson, the long time executive editor, becoming general manager. Richard (Rick) Thomas had been brought in from Tallahassee, another Knight-Ridder newspaper, to succeed Watson as executive editor. Almost immediately the new executives faced the task of deciding how the merger would be handled and how the duplicated staff positions — particularly in the news departments — would be resolved.

Thomas examined some of the decisions that had to be made in the following column, published on August 14:

> Faithful readers know that *The Macon Telegraph* and *The Macon News* will merge into a single morning newspaper on Sept. 6. What they may not know is just how complicated a process it is.
>
> In fact, many readers in Macon already think of *The Macon Telegraph* and *The Macon News* as one newspaper, because they are owned by the same company. Granted, there are a number of people who work for both newspapers. Publisher Ed Olson is responsible for both. As executive editor, I'm responsible for both news operations. Similarly, production, advertising, circulation, personnel and other functions for both *The Macon Telegraph* and *The Macon News* are headed up by the same people.
>
> But make no mistake: *The Macon Telegraph* and *The Macon News* are two distinctly different newspapers with, for the most part, two distinctly different staffs. Because the newsroom is my area of expertise, let me use the news operation as an example of what goes into bringing those staffs and those newspapers into one.
>
> It's a good example, because nowhere in *The Telegraph* and *News* building is the sense of separation more distinct than in the newsroom. Although several newsroom departments — photography, sports, features and state news — work for both papers, the competition between the city staffs and the editing desks of *The Telegraph* and *News* is fierce.
>
> *The Macon Telegraph*, published in the mornings, has its own managing editor, its own city editor, its own staff of reporters and editors. *The Macon News*, published in the afternoon, has the same. And each staff is determined to do a better job than its counterpart across the room in bringing the news to its readers.
>
> So among the first items of business was to find a way to bring those two staffs together, utilizing talent as best we could while trying to make it possible for everyone to be happy with his or her assignment on the new merged newspaper. It has been a tough job, and we have a long way to go.
>
> Another important task: to sort out all the features currently running in *The Telegraph* and *The News* and to decide which ones to keep and which ones to discard. That job was a bit easier, because we had promised from the start to keep as many features as possible from both papers.
>
> For example, *The Macon Telegraph* carries popular advice columnist Ann Landers; *The Macon News* carries Dear Abby. Because both have loyal readers, we decided to run both in the

merged *Telegraph* and *News*.

> On the other hand, we won't need two crossword puzzles or two horoscopes in the new newspaper, so we had to decide which one to keep. We decided on the crossword that appears in *The News* and the horoscope that runs in *The Telegraph*.
>
> Then there was the matter of the newspaper's appearance. Would the new *Telegraph* and *News* more closely resemble *The Telegraph* or *The News*? (Compare the two some time; they are quite different in looks.) What kind of headline type would we use? Would we need new signs for the newspaper's features? These are tough, time-consuming matters, and they haven't been resolved completely. But they have to be resolved by Sept. 6, or the result will be a sloppy-looking newspaper.
>
> The newsroom itself also had to be considered. Currently, reporters and editors for *The Telegraph* work at one end of the room, and their counterparts on *The News* at the other. They must be brought together into a logical workspace, and that will require moving desks, changing telephone extensions and rerouting computer cables. No small chore and not much time to accomplish it.
>
> The planning and execution of such an undertaking can be tedious, frustrating and, at times, even painful. But it's also exciting. Here in the newsroom and in the other divisions of *The Telegraph* and *News*, we're in the process of creating a bigger, better newspaper for Middle Georgia readers. We'll try to keep you informed of the major decisions as they're made.

Here's how the key news staff positions were resolved:

Thomas, of course, was executive editor of both newspapers, and for some years the executive editor had also nominally been editor of *The Telegraph*. So there was actually no editor on *The Telegraph*, making that decision fairly simple. Ed Corson, who had been editor of *The News*, became editor of *The Macon Telegraph and News*, with main responsibility for the editorial and op-ed pages. Jim Chapman, who had been senior managing editor of both papers, retained that post, with duties in newsroom administration, production coordination, computer systems and the photography department.

Ron Woodgeard, managing editor of *The Telegraph*, was named managing editor for news on the merged paper, while Barbara Stinson, managing editor of *The News*, became managing editor for features.

The most extensive changes probably took place in reporting assignments since there was more duplication on the two staffs in that area. One interesting change was the appointment of George Doss to the new post of Accuracy Editor, which may be a first on Georgia newspapers. Doss' new duties call for him to work closely with the city desk and editorial page staff to make sure stories and editorials are factually correct. Doss came with strong credentials for the job as he had spent 34 years as a reporter on *The Macon News*, covering almost every beat in Macon and Bibb County. In his new job he also writes analytical articles and editorials.

When the first edition of *The Macon Telegraph and News* appeared on Tuesday, September 6, the headline type and general makeup closely resembled *The Telegraph*, which was understandable since nearly 80 percent of its readers were accustomed to *The Telegraph*. The new op-ed page was actually half a page of letters and columns and a half page of ads. There were several wide open news pages, however, including two full pages of comics and features. Twenty-nine comic strips or panels were carried on these pages. The sports section had three wide-open pages.

Little was mentioned about advertising rates or circulation rates in the stories and columns leading up to the merger. Presumably there was no change since virtually all ads were already sold for both papers at a combination rate.

The decision to merge *The Telegraph* and *News* was made by the executives in Macon and recommended to Knight-Ridder headquarters in Miami where it won support. It was not a decision made in Miami and passed on to Macon.

Undoubtedly, there will be a close watch on what happens in Macon from Columbus, in particular, which is another Knight-Ridder property and also Augusta, Savannah and even Atlanta.

The Anderson Era

In addition to September 6, 1983, which brought the first edition of *The Macon Telegraph and News*, two other dates are especially significant in the history of the Macon newspapers since World War II. The first was January 3, 1951, when Peyton Anderson Jr. became the sole owner of the newspapers which had been published earlier by his father and uncle. Anderson, 43 at the time, had been publisher of the papers since 1948 and a one-third owner since 1940. He acquired the other two-thirds of the stock from General Newspapers in late 1950.

Under Anderson's leadership the papers expanded their coverage, facilities and size during the post-war years. The year he took full control the papers started running "Parade," the national Sunday supplement. They reactivated their Atlanta bureau in 1955, with Reg Murphy handling the job for the first four years. (He later went on to be editor of *The Atlanta Constitution* and publisher of papers in San Francisco and Baltimore.)

Also in 1955, Thomas Johnson, a high school student, became a *Telegraph* sports correspondent. He was a part-time reporter during college days, then later a White House Fellow, TV station president, and successively publisher of *The Dallas Times-Herald* and *The Los Angeles Times*.

A Warner Robins bureau was established in 1958 with two reporters. Three more reporters were added within the decade.

In 1961 the papers left their old quarters on Cherry Street for a brand-new building at the corner of Broadway and Riverside. Printing had begun there in 1960 and the 44,000-square-foot main building was occupied in 1961. The building had a helipad on the roof and Anderson experimented with delivering *The Macon News* by helicopter, through a subsidiary company, Newscopters, Inc., which employed a full-time pilot.

In 1966 a weekly food section was begun, but the farm page disappeared a year later with the retirement of farm editor Susan Myrick. And in 1965 Mildred Henderson, who had taken over a decade earlier as the last editor of the "colored pages," moved into the main newsroom from her segregated quarters on Cotton Avenue.

Several outstanding newsmen began their executive careers on *The Telegraph* and *News*. Joe Parham became editor of *The Macon News* in 1949, the start of a 31-year tenure in that post. Bert Struby became executive editor of the two papers in 1948, moving to the business side as general manager in 1957, a position he was to hold for 20 years before becoming publisher. Bill Ott succeeded him as editor of *The Telegraph* in 1958.

The paper's editorial positions were moderate-to-liberal for their times. In the furor over the beginnings of school integration nationally, the papers took a moderate, "abide-by-the-law" stand well in advance of many of their readers. They strongly supported keeping Georgia's colleges open during the University of Georgia desegregation crisis in 1961. They applauded Mercer University's voluntary desegregation in 1963. They also took a moderate stance on the Vietnam War and the opposition to it. Locally they pushed hard for interstate highways through Macon.

The Knight-Ridder Era

The next significant day came on March 3, 1969, when *The Tele-*

graph and *News* joined the growing move toward group ownership. The newspapers, along with *The Milledgeville Union-Recorder* and Drinnon's, a commercial photo studio, were sold by Anderson to Knight Newspapers, Inc.

This group, which merged with the Ridder newspapers in the mid-1970s to become Knight-Ridder Newspapers Inc., with the largest total paid circulation in the country, went on the New York Stock Exchange shortly after the Macon purchase. Knight policy gave its papers "full editorial independence and autonomy," with complete separation of editorial and financial functions. Much of the public, unfortunately, held to the mistaken notion that editorial policies were dictated outside of the local community.

Also in 1969 a $1.5 million, 300-ton Hoe Colormatic press went into service. The papers remained committed to the letter-press method. Now able to produce four-color process color, the papers won recognition as one of the best letterpress reproducers in the nation.

Mirroring social changes, the news columns of the papers were fully integrated in 1969 as the "Negro news" pages were dropped in response to a petition. Two years later, the news staff was racially integrated with the hiring of Freddie Bentley, a black photographer. Sports reporter Mike Sheftall came aboard the same year, and in 1973 Tethel White became the pioneer black news reporter. (At the end of 1982 she headed the large feature department as feature editor.) Kaijer Lee became the first black division director (circulation) in 1982.

A major technological shift began in 1972 with the phasing in of an optical character reader/scanner typesetting system. It "read" newsroom copy typed with coding on electric typewriters and converted the letters into punched tape. And in 1974 a full "cold type" operation was phased in. The punched tape ran through a Photon machine, which provided the "type" on photographic paper ready for paste-up. After paste-up a Merigraph process produced a one-pound plastic plate. Four years later, upon the completion of extensive remodeling and expansion of the building, the unwieldy scanner system was replaced by use of CSI video display terminals hooked directly to computers and typesetters; in the 1980s came reception of AP "wire" copy from a satellite.

Thus, in a few years the Macon papers got rid of teletypes, linotypes, hot metal and heavy printing plates; in came photographed type, plastic printing plates, the video terminal and the computer. Access to this new technology, previously out of reach, was made possible by the greatly expanded resources and financial support provided by group ownership. Such improvements meant that more money could be put into the news product, with funds shifted from the production to the editorial side.

The Telegraph added full stock tables, *The News* took on Action Line, and the newshole grew to be 40 percent larger than it had been two decades previously when it was the smallest among Georgia's large dailies. There were more reporters and editors, less labor in production. In 1973 the locally edited "TV Teletime" appeared, one of the first weekly TV quarterfolds in Georgia. In 1974 a combined Saturday paper made its appearance. Also in the 1970s the papers established bureaus in Baldwin and Laurens counties. And in 1976 they stationed their first correspondent in Washington. Zoned advertising and editioning began in these years, offering greater reach and flexibility.

Just as blacks entered the newsroom mainstream, women also moved into jobs formerly considered a male preserve. On *The News*, Roger Ann Jones, who started as a *Telegraph* copy editor, became state editor, then *News* city editor and managing editor. By the end of 1982, Barbara Stinson was *News* managing editor, Lee Ann Schlatter and Mary Burdette had been its city editors; and Helene Lorber was news editor.

There was some movement among key personnel during the period. Bert Struby became publisher in 1977, to retire in January 1983. Meantime Don Carter became executive editor in 1971, after *Telegraph* editor Bill Ott moved on to another Knight newspaper. Carter was succeeded in 1975 by Frank Caperton, who in turn gave way to Billy Watson as executive editor in 1977. Joe Parham died suddenly in late 1980, to be succeeded as editor of *The News* by Ed Corson.

Editorially, the papers gradually turned against the Vietnam War. Later they soured on Pres. Richard Nixon (whom they had supported for president in 1972 — the first time *The Telegraph* had ever endorsed a Republican for that post). The papers gave staunch support to Georgian Jimmy Carter in 1976 and 1980.

Locally, the papers carried on a running battle with two-term Mayor Ronnie "Machine Gun" Thompson from 1967 to 1975. When his political career ended, he became a columnist for *The News* in 1981. The papers tried to calm public feeling during the local school integration crisis starting in 1971. They did a major investigative job on the racial/political mess in Hancock County; later they did impressive series such as "Who Runs Macon?" and printed the salaries of all local public servants. They crusaded for gun control (to the chagrin of a majority of their readers), sex education and fluoridation; *The Telegraph* mounted an onslaught against smokers. The two papers differed on various subjects, too, such as the death penalty and the rights of homosexuals.

Before the big changes of mid-1983 the newspapers were under the joint leadership of general manager Ed Olson and executive editor Billy Watson. Division directors included: Editor of the News, Ed Corson; Production Director, Bob Lawson; Advertising Director, Paul Burley; Circulation Director, Kaijer Lee; Personnel Director, Jo Ann Green; Comptroller, John Kelly; and Data Processing Director, Mike Cox. Senior Managing Editor was Jim Chapman. Newsroom department heads included Ron Woodgeard, managing editor of the Telegraph; Barbara Stinson, managing editor of the News; Tethel Brown, feature editor; Ed Grisamore, sports editor; Cecil Bentley, state editor; R. L. Day, Sunday editor; Danny Gilleland, photo chief and Mike Morgan, newsroom artist and cartoonist.

People of The Telegraph and News

Following are short sketches on some of the important personalities associated with the Macon newspapers during the past 40 years:

PEYTON ANDERSON JR., born in 1908, was the son of the paper's long-time business manager and nephew of its publisher. He started work for *The Telegraph* as a nine-year-old delivery boy. Forced by an injury to leave the U.S. Naval Academy after two years, he joined the national advertising department in 1927 and was made circulation manager in 1929. A year later, when *The Telegraph* bought *The Macon News*, he became assistant general manager of the merged papers.

Business manager in 1935, he moved up to become president and one-third owner in 1940. After wartime service in the Navy, he returned to be publisher of a paper in Gadsden, Alabama, owned by the company which held the other two-thirds of the stock, then came back to Macon in 1948 to become publisher. He bought the other two-thirds of the stock in 1951, becoming, at the age of 43, publisher and owner.

"I gave the editors free rein," he said. "I was only concerned that we put out a good, progressive newspaper . . . Newspapers can't have character without money in the bank." With the turmoil of the later 1960s, and technological changes requiring enormous capital investment on the horizon, he sold the papers in 1969 to Knight Newspapers, Inc. He continues on the board of directors of Knight-Ridder Newspapers, Inc.

BERT STRUBY, a Macon native, retired as publisher in January 1983 after 44 years with the newspapers. He began his journalistic career as a pre-teen, when he put out a neighborhood newspaper, ceasing publication "when I started to get interested in girls." He graduated from Mercer University with a magna cum laude degree in journalism in 1938. Unable to find a job, he worked a couple of months for *The Telegraph* without salary to gain experience. When a $17.50 per week job opened as cub reporter, he got it, but the business manager insisted the paper could afford only $15. After two years as a reporter and a year as state editor, he put in a five-year Navy stint during World War II.

He returned to *The News* as state editor, then assistant city editor. In 1947 came a giant step up to executive editor of both papers (he also assumed editorial page duties for *The Telegraph*). In 1957 he shifted to the business side to become general manager. He was reluctant to make the move but reasoned that "any other guy Anderson got as general manager and I might not have been able to get along with each other." He served in the post until 1978, when he was named publisher, a title which had been vacant since the sale to Knight in 1969.

Like Anderson before him, he maintained a policy of non-interference with the editorial columns of the newspaper. He was active in a wide range of civic activities: chairman of the Macon Housing Authority, president of the Greater Macon Chamber of Commerce, chairman of the United Givers Fund and chairman of the Mercer University board of trustees. He served the Boy Scouts most of his adult life, winning high regional positions and many awards. He also served as president of the Southern Newspaper Publishers Association and is credited with starting the SNPA Foundation.

He was a good churchman, too. He recalls that at one time, he was chairman of the deacons at Highland Hills Baptist Church, *Telegraph* editor Bill Ott was chairman of the board at the Mulberry Street United Methodist Church, and *Telegraph* associate editor Nathan Gans was president of his synagogue, which seemed to refute the popular stereotype of newspapermen as profane carousers.

JOSEPH PARHAM edited *The Macon News* for 31 years. He was born and reared in Winder; his "lifelong love affair" with the newspaper began at the age of nine when he helped out at the country weekly where his father worked. He had to go to work instead of college when he graduated from high school during the Depression, but despite his limited formal education he made himself a very well-read and educated person. At 22 he was working for a little weekly paper as "linotype operator, sports editor, job press operator, general reporter, single wrapper specialist and chief sweeper."

He came to Macon in 1941 to start his daily newspaper career. After serving in the Army Air Corps during World War II as a maintenance sergeant, he returned to Macon in 1946 as *News* sports editor. Named managing editor in 1949, he became editor the same year. That was, he said, "as high a title as a man would ever want to aspire to." He made an unsuccessful race for the state senate in 1958 and later wrote humorously about the magnitude of his defeat.

A superb story-teller, Parham was best known to the public for his columns. He wrote more than 6,200 in his career, starting in 1946. In the 1970s he won the Georgia Press Association's "Best Daily Newspaper Column" award five times, four in a row. He could handle many different kinds of subject matter. He could pen uproarious tales (such as the story of the mule and the hunting horn, or the man left on the Interstate in his underwear), but he could also write tenderly about his four sons, the death of his first wife, or about life with "my bride," Hazel. He could also comment seriously or indignantly on current events, or write nostalgically about growing up in North Georgia or his wartime experiences. He could write informatively about the travelling he loved to do. He died suddenly, after several years of uncertain health, in December 1980, at the age of 61.

DON E. CARTER, native of Plains and first cousin of former President Jimmy Carter, came to *The Telegraph* and *News* in 1971 as the paper's first executive editor since Bert Struby moved to the business side 14 years earlier. He says he decided on a newspaper career as a schoolboy when he heard *Telegraph* owner-editor W. T. Anderson make a speech about newspapers. Editor of the Sumter County weekly at 17, he went to the University of Georgia where he was a Phi Beta Kappa graduate of the Henry Grady School of Journalism. From 1938 to 1959, he was a reporter, then for eight years city editor, at *The Atlanta Journal*, with a break for World War II service in China and India.

In 1959 his career shifted to the New York City area — first as executive director of the Wall Street Journal Newspaper Fund, then as founding managing editor of *The National Observer.* From 1967 to 1971 he was executive editor of a major suburban daily, *The Bergen, New Jersey Record*. He served as executive editor of the Macon papers for four years, overseeing the change to new technology and integration of the staff, while exercising firm control over coverage and a newshole expanding in quantity and quality.

In July, 1975, he left Macon to become publisher of another pair of Knight-Ridder papers, the Lexington (Ky.) *Herald* and *Leader*; two years later he moved to corporate headquarters in Miami, where he supervised the news operations in the KRN group's 17 smaller and medium-sized papers (of which *The Telegraph* and *News* were members) as vice-president for news, city group. He retired from this position at the end of 1982.

WILLIAM A. OTT served as editor of *The Telegraph* from 1958 until 1971. A native of Moultrie, he was a Phi Beta Kappa graduate of the Henry W. Grady School of Journalism in 1949. He served as an Army Criminal Investigation agent in Korea. On his return, he became city editor of *The Moultrie Observer*, then came to *The Telegraph* in 1950. After serving on the copy desk and as county reporter, he moved up to the managing editorship in 1953, filling the vacancy left by Bert Struby the year before. He became editor in 1958.

He was a dedicated and astute newsman who could quickly size up a situation and — with eloquence and wit — support his decision. He was active in civic affairs as president of the Greater Macon Chamber of Commerce and also of the Boys Club, the Mulberry Street United Methodist Church and The Macon Rotary Club. In 1971 he left for a much larger Knight newspaper, the *Akron Beacon-Journal*, where he moved quickly into the general managership.

He moved to Miami in 1975 as vice-president for operations (metro group) of KRN, overseeing the business operations of the group's 14 larger papers; in 1982 he was appointed senior vice-president, operations, with overall responsibility for the entire Knight-Ridder newspaper business operations.

BILLY WATSON, from Pitts, became executive editor of *The Telegraph and News* in January 1978. He did his college work at Georgia Southwestern College and the University of Georgia, graduating from the Henry W. Grady School of Journalism in 1960. There he was editor of *The Red and Black* and worked part-time with *The Athens Banner-Herald*. After graduation he worked for *The Cordele Dispatch* and *The Wilcox County Chronicle* before spending two years in the Army.

He returned to join *The Macon Telegraph* in 1963 as a county beat reporter, but quickly moved to Atlanta as chief of the paper's bureau there, where he covered state politics and government for four years. He returned to Macon in 1967 to work as a copy editor and special assignments editor. He was named Sunday editor in 1970 and managing editor of *The Telegraph* in 1972. He became editor in 1975 and executive editor in 1978. He was named general manager in June 1983. Watson has been active in civic affairs; is a deacon in the Northminster Presbyterian Church and has served on the boards of the Cerebral Palsy Unit, the Middle Georgia Council on Human Relations and the Red Cross. He is a member of the state board of the American Cancer Society and has served as president and chairman of the ACS Bibb-Jones unit.

JAMES A. CHAPMAN, managing editor of *The Telegraph* since 1958, became senior managing editor of both papers in 1972. He took on numerous budget responsibilities, supervision of several departments, and the brunt of the task of bringing the newsroom into scanners and then VDTs. An Atlantan, he graduated from Emory University with an A.B. in journalism and served as an Army Signal Corps photographer during World War II. After a year with *The Jacksonville Journal* he joined *The Telegraph* in 1951 as a reporter, later serving on the wire and city desks.

SUSAN MYRICK, who became associate editor of *The Telegraph* in 1948, held that post until her retirement in 1966. Her total career with *The Telegraph* spanned 54 years. A charming and gracious lady who could be at home with a wide variety of people, she was born in Milledgeville in 1896. She came to Macon as a college-trained physical education teacher at Lanier High School for girls.

Her byline first appeared in 1924 over a "Saner Eating" column. By 1928 she was working for *The Telegraph* full time. Her long-running "Life in a Tangle," a unique local column of advice to the lovelorn and lifeworn under the name of "Fannie Squeers," began in 1929. She kept writing these columns weekly even during an eight-month leave of absence in 1939 in Hollywood as technical advisor for *Gone With the Wind*. In 1940 she worked for *The News*, then in 1941 became editor of the Sunday paper's "Georgia Magazine" until the wartime newsprint shortage forced its discontinuance. She became *Telegraph* "war editor" and in 1946 was made farm editor, producing a Sunday page. This was an unusual assignment for a woman at that time. She became widely known for significant contributions to soil conservation.

In 1949 she began the twice-weekly editorial page columns which continued until only three weeks before her death at 82 in 1978. She was engaged in many civic activities, was a founding member of the Macon Little Theater and became a late-blooming water-colorist.

NATHAN ALFRED GANS became associate editor of *The Telegraph* in 1951, serving until his retirement in 1974. Born in Albany in 1910, he graduated magna cum laude and Phi Beta Kappa from the University of Georgia in 1930. After working briefly with *The Albany Herald*, he joined *The Telegraph* the same year — first as a sportswriter, then as state editor. He became sports editor of *The Macon News* in 1933 but in 1936 left newspapering to become sales promotion manager of Happ Brothers Company, then entered business for himself. However, he maintained his ties with the paper, and often worked part-time to fill in on various editorial staff positions, especially during and after World War II. He is remembered as a lightning-fast wire editor and layout man. As associate editor from 1951, when he re-entered full-time newspaper work, he won a reputation for integrity and fairness of his editorials, handling most of the national and international matters. He died in September 1982.

BLYTHE MCKAY edited the women's pages of *The Telegraph* and the Sunday paper from 1939 until her retirement in 1972. Prior to that span of service the Wesleyan College graduate had pinch-hit for her mother, who was often ill, as women's editor of *The News*, starting when she was a teenager in 1927. In 1935 she and Emily Tribble handled *The Telegraph* women's page as a shared full-time job, working alternate weeks. She replaced her mother as *News* women's editor in 1936, but soon returned to *The Telegraph* as reporter, then picture editor. She succeeded her mother at *The Telegraph* when the latter left the paper in 1938. She was known as a stickler for accuracy, especially where Macon and family history were concerned.

SAM GLASSMAN, Baltimore-born, arrived in Macon in 1944. He was a *Telegraph* staffer until his sudden and unexpected death of a heart attack in 1959. He brought stability and brilliance to the post of *Telegraph* sports editor, which had been a revolving door for 25 years. Short, stocky and friendly, Glassman was an aggressive newsman who fought hard for breaks on news stories. He was a charter member of the Southern Football Association and officiated football and basketball games for 25 years. An avid sports promoter, he was responsible for launching a strong elementary school athletic program in Macon.

WALTER HARLEY BOWERS succeeded Glassman. The Moreland native had been named outstanding graduate of the 1942 University of Georgia journalism class. He served three years with the Army Air Corps during World War II, seeing combat as a B-24 crewman in Italy. In 1946 he joined *The Atlanta Constitution* as wildlife editor, later moving to *The Columbus Ledger* and then to *The Albany Herald* in 1948, where he spent 11 years as sports editor. He joined *The Macon Telegraph* as sports editor in

1959. After 15 years in that post, he was named executive sports editor of *The Telegraph* and *News* in 1974. He was named Georgia sportswriter of the year in 1979 and 1981, and is a former president of the Georgia Sports Hall of Fame.

EDMUND S. OLSON, who came to the Macon papers as assistant to the publisher in 1978, became general manager in 1980 and publisher in 1983. He is a graduate of the University of Florida's College of Business and College of Law. After serving three years as a special agent for the Federal Bureau of Investigation, he began his newspaper career at *The Tallahassee Democrat* in 1972, moving on to *The Charlotte Observer* and *News*, working in circulation, production and advertising. Among his civic activities in Macon have been the presidency of the Bibb County Cancer Society, chairmanship of the United Way campaign and membership on the board of directors of the Greater Macon Chamber of Commerce.

EDWARD W. CORSON, who succeeded Joe Parham as editor of *The Macon News* in January 1981, started his journalism career as a correspondent with *The Raleigh Times* in 1965 while attending theological seminary. He did part-time and fill-in work for *The Macon Telegraph* and *The News* from 1970, starting as a drama reviewer. Corson, who has degrees from Amherst College, Southeastern Baptist Theological Seminary and the University of Georgia (Ph.D) spent nine years as an Air Force navigator, then nine years as an English professor at Mercer University, before going full-time with *The Macon News* in 1977 as associate editor. He became managing editor in 1980 and editor in 1981. He was selected to be editor of the combined *Telegraph* and *News* in 1983.

In civic activities he has been president of the Macon Civic Chorale, a deacon in Vineville Baptist Church, and is a board member of the Red Cross and the Booker T. Washington Community Center. He serves on the Education Committee of the Greater Macon Chamber of Commerce.

William S. Morris Jr. . . . He founded the dynasty.

William S. (Billy) Morris III . . . He extended the empire.

Billy Morris in Chronicle-Herald *pressroom, 1969, with Production Manager Robert (Red) Norris and General Manager Beverly R. Carter. Norris went on to become publisher of Lubbock, Texas papers; Carter became publisher of* The Miami Herald.

Paul S. Simon has been Billy Morris' right-hand man since 1969.

Edward B. Skinner has been Chronicle-Herald *general manager in 1970s and 1980s.*

Howard Eanes became Chronicle *managing editor in 1974.*

David Playford, Herald *managing editor has been on staff since 1951.*

Longtime Chronicle-Herald *news executive Louis C. Harris sells Cracker Crumble tickets to Governor Lester Maddox.*

Patrick H. Rice Jr. was business manager and general manager of Augusta newspapers and radio station until his death.

R. L. M. Parks was editor of Chronicle *for 25 years until his death in 1959.*

Savannah News-Press *executive editor Wally Davis and general manager Donald Harwood hold copy of July 4, 1976 Bicentennial edition, which was judged Georgia's best.*

Charles Morris was News-Press *publisher, 1965-70, then formed own corporation in Savannah.*

Tom Coffey, a Savannah newspaperman since 1930s, is popular columnist, one-time assistant city manager.

Building in right foreground was erected in 1819 by Col. James Johnston, nephew of Georgia's first newspaper publisher. In 1979 it was made a part of The Savannah News-Press *building and houses the classified ad and accounting departments. Building at left dates back to late 19th century.*

This is the famed Oliver Sturges house when it was being used as a boarding house in 1936. In the 1970s it was bought by Charles Morris and restored for use as the headquarters of his nationwide communications company.

Editor Albert Scardino and Publisher Marjorie Scardino in front of Georgia Gazette *building in Savannah. He was 1984 Pulitzer Prize winner for editorial writing.*

The Georgia Gazette *name was revived after 176 years from Georgia's first newspaper, published by James Johnston, whose gravestone is shown here. Markings tell of his role in state journalism.*

An interesting used-car sale

See Page 1B

Allison outpaces challengers to win the Southern 500 race

See Page 1C

Bobby Allison

Macon Telegraph and News

OUR 157th YEAR — No. 249 ©Macon Telegraph Publishing Co. 1983 MACON, GEORGIA, TUESDAY MORNING, SEPTEMBER 6, 1983 HOME EDITION 5 SECTIONS — 56 PAGES — 25¢

Introducing the new Telegraph and News

Good morning, Middle Georgians.

Welcome to the first edition of the new *Macon Telegraph and News*, a merger of *The Macon Telegraph* and *The Macon News*. Besides our new look, please notice that we have included most of the regular features of the morning *Telegraph* and the afternoon *News*.

The stock markets were closed due to the Labor Day holiday, but in this issue you will find expanded business coverage and enlarged sections for national, international and sports news.

Also, there are two pages of comics on 6 and 7B and two crossword puzzles.

Reagan demands accounting, apology over downing of jet

The soviets still blame the U.S. for incident with the jetliner, see page 2A; Thousands protest the deaths of the jetliner's passengers, page 3A.

By James Gerstenzang
Associated Press Writer

WASHINGTON — President Reagan, mixing tough talk with soft sanctions, unveiled a series of diplomatic and aviation restrictions on Moscow Monday night in response to the downing of a South Korean airliner and said, "this crime against humanity must never be forgotten."

Using a tape recording of a Soviet pilot announcing to a ground controller that "the target is destroyed" two minutes after a missile was launched, Reagan demanded an accounting and an apology from the Soviet Union.

Speaking to the nation by television and radio from the Oval Office, the president referred four times to "what can only be called the Korean Air Line Massacre."

"Our immediate challenge to this atrocity is to ensure that we make the skies safer and that we seek just compensation for the families of those who were killed," Reagan said.

(See REAGAN, Page 6A)

Last-minute participant Sweeps field

Another story, more pictures and a listing of race participants are on Pages 1C, 4C and 5C.

By Paul Marks
Telegraph-News Bureau

Tony Bateman of Auburn, Ala. strolled over to Macon to meet his girlfriend and wound up winning the 10,000-meters 1983 Macon Labor Day Road Race Monday in a time of 30:51.8.

Mike Mead of Carrollton was second in 31:09, and third place was taken by Adam Pinkston of Macon who set a personal best time in the race of 31:18.

Barbara Balzer, a lawyer from Tallahassee, won the women's division with a time of 38:13.

A record turnout of [illegible] runners competed in Monday's race which was held under warm, very humid conditions. There were four runners who had to be taken to hospitals for heat-related injuries.

Bateman, a former track coach at Vanderbilt University, came to Macon with the original intention of watching his girlfriend, Edie Brantley of Dublin, run the labor Day Race. Brantley surprised Bateman Friday with the news he would be running in the race.

Tony Bateman

"She met me at the bus station with a hug and a race packet," the 27-year-old Bateman said.

BATEMAN RAN track at North Carolina State University, and he listed a previous best 10,000-meter time of 28:40 at the Dogwood Relays in Knoxville, Tenn. Bateman said after he left Vanderbilt in June, he decided to devote more time to training for a shot at making the United State Olympic team at 10,000-meters.

Bateman's entry into the race Saturday made him the top seed for Monday's race. Since he was the only sub 29-minute runner in the field, Bateman was the class of the field which had no other runners with previous times below 30 minutes.

Bateman treated the race as a training exercise.

"I just wanted a good, hard effort," he said. "I really didn't want to kid myself into thinking I could race."

Bill Kvaskay of Fort Valley takes a drink at water station Photo by DANNY GILLELAND

Bateman was out of the picture early, but by the midway point of the race he had everything locked up.

WHEN THE runners broke from the starting line on Vineville Ave. near Wesleyan, Bateman laid back behind a pack which included Mead, Macon's Pinkston, Dan Lasseter of Atlanta, Wes Wesseley of Atlanta and Rick Miller of Tallahassee, Fla.

Pinkston led the charge up the initial hill near Rivoli Dr. at the one-mile mark. At the crest of the hill, Pinkston gave the first-place position to Lasseter, who held it until about halfway through the race.

(See RACE, Page 7A)

Forsyth native was passenger on Korean jet

By Janet Groat
Staff Writer

Jessie P. Green's fondest memories of Jessie P. Slaton are of the times the two would go to court together and Green would listen to her older cousin rule from the bench.

"[illegible]," Green recalled. "Being in the minority, I feel that she had to hold her ground and be firm and let her light shine. And this I feel that she did."

Slaton, a native of Forsyth, was one of 61 Americans on board the ill-fated Korean passenger jet shot down by a Soviet jet fighter Wednesday.

Green, a secretary at Unionville Elementary School, remembers frequent childhood visits with her cousin, whose accomplishments and [illegible] always an inspiration to her.

Slaton practiced law for many years in Detroit and went on to become a traffic court judge and a civic leader there.

GREEN REMEMBERS their frequent trips to Canada when she was visiting her in Detroit. Slaton also loved to travel to other parts of the world.

But Slaton took her last trip Wednesday. All 269 persons aboard the Boeing 747 are believed to have died in the incident.

While the U.S. government and its allies haggle over an appropriate response to the Soviet Union, Green says she can only grieve over her personal loss and the loss to her family.

She is concerned about recovering the bodies of the victims so her family will have "at least some remains" for a memorial service in Detroit Sept. 16.

She wonders what happens when the missile downed the plane. "Were they blown to pieces or did the sharks eat them up?"

But watching the news on television is painful now. Green's main interest is helping her mother and aunt get through a difficult time. When the mourning is over, maybe she'll begin to think about the politics of the incident.

(See MEMORIES, Page 6A)

Shot man dumped behind school, dies

From staff reports

An unidentified man was dumped behind Metta Danforth Elementary School Monday afternoon after being shot once in the chest. He was taken to the emergency room at the Medical Center of Central Georgia but died.

Police thought they had found the man's wife, but as of Monday evening she had not seen the body to identify it, Assistant Bibb County Coroner Jimmy Fain said. The dead man, who appeared to be in his early 20s, was clad only in a pair of jogging shorts, Fain said. He had no identification with him.

POLICE WERE searching Monday afternoon for a large, yellow car that witnesses said the man was dumped from. The car reportedly came up a dirt road out of the woods about 2 p.m., dumped the body behind the school and left the scene.

Pope strongly reaffirms women can't be priests

By Kevin Costelloe
Associated Press Writer

VATICAN CITY — Pope John Paul II took his strongest stand yet against ordaining women as priests and told U.S. bishops Monday to reaffirm traditional church views on sex and marriage — even if they are unpopular.

Pope John Paul II

But the pontiff also called on the bishops to oppose "discrimination of women by reason of sex."

The pope, addressing 23 U.S. bishops at his summer residence at Castel Gandolfo south of Rome, said they must strongly reaffirm church stands against contraception, divorce, homosexuality, pre-marital sex and abortion.

Archbishop Patrick F. Flores of San Antonio, Texas, one of the participants in the meeting, called the talk "challenging."

"He gave us food for thought," Flores said of the meeting.

THE PONTIFF USES the traditional meetings he holds with bishops every five years to address particular problems in their home countries. An eight-page statement on his comments to the bishops was delivered in English and made available here.

"The bishop is called upon to oppose any and all discrimination against women by reason of sex," the pope said.

(See POPE, Page 7A)

Good Morning

Thundershowers

	High	Low
Yesterday	93	75
Today	95	72
Tonight		72

Details on Page 2A

Today's Chuckle

People are like tea bags; you never know their strength until they're in hot water.

Index

Shuttle's performance garners highest praise

By Robert Locke
Associated Press Writer

EDWARDS AIR FORCE BASE, Calif. — *Challenger* returned home from the void to a concrete carpet of light early Monday, and its six-day trip drew high praise from the boss of the shuttle program, who called it "just a fabulous mission."

"The cleanest mission yet," added Lt. Gen. James A. Abrahamson, after the shuttle and its five-man crew accomplished the first night shuttle landing at 3:40 a.m. EDT Monday.

It was a triumphant conclusion for a near-flawless eighth flight that began with the first night launch of a shuttle, from Cape Canaveral, Fla., and counted among its crew the first black to fly in space.

Nothing, however, summed up the flight as well as commander Richard Truly when he brought the 100-ton spaceship out of space, out of a black, starlit sky to a landing as perfect as any of the seven that preceded it in daylight.

> *'That was fun. Let's do it again.'*
> —**Richard Truly**
> **Shuttle Commander**

"That was fun," he said. "Let's do it again."

LATER HE TOLD a welcoming crowd that "the real hero tonight is the *Challenger*. Already she has been

(See SHUTTLE, Page 7A)

Day One of The Telegraph *and* News, *Tuesday, September 8, 1983*.

1884 1885 1886 1887 1888 1889 1890 1891 1892 1893
1894 1895 1896 1897 1898 1899 1900 1901 1902 1903
1904 1905 1906 1907 1908 1909 1910 1911 1912 1913
1914 1915 1916 1917 1918 1919 1920 1921 1922 1923
1924 1925 1926 1927 1928 1929 1930 1931 1932 1933
1934 1935 1936 1937 1938 1939 1940 1941 1942 1943
1944 1945 1946 1947 1948 1949 1950 1951 1952 1953
1954 1955 1956 1957 1958 1959 1960 1961 1962 1963
1964 1965 1966 1967 1968 1969 1970 1971 1972 1973
1974 1975 1976 1977 1978 1979 1980 1981 1982 1983

FINAL EDITION

WEATHER
Thundershowers
Sunrise 8:10 a.m.
Details on 2A

THE MACON NEWS

Home Edition

Our Beat Is the Heart of Georgia

99th Year, No. 245 — ©Macon Telegraph Publishing Co. 1983 — Macon, Georgia, Friday Afternoon, September 2, 1983 — 4 Sections, 40 Pages — 25¢

To our readers

This issue of the *The Macon News* raises all kinds of conflicting emotions among those of us who work here.

In one sense, it's an issue that none of us really wanted to see, because it represents the end of afternoon newspaper publication in Macon. But in a more important sense it's exciting, because it means the beginning of a new, bigger and better newspaper for Middle Georgia.

On Tuesday, the *News* and the morning *Macon Telegraph* will merge into a single morning newspaper. It will bring together two professional news staffs which, for nearly 100 years, have competed with each other to be first to bring the news to Macon area readers.

The reasons for the merger have been outlined a number of times since it was announced more than a month ago. Among them: declining afternoon readership, the need to use personnel and resources more efficiently and the desire to bring more news and information to readers through expanded news space.

The new *Macon Telegraph* and *News*, quite simply, will be a better newspaper than either of its predecessors, good though they may have been through the years. Readers will lose few, if any, of their favorite features from either paper. The same number of reporters and editors will be working on one newspaper instead of splitting their efforts between two. An average of three full pages of new space per day will be added, allowing us to provide more business news, more features, more commentary, more sports coverage.

It's a good move, and we're excited about it.

Still, there is a certain sadness in putting *The Macon News* to bed for the last time. There will be those readers who will miss receiving their paper in the afternoon. There will be others who will miss that very special style that was the mark of this publication. And there will be many in our newsroom who will miss the excitement of racing against early morning deadlines to get a big story on the street by noon and the challenge of friendly competition with the older, bigger sister across the room.

To those loyal readers who have shared our successes and our shortcomings through the years, we extend our heartfelt appreciation. To those same readers, and to readers of *The Macon Telegraph*, we pledge our continued dedication to publishing a newspaper that is energetic, useful and informative: the new *Macon Telegraph and News*.

Rick Thomas
Executive Editor

Today

On inside, more on plane attack

- President Reagan and members of Congress have united in demands for a full accounting from the Soviet Union. Page 3A.
- Governments around the world expressed outrage over the Soviet attack on the airliner. Page 2A.
- An account of the plane's final flight is on Page 3A.
- Kathryn McDonald says she's considering running in a special election to fill the congressional seat her husband held. Page 1B.
- The John Birch Society has largely been unheard from lately until the tragedy which struck its leader, Larry McDonald. Page 1B.
- On Page 9A: astronauts orbiting the Earth aboard space shuttle *Challenger* learned of the crash in a news summary sent by Mission Control; the United States is calling for an urgent meeting of the U.N. Security Council to denounce the downing; a minute-by-minute account of the destruction of Flight 007 is given; and military sources say that nothing flies "from, over or near" the strategic Soviet island where the disappeared without U.S. intelligence monitoring by radio and radar.

WILLIAM BERRY/Macon News

Frank Wrye says he's sorry to see afternoon paper end

Local resident has read Macon News *for 66 years*

On Page 6A and 7A we conclude our series on the history of The Macon News. *There also are several other stories related to the past years of the afternoon paper.*

By Cynthia George
Macon News Writer

Sitting on a stool at the counter, with his cigar dangling from his fingers, the man glanced over Tuesday's front page of *The Macon News*.

"*News* survived hard times, achieved stability," he read aloud.

"That's true," he said. "It sure did."

Frank Wrye considers himself knowledgable about the *News* — he's been watching the action from the sidelines since before 1917 — more than 66 years ago.

"My mama started taking the paper before I was old enough to recognize it," he said, adding that he became an avid reader during World War I.

"**WHEN I GET** home, shuck off my shoes and get a drink — I want my *News*," Wrye said.

Wrye, 76, has been a Macon resident most of his life. He's seen many changes in the town, the politicians, the attitudes of people and the newspapers.

"My friends say I came in with the Indians," he said. "But I tell them I came in right behind them."

Wrye, who also subscribes to *The Macon Telegraph* "because my sister-in-law prefers it," said he is saddened by the demise of the *News*.

The two newspapers will merge to form the *Macon Telegraph and News* beginning Sept. 6.

"I'm sorry to see it go. It's another marker we're throwing on the side of the road," he said, waving a copy of the *News* in the air. "They're looking at it from a standpoint of making money, not what the readers want."

Wrye said he's seen a lot of reporters go to the *News*, "learn the business and then get out and make some money."

"**IT'S TRAINED** a lot of workers all over the county," he said, rattling off acquaintances who had worked at the *News* over the years — Hugh Parks, a reporter; Foy Evans, now mayor of Warner Robins and Jimmy Jones and Ben Chatfield, both former sports editors.

Wrye works at Washburn Storage Co. "doing what I want, when I want — that's what I was hired for." Actually, Wrye works in sales. During his years in Macon, he also worked at several downtown drugstores and also worked his way from delivery boy to assistant manager at Western Union.

"People from the paper would come over there (Western Union) and tell us things they wouldn't tell anyone else," he said. "They knew it wouldn't go any farther than over that counter."

Wrye said his biggest gripe about the changes over the years is the attitude of newspaper deliverers.

"They used to walk up on the porch and hand it to you," he said. "Now when I get home at night, I pick it out of the bushes. If it's been raining and the paper lands in the driveway, I have to put it in the oven and cook it before I can read it."

THE PRICE of the paper is a major change, he said, noting that when he first began buying the paper the cost was 15 cents a week, including Sundays. It now costs $1.80 per week.

Wrye said he enjoys the editorials in the *News* the best, and hopes the slogan "Our Beat is the Heart of Georgia" lives on "because it's true".

He said he'll subscribe to the *Macon Telegraph and News* "unless someone opens another paper — and I hope they do. I enjoy my afternoon paper."

Reagan mulls U.S. response

By The Associated Press

President Reagan accused the Soviet Union on Friday of "a terrorist act" in the downing of a Korean jumbo jet, and said the episode raises new questions about the credibility of Moscow statements on peace and arms control.

"What can be the scope of legitimate mutual discourse with a state whose values permit such atrocities?" Reagan said, as he cut short his California vacation to return to the White House and consider the U.S. response to the episode.

At least 51 Americans were aboard the airliner, Korean Air Lines said today in Seoul, and searchers found a large oil slick in waters where it was believed to have crashed.

President Chun Doo-hwan accused the Soviet Union of "a barbaric act."

At a conference room in Seoul, an empty chair marked the absence of U.S. Rep. Lawrence P. McDonald, one of 269 people aboard the plane who are presumed killed.

McDonald

KAL left open the possibility that more than 51 Americans were aboard by saying some of the others on the flight may have held dual nationality.

KAL initially reported 269 people aboard the flight, but said four crew members got off at a refueling stop in Anchorage, leaving 265. However, KAL said today the four who got off were replaced in Anchorage by four fresh crew members, bringing the total back up to 269.

KAL gave the following breakdown: 29 crew members and 240 passengers. Of the passengers, 82 were Korean, 28 Japanese, 21 Taiwan Chinese, 14 Hong Kong Chinese, 51 American, 16 Filipino; 10 Canadian, 6 Thai, 4 Australian, 1 Swedish, 1 Malaysian, 1 Indian, and 5 undetermined.

THERE WERE calls for retaliatory action as search boats and planes, including two U.S. military aircraft,

Please see PLANE, 3A

U.S. denounces Soviet attack

By The Associated Press

Two states canceled trips to Moscow, a well-known lawyer said he'll sue the Kremlin, and outraged Koreans wired President Reagan as denouncements of "cave-man tactics" swept the country after the reported Soviet destruction of a commercial airliner.

One Minnesota legislator urged the state to call off a planned visit from a Soviet trade delegation and other officials said the downing of Korean Air Lines Flight 007 may severely cripple U.S.-Soviet relations.

Attorney Melvin Belli said he plans a suit in New York against the Soviet Union and the airline, on behalf of the husband of one of the passengers.

"**YOU DON'T KNOW** what to do, you're devastated, you want to punch death, but you can't, so you sue the ... (people) responsible," Belli said Thursday. He represents Michael Kole of Loudonville, N.Y., whose 40-year-old wife Muriel was aboard the plane.

Arthur Hartman, U.S. ambassador to Moscow, said shooting down the plane "definitely was a mistake, both from their point of view and the whole process of relations with the Soviet Union, but this must have been considered action by someone at some level ... They certainly had adequate time to get to a higher level." Hartman spoke today on ABC's "Good Morning America."

Please see REACTION, 3A

Heart attack kills Sen. Henry Jackson

EVERETT, Wash. (AP) — Sen. Henry M. "Scoop" Jackson, the powerful Democrat who combined hardline anti-Soviet stands with liberal views on social issues, is dead after suffering a massive heart attack at his home. He was 71.

Jackson, who failed in two bids at the presidency but never lost an election in his home state of Washington, died Thursday night, just hours after holding a news conference to condemn the Soviet Union for shooting down a Korean jetliner the day before.

HE WAS KNOWN as an advocate of a strong national defense, a friend of Israel and supporter of emigration for Soviet Jews. He played a major role in the creation of the Environmental Protection Agency and was considered a champion of organized labor and of civil rights for minorities.

The 43-year congressional veteran who came to Congress when Franklin Roosevelt was president, died within an hour after being brought to Providence Hospital, just 12 blocks from his Everett home. Jackson, whose death stunned those who knew him for his hard-driving schedule and energetic lifestyle, had never been in the hospital before, except to meet with its board of directors and sip tea with its Catholic nuns.

"I always thought he was indestructable. ... He took exceptional care of himself," said former Sen. Warren G. Magnuson, D-Wash, who served 28 years in Congress with Jackson. "I lost a great personal friend. We were very close."

Henry Jackson

Denny Miller, Jackson's administrative assistant, said Jackson had been at home with his wife, Helen and had retired early at about 7:30 p.m. "complaining of not feeling too well."

Miller and a family friend, Dr. Haakon Ragde, later came to the house and found Jackson stricken in bed. He was rushed to the hospital and pronouced dead of a massive heart attack at 9:25 p.m., after attempts to revive him failed.

The senator did not smoke, drank little and exercised religiously. The son of Norwegian immigrants, he delivered newspapers while in school, earning him the nickname "Scoop."

Please see JACKSON, 2A

Final front page of The Macon News, *Friday, September 2, 1983.*

Peyton Anderson was owner and publisher of Macon Telegraph-News, *1951-69.*

Bill Ott, editor of Macon Telegraph *(1958-1970) later became vice-president of Knight-Ridder Newspapers.*

Don Carter was the best-known Carter from Plains until his cousin became governor and later U.S. president. He was executive editor in Macon during 1970s.

Bert Struby was Macon's most enduring newspaperman: editor, general manager, publisher over 43 years.

Ed Olson became Telegraph *and* News *publisher in 1983.*

Billy Watson has served as executive editor and general manager of Macon newspapers.

Harley Bowers is a longtime sports editor and columnist in Macon and Albany.

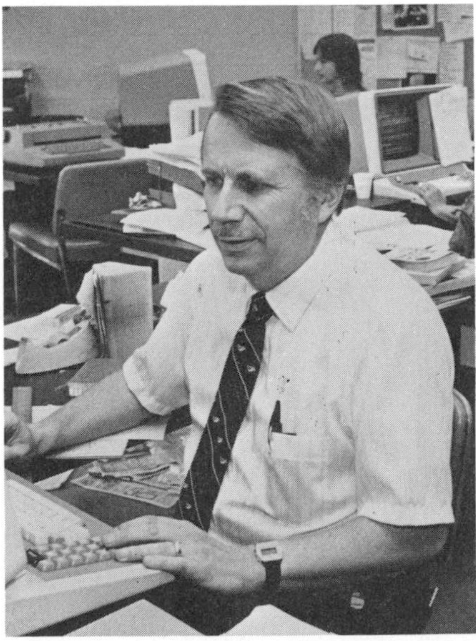

Ed Corson was named editor of merged Telegraph *and* News.

Joe Parham, editor of Macon News *for 31 years, is shown receiving one of his many best column awards from 1972 GPA President Sam Griffin.*

Susan Myrick, a Telegraph-News *writer for 50 years, is shown with Jere Moore of Milledgeville* Union-Recorder.

Chapter V

Portrait of a City and Its Newspapers: Columbus and The Ledger-Enquirer

Georgia's "Second City"

There is an old story about a man who went to a carnival sideshow which advertised a "real-live midget." The man paid the barker and went inside the tent to see the midget. He came back out complaining bitterly to the barker that he'd been fooled. "That's no midget in there," he said, "That man is at least five feet tall. He's just plain short."

"Oh no," said the barker, "he's a midget all right. He's just a very large midget."

That story has been told on occasion about Georgia's second largest city, which has been accused of being a "big town" rather than a real city. Actually Georgia's second largest city is neither a city nor a town. It is a county. When Columbus and Muscogee County consolidated their governments in 1971, the county lines became, in effect, the city limits, and thus the entire population of the county (170,000 in 1980) was the population of Columbus-Muscogee, pushing it ahead of Savannah (141,000) in city limits population, and making it the second largest municipality in Georgia.

But for years Columbus had been either the third or fourth largest city in Georgia, and arguably the state's second most important city for the past 50 years. Most of its citizens have never felt that Columbus gets the respect it deserves. It is a municipal Rodney Dangerfield, referred to often as "Georgia's Best Kept Secret," and for a time even overshadowed by its tawdry Alabama neighbor, Phenix City, which enjoyed nationwide notoriety as the South's worst "sin city" of private vice and public corruption.

Columbus' principal competitors among Georgia cities, Savannah, Macon and Augusta, became cities earlier than Columbus, but none of them kept pace with Columbus' growth in the middle decades of the twentieth century. Bolstered by Fort Benning and three wars, Columbus finally realized the expectations of its founders, who laid out the state's western-most city at the head of navigation of the fabled Chattahoochee River, which turns sharply south near Columbus on its long journey from the hills of Habersham (county) to the Gulf of Mexico.

Columbus was supposed to become a great inland port, and as recently as the 1970s its city limits signs proclaimed it as "A Port City." The state built elaborate docks in the middle-1960s, and the federal government spent billions of dollars to make the Chattahoochee navigable from the gulf to Columbus. But the boats and barges have never come in large number, at least not in the twentieth century, and the funds invested in the several dams along the Chattahoochee have mainly created a playground for boaters and fishermen.

The river was always vital, however, because it provided industry with needed water, and at the time of the Civil War, Columbus was one of the chief industrial cities in the Confederate states. The last official land battle of the War was fought in Columbus when Union General Lewis Wilson's army came through a few weeks after Appommatox. Word of Lee's surrender hadn't reached that far south.

In 1918, Camp Benning was established in Columbus, just before the end of World War I. Benning grew to be a fort between the world wars, and during World War II it became the world's largest training base for infantrymen. Ironically, this major U.S. army post is named for Henry L. Benning, a confederate general who was a bitterly unreconstructed rebel.

Fort Benning was important for more than just the economic and population impetus it provided. Through its gates passed thousands of American soldiers on their way to North Africa, Sicily, Normandy, Okinawa, Korea, Vietnam and every other corner of the world during the past 60 years. Many of them returned to Columbus or to Georgia to make their home, and even more found wives in Columbus and the surrounding area. During World War II Columbus earned the nickname of "mother-in-law" of the army because so many Columbus girls married soldiers at Benning.

Columbus was the first Georgia city to add kindergarten to its public schools, and in 1950 Columbus and Muscogee County were the first Georgia city and county to consolidate their school systems, a step many other communities have followed.

These would seem to be achievements enough to delight any city's Chamber of Commerce, but Columbus still suffers a puzzling civic inferiority complex. For several years the Chamber of Commerce distributed auto tags bearing the slogan, "America Discovers Columbus, Ga.," as if it were still not well-known in the state and nation.

In truth, there is some substance to that suspicion. Given Columbus' considerable attributes, many Georgians who live east of the Chattahoochee do seem unfamiliar with where or what it is and certainly unaware that it is the state's second city in size, influence and other aspects. Part of this syndrome has been blamed on the fact that the nearest interstate highway passes 30 miles from Columbus. It was the largest city in the country not located on the original interstate routes mapped out in the 1950s, and this has been a sore point with Columbus civic leaders for three decades. By contrast, Atlanta is the junction for no less than three interstates; Savannah and Macon have two interstates passing close by; and Augusta has one.

Columbus finally did gain a "leg" to an interstate with the completion in 1980 of I-185 which runs from Columbus to I-85 just north of LaGrange, providing a four-lane highway from Columbus to Atlanta. This has proved a mixed blessing, however, since it reduced the number of passengers using the Columbus airport, just at the time the airlines were looking for excuses to cut down flights at secondary locations. Many Columbus travelers now find it more convenient and economical to drive the interstate to Hartsfield International — about 90 minutes away — instead of taking a connector flight from Columbus to Atlanta.

Another reason other Georgians may overlook Columbus and its importance is because of its strong associations with Alabama. When it was founded in 1828, Columbus was Georgia's frontier town, but it also was the gateway city to eastern Alabama, and in this century the surrounding counties in Alabama have been more populous and prosperous than the surrounding counties in Georgia, tending to give Columbus an Alabama flavor.

That has been a problem for its newspapers through the years, as they tried to serve readers in both states, a task not uncommon for border newspapers but especially difficult in middle-west Georgia. The task was complicated for the Columbus papers because so much news was generated by prominent Alabama leaders living in their circulation area. Every elected governor of Alabama — mainly George Wallace — since 1958 was at one time a regular subscriber to *The Columbus Enquirer*, not to speak of one governor of Georgia who went on to become president of the United States.

But *The Enquirer* can claim an even closer tie to political leaders than readership. Its founder became the second president of a sovereign nation, the Republic of Texas.

The Founder of The Enquirer

Mirabeau Bonaparte Lamar, founder of *The Columbus Enquirer* and second president of the Republic of Texas, was born in Warren County, Georgia in 1798, near Louisville, which for a brief time was the state capital.

When Lamar was 12 his family moved to a plantation in Putnam County, near Eatonton, carrying with them 12 slaves. Lamar never liked plantation life, preferring literary pursuits even as a youngster. In his early 20s, he obtained the coveted post of executive secretary to Gov. George Troup, one of the most powerful Georgia political figures of the early 1800s. In 1827, Lamar wrote a review of the four years of Troup's governorship, defending him against his many enemies.

In early 1828 he found his way to the settlement of Columbus and decided he would start a newspaper for the new city. Lamar published the first issue of the paper, which he called *The Enquirer*, on May 29, 1828, six months before Columbus received its official charter of incorporation. The surveyors were still marking off the streets and lots of Columbus, which was as carefully planned as Savannah had been on the other side of Georgia nearly 100 years earlier.

Lamar pledged that his *Enquirer* would adhere to the principles of Thomas Jefferson at the federal level and to the "defense of the union of the states and the sovereignty of the states.

"But it will not be wholly devoted to these matters," he wrote. "A large portion will be filled with such miscellaneous selections as are calculated to please and instruct; to gratify fancy and to increase knowledge, making it a literary as well as a political paper."

As the city grew, Lamar and his newspaper prospered. He was a pioneer in the field of education, at a time when education did not enjoy broad support, and he was constantly in demand as a speaker at schools in the area. His editorials and speeches grew stronger and stronger in support of states rights. In the summer of 1833, Lamar announced that he would like to represent the district in the U.S. Congress. The custom at the time was for a caucus of party leaders in the state legislature to select nominees for Congress. When the nine nominees were announced, Lamar was not among them. Even when a vacancy occurred among the nine, he was passed over again.

Thoroughly angry and disgusted with the caucus system, Lamar thundered: "If my political bark cannot sail upon the sea of correct principles, let it flounder; it shall never float upon the waves of triumphant error."

He had already decided to leave Columbus and seek opportunities further west when his young wife was stricken with typhoid and died. Heartsick over her death and his political failures, Lamar left Columbus and the state of Georgia in 1835, never to return again.

In his subsequent career Lamar proved that he was indeed an exceptional man, and one of the great leaders produced by Georgia during that period. He went to Texas where he joined the Texas army in its fight for independence against Mexico. He was soon asked by the officers of the cavalry to take command of their regiment because of the bravery and leadership he exhibited in several battles.

When Texas declared itself an independent republic after winning its revolution against Mexico, Lamar was selected to run for vice-president with Sam Houston who became Texas' first president. In 1838, Lamar was elected president succeeding Houston. As president, Lamar was known as the "father of Texas education" because of his strong support for public schools.

For many years *The Enquirer* — the newspaper he founded and left behind in Georgia — carried in its masthead each morning the following quotation from his first presidential message to the Texas Congress: " The cultivated mind is the guardian genius of democracy, and while guided and controlled by virtue it is the noblest attribute of man. It is the only dictator that free men acknowledge, and the only security which free men desire."

Lamar served a three-year term as president and later was a U.S. senator from Texas when it became a state.

After his political career Lamar enjoyed a successful career as a poet. Thus in his lifetime he was a farmer; executive secretary to one of Georgia's most influential governors; a newspaper founder, editor and publisher; a soldier; an educator; a nation's first vice-president and second president; and a recognized man of letters in both prose and poetry.

Lamar died in 1859 at the age of 62, shortly before the outbreak of the Civil War which he had seen coming for many years.

A true renaissance man, Lamar is in the Georgia Newspaper Hall of Fame, but his name and achievements are not familiar to most Georgians, perhaps because he achieved his greatest fame in Texas. Lamar proved to be only the first of many Columbus area leaders who would play influential roles in the history of Georgia, Alabama and the nation.

Two of the most important — who also are little known in the state generally — were instrumental in setting Georgia's course during the critical period following the Civil War.

James Johnson, a Columbus lawyer, had been courageously outspoken in his opposition to secession, and he remained a loyal unionist throughout the Civil War. He had served one term in Congress and was thus a logical choice by President Andrew Johnson to be Georgia's provisional governor after the War ended.

Johnson served for only six months, but he presided over several historic developments. Among these were repeal of the secession ordinance, adoption of a new constitution and adoption of the thirteenth amendment to the U.S. constitution, which abolished slavery.

In a speech during his brief tenure, Johnson declared that the war "had been a tremendous folly," and that Georgia would increase in prosperity and civilization without slavery. Johnson sought a U.S. Senate seat but the legislature, which then elected senators, rejected him. His leadership had cleared the way for Georgia to return to the Union, but the lingering bitterness of the war soon wiped out the healing process he began.

It was left to another Columbus lawyer, James M. Smith, to bring about both a return to the Union and a return to state control of elective offices. Smith was elected governor in December 1871, ending three years of Republican domination of Georgia politics. During Smith's two terms (1872-1877), Reconstruction and its excesses were ended. Smith, a former blacksmith, held strong opinions and spoke them bluntly, which made him many enemies. Like Johnson, he sought to move into the Senate, but was rejected by the legislature.

Smith was the last Columbus resident to be governor of Georgia, and through the late 1800s and early 1900s Columbus' influence seemed to wane in the state at large.

But the little-noticed establishment of an army camp in 1918 was the turning point which elevated Columbus and Muscogee County to metropolitan status along with Georgia's older cities. Muscogee's population rose from 44,000 in 1920 to 57,558 in 1930 and then in the decade of the Great Depression jumped to 75,000, when the population of many counties declined. By 1950, with 118,000, Muscogee was the fourth largest county in Georgia, behind Fulton, Dekalb and Chatham.

It was also in that year that Muscogee County and the city of Columbus combined their school systems, a step which many other Georgia counties and cities would follow.

The consolidation 20 years later of the city and county governments was expected to be another pace-setting innovation, eliminating duplication of government agencies and providing more efficiency and economy for citizens who usually say they want less government and lower taxes. But in the more than 10 such referendums held in other Georgia cities and counties since 1971, consolidation has been defeated each time.

The Columbus daily newspapers, *The Ledger* and *The Enquirer*, played an essential role in bringing about Georgia's only successful city-county consolidation. Their editorials and articles originated the idea in the early 1960s and were responsible for legislative action which provided the first public referendum in 1962. The voters rejected consolidation at that time by a substantial margin, and the movement seemed to be dead. But four years later, in 1966, an *Enquirer* editorial revived the idea, and Jesse Binns, a Columbus city councilman, and Mayor J. R. Allen became staunch advocates of another referendum. Allen was especially effective, since he had opposed consolidation in 1962 when he was a county commissioner. When the second referendum was held in 1970, consolidation was approved by a vote of 5-1, a tribute not only to courageous political leaders, but also to the determined and unrelenting efforts and support of *The Ledger* and *Enquirer*.

In many respects the victory for city-county consolidation was a greater achievement by the Columbus newspapers than their role in the cleanup of political corruption in Phenix City, Alabama, 15 years earlier, for which *The Ledger* won the 1955 Pulitzer Prize for community service.

The Columbus newspapers have been read by an unusual number of present and future political leaders who grew up or lived in the surrounding counties. President Franklin D. Roosevelt, who established a "Little White House" in Warm Springs, 35 miles from Columbus, often read *The Enquirer* during his visits to the area.

During the 1950s and 1960s a regular subscriber of *The Enquirer* was a peanut farmer and warehouse manager in Plains, Georgia (50 miles from Columbus) named Jimmy Carter. In those same years other regular *Ledger-Enquirer* subscribers included a Phenix City attorney, John Patterson, who was governor of Alabama from 1959-1962; a circuit judge in Barbour County, Alabama, named George Wallace, the ongoing governor of Alabama (1963-67, 1971-78, 1983-); a Pine Mountain businessman, Bo Callaway, who was almost elected governor of Georgia and later served as President Nixon's Secretary of Army; and an Opelika, Alabama barbell manufacturer, Fob James, who would become the only person elected governor of Alabama (1978) other than a Wallace in a 24-year period.

Journalists Passing Through

Journalists have always been prone to change jobs at the hint of a raise or the promise of a title or a bigger office. This tendency reached its peak in the post-World War II decade as newspapers expanded their staffs and there was a blending of the "old-time" practitioners, most of whom were not college-trained, with the flood of graduates from the journalism schools. At one time in 1947 the staff of *The Ledger* included Jim Fain as city editor; Jim Bellows, Carlton Johnson and Joe Hall as reporters; Millard Grimes as copy boy; and Jim Hobgood as a photo engraver. Alvah Chapman Jr. was in the front office as business manager.

Fain, son of the district superintendent of Methodist ministers for the Columbus area, was at the beginning of a brilliant career which would take him to Atlanta, Dayton, Ohio, and Austin, Texas, as editor, publisher and syndicated columnist.

Bellows, a Yankee come south, followed Fain to Atlanta and went on to one of the more remarkable careers in contemporary U.S. journalism, serving at various times as editor of *The Miami News, The Washington Star, The New York Herald Tribune* and *The Los Angeles Times*. Bellows, who later got into television as a producer of the "Entertainment Tonight" program, was known as "Mr. Fixit" because he was summoned to save so many dying newspapers in the 1960s and 1970s. Sadly, most of the patients died, but Bellows' efforts made them go more grudgingly, and his innovations left the survivors better newspapers.

Carlton Johnson later became editor of *The Ledger* and executive editor of *The Ledger-Enquirer*; Grimes became editor of *The Enquirer* and then a publisher and president of his own newspaper group.

Joe Hall and Jim Hobgood soon left the daily field and spent the rest of their careers on weeklies. Hall, who had the looks and style of the classic big-city reporter and city editor, went back to his native town of LaFayette and operated his family's newspaper for more than 30 years until his death in 1978. Hobgood bought a weekly newspaper in Calhoun, was president of the Georgia Press Association in 1962-63, and is now retired in Calhoun.

In the "front office" as general manager in those years was Alvah Chapman Jr., who would become president and chief executive officer of Knight-Ridder Newspapers. At that time, in addition to being general manager, he was the son of *The Ledger-Enquirer* president and grandson of the man who developed *The Ledger*.

The Copy Boy

The position of copy boy is now virtually extinct, but it was so important on medium to large-size newspapers in the two decades after World War II that most editors said they could endure the unexpected absence of anyone on the staff more easily than the copy boy's. His duties were essential to "getting the paper out," and usually no one else on the staff could or would do what the copy boy did.

The copy boy's job was also an important entry position for newspaper work and was considered a coveted plum on the metropolitan papers of New York and such cities, even for college graduates.

Many sportswriters, in particular, got their start as copy boys on the Columbus newspapers, and that was probably true at other Georgia newspapers in the larger cities.

Grimes recalls that when he became a full-time copy boy on the *The Ledger* at the age of 17, he replaced a 29-year-old who was "promoted" to the composing room. Composing room jobs, on the whole, paid more than newsroom jobs in hot-type days, a condition that prevailed well into the 1970s and still does in some situations.

The copy boy's pay at *The Ledger* in 1947 was $18.75 a week for six days, Monday through Saturday. Reporters made from $26 a week to $50 a week for the more experienced such as Bellows. These salaries were common on newspapers in those days, even at the Atlanta newspapers. Four years later, in 1951, Grimes was offered only $50 a week as a starting sports reporter on *The Constitution* when he graduated from college, which was the same salary the Columbus paper offered him.

Copy boys had a variety of duties, of course, but as their title implied, the main one was to take copy from the spike and get it to the composing room. In 1947 at the Columbus papers this was done by means of a wire basket which was lowered from the second floor newsroom to the first floor composing room. A pneumatic tube system replaced the basket in the late 1940s.

The copy boy ran any errands that an editor ordered, and in the days before coffee machines, he was responsible for going to the nearby coffee shops and returning with the number of cups necessary to keep the news staff operating. At times this could range up to 20 cups of hot coffee, requiring sure hands on the sacks as the copy boy walked the distance from cafe to office and up the stairs.

Grimes recalls his most unusual assignment as a copy boy was from a city editor who told him to go to his downtown apartment, knock on the door and ask the young lady who answered to please leave before the maid came.

The advent of wire service tape in the late 1940s and early 1950s made copy boys even more valuable to the newsroom operation. This tape, of course, corresponded with the written text on the machines, and when run through the linotype would set the type without need of a human operator, saving much time and labor.

The copy boy came in at about 5 a.m. and began winding the tape that had accumulated during the night, separating the stories, and hanging individual tapes on a numbered peg board. This procedure varied from paper to paper, but the proper handling of wire tape was essential for a smooth operation and for "getting out on time."

If the copy boy didn't show up, there often was no one else in the newsroom who knew the wire tape procedure — or wanted to do it. In later years, composing rooms took charge of the tapes and usually handle them today where tape is still used.

Copy boys also got a chance to take stories on the phone if no reporter was handy, and to cover stories, usually sports stories.

Although there may have been copy girls at some papers, there were none at the Columbus papers in the 40s, 50s and 60s.

Turnover was rapid in most newsroom jobs at medium-sized dailies in the post-war years. *The Ledger* changed managing editors every year from 1946 through 1951. The morning *Enquirer*, by contrast, was a model of stability. Edge Reid, who would work for the company nearly 50 years before retirement, was *The Enquirer's* ME through all of the years of change on *The Ledger*.

An Editor Who Made a Difference

In 1948 a young (35) editor-in-chief came to *The Ledger* who would have a profound impact on the newspaper and the community and would be the dominant news personality in Columbus for the next eight years. Among the many who passed through Columbus in those days, he was truly one who made a difference.

His name was Robert W. (Bob) Brown, a native of Mississippi who got his early newspaper experience working on *The Delta Star* of Greenville, Mississippi, when it was owned by the elder Hodding Carter.

In his book, *Where Main Street Meets the River* Carter writes fondly of Brown as a young reporter. Carter had started *The Delta Star* in competition with the *Delta Democrat* in 1936. Then, as now, the odds against a new daily overcoming an established daily were extremely long. But *The Star* did overcome, and Carter gave much of the credit to the staff he had assembled. "Especially," he wrote, "there was Bob Brown. His letter of application, which arrived about a week after we had put out the first issue and were beginning to wonder why, read: 'Young, alert, aggressive, experienced, Ninety Bucks.' I telephoned him, confirmed my hopeful suspicion that the ninety bucks salary was for a month, not a week, and told him that unless he could get to Greenville from Hattiesburg in 24 hours he needn't come because I'd be dead and *The Star* fallen.

"Bob arrived at midnight that same night, 22 years old with deceptively sleepy eyes, a slow-breaking grin and the biggest bagful of untried tricks that ever bewildered another newspaper . . . Bob haunted the police court and the fire stations, the courthouse and the hotels. Some fortunate reporters have the ability to dig up and write readable stories and write them fast. Bob was one of them, a newsman who could — and almost every day did — gather and write from 25 to 35 stories, ranging from one paragraph briefs to exclusive tales he developed himself. Just before we won out (over the competing paper) Bob went on to the Associated Press, then to the *New Orleans Times Picayune*, to Washington, to a radio stint in New York, and to the editorship of the Columbus, Georgia *Ledger*. I'm thankful for the two years he spent with us . . ."

At *The Ledger*, Brown replaced scholarly, urbane and aloof Bryan Collier, who had been editor since 1942 and who had decided to seek a position in which he would have more writing duties than administrative ones.

Brown had been out of newspaper work for several years when Publisher Maynard Ashworth went to New York City and personally recruited him for Columbus. It was one of the more elaborate "searches" the Columbus papers ever made for an editorial position.

But Brown brought to his post an assurance that inspired the constantly changing faces on the news staff, plus strong ideas about news presentation. *The Ledger*, for instance, was the first Georgia daily to have a "second front page," with all local news, which has now become standard for larger dailies. Brown believed in separate, distinct pages for business, features, and entertainment before that became common practice.

He also had some idiosyncracies which made life more trying for copy desk personnel. The Page 1 banner was never to be less than five columns, two lines, 72 point type, and he insisted that every headline have a verb in its top line. That was especially difficult on the 1-column, 42 point headlines which were a standby on *The Ledger* in those days and counted less than 10 units per column.

But Brown was mainly a promoter — of the newspaper, of his staff, of his community, and not least, of himself.

Brown's promoting paid off. In 1951 he was selected for a Nieman Fellowship, the prestigious award given to a handful of journalists each year, allowing them a year's study at Harvard, with all costs paid, including the salary they are then earning.

The link with the Niemans was to prove useful to other Columbus newsmen as Brown helped get Niemans in later years for three other members of the 1951 staff, Carlton Johnson (1954-55), Marvin Wall (1956-57) and Ray Jenkins (1964-65). No other comparable size newspaper in the nation had as many Nieman selections in so short a period.

Brown later secured a U.S. Information Agency grant which allowed him to go to India for a three-month study, and he obtained similar study trips for other staffers.

But Brown's crowning achievement in his years as *Ledger* editor was the 1955 Pulitzer Prize for community service, awarded to *The Ledger* for its role in the cleanup of public and private corruption in neighboring Phenix City, Alabama.

The Pulitzer was for a staff effort, but Brown was generally regarded as the driving force in *The Ledger's* performance. He became a sought-after speaker, and by 1956 he was probably the best-known newspaper editor in Georgia outside of Ralph McGill.

Ironically, but not uncommonly, that proved to be the apex of his career. In November 1956, Brown resigned from *The Ledger*, for reasons never quite explained. Money was probably one reason. In those years newspaper editors — even popular, aggressive ones — on medium-sized dailies drew salaries ranging from $150 to $200 a week. Brown, despite his globe-trotting, his Niemans, and even the Pulitzer Prize, never made more than $11,000 a year in Columbus. He also felt he'd gone as far as he could at *The Ledger*.

Brown left the newspaper field for his next job, and became associated with the federal government's Point 4 program on assignment in India. While he was in India, Nelson Poynter, publisher of *The St. Petersburg, Florida Times*, came through on a visit. He remembered Brown as an effective, hard-hitting editor. "What are you doing here?" Poynter wanted to know.

"I couldn't make a living in the newspaper business," Brown reportedly told him.

"Well, come on back and I'll see that you do on my paper," Poynter offered.

So after less than two years away from newspapers, Brown returned as editorial page editor of *The St. Petersburg Times*, which at that time had about 90,000 circulation but was already regarded as the up-and-coming newspaper in the crowded, competitive Florida field. (In 1983, *The Times*' circulation had reached 250,000 under the leadership of another former Georgia editor, Eugene Patterson, who succeeded Poynter as publisher and president.)

But while in India, Brown contracted yellow jaundice, a disease which kept coming back to plague him and almost took his life in 1962 when doctors gave him up for dead. Miraculously, Brown recovered but he felt a smaller newspaper would put less strain on him in his weakened condition. So he moved on from St. Petersburg in 1963, working for a time on the copy desk at *The Montgomery Advertiser* (where Ray Jenkins, one of his young proteges on *The Ledger* 10 years earlier, was editor of the afternoon *Journal*), and then to the Rock Hill, South Carolina *Herald*.

In the final five years of his life Brown returned to Georgia as managing editor of *The Augusta Chronicle*, the post he held until his death in April 1974.

Brown was an effective writer who did not especially like to write, often soliciting editorial contributions from any staff member who would provide them. His air of self-assurance masked a basic shyness and a stage fright which he worked hard to overcome as a public speaker.

He inspired several members on *The Ledger* staff in the 1950s to their greatest achievements, although he was given neither to inspirational talks nor the abusive tirades which at least one of the managing editors of that period resorted to regularly. He mainly exuded a sincere sense of mission which was impressive to his young employees.

The Ledger news staff stabilized during Brown's tenure, compared to the revolving-door turnovers of the earlier post-war years.

L. P. Patterson was the managing editor for the first four years that Brown was editor, and John Bloomer held the post for the last four years, including the Phenix City cleanup period. Just before Brown resigned he appointed Carlton Johnson as managing editor.

Patterson, who was acting editor during Brown's Nieman year at Harvard, had trouble adjusting when Brown returned. He took a step downward when he left Columbus, going to the smaller Dothan, Alabama *Eagle* as executive editor, but a few years later he became managing editor of *The Montgomery Advertiser*, at that time Alabama's most prestigious daily.

Bloomer, his successor, also ended his career in Alabama, becoming managing editor and then executive editor of *The Birmingham News*, the state's largest daily.

Several other members of *The Ledger* staff during its Pulitzer Prize year migrated to Alabama. Ray Jenkins, one of the Phenix City reporters, went to Montgomery as city editor in 1959 and eventually was editor of both *The Advertiser* and afternoon *Journal* during his 20 years with the Montgomery papers. He left to become deputy press secretary to President Carter in 1979, and in 1982 was named editor of *The Baltimore Evening Sun*, filling the post once held by the famed iconoclast, H. L. Mencken. Another former Georgia newsman, Reg Murphy, is publisher of the Baltimore Sunpapers.

Tom Sellers, who was the chief reporter on the Phenix City story, also migrated to Montgomery, serving as city editor of the *Advertiser*. He later returned to the Columbus newspapers where he wrote a popular front page column in the 1960s. Then, for 16 years, he was science editor at Emory University, before retiring in 1983.

Other *Ledger* staffers during the Pulitzer year included Johnson, city editor; Don Wasson, news editor, who also went to Montgomery where he covered the state capitol for *The Advertiser* for 10 years; and Marvin Wall, later an associate editor for *The Constitution* and an aide to U.S. Attorney General Griffin Bell.

The assistant news editor was Grimes, the former copy boy, who along with Johnson was one of the few holdovers from the 1940s. Grimes left *The Ledger* staff on May 2, 1955, the day the Pulitzer Prize was announced, to become editor and publisher of a weekly newspaper which he founded in Phenix City following the cleanup. His replacement was Glenn Vaughn, who had been wire editor of *The Albany Herald*.

Of all *The Ledger* staff members in that remarkable year, Vaughn's career on *The Ledger-Enquirer* would prove the most remarkable. From the rim of the copy desk, with several detours on other newspapers, he would eventually succeed Maynard Ashworth as the company's president and publisher.

The Enquirer also did a commendable job on the Phenix City story, winning the National Headliner Award for its coverage. Compared to *The Ledger*, there was stability at *The Enquirer* helm. W. C. (Cliff) Tucker would serve 24 years (1937-61) as its editor, and Edge Reid was the managing editor from 1945 to 1956. Among its staff members in those days was Harold Davis, later to be Dean of Journalism at Georgia State University.

In newspaper circles, the winning of a Pulitzer Prize has become a symbol of achievement that forever marks those involved with an aura of success, as in "the Pulitzer-Prize winning reporter (editor, photographer, or what have you) . . ." No business, with the possible exception of entertainment, is so enamoured of awards, or provides so many opportunities for awards.

Just about everyone on newspapers except the cold, calculating accountants are enraptured by awards. The accountants, quite correctly, have put their pencils to the balance sheets and discovered that through the years awards have a minimal effect on a newspaper's financial success and can even prove a detriment.

In fact, *The Enquirer* had won the 1926 Pulitzer Prize for Public Service and a couple of years later had to sell out to its competitor, *The*

Ledger, which had won no Pulitzer but carried the most ads.

Then, almost 30 years later, *The Ledger* got its Pulitzer for Meritorious Public Service, which is the most coveted Pulitzer since it honors the efforts of the entire staff, not just a single reporter, editor or photographer.

For the staff, such an award is definitely an exhilirating tonic, as well as a kind of justification for many hours of low-paid efforts, sometimes in dangerous circumstances, which was certainly the case for several of *The Ledger's* staff in its Pulitzer year of 1954.

Nor is the Public Service Pulitzer a common happening for Georgia newspapers. Only three times have Georgia newspapers won the award, and the Columbus papers account for two of those times. The other Public Service Pulitzer went to *The Atlanta Constitution* in 1931.

The New York Times, on which Pulitzers are often bestowed because it is *The Times*, has won the Public Service award only three times.

So it was a proud Columbus *Ledger* staff which greeted the news of the award in May 1955, and no one was prouder than six-foot-six Tom Sellers, *The Ledger's* chief Phenix City reporter before and during the murder, National Guard takeover and vice cleanup which occurred in 1954-55.

Sellers, who now lives in Decatur, recounted his memories of that year in an article written especially for this history of Georgia newspapers. He tells of both the conditions that prevailed in Phenix City and of the role which *The Ledger* played in the cleanup.

Following is Sellers' account of that unique newspaper adventure:

THE PULITZER PRIZE YEAR
by Tom Sellers

It was late afternoon on Thursday, July 22, 1954, when the phone rang on *The Ledger* city editor's desk. I was seated across the room, typing an overnighter on the so-far fruitless search for the killer of Albert Patterson, a prominent Phenix City attorney who'd been nominated to be Alabama's next attorney general. My boss, normally a mild-voiced man, suddenly barked at me so loudly it rattled the window next to my head: "Get over to Phenix City, Tom, all hell's breaking loose!"

I picked up a wad of note paper and ran out the door. These were unreal, dramatic days at *The Columbus Ledger* and *The Sunday Ledger-Enquirer*. Since the Patterson assassination a month earlier, we'd begun to feel like shell-shocked combat correspondents, and indeed, it would become more like a war than we could then imagine.

The special note of urgency in my city editor's voice made me forget my car. I sprinted the three blocks up to the 14th Street bridge, which spanned the muddy Chattahoochee, and jogged up the hill to the big red-brick Russell County courthouse, which dominated the high ground overlooking the river.

A platoon of combat-clad National Guardsmen had surrounded the building, holding their M-1 rifles in readiness like an infantry unit on patrol. My first thought was that they had tracked the Patterson killer to the courthouse and were about to smoke him out. What I learned in the next few minutes was even more astonishing: The governor of Alabama, Gordon Persons, had declared a "qualified" state of martial rule. The state adjutant general, Major General Walter (Crack) Hanna, and a hundred citizen-soldiers from all parts of the state, were seizing control of the law-enforcement machinery in both Phenix City and Russell County. It was an action without precedent in the 20th century for an American city and county.

It was then about 5:30 p.m., Eastern Standard Time. As the Guard was making history in Phenix City, the governor was reading his proclamation at the State Capitol in Montgomery. The Guard immediately impounded all weapons and vehicles at the sheriff's office in the courthouse and at the Phenix City police department a few blocks away. They prohibited the carrying of guns by anyone except themselves. Lieutenant Colonel Jack Warren, a Birmingham police lieutenant, took over as sheriff, and Colonel James (Boxjaw) Brown became the Phenix City police chief.

One disbelieving Phenix City policeman, as he was relieved of his authority and gun, told a *Ledger-Enquirer* photographer: "It's your newspaper's fault that the city is in the shape it's in."

I was on the phone within five minutes, dictating what I'd found out to a rewrite person on the city desk, and back at the *Ledger* office, every warm body was being put into action. It was long past the final deadline, but the editors decided to publish an EXTRA edition, the first for *The Ledger* in years. It sold more than 8,000 copies. (Television news in 1954 was in its infancy; the printed word was still the primary source of news.)

It didn't occur to most of us during the next few unforgettable months that our efforts would bring us journalism's highest award — the Pulitzer Prize for Meritorious Public Service. It was true, however, that over the years *The Ledger* had been the most persistent journalistic foe of the corrupt alliance of hoodlums and politicians across the river, especially in its news coverage. Our sister newspaper, the morning Columbus *Enquirer*, focused much of its attention in those days on the outlying regions, an area we called the Chattahoochee Valley, and left the leadership in metro Columbus and Phenix City to the afternoon *Ledger*.

In 1946, *The Ledger's* Carlton Johnson, later an executive editor of the Columbus newspapers, had exposed a method of payoff by the criminal element of the Phenix City government through bond forfeitures, and *Ledger* Editor Bryan Collier had challenged the subsequent closing of public records. In 1952, Ray Jenkins and I, both *Ledger* staffers, were attacked in the streets of Phenix City during a hotly-contested city election. I found myself exchanging blows with two of the meanest-looking men I'd ever met, and due to my size (six feet, six inches; weight about 200 pounds) I managed to stay on my feet.

Robert W. (Bob) Brown, who was *Ledger* editor in the cleanup period, often chastized officials who failed to prosecute prominent gamblers. I was a friend and confidant of cleanup leaders including Albert Patterson, Hugh Bentley, Hugh Britton, Howard Pennington and Hilda Coulter. On several occasions, Ledger reporters, myself among them, were threatened with bodily harm, both on the telephone by anonymous callers and face-to-face by Phenix City hoodlums. In 1952 L.P. Patterson (no relation to Albert Patterson) waged a no-holds-barred editorial campaign against the racketeer regime while Bob Brown was at Harvard as a Nieman Fellow.

But in mid-1954, we didn't have time to think about a Pulitzer Prize. Only two Georgia papers had won the prestigious gold medal for "distinguished and meritorious public service by a United States newspaper" since the prize was first given in 1918. One of these was *The Columbus Enquirer*, which received a Pulitzer in 1926 for Editor Julian Harris's castigation of the Ku Klux Klan, and the other was *The Atlanta Constitution*, in 1931.

Unlike some prize-winning campaigns, no single individual can be given credit for *The Ledger's* 1955 Pulitzer. Editor Bob Brown provided forceful leadership and wrote brilliant front-page editorials in the months after the Patterson murder, but his editorial performance before that time had not been notable. Ray Jenkins became a *Ledger* star during the cleanup period, writing superb exposes of the unholy relationship between vice kingpins and law-enforcement officials, but these articles came at a time when the presence of the Alabama National Guard made the Phenix City environment relatively safe.

My main contribution was in the period of 1950-54 when I was *The Ledger* reporter assigned to the Phenix City beat. My best work dealt with the organization of the Russell Betterment Association, the efforts by RBA members to gather evidence of crime and corruption, their confrontations with corrupt public officials, and their unsuccessful attempts to get rid of crooked politicians by impeachment and at the ballot box.

Carlton Johnson was a strong and helpful *Ledger* city editor in this period, with a distinguished track record of crusading vigor in Phenix City. L. P. Patterson, *Ledger* managing editor and acting editor in 1952, gave the paper fire and spirit at a time when the cleanup movement sorely needed our help. And the two top officials of the *Ledger-Enquirer* newspapers, President Alvah Chapman Sr., and Publisher Maynard Ashworth, did not falter when the going got hardest. Many others contributed to *The Ledger* crusade, which was vital to the ultimate victory of decent government in Phenix City.

The problems in the Alabama border town had festered for more than a hundred years. Vice and violence dated from the early part of the 19th century when the area that later became Phenix City was a haven for "disreputable white men, Indians and runaway negroes" who often crossed the river one step ahead of the Georgia law.

One of the first settlements was called Sodom, and it was described as "a wild-looking village, scattered through the edge of the forest." Illegal liquor was the main attraction in the 19th and early 20th centuries. State agents converged on Girard, the town that grew out of Sodom, in 1916, and seized an estimated million dollars' worth of bootleg whiskey. The county sheriff was impeached, but not long afterward the townspeople reclaimed most of their illicit alcohol by digging a tunnel from the river bank to a guarded warehouse. The impeached sheriff later was re-elected, and moonshining again became a major industry.

In 1923, during Prohibition, a second raid was conducted by federal agents in Girard and Russell County, and that same year Girard was incorporated into the more respectable Phenix City.

The area's sordid reputation failed to improve, however. Prostitution thrived in Phenix City in the 1930s and early 40s when World War II brought 50,000 young men into nearby Fort Benning. Fed by GI dollars, honky-tonks like Ma Beachie's and the Bama Club prospered, as did the little shotgun houses where loose and lissome ladies plied their trade.

Slot machines and wide-open gambling became an even more lucrative means of relieving the Fort Benning soldiers and other visitors of their hard-earned cash. Some 1,500 gambling devices, many later found to be rigged, were estimated to be in the bars and clubs. The city had about 200 professional gamblers and 275 lottery writers.

Altogether, the annual take from vice in Phenix City was conservatively estimated at $15 million. For soldiers, the 14th Street bridge across the Chattahoochee was a gateway to booze and sex and, too frequently, a mess of trouble. The Army tried to keep the worst dives off-limits, but venereal disease was so rampant a tough Fort Benning tank commander named George S. Patton once threatened to move his armored troops across the river and straighten Phenix City out.

All this permissiveness required a cooperative city government, of course. During the investigations that followed Patterson's death, it was shown that top public officials had close ties with the gambling czars. They picked candidates and rigged elections to their liking, trial testimony showed.

One way they controlled the government was to keep a tight rein on the jury lists. Many jurors were local toughs employed by the honky-tonks as bouncers and bartenders. It was noticed during the cleanup that less than 2,000 of Russell County's 40,000 citizens were on the jury list, and of those, about 1,000 had served from two to nine times each.

B-girls, soldiers, rowdies, and sometimes a law officer who became too inquisitive would disappear. Bodies were buried in unmarked graves in the Russell County countryside; others drifted downstream in the Chattahoochee. While this was going on, law-abiding, church-going Phenix Citians went about their business as though nothing was wrong.

The two men who did most to destroy the Phenix City vice empire made an unlikely pair. One was Hugh Bentley, a Phenix City resident who owned a sporting goods store in Columbus. Bentley was a meek-seeming man with a fierce determination that baffled his opponents. A devout Christian, he became dedicated to his goal of a better city and county at the height of the war in 1944. On a Sunday night, he wandered down to the honky-tonk area near the 14th Street bridge and up Third Avenue along the strip. The joints were open and jumping, even on the Lord's Day. Everything he saw had been there for years, but now it was particularly obscene.

"I went straight over to see a city commissioner friend of mine," Bentley told a reporter for the Atlanta Constitution in 1974, 20 years after the cleanup. "He was sick in bed but I told him what I had heard and seen and asked 'What can we do?'

" 'Why nothing,' he told me. 'The juries won't do anything. The mayor's in on it. Didn't you know all this? What's wrong with you, Hugh?' " The ensuing years for Bentley brought more of the same: a series of frustrating putoffs by indifferent citizens, intimidation, and finally violence.

His Christian Laymen's Association, which began with three representatives from each church in town, dwindled from 66 men to five within a year. He recalls the day a Phenix City girl in his Sunday school class came to him weeping after her school band had given a concert in Columbus. "They told me to get back across the river to our gamblers and whorehouses," the girl told Bentley. "She wept and it broke my heart," Bentley said. "It was happening because men like me didn't have the guts to stand up and fight it."

In 1951, Bentley joined forces with Albert Patterson, a graying, crippled attorney whose limp was due to German machine-gun bullets that stitched through his left leg in World War I. Patterson had served in the Alabama State Senate and had run for lieutenant governor; once he represented gambling kingpin Hoyt Shepherd in a murder case. Because of his former ties with men like Shepherd, Patterson's motives were questioned — until he proved his case decisively on the evening of June 18, 1954.

Patterson had an idea of how to beat the vice clique; he laid out a plan to Bentley for a group he called the Russell County Betterment Association. I attended one of the earliest RBA meetings in Patterson's law office in Phenix City. There were 10 men there who were listed as founders and directors, and not one believed he would emerge from the upcoming fight alive. Bentley was the group's president; his first lieutenant was Hugh Britton, a gutsy World War II veteran; and Howard Pennington, a bricklayer, also played a leading role. Patterson served as the RBA's attorney.

In the months that followed, the RBA showed its mettle. It was more than just another cleanup effort doomed to failure. The group brought impeachment proceedings against Sheriff Ralph Mathews, only to see them thrown out in Montgomery by the Alabama Supreme Court. There were citizens' arrests, confrontations with the mayor, voter registration drives, and the formation of a women's auxiliary.

The gangsters reacted to the RBA with disdain, irritation, and then dynamite. Bentley returned home one night in January 1952 and found smoke billowing from his shattered house and his son Hughbo sitting dazed where a bomb explosion had hurled him 40 feet from the bedroom. Miraculously, no one was seriously hurt. In May of that year, Bentley, Britton and Hughbo were bloodily beaten on their faces and bodies at a Phenix City voting place while the RBA was conducting a poll watch. That was the day that Jenkins and I were also attacked; we had been talking with the cleanup leaders when the thugs suddenly gathered around us and moved in, swinging their fists.

In 1954, Albert Patterson ran for attorney general of Alabama on a promise to do whatever it took to clean up Phenix City. He was often threatened with death and told associates he did not believe he would live to take office. Howard Pennington left his job and traveled the state with the Phenix City lawyer, serving as his driver and bodyguard. Patterson won the Democratic nomination and came home in June to catch up on his law practice and send thank-you notes to political supporters.

At about 9 p.m. on the night of June 18, the 57-year-old man got up from his desk, took his cane, and limped down the stairs of the Coulter Building. He stepped out onto Fifth Avenue and slowly made his way to his car in a dark alley. As he slipped behind the wheel, someone poked a .38 caliber pistol to his face. Four shots were fired, two ripping into his chest, a third through his mouth and lodging in his brain. Patterson staggered out of the alley and into the street, sank to the pavement and died.

That was the spark which caused *Ledger* Editor Bob Brown to mount an all-out newspaper campaign against the situation in Phenix City, more extensive than anything the community had seen before. Front-page editorials and cartoons blasted the Phenix City regime for its failure to press the search for Patterson's killer, and after the Alabama Guard took over law enforcement, we published a series of hard-hitting articles on the backgrounds of suspected vice leaders. A special Phenix City news desk was established under the direction of Carlton Johnson.

Finally, three men were indicted and arrested for the murder of Patterson. One of them, surprisingly, was Si Garrett, the attorney general of Alabama, whom Patterson had been nominated to replace. The other two were Russell County District Attorney Arch Ferrell and Deputy Sheriff Albert Fuller. Fuller and Ferrell both were tried in Birmingham; Fuller was convicted and received a life sentence; Ferrell was acquitted, and Garrett never came to trial, having been declared mentally unfit for a trial.

The National Guard remained in control of the government and law enforcement agencies for the remainder of 1954 and into 1955. Citizens of Phenix City, Russell County and neighboring Columbus were shocked as one spectacular event followed another. Gen. "Crack" Hanna canceled all liquor and beer licenses and voided all gun permits. The Guardsmen broke down doors when owners refused to cooperate, found secret rooms, one-way mirrors and tons of illegal slot machines and other gambling paraphernalia in basements, attics, barns, closets, ponds, haylofts, and private bedrooms. All of the unlawful equipment was later destroyed. There were hundreds of arrests and convictions.

The Guard closed its books on Phenix City in January, 1955, six months after it took over the town. Honest elections had been held, new leaders were in control of the city and county, and the community was so clean and progressive that Phenix City won an All-American City award in 1956.

John Patterson, son and law partner of the martyred Albert Patterson, was elected to serve his father's term as Alabama attorney general and then won election as governor in 1958.

A movie, *The Phenix City Story*, starring Richard Kiley, Kathryn (Crosby) Grayson, Edward Andrews and John McIntyre, was released in 1955. It offered a dramatic account and used many actual names and events, although it was considerably fictionalized. John Patterson, played by Kiley, was the hero, and the movie's popularity in Alabama undoubtedly helped Patterson defeat the favored George Wallace for governor in 1958. It was the only election Wallace ever lost in Alabama.

In December 1966, Roland J. Page, a former Columbus reporter, spent a year investigating *The Ledger* coverage which earned the 1955 Pulitzer Prize for Meritorious Public Service. His findings were put down in a master's thesis for the Graduate School of Florida State University, and it is still the best and most complete account of the story yet written. At the close of his manuscript of 184 typewritten pages, Page concludes that *The Ledger* did indeed earn the Pulitzer.

He wrote:

"Seldom has a newspaper the size of *The Ledger* used so many different tools with which to conduct a campaign. News stories flooded the front pages with accounts of daily developments from across the river. Countless expose columns, gleaned from back files, reminded both public and officials of the border town's past and the character of its rulers. An incessant flow of front page editorials demanded that no issue be neglected, no transgressor spared, and no question unanswered in the campaign. Photographs illustrated the news coverage. Cartoons reinforced the editorial crusade. The Phenix City story dominated *The Ledger's* news and editorial columns for nearly seven months, from assassination night through late December, 1954."

Of all the events that marked the cleanup years, my recollection of Albert Patterson and his Gall Club are most vivid. Shortly after he organized the RBA, a member of the courthouse gang asked Patterson, "How could you have the gall to get involved with that crowd?" Soon afterward, in Patterson's law office one day, I was inducted as a member of the Gall Club along with Bentley, Britton, Pennington, and several *Ledger* staffers who had paid their dues in Phenix City. And every time I visit the street where Patterson was killed, I can imagine that I see his ghost tapping its cane along the sidewalk, walking into everlasting glory.

Postscript: While most of the information in this account represents the author's own recollections, I am also deeply indebted to the following sources: Roland Joseph Page's *The Columbus Ledger and the Phenix City Story: On Winning a Pulitzer Prize*, a thesis submitted to the Graduate School of Florida State University in partial fulfillment of the requirements for the degree of Master of Arts, December 1966; Jim Stewart, "Phenix City Living Down Its Raunchy Past," in *The Atlanta Constitution*, April 8, 1974; and Colonel W. D. McGlasson, "Phenix City 1954: Putting Out the Flames of Corruption" in *National Guard* magazine, June 1981.

After the Pulitzer

For *The Ledger*, the 1955 Pulitzer was high noon. Its sun would never be so bright again. The staff had been remarkably stable during the 1951-55 period. But within 18 months after the Pulitzer announcement, Editor Brown, Managing Editor John Bloomer, Tom Sellers and Hal Allen, acting city editor for much of the Pulitzer year while Carlton Johnson was away on a Nieman, were all gone. Oddly, none of them left for especially better jobs, nor were *Ledger* staffers in demand by other newspapers because of the Pulitzer. Honor and satisfaction had to be reward enough.

With Brown's departure, *The Ledger-Enquirer* management retreated from the more flamboyant paths which Brown had blazed by replacing him with Edge Reid, the *Enquirer* managing editor, a man very different in outlook, temperament and ambition.

At that time *The Ledger* staff tended to look on *The Enquirer* as *The Ledger's* ugly stepchild, and they did not take warmly to having an "Enquirer man" become the chief news executive on *The Ledger*. They feared *The Ledger's* dominance would decline, which it did, but for reasons not then suspected. Reid in fact, proved himself an unrelenting *Ledger* partisan, even after he became executive editor of both newspapers. Although *The Ledger* remained higher in circulation for another seven years, the circulation odds were beginning to shift toward the morning side, for the simple reason that *The Enquirer* could be more easily distributed in the surrounding areas where circulation growth would have to come.

Reid was the consummate company man. He joined the newspapers in 1928 as sports editor of *The Ledger*, and he stayed for the next 47 years, except for military service in World War II. A lifelong bachelor, Reid was a courtly southern gentleman, who grudgingly surrendered the past. As managing editor he was noted for still wearing the green eye shade which was familiar in newsrooms in the early part of the century.

He was a stickler for accuracy, down to the slightest typographical error, a worthy trait which occasionally led him to agonizing over molehills while ignoring mountains.

But unlike Brown, Reid was satisfied with his station and satisfied with the newspaper. In neither case did he appear to envision any horizons beyond getting out the day's edition.

He was a sound and competent newsman, and an even-handed supervisor, which accounted for his long career at *The Ledger- Enquirer*. But he was a pedestrian editorial writer, and writing editorials was the editor's first responsibility in those days.

In that regard, he was somewhat like his *Enquirer* contemporary, W. C. Tucker, another good newsman, who could grind out an incredible volume of words for editorials and a personal column each day.

But change was coming. The 1960s in Columbus would be very unlike the 1950s.

Ashworth, The Legendary Colonel

In the spring of 1961 two deaths started the period of change on *The Ledger-Enquirer*. Alvah Chapman Sr., who had been president of the company since 1937, died in March. Chapman, who had married the older daughter of *Ledger* owner R. W. Page, shared the top management with his brother-in-law, Maynard Ashworth, who married Page's younger daughter. Page's son, W. E. Page, had been both president and publisher until his untimely death in an automobile accident in 1937.

Following Chapman's death, the question for the board of directors, which was composed of members of the Ashworth, Chapman and Page families, was whether to appoint Ashworth president and bring in a publisher which would continue the divided authority, or whether to allow Ashworth to become both president and publisher.

During the period before the final decision, *Enquirer* Editor Tucker died unexpectedly of a heart attack at the age of 61.

Chapman's son, Alvah Jr., as heir apparent, had left his family's business in 1953 after six years as business manager. The younger Chapman was one who definitely looked for new horizons, and he first went to St. Petersburg, Florida, as business manager of *The Times* for four years.

He then formed a partnership with Mills Lane, Georgia's most prominent banker, to buy the Savannah newspapers (see section on Savannah). That venture lasted only three years and Chapman then joined the Knight newspaper organization and was one of its rising stars in 1961 when he came to the board meeting in Columbus shortly after his father's death. There was speculation that he might want to return home and become a third-generation publisher of the Columbus newspaper.

But Chapman turned away from that path, kept on the one which would one day take him to the presidency of the largest newspaper group in the county, and ironically allow him to engineer the purchase of his family newspaper for that group.

The board's decision was to make Ashworth both president and publisher, giving him the full management authority he had long relished.

In April 1961, Ashworth was already 66 years old, a year past the retirement age for regular *Ledger-Enquirer* employees, but he was to wield power as president and publisher for 12 years, and in those years *The Ledger-Enquirer* reached new heights in circulation, advertising and news coverage.

A native of Missouri, Ashworth had served in the Army in both world wars, earning the rank of colonel in World War II. Most of his employees always addressed him as "Colonel," and he seemed to model himself after two other prominent publisher-colonels, Robert McCormick of *The Chicago Tribune*, and Frederick Bonfils of *The Denver Post*.

Indeed it might have been said of Ashworth as one prominent Denver citizen said of Bonfils: "When they made Frederick Bonfils, they broke the mold . . . Thank God, they broke the mold."

Ashworth was unswervingly dedicated to the proposition of having good newspapers in all respects, editorially, financially, and mechanically. He was a man driven by his passions, which made life extremely nerve-wracking for department heads on whom his wrath would frequently descend, sometimes for a good reason, sometimes for trivialities, sometimes for imaginary faults.

Ashworth's favorite means of communication was to write with a red crayon on the page or pages which had offended him — or in rare cases which pleased him — and send them to the appropriate editor or other department head.

The problem was that Ashworth's handwriting was hard to decipher under the best of conditions and almost impossible to decipher in heavy red crayon, usually written in haste and anger.

Editors would sit for long periods studying the scrawl of red words, fearful of their message, but striving mightily to resolve the puzzle which they presented. "Hey, I've got it," would come a cry, as an editor realized that the message related to a typo, or he discovered the clue to which story, word or headline the message was linked.

When Ashworth was upset to the point of brooding and reflection, he would send lengthy, typed memos, which editors received gratefully even if they were critical. At least they could read them.

One of his more notable and brilliantly wrought memos was sent to the editors of *The Ledger* and *The Enquirer* on the occasion of the 26th anniversary of the Japanese attack on Pearl Harbor. Neither editor had written an editorial that year to commemorate the anniversary.

Ashworth's onslaught against this alleged oversight questioned both the patriotism and the judgement of the two editors for failing to take note of the anniversary.

"I sometimes wonder if our editors have any comprehension of the responsibility of editors of a newspaper of consequence," the memo began. It continued for a page and a half, stressing the importance of reminding readers of historical days in U.S. history, and how the editors had failed to meet this responsibility. "None of our editors thought enough of Pearl Harbor Day to mention it on our editorial pages. This, I think, is a deplorable and unforgivable omission — not so much because of the omission but because of what it spells out to me concerning the thinking of the editors and the lack of sensitivity to historical facts which is prevalent in the minds of our editors.

"Are we too engrossed, or too busy, or is it a lack of alertness of mind? Let us not forget Christmas — remember it is the day of the birth of Christ, and this, I think, was an important event in history."

The two editors — Johnson on *The Ledger*, Grimes on *The Enquirer* — were naturally taken aback. If there was anything they knew for sure about their responsibility it was that they must reflect the deep and sincere patriotism of their publisher. On the previous Dec. 7 — which was the 25th anniversary of Pearl Harbor — they had both written extensive pieces on its meaning for the United States in 1966. Not wishing to be repetitious they had decided to let the 26th anniversary go without editorial notice.

In an effort to defend themselves, they searched the exchange newspapers for editorials on the Pearl Harbor anniversary and found only one. That merely convinced Ashworth that the whole newspaper business was remiss in patriotism, which he already suspected. But a lesson was learned.

Pearl Harbor was thereafter always remembered in *The Ledger* and *Enquirer* while Ashworth was publisher.

Sometimes the oversights or errors on the part of editors or managing editors were more imagined than real, which did not necessarily spare them from Ashworth's wrath.

One of the most crucial daily duties of *The Ledger* managing editor was to make sure that the U.S. flag was flying over the newspaper building each day. The actual raising of the flag was done by the copy boy, but the managing editor was held responsible for making sure the copy boy was diligent, and that he observed the various rules and regulations regarding the flying of the flag. The managing editor was certainly supposed to know all those rules.

At one of the regular weekly meetings of the editors, managing editors, and city editors of the two newspapers, Ashworth began castigating *The Ledger* managing editor because the flag had not been flying on the previous day, which happened to be November 11, then called Armistice Day.

The managing editor explained that it had been raining that morning and that the rules say you don't fly the flag in the rain. But the ME hadn't looked far enough. Ashworth retorted that the controlling rule was that you raise the flag on Armistice Day no matter what the weather conditions.

Editors present at that meeting could not recall a more prolonged and intense chewing-out for any journalistic offense as that *Ledger* ME received for failing to get the flag up on a rainy Armistice Day.

The managing editor happened to be Glenn Vaughn, whom Ashworth would 10 years later appoint as the company's general manager, paving the way for him to succeed Ashworth as *The Ledger-Enquirer* publisher.

Something else Ashworth felt strongly about was the stock market report. In the 1960s *The Enquirer* carried the most extensive stock market report in Georgia. Every market item offered by the wire services was taken by *The Enquirer*, and its market and business pages were far ahead of the trend to more extensive business news which other large dailies followed in the 1970s.

Omissions on the stock pages were almost akin in Ashworth's view to not flying the flag. The gravest sin was to neglect running a page one box on days when the market had been closed explaining why there were no stock pages in that day's edition.

After one stock market holiday Ashworth came storming into *The*

Enquirer newsroom, waving a front page covered in broad red crayon strokes, wanting to know why there had been no page one box story about the stock market being closed.

The managing editor, shaken and uncertain, stared balefully at the page of print and crayon, silently cursing the composing room gremlins whom he assumed must have left out the story. But then his eyes brightened as he spotted at the bottom of the page the headline and the story explaining that there were no stock pages because the market had been closed.

"But we did carry the story about the stock market," he cheerfully informed the fuming Ashworth. "There it is, right there."

Ashworth gave the page a disgusted look and threw it on the ME's desk. "That doesn't matter," he bellowed, "I didn't see it."

Working at *The Ledger-Enquirer* in the 1960s in upper echelon jobs could be harrowing and hectic but there were compensations. Ashworth's eccentricities had their good side. His department heads knew that he CARED. Because he was so determined to eliminate every typographical error they tried a little harder. Because he wanted desks neat and orderly, the news rooms were more neat and orderly. Because he truly wanted superior newspapers in every aspect, *The Ledger* and *Enquirer* were better newspapers.

His memos were not always critical. He also commended what he considered a good job. Despite his tirades he was slow to fire an employee. He was generous with the "news hole," which many publishers were not in those days.

Perhaps most importantly, he cared about the community. He cared whether Columbus and Muscogee County had a consolidated government, and his tenacity on this issue was a major reason that Columbus and Muscogee have the only consolidated city-county government in Georgia.

Ashworth was farsighted in terms of equipment and plant capacity. *The Ledger-Enquirer* had cold type machines for advertising as early as 1956. There was constant remodeling and expansion in the Spanish-style building which had been erected on 12th Street (giving rise to the derisive term '12th Street Rag') and Front Avenue in 1930.

In 1971 a six-story addition to the building was completed, which extended *The Ledger-Enquirer* building for the entire block of 12th Street between Front and Broadway.

The main attraction of the addition was the ornate third-floor office for Ashworth, probably the finest and largest publisher's office in the South. Its windows provided a view in all directions of what was then

Downtown Columbus, and which was already showing signs of serious decline.

Ashworth's philosophy and driven nature were summed up in a memo sent to department heads on the occasion of his 71st birthday in 1965. He wrote:

> Values of life are different — less confusing — as one gets older. Many values, considered paramount when younger, fail to have reason for important value when looked at through eyes of experience — many years of testing, evaluating.
>
> We all do, or should, have ideals — a burning desire for perfection of accomplishment — accomplishment of an overriding, single goal — and this ideal, or goal, should be established in one's mind and heart early in life.
>
> From the time of this decision, from this point on, throughout life, every move, every calculation, should be to achieve this goal, this ideal, by honorable means — by nothing short of all the hard work and effort needed to accomplish this goal.
>
> It is achieving this goal, the effort to achieve it, that is incentive to do things which thrill, which stimulate life, this is the driving force which keeps us on-course — with determination — with refusal to be frustrated, or to be denied. Most always there is achievement of a portion of our goal — if we but stay with it.
>
> It is this struggle which keeps life interesting, keeps it exciting, and keeps our minds active, clear of false intrusions, worrisome thoughts, and too often, complete misunderstanding of life — which ends in disappointment, disillusionment, in life defeating us.
>
> My philosophy has been to strive constantly to achieve a chosen goal — these newspapers are a symbol of this desire — to make of these newspapers the finest, the best, the proudest, in their field.
>
> It is not money — one must have economic security in order to have a free mind, but the greatest compensation is achieving a goal of consequence which is worthy.
>
> In newspaper publishing, we are serving people, we are striving to better people's lives — their living conditions, economic conditions, moral standards — every facet of daily living of this life; this is a newspaper's paramount reason for being, for continuing the struggle of accomplishment each day. And, this should not be forgotten in the day to day effort — when at times humdrum seems to be the order of the day.
>
> No one alone can reach a goal; there must be, depending on dimensions of the goal, an organization of people — a team — people who see alike, feel alike, who have the same vision and

> determination.
>
> Last evening, there was a demonstration of this, I think, evidenced by the birthday party at the Chickasaw Club — here was evidence of the existence of such a team — this is the point I want to bring to the heads of our departments, and others who were present, to have my point understood. I want the members of all families of department heads to know this too.
>
> It is so essential that all department heads — all of their families — know and understand this. They, too, the families, must feel these things — be a part — always . . .

Ashworth's willingness to try new methods was quickly evident after he assumed full control in 1961. The vacancy in *The Enquirer*'s editor's position provided an opportunity to revamp the hierarchy of the two news departments and to move toward their consolidation. Ashworth was years ahead of a trend that would become common — even to merging entire newspapers — but in 1961 the resistance to staff consolidation was to be stubborn — and ultimately successful.

The consolidation plan was put into effect in the summer of 1961. The position of editor was eliminated on the two newspapers and an editorial board was established with responsibility for all editorials, morning, evening and Sunday. An executive editor was named, with authority over the news and editorial staffs of *The Enquirer* and *Ledger*. The sports and women's news departments were also consolidated, although the city news staffs remained separate.

The new arrangement was introduced with a front-page story, photos and bios of the people involved, and a promise to the readers that the newspapers would be better news products because of the changes.

For the Columbus newspapers, the 1961 "shuffle" was the most thorough restructuring of the news staffs during that decade, but it proved to have a more far-reaching effect on the individuals involved than on the newspapers, which 18 months later reverted to their old, separate ways.

To create the editorial board, the editor of *The Ledger*, Edge Reid, was made executive editor of both *The Ledger* and *Enquirer;* the two managing editors, Carlton Johnson of *The Ledger*, and Dave Miller of *The Enquirer*, became associate editors of both papers, and Millard Grimes was taken from *The Ledger* copy desk to be an editorial assistant for both papers.

Grimes was already a regular Sunday editorial page columnist, and a frequent contributor of editorials to *The Ledger* daily page. Although he had been on the staff off and on since he was a 16-year-old junior at

Columbus High, Grimes had left the organization twice in the previous six years, (in 1955 and 1959) to become editor of smaller newspapers in the area. On his second return in April 1960, he had been relegated to the rim of the copy desk, from which he was plucked by Ashworth for the editorial board position.

Johnson and Miller had worked their way up the ladder from reporter to managing editor of their respective newspapers during the past 15 years.

The 1961 changes also included the promotion of Glenn Vaughn to replace Johnson as managing editor of *The Ledger*. For Vaughn, that was an early step toward his eventual succession of Ashworth as publisher, although such a development was wildly improbable in the family-operated *Ledger-Enquirer* company of 1961.

Old habits die hard, of course, and most of the staffers in the combined departments still tended to favor the newspaper on which they previously worked, and in some cases did little or nothing for publication in the other paper. Miller seldom wrote an editorial for *The Ledger*, Johnson seldom wrote one for *The Enquirer*. Grimes was the only real swing man in the editorial department.

Miller, who had spent years working into the wee hours of the night as an executive on a morning newspaper, never adjusted well to the different demands of the editorial board post.

He was a victim of the common practice among newspapers throughout the nation, then and now, to take competent, experienced newsroom personnel and put them in editorial page positions, which are basically research and writing jobs, and for which many of them are unsuited, both in temperament and ability.

An additional trauma, in Miller's case — as it usually is for former managing editors — was the loss of authority over a large staff, which a managing editor has but an associate (or editorial page) editor does not have.

A columnist and editorial writer mainly has charge of himself, a difficult and lonely authority.

Miller became emotionally involved in the editorial campaign for consolidation of the city and county governments, and its defeat in the 1962 referendum left him even more despondent.

By mutual agreement he left *The Ledger-Enquirer* in May 1962, and soon found a position which allowed him to return to the news room, first as city editor and then as news editor of the Huntsville, Alabama *Times*. Later he was news editor of the Decatur, Alabama *Daily*. A young reporter's tribute to Miller for his guidance and enthusiasm for news was a prize-winning column in the 1983 Alabama Press Association contest.

Miller's departure for all practical purposes ended the experiment of joint staffs at *The Ledger-Enquirer*. Johnson was soon appointed editor of *The Ledger*, and Grimes became editor of *The Enquirer*, with authority over the entire news operation of their respective newspapers.

Separate sports departments were later restored although the women's departments remained combined.

As it happened, the renewed competition between *The Ledger* and *Enquirer* came at an opportune time, as both newspapers were on the threshhold of their peak years of circulation growth, and the efforts by the two staffs to outperform each other carried over to the circulation department in the middle and late 1960s.

Home-Town Boy Makes Good

Carlton M. Johnson, the new *Ledger* editor, was a home-town boy who went to work as a reporter on *The Ledger* in 1946, after serving in the Navy during World War II.

His intensity and determination quickly gained notice, even on the all-star cast which wandered through *The Ledger* newsroom in the early post-war years.

Johnson graduated from Georgia's first vocational high school, Jordan of Columbus, but he managed to get in only a month of college. That fact always bothered him, even years later when he was the top news executive on the Columbus newspapers, had been a Nieman fellow, and had long since surpassed his contemporaries who spent four years at college.

In September 1947, he had enrolled at the University of Georgia, with the intention of getting a degree, but one month later the illness of his father forced him to return to Columbus and ask for his reporter's job back, so that he could help support his family.

When Bob Brown came on as editor of *The Ledger* in 1948 he took an immediate liking to the youthful, redheaded reporter. Johnson then got a break of sorts when he and fellow reporter Jim Bellows and photographer Joe Talbot were seized by Ku Klux Klansmen while they were covering a Klan rally on Pine Mountain.

The Klansmen forced them to drink large quantities of moonshine whiskey and then left them gagged and bound on the mountain. The story received nationwide attention, and was featured in *Time* magazine. Johnson, whose compassion for the less fortunate was always an integral part of his personal and professional philosophy, was deeply affected by the incident, and the memory still burned in his heart years later when the civil rights struggle erupted across the South and nation in the 1960s.

In 1950, at the age of 23, Johnson was named city editor of *The Ledger*. Brown sponsored him for a Nieman Fellowship, which he was awarded for the 1954-55 year at Harvard. A week before leaving for his Harvard sabattical, City Editor Johnson surprised the staff by marrying its only female reporter at the time, tall and attractive Constance Pilkington, a Mississippi belle, who had joined the staff in 1951.

One of Brown's last acts as editor in late 1956 was to name Johnson managing editor, replacing John Bloomer. Six years later, Johnson succeeded to *The Ledger* editor's post. First, however, he had to get the position reinstated.

Johnson never quite overcame a serious stage-fright when forced to speak or preside at large gatherings, but in small groups, or with individuals, he had a warm and intense manner which served him well with the employers who helped him up the ladder. He also possessed the ability to rise above his insecurities at decisive times, and make a case for what he believed. That was what he did in late 1962, as he told Ashworth that he felt the former system of separate editors and separate editorial staffs should be restored for *The Ledger* and *Enquirer*. Ashworth, who appreciated boldness and courage, surprisingly agreed with him.

Edge Reid retained the position of executive editor of both newspapers, as Johnson took over direction of *The Ledger*, and Grimes was given the reinstated position of editor of *The Enquirer*.

Johnson was a vigorous editor, as he had been a vigorous managing and city editor, and he was the point man in the newspapers' campaign for a new courthouse and a consolidated government.

In 1967, in a puzzling move by Ashworth, Johnson was named executive editor of *The Ledger-Enquirer*, while also continuing as editor of *The Ledger*, and Reid was given the title of associate publisher. At the time Ashworth said he wanted another person in administration of the entire newspaper operation and felt Reid was the appropriate choice.

Johnson's name was added to The Enquirer's masthead, but he continued mainly to function as *Ledger* editor, while Grimes and his successor Vaughn, supervised *The Enquirer*.

Johnson was a strong supporter of Carl Sanders for governor in 1970, but he did not insist that *The Enquirer* follow his lead, and *The Enquirer* endorsed Jimmy Carter, the eventual victor. It was one of the rare splits on a major endorsement by the two newspapers.

Shortly before *The Ledger-Enquirer* was sold to the Knight Company, Johnson suffered a major disappointment when Vaughn was selected by Ashworth to be general manager of the newspapers. Following the sale, he briefly regained full authority over the news departments under the Knight system but then had another setback when Carroll Dadisman was brought in to replace him as executive editor in 1974. He had earlier relinquished the title and duties of *Ledger* editor to Carrol Lisby, but to make room for Dadisman, Johnson became editor of *The Ledger* again and Lisby moved to *The Enquirer* editor's position.

The Johnsons, Carlton and Connie, were a constant and vital part of the Columbus literary, cultural and civic scene for more than a quarter of a century, each complementing the other in striving for better newspapers and a better community.

Johnson suffered an aneurism while he and Connie were vacationing in North Carolina in August 1977, and he died a few days later at the age of 51.

Connie Johnson has remained in the reporter's job she has held since 1951, and in April 1985, she marked her 34th year on *The Ledger* staff.

Because of Carlton Johnson's deep and abiding interest in education, *The Ledger-Enquirer* established a memorial award in his name, which is given to a deserving student in the Columbus school system each year for college expenses. He was inducted into the Georgia Newspaper Hall of Fame in 1982, the only Columbus journalist so honored except for Mirabeau B. Lamar.

On Less-Traveled Paths

Johnson's rise to the editorship of his home-town afternoon daily was fairly traditional. He started as a reporter when he was 20 years old and spent his entire career with *The Ledger-Enquirer*, moving up the ladder to city editor, managing editor, associate editor and editor.

But his counterpart on the morning *Enquirer* in the 1960s arrived at the editorship of his home-town newspaper in far less orthodox fashion, a tactical characteristic which has led his career down several "less-traveled paths."

When he was named editor of *The Enquirer* in January 1963, Millard

Grimes was 32 years old, and had never spent a day actually working in *The Enquirer* newsroom. What was worse in the eyes of *Enquirer* staffers was that he had spent all of his Columbus career on the afternoon *Ledger*, which they felt made Grimes a "*Ledger* man," who was being moved in to head *The Enquirer*.

Ironically, it was the same feeling that Grimes and other *Ledger* staffers had when Edge Reid came from *The Enquirer* to be editor of *The Ledger* five years earlier.

Aside from his *Ledger* antecedents, Grimes had also missed most of the rungs on the ladder up, having never held any supervisory positions, such as sports editor, news editor, city editor or managing editor.

Twice in the past 12 years he had left *The Ledger-Enquirer* to work on smaller papers in the area, and when he came back to *The Ledger* in April 1960, he was relegated to a rim job on the copy desk.

But Grimes achieved visibility in the most effective way for a would-be editor. He wrote editorials and editorial page columns. He had done that throughout his *Ledger* career, and not long after his most recent rehiring he began writing a Sunday column again. Symbolically, when *Enquirer* Editor Tucker died, Grimes' column was moved into the space Tucker's Sunday column had occupied.

Despite his lack of supervisory experience on *The Ledger-Enquirer*, Grimes had been preparing for the editor's duties virtually all his life.

As a 16-year-old high school junior in 1946, he applied for a summer job on *The Ledger* and was surprised to find himself a proofreader, along with three middle-aged ladies. That contact led to a Saturday copy boy position during the fall. But on the Saturday before Christmas that year the managing editor told Grimes that his services would no longer be needed since he was being replaced by the city editor's younger brother.

Grimes' pride and wallet were both damaged by that dismissal since his father had recently been forced to quit his job because of an illness which would take his life a few months later. But it was a memorable experience which in later years made Grimes a sensitive and thoughtful employer, if not always a forceful one.

He was called back the following summer to the regular copy boy's job, and thereafter his several departures from *The Ledger- Enquirer* were all of his own choice.

Grimes worked at *The Ledger* in each of the summers during his four years at the University of Georgia, and on graduation in 1951 he came on full time. After only two months as a reporter he moved to the copy desk as makeup editor. He was in his favorite element on the desk, selecting stories, laying out pages, writing headlines and "getting the paper out." For most of the next 10 years he was the *Ledger's* chief news representative in the composing room, cajoling and wrestling with the hard-bitten denizens of the hot-type process, who liked to eat editors for breakfast and lunch in the 1950s.

Also from his earliest days following college, Grimes wrote editorials after regular work hours and contributed them to the editor, who usually appreciated and printed them. Soon, in fact, the editor was assigning him subjects.

Like his editor, Bob Brown, Grimes was ambitious. Although he had lived in Columbus since he was 10 years old, his childhood years were spent in LaGrange and Newnan, and unlike most journalists he always yearned to return to smaller cities and newspapers rather than moving up to larger ones.

In 1955, just after the publicized cleanup of corruption in neighboring Phenix City, Grimes formed a partnership with a Phenix City attorney, Roy Greene, who put up $2000 to start a weekly newspaper in that city.

Phenix City, of course, is actually an extension of Columbus, despite being in another state. Its downtown is only two blocks from downtown Columbus, both of them hugging the Chattahoochee River. *The Phenix Citizen*, which Grimes called the new paper, was Alabama's first "suburban" weekly, and Grimes' experience with it foreshadowed his role with Atlanta suburban newspapers some 25 years later.

Grimes was replaced on *The Ledger* copy desk by Glenn Vaughn, a friend from his University days, the first junction in their two careers which were to cross each other at regular intervals.

The Phenix Citizen did well for a new paper (and is still going strong 30 years later) but Grimes soon discovered that while he liked being an editor and publisher, he preferred a daily's pace, and the broader variety of news which a daily handled.

In July 1956, he sold his interest in *The Phenix Citizen* to Vaughn, and they swapped jobs, with Grimes returning to *The Ledger*.

Vaughn's tenure at *The Citizen* was distinguished by its becoming one of the early offset newspapers in Alabama, even to the extent of having its own press, which was an old mapmaking press which Greene picked up at a Fort Benning auction.

In the spring of 1959 Grimes resigned again from *The Ledger*, this time to take a job as editor of *The Valley Times-News*, a small daily in nearby West Point, which had just converted to cold type composition, but was still using a letter press. (See Chapter II, The Last Linotype).

Grimes liked the small daily operation, despite the tribulations of early cold type equipment, and the long hours required of a daily editor with only three staff members. But family considerations dictated a return to Columbus. Money was also a factor. He was making $110 a week in West Point, and had been making $106 in Columbus, but his wife could work more easily in Columbus.

When he left the second time from *The Ledger*, he had been told, in effect, don't come back, so he returned to *The Phenix Citizen*, but not as a part-owner. It was at a time (late 1959, early 1960) when *The Citizen* had slipped from its early promise (12 to 16 pages a week) to 6-8 pages. The nation was in a recession and Phenix City was still waiting for the progress that was supposed to follow the cleanup. (In fact, it was still waiting 30 years later.)

Then one day *Ledger* Managing Editor Johnson called and told Grimes he'd like to have him back on the copy desk. At this time, Vaughn, after his stint on *The Citizen* and several years in Atlanta, was *Ledger* news editor.

Grimes, now 30 years old, returned to the same job he'd held just after graduating from college nine years earlier. He'd founded a newspaper, been a publisher and an editor, and would-be fiction writer along the way (one story published in *Planet Stories*, 1954) and he still had dreams of creating a newspaper chain of his own, but he was virtually broke, in a $115-a-week job, with a growing family to look after.

It was the kind of low ebb that many journalists reach in their careers at one time or another, but from that low point Grimes rose to become editor of *The Enquirer* just 20 months later. When the editorial board was formed in 1961 Grimes was a logical choice to be one of the writers since he had been writing editorials for 10 years, both at *The Ledger* and in his two intervals away. He had also been a regular Sunday editorial page columnist for two years.

When the positions of editor were reinstated he was already writing most of *The Enquirer*'s editorials and handling the editorial pages, so the main change was that he gained authority over the rest of the news operation.

Grimes moved in with more changes than any Columbus editor since Brown. Two immediate goals were to reduce the number of jumps (*The Enquirer* routinely jumped every story on page one) and to give *The*

Enquirer a second front page for local and area news, something *The Ledger* had carried for a decade.

The old time *Enquirer* staffers gave ground grudgingly, and sometimes not at all, but *The Enquirer* changed, perhaps not as much as Grimes wanted, but noticeably. As he explained to the department heads, he didn't want *The Enquirer* to be "another *Ledger*," he just wanted it to be a better newspaper.

Soon, most of the staff came over to his side, mainly because *The Enquirer* began moving up on *The Ledger* in circulation. There were many reasons for the increase, mainly the simple one that the morning newspaper was in position to gain more circulation in the surrounding counties.

Grimes was a tireless promoter of *The Enquirer*, traveling to club meetings throughout the circulation area to tell its story. He did not come easily to that task, having at earlier times in his life gotten physically ill when facing a talk before even small church groups. Later, however, he used to say he was so relaxed the audience sometimes went to sleep.

When *The Enquirer* passed *The Ledger* in circulation for the first time in the 20th century, *The Enquirer* staff proudly announced the achievement in a page one story.

Both *The Enquirer* and *The Ledger* reached their peak circulation in 1967, during the buildup at Fort Benning for the Vietnam War. Another factor was that the newspapers still sold for five cents daily, and 15 cents Sunday, with correspondingly low weekly and monthly rates.

Grimes was proud of *The Enquirer*'s progress, and enjoyed the main duties of an editor, which included producing two editorials, plus a column every day.

In that period, he was effective at articulating the moderate-to-conservative views of most Columbus area readers, especially on racial unrest and the spreading demonstrations on college campuses. Those also happened to be the views Ashworth wanted the newspapers to promote, although he was personally more conservative than the editorials in his newspapers.

Readership polls showed Grimes' daily and Sunday editorial page columns ranked with Snuffy Smith and Ann Landers in popularity among readers in the 30-60 age range. One critic, however, was *Enquirer* subscriber Jimmy Carter of Plains, whose relationship with the Columbus newspapers was tenuous throughout the 1960s.

In 1962, when Carter ran for the state Senate the final vote count showed him losing to his opponent in the Democratic primary. But Carter contested the outcome, charging that numerous incidents of vote fraud in Quitman County, a small county south of Columbus, had cost him the election. He first contacted the *Enquirer's* state editor, Luke Teasley, asking him to investigate the Quitman vote returns.

Apparently getting no satisfaction, Carter telephoned Grimes, who was then associate editor and had no authority over the newsroom, wanting to know why the state editor was unwilling to expose the vote fraud.

Grimes turned Carter over to the newsroom instead of following up the complaint himself, an oversight he often agonized about in later years.

In his book, *Why Not The Best?*, published by Broadman Press in 1975, Carter writes of his frustration with the Columbus newspapers during the primary and his subsequent challenge of the results:

> On election day I visited as many of the polling places as possible, and everything seemed to be in order until I arrived in Georgetown, a small town on the Chattahoochee River. There were no voting booths in the courthouse and the voters were marking their ballots on a table in full view of the voting officials. The local state legislator and dominant political boss of the county was supervising the election. Campaign cards of my opponent were on the voting table, and the supervisor would point to the cards and say to each voter, 'This is a good man and my good friend.' . . . On several occasions he reached into the box and extracted a few ballots to be examined.
>
> It was an unbelievable scene. He completely ignored my protests. All the other poll workers seemed to obey his orders. I drove to a cafe and telephoned the newspaper office in the nearby city of Columbus to describe what was occurring. They promised to send a reporter. When I returned after a couple of hours from a visit to another county (in the Senate district) I saw the reporter and political boss chatting on the steps of the court house. It was obvious that they were old friends, and the reporter was not interested in writing any story critical of election procedures in Quitman County.

Carter goes on to describe how the results that night showed him ahead by 70 votes with the Georgetown box still to report. When it came in he lost by less than a hundred votes. He immediately began a legal challenge of the outcome, on the basis that voting irregularities had occurred throughout the day at the Georgetown polling place.

John Pennington of *The Atlanta Journal* eventually came to investigate the case, which also led to Carter's first contact with Atlanta attorney Charles Kirbo. A new election was finally ordered which Carter won by a comfortable margin, putting him on the road to the White House.

In 1966, when Carter first ran for governor, neither *The Enquirer* nor *Ledger* supported him editorially, and in fact were critical of him for splitting the moderate vote in the Democratic primary, allowing Lester Maddox to make the runoff.

Carter's neutrality in the Democratic runoff between Maddox and Ellis Arnall also drew criticism from the Columbus newspapers — and most others in the state. *The Enquirer* editorially proclaimed that, "Carter has written his political obituary," since it was assumed that liberals and moderates would never forgive him for not taking sides in the Arnall-Maddox runoff, which Grimes and most editors viewed as a "choice between the law and axe-handles."

Carter's gamble paid off for him, however, as Maddox won the runoff, and then was elected governor by the state legislature after Republican Bo Callaway failed to win a clear majority in the general election.

Some months after the election, *The Enquirer* speculated that Carter would not run in 1970 if former Gov. Carl Sanders or the popular attorney general, James Bentley, were candidates. That editorial brought a handwritten message on Carter Insurance Company scratch paper in a Carter's Warehouse envelope to Editor Grimes, which read:

"Subject: Erroneous editorial. I read your editorial this morning and, off the record, you are completely in error about me. If I decide to run, the candidacy of Sanders, Bentley, etc., would not affect my plans at all. This is not for publication but I just thought you should know that I'm making plans . . . . Jimmy Carter."

The determination reflected in that terse note was Carter's great and enduring asset, and when he decided to run for president, he viewed the possible opposition of Edward Kennedy, Hubert Humphrey, Harry Jackson and better-known Democrats in the same light as he had viewed state opposition from Sanders and others. (See Carter and the Georgia Press, Chapter I.)

During the 1960s, the Columbus newspapers backed Carl Sanders for governor in 1962; Barry Goldwater for president in 1964; Ellis Arnall for the Democratic nomination as governor in 1966; then Bo Callaway, the Republican, in the general election; Richard Nixon for president in 1968.

Grimes covered the 1964 and 1968 national Republican conventions for *The Ledger-Enquirer*, and was a strong supporter of a two-party system in Georgia and the South. He felt that Goldwater's candidacy, whatever its failure at the national level, opened up the South for Republicans.

Also in those years, the two newspapers strongly promoted and endorsed Erle Cocke Jr. for the Democratic nomination for 3rd District congressman in 1964 and 1966, which seemed at variance with their prevailing editorial direction.

Cocke, a former national president of the American Legion, was a competent and experienced Washington hand. The problem was that he had lived away from Georgia for many years, and his former home town of Dawson was in the 2nd Congressional District. But Cocke was a good friend of Publisher Ashworth, and although Ashworth generally preferred Republican candidates in those days, he wanted to be the king maker who put Cocke into Congress.

It was the only endorsement during that decade which Grimes felt uncomfortable with, even though he recognized that Cocke would be a good congressman. In addition to his residency problem, Cocke's main Washington connection was a long and close relationship with then-President Lyndon Johnson, and that was no political asset in Georgia's 3rd District in 1964 and 1966.

Bo Callaway was seeking to become the first Republican congressman from Georgia since Reconstruction, and he was counting on *The Ledger-Enquirer's* help in the 1964 general election. If Cocke should be his Democratic opponent, that would put the newspapers in an awkward philosophical bind of being for Goldwater and Cocke against Johnson and Callaway.

But Cocke lost to former Lt. Gov. Garland Byrd in the primary, which cleared the way for *The Enquirer* and *The Ledger* to support Callaway for Congress and Goldwater for president in the general election.

In 1966 Cocke bought a house in Columbus and moved there for the election campaign. But this time he was up against a Columbus resident, Jack Brinkley, and once again he lost in the primary. Brinkley was elected in November, easily defeating the Republican candidate, Billy Mixon, and going on to serve 16 years in the U.S. House.

By the spring of 1965, Grimes was afflicted anew by his old dream of being a small-town publisher. The city where he most wanted to be a publisher was Athens, which he considered ideal in all respects.

While in Athens for the 1965 Press Institute, Grimes came across a copy of the weekly *Athens Advertiser*. He contacted the publisher, Claude Williams, to see if he had any interest in converting the *Advertiser* to a daily. Williams was definitely interested, so all that was needed was money, of which neither Grimes or Williams had any. They soon found financial backing however and began to order equipment and a press. Grimes was to resign from *The Enquirer* and move to Athens and be editor and publisher of the new daily, which he planned to call *The Athens Daily News*.

But Ashworth heard of the venture from a feature syndicate salesman while he was attending a national convention in New York. He immediately called Edge Reid in Columbus and told him to confront Grimes with the information and demand to know immediately if he was planning to leave *The Enquirer*.

Grimes, faced with an ultimatum, backed down. There were family considerations, and he also had second thoughts about leaving the editorship of a large daily for a high-risk venture on a new daily in a smaller market.

Fortunately for Williams and others who were far along on the deal, there was a capable substitute available. Glenn Vaughn, at that time managing editor of *The Ledger*, was eager to take the opportunity Grimes was giving up. (See Chapter VIII.)

Grimes stayed, but his relationship with Ashworth was never as close again. *The Enquirer* continued upward in circulation during the next few years, and coverage of the Vietnam War by its famed correspondent, Charlie Black, brought prestige and acclaim rare for a newspaper of its size.

Grimes was more puzzled than upset when Johnson was appointed executive editor of both newspapers, placing him theoretically over Grimes and *The Enquirer* news operation. Ashworth never offered any explanation, and although Grimes and Johnson had lunch together nearly every day as well as conferring professionally, they never came up with the reasons or the meaning for the change. One effect, however, was to increase Grimes' inclination to stare out his second floor office window at the horizon across the Chattahoochee River which flowed just a block away.

In September 1967, a group of businessmen in Opelika, Alabama asked Grimes to come speak to them about how *The Athens Daily News* had been financed and started. The group was interested in a similar venture for Opelika and its adjoining city, Auburn, site of Auburn University.

Grimes advised them that the best course would be to try and buy the existing five-day daily in Opelika, before attempting a new paper. Grimes knew the owners of the Opelika newspapers, and had gone to them for information on equipment two years earlier when the Athens operation was being set up, so he approached them personally about the possibility of selling. The response was encouraging.

Only a few of the original group of interested parties stayed the course after Grimes explained to them the amount of money it took to buy newspapers, or to start them. But by the summer of 1968, a tentative agreement had been reached with the owners of the Opelika daily, and Grimes again faced the decision of swapping the editorship of his hometown morning daily for a risky venture on a small-town daily. This time the newspaper did already exist, and Opelika was only 27 miles from Columbus, a consideration for Grimes because of his responsibility for elderly relatives who lived in Columbus.

But 1968 brought another presidential campaign, and the racial and political turmoil of the 1960s reached their peak during that summer. Grimes did not feel he should leave *The Enquirer* during the campaign. Ashworth had stressed many times that he felt editorial continuity was important during a political campaign, and Grimes knew he owed that consideration to the newspaper which had given him so many opportunities. So he put the Opelika deal on hold until after the November election.

Newspaper values were going through a dramatic transition in the late 1960s, and within the next 10 years the values would reach levels to make publishers blink in disbelief. The predictable result has been a massive shift in ownership of daily newspapers from families to corporate groups.

Even in 1968 it was rare that a small daily newspaper was sold to any buyer other than a sizeable newspaper group. Local businessmen who might be interested couldn't understand why newspapers were so expensive, and thus the only buyer usually willing to pay the price was a newspaper group.

Several groups had designs on the Opelika newspaper when Grimes put together the investors to buy it in late 1968. It was not a highly profitable operation at the time, and its gross income for 1968 was only $375,000, low for a daily even in those days.

But Grimes, who had learned something about values and negotiating during his Athens dealings, offered the owners — whose families had operated the paper since 1892 — more than three times the most recent annual gross. The attractive part for the buyers was that a substantial amount was to be paid to the seven current stockholders in the form of noncompete covenants, which would be deductible expense for the new corporation.

Finally, after one key investor dropped out, Grimes with the help of John Denson, an Opelika lawyer, persuaded three other lawyers to come up with the money for the down payment. The transaction was made with an initial investment of $260,000, with the rest due in notes or covenants.

Announcement of the sale was made in *The Opelika Daily News* on January 20, 1969, and by the wire services the following day. But Grimes' name wasn't mentioned as one of the buyers, or as the man who would be the chief executive. The reason was that he still hadn't submitted his resignation at *The Ledger-Enquirer*. But he knew he'd left himself no way to back out this time.

His meeting with Ashworth was less stormy if not any more comfortable than four years before. Grimes suggested that he work a six-weeks notice, and Ashworth agreed. In that same week, Paul Miles, who had been city editor for seven years, also resigned. Miles went to Cartersville as assistant to the publisher, and in 1976 he would become publisher of *The Calhoun Times* and *Gordon County News*.

The six-week notice period allowed Grimes to fulfill another obligation he felt strongly about, which was serving as chairman of the Georgia Press Institute that year. He and the committee had lined up a program that included syndicated columnists Sydney J. Harris, James Kilpatrick and Dick West, and two prospective gubernatorial candidates, Carl Sanders and Bo Callaway — but not Jimmy Carter who would be the 1970 winner.

On February 28, his last day at *The Enquirer*, Grimes was cleaning out his desk when Ashworth came to the door of his office. It was their first verbal communication since Grimes had resigned six weeks earlier. Ashworth glanced around the office and finally said tersely: "Will you be out of here tomorrow? I want to have this office redecorated."

As usual, it was long past nightfall when Grimes left the building. He was 38 years old, and once more he was walking away from the newspapers on which he had worked for most of the past 22 years. He had a wife and three young children, and he was exchanging the editorship of a distinguished daily with 37,000 circulation for a job on a 7,000 circulation five-day daily which was less respected in its own county that the weekly *Bulletin* in adjoining Auburn. Many journalists have made similar decisions since World War II, and many others have pondered them.

But at the time of the break there is always the fear of the unknown; the sudden free-fall of no longer having the safe, secure paycheck, no matter its size; and in the case of editors or reporters leaving large newspapers to go to smaller ones, there is the very real sense of loss of influence and an audience that has been supportive and familiar. Sometimes it takes years to build a personal audience. Grimes thought about that as he walked away.

But during his eight years as editor and associate editor, Grimes' weekly salary had ranged from $129 to $250, which he'd just reached in January, up from $225 in 1968. In those years he had regularly worked six days a week, and usually made a visit on Sunday night to check the Monday editorial page. There had been few Saturdays off; the only Christmas bonus was a ham, a turkey, or a Christmas party for your department. You had to choose one. *The Enquirer* news room solved that choice some years earlier by putting the Associated Press payment for local stories into a Christmas party fund so that the staff members could have the party and still get a ham or turkey.

What really bothered Grimes was that everyone else on the news staff made less than he did, and *The Ledger-Enquirer* was one of the largest newspapers in Georgia. Its management, in fact, was an enlightened one for those times, and the problem of low pay in the newspaper business has remained almost as serious since then as it was in the 1960s.

Grimes immediately defined the difference between being an editor and a publisher-stockholder. On his first day as publisher of *The Opelika Daily News* he gave himself a $100-a-week raise. That made it easier to go from a 37,000 circulation paper to a 7,000 one.

Charlie Black, War Correspondent

The most widely-known writer on *The Ledger-Enquirer* during the 1960s was a reporter who made considerably less money than the editor, although he did get one publicized "battlefield pay raise." His name was Charles L. (Charlie) Black, and his personal story was more fascinating than any of the stories he wrote.

Black was looking for a full time job when he happened through Columbus one Saturday afternoon in 1963. He was hired, and at age 40, he was the oldest member of *The Enquirer* news staff at that time. For awhile the editors couldn't find the right niche for the elfish, affable Black, who spent most of his life looking for a place to fit. His problem was that he set his own terms.

But by one of those fortunate turns of fate, Black had come to the right place at the right time to fulfill a mission that set him apart from thousands of other average journalists, not that he could have ever really been called average.

Black had served in the U.S. Marines during World War II and the Korean War. His first contact with Columbus came when he was a steel hanger, working on the new city auditorium in the middle 1950s. He got journalistic experience on newspapers in his native Missouri, and then as a reporter on *The Cobb County Times* during the time Leo Aikman was also on the staff. Aikman later was one of the state's most popular columnists in *The Atlanta Constitution*.

Black's first assignment on *The Enquirer* was to cover the Miss Georgia pageant, which is held in Columbus each year. As always, he did it imaginatively, finding one contestant who like himself had Indian ancestors. She didn't win but Black's interview transformed her into a distinct personality rather than just another anonymous entry. That was Charlie Black's particular talent, turning ordinary people into news personalities. But he was still looking for the right beat.

About that time Vietnam was becoming a frequent dateline on newspaper front pages, Fort Benning was filling up with soldiers again as the air assault concept was developed there and the Air Cavalry Division was being organized. Black's military background, and his adventurous nature, made him the logical person to cover the buildup at Fort Benning. *The Enquirer* didn't have a full time military reporter, but Black could turn out so much copy on any beat he chose to cover that he singlehandedly created the position.

The Enquirer and *The Ledger* were in a decisive stage of their circulation war, with *The Enquirer* still trailing *The Ledger* by about 2,000. Charlie came up with an idea that when the Air Cav division went on maneuvers in North Carolina, he'd go along to report on their activities, and he'd make an arrangement with the general to have several hundred *Enquirers* flown to the maneuvers site each morning on one of the transports that made daily trips.

So Charlie's first "foreign" assignment actually was the result of a circulation scheme. A next logical step was to send Charlie to Vietnam with the Air Cav Division when it went there, and that's how he ended up covering a much bigger story than anyone in the nation recognized in 1964, the year he made his first Vietnam trip.

No one else told the story of the American soldier in Vietnam as well as Black did. And eventually he also came to understand and interpret the U.S. role in Vietnam better than the correspondents who mainly stayed in Saigon looking for political angles. Black went into the field with the troops. Charlie bluntly said, "I'm covering this war as an American." He was a friendly observer of a mission that sorely needed a journalistic friend.

The sending of a correspondent to Vietnam for long periods was unusual for a newspaper the size of *The Enquirer*, but as the war continued other relatively small newspapers dispatched their own editors and reporters to Vietnam. *The Enquirer* was the first, however, except for the wire services and the largest newspapers.

In 1965, Black's weekly salary was only $150 a week, a fact which was embarrassingly exposed in an article about Black in *Newsweek* magazine. When the article appeared, Publisher Ashworth called managing editor Ben Walburn to inquire if that was all Black was being paid. Told that it was, Ashworth ordered that Black be sent a telegraph informing him that he was getting an immediate $20 a week raise.

The article pointed out that Black often dodged enemy bullets on his trips with the soldiers and carried a rifle of his own.

In all, Black made seven trips to Vietnam, sending back thousands of words about the soldiers, what they were doing and where they were fighting. He also wrote dozens of columns, but he emphasized strategy and personalities more than the politics. He was a military reporter in the strictest sense, and he became so informed on military strategy in Vietnam that he was invited to give briefings at the War College in Washington on several occasions. *The Ledger-Enquirer* received requests from throughout the country for Black's articles because of the information they contained about individual soldiers.

Back in Columbus he became the most sought-after speaker in the Chattahoochee Valley and Charlie was as prolific at the podium as with a typewriter, often talking for more than an hour, always without any notes, and usually without much planning. He would just start talking about Vietnam and let his thoughts take him where they would. But somehow he made sense, although some of his listeners probably learned more about Southeast Asia than they really wanted to know. Editor Grimes accompanied Black on many occasions and he never recalls hearing him make the same speech twice.

Black many times said the American soldiers who fought in Vietnam were superior to those he fought with in World War II and Korea. He thought they fought valiantly and well, and fulfilled the mission they were sent to accomplish, which was holding the North Vietnamese at bay until the South Vietnamese could defend themselves.

During this period Black was truly a celebrity, a friend of generals, as well as privates, a respected authority on strategy whose advice was sought by the Pentagon, a reporter whom other reporters in Vietnam, from larger newspapers, went to for information.

In 1968 Black was given the title of associate editor, and he settled into writing a regular column, covering military affairs and whatever else struck his fancy. This also removed him from the supervision of the managing editor, Walburn, who was never comfortable with a "star" on his staff, and who on at least one occasion wanted to fire Black for some alleged misconduct. Grimes, who thought Black was the best thing that had happened to *The Enquirer* since Mirabeau B. Lamar, stifled that move, and suggested the promotion to associate editor. Grimes, who knew he would probably be leaving soon, also wanted Black in a position where he would be considered as his successor.

When Grimes left, however, the unconventional Black was passed over even though he had many of the attributes of a good editor, including a sincere enjoyment of working with young journalists. He also was a voluminous reader whose knowledge was deep and broad on many subjects.

But Black's time in the journalistic sun was nearing an end. He made a visit to the Mideast and wrote knowledgeably of that complex, tragic area. He returned again to Vietnam, when the U.S. role in the war was winding down.

In the early 1970s, Black did some brilliant stories on crime in the Columbus area, as he searched for a "Mr. Big", who was never identified. His stories were an echo of the Phenix City exposes of 20 years earlier.

By 1974, Charlie was becoming bored with his routine. That elusive niche, which briefly he'd found in Vietnam, was missing again. He moved into a mobile home in Quitman County, some 45 miles from Columbus, and asked that his hours and salary be reduced so he could just contribute a column several days a week.

He began missing deadlines for his columns; his always rough copy became rougher. Finally he was fired outright, even as a part-timer. It was a bad period for Charlie. He had also just been divorced from his second wife.

For a time he worked as a clerk in Little Joe's Liquor Store in Columbus. At other times, he had no regular job, and a back injury handicapped him for several months. But Charlie did find some consolations in those years, despite the blows that fate continued to land on him. Most importantly of all, he found a new wife, a bright, 28-year-old journalist he had met while still on *The Enquirer* named Priscilla Hedges. They were married in 1975.

Finally, in 1978, Charlie got the kind of newspaper job he'd always wanted. He became editor of *The Valley Times-News*, a small daily in Lanett, Alabama. Black immediately filled the editorial page with his writings, and he became the teacher, friend and confidante of the young staff members.

He made this change at a time when a doctor had told him that he only had six months to live because of heart problems. Charlie didn't believe him. He had looked death in the face too many times before. So he kept looking for a doctor who had a better solution. He found one, and managed to stretch the six months into more than four years.

He might have cheated death even longer except for an automobile accident in late 1979 which left him in critical condition. He recovered but was partially crippled and never was able to resume his duties at *The Valley Times-News*.

Charlie died of a heart attack in October 1982, while working on the house where he and Priscilla lived near Phenix City.

Bob Poos, who was an Associated Press reporter in Vietnam and knew Charlie well from those days, wrote of him in a magazine article: "The wonder of it all is that Charlie Black lived long enough to die peacefully at home. How strange that his bones weren't left to whiten amid the coral of some Pacific island, or on the slope of a cold, barren Korean hill or upon a field of fire and futility in Vietnam. That, I think, is what Black would have preferred, perhaps what he sought." Poos was poetic but off the mark. He only knew one side of a many-faceted man.

Black, knowing he was living on borrowed time, had written down the plans for his own memorial service and given them to Priscilla. The service was to be held at Main Post Chapel, Fort Benning, and Charlie even listed the songs he wanted played, which included "Marine Corps Hymn", "Garry Owen," a marching song, "Shenandoah", "Born to Run", and "Onward Christian Soldiers".

Eleven of his friends and co-workers came to tell their thoughts about Charlie, and Priscilla bravely and with considerable poise introduced the service before a large crowd at the Chapel.

Ashworth, Vaughn, Grimes, Walburn, Tom Walls of *The Valley Times-News*, and Peter Arnett, the Pulitzer Prize-winning AP reporter, were among those paying tribute.

Grimes, who had been Charlie's chief editor and enthusiastic fan during his Vietnam period, said:

> What I remember best about Charlie Black is that he was always trying to make some sense out of an illogical world that

never quite accepted him.

My main association with him was during those years of his journalistic eminence, but the memories I hold most fondly are of our random meetings during the past 10 years when the sound of trumpets had faded for Charlie. He no longer stood with presidents, generals and congressmen; at times he was a clerk in a whisky store; often unemployed; then the editor of a small daily newspaper, covering zoning cases instead of dramatic military battles. And at times he was critically ill and crippled.

But what was remarkable was that I never detected a change in Charlie's spirit. The mischievous smile still came swiftly, the questions, the eager desire to explain, to teach. The spirit never wavered in the face of tribulations so fierce that surely they tested even Charlie's determined efforts to make life work.

I'm proud to have been the editor for Charlie Black, the greatest reporter of the Vietnam War, and I'm even prouder to have been the friend of Charlie Black, the cheerful philosopher who always looked for answers no matter how harsh the questions had become.

The Improbable Successor

The Ledger-Enquirer newspapers have had only two publishers since World War II. The first was Maynard R. Ashworth, an advertising salesman who married Annie Laurie Page of Columbus and soon began a rapid ascent to the newspapers' hierarchy.

Ashworth, as it happened, was an exceptional newspaperman and executive, but there can be little doubt that he benefited from the fact that Annie Laurie was the daughter of *The Ledger's* owner, Rinaldo W. Page. Marrying the boss's daughter is a proven and respected path to power in many fields, and most especially in the newspaper business, where the publishers who built the modern *New York Times* and *Washington Post* were both sons-in-law of the owners. (C. L. Sultzberger, *Times*, 1935-1961, and Phillip Graham, *Post*, 1945-1963.)

The Ledger-Enquirer and its parent company, the Page Corporation, was very much a family enterprise. W.E. Page, son of Rinaldo, was the publisher until his death in an automobile accident in 1937. Alvah Chapman Sr., husband of the oldest Page daughter, was publisher of the Bradenton, Florida *Herald*, one of the corporation's other holdings at that time. He was called to Columbus to replace Page as president of *The Ledger-Enquirer* and the Page Corporation. Ashworth, husband of the younger daughter, was given the title of publisher of *The Ledger-Enquirer*, and he and Chapman shared the management duties for the next 24 years.

Alvah Chapman Jr. was business manager for six years, but left to make a way on his own, and it was quite a way he made. Maynard Ashworth Jr. preferred a field other than newspapers and moved to San Francisco where he is in the real estate business.

For several years in the 1960s, an heir apparent seemed at hand in the person of James E. Hickey, who was married to the Ashworths' daughter, Peggy. Hickey, son of a prominent Atlanta doctor, worked his way through several departments at *The Ledger-Enquirer*, putting in time as a reporter, ad salesman, compositor and circulation supervisor. He was then named business manager and after an appropriate interval was given the title of general manager, which had been vacant for several years.

Hickey's rise at *The Ledger-Enquirer* ended abruptly in 1967 when he and Peggy were divorced. He voluntarily left the company and moved to Atlanta. Hickey has continued to be involved in the newspaper business, owning several weekly newspapers, for a time publishing the weekly *Buckhead Atlanta*, and serving briefly as business manager for The Marietta Daily Journal and the Neighbor newspapers.

Hickey's departure left no family members as potential successors to Ashworth who by then was in his 70s. His grandsons, the children of Jim and Peggy, were still teen-agers.

Edge Reid had been given the title of associate publisher, but he was in his 60s, too old to be a potential successor to Ashworth. Mike Bruni, who rose through the accounting department, had become the business manager and was considered the second-in-command on *The Ledger-Enquirer* after Hickey left.

But the reach of Bruni's authority was more apparent than real. He had the office other general managers had used — Hickey, Chapman Jr., and Louis Eidt, who came in for a few years in the 1950s — but he did not have the final word on any department's budget. He was just one among equals, along with Johnson, the executive editor, and other long time department heads.

The general manager's title had been vacant for nearly six years when Ashworth finally filled the job, putting the man he selected in line to eventually become publisher.

Ashworth's choice was a surprise in two ways. First, he stayed within the company. Secondly, he reached down past the long time loyalists such as Bruni, Johnson and Reid, and elevated Glenn Vaughn, the editor of *The Enquirer*, to be the general manager, with authority over all departments at the newspapers.

Vaughn was married to Nancy Weeks of Ellijay, who had no connection with the Page family of Columbus, which made him only the second general manager in *Ledger-Enquirer* history without a family tie, Eidt being the other.

His rise to eventually be both president and publisher (he was actually president before he was publisher) is one of the more remarkable success stories in Georgia journalism in the past 30 years.

Vaughn is a native of Newton County (Covington). He spent two years in the Marines after World War II, and then attended the University of Georgia, where he was editor of *The Red and Black*, met Nancy, his future wife, and acquired an affection for Athens and Clarke County which would have a lasting effect on his life and career.

He worked on *The DeKalb New Era* and *The Albany Herald* before finding his way to Columbus for the first time in May 1955, where he replaced Grimes on *The Ledger* copy desk when Grimes left to start a weekly newspaper in Phenix City.

Fourteen months later Vaughn and Grimes swapped jobs again, with Vaughn moving over to become editor and publisher of the Phenix City weekly, and Grimes returning to *The Ledger* copy desk.

During his brief time in Phenix City, Vaughn installed the first cold type operation on an Alabama weekly. In fact, Phenix City even had its own press, and was printed on a high-grade, thicker paper that produced a sharpness in photos and type perhaps unexcelled by any other Georgia or Alabama newspaper since then.

But a new opportunity beckoned to Vaughn. John Bloomer, managing editor of *The Ledger* for four years, had left in 1956 to become editor of a daily newspaper being started in Portsmouth, Virginia, as a competitor to the Norfolk, Virginia newspapers in the adjoining city. Bloomer called Vaughn in mid-1957 and asked him to come up and be his managing editor. So the struggling *Phenix Citizen*, always in financial straits, lost its second publisher-editor in less than a year (although it managed to keep on struggling through many others) as Vaughn again answered the challenge of a new venture.

Things didn't work out in Portsmouth for either Bloomer, Vaughn or the newspaper. Vaughn stayed just long enough to fire the city editor and then returned to Georgia where he took a job on the copy desk of *The Atlanta Journal*.

Nancy Vaughn got her first real taste of the newspaper business during their two years in the Atlanta area when she started a weekly newspaper called *The Tucker Tattler* to serve the growing community in which they lived in DeKalb County.

Suburban newspapers for specific communities were still rare in the late 1950s, but *The Tattler*, which was printed in *The Rockdale Citizen* plant at Conyers, managed to survive — later as *The DeKalb Tribune* — until the Neighbors and Suns took control of the community market in DeKalb County in the 1970s.

But Columbus seemed to have an appeal for the Vaughns, and Glenn seemed to have an appeal to the editors at the Columbus papers. He returned to *The Ledger* as news editor in 1959, and a few months later, his job-swapping buddy, Grimes, came back in a rim position. On coffee breaks at the old Lane's Drug Store on the corner of 12th and Broad, where *The Ledger-Enquirer* tower would one day stand, Vaughn and Grimes discussed their past adventures and future hopes, which were to have a profound effect on a number of Georgia and Alabama newspapers.

Vaughn moved over to the city editor slot on *The Ledger*, and then to managing editor during the extensive staff shakeup of 1961-62. He served with distinction in that post for more than three years as *The Ledger* sought to maintain its dominant position over *The Enquirer*. Then in May 1965, Vaughn made a stormy exit to embark on the great adventure of his journalistic career, the launching of a new daily newspaper in Athens (see Chapter VIII).

The exit was stormy because Ashworth was extremely angry with Vaughn, as he had been with Grimes. Like most publishers, he didn't relish the idea of competitive newspapers being started, since a success might give somebody the same idea in Columbus.

Vaughn no doubt felt he'd never return to Columbus again, but by a remarkable turn of fate, he was back on 12th Street less than four years later. Ashworth forgave him, Carlton Johnson remembered him, and for the fourth time in 14 years Grimes vacated a position into which Vaughn moved.

Vaughn's Athens venture was both a success and a failure. It succeeded to the point of forcing a buy-out by the Morris Corporation, which owned the afternoon *Banner-Herald*, and it succeeded in the broader sense because *The Athens Daily News* was one of the truly innovative offset dailies in the South during the 1960s. Perhaps its most enduring legacy is the remarkable number of journalists who got their start in the frantic, exciting competitive newspapers wars of Athens in the 1965-1968 period.

Lewis Grizzard, Jim Wooten, Chuck Perry, Collen Teasley, Mark Smith, Bob Fort and Johnny Futch were among the many who served and learned well.

But there was failure to the extent that *The Banner-Herald* finally won the war.

After *The Daily News* was sold to the Morris Corporation, Vaughn stayed on as editor, while N. S. (Buddy) Hayden became publisher of both *The Daily News* and *Banner-Herald*. The two-and-a-half-year struggle with *The Banner-Herald* had left scars too deep to fully heal, especially for Vaughn, who wept as *The Daily News* offices were uprooted and moved from their location on North Clayton to the renovated *Banner-Herald* quarters at Press Place.

Vaughn still had many friends on *The Ledger-Enquirer*, one being the circulation manager, Curtis Adams, who spotted an article written by the Athens Chamber of Commerce manager, praising Vaughn for his role in civic affairs while he was operating *The Daily News*. Adams brought the article to Ashworth's attention, and Ashworth was impressed. He liked for his editors to be good citizens.

Grimes was leaving *The Enquirer* editor's job about that time, and Johnson, now the executive editor for both *Ledger* and *Enquirer*, put in a call to Vaughn to ask if he'd be interested in coming back to Columbus as an editor. Vaughn wanted to make the move, but felt he had to get at least $270 a week, which was more than Grimes was making.

Johnson approached Ashworth about taking Vaughn back and found him receptive. So Vaughn returned to Columbus in March 1969, as editor of *The Enquirer*, and got the $270 a week.

The experience Vaughn gained in Athens on the business side, and as a recruiter and organizer of talent served him well now that he was back on a large and secure operation where he could put to use some of the ideas and managerial strengths he developed in Athens.

He brought Wade Saye in as *Enquirer* managing editor, and Bob Fort as a governmental reporter. Saye had been the first person hired on *The Daily News*, and Fort had been a reporter for both *The Daily News* and *Banner-Herald*.

Johnson continued for awhile as both executive editor of *The Ledger-Enquirer* and as editor of *The Ledger*, but eventually turned over the title and duties of *Ledger* editor to Carrol Lisby, a veteran *Ledger* staffer, who had held every executive position in the afternoon newsroom, despite being crippled by polio since 1955.

Vaughn and Johnson split on the 1970 Georgia gubernatorial primary, with Vaughn in *The Enquirer* supporting Jimmy Carter, and Johnson in *The Ledger* supporting Carl Sanders. It was one of the rare disagreements on gubernatorial candidates by the two newspapers, and indicated that Ashworth did not feel strongly for or against either of the candidates.

In 1966 Vaughn had been one of only two Georgia daily editors to endorse Carter in the first Democratic primary.

By the spring of 1973 Vaughn was becoming restless for a new challenge and he was on the verge of considering a move to the Atlanta newspapers when Ashworth called him in one day and asked him if he'd like to be general manager of *The Ledger-Enquirer*. At that time, in May 1973, Ashworth told Vaughn that he was still looking outside the organization for a publisher, and he also indicated that the Page Corporation did not plan to sell the newspapers.

The announcement of Vaughn's appointment as general manager was a bitter shock to Johnson, the executive editor, and Bruni, the business manager, both of whom out-ranked Vaughn in the hierarchy. But worse disappointments were in store for them.

Vaughn immediately began upgrading salaries for long-time employees, some of whom had not had a raise in several years. He decided they hadn't asked, and their department heads had not asked for them. He found that Ashworth did not object to most of the requests.

But 1973 was to see much greater change on the Columbus newspaper scene than appointment of a general manager. The next big wave of that epochal year was the announcement of the first competing newspaper for *The Ledger-Enquirer* since the 1930s.

The Short, Unhappy Life of *Thursday*

In July, an ambitious new weekly newspaper named *Thursday* was announced for Columbus. The driving force behind *Thursday* was John Amos, a wealthy insurance man, who in just 12 years had built his American Family Life Assurance Company into the largest cancer insurance provider in the world.

The symbol of Amos' success was a 22-story building on Wynnton Road, the tallest building in Columbus, which loomed even taller because of its location on one of the highest points in the area.

Amos, who was also active in politics, had once been close to the Columbus newspapers, especially in their support of city-county consolidation. But he had lately come to feel that the newspapers were unfair to his business and to his political activities.

For his venture into newspapers, Amos had enlisted the aid of a well-known midwestern publisher, John McGoff, who was announced as chairman of the company which would publish *Thursday*. To gain more credibility, Amos raided *The Ledger-Enquirer* staff and hired the advertising manager, James Whaley, two assistant ad managers, Jim Register and Richard Heath, and the *Enquirer* city editor, Ron Feinberg. He also brought in former *Ledger-Enquirer* circulation manager Curtis Adams, who had been working on the Chattanooga papers.

For editor-publisher he selected J. Edward Wilson, a well-known radio personality in Columbus, noted for his hard-hitting broadcast editorials. *The Ledger-Enquirer*'s best photographer, Ken Hawkins, also switched to *Thursday*.

Ashworth, Vaughn and other *L E* officials were worried, of course, but they might have been even more concerned if their minds hadn't been on a development of even greater impact for their company and jobs.

The Page Corporation had decided to sell the newspapers. A gala country club dinner had been planned for the announcement, and by an odd coincidence, the dinner was scheduled on Thursday, September 20, 1973, which was the day that the first issue of Amos' weekly, *Thursday*, was to come out.

Thursday's first issue had 48 broad-sheet pages, and its banner headline proclaimed: "Thursday New Day for City; Long-Standing Newspaper Monopoly Broken by Competitive Publication."

Editor Wilson wrote: "I have never heard of a city where the public attitude is as favorable to the publication of a new newspaper as it is in this city right now."

Amos, listed as secretary-treasurer of the publishing company said, "It's time for some competition here in the newspaper business. An alternative voice is needed. The people have indicated they are tired of one-sided, managed news reporting."

Never had a new newspaper been launched in Georgia with such impressive financial backing, modern equipment and experienced personnel. The ill-fated *Atlanta Times* of nine years earlier did not have either the leadership or the equipment with which *Thursday* started.

Thursday was printed on a five-unit King offset press; composed on the best cold type equipment available at that time; it had 300 tons of newsprint in its spacious warehouse when publication started, with commitment for more, and this was at a time when long-established newspapers were strapped for newsprint and paying black market prices for a few extra pounds.

The corporate structure included McGoff, then a prominent and affluent publisher; Mark McKee, a Connecticut publisher; and Amos, already well on his way to becoming one of the highest-paid executives in the nation as well as the major stockholder of a dynamic insurance company. Four former *Ledger-Enquirer* department heads were on *Thursday's* management team.

The first edition's press run was 45,000. The front page was full of color, and resembled Gannett's *USA Today* of nine years later. The content was strong and varied. There was a page of letters from local officials and other citizens, most of them criticizing *The Ledger-Enquirer*. A typical example: "I am very happy over the idea of Columbus having another newspaper . . . hope it will give Columbus readers the kind of news they need . . . I am tired of seeing news about sports in New York and Chicago and not a mention about our youngsters and their activities . . . There is no doubt that your newspaper will be a tremendous success. It is needed . . . I salute *THURSDAY* for bringing to Columbus a factual, objective medium that will without prejudice or bias fully inform the populace of the news of the community . . . (This was written before the first issue had even been printed) . . . There is a crying need in this community for objective reporting, without slanted phraseology designed to control the thinking and opinions of our citizens. Our citizens have a right to know all the facts, not just a few as has been the case in years past."

Then, as if to make prospects even better for *Thursday* as a local-oriented, local-owned newspaper came the announcement a few hours after its first issue was on the streets that *The Ledger-Enquirer* had been sold to Knight Newspapers, one of the largest newspaper chains in the country.

Knight's president at the time was Alvah Chapman Jr., whose connections with the Page Corporation, Columbus and the newspapers were lifelong and strong. It seemed logical that if *The Ledger-Enquirer* were to be sold to a chain or group, that Knight would be the choice. Knight had bought the Macon newspapers in 1969 and thus had a nearby connection.

Thursday's staff and investors were jubilant about the surprise turn of events. The second issue emphasized with words and cartoon the fact that *The Ledger-Enquirer* was now "foreign-owned", and even hinted that the pending advent of *Thursday* influenced the former owners to sell.

But the joy at *Thursday* lasted for only a few weeks as it quickly dawned on both the staff and the backers that the struggle for survival would be long and hard, not a short, dramatic leap to a position of acceptance and financial stability.

The fact was that *Thursday* peaked on its first publication day. It went swiftly downhill from there. Despite the formidable array of talent, financial support, equipment, and the so-called surveys which showed the need for another newspaper, *Thursday's* creators fell into a trap familiar to anyone who has been in the newspaper field for long — that there is a thin but usually vocal crust of people in any community who have personal grievances against the existing newspapers. Some grievances are as deep as a major political difference or a story which put the offended party in a bad light; some as minor as an unreported tea party or little league game. In addition there are a great many other people who when asked their opinion consider it fashionable to criticize the newspaper, just as they criticize the government or the hospital or the utility companies or the post office.

But when it comes to putting money on the line, even the thin crust with real grievances gets much thinner, and decides to "wait and see".

The money disappears fast in a new newspaper operation, even for those who have lots of it. *Thursday* started on a grand scale and its fall was all the more rapid because of that.

By November Wilson, the editor and publisher, was gone. Adams was named general manager, and was nominally in charge. McGoff and McKee's names disappeared from the masthead during this time and Amos was now listed as the publisher.

By December *Thursday* had changed to a tabloid format, and on January 3, 1974, in its 16th issue, Amos announced in a Publisher's Statement that "with this issue, *Thursday* comes to an end." Amos mainly blamed the economic downturn for *Thursday*'s failure.

"Between the time our plant was ordered and the first publication, Watergate tore our nation asunder," Amos wrote, "followed by the war in the Middle East, the oil boycott, and subsequent oil shortage." He also mentioned the spiraling cost and scarcity of newsprint, which in fact was a critical problem for all newspapers in the winter of 1973-74. Ironically, the large supplies which *Thursday* had managed to accumulate helped some nearby publishers get by when Amos sold it off.

The equipment and plant which had been assembled for *Thursday* continued to do commercial job printing for several years, and partially recovered some of the funds poured into the brief but flamboyant experiment that was *Thursday*.

Amos later expanded into television stations, where his luck was much better, and his American Family Life Company kept growing. His personal salary in 1983 was reported to be more than $1 million annually, one of the highest — if not the highest — in Georgia.

Years later, he said of the *Thursday* experience, "I should have been doing something else that day."

The Knight-Ridder Era

The Ledger-Enquirer was certainly not indifferent to the threat posed by *Thursday*, especially since several of its key department heads and long-time employees defected to the fledgling challenger. But the management was understandably distracted at the time by internal changes and challenges during 1973, which was an unprecedented year of transition for the company.

Vaughn, who had been merely the editor of the morning newspaper as recently as May, under several layers of authority in a family-oriented property, found himself in charge of the entire newspaper operation as general manager, answerable only to Ashworth, who was now almost 80 years old and ready to relinquish some of the daily supervision.

Then in September, with the sale of *The Ledger-Enquirer* to Knight Newspapers, Vaughn was suddenly in another situation altogether. He was still general manager, and with Ashworth moving aside, he had no one to answer to on the Columbus scene. But in place of Ashworth, Vaughn had the managerial hierarchy of Knight Newspapers to answer to. These managers included Don Carter, his onetime boss at the Atlanta newspapers, who was now executive editor of the Macon newspapers, and a Knight news group leader for the southeast. Others included Derick Daniels, who later went on to become a top official in the *Playboy* publishing empire, and John McMullan, who was to gain fame as executive editor of *The Miami Herald*.

But that was expected and accepted by Vaughn, who recognized that Knight's guidance and procedures were among the best in the newspaper business. In addition Knight offered incentives to executives that were far more lucrative than the previous ownership had provided.

The more difficult adjustment for Vaughn was that under Knight ownership he lost authority over the news operation of the two newspapers. At that time Knight was using a divided-management concept on most of its newspapers which eliminated the position of publisher. A general manager presided over the business operation of the newspapers, and an executive editor was over the news operation. The executive editor was not answerable to the general manager, only to his group leader in Miami, where Knight is headquartered.

The immediate result of this change was to return Carlton Johnson, the executive editor, to full authority over the two newsrooms and the editorial policy, while Vaughn concentrated on the business departments, which included advertising, circulation and production.

Several other far-reaching changes were also taking place. The newspapers were already in the process of converting completely to cold type before the sale. For metropolitan newspapers, the conversion was much harder and more complicated than for smaller dailies and weeklies.

By 1973, of course, many of the bugs which Vaughn had encountered on *The Phenix Citizen* 17 years earlier, had been ironed out of cold type. Most importantly, there were photocomposition machines which provided a clearer type than was available for many years, making the change easier on the reader's eye.

Most newspaper readers subconsciously know whether type or makeup is appealing and pleasing to the eye, although they seldom comment or complain about poor typography. What readers mainly don't like is abrupt changes, and in the latter part of 1973 and the early part of 1974 they detected too many changes in *The Ledger* and *Enquirer*.

First, Ashworth was gone from the management scene after nearly 40 years, and whatever his faults, there was no question that he was a presence on the newspapers and in the community who provided a clear and certain identity, especially to the most vocal group of readers and advertisers.

Secondly, the addition of the Knight News Service wire was like a new toy for the editors, who previously had only AP and UPI. They tended to run more Knight News Service stories than was wise during an adjustment period for readers, raising the complaint, largely unjustified, that the newspapers were no longer carrying as much local and area news.

But the worst hurdle during this period was the changing of the body type from Linotype's tried and true familiar letters to a cold type face which was unfamiliar and not as easy to read.

Vaughn had stayed out of the body type selection since body type is mainly used for news stories. The editors did the selecting and their choice created an uproar among many readers, who probably were looking for a reason to complain.

It was a problem easily corrected, and within a few weeks, a new type face was substituted, which was closer to the old hot type text face, and which gained broad acceptance.

The fact is, of course, that there is a difference in hot and cold body type, although the difference is less noticeable in some faces and from some machines. Justification and hyphenation are a real problem for the automatic computers, as compared with linotype machines, and when words are hyphenated in the wrong place, or there is excessive spacing between letters or words, the readers notice.

Whether because of the type fiasco or other reasons, Knight's hierarchy decided there was one major change it wanted to make in *The Ledger-Enquirer* management team. It wanted a different executive editor. The post was first offered to Vaughn, with the explanation that he would become a vice-president and could return to the phase of newspapers with which he was most familiar. But Vaughn felt that would be a step backward, and he also wanted to prove that he could handle the business side, so he declined, and the Knight managers accepted his decision.

They then turned to a journalist who already had a distinguished career on Georgia newspapers, and who had given up a promising editorial future with *The Marietta Journal* and Neighbor Newspapers because he'd always wanted to work for the Knight newspapers.

His name was J. Carrol Dadisman and in the spring of 1974 he was managing editor of *The Macon News*, the afternoon paper in Macon, and definitely the weaker of the Macon papers. A native of Jefferson, Georgia, Dadisman was a 1956 graduate of the University of Georgia, where he had been editor of *The Red and Black*, and had become friends with another editor of that era, Billy Morris of the Augusta newspaper Morrises. Dadisman started his career in Augusta and spent 10 years as a reporter, editorialist and managing editor on *The Augusta Chronicle*. He was then editor of *The Marietta Daily Journal* from 1966 to 1972, during the period when Publisher Otis Brumby was starting his chain of Neighbor newspapers in the Atlanta suburbs.

But Dadisman was a long-time admirer of the newspapers which the Knight group published. One of his duties as an editorial assistant in Augusta in the early 1960s was to look through the exchange papers and select editorials worthy of reprinting. He noticed that the newspaper he found most readable was Knight's Charlotte, North Carolina, *Observer*.

In 1971 Dadisman was among a group of editors invited to a function at the governor's mansion by then-Governor Jimmy Carter. Another guest was the governor's first cousin, Don Carter, who had just returned to Georgia to be executive editor of the Macon newspapers. Dadisman mentioned to Carter his admiration of Knight operations and Carter (Don, that is) remembered. A year later he asked Dadisman to come to Macon as managing editor of *The News* and Dadisman accepted. In 1974, Carter, who was now the liaison for news operations of several Knight newspapers, including Columbus, felt it was time to give Dadisman a chance to move up.

Dadisman recalls that he was summoned from Macon to the Miami headquarters and offered the job as executive editor of *The Ledger-Enquirer*. There were some obstacles to be cleared, however, since Johnson, whom he would replace, was going to be asked to become editor of *The Ledger* again, and Carroll Lisby, who had that job, would be asked to move over to become editor of *The Enquirer*. Wade Saye, who was editor of *The Enquirer*, was to be offered a position on another newspaper.

Dadisman and Carter went to Columbus the next day and Carter told Johnson and Lisby of Dadisman's appointment and of their new roles in the structure. The four of them — Carter, Dadisman, Johnson and Lisby — then went to dinner together at Columbus' century-old Goetchius House, for what must have been one of the more uncomfortable social gatherings in its history. "I remember a sense of relief when the dinner was over," Dadisman recalls, "although both Carlton and Carroll were very cordial and pledged their cooperation to improve the Columbus newspapers."

At a luncheon the next day, the announcement was made of Dadisman's appointment and he and Vaughn were also named vice-presidents of *The Ledger-Enquirer* company. Vaughn had learned of the changes in the news department only that morning. He had not been consulted about them.

The changes were effective immediately, so Dadisman arranged to move into a room at the old Ralston Hotel and went right to work. "We made a lot of changes over the next few years," Dadisman recalls, "too many too fast for some readers and community leaders, too few too slowly for some on the staff. I tried to steer a middle course, moving at a pace that produced progress without too jarring an effect on organization or the community. We had two good newspapers with solid reputations, but we had a lot of opportunities to improve them in both personnel and content."

The editorial policies of the two papers were mainly left to the editors although Dadisman sat in on editorial conferences and read most of the editorials before publication. He encouraged the editors to go their separate ways on editorial positions if they were so inclined.

Both *The Ledger* and *Enquirer* called for Richard Nixon's resignation as president several months before he resigned, and in 1976 they both supported Jimmy Carter for president, perhaps more enthusiastically than any of his home state's larger newspapers with the possible exception of *The Atlanta Constitution*, which now had a Carter supporter, Hal Gulliver, as editor in place of Reg Murphy, Carter's old antagonist.

The editorials were marginally more liberal than under the Ashworth regime, but actually he had allowed his editors wide latitude even to the point of endorsing different candidates for governor on at least two occasions. Politically, the Columbus papers had usually been more liberal than Augusta and Savannah, more conservative than Atlanta and Macon.

Several major content and packaging changes were made during Dadisman's first year as executive editor. The combined Saturday paper was renamed *The Weekender*, and special entertainment and gardening sections were added. *The Ledger-Enquirer's* Sunday magazine was renamed *Chattahoochee* and among other things a "Dining Out" column was added, which was a critique of area restaurants. Although this was to become a popular and widespread feature in many newspapers and magazines in the late 1970s it was a relatively new idea when Columbus initiated it in 1976 and it quickly became one of the most talked-about items in the Sunday edition. It was written first by Beverly Grier, whose distinct and personal approach made her perhaps the best-known writer on the Columbus papers for a brief period. Mildred Dadisman, Carrol's wife, wrote the feature in its last year 1979-80.

A local feature columnist was added to the second front page of *The Ledger* in 1975. Jack Swift, who had been a reporter and city editor on *The Enquirer*, was selected for the task by Dadisman, and he proved to be an immediate success, with a light and pugnacious style that soon made him the most visible newspaperman in Columbus since Charlie Black's Vietnam days.

Richard Hyatt, a former *Enquirer* sports editor, soon evolved a similar column in *The Enquirer*, from his position as associate editor. Hyatt was an early reporter of the 1975-76 Carter campaign for president, traveling to New Hampshire with the Peanut brigades, and following the president-to-be on many campaign tours. For Hyatt, the coverage led to a book on the Carter family called *The Carters of Plains*. For *The Enquirer*, the coverage payoff came on the morning after the general election when Carter returned to Plains in triumph and held up the front page of *The Enquirer* for photographers to display its large headline, "Carter Wins".

Bureaus were established in Atlanta, Montgomery and the Opelika-

Auburn area, and a Washington bureau was shared with the Macon newspapers.

Ironically, by the end of Dadisman's six years in Columbus many of the innovations had been abandoned for one reason or another. *The Weekender* format was changed back to simply a Saturday edition; the magazine folded in 1980; and the bureaus were dropped during an economy move in the late 1970s. A Sunday TV book did take root and became a financial as well as informative success.

The changes that were most influential came about in personnel. When Johnson died in August 1977, Mary Margaret Byrne became *The Ledger* editorial page editor, the first woman in an editorial policy position for *The Ledger-Enquirer*. A Columbus native, Ms. Byrne had worked for the newspapers for 27 years, mainly in the position of woman's editor and columnist.

Baxter Omahundro was brought in as *Ledger* managing editor shortly after Dadisman arrived, and in 1976 William (Bill) Brown came from Tallahassee to be managing editor of *The Enquirer.*

Time of Terror: The Stocking Strangler

The news staffs which had evolved on *The Ledger* and *Enquirer* in the mid-1970s soon found themselves challenged by a story that was as big in its decade as Phenix City had been in the 1950s. In some respects it was a story that attracted even more national interest, and its impact on Columbus was more intense.

In mid-September 1977, Ferne Jackson, director of education for the Columbus Health Department, was found in her home strangled to death with a stocking. Mrs. Jackson, 60, was a widow who lived alone in the fashionable Wynnton section of Columbus. The condition of her house indicated that a violent struggle had taken place. She had been both beaten and raped. Her car was found several blocks away where the killer had apparently driven and then abandoned it.

The city was shocked, both by the brutality of the murder and the loss of a valuable citizen. It was a murder unlike any other in the memory of most Columbus residents. Indeed, no one could recall a murder in the Wynnton residential section. Certainly no one could imagine the nightmare of unprecedented dimensions which was just beginning.

There were assurances from the authorities that the investigation was proceeding well and that an arrest was anticipated soon. Then, just 10 days later, in the same Wynnton section, another woman who lived alone was found strangled — again by a stocking. She was Miss Jean Dimenstein, retired co-owner of a local department store. The murders were almost identical. She had also been beaten and raped, her car had been taken and found a few blocks away in the Carver Heights area. Both Miss Dimenstein and Mrs. Jackson had been wearing diamond rings which the killer did not take. Robbery was obviously not the motive — only murder.

Fear now joined horror and shock. Gun sales began to climb. Special locks and bolts were installed at many homes, especially in the Wynnton area. "The Stocking Strangler" became a familiar term in news stories.

But in those early autumn days of 1977 the full scope of the terror to come was still beyond comprehension. Several weeks passed. Then on Friday, October 21, about 11 a.m., a third victim was found. Mrs. Florence Scheible was just one day short of her 90th birthday, and was partially blind. But she lived alone, in a Wynnton apartment complex. The murder apparently had occurred in the daytime. She had been strangled with a stocking.

Only four days passed before the Strangler struck again. Mrs. Miriam Thurmond, a retired school teacher, was found in her home a few blocks from the other murder sites — strangled with a stocking. On the weekend before, her son, who lived in Atlanta, had visited and was quoted as saying that he nailed down the windows and installed dead-bolt locks. The killer dismantled one of the dead-bolts to gain entry.

Thus within 40 days four elderly women, all who lived alone, had been murdered by strangulation with a stocking. Their homes were within 1.5 miles of each other. A madman was obviously loose, and despite a massive police investigation, aided by the Georgia Bureau of Investigation, there were few real clues.

The newspaper editors and staffs were also in a dilemma. They didn't want to add to the hysteria which already gripped the city, or appear to be exploiting what was becoming a series of numbing tragedies, acted out in agonizing repetition. So on perhaps the most dramatic story in the city's history, *The Ledger* and *Enquirer* provided what amounted to undramatic coverage.

The Strangler Murder cases never attracted the national attention they warranted, which was just as well, but in many respects the Columbus stranglings were unique among the country's mass murder cases during this century.

First, they took place in a relatively small section of a relatively small city. Columbus had about 170,000 people at the time; the Wynnton section, in which all but one of the murders occurred, covers less than two square miles.

Second, the victims were well-known persons in the city. They were mothers, friends, teachers, social and business leaders, familiar faces who suddenly became murder victims, not faceless names in a large metropolitan area, little-known outside their families and immediate circle.

Third and most unique, the seven murders and one attack generally attributed to the Stocking Strangler all took place inside the victim's home, where Americans expect to have the highest sense of security. The most terrible fear spawned by the Strangler was his ability to pierce even the strongest locks and barriers, and to find his victims in their sanctuaries, not on a lonely dark street or parking lot, or in a bar or through some subterfuge by which they were lured into his trap.

That was what set the Columbus murders apart from other such multiple murders as the Atlanta child slayings of a few years later, or the Los Angeles freeway slayings of about the same period.

And, of course, the terror was concentrated in the most vulnerable of society's members, elderly women living alone, often by necessity, usually fearful already of the creaks in the night, the falling limbs, and now suddenly finding themselves on the murder list of a maniac who seemed to have no logic or motive.

The search for meaningful clues was frustrating. After the Jackson murder, the Strangler had apparently taken a bath to clean away the blood before leaving the house. He always wore gloves. There were no fingerprints. His pattern was gruesomely evident but nothing else provided a glimpse of the elusive killer. Nor could police find a connecting link among the victims which might indicate why the killer had chosen them.

On Halloween night, 1977, there was no trick or treating in Columbus. The murders had produced a fortress city.

As the weeks went by during the Thanksgiving and Christmas seasons, the Strangler was not heard from. Although the police reported no progress on the investigation, people began to relax a bit. Then, three days after Christmas another victim was found, this one the most prominent and well-known of them all, Mrs. Kathleen Woodruff, widow of George (Kid) Woodruff, a Columbus industrialist who had served as the University of Georgia's head football coach during the 1920s.

Mrs. Woodruff, 74, lived alone, and within a mile of the homes of the other victims. She was found in her bedroom with a scarf, rather than a stocking, around her neck. She had been strangled and beaten, but not as brutally as the others, according to police and the coroner's report. Although the most familiar trademark of terror was missing — a stocking — police concluded that Mrs. Woodruff had been murdered by the same person who murdered the four earlier strangulation victims.

After the two-month respite, this fifth murder set off a new wave of frustration and fear. The news media were beginning to meet more resistance and hostility from the police and other officials, who believed their conversations would be sensationalized and that evidence would be revealed which would hamper the investigation. Throughout the period of the strangling cases, very little information was revealed about clues, the murder scene or the condition of the victims.

The main result was a barrage of rumors, ranging from the absurd to the logical, but all without any real foundation of facts. Since the people, desperate for some hint of hope or solace in the cases, were getting little from official sources, they made up their own.

Actually the Columbus news media acted with a restraint and responsibility unusual for these years when competition between newspapers and TV, and among newspapers themselves, often leads to over-zealous pursuit of news angles.

Adding to the burden for the news media was a resurgence of racial animosity, always just below the surface in most southern cities. Columbus had been a virtual oasis of racial cooperation during the turbulent 1960s. There had been a brief eruption in 1971, followed by intensified efforts of both white and black leaders to restore a consensus.

But the fear and suspicion roused by the Stocking Strangler was sorely testing the city's racial harmony. Most of the rumors assumed that the Strangler was a black man, although the police never said for certain. A coroner's report revealed that pubic hairs found at one murder scene had "negroid characteristics".

Two of the stolen cars were found in or on the edge of black neighborhoods. This led to an announcement by the head of the Columbus Ku Klux Klan that Klansmen were going to start patrolling the streets in Wynnton. Since the Klan barely existed in Columbus that was an announcement that probably got more attention than it deserved but it did increase the tension. The police chief strongly discouraged the Klan's patrols, and after a few days no more was heard about them.

Again there was a pause in the slayings, but the strangest night of all in the Strangler's reign of terror was coming in the early hours of Saturday,

February 11, 1978. It was also the night when the police came within seconds of apprehending their elusive prey.

On that night the killer made two attacks; one of them resulted in his only known survivor.

Police were patrolling the Wynnton section heavily during this period and at 5:44 a.m. a call was received to go to the home of Mrs. Ruth Schwob, which was in the very heart of the area where the Strangler operated. The call had come from a neighbor of Mrs. Schwob, and apparently followed this sequence of events:

Mrs. Schwob, 74, a widow who lived alone, had awakened about 5:30 and found a man on top of her choking her with a pair of pantyhose. According to police reports she fought back at her assailant and managed to reach an alarm button at her bedside which alerted a neighbor to check on her. The neighbor was awakened by the alarm and dialed Mrs. Schwob's number, letting it ring 10 times before then calling the police.

According to a statement made later by Ronnie Jones, head of the special police unit assigned to the Strangler cases, two police officers — one male, one female — arrived at the Schwob house "within 15 to 20 seconds, and I wouldn't put it a second beyond that . . . When they got to the house they knew beforehand that the Strangler was supposed to be inside at that very moment killing the woman. So they went straight on into the house to save the woman's life. The officers went in through the front door allowing the attacker to escape — only by seconds — out the back of the house."

In an interview with T.W. Moody Jr., of Fort Valley, who researched the Strangler case for a book — which was printed but never released for sale — Jones said he believed the Strangler went straight from Mrs. Schwob's house, hiding in the hedges and shrubbery in the area, about two blocks to the home of Mrs. Mildred D. Borom on Forest Drive, entered that house and killed Mrs. Borom about 6 a.m.

Because the area was now swarming with police officers checking the Schwob attack, Jones speculated that the Strangler hid in Mrs. Borom's home for several hours and then left when things quieted down.

Mrs. Borom's body was discovered on Saturday afternoon. She had been strangled with a piece of curtain cord. Like Mrs. Schwob and Mrs. Woodruff, she was the widow of a prominent Columbus businessman, in her 70s, and well-known in the community.

The double attack brought the largest headlines of the period in the Sunday *Ledger-Enquirer* of February 12. Because there was now a surviving victim who had actually been in contact with the Strangler, hopes were raised that there would be some definite clue to aid the investigation.

But instead there was only deepened frustration. *The Ledger-Enquirer* quoted Mrs. Schwob as saying she could not give a description of her attacker because he had on a mask. A police spokesman said that she could not see him because the room was so dark. In any event no substantial clues were reported from the Schwob case that helped police in their continuing search for the killer.

There was much frustration that the police had come so close to catching him at the scene of an attack. Questions were asked as to how the killer managed to elude the cordon of officers that descended on the area, and commit another murder only two blocks away within the same hour.

Jones, in his interview with Moody, defended the action of the two officers at the Schwob house, pointing out that their first responsibility was to save the woman's life. Usual police procedure, he admitted, would have been for one officer to cover the back of the house while one went in the front. "They chose to save the woman's life," he said.

Even for a population now numbed to the tragedy of the stranglings, the events of February 11 intensified the terror and suspicion. The Strangler seemed to lead a charmed life, almost like one of the supernatural beings who inhabited the horror movies then currently in vogue.

The apprehensive days turned into weeks, then months. Spring came. There were no new clues, but no more murders. Then on April 20, the body of Mrs. Janet Cofer, 61, a teacher and a widow who lived in the Steam Mills Heights area, was found in her home. She had been strangled with a stocking and sexually assaulted. Her home was several miles east of the Wynnton area but the pattern of the murder convinced the police that she was another victim of the Stocking Strangler.

Because he had now struck in another section, the fear widened in Columbus. The pressure on the police to make an arrest grew fiercer. Many people seemed to feel an arrest would at least ease the fears. But the police had no one to arrest. They had questioned hundreds of potential suspects and come up empty.

Then, as abruptly as the stranglings began, they ceased. Seven murders in seven months were attributed to the Columbus Stocking Strangler. But six years after Mrs. Cofer's death, there have been no similar slayings in Columbus. From whatever evil pit the Strangler had emerged, he suddenly seemed to return. But in Columbus, the fear, suspicion and siege mentality were slow to subside.

Nearly seven years after the first strangling the cases were still open on the Columbus Police Department's books and there had been no arrests, no real suspects, no new clues since the last strangling in April 1978. Nor is there any explanation for the brief but unprecedented rampage by a killer who struck only at elderly women living alone, in a limited geographic area, and who strangled them all, usually with stockings.

He never entered homes with dogs, nor ever attracted barking dogs on his nocturnal wanderings through the neighborhoods. He always attacked women only when they were alone, although some of them had relatives — and sometimes even policemen — who stayed in their homes on other nights. Footprints were found in some yards, usually of a tennis shoe, but no fingerprints were ever reported.

If he was a black man, as the meager evidence indicated, he managed to move about in a largely-white neighborhood without attracting notice, even in a time when any stranger was instantly under suspicion. There is no evidence that he ever invaded a home when the occupant was not alone, or was not a white woman 60 or older. He knew where his victims lived, and seemed to know something of their habits, but there was no indication that he actually knew them personally, nor any clue as to why he selected them.

Curtis McClung, who was the Columbus police chief during the strangling period, was also interviewed by T. W. Moody in connection with research for his proposed book. McClung, who retired soon afterwards, told Moody: "I don't believe anything could have been done that wasn't done in the investigations of these crimes, and in that regard I have no apology. My deepest regret is that we were not able to solve the crimes, but we did accomplish the second best objective, which was stopping the crimes. Going back to the behavioral scientists, they suggested that the person would continue with this type of crime unless he died or was incarcerated. So, playing the odds, chances are this person is either dead or is incarcerated. We pursued every avenue that was open to us to verify either possibility, but were unable to come up with anything we felt was significant."

So there the cases rest. No similar series of murders have been reported in the nation before or since. The mystery remains, a haunting reminder that life provides many questions that have no answers. Slowly the fear subsided, but for many Columbusites it would never fade completely. They could never again be as easy about what the shadows hide.

Editor's note: On May 4, 1984, Carlton Gary, a 33-year-old black man, was arrested in Albany, Ga. and charged with three of the Columbus

stranglings. He was indicted the following day in all three cases, which involved the rape and killing of Mrs. Scheible, Mrs. Thurmond and Mrs. Woodruff.

Gary, who lived in Columbus as a child and young man, had a long record of arrests and burglary charges, dating back to 1967. He was charged with the armed robbery of five restaurants in Greenville, S.C. in late 1978, pleaded guilty in 1979, and had served most of the past five years in a prison in Columbia, S.C.

Gary escaped from the prison in March, 1984, and apparently returned to the Columbus area. Columbus police say he also was in Columbus during the period of the stranglings after escaping earlier in 1977 from a prison in Jamesville, N.Y. where he was serving time for armed robbery and prison escape.

He was scheduled to stand trial in the strangling cases sometime in 1985. Police have not revealed the main evidence against him, except to say that he was traced through a gun stolen from a home in the Wynnton area in October 1977.

Columbus police arrested Gary in April 1984 on two misdemeanor charges but released him on bond because he gave an alias which they did not identify with his long record of violations. Later, through fingerprints, they realized who he was and traced him to the Albany motel.

The Challenge of the 1980s

In March, 1980, Dadisman was offered the post of general manager on *The Tallahassee, Florida Democrat*. A lifelong Georgian, Dadisman, who at the time was serving as president of the advisory board of the School of Journalism at the University of Georgia, was reluctant to leave his home state, even to so close a site as Tallahassee. In addition, the general manager's post was equivalent to the one he held in Columbus, and would move him out of the news-editorial side where he had spent all of his career. But he realized that it was probably an essential step to eventually being a publisher, so he accepted the offer and left Columbus in May 1980.

Just 16 months after Dadisman became general manager of *The Democrat*, W. H. Harwell, the publisher, was promoted to Knight-Ridder's headquarters in Miami, and Dadisman was named president and publisher.

In Columbus, Dadisman's move to Tallahassee cleared the way for the naming of Vaughn as publisher of *The Ledger-Enquirer*, with full authority over both the news and editorial departments. Bill Brown, managing editor of *The Enquirer*, succeeded Dadisman as executive editor, and Roger Ann Jones came from Macon to be the first female managing editor on *The Ledger-Enquirer*.

Vaughn had been named president of *The Ledger-Enquirer* in 1977 but the title and authority of publisher, which he had briefly wielded in 1973, had eluded him until Dadisman's departure.

Vaughn had little chance to savor his new position and the opportunities it offered because in May 1980, he was in the midst of the most serious financial crisis he'd faced since moving over to the business side. It had begun innocently enough when Vaughn was chairman of a Knight-Ridder study committee looking into the feasibility of using full time employees to deliver the newspapers each day in place of the independent "little merchant" system most newspapers had favored for years.

Vaughn's committee came up with a strong recommendation for changing to employee-carriers. It made so much sense to Vaughn, in fact, that he told Knight-Ridder he'd be willing to give the idea a trial run in Columbus.

This was a major change for two newspapers with a combined circulation of more than 60,000, and it entailed several crucial transitions. First, there would be the switch from independent carriers to company-employed carriers. Secondly, there would be a switch from hand-billing to computer-billing, with all bills sent out from the main office and all payments received there. Thirdly, there would be the perception of change for the customer from dealing with the neighbor kid down the street to dealing with a large corporation.

Obviously there were advantages to be gained, a major one being that the company would realize more of the financial benefit from any future additions to circulation.

The changeover began in the early spring of 1980. A pilot program had been rehearsed, and the modest goal was to convert only the routes in the immediate city zone, leaving routes outside the city zone with independent carriers.

A number of carriers with cars were offered jobs with the company, although most younger carriers, who used motorbikes or bicycles, were replaced after adequate notice. There was a rippling effect, however, when the first notices of the change got out, and carriers expecting to lose their routes began abandoning them faster than the company could adequately keep up with filling them. Some former carriers were critical of the system to their customers, adding to the discontent generated by the slower, less certain service which was inevitable in the early weeks of the experiment.

The worst hurdle, however, turned out to be the computer billing system. As anyone who has ever thrown newspapers (and that's a good percentage of the American population) will tell you, people are very cantankerous about their newspaper bill, and in Columbus during 1980 most of the bills were going out wrong.

In the changeover to the computer, names were often not listed specifically enough. The computers had to learn to make "stops" and "starts", and it wasn't an easy task. One subscriber called to complain that he had stopped getting his paper even though he was paid up. A few days later he called to say that now he was receiving three copies of the paper each day. Those kind of snafus were commonplace.

The company also found that several thousand subscribers being billed to the carriers and thus listed as paid actually weren't paying the carriers. Those subscribers were dropped under the new system, which reduced circulation and net income since part of their subscription price had been paid by the former carriers.

But there were also some very real declines as the new arrangement spread through the city-zone circulation area. Poor service, computer foul-ups of bills, new carriers — all contributed to the problem, and to make matters worse, Columbus was feeling the effects of an economic slump and the huge jump in fuel costs of that period.

At the low point in 1980, the combined circulation of *The Enquirer* and *Ledger* dropped below 50,000 for the first time in 30 years, and the total loss since the beginning of the changeover was 20 percent of the paid circulation. *The Ledger* had borne the brunt of the loss because more of its subscribers were located in the areas where the change was made, while most *Enquirers* were in the unaffected zones beyond the city. The financial loss was also substantial, estimated at nearly $500,000 counting higher costs and reduced revenue.

But finally the figures began to turn. The bottom was reached in the fall of 1980. The computers began turning out the proper bills, and the new employee-carriers became more comfortable with their tasks, and the customers with them. Soon service was actually better than under the previous system. As expected, the company began realizing more income from circulation per subscriber, and circulation began to climb.

By the end of 1983, the combined circulation stood at 60,560 (34,060, *Enquirer*, and 26,500, *Ledger*), above the 1979 figure, and still rising. Sunday circulation was close to 70,000, highest since the Vietnam period.

Vaughn had survived a stern test and *The Ledger-Enquirer* experience had shown that employee-carriers were feasible. Many of its problems were avoided in similar changeovers on other Knight-Ridder papers. At a meeting of Knight-Ridder executives in 1981, Vaughn was presented the ''Golden Guinea Pig'' award in recognition of his trials and tribulations.

View From the Tower

The six-story tower, which Ashworth added to the building in 1971, still had three vacant floors in 1984. Standing at the former crossroads of Columbus, 12th and Broad, it looks out over a downtown far different than the one which flourished some 20 years earlier.

As recently as 1964 Downtown Columbus, and particularly Broadway, was still the main shopping destination of people in a 16-county area in West Georgia and East Alabama. The city's business, theatre and governmental activity was centered in the downtown area.

All the major department stores were still on Broadway in 1964. The city's three main movie houses were in downtown. In the three square blocks bounded by 13th Street and 10th Street on the north and south, and Front Street and 2nd Avenue on the west and east, there was seldom a vacant store, or a vacant parking space during the daytime hours. But perceptive leaders saw trouble ahead. They came forth with a new "redevelopment" plan for downtown every few years. They wanted to take parking off the streets completely, even though the early planners of Columbus had the foresight to include a large median down the middle of Broadway, which was not only decorative but separated the traffic and provided space for one-way travel on each side, with room for angle parking on the curbs.

The center of Columbus population had long-since moved to the residential areas five miles east of downtown, which bounded Macon road, and that was where the city's first enclosed shopping Mall was built in 1965. It attracted two of downtown's oldest and most popular stores, Sears and Penney's.

About that same time Davison's closed its downtown store and moved to Cross Country Plaza, which was across Macon Road from the new Mall. By 1970 all three of the downtown movie houses had closed. Montgomery

Ward's closed its store at 12th and Broad, across the street from *The Ledger-Enquirer* tower. The tower itself had replaced an important focus of downtown appeal, Lane's Drug store, a coffee-break spot of area businessmen for four decades. Lane's demise was sudden and without warning. One February day in 1969, a sign appeared on its front door declaring that it was closed.

A central business district which had virtually no vacancies in 1960s was pockmarked with them by 1970, and the trend accelerated during the next few years. Another Mall opened in 1975 on the northern outskirts of Columbus. By that time there was only one major retailer left in the downtown area. That was Kirven's Department Store, which for more than a century had been the leading retailer in Columbus and the Chattahoochee Valley. Kirven's is to Columbus what Rich's is to Atlanta. At its peak, Kirven's stretched a block from Broadway to First Avenue, with four floors, a basement, and entrances on 12th Street, Broadway and First. As the major chain stores left Downtown, Kirven's, a home-owned, home-operated business, stayed the course, keeping all of its business under one roof, with no branches in the malls or centers.

It was not easy on several counts. Accusations that Kirven's discriminated against blacks in its hiring policies brought on a black-organized boycott of the store in the 1960s at a time when blacks made up a significant percentage of downtown customers.

Finally Kirven's had to change also, and it established a large store in Columbus Mall on Macon Road, and then later put a store in West Georgia Commons Mall at LaGrange. The basement was closed at the downtown store and in the 1980s Kirven's extensively remodeled its Broadway front by converting a large amount of its inside floor space into an open-air, mall-type entrance.

By 1977, the Columbus central business section touched bottom. While the central sections of nearly every Georgia city faded during the decades of the 1960s and 1970s, Columbus had a strong claim to being the most faded.

The Stocking Strangler didn't help, of course. Although he operated in a residential area, the pall cast by the murders affected the entire city, and the fear of "going Downtown," which already existed, was simply intensified.

Unlike many comparable cities, Columbus did not even have any large restaurants in its downtown area. The 10-story Ralston Hotel, which had been the city's tallest building from 1914 to 1969, and was its civic and social hub for most of those years, had been converted into a home for the elderly. The other downtown hotels had long-since closed, and the newer, nicer motels were being built on the outskirts of the city.

The consolidation of the city and county into a single political entity had made Columbus-Muscogee the state's second largest city in the 1980 census, but the figures were not otherwise encouraging. Muscogee County increased its population by 83,000 in the 20 years from 1940 to 1960 but in the following 20 years, from 1960 to 1980, the population increased by only 12,000 — to 170,000 — and only 3,000 of that increase had come in the decade of the 1970s.

The major economic bases of textiles and Fort Benning had both declined in the 1970s.

But Columbus was not without its strengths and those strengths began to assert themselves in the late 1970s. Downtown, or "uptown" as it was renamed, began to move south on Broadway and adjoining streets. That was natural in some respects since the governmental center of the city had always been around the courthouse which was between 9th and 10th streets. The historic Springer Opera House, which had been saved from the wrecking ball and restored in the 1960s, was on 10th street, and it had become one of Columbus' stellar attractions. The towering new government center — 11 stories high — had opened in the early 1970s. The historic preservation effort, although modest by Savannah standards, had concentrated on the ten blocks of Broadway south of the traditional "downtown".

The block between 11th and 10th was bought by a group of local businessmen and transformed into what they called "Rankin Square", with new restaurants, office buildings and shops. While not an outstanding financial success, it had rescued a block that was on the verge of becoming a business slum.

Another group bought an old iron works building even further toward the river, and transformed it into perhaps the most unique trade and convention center in the state.

A few years later, in 1982, a six-story hotel was completed nearby, providing Columbus with both an appeal for conventions and tourists, and a place for them to stay.

The Ledger-Enquirer newspapers played a major role in encouraging the rescue effort designed to make Columbus at least a competitive city for state conventions. The climatic event in this effort came in March 1983, when *The Ledger-Enquirer* sponsored Expo '83 at the Iron Works Trade and Convention Center, with more than 100 local exhibitors displaying what the city had to offer. *The Ledger-Enquirer* provided much of the impetus for Expo, and also the chairman, Rick Kaspar, who had become general manager in 1980 after Vaughn was named publisher.

The main speaker for the occasion was a former *Ledger-Enquirer* business manager named Alvah H. Chapman Jr., who by then was chairman of the board of Knight-Ridder Newspapers.

Chapman was speaking in his old hometown 10 years after his family had sold *The Ledger-Enquirer* to Knight Newspapers, and he had to be pleased that both the city and the newspapers were in much better health than a few years earlier. In his speech, he told of the problems of his current hometown, Miami, Florida, and how a concerted effort was being made to meet those problems . . .

Vaughn, in his 10th year as *The Ledger-Enquirer's* chief executive, walks down a hall to his office each morning which is lined with portraits of former editors, starting with Mirabeau B. Lamar, the young pioneer who later became president of Texas, and continuing on with many others mentioned earlier in this history — Brown, Tucker, Reid, Johnson, Grimes, Dadisman, Vaughn himself. In the elaborately-appointed conference room on the second floor are portraits of Ashworth, Mrs. Ashworth, Rinaldo Page and Alvah and Mrs. Chapman Sr. In *The Enquirer* newsroom a portrait of Charlie Black in his Green Beret cap watches grimly over the proceedings. There are signs of past glories throughout the building in the form of plaques, framed front pages, even lead molds of several famous front pages.

The Ledger newsroom remains where it has been since 1930 when the older portion of the building was completed, overlooking the Chattahoochee River, with the streets and hills of Phenix City, Alabama easily visible in the distance. It is the room with an outside view. *The Enquirer* newsroom, by contrast, has no windows, and although remodeled extensively, it is still where it was moved in 1951 when the newsrooms were separated.

(Editor's note: The news staffs were combined in late 1984, and separate newsrooms are no longer maintained.)

Vaughn's office, on the third floor of the tower, is as elegant as any to be found in a Georgia newspaper building. Ashworth designed it as a showcase, for his use and his heirs. Its windows provide a view of where the action used to be in Columbus — the central business district which was vibrant before and after World War II. It is a view that easily summons up yesterday's glories, and prompts a few tears for its present decline.

Among the recent additions to Vaughn's office is his own personal computer. With a touch of his finger he can call up a summary of the items moving on the wire machines in the newsrooms. Briefly, he must ponder if that is the future of the business in which he has spent his career — a machine spewing out information and news at a rate sufficient to satisfy the most curious mind.

He can look out the windows at the deserted downtown buildings which once seemed so important and permanent, now all cast aside for new and better ways and places. In the lobby of *The Ledger-Enquirer* sits its last linotype machine, an antique displayed for visitors interested in history and obsolescence. The linotype too once seemed secure against the tides of change.

Vaughn turns from his computer with its generous and constant summaries and finds the latest edition of *The Ledger* which has just been delivered to his desk. He picks it up, and holds it in his hands and it reassures him that the newspaper is still a unique product. No computer can encompass the variety of information and items that crowds into a newspaper page. The newspaper's format defines the news as well as conveying it. The headlines give the news its life and its place.

The newspaper is a new product every edition, constantly changing yet reassuringly the same. The machines that compose it have changed; the presses that print it have changed; the people who produce it are constantly changing. And, of course, the readers are changing, just as they have changed in every generation. But the irreplaceable link between Gutenberg's first movable metal letters and the latest miracle computer is the intimate relationship which the printed word establishes between an individual and information, and which only the newspaper still transmits in such volume, flexibility and convenience.

In Columbus and its trade area, in some 60,000 tubes, doorsteps and assorted other sites, someone is reaching for the "new" edition of the newspaper each morning or afternoon, wanting it to be there, and disappointed — even angry — if it is not . . . the surest proof of the newspaper's continuing vitality.

Publisher Maynard Ashworth shown presiding at a 1949 Georgia Press Institute luncheon in Athens. At left is Ledger *Editor (1948-56) Bob Brown; at right,* Enquirer *Editor (1937-61) W. C. Tucker; and* Christian Science Monitor *Editor Erwin Canham, who was president of ASNE.*

Maynard Ashworth, center, at 1976 luncheon marking his 50 years in newspapers. At left, James Knight of Knight-Ridder newspapers; right, 1976 GPA President W. H. Champion, Dublin Courier-Herald.

A fight broke out at a Phenix City polling place in May 1952. Ray Jenkins, left, a Columbus Ledger *reporter on the scene, was splattered with blood, as anti-vice crusader Hugh Bentley, right, was beaten up.*

Editor Bob Brown, reporter Tom Sellers (see his article in this chapter) and managing editor John Bloomer look at telegram informing them The Columbus Ledger *has won the 1955 Pulitzer Prize for Community Service for its coverage of corruption in Phenix City.*

Alvah Chapman Sr., president of Ledger-Enquirer, *1937-61; had earlier been publisher of* The Brandenton, *Florida* Herald.

Alvah Chapman Jr., Ledger-Enquirer *business manager (1948-53); later, publisher of* Savannah News and Press; *president and chief executive officer, Knight-Ridder Newspapers.*

Mirabeau B. Lamar, founder of Columbus Enquirer *in 1828, and second president of the Republic of Texas.*

Glenn Vaughn succeeded Ashworth as chief executive officer of Ledger-Enquirer *in 1973. He started on Columbus papers as copy editor in 1955.*

Carlton Johnson (in portrait) was the second Columbus newspaperman inducted into the Georgia Journalism Hall of Fame. Mirabeau Lamar was the other. Johnson was editor of The Ledger *for 15 years and executive editor of* The Ledger and Enquirer *for seven years. L to R, Constance Johnson, his widow, and W. H. NeSmith, 1982 GPA president.*

Millard Grimes, Enquirer *editor during the 1960s, is shown receiving 1962 Best Column plaque from Kirk Sutlive, master of ceremonies at many GPA Award Nights.*

Glenn Vaughn, then general manager of Ledger-Enquirer, *spoke at LaGrange College convocation in 1973. He is shown with L C President Waights Henry, right, a* Ledger-Enquirer *columnist for more than 30 years, and 1973 student body President Bill Nall.*

Carroll Lisby held every major news position on Ledger, *then moved over to become editor of* The Enquirer *in 1974. Started with company in 1955.*

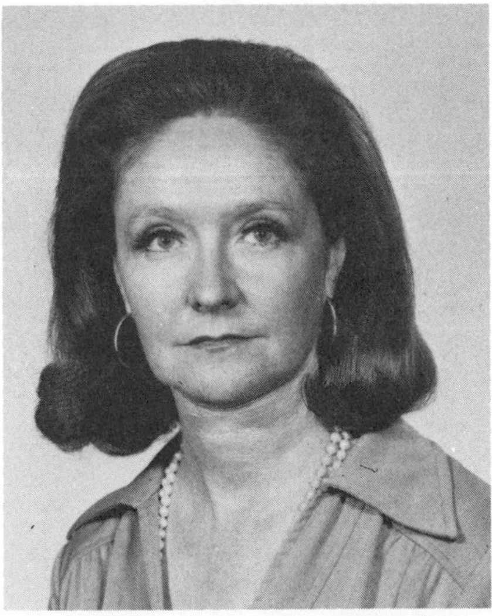

Mary Margaret Byrne is another long time L-E employee, starting in 1950. She was named editor of the editorial page of Ledger *in 1977.*

Charles Black found his niche in the 1960s covering the soldiers of the Air Assault Division in South Vietnam.

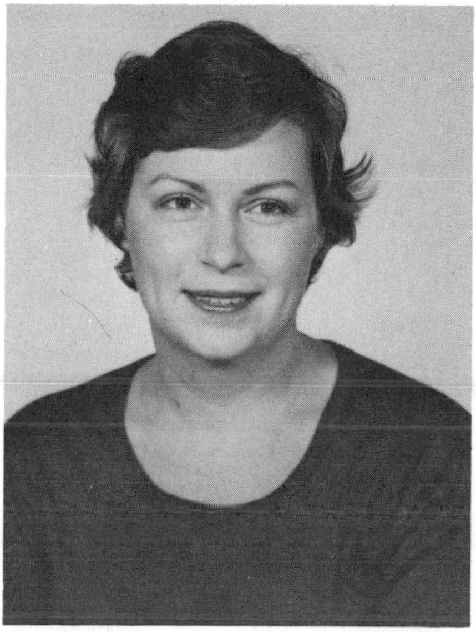

Priscilla Black, who married Charlie in 1975, became city editor of The Enquirer *after his death.*

Artist Angelo Franco drew many scenes such as this one to illustrate Black's reports from Vietnam.

This portrait of Charlie Black, also by Franco, now hangs in The Columbus Enquirer *newsroom.*

Edge R. Reid worked on Ledger-Enquirer *for 47 years (1928-75) serving as managing editor, editor, executive editor and associate publisher.*

W. C. (Cliff) Tucker was editor of The Enquirer *for 24 years (1937-61), holding the post until his death.*

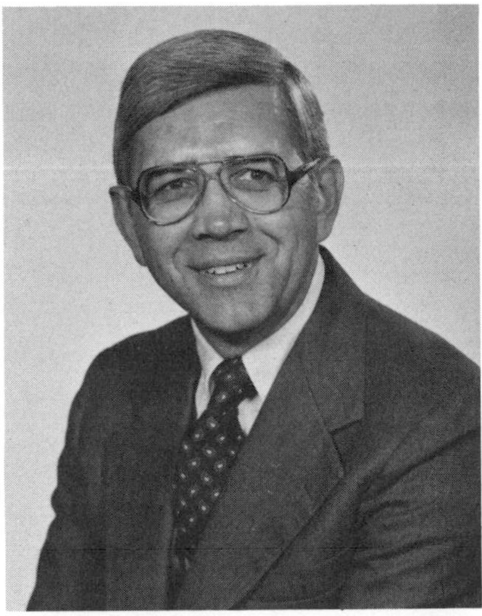

Carrol Dadisman was executive editor from 1974-80. He later became publisher of The Tallahassee, *Florida* Democrat.

William C. (Bill) Brown, shown during his bearded days, was managing editor of Enquirer *and succeeded Dadisman as executive editor in 1980.*

This Christmas season scene of 1970 shows steel skeleton of Ledger- Enquirer *Tower under construction. Main building at right was completed in 1930. Photo below shows tower when completed at corner of 12th and Broad.*

THURSDAY — THE PEOPLE'S NEWSPAPER

Published in Columbus, Georgia, each Thursday by TARGET COMMUNICATIONS CORPORATION

VOLUME 1 / NUMBER 1 / THURSDAY, SEPTEMBER 20, 1973

Here is THURSDAY! Look us over. We think you will like what you see. A newspaper that cares more about people. That's what we wanted to print. And that's why we decided to call it "The People's Newspaper." But calling it that won't make it that. That's where THURSDAY'S people come in.

THURSDAY'S people have been hard at work. And they will continue working to produce a colorful, newsy, reliable, readable, modern, full-sized newspaper. It's a big order. But our people are professionals. And they are not afraid of the challenge. The THURSDAY team includes people of many skills — journalism, advertising layout, circulation, typesetting, photography, press operation, and more. And the entire team is dedicated to producing a new kind of newspaper for Columbus-Phenix City-Fort Benning.

A new kind of paper? Yes, indeed! *Here's how:* You will find THURSDAY packed with local news. In fact, THURSDAY is a *local* newspaper, designed and built especially for this community. The news you will read in THURSDAY is "people news". It's the interesting, exciting news too often overlooked by big, over-staffed newspaper factories. Nothing wrong with being big, mind you.

See THURSDAY Special, Page Four

THURSDAY NEW DAY FOR CITY

Fairchild Color King Offset Printing Press Provides Full Color Capability for Printing of THURSDAY

Long Standing Newspaper Monopoly Broken by Competitive Publication

By The THURSDAY News Staff

The THURSDAY newspaper publishing enterprise comes to Columbus-Phenix City-Fort Benning in the midst of an acute paper shortage, in the face of competition from an entrenched daily, and against a nationwide trend toward one-newspaper cities.

But the people behind THURSDAY, Target Communications Corporation, say the paper is destined for success—that the supposed liabilities are, in this instance, actually assets.

Editor and Publisher J. Edward Wilson says he has ". . . never heard of a city where the public attitude is as favorable to the publication of a new newspaper as it is in this city right now."

As to the paper shortage, Wilson says he is not worried. He points to more than 300 tons of newsprint in the warehouse, and says the corporation has commitments for a continuing supply. Newspapers across the nation are curtailing advertising and news in efforts to cope with the shortage. Some papers have had to delete pages. A few have shut down.

The publication of THURSDAY ends a newspaper monopoly in Columbus. John B. Amos, Target Secretary-Treasurer and major moving force in the publishing project, thinks the existing paper created the need for a new newspaper voice. "It's time for some competition here in the newspaper business," says Amos. "An alternative voice is needed. The people have indicated they are tired of one-sided, managed news reporting."

In spite of the trend toward one-newspaper cities, THURSDAY publishers say they are convinced the people of the bi-city metro area will welcome the new newspaper and make it a success.

Target Communications Corporation was formed in July this year, for the specific purpose of publishing a newspaper in Columbus. The officers of the corporation are:

John P. McGoff, Lansing, Michigan, Chairman; Mark T. McKee, Oxford, Connecticut, President; John B. Amos, Columbus, Secretary-Treasurer; and J. Edward Wilson, Columbus, Executive Vice President.

Formation of the corporation came after months of local planning and discussion. McGoff and McKee, both veteran publishers, joined the endeavor after extensive consultation with local participants.

Office and production facilities, as well as warehousing, are located at 1620 Fifth Avenue. The property is being leased from the former owners and operators of United Builders Supplies, Inc. These include B. J. Beech, Richard Lane, and Wilson Lane.

Wilson says, "The property is remarkably suited to our needs." He says necessary renovations have been relatively minor, and notes that a railroad siding is convenient for the delivery of newsprint.

Consultation on Delivery Techniques

The initial circulation of THURSDAY is 45,000, more than any other publication in the metropolitan area. Circulation Manager Curtis Adams set up a home delivery system, which utilizes a force of special supervisors and carriers.

Advanced offset printing equipment—the only set-up of its type in the area—is used in the printing of the newspaper. Computerized, photo typesetting equipment is used to produce copy in a composition department headed by Sam Shirah. The printing is done with a Fairchild Color King press.

Advertising Manager Jim Whaley says the modern typesetting and printing methods offer many advantages to advertisers. Whaley cites elimination of most engraving costs, greater freedom in layout, and superior reproduction of both photographic and word copy.

Editorially, Wilson says THURSDAY will be broader in scope than most Columbus newspaper journalism of the past. He notes that material from other writers will supplement that produced by the paper's news staff. Most of the newspaper will be devoted to local news. An exception to this is the features of National Editorial Associates, a widely-used service which supplies comics, horoscopes, crossword puzzles, a doctor column, sports features and other special items.

THURSDAY officals predict the paper will go daily sometime. And they concede that when it does the name will have to be changed for the daily editions. But the plan is for THURSDAY to continue as a special edition, even if joined by issues of another name on other days of the week.

Meanwhile, Wilson says the staff intends to make full use of the advantages of a weekly publication. "One advantage of a weekly," says Wilson, "is that a better perspective is possible. We can avoid some of the pitfalls of instant news reporting."

Computerized Photo Typesetting

What about that line, "The People's Newspaper"? THURSDAY staffers say it means they'll be more sensitive to the activities and desires of people.

The first edition grew from a projected minimum of 32 pages to the 44-page newspaper which rolled off the press September 20th, 1973, the day Columbus got its colorful new newspaper.

Under the THURSDAY circulation plan, the Columbus-Phenix City-Fort Benning metro area is divided into ten divisions, and these divisions are divided into an average of 21 routes each.

Bundled newspapers will be delivered by truck to the carriers' homes. Each carrier's route is in his own neighborhood. Plastic bags will be furnished the carriers for dry delivery on rainy days.

Adams says, "We are determined to give excellent delivery service; but if anyone has a complaint we hope he will call us." And he added that the circulation office will be open for telephone calls until 8:00 p. m. every Thursday. The plan, he explains, is to deliver the newspaper by 5:30 p. m.

To stimulate the purchase of subscriptions, Adams has set up a contest in which carriers can win prizes — including such items as motorcycles, trail bikes, and inflatable rafts — according to the number of subscriptions they obtain.

Editor and Publisher J. Edward Wilson says, "We are proud of the organization Curtis Adams and Ken Gruschow have put together, and we look upon the carriers and supervisors as key individuals in the publication and distribution of THURSDAY."

THURSDAY officials say they intend for the paper to be a fair and impartial source of news, as well as of other worthwhile information and entertainment.

To Subscribe to THURSDAY
Call 324-2378 during
regular business hours (9 to 5)
Monday through Friday

Controlled Circulation Assures Efficient Home Delivery

Home delivery of THURSDAY will be accomplished through *controlled circulation* — a method of newspaper distribution unique in this city, which officials of the newspaper say will insure dependable home delivery.

Controlled circulation has been used successfully in other parts of the country. It differs from the distribution of a shopper in that it is carried out by trained carriers, and THURSDAY stands behind the delivery plan. It differs from old fashioned newspaper delivery methods by removing collection problems and possible losses from the shoulders of youthful carriers.

Curtis Adams, an experienced newspaper circulation man is THURSDAY'S Circulation Manager. He and his assistant, Ken Gruschow, set up the THURSDAY delivery organization.

Adams says, "One of the big advantages I see in controlled circulation is that the newsboy gets paid by the newspaper, regardless of the condition of the customer's subscription account. "This," says Adams, "provides a more dependable carrier force."

On September 15th, Adams and Gruschow staged a "kick-off" for the THURSDAY carrier program at the newspaper's Fifth Avenue headquarters. More than 200 youngsters crowded THURSDAY'S office to hear the Proprietors rock musical group and get instruction on delivery methods.

Adams' reaction: "In more than 20 years experience with newspaper carriers, this is by far the most enthusiastic group of young people I have encountered."

Adams has high praise for his division managers — "men and women of experience and dedication" — for building the carrier force of boys and girls.

In City Drug Bust

COLUMBUS CITY STREETS CLEARED OF DOPE PEDDLERS

By RON FEINBERG
Thursday Staff Writer

The recent drug-related arrests of ten Columbus men labeled "street lieutenants," have cleared the city of dope peddlers and cut off the supply of heroin into the area, according to Columbus Police Chief Curtis McClung.

The roundup two weeks ago climaxed a six-month investigation aimed at the major suppliers of heroin here, in an effort "to cut off the flow of hard drugs into Columbus," police said.

The arrested men, characterized by police as "wily, careful criminals," who wear "hundred dollar shoes and drive around in big cars," were held over to Superior Court without bond following preliminary hearings in Recorder's Court.

The men, all charged with selling narcotics, were identified by police as:

Eugene Pyatt, 22, 2823 Baldwin Street; Henry Frazier, 2705 Willow Street; Robert Barnes, 22, 530 Annette Avenue; Henry Johnson, 21, 2965 Brookhaven Road; Michael Mingo, 21, 2912½ Thomas Street; Melvin James, 29, 2707 Spenola Street; Willie Lee Sampson, 548 Clover Avenue; Joseph L. Boswell, 18, 2715-B Willow Street; Larry Jones, 22, 2715-C Willow Street; and Terry J. Scott, 20, 534 Roosevelt Street.

Several more warrants have been issued in connection with the lengthy investigation, and additional arrests will be made "as the people can be found," McClung said.

"Some of these people were looked upon by pushers and addicts as being extremely cool and smart, almost untouchable," according to the police chief.

"But now that these arrests have been made," he said, "there is confusion and lack of confidence" in the drug underworld, "that is causing them (addicts and pushers) to take a second look and back off."

It was such "confusion," and "lack of confidence," following the massive drug bust last March that forced "these street lieutenants" into the open, city police vice squad director John Vasquez said.

According to Vasquez, the ten men arrested last week would sell only in large quantities, usually to smaller pushers and addicts who resold the dope on the streets of the city.

But he explained that when the city was cleared of the "smaller fish," the "biggies" were forced to hit the streets themselves.

In connection with the investigation, police indicated they were looking into the financial backing of the local drug operation, which Vasquez said is being provided by "prominent" members of the community who belong to "civic clubs," and "lead comfortable lives."

"We know where the money is coming from," he said. "We just haven't been able to make any cases yet, but we're continuing our investigations in this area."

McClung said he expects the city to remain clear of hard drugs "for at least a

See Drug Bust, Page Three

". . . now there's not much left, and I don't know what I'll do when the cash runs out."

". . . who knows or cares, where I'll be two years from now?"

Life Between 'Trips' Is Dreary for Drug Addict

By RON FEINBERG
Thursday Staff Writer

For Robert Daniels (not his real name) each day is not much more than an endless span of time that leads into chilling nights filled with dreams of demonic characters.

Nothing much is important to him "anymore" except knowing where the next fix is coming from — and how much he's going to have to dish out for it.

Daniels, his slight frame draped in a drab, lifeless suit, bent and trembling as he talked in the stifling confines of his one-room apartment in downtown Columbus, is approaching thirty — although he looks like he's already reached middle age.

And it's not as if he doesn't

See Addict, Page Three

Inside THURSDAY

Miss Columbus Photos and Story - Page Seven

Kieven's Builds at Columbus Square
Read about it on Page Nine

Business News is in the THURSDAY
Metro Newsbeat - See Page Eleven

SPORTS! Of course! see Borderview on Page Twenty-One, and more Sports beginning on Page Twenty-Eight

THRIFTY THURSDAY WANT ADS
The "people kind" of classified - Page Thirty-Seven

Read about The Clown and all kinds of interesting things in THURSDAY Nitelife - Page Twenty-One

Front page of Thursday's *First Edition*

Chapter VI

Where The People Are: Rise Of The Suburban Press

The Dynamic Ten Counties

Georgia, after several decades of mediocre population growth, suddenly surged forward during the 20 years from 1960 to 1980 to become one of the nation's fastest growing states. The 19 percent increase from the 1970 to the 1980 census compared to an average for all states of 11.4 percent, and Georgia jumped from 19th to 13th among the states in population. By 1990, it has a good chance to become the 10th most populous state since three of the states ahead of Georgia in the 1980 count — Indiana, Massachusetts and North Carolina — were all growing at slower rates.

East of the Mississippi, only neighboring Florida and South Carolina exceeded Georgia in growth rate during the 1970s, and a significant part of South Carolina's growth was in the suburbs of Augusta and Savannah.

In raw figures Georgia's population went from 4,587,930 in 1970 to 5,464,265 in 1980, a net of 876,335. Coupled with an increase of 644,000 during the 1960s, this meant that more than a million-and-a-half more people lived in Georgia by 1980 than had lived in it in 1960, and this large gain had come during 20 years of declining birth rate.

What is most remarkable about the change, however, is the limited geographic area in which most of the gain occurred. Georgia, which observes county boundaries that long ago became meaningless and obsolete, still has 159 counties. But more than half of the 20-year population gain occurred in just 10 of those 159 counties.

From 1960 to 1980 the counties of DeKalb, Cobb, Gwinnett, Clayton, Douglas, Rockdale, Fayette, Cherokee, Forsyth and Henry had a net gain of 835,000 in their populations — almost evenly divided between the two decades, 420,000 in the 1970s, 415,000 in the 1960s. Georgia's other 149 counties had a net 20-year gain of 686,000, or 150,000 less than the dynamic 10.

The 10 counties with the big gains had one common factor. They were clustered around elongated Fulton County, within a 15-30 minute drive on the new interstate highways to Downtown Atlanta.

These counties were where the people came in the 1960s and 1970s, and to some extent in the 1950s. Fulton itself accounted for 35,000 of the statewide increase, rising in population by 50,000 in the 1960s, then declining by 15,000 in the 1970s.

The increase in some of the suburban counties was even more spectacular than the raw figures show. Clayton, for example, was a sleepy rural county of only 11,000 people in 1920, and had grown to only 22,000 in 1950. By 1980, it had 150,000.

Cobb jumped from 61,000 in 1950 to 297,000 in 1980. DeKalb, at 450,000, was 10 times as large in 1980 as it had been in 1920. Gwinnett, a late bloomer, had the biggest gain in the 1970s, but was only five times as populous in 1980 as it had been in 1920, when it was larger than Clayton or Cobb. Fayette County had actually declined to 7,900 in 1950 from a 1920 population of 11,296, and by 1970 Fayette was still not quite up to that 1920 total. Suddenly, Fayette's growth took off for a 156 percent gain in the 1970s to a 1980 census figure of 29,043, and still moving.

In this 10-county area of such remarkable population growth there was naturally a corresponding amount of rapid newspaper growth and activity. The suburban press is almost entirely a product of the post-World War II years. It was in the suburbs that many of the advances in printing technology were first tried. It has been there that the battle is most fiercely joined between paid weeklies, shoppers, free distribution papers, new dailies, and the old dailies which are mainly *The Atlanta Journal* and *Constitution*. The struggle for the hearts, minds and pocketbooks of the suburbanites is a dramatic story on many fronts, and none more so than in the newspaper field.

In 1950, the 10 counties which were to account for more than half of Georgia's population growth in the 1960s and 1970s could boast of but one daily newspaper published within their borders. That was *The Marietta Daily Journal*, which had only 6,000 circulation and was losing the battle for its home county against the weekly *Cobb County Times*.

By 1984, four of the 10 counties had daily newspapers based within their borders, while six of them are still served by weeklies. The three additional dailies are *The Gwinnett Daily News*, Lawrenceville, started in 1965; *Clayton News/Daily*, Jonesboro, started in 1971, and *The Rockdale Citizen*, Conyers, which went daily in 1978.

In all, nine newspapers have been started or converted from weekly to daily in Georgia since 1950. One of those, *The Warner Robins Sun*, which went daily in 1969, can also be listed as a suburban newspaper, being located 18 miles south of Macon. Houston, its home county, had a growth as remarkable as some of the Atlanta Metro 10, going from 11,280 in 1930 to 77,605 in 1980. Houston even suffered an unusual detour in its growth, if you go back to 1920 when the census listed it with 21,964. During the 20s more than half of Houston was carved away to form Peach County, the last county established in Georgia.

But Houston came on strong after 1950 with the establishment of Warner Robins Air Force Base, doubling in population in the 50s. Its newspapers will be included in this chapter.

Another new daily in the Macon area is *The Union-Recorder* of Milledgeville, which began a daily (Tuesday-Saturday) schedule in March 1982. But Milledgeville was a city before Macon, and *The Union-Recorder* is one of the state's oldest newspapers, and thus will be covered in the chapter on small dailies beyond the suburban areas.

The other new dailies since 1950 are *The Dalton Citizen-News* (1962); *The Athens Daily News* (1965); *The Statesboro Herald* (1971) and *The Carrollton Times-Georgian* (1980). One 1950 daily, *The Cedartown Standard*, reverted to weekly publication and *The Macon News* was merged with *The Telegraph* in 1983.

In the Atlanta Metro market, there are also a large number of paid and free weeklies. Two weekly chains operate in the area, the Neighbor Newspapers, based in Marietta and associated with *the Daily Journal*, and the Sun papers, based in Decatur.

The Neighbor group is the most numerous and extensive with 27 free-distribution weeklies in eight of the 10 high-growth counties, plus Fulton and Paulding.

The News/Sun papers are centered in populous DeKalb County, with a strong presence in the south metro area of South Fulton, Clayton and Fayette. These newspapers are also distributed free except for one DeKalb County edition.

The Marietta Daily Journal and *The Neighbors*

With a listed free distribution of 325,000 plus the 25,000 paid circulation of *The Marietta Daily Journal*, the Neighbor group has made a strong bid to compete for the metro area's print advertising against *The Atlanta Journal-Constitution*. This group, the brainchild of Otis Brumby Jr., was launched about 17 years after his father, Otis Brumby Sr., bought *The Marietta Daily Journal* from Stanley Whitaker and Brooks Smith and merged it with his *Cobb County Times*. Brumby Sr. served as chairman of the board of the new organization until his death in 1954. His widow, Elisabeth Dobbs Brumby, succeeded him as chairman, a position she still held 30 years later.

Brumby Jr., the present president and publisher, joined the newspaper in 1965, after graduating from the University of Georgia Law School, and became publisher in 1967.

Brumby is also a graduate of the University of the South in Sewanee, Tennessee, and a member of the Cobb County and Georgia Bar Associations.

It wasn't long after Brumby assumed the publisher's post that he launched the company on a major expansion project — the publishing of community newspapers to serve the suburbs of metro Atlanta. The move put the company in the forefront of what has become a national trend in the newspaper industry.

"I had seen the expansion of newspaper operations in Chicago and other urban/suburban areas and decided the world was not upside down in Atlanta, Georgia," Brumby recalls.

"The move to the South was on. Everything and everybody seemed to be moving to Atlanta so I decided if they could do it [publish suburban newspapers] in Chicago, we could do it here. Atlanta was becoming a major league city and deserved a large suburban operation."

So, with an eventual goal of surrounding the city of Atlanta with a string of newspapers, Brumby started the first Neighbor Newspaper — *The Northside Neighbor* — in February 1968, serving the north side Atlanta/Buckhead area. With a strong mix of all-local news, features and sports, highlighted with full-color photos, *The Northside Neighbor* gained community acceptance and other Neighbor newspapers were soon launched in south Fulton and DeKalb County.

More Neighbors were started as the years went by and by 1984 27 Neighbor Newspapers were published in communities in Cobb, Fulton, DeKalb, Rockdale, Clayton, Fayette, Henry, Douglas, Paulding and Cherokee counties.

At one time, the company also published three other daily newspapers — *North Fulton Today, South Fulton Today* and *South Cobb Today. North Fulton Today*, the first to begin publication in August 1973, was also the last to cease publication in September 1979. High gasoline prices were given as the reason for discontinuing the dailies.

A key factor in *The Marietta Daily Journal*/Neighbor Newspapers growth is its central production facility, located at the headquarters office in Marietta. While the Neighbor Newspapers have 13 district offices, with video display terminals linked to Marietta, all production, data processing and printing is done in Marietta.

The heart of the production operation is the Goss Urbanite press, installed in 1966 in a production facility on Fairground Street near Marietta's Lockheed-Georgia plant. Four years later, the editorial and business offices of *The Marietta Daily Journal* and Neighbor Newspapers moved into an adjoining 33,000-square-foot building.

The first offset edition of *The Marietta Daily Journal* was published in January 1967.

The Goss press has one three-color and seven black units. It is equipped with two folders so it can print two small newspapers at one time or one large (56-page) newspaper.

Another major technological change for the newspaper came in 1975 when computers entered the newsroom, bringing a new way of life for editors and typesetters. The Itek CPS-720 system installed at the time gave editors the chance to put up their red pens and spend their time instead looking into a screen with green letters.

The system, which originally came with eight terminals and two optical scanners, grew to 12 VDTs a year later, and it gave the news and composition departments more flexibility. Reporters at the time made the change from manual to electric typewriters, required to prepare scanner-ready copy, but they too have now forsaken the old ways for the new.

In December 1982, *The Marietta Daily Journal* and Neighbor Newspapers installed a highly automated computerized processing system with 50 terminals, including two in each of the outlying Neighbor offices and one at the company's Atlanta bureau at the state capitol.

Circulation has kept pace with the technological changes at *The Marietta Daily Journal*. From the 13,000 at the time of the merger with *The Times* in 1951, *The Journal's* circulation grew to 17,000 in 1960, 22,000 in 1970, 24,000 in 1975 and 26,000 in 1980. In 1983, daily circulation topped the 26,000 mark, and the Sunday edition had more than 28,000.

In addition to Brumby, key personnel at the newspapers include General Manager Harris Kettles, Associate Publisher Jay Whorton, Executive Editor Bobby Nesbitt, Advertising Director Terry Smith, News Editor Susan Miles and Associate Editor Bill Kinney.

Kettles got his start in the newspaper business as an apprentice printer at *The Citizen-News* in his hometown of Dalton, Georgia. He worked at *The Columbus Ledger-Enquirer* from 1948-1968 where he was composing room foreman. Kettles joined *The Marietta Daily Journal* and Neighbor Newspapers in 1968 as production manager and was named general manager in 1975.

A graduate of Jacksonville State University in Jacksonville, Alabama, Whorton came to *The Marietta Daily Journal* and Neighbor Newspapers in 1971 after working with the Carroll Publishing Company in Carrollton for 12 years. After serving as advertising director, Whorton was named associate publisher in 1977. In addition to handling the national and major advertising accounts, Whorton directs the company's promotions and public relations activities.

Nesbitt, a journalism graduate of Georgia State University, joined the company in 1968 as editor of *The Northside Neighbor*, the first Neighbor publication. He was subsequently named managing editor of the entire Neighbor group, and then, in 1975, was named to head the 100-plus-person news operation for both the Neighbor Newspapers and *The Marietta Daily Journal*.

Smith was named advertising director of the newspaper in December 1982 after heading the advertising departments in several of the outlying counties. A graduate of Auburn University, he was formerly with a group of newspapers in Florida.

Marietta Daily Journal News Editor Susan Miles continues a family association with the newspapers. Her father, the late Leo Aikman, was editor of *The Cobb County Times* in the 1940s and later became a well-known columnist with *The Atlanta Constitution*. Mrs. Miles, an Agnes Scott graduate, joined *The Marietta Daily Journal* after working in the Atlanta office of a national publishing company.

Following is a list of the Brumby newspapers on January 1, 1985:

Cobb County:
The Marietta Daily Journal
The East Cobb Neighbor
The Kennesaw Neighbor
The Acworth Neighbor
The Powder Springs Neighbor
The Mableton Neighbor
The Austell Neighbor
The Smyrna Neighbor
The Vinings Neighbor

DeKalb County:
The Dunwoody-DeKalb Neighbor
The Chamblee-DeKalb Neighbor
The Doraville-DeKalb Neighbor
The Decatur-DeKalb Neighbor
The Tucker-DeKalb Neighbor
The Stone Mountain-DeKalb Neighbor
The South DeKalb Neighbor

Douglas County:
The Douglas Neighbor

Paulding County:
The Paulding Neighbor

Rockdale County:
The Rockdale Neighbor

Fulton County:
The Northside Neighbor
The Sandy Springs Neighbor
The Roswell Neighbor
The Alpharetta Neighbor
The South Fulton Neighbor

Clayton County:
The Clayton Neighbor

Fayette County:
The Fayette Neighbor

Henry County:
The Henry Neighbor
Cherokee County:
The South Cherokee Neighbor
The Cherokee Tribune

Brumby's Neighbors, of course, were not warmly welcomed by the paid circulation dailies and weeklies in the counties where they circulate. Not only do they provide competition for advertising dollars, but they are a damper on efforts by the paid newspapers to sell subscriptions since they provide a relatively large weekly newspaper at no expense to the reader. A Neighbor newspaper must have at least 24 pages to qualify for the second-class "controlled circulation" rates which are the key to holding down the Neighbors' distribution costs. The "controlled" rate is several cents per copy less than the third class rate which is levied on most unpaid mail.

The formats are identical on the 27 Neighbors, all patterned after *The Marietta Daily Journal*, the record-holder for number of GPA awards for content and appearance. As a rule, each Neighbor has four sections with four "cover fronts," the main page one, a sports front, a business news front, and a people or feature front. The inside pages are fairly tight with advertising. For years there was only a semblance of an editorial page, but in 1983 each Neighbor began running a full editorial page with local editorials and columns.

With the 27 Neighbor papers, *The Marietta Daily Journal* and *The Cherokee Tribune*, which is the paid weekly in Cherokee County, Brumby's company publishes more separate newspapers than any other Georgia newspaper company. Their aggregate circulation of 350,000 (90 percent unpaid) is exceeded in exposure in Georgia only by the combined paid circulation of *The Journal* and *Constitution*.

Although there are advertising staffs in each Neighbor office which solicit in the individual counties, the majority of advertisements in the Neighbors are sold through combination rates, which give the advertiser a choice of the entire circulation of the 29 papers, or in specific areas which several Neighbors cover, such as DeKalb, Cobb or the South Metro.

For example, a supermarket chain with outlets in all of the counties covered by Neighbors would buy the whole "package." The addresses of the outlets in the specific county or community are listed only in that area's edition.

The growth of the Neighbor group since 1969 has had a diminishing effect on paid circulation weeklies in the Atlanta metropolitan market. In

Fulton County, for example, five weekly newspapers listed as members of the Georgia Press Association in 1956 are no longer published. They were *The Metropolitan Herald*, Buckhead; *The Suburban Reporter*, East Point; *The Advertiser*, Atlanta; *The South Fulton Recorder*, Fairburn; and *The North Fulton Herald*, Roswell.

In Cobb County, the Neighbors are now the community newspapers for Austell, Acworth and Smyrna, all of which were once served by paid weeklies. But in the counties other than Cobb there is plenty of print competition, both from the Atlanta dailies and their Extra editions, from long-established paid circulation weeklies or dailies, and in several cases, from various editions of the Sun/News papers.

The Neighbors and the Suns clash most directly in DeKalb County where the Suns are based, and where seven Neighbor mastheads are distributed. *The DeKalb Sun News* is the paid circulation newspaper for DeKalb and *The Sun-News* offers saturation circulation with its free North DeKalb edition and South DeKalb edition. The same company also publishes *The Lithonia Observer*, a paid weekly.

The other area in which the Neighbors and Sun-News compete most directly is South Fulton County. *The Southside Sun* is the oldest of the Sun/News operations outside of DeKalb County. *The South Fulton Neighbor* replaced one of the Brumby dailies, *South Fulton Today*, which started in February 1975 and was terminated three years later. A paid weekly, *The South Fulton Recorder*, which was based in Fairburn, was started by Bill and Kate Jones in 1954 and became a daily for several months in 1975-76. *The Recorder*, by then a property of Woodprint in Jonesboro, suspended publication in early 1980.

In Paulding, Douglas and Henry Counties, the Neighbors compete with long-established paid circulation weeklies. In Fayette County, the Neighbor is one of four weekly publications, two free and two paid. The century-old *Fayette County News* is the paid-circulation legal organ. Then there is *This Week In Peachtree City*, a paid weekly which has served Peachtree City and the western part of the county since 1974. The fourth paper is *The Fayette Sun*, a free-distribution offshoot of *The Southside Sun*.

In Clayton and Rockdale counties, the Neighbors face paid daily newspapers which have Total Market Coverage editions on Wednesday. Clayton also has a Sun/News paper, giving that county three mass-delivered papers on Wednesday.

The two Atlanta metro counties which don't have Neighbor papers are Gwinnett and Forsyth where Brumby's first cousin, Robert Fowler, publishes a paid circulation daily and weekly. Despite the family ties, dynamic Gwinnett poses a tempting target for The Neighbors and could become an essential piece of the market which Brumby proposes to sell.

The Neighbor papers often surpass the traditional paid-circulation weeklies and dailies in appearance. Since they are all produced at the Marietta plant they have the benefit of more advanced equipment than most weeklies. They also get the benefit of supervision by Editor Bobby Nesbitt, who assures strong layout and makeup in all of the Neighbors. Another outstanding feature of the Neighbors are imaginative, sharp, well-cropped photographs. Facial expressions and unusual angles are emphasized.

Neighbors are "tighter" on inside pages than most paid circulation newspapers, although their section fronts are usually free of ads. The Neighbors carry fewer obituaries, weddings and engagements than traditional paid weeklies. They also stress upbeat news, personality portraits, and business news, thus tending to carry less "hard" news than the paid newspapers.

Brumby believes the Neighbors can coexist and prosper with their in-county competition as well as against *The Journal* and *Constitution*, with which they compete for metro-wide advertising. He points to his own Cobb County as the prime example of a home-county daily competing successfully with eight Neighbors scattered throughout its market. "The Neighbors are *The Marietta Journal's* strongest competition," he says, but he believes *The Daily Journal* and Neighbors serve distinctive roles for the advertisers. Brumby exerted a major effort to increase *The Marietta Journal's* paid circulation during the early 1980s, realizing that paid gains come hard when most of your potential new customers are getting a free Neighbor.

Brumby, of course, is competing with himself in Cobb County, somewhat as morning-evening combinations owned by the same company compete with each other. In the other counties the Neighbors are competing for advertising, news and — very importantly — for reading time, against newspapers based in those counties, which have staffs that live and work there, and which are usually the legal organ.

In most of these cases, the older, paid publications have not only survived but in general have increased their ad volume since the introduction of a Neighbor into the market. This is partly a result of the growth in the particular counties but also is a sign that advertisers recognize the specific function of the various print media, and the importance of using all the print exposure that is available.

The Sun/News Publications

The closest parallel to the Neighbor Newspapers is the Sun/News group, headquartered in Decatur. This company was started modestly in 1949 by William Crane, a former linotype operator at the Atlanta newspapers. Crane had $500 and a used typewriter, and he was the first Georgia publisher to use free distribution in the modern sense. The newspaper was called *The Decatur News*, and it was the foundation of a commercial printing and newspaper company that grossed close to $15 million in 1983, most of which — more than 80 percent — came from commercial printing.

Crane's concept of the "free" newspaper has been widely copied in the past 35 years, most notably by his company's main competitor, the Neighbors.

The major in-county weekly newspaper in DeKalb County in 1949 was *The DeKalb New Era*, which was probably Georgia's original suburban newspaper, dating back to the 1870s.

For many years, *The New Era* was run by W. Hugh McWhorter, who owned the newspaper along with four other DeKalb businessmen.

They included Scott Candler Sr., who for some 16 years was DeKalb's one-man commissioner of roads and revenues and later was Secretary of Commerce for Georgia. He also served a stint as executive director of the Stone Mountain Memorial Association during the early stages of development of the mountain as a state park.

McWhorter was a member of the Georgia General Assembly from DeKalb for several terms, first as a state representative and later as a state senator, and was president of the Georgia Press Association in 1951.

When Georgia's first "bona fide" free newspaper was founded in competition with *The New Era* by Crane and his wife, Mary, free newspapers were already common in the northeast and mid-west states, where they had emerged during the Great Depression as a way to give advertisers saturation coverage of their markets.

Unlike some of the "shoppers" which already existed around the southeast, the Cranes insisted that their newspaper be competitive not only as an advertising medium, but also in coverage of local news.

Saturation coverage of the City of Decatur was the first goal of the Cranes, at the insistence of at least one large chain-store advertiser which did not think it was getting enough penetration of its market in the existing paid-circulation *New Era*.

About 5,000 copies were printed of *The Decatur News*' early issues. These were all mailed but as the number grew the method of delivery was changed to a distribution firm with door-to-door delivery.

Crane continued to hold his job as a supervisor in the composition department at the daily Atlanta newspapers, with Mrs. Crane selling advertising and also directing most of the news coverage. But Crane soon left *The Journal-Constitution* to devote his full time to his own newspaper.

The Decatur News showed definite signs of strength, which ruffled the feathers of the tradition-bound, close-knit Decatur establishment. But advertisers loved it, and many of the newcomers to the community looked upon it as "their" newspaper.

The News was aggressive, and as a newspaper that printed both sides of a controversy, it served as a voice to a coalition of newcomers and disgruntled voters who joined together to defeat Scott Candler for the powerful commission chairman's post.

The paper continually expanded its free distribution to the developing suburban areas around Decatur as new subdivisions were built and shopping centers began to appear in what had previously been farm and dairy country.

By the mid-1960s, *The News*, which had expanded its name to *The Decatur-DeKalb News*, was matching its older competitor, *The New Era*, page for page in advertising volume and far outstripping it in distribution.

In 1972, the company absorbed *The Tucker Tribune*, a paid circulation paper serving a portion of DeKalb County. *The Tribune's* subscription list was merged with the paid subscribers of *The Decatur-DeKalb News*. At the same time, the free circulation newspapers in DeKalb were renamed *The DeKalb News/Sun* and divided into North and South editions. The circulation was increased and the pattern was enlarged so that almost all homes in the county were reached.

The Decatur-DeKalb News was chosen to be the county's legal organ, effective July 1, 1974, and it became the first Georgia newspaper to publish a tabloid insert containing the legals and focusing on the legal, business and professional events within the county. This weekly tab within *The Decatur-DeKalb News* was named the "Business and Financial Review."

The Southside Sun had been started in 1967, covering the South Fulton area of suburban Atlanta, and *The Clayton Sun, Fayette Sun* and *Henry Sun* were launched in 1976.

The News/Sun, the flagship newspaper, had a total distribution in 1984 of more than 95,000 copies each Wednesday and is zoned for north and south DeKalb with several pages, including the front, changed to localize the news to those areas of the county. It is distributed by the firm's own fleet of vehicles. *The New Era*, acquired in 1978, was combined with *The Decatur-DeKalb News* to form the *Decatur — DeKalb News/Era* and has a paid circulation of more than 7,500 copies weekly. It includes the weekly business tabloid which contains the legal advertisements.

The six News/Sun Publications, both paid and free, reach more than 178,000 homes and businesses weekly in DeKalb, Fulton, Clayton and Fayette Counties.

The growth of the publications required heavy capital investment in web presses to produce the large page-count editions generated by the high circulation. After their initial investment in offset presses, the Cranes decided to enter the web offset commercial printing field.

This activity, under the guidance of Rick Sauers, son-in-law of the founders, grew within a few years to produce significant volume for the company. Using different marketing techniques and organizing internally as a separate operation, sharing only business management and production facilities, it established its own identity, *NEWSprint*.

Jerry Crane, son of the founders, is president and chief executive officer of the company. He joined the operation in 1959. He has been active in the Suburban Newspapers of America, which represents more than 1,000 suburban newspaper members, and served that organization as president in 1980.

The firm's three buildings on Dekalb Industrial Way in north Decatur total 60,000 plus square feet, and in addition to the fleet of 11 Motor Media distribution vehicles, the company operates two 18-wheel-over-the-road transports to deliver inserts and printing from its NEWSprint division throughout the southeast.

Long time employees include Linton Broome, executive editor, Steve Teasley, editor and Mike Traynor, advertising director.

The decisive advantage in *The News*' long struggle with *The New Era* came in 1974 when it became the county legal organ, and thus gained not only the additional prestige, but also some $300,000 in annual revenue which the legals in a county as populous as DeKalb can generate. The legals still give *The News/Sun* an advantage over its new rival, the Neighbors.

Loss of the legals was crucial for *The New Era*. Like *The News, The New Era* also was part of a large printing operation, and Britt Fayssouix and Jim Boatright, the owners, decided to devote full time to their printing and mailing business after losing the legals. By the time they sold *The New Era* and *Lithonia Observer* to the Crane operation in 1978, the two papers had declined to tabloids that carried only a few token ads.

In Georgia, a county's Legal Organ is determined by three officials: the probate judge, the circuit court clerk and the sheriff. They designate a newspaper as the official legal organ for the county, and legals are placed in that newspaper by most lawyers and agencies. The main condition in the past was that the newspaper must be a paid circulation publication.

Because of the condition *The Decatur-DeKalb News* was not eligible for legals for nearly 25 years of its existence. But by virtue of absorbing *The Tucker Tribune* (a descendant of *The Tucker Tattler* — See Chapter V), *The News* began to acquire paid circulation and became qualified for the legals.

A Republican, Robert Guhl, was elected chairman of the county commission in 1972, defeating the Democrat, Walt Russell, who had been supported by *The New Era*. On taking office, Guhl used his influence with the other officials to bring about a change in the legal organ. In 1973, the designation was switched from *The New Era* to *The Decatur-DeKalb News*. Not only did a considerable amount of revenue thus move from *The New Era* to *The News* but also the prestige and status of being the newspaper read by lawyers, county officials and others interested in the legal advertisements was gained.

The New Era never really recovered. Fayssouix and Boatwright, its principal owners, as mentioned, had a large printing and mailing business, and after a few lean years on the newspaper side of the operation they sold *The New Era* and *The Lithonia Observer* to a group headed by two former *Atlanta Journal* newsmen, Harry Murphy and Bill Hughes. Murphy and Hughes also bought *The Monticello News* at this time, with Hughes becoming the publisher in Monticello while Murphy concentrated on the DeKalb county newspapers.

By then — 1977 — *The New Era* and *Observer* were not major contenders in the battle for newspaper readers and advertisers in DeKalb County. That struggle was between the *News/Sun* and the invading Neighbors, and, of course, the Atlanta dailies.

Murphy changed the papers to a tabloid format and made a gallant effort to inject strong reader appeal columns and features, but by 1978 the two papers had little advertising or paid circulation. Fayssouix and Boatwright took them back in late 1978 and then sold them to *The News/Sun* which combined *The New Era* with its DeKalb weeklies and continued to publish *The Lithonia Observer* as a separate paid newspaper.

A seventh Neighbor masthead was added in DeKalb in 1980 when

The South DeKalb Neighbor was started along with a *Rockdale Neighbor.*

Atlanta's Something "Extra"

Additional competition for advertising dollars in DeKalb came from the Atlanta Newspapers' *DeKalb Extra*, one of four suburban tabloid editions launched in 1979. The others were *Intown Extra, Cobb Extra* and *North Fulton Extra*. These editions, which are inserted into the Wednesday or Thursday *Journal* and *Constitution*, resemble weekly newspapers for the particular areas, carrying only local news, photos and editorial comment, with advertising sold at a discounted rate for the circulation in the specific area.

To make the package even more appealing for advertisers, the *Extras* were divided into three separate editions in DeKalb (north, middle and south) and two editions in Cobb. In their first four years, the *Extras* did not attract a significant amount of advertising, although the Atlanta management does feel they served as an entry-point for some advertisers to the full-circulation *Journal-Constitution*. The average number of pages range from as few as 12 (tab-size) in South DeKalb and In Town to 36 in the North DeKalb edition.

More *Extras* were planned, but almost four years passed from their first introduction until another *Extra* made its appearance, this one being a *Gwinnett Extra* in March 1983. Two more *Extras* soon followed, *Clayton Extra* and *South Fulton Extra*, both launched on December 1, 1983.

The *Journal-Constitution* also offers a section called "Reach," which is essentially a four-page wrap-around with selected stories and features, that contains pre-prints. It is mailed weekly to homes not subscribing to one of the dailies.

The Gwinnett Daily News

The Marietta Daily Journal, which changed from weekly to daily publication in 1935, was Georgia's first suburban daily, although in 1935 Marietta probably didn't consider itself a suburb. It was a very substantial city in itself, separated from Atlanta by 20 miles of bad roads, the Chattahoochee River and uninhabited countryside. Cobb County's population at the time was about 35,000, and Marietta had about 15,000 of that.

It was the growth of both South Cobb and North Fulton that eventually made Marietta and its newspapers part of the suburban sprawl.

That was also the experience of the second daily to be started in what is now a suburban county. It was a small-town daily which got swallowed up in the expanding metro area. Its home base of Lawrenceville was much smaller (about 7,500) than Marietta in 1935 but Gwinnett, the county it serves, was on the verge of becoming Georgia's fastest growing, in both percentage and real numbers, and one of the most dynamic in the nation.

It was also appropriate that Robert D. Fowler, a former editor of *The Marietta Daily Journal*, would be the driving force behind the second daily in the Atlanta metro area and its founding editor and publisher.

The Gwinnett Daily News began six-day publication on September 12, 1965, launching a venture which saw the small, county-seat daily grow into one of the most successful suburban newspapers in the Southeast. *The Daily News* was the result of the merger of three weekly newspapers which had served Gwinnett. Groundwork for thc daily began in 1964 when Fowler purchased *The Lawrenceville News-Herald* from the estate of Marvin Allison.

Five months later — in November 1964 — Fowler's Gwinnett Publishing Company formed a joint venture with Georgia Community Papers, Inc., which was already publishing *The Buford Advertiser* and the newly-founded *News* of Gwinnett. By agreement, Fowler and Georgia Community Papers owner Charles Smithgall established "The News Company" to publish the three weekly newspapers.

Some 10 months later, *The News-Herald* became *The Gwinnett Daily News*, with *The Weekly Herald* continuing to serve Lawrenceville, *The Buford Advertiser* serving Buford and *The News* of Gwinnett serving the Norcross-Duluth area. The weeklies were later combined into *The Gwinnett Daily News*.

In converting *The Lawrenceville News-Herald* into a six-day publication, The News Company promised its readers a "complete newspaper." The county-seat daily concentrated heavily on coverage of its city and county, but also offered state, national and world news from United Press International.

Though not established as a suburban daily newspaper, *The Gwinnett Daily News* soon became one. Located in a county which was to jump from 43,500 population in 1960 to an estimated 220,000 in 1985, *The Daily News* also made impressive gains in circulation.

In 1966, just a year after converting to daily publication, the newspaper moved into a new building a block off the square in Lawrenceville. That same year, a used three-unit Vanguard press was installed. The paper previously was carried 25 miles each day to the *Walton Tribune* plant in Monroe to be printed. Continuing growth led to the installation of a five-unit V-15 Harris press in 1968.

As new residents began pouring into Gwinnett County, *The Daily News* found that its subscriber penetration was not keeping pace with the market. Many of the new families were Atlantans moving to the suburbs and their newspaper allegiance remained with the familiar Atlanta dailies rather than the local paper.

In 1970, Fowler decided to start a total market coverage program, one of the first in the Southeast. Each Wednesday, a free newspaper was left at the homes of non-subscribers in the county, thus assuring advertisers of near-saturation coverage for their ads. This successful move resulted in increased advertising and probably discouraged other newspaper competition in other sections of the sprawling county.

One weekly competitor was launched in 1970 by a former *Daily News* advertising manager, Bruce Still. That paper, *The Home Weekly*, continues to be published in Lawrenceville with a paid circulation of 3,242, plus additional free circulation in parts of the county.

The Daily News' TMC program was expanded to twice a week in 1979, and in 1983 it reached 56,500 homes. This steady growth of *The Daily News* led to expansion of the newspaper plant in 1973, when circulation climbed past the 10,000 mark, and again in 1979 when a new 10-unit Rockwell-Goss press was installed.

The circulation growth of the newspaper, coupled with the rapid suburbanization of the Gwinnett market, led to changes in the newspaper's editorial concept between its conversion to a daily and the boom years of the 1970s. The weekly flavor of the product, perhaps best exemplified by the publication of social columns from various communities around the county, gradually gave way to a more sophisticated content. Social columns were replaced with expanded coverage of city and county government, features on community organizations and events, and comprehensive reports of zonings and education. While retaining its emphasis on local news, *The Daily News* moved toward producing a complete news product.

Growth in circulation was accompanied by growth in the number of pages. From a weekly averaging 16 pages per issue in 1964, *The Daily News* grew to an average of 36 pages per issue by 1983.

A milestone in the progress of *The Gwinnett Daily News* came in the fall of 1979 when the newspaper introduced an expanded Sunday edition. It included news, sports, lifestyle and business sections, as well as a quarter-fold television magazine, a quarter-fold, full-color comic book and a Sunday magazine supplement.

In January 1983, *The Daily News* added the services of the Associated Press to its United Press International wires and also offers readers the supplementary wire services of *The Christian Science Monitor*.

A third expansion of the Clayton Street plant was begun in the Spring of 1983 to house an expanded inserting department and to provide more space for the news and advertising departments. The addition increased the plant's total square footage to 30,000.

Benefiting from the rapid population growth of Gwinnett County during the past 15 years, *The Daily News* in 1982 became the fastest-growing Evening/Sunday newspaper in the nation, based on percentage gain. Circulation surpassed 23,000 daily and 25,000 Sunday. Circulation grew more than 15 percent during 1982-83.

Fowler, a former president of the Georgia Press Association, held the title of editor and publisher until 1971 when Gainer Bryan took over the responsibilities of editor. Bryan was succeeded in 1975 by Steve McMullan, another former editor of *The Marietta Daily Journal*. In 1984 Jim Osteen was named the fourth editor of the Gwinnett paper.

Elliott Brack became the newspaper's first general manager in 1974 and has served in that capacity for more than 10 years.

Except for Fowler, Brack has probably played the biggest role in making *The Gwinnett Daily News* the outstanding success story among Georgia's newer dailies. But his coming to *The News* resulted from an unusual series of coincidences. Brack, a native of Macon, had bought into an opposition newspaper in Jesup, Georgia, in 1962. Brack's paper, *The Wayne County Press,* was a tabloid, and in the face of tough odds, it managed to survive and grow. About 1971 he took in a partner, W. H. (Dink) NeSmith.

In September 1973, Wallace Eberhard, head of the editorial sequence at the University of Georgia's journalism school, called Brack and said he had an unexpected opening on the faculty. He asked if Brack could come to Athens as a visiting lecturer for a year and teach the newspaper management course. Brack was trying to give NeSmith a larger role in the newspaper operation and he decided that the best way to do that might be for him to get completely out of the picture for awhile. So on short notice he accepted the nine-month teaching assignment at Georgia, intending to return to Jesup at the end of that time and resume his duties on *The Press*.

The following April, as Brack recalls it, he took his management class on a tour of *The Gwinnett Daily News* plant, and during the tour Publisher Fowler asked him to step in his office. "How would you like to come here and be general manager?" Fowler proposed to Brack.

Brack, after more than 12 years as publisher of a struggling competitive rural weekly, decided he might like that. In addition the University offered to let him continue teaching the management class on a part-time basis, and Lawrenceville was only 30 minutes from the campus.

Brack became general manager and eventually sold his interests in the Jesup operation when the two weeklies there were consolidated under NeSmith's leadership. In addition to his duties at *The Gwinnett Daily News*, Brack continued to be a visiting professor at the University of Georgia until 1982. He also helped organize and was the first chairman of the Board of Advisors to *The Red and Black* when it became independent of the University in 1980. For a number of years he was the GPA chairman of the annual Cracker Crumble, the satirical show which is the main fund-raising event for the Georgia Press Education Foundation.

The Gwinnett News Company owns two weekly newspapers in adjoining counties, *The Winder News*, purchased in 1972, and *The Forsyth County News*, purchased in 1973. Both are printed in the plant in Lawrenceville. *The Forsyth News* added a Sunday edition in April 1984, and Publisher Eddie Stowe observed: "We hope to publish daily at some point in the future." The Forsyth Sunday edition carries the TV booklet and the special Sunday women's section from *The Gwinnett Daily News*' Sunday edition.

The Daily News is the only newspaper in Georgia history to win the GPA's coveted "General Excellence" award for four consecutive years.

Clayton News/Daily and Woodprint

A county with many similarities to Gwinnett in growth and proximity to Atlanta is Clayton, in the south metro area. Clayton is much smaller geographically (149 square miles to Gwinnett's 436) and its population growth was most spectacular in the 1950s and 1960s, doubling in both decades, whereas Gwinnett's great surge was in the 1970s.

Two interstate highways (I-75 and I-85) pass through Clayton; it is the site of the State Farmers' Market; it is the legendary setting for most of *Gone With the Wind*, Tara supposedly having been located in the Jonesboro area; and most importantly, the new mid-field terminal of Hartsfield International, the nation's second busiest airport, is located within

Clayton's borders, although it is still under the authority of the City of Atlanta.

Clayton contains all or part of nine communities or municipalities: Forest Park, Riverdale, Jonesboro, Morrow, College Park, Lake City, Rex, Conley and Lovejoy. In the 1980 census it reported 150,357 residents, up from 11,519 in 1920, the largest percentage increase for that 60-year period of any Georgia county.

Clayton's newspaper history has been varied and oft-changing, reflecting its rapid growth, its rural antecedents and its present urban nature.

In 1950 the only paid circulation newspaper listed in Clayton County was *The Clayton County News and Farmer* at Jonesboro, W. Lloyd Matthews, editor and publisher. It was joined in the early 1950s by two weeklies in Forest Park, which at that time was the most dynamic part of the county. Forest Park attained a city-limits population of more than 20,000 by 1970. The papers were *The Forest Park Free Press* and *The Forest Park News*, both owned and published by Jack Troy, a former sports editor of *The Atlanta Constitution*. Troy bought out *The Clayton News and Farmer* in the early 1960s and merged it with his *Free Press*, which was published on Tuesdays. *The News* came out on Thursday, giving the county what amounted to a semi-weekly newspaper, although the names were different.

Another weekly, *The Clayton County Journal*, was started in Jonesboro in 1962. Its existence was precarious from the beginning, and it changed hands three times in its first two years, passing from Herman House to M. M. Buice, and then to a new corporation which had been formed by George Kilpatrick, then chairman of Clayton Federal Savings and Loan, and Jim Wood, a newspaper publisher from neighboring Fayette County. But *The Journal* laid the foundation for the home-county daily newspaper, *Clayton News/Daily*, which still serves the county 20 years later.

Wood, one of the most versatile and innovative newspaper executives in Georgia during the past 30 years, had been recruited by Kilpatrick to take over *The Journal*, which was in suspension by 1964.

Wood, writing years later, recalls the circumstances of how he came to publish a paper in Clayton County:

"George Kilpatrick, chairman of the Clayton Federal Savings and Loan Association, inquired if I'd be interested in coming to Clayton County to operate a weekly newspaper. At that time I was publisher of *The Fayette County News*, and his bank was one of our better advertisers.

"Mr. Kilpatrick said he had observed our operations in building up the bankrupt Fayette newspaper and he and a group of business friends (most of whom were active directors of the savings and loan) were concerned about the sad state of newspaper affairs in Clayton County. He felt the bickering of the two Clayton County weeklies was projecting a bad image for the county."

The new firm purchased the name and rights to *The Clayton County Journal*, and Ruby Royal Quick was named news editor.

In June 1968 the directors declared in the corporate minutes that a daily newspaper in Clayton was the eventual goal of their publishing operations. An old warehouse on Church Street in Jonesboro was purchased from Hugh Dickson, the city's long-time mayor, and John Whatley, and was renovated for use as offices.

Jack Troy's *Forest Park Free Press* was still the county legal organ, but he was in ill health at the time. His business manager, Mrs. Frederick Lee, suggested that Troy sell his newspaper to Wood's company.

The sale price was $50,000 for Troy's paper, which at the time was grossing $94,000 a year. The purchasing firm, Woodprint, Inc., was grossing $141,000 and printing eight other weekly newspapers in its plant which was then at Grantville, some 50 miles from Jonesboro.

Wood had acquired the Grantville plant from Leo Bowen, a legendary figure in Georgia newspaperdom, who befriended Wood during the time he was printing *The Fayette County News*. He later made it possible for Wood to purchase the printing concern. The plant moved from Grantville to Jonesboro in 1969.

Plans were begun at that time for a five-day daily newspaper in Clayton County. The first daily edition was published on August 3, 1971, with subscribers of the twin weeklies given the opportunity to become "Charter Subscribers" of Clayton County's first daily newspaper, which was called *News/Daily*.

In early 1971 Woodprint, Inc. had acquired Martin-Johnson Printing Company of East Point, including its printing and office supply business and its weekly newspaper publication, *The Atlanta Suburban Reporter*. The firm later divested itself of the printing and office supply operations when they proved to be unprofitable.

The Fayette County News was sold to Quimby Melton Jr. of Griffin in March of 1975 in exchange for stock he owned in Woodprint. *The Fayette County News* was the newspaper from which Jim Wood started the firm, acquiring it while the paper was in bankruptcy in 1963. Wood operated the newspaper for 12 years, the longest period of continuous ownership in its history.

The stock reclaimed from Melton was sold to Millard Grimes and his Opelika-Auburn, Alabama Publishing Company, with the money from the sale being used to finance expansion and the operation of a new daily which Wood had started in South Fulton that year.

The years of 1974-76 witnessed an unprecedented surge of competition in the newspaper scene of South Metropolitan Atlanta, with repercussions which would determine the surviving players and competitors. Growth and prosperity had been prevalent for so long that the recession of 1975 and early 1976 in the Atlanta area was not anticipated by the newspaper companies which decided to make decisive moves into the south metro about that time.

In 1974 *The Southside Sun* out of Decatur was already a presence in the tri-city area of East Point, College Park and Hapeville. Also in the tri-cities was Wood's *Atlanta Suburban Reporter* in East Point. The other paid weekly newspaper in South Fulton was *The South Fulton Recorder*, then owned and operated by Stanley Parkman's Carroll County Publishing Company of Carrollton. Kate Jones was still editor and publisher in 1974, but was ready to step aside after 20 years.

The first stirrings of additional newspapers in the area was appropriately enough in its newest town, Peachtree City, which was incorporated in 1959, and by 1974 had become a community of about 4,000 people. In August 1974, Jimmy and Margo Booth launched a tabloid newspaper, *This Week in Peachtree City*, to serve Peachtree City and the western part of Fayette County. (See later section in this chapter).

Wood, who still owned *The Fayette County News* at that time, also started a newspaper specifically for Peachtree City, feeling his position in Fayette County threatened by Booth's new paper. The two papers competed for about six months before Wood closed down his *Peachtree Press* shortly before selling *The Fayette County News* to Melton.

Meanwhile big changes were occurring in South Fulton in the opening months of 1975. Rumors were rampant that THREE daily newspapers were about to be started in the South Fulton area. Several billboards advertised the imminent appearance of one, which was to be headed by a former employee of Wood's named Bill Muller. The billboards and the rumor were all that ever came of that venture.

But incredibly the rumors were right about two other dailies. In February, Wood converted *The Atlanta Suburban Reporter* into a Monday through Friday newspaper called *South Fulton News/Daily*. A week later Otis Brumby's company in Marietta jumped into the field with a Monday through Friday afternoon paper called *South Fulton Today*. Brumby's group was then publishing two other similar dailies — South Cobb and North Fulton — in addition to the weekly Neighbors and *The Marietta Daily Journal*.

Both dailies had sizable news and ad staffs and were impressive products. Ken Wynn, a former sports editor of *The Marietta Daily Journal*, was editor of *South Fulton News/Daily*, and Rob Richardson was the original news editor for *South Fulton Today*. Richardson would later be executive editor for all of the *South Metro Neighbors*. *South Fulton Today's* first edition was 32 pages, and benefited from the tie-in with several Neighbors which had been published in the area.

During that same month — February 1975 — Parkman and Mrs. Jones closed a deal to sell the weekly *South Fulton Recorder* to Grimes. *The Recorder* was running about 10-12 pages, with a paid circulation of 3,000. It had no on-premise composing equipment, as all the work was done in Carrollton. But it had a 20-year history, and a familiar office location on the main street of Fairburn, and Grimes, then living and working in Alabama, very much wanted a Georgia connection, especially one in the Atlanta metro area.

Grimes and Parkman had discussed the sale of *The Recorder* since the previous summer, but when the rumors of new dailies began floating, Grimes naturally was concerned. What was attracting him, and possibly the other publishers crowding into South Fulton at that time, was a huge cleared area on I-85 near Union City where a regional mall was planned that would have a Davison's, Rich's, Sears and many other stores, bringing retail trade to an area then short of outlets. (Shannon Mall finally did open on that site, in November 1980, almost six years after the first announcement.)

After taking over *The Recorder*, Grimes hired Neil Monroe, a reporter on *South Fulton Today*, and a former editor of *The Recorder*, to return as editor and general manager.

Obviously the newspaper field was overcrowded in South Fulton during those hectic months of 1975. First, of course, it was still Fulton County, home county of *The Atlanta Journal and Constitution*. Then there were the two South Fulton-oriented paid dailies, *News/Daily* and *Today*; the free distribution weeklies, *The Southside Sun* and the weekly neighbors on Wednesday or Thursday; and *The Recorder*, a paid weekly which carried the motto on its Page One masthead: "More than a newspaper . . . a community service." Certainly it needed something to distinguish it.

Wood and Grimes had known each other since their days on the copy desk of *The Columbus Ledger* in 1951, and their paths had often crossed since. As soon as Wood got Melton's stock in exchange for *The Fayette County News* he offered to sell the 12 percent interest in *Woodprint* to Grimes for money plus the weekly *Recorder* which Wood wanted to merge with his daily.

The deal was made in the summer of 1975 and in October Grimes became a director of *Woodprint* along with Wood, Dr. Walter Spivey, Dr. Needham Bateman and Grady Lindsey, a realtor. On October 1, the weekly *Recorder* was merged with *South Fulton News/Daily* which became known as *The South Fulton Recorder-News/Daily*, one of the longest names for a daily in Georgia history. It was later shortened to *The Daily Recorder*. Neil Monroe became managing editor of the merged paper, Ken Wynn having departed.

In March 1976, Wood added a Sunday edition which carried the mastheads of both the Clayton and South Fulton *News/Dailies*. Wood said he felt a Sunday edition would give his newspapers an advantage in their inter-county battle with *South Fulton Today* and put them in a better position to serve the large shopping mall, Southlake, which was scheduled for completion at Morrow that summer.

What the Mall mainly brought was more competition in Clayton , where *The News/Daily* had enjoyed a local monopoly for six years. Both a *Clayton Neighbor* and a *Clayton Sun* were started that year (1976), soon followed by Neighbors and Suns in Fayette and Henry counties.

The newspaper battles in south metro Atlanta during 1974-1976 were unique in their variety and complexity, if not in their ferocity. In South Fulton there were no survivors among the paid circulation papers, and the people hurt the most were the hard-working staff members, who were on the front lines against the competition, and whose jobs were whittled away as the combatants fell by the wayside. An oddity was that the public did not seem to notice very much, which may have been the most telling clue to the eventual outcome.

The ranks began to thin out in the fall of 1976. Wood dropped his daily in South Fulton and let *The Recorder* revert to weekly publication. The following year Brumby folded *South Fulton Today*, replacing it with a single South Fulton Neighbor, distributed free each week.

Wood continued his Sunday or weekend edition in Clayton, and in the fall of 1978 he came up with another publication idea which proved much more successful than the venture into South Fulton. This was a weekly newspaper for employees at Atlanta Hartsfield International Airport. It was a free distribution newspaper, left at various places in the airport complex to be picked up by employees. Advertising was sold in combination with *News/Daily*.

Called ATL, for the airport's call letters, the tabloid's first editor was Neil Monroe, a flying enthusiast, who had been editor of *The Recorder*. ATL proved a valuable ally to *News/Daily* in its battle to maintain advertising and circulation totals against the Atlanta newspapers and the two free weeklies in Clayton.

At this time Wood also began soliciting large commercial printing jobs, some running into the millions of impressions. He felt the company had to have the additional income to maintain enough cash flow to support the newspaper operation.

In 1976, Wood had also taken another important step. He offered as a candidate for the state legislature and was elected after a tough runoff and general election. The following summer he was elected president of the Georgia Press Association, and thus found himself a state legislator, president of one of the state's most important trade associations, as well as facing time-consuming problems in his own businesses.

Wood was reelected to the state legislature in 1978 and 1980, serving six years in all. His 1978 opponent attacked him in ads for serving as both a legislator and president of the GPA, which the opponent (an attorney) called a "lobbying group," offering as evidence that the GPA was seeking an increase in legal rates. Wood, a tee-totaling active layman in the Methodist church, who used tomato sandwich rallies to meet the voters, won easily in his second race. By an odd coincidence, Wood and one of his former partners, Quimby Melton Jr., are two of only four GPA presidents since World War II to serve in the legislature. C. J. Broome and W. H. McWhorter were the others.

Among the editors and ad managers who passed through the doors of *News/Daily* during this period were Jimmy Booth (first managing editor); Jimmy Stewart, later an editor in Griffin; Terri Bakken, who wrote a history of Clayton County; Brent Carroll, who was later ad director for all of the Neighbor papers; Frank Robinson, also a Neighbor executive later on; and Jim Register, a former ad manager with the Columbus newspapers, who briefly went over to the weekly Thursday, and was later ad manager in Thomasville. The constant presence was General Manager Bill Wadkins who came to Jonesboro from *The Cartersville Tribune-News* in 1969 and stayed on through the several transitions.

In 1980, when commercial printing began to decline, Wood took two important steps to shore up his operation. In February he reluctantly folded the 26-year-old weekly *South Fulton Recorder*. Joe Hiett, who had come up from Perry to be *The Recorder's* last editor and publisher, moved over to *News/Daily*, and became managing editor later that year when Jim Arnall took over ATL. Arnall was a veteran newspaperman with stints at Associated Press, The Montgomery Advertiser, and the University of Tennessee where he was advisor to student publications. His original home was in Senoia and he wanted to return there to care for his aging mother, which led him to accept the job on *News/Daily*. In his 50s, he found his true journalistic mission on ATL, covering and reporting the activities of the people and companies at Georgia's single largest site of employment, the Atlanta Hartsfield Airport.

Monroe, first ATL editor, left the newspaper business for a public relations post at Georgia Power.

Wood then changed *News/Daily* to a mail-delivery system, which for a daily means putting out a morning newspaper (produced at night, in other words) and mailing it at the appropriate post office so that it is delivered to the subscriber with the day's mail. The time of delivery depends on the time the mail is delivered. This system has been used by daily newspapers in large rural areas where it is impractical to have carriers because of the long distance between subscribers. It is, of course, used by virtually all weekly newspapers and by many free distribution papers such as the Neighbors. Most carriers are phased out under this system, and all subscribers are billed from the main office.

In January 1981, Wood brought in a new circulation manager, Van Dozier, who did not like the system, and immediately set about to switch back to carrier-delivery, but as a morning paper instead of afternoon.

Woodprint was started with a small financial base, and it had proceeded through expansion of its building, its press and composition equipment, property acquisition, and several publishing ventures such as South Fulton and commercial printing, with little additional financial investment.

During most of this time it had also operated an office supply business in East Point; a print shop in its Jonesboro building; an office in Forest Park, and a small shopping center on Georgia 139 in Riverdale. The shopping center had been obtained partly as payment for ads. Wood had aggressively expanded the old warehouse bought in 1969, adding an adjoining metal building for the pressroom, newsprint storage and business offices. The press had been increased to six units, and a second rotary press was bought for commercial web work.

Several magazines which had been included with the purchase of the Martin-Johnson Printing Company in the early 1970s had proven to be financial failures and had to be folded. But Wood and his associates had been fortunate in one area: real estate purchases. When money got tight in the business operation, they sold a lot, a building, and the Riverdale shopping center to make ends meet. Eventually the job printing shop and the office supply business were also sold to obtain operating capital.

But by mid-1981, Wood was down to the basic business, and was becoming weary of the day-to-day hassle of keeping it financially sound. As a legislator he had to spend many long days at the Capitol that year because of the reapportionment and redistricting battles resulting from the 1980 census. He also had been bitten by a political bug of a different nature. He felt his district needed a different U.S. congressman and he didn't see anyone else on the political scene standing up to run.

In the six years since Grimes had become a partner in Woodprint, he and Wood had a monthly routine which seldom varied. Grimes would drive over from Opelika (about 90 miles) on the third Monday in each month for a 7 p.m. stockholders' meeting in Wood's office. Spivey, Bateman and Lindsey were usually present to go over the monthly statements and hear Wood explain the company's current condition. Grimes recalls that the discussions seldom centered on the most relevant matters, such as the fact that the bank account was usually overdrawn.

Then Wood and Grimes would go to the Sambo's Restaurant in Jonesboro for an evening snack (Wood had usually already had dinner; Grimes had not) and discuss various matters, a frequent one being how they could merge their operations, or expand.

During this six-year period, Grimes' own situation changed considerably. His company had sold *The Opelika-Auburn News* in late 1977, and he had formed a new corporation, Grimes Publications, which subsequently bought and operated *The Rockdale Citizen* in Conyers; *The Houston Home Journal* in Perry (for two years), and the Enterprise, Alabama, *Ledger*, a daily and Sunday publication.

In the summer of 1981, Grimes sold the Enterprise paper to the Thomson chain, and acquired Wood's old paper, *The Fayette County News*, plus Jimmy Booth's *This Week in Peachtree City*. Grimes, although he still lived in Opelika, told Wood he had decided he wanted to concentrate all of his businesses in one state, and the state he preferred was Georgia.

That brought up an old question for the two long-time friends: Could they form a company that would have newspapers in Clayton, Rockdale, Fayette and other metro counties, and share the authority and responsibility of running them?

Grimes had been reluctant to pose the question because he did not really believe Wood wanted to sell out or have less authority in the operation of his businesses. But on a July night in Sambo's that year, Wood said he felt the time had come when he truly did want to sell.

First, the other stockholders had to be bought out, and they were agreeable. Then Grimes and Wood decided that it would be best if Wood stepped aside completely from the management and pursued his political ambitions. The transactions were completed on November 2, 1981, with Grimes Publications buying all of Wood's stock (51 percent) but agreeing to let Wood buy back ATL and then lease it to News/Daily.

Grimes named Bill Wadkins as the new publisher. He switched back to Monday through Friday afternoon publication; dropped the Sunday edition, which had actually been published on Saturday morning, and generally reduced operating expenses all along the line.

"Any subscribers who stick with us will have to be loyal," he remarked, "since we must have thoroughly confused them during the past two years, going from afternoon to mail to morning and now back to afternoon." Grimes felt the afternoon schedule was necessary for reducing expenses. By January 1984 there were 42 persons on the payroll, compared to 60 on payroll at the time of the sale.

Wood, meanwhile, declared his candidacy for the Democratic nomination to Congress from the Sixth District. He won the nomination easily and then went against the two-term incumbent, Republican Newt Gingrich. Wood ran a strong race, with little financial help from the Democratic party, but Gingrich bucked a strong Democratic trend in the November 1982 general election and won with 55 percent of the vote.

In early 1983, Wood and Jimmy Booth formed a public relations company in Jonesboro. Wood also bought the airport newspaper in Dallas, Texas, and he and Booth began publishing a magazine for the south metro area.

Clayton County remains Georgia's most competitive county for newspapers. Many residents receive three free newspapers a week: *The Clayton Neighbor*, which has the largest distribution of any single title in the Neighbor chain; *The Clayton Sun*, a formidable publication, although with fewer pages or ads than *The Neighbor*, and a free circulation Wednesday edition distributed by *Clayton News/Daily*.

Of course, there are also *The Journal and Constitution*, including their weekly Clayton Extra on Thursdays, and because the nation's second busiest airport is in Clayton County, it was one of the first areas in the nation to receive the full impact of *USA Today*, the colorful national newspaper from Gannett Newspapers, which is aimed in large measure at air travellers.

Clayton's several separate municipalities and communities tend to dilute its county identity, and identity is an important factor for a local-based daily. Of the four Atlanta metro counties which have local dailies — Cobb, Gwinnett and Rockdale being the others — Clayton's county seat of Jonesboro is the closest (18 miles) to downtown Atlanta, and most of the county's population lives within 12-15 miles of downtown Atlanta. In nearly every respect, *Clayton News/Daily* provides the classic example among Georgia's newspapers of the handicaps in a suburban market and how survival is measured by battles won each week, in a war that never ends.

Gwinnett, richer and faster-growing, is 15 crucial miles further from downtown Atlanta (although in the future, its proximity to the expanding Lenox Square area may prove a vulnerability) and Gwinnett has no Neighbor or Sun newspaper to contend with. Rockdale has only one municipality and a stronger identity. Marietta, of course, is an older city, an older paper, and has no in-county competition at all except from its own publications.

But despite its handicaps, *Clayton News/Daily* by early 1985 had increased its paid circulation to 9,000, up from 5,000 in January 1982; its 1984 ad revenue was the highest in its history, with 1985 totals running well ahead of the previous year totals; and it continued to provide by far more news about Clayton County activities than any of its weekly competitors.

As a small fish in a big pond, *News/Daily* keeps swimming, while slowly working to expand its part of the pond.

Georgia's Richest County

It is not surprising that Jim Wood, Quimby Melton Jr. and his son Quimby III, Millard Grimes and Jimmy Booth have all played prominent roles on the Fayette County newspaper scene as well as Clayton County's.

Fayette County closely adjoins Clayton and Spalding (Griffin), and its sudden emergence as Georgia's fastest growing and richest county is one of the state's most fascinating success stories. Fayette, like Clayton, is a small geographic county, only 199 square miles. Their combined size of 350 square miles is nearly 100 square miles less than Coweta (443) or Gwinnett (436), and when comparing populations, the amount of land area covered is a factor to be considered. Clayton and Fayette together have more people than Gwinnett — in a smaller land area.

Fayette is one of the older counties in the Atlanta metro area, having been created in 1821, which may account for why it has the oldest surviving courthouse in the entire state.

In 1920 Fayette reached a population of 11,396, which was more than Clayton had in that census, but a decline set in that reduced its population to 8,199 in the 1960 census (while Clayton in that year reached 46,000). As the rest of the Atlanta metropolitan area surged in population in the 1960s, Fayette picked up but not dramatically. The 1970 census total was 11,364, still below the 1920 population. But then came a 10-year population explosion that is unique in Georgia during the past 50 years. During the 1970s Fayette's population increased by a remarkable 159 percent, the biggest 10-year percentage jump recorded by a Georgia county in this century and probably in any other. In addition, Fayette attained the highest per capita income of any county and still holds that distinction in the 1980s, according to Emory University economic surveys.

Fayette is projected by the State Office of Planning and Budget to continue its phenomenal growth, rising to a population of 62,000 in 1990, and becoming the 20th most populous county in the state. In 1970 it had ranked 89th.

All this was difficult to see for the publishers and editors who tried to keep alive various newspapers in Fayette County during the past century. *The Fayette County News* claims its roots go back to 1886, but it was not listed in *Georgia Journalism*, the history of the state's newspapers published in 1950. The newspaper listed for Fayetteville was called *The Enterprise*. However, *The Fayette County News* does turn up in the 1953 Georgia Press Association directory, with Sid Williams, a former executive manager of the GPA, as the publisher. Williams, who left the GPA post in 1947, published several weeklies in the Atlanta area during that period.

Ed Bernd, a journalist who spent several years as managing editor of *The Rome News-Tribune*, took over *The Fayette County News* in the early 1960s, but the business just was not there. In 1963, a Chapter 11 bankruptcy was filed for the paper and Jim Wood, who was looking for a chance to get back into the newspaper business after a stint at Emory University, bought

The News' assets and assumed its debts for about $8,400.

This indirectly brought about his association with Leo Bowen's printing shop in Grantville. *The News* was being printed there on a two-page, flatbed press, and the average issue was four pages. Wood joined Bowen in the printing business in 1964, moving to Grantville, and it was from there that he later expanded into Clayton County and started *Clayton News/Daily*.

Another newspaper which Wood bought during that period was *The Hogansvile Herald*. Thorne Lane, a veteran newspaperman who also conducted circulation drives throughout thc South, was publisher of *The Herald* for several years. Wood sold *The Herald* to Bob Tribble in the early 1970s when Tribble was forming his group of small weeklies, most of which no one else wanted.

In 1975, *The Fayette County News* became the means by which Wood helped boost the finances of his Woodprint operations in Jonesboro. One of his partners, Quimby Melton Jr. of Griffin, swapped his stock and other considerations for *The Fayette County News*, clearing the way for the stock to be sold for nearly $200,000, which was infused into the Woodprint coffers. Melton's son, Quimby III, became the Fayette publisher, assisted by his wifc, Louisa. Quimby III and Louisa brought imagination and flair to the suddenly-growing community and newspaper.

From a county which had one bankrupt weekly in 1963, Fayette County in 1975-76 had no less than four weekly newspapers — and all of them are still operating in the mid-1980s.

Peachtree City, The "New Town"

The founding of Peachtree City in western Fayette County in 1959 was the most significant step toward transforming Fayette from its long-time role as a stagnant rural area into Georgia's fastest growing county. Atlanta's Hartsfield International Airport was expanding rapidly during that period and Fayette offered convenient homesites for the airport's affluent workers. Peachtree City is unique among Georgia's "new towns," almost hidden from regular highway traffic patterns, some 12 miles off I-85, between Fayetteville and Newnan. The first planned city in Georgia since Savannah, Peachtree City encompasses 15,000 acres, and is a community of surprisingly large, lovely and expensive homes and neighborhoods. Some of its homes range toward the half million mark in price. Most of these are off its main highway, and not visible to the passers-through who see only the business section, which is built in an attractive and uniform style and pattern, specified by the city government.

Peachtree City's distinction is that it is not just a neighborhood; it is an incorporated city. It also is not part of the continuous urban area. It is 26 miles from downtown Atlanta, and a lot of countryside lies between it and the nearest other commercialized areas, which would be Fayetteville to the east, and Newnan to the west. The architecture of the homes varies, and each home sits on a minimum one-acre site. From zero in 1959 Peachtree City had reached a city limits population of 8,000 and rising by 1980. In addition it has generated residential growth throughout the western side of Fayette County. It is not surprising that a new town soon attracted a new newspaper, one that like the town had some distinctive features.

This Week in Peachtree City was launched in August 1974 by Jimmy and Margo Booth. Jimmy had grown up in Fayetteville, the county seat, and had closely observed the early growth of Peachtree City. He saw people there who believed they could create a model city and could find a special quality of life. He moved there himself in 1965.

Caught up in the optimism and confidence around him, Jimmy had a dream of his own — to publish a newspaper to serve this unique new community. "As the city grew in size, it developed a character all its own," Jimmy says. "It needed a newspaper especially designed for that character." And so in 1974, when Peachtree City's population had reached 4,000, the Booths decided the time was right.

Jimmy had worked as a newspaper editor for 15 years, including five at *The Fayette County News*, legal organ of the county. In addition, he had three years' experience as public relations/advertising director for the parent company of the prime developer of Peachtree City. "I felt I knew the community I was working with. I knew its personality, its history, its politics, its people. I knew its strengths and weaknesses. I believe this intimacy I already shared with the city and the county was the key to what turned out to be an overwhelming acceptance of our newspaper from the start," Jimmy explained.

And Margo, though having no actual newspaper experience of her own beyond a few freelance writing assignments, did have a degree in English and five years of living and working in the county.

"We had several major decisions facing us," Jimmy recalls. "Peachtree City did not have a large enough business base to support a newspaper. We considered attempting a countywide paper, but that could not be accomplished while focusing on the flavor of Peachtree City. So we decided to limit our active news coverage to the Peachtree City area.

"We also had to decide on format, and for several reasons, we went to a tabloid. We intended to offer sophisticated layouts with good photography. Also, we were in a competitive situation from the very beginning, and a tab gave us an appearance of bulk because it had twice as many pages. Later, when we found ourselves as one of four papers trying to serve the county, we were grateful for the distinctive identity of the tabloid format."

Another early decision the Booths faced was whether circulation should be free or paid. "In the beginning all of our circulation was free. Then, we gradually converted to paid circulation, first in Peachtree City and later in the outlying areas. Eventually, we had from 93 to 95 percent paid coverage in Peachtree City, our primary market," Margo says.

The Booths started the operation as the only investors and with only $10,000 in the bank. "This was money Margo and I had saved, and we realized we were taking a big risk," recalls Jimmy. "August of 1974 was not the best time to go into business. The economy was suffering from a slump in the real estate industry and a fuel crisis, but we felt we needed to make our move then before someone else recognized Peachtree City's potential. And though we didn't have much cash on hand, we did have a friendly bank which provided us with small loans on a couple of occasions when they were needed."

Compiling a staff was an easy job. "We learned of a woman who was new to the community who came here with experience in typesetting and paste-up. We hired her and a receptionist/bookkeeper, and our budgeted positions were filled," Margo said. "Jimmy and I were the writers and editors, photographers, and ad reps. This habit — set at the beginning — of us personally doing such a large proportion of the work never changed during the years we owned the paper." She added, "In retrospect, I see that as both the factor which contributed most to the paper's success and also contributed most to our eventual decision to sell the paper."

"We began publishing in four rooms of rented office space equipped with a Compuwriter Junior and a Compugraphic 7200 headliner," said Jimmy. "Bursting at the seams and with no reasonable rental space to move to, we built our own building about four years later. Our typesetting equipment, though inadequate for producing an average of 48 tabloid pages per week, was never expanded during our ownership."

Peachtree City presented a unique challenge. A weekly newspaper had to satisfy a highly-affluent and well-educated readership which had no roots in the community. The news common in most rural weeklies had little appeal to such an audience. Because of the closeness to Atlanta's Hartsfield International Airport, Peachtree City has a large number of residents who are airline officials, pilots or other highly-paid personnel at the airport. Added to these are the top executives of local industries and local entrepreneurs. With this kind of residential base, Peachtree City soon evolved into the town with the highest income level in Georgia.

But the biggest challenge confronting the fledgling *This Week* from the outset was competition from other newspapers. When the Booths first published *This Week* on August 7, 1974, *The Fayette County News* was the only other paper based in the county. Because Peachtree City, which had no newspaper, was becoming the largest population center in the county, the Booths felt Fayette County could be a two-newspaper market. However, when *The News'* ownership (Jim Wood) learned of the Booths' plans, it started its own Peachtree City newspaper, *The Peachtree Press*. "Fortunately for us, we were able to win this battle," said Jimmy. "*The Press* was closed down after only six months." (Ironically, in 1982 Booth would be former competitor Wood's campaign manager when Wood ran for Congress. They later became partners in a public relations company.)

As the years passed, the Booths found themselves with other competitors, as both News/Sun Publications and Neighbor Newspapers expanded into Fayette County with free circulation publications.

"Being in a four-newspaper market was tough," Jimmy admitted. "Fortunately, we remained the only paper actually published in Peachtree City and therefore the only one able to devote nearly 100 percent of its news coverage to Peachtree City. As long as we stayed on top of everything going on around us, we could come out ahead."

But "staying on top" meant an expanded news staff, and quality in layout and appearance required an expanded production staff. "We ended up with about 17 employees and a payroll that ran close to 60 percent of our revenue," said Margo. "Anyone who has published a newspaper knows that is an unrealistic figure, but as long as we were able to keep our heads above water, we lived with it."

The economy, which had been in a slump at the time the paper was started, went up and down but was generally depressed during the years the Booths owned the paper. Margo commented, "I attribute our success in ad sales during this period to a number of things. To begin with, our three ad people were paid on commission. There was no ceiling — it amounted to about a straight 15 percent. We averaged as many as 120 ads per issue, and that required a lot of legwork." The ad territories stretched far beyond the circulation area, covering a radius of approximately 30 miles around Peachtree City. "I believe we would never have made it without those ad people out there knocking on doors," Margo said. "The result of a very aggressive ad team was that we had lots and lots of small customers and a few big ones. In a way, this worked to our advantage. We never found ourselves dependent on any one or two advertisers, and during times when full-page advertisers would drop out, their overall impact on our revenue was not as damaging."

As *This Week* grew in reputation, it grew in value, and a number of newspaper groups showed an interest in acquiring it. "While we didn't want to give up control of the paper, there were several compelling reasons to consider a sale," said Jimmy. "Our operation was still very small and while we were by then able to show a small profit, we knew we would never be able to install the practices utilized by groups to turn a big profit. Our financial condition also prevented us from making equipment purchases to keep up with technological advances. So we felt a sale to a larger organization could assure the future of the newspaper and allow it to keep pace with the growth of the town. Most of all, we hoped it would give us some relief from what had become by that time an overwhelming and tremendously continuing sense of responsibility for the operation of the paper."

In July of 1981, the Booths sold *This Week* to Grimes Publications of Georgia which had, only months before, purchased *The Fayette County News*. Jimmy remained publisher/editor of *This Week* and Margo remained as business manager.

In January of 1982, Grimes sold *This Week* and *The News* to Bob Tribble's Tri-County Newspapers of Manchester. The two papers were brought into a new company, Fayette Newspapers, Inc., with Jimmy as publisher of both. But three months later, because of sweeping changes in format, in philosophy, and in production methods, the Booths left the company.

In a farewell column on March 31, 1982, Jimmy wrote: "All things change, I suppose. This is particularly true in the world of business. At the present time, this is what is happening at *This Week* newspaper.

"For business reasons, *This Week* has been making some changes in direction. It is a direction Margo and I don't choose to travel, so we are leaving the staff, effective this Friday.

"The decision to leave the newspaper which Margo and I originated back in late summer 1974 was not an easy one. However, we are convinced that the decision is best for ourselves and for the newspaper's new ownership."

One year later, Margo summed up the publishing experience in Peachtree City by saying, "Looking back, I believe that our knowledge of the community, our appreciation of it, and our caring for it were the keys to the success of *This Week*. I don't know if it makes sense to talk about a paper having a relationship with a community, but that is what we built at *This Week*. The paper was a source of pride for the community. It was welcomed into homes, missed if it didn't come, and shared with relatives. Those are the things I will remember about it, that and the fact that it was a lot of hard, hard work."

In November 1983, Jimmy Booth was named editor of *Clayton Extra*, another of the *Journal-Constitution* weeklies devoted to news and ads in specific areas. Because of a non-compete covenant with the owners of the Peachtree City weekly, Booth cannot work for a competing paper in Fayette County, so *Clayton Extra* does not circulate in Booth's home county. Fayette subscribers of the *Journal-Constitution* receive instead *South Fulton Extra*, edited by Katherine Gibney, a former news editor of *This Week in Peachtree City.*

Some of the other journalists who worked at *This Week* during the Booth years included:

Keith Graham, later with *The Atlanta Journal-Constitution;* Burt Roughton Jr., later with *The Atlanta Journal-Constitution;* Lisa Richardson, later editor of *The Fayette Neighbor,* Fayetteville; and Ginger Blackstone, later director of public affairs, State Department of Natural Resources.

The Fayetteville Transitions

Four separately-owned weeklies in Fayette County did seem a bit much, despite its phenomenal growth. In early 1981, Millard Grimes was looking for an opportunity to expand his holdings in the Atlanta metro area. He talked to Quimby Melton about the possibility of buying *The Fayette News* and found him responsive. Melton III, the publisher, wanted to move to Griffin, and the Meltons had several other weekly newspapers which were in less competitive markets than Fayette. Grimes felt the key to success in Fayette was a common ownership of the two paid circulation papers. So he also talked to Booth, who he knew was interested in selling.

Grimes Publications bought *The Fayette County News* in April 1981, and then added *This Week in Peachtree City* in July 1981. Booth remained as publisher of *This Week* and Tom Kerlin became publisher and editor of *The Fayette County News*. The two papers were printed at *The Rockdale Citizen* plant in Conyers.

Later that year, Grimes had the opportunity to become the majority stockholder in Woodprint *(Clayton New/Daily* etc.) and he chose to pursue that course. Feeling he did not have the time or financial depth to also publish the Fayette County weeklies, he sold them to Robert Tribble of Manchester, who consolidated the composing operations of the papers at the Peachtree City building, and made Booth publisher of both papers. The combined price of the two properties was about $530,000. or slightly more than one times their 1980 gross income. Neither had been really profitable under separate ownership.

After Booth resigned in April 1982, Gary Cornwell, a long-time Tribble executive, moved to Peachtree City and became general manager of both papers. Kerlin left in September 1982, and Cal Beverly was named editor of the two papers.

Although a definite separate identity has been maintained for *The News* and *This Week*, Tribble reluctantly abandoned the tabloid format of *This Week* so that ads could be sold jointly and picked up more easily from one paper to the other. By mid-1983, the use of combination rates had increased the number of pages and ad inches over their two-ownership days. The papers were also holding to their paid circulations of about 3,300 in Peachtree City and 3,800 for *The Fayette County News*. In the spring of 1984 the two papers moved to a larger building in Fayetteville, and in 1985 a five-unit press was installed at the Fayette plant.

East Metro: Rockdale and Newton

Another relatively new daily newspaper being published in the metropolitan Atlanta counties is *The Rockdale Citizen,* which converted from semi-weekly to a Monday-Friday, five-day-a-week schedule on August 1, 1978. It is based in Conyers, a town of about 8,000, 25 miles from downtown Atlanta. Rockdale County was just another small rural county until an interstate highway passed through and provided a link that brought sudden development and population growth. In the 1960 census, Rockdale had only 10,572 residents; by 1970 it had climbed to 18,152, and then in the 1970s its population more than doubled to 36,747.

In land area, Rockdale is the second smallest of Georgia's counties, next only to Clarke, with 128 square miles, so its population growth is concentrated in a 10-mile radius of Conyers, which is its only incorporated municipality.

Until 1953, Rockdale was one of the state's most unstable newspaper markets. In Rockdale's past were the graveyards of many newspapers which had flared brilliantly for a few years and then disappeared, without even a semblance of their name or masthead left to recall them. Among them was the *Conyers Solid South* in the 1880s and 1890s, whose editor of that period, M.D. Irwin, was the main force in organizing the Georgia Press Association. Irwin was the first GPA president, in 1887, and served another term as president in 1891.

Irwin and *The Solid South* both disappeared from the Conyers scene in the 1890s, and information about Irwin's subsequent career is meager. *The Solid South* just changed its name, and became known as *Hale's Weekly*, after J. N. Hale who had bought it from Irwin.

There were a number of other weekly newspapers before and after *The Solid South* that served the city and county. The first one, apparently, was *The Rockdale Register*, started in 1876 by Judge A. C. McCalla. A *Conyers Courier* appeared in 1878, published by W. P. Reed, a former employee of *The Register*. That same year another weekly, *The Examiner*, started publication, although it seems to have been *The Register* under a different name.

In 1883, *The Conyers Weekly* appeared, with J. N. Hale as an assistant editor. Hale would be associated with several Conyers newspapers in the next few years. Then came *The Solid South* in 1885, published by John R. Maddox and Irwin. Two years later both *The Conyers Weekly* and *The Solid South* would send representatives to the first meeting of the Georgia Weekly Press Association. Both Marcus D. Irwin and J. R. Irwin were listed among the charter members representing *The Conyers Solid South,* and R. J. Guinn was listed from *The Conyers Weekly.* (See Chapter X).

Later *The Weekly's* name was changed to *The Rockdale Banner*, and under the ownership of W. S. Wardlow it became the leading weekly in Rockdale's crowded newspaper field at the turn of the century. *The Weekly* and *The Banner* were merged in the 1900s and for a time were published semi-weekly.

But it was *The Conyers Times*, started by the Harper Brothers in 1909, which became the dominant newspaper in the county for the next 30 years. By 1911, it was the only newspaper being published in Conyers.

Edward Augustus Harper, know as Guss, was editor and publisher of this paper for about six years until his untimely death on New Year's Eve,

1914, at the age of 44. Based on reprints of editorials from throughout the state, which are preserved in an old issue of *The Times*, Harper had quickly become one of the most respected editors in Georgia. *The Clarkesville Advertiser* called *The Times* "one of the state's brightest newspapers." *The Walton News* said "*The Conyers Times* is one of the most interesting exchanges that comes to our table and we read it weekly with pleasure." *The Lawrenceville News-Herald* praised Harper for having "established *The Times* so firmly that it drove able competition from the field and sustains its reputation as one of the best Georgia weeklies, and is the only newspaper in Rockdale County."

From these comments, it seems that Harper and *The Times* had a strong impact in newspaper circles despite the short period in which he was associated with the paper. *The Times* continued as the only newspaper in Rockdale County from 1911 until 1928 when *The Rockdale Record* began with J. M. Towns as editor. *The Times* and *Record* were merged just two years later in January 1930, with Towns continuing as editor for nearly 20 years.

Another new weekly came on the scene in 1941 when *The Conyers News* was established by Belmont Dennis of Covington. Dennis operated several newspapers, including *The Covington News*. His general manager, W. Thomas Hay, lived in Conyers, providing an advantage in the competition for the meager advertising market in a county which then had only 8,000 residents. Dennis bought *The Conyers Times-Record* in 1952 and it soon disappeared from the scene, adding another tombstone to Rockdale's huge newspaper graveyard.

Hay sold ads for *The Covington News* and *The Conyers News* as a combination to advertisers wanting to cover both counties. Before I-20 extended into these counties, they were not considered suburban.

Dennis and Hay were a successful team for nearly 20 years before they came to a sudden parting of the ways in 1953. Hay had gone to work for Dennis in 1933, two years after Dennis took over *The Covington News*. Dennis, who had only a grade school education, was one of Georgia's most colorful and inventive publishers for nearly three decades. He had joined the U.S. Navy at the age of 13 by telling officials he was 18. He was selling intertype machines when he got a chance to buy *The News* for $10,000. Dennis had also been press foreman for the Charleston, South Carolina *Evening Post*, and in 1935 he contracted to buy a 32-page rotary press from the *Post*. In those days few weekly publishers in Georgia had rotary presses, as they mostly used flatbeds, but Dennis was planning to get into the printing business in a big way.

Soon he managed to land a contract with Sears Roebuck Department Store to print a million-plus circulars on a regular basis. Hay recalls that the Covington plant was not large enough to handle the printing, packaging and shipping of such a large job. "We worked on the sidewalks, in empty buildings across the street and anywhere we could find space," he says.

Later Dennis got the printing contract for the weekly Georgia Market Bulletin plus other printing jobs which soon made his plant one of the busiest and most prosperous in the state.

The Covington News also grew as a newspaper, and Dennis became active in state politics, twice running for lieutenant governor. He spent more and more time away from the office, always wintering in Florida and sailing on his 65-foot yacht, which was the third and largest yacht he owned.

Hay, as general manager, supervised the Covington and Conyers newspapers, and was also manager of the Dennis-owned Covington radio station. "During this time I felt quite secure in my position," Hay recalls. But events were building for a split in the working association of Hay and Dennis, with consequences that would greatly affect the newspaper business in Newton and Rockdale counties.

Dennis' brother-in-law, Leo Mallard Sr., had joined the company about 1950 and took an increasingly active role in its management. Hay asked Dennis for some assurance that his future with the company was secure in the event Mallard took over, but Dennis said he couldn't offer any. So in the summer of 1953, Hay plunged out on his own and started weekly newspapers in both Conyers and Covington, in competition with the two Dennis papers.

Hay called his Covington weekly *The Citizen-Observer* and his new Conyers paper *The Rockdale Citizen*. Its first edition appeared in July 1953.

Thus was joined a unique battle in Georgia newspaperdom, two new paid-circulation weeklies battling two established weeklies in counties adjacent to each other. Of the four newspapers in the battle, the one which was weakest at the time and seemed to have the most doubtful future was *The Rockdale Citizen,* which 30 years later would not only be one of the survivors but a daily and the strongest of the survivors. Recalling the all-out battle, Hay wrote years later:

> It was dog eat dog for five years, with Dennis and me trying to better the other. Dennis started running a box on Page 1 that said '20,000 readers.' We came back with a box that said '20,001 readers.'

> Prices for ads dropped as low as 15 cents an inch. When I left *The Covington News* it was running 32 to 36 pages a week, and the number rose to more than 40 pages later on. We started out in Covington with 24 pages a week but soon dropped to an average of 12 pages and hung on. We got the services of a professional circulation company, gave away two automobiles, started a paper in Lithonia and ended up with about $800 in the bank from the circulation drive. That got our combined (Covington and Conyers) paid circulation up to about 5-6,000.
>
> In 1958 both of us were losing money and Dennis approached me about a settlement. About that time my papers got a big break by receiving a trial series of ads from Colonial Stores (now Big Star). They alternated between the two competing papers in each city, and the legal advertising was also on alternating years between the papers.
>
> That brought things to a head. Dennis and I met one night in his office and struck a deal. He offered me the Conyers papers and $10,000 in exchange for closing down my Covington paper. At that time, of course, the Covington market and papers were the largest.
>
> Dennis and I remained good friends. He often stopped in Conyers to visit and showed a genuine interest in my success or failure. There was always a sort of father-son relationship between us despite our five-year battle.

Hay now had the only newspaper in Rockdale County, and he added a commercial printing shop and an office supply business. The newspaper was still small, compared to *The Covington News*. Newton County had twice the population of Rockdale at that time, and Covington had been a major trade, industrial and educational center for years.

But Interstate 20 was coming to both counties, and the one it helped most was the one closest to Atlanta, which was Rockdale.

Hay and his brother, S. M., his wife Jewell, and later his daughter, Elizabeth, were the key management personnel on *The Citizen* and its related operations from 1958-1977, as the county more than doubled in population, and most important for the newspaper, many new retail businesses opened. The open fields around the I-20 intersections began filling up with shopping centers.

The Citizen became a semi-weekly (Tuesday and Thursday) in 1972 and by 1976 Hay had ideas of turning it into a daily. In preparation he employed two circulation men to convert *The Citizen* from mail-delivery to carrier-delivery.

Hay by now was 66, however, and he had built *The Citizen* into a valuable property. Several companies had contacted him about a possible sale. One contact was from Millard Grimes, who in 1976 was head of a newspaper group based in Opelika, Alabama. Grimes had bought *The South Fulton Recorder* in February 1975 and had noticed among the exchange papers at Fairburn that the Atlanta suburban newspaper which seemed to have the most ads was *The Rockdale Citizen*.

One day he dropped by *The Citizen* office in Conyers and introduced himself to Hay. They had a friendly talk and Grimes told Hay that his company would like to make an offer if Hay ever considered selling. "In about 18 months, I might be interested," Hay said. That was in February 1976. In August 1977, Grimes got in touch with Hay again. At that time Grimes was forming a new company, Grimes Publications, and was in the process of selling *The Opelika-Auburn News*. He told Hay *The Citizen* would be the flagship of his new company. An agreement was reached on virtually the exact offer Grimes first made. Hay kept the commercial printing company and Grimes got the newspaper, which included a Total Market edition on Wednesday called *This Week in Rockdale*.

Grimes, primarily a daily-oriented publisher, hoped to follow through as soon as possible on Hay's plan to go daily.

Hay had been publisher and his wife, Jewell, was the bookkeeper or business manager. Their daughter, Elizabeth (Libby) Staples, served as editor for several years and was the general manager at the time of the sale. Grimes, a strong believer in local-oriented publishers, asked Ms. Staples to succeed her father as publisher, putting her in line to become the first woman publisher of a general circulation daily newspaper in Georgia.

The sale was completed on December 9, 1977, and less than nine months later, on August 1, 1978, *The Rockdale Citizen* published its first daily (Monday through Friday) edition. Staff members at the time included Fred Turner, editor; Jane Patterson, advertising manager; Jenell Orr, business manager; Tom Barry, sports editor; Harvey Cowan, photographer; Roger Young and Vickie Garner, composition. All of these, including Ms. Staples, the publisher, had been with *The Citizen* virtually all of their adult careers and had never worked on a daily. They were worried that, first, there would not be enough advertising to justify the number of pages for five editions a week, and secondly, that there would not be enough news to continue an all-local, staff-produced front page, which they had agreed would be needed for a suburban audience.

Grimes had never been involved in changing a semi-weekly to a daily, and neither he nor Hay had done any real research on whether Rockdale was ready for such a move. The semi-weekly was averaging about 56 pages a week in 1978 (36 on Thursdays, 16-20 on Tuesdays) and paid circulation was about 6,000. Grimes had been told by others who had converted that it would take at least two years to make a profit and regain lost circulation.

But the factor Grimes considered most strongly was timing. He felt it was better to establish a daily in the early stages of the county's growth so that the new residents coming in would be accustomed to a local daily newspaper. In an editorial for the first daily edition, he wrote: "We don't believe that Rockdale is a 'weekly county' any longer. A daily newspaper will provide another point of identity for the county, and make communications and information easier and quicker. It will put Rockdale County more firmly on the map. Only 26 of Georgia's 159 counties had a home-county daily newspaper on July 31, 1978. Rockdale is now the 27th."

Publisher Staples, in a column of amusing candor, wrote in that issue: "Twenty-five years ago as I stood in the little Covington plant my father had built and ran the folder into the middle of the night for the first issue of *The Rockdale Citizen,* I would have been astounded had anyone suggested it might ever be a daily, and particularly if they had said I'd be a part of it. At that time my mind was on Stephens College which I was to enter in the fall and from whence I never expected to return to Conyers other than as a visitor. I saw that college as my passport out of this little hick town that I thought held no future for me. Twenty-five years later, if I have learned one thing it is that one's future is totally unpredictable."

As with most new dailies, *The Citizen* experienced rough going in its early months. The staff had to become familiar with a daily routine, with selecting the best wire stories, with producing five front pages a week instead of two. Fortunately the advertising did increase and *The Citizen* jumped to 90 to 100 pages a week in the fall of 1978. One reason for this was a generous rerun policy on classifieds which was instituted to assure a strong classified section each day. Another tactic, continued from Hay's time as publisher, was the running of all supermarket advertising on Monday as well as on Wednesday, but at the price of one run. Hay started that policy when *The Citizen* became a semi-weekly, to assure enough pages in the Tuesday edition. As a daily, *The Citizen* added a pickup rate for camera-ready ads that ran twice in the same week, and soon made the two runs a paying proposition. The supermarket ads bolstered a usually slow day, providing both bulk and readership to the Monday edition.

Only one news staffer was added for the daily schedule, which was cutting it rather thin, and matters got worse when Editor Turner broke his leg while playing soccer two months after the daily schedule began.

The Citizen's task also was complicated by an unusual printing arrangement for a daily newspaper. The press room, with press and plate maker, was located approximately a city block away, making it necessary to walk the page negatives over in rain or shine. It also divided the small press and camera staff between two buildings. The 16-page press was one of the earliest News Kings designed for newspapers. By 1979 it was very tired, having turned out millions of circulars as well as thousands of newspapers.

Late press runs were a common occurrence which hampered the circulation effort and the need to establish a regular afternoon identity. In early 1980, however, a rebuilt 16-page Goss Community press was installed in the main building, which was extensively remodeled at the time, providing a press room and circulation preparation area in the part that had previously held the commercial shop, and moving the executive and advertising offices into an adjoining old house which had previously held a gift shop. *The Citizen* has the only daily newspaper office in Georgia with fireplaces and mantelpieces in the publisher's and ad manager's offices, as well as in the reception area which was once a living room. About that time *The Citizen* got in-county competition from the introduction of *The Rockdale Neighbor* in February 1980. This was the first time two newspapers had carried Rockdale in their mastheads since Hay and Dennis had settled their bitter struggle 22 years earlier.

But as in other metro counties, the paid-circulation daily and the free-distribution weekly have managed to coexist, and in 1985 *The Citizen* was into its eighth year as a daily, with close to 8,000 paid subscribers, and a consistent record of ad revenue gains in each year as a daily.

Libby Staples is a native of Conyers and thus fairly rare among its current residents. She is also a rarity in Georgia journalism. Although women have moved into nearly every area of newspaper work during the past 30 years, and actually dominate many departments in which they were scarcely seen in 1950, Ms. Staples was still the only woman publisher of a general circulation Georgia daily in 1985. (Frances Beck is publisher of *The Fulton Daily Report*, which carries the legal notices for Fulton County.)

She is quick to admit that being the daughter of the former owner was undoubtedly a big help, but for seven years, through conversion to a daily schedule, and numerous other trials and tribulations, she has been the chief executive on the scene, handling the public on a daily basis, representing the newspaper at functions and on boards, and writing most of the editorials and a weekly column. Her editorials have won a first place award in the

Georgia Press Association competition and she has also won awards for feature writing and her personal column.

In civic work, she has been a Chamber of Commerce board member and chairman of the Rockdale United Fund. It hasn't been all that smooth, however, either in her career or personal life. Divorced and remarried, Ms. Staples and her second husband have eight children between them, four of hers and four of his. All of the children have been part of her household at various times since she became publisher, and she also took in as boarders other young people who were working at the newspaper until they could find places of their own. Her two youngest children were still in high school during her years as publisher and they required the mother's attention that teen-agers must have. Her oldest son is a pilot in the Air Force, and her second son is a pressman at *The Citizen*.

Commenting on her status as a woman publisher, Ms. Staples writes:

> Actually I've never given much thought until right now about being the only woman publisher of a daily. I guess I never had to and I feel vaguely guilty, as if I should be using the distinction as a forum to promote women's rights. I'm a believer in women's rights, though the more radical manifestations of that cause leave me cold.
>
> I think that women as a gender have capabilities that have been badly underrated in our culture, by both sexes. And the real tragedy is that this world certainly isn't in any shape to ignore its resources. Yet, the issue is not about women as a group. It is about choices. It is a shame that one's abilities and ambitions have to be determined by someone else's idea of what they should be. Both males and females should have the freedom, both in law and social acceptance to be what they are capable of being.
>
> But I must confess, that in my particular situation, if I have ever encountered any handicap to doing the job I love because of sexism, I didn't know it was happening.
>
> Perhaps if I had not had the special opportunities that were offered me, things might have been different. My father founded *The Rockdale Citizen*. Before that, he was general manager of *The Covington News*. So, not only was I "born under a press" as I like to say, I was, in later years, to find an easier access to the management level of the business, though, for a period of time, I was not enthusiastic about taking advantage of the opportunity.
>
> As I tried to learn my craft by covering politics, sewer grants, elections, government budgets and zoning and police reporting (the latter consisting mostly of running to the sheriff's office and going through accident reports with the full cooperation of

Sheriff Wallace). I decided the newspaper business was like a short course in everything.

And of course, as on most small papers, I also had several advertising accounts, working, incidentally, with a woman, Jane Patterson, who I consider the best ad manager in the state. So my involvement in the business of putting out a newspaper expanded and deepened. I finally had to admit I was hooked.

When my father sold *The Citizen* I was kept on as publisher. I must confess, that as I moved into the publisher's office and sat down in my Dad's big black executive chair, I was scared. But I don't think that has anything to do with being a woman. Anybody probably would have been at least a little nervous under the circumstances.

An Employee-Owned Newspaper

Meanwhile, in Covington, after the death of Belmont Dennis on Christmas morning, 1961, Mrs. Dennis assumed the publisher's title, and Mrs. Mallard, her sister, became an associate. Leo Mallard, her husband, continued as advertising manager. The Mallards' son, Leo S. Mallard, who had worked on the Carrollton papers for a time, returned to Covington and was named assistant to the publisher. The younger Mallard soon moved into more and more responsibility for the overall operation, as well as being active in the community. In 1974 he was named president of The Covington News, Inc. and given the title of editor.

According to a special edition published by *The News* in 1975, Mrs. Dennis and Mrs. Mallard had actually been the majority owners of the company since 1931, with Mr. Dennis being a minority stockholder. Dennis, however, had obviously been the leading figure in its development, as well as a pioneer in weekly commercial printing on web presses.

By 1964, the volume of commercial work at the Covington plant had dropped sharply, although *The News* still printed the *Georgia Market Bulletin*. But in that year *The News* changed to cold type and offset, boosting its commercial business considerably. In 1975, *The News* company moved from its long-time location in downtown Covington to a spacious new building and began the expansion of its press units to a 48-page capacity. In the early 1980s *The News* plant was turning out a huge volume of pre-prints, having again gotten much of Sears printing, which ran into the millions of copies per week.

On the newspaper side, a free distribution paper called *The Multi-County Star* was started in 1976, going to some 24,000 homes in Newton, Walton, Morgan, Jasper and Rockdale counties each week. *The Star* was published on Tuesday and *The News* was published on Thursday, reverting to once a week from semi-weekly when *The Star* began.

But the commercial web printing business was becoming even more competitive in the Atlanta metro area. In 1981-82, two new web-printing companies were launched, and Phil Pruitt, the long-time production manager of *The News*, went with one of them, taking with him two of *The News'* larger jobs. The loss had a severe financial impact on the overall *News* operation. By this time the majority of its stock had been placed in a trust fund, handled by the Citizens and Southern Bank, and the bank's trust department decided in late 1982 that it would be in the best interest of the trust to sell the entire Covington operation.

In the August 4, 1983 edition of *The Covington News,* a two-line, eight-column headline announced: "*Covington News,* Press Purchased by Employees."

The story read:

> The Covington News and Covington Press, owned by the families of Mary S. Mallard and Mable S. Dennis, was sold Wednesday to the employees of the company.
>
> In making the announcement, company vice-president of finance Lloyd G. Barnard explained that the employees had used the funds from their profit-sharing plan to purchase just over half the company stock. The remaining shares are owned by existing department heads and officers of the company as well as two new people — Mike Tatham and Larry Nuckols — who recently joined the company.
>
> The ESOP (Employee Stock Ownership Plan) was formed immediately following the closing of the sale Wednesday afternoon. Funds which were being invested in outside corporate stocks and bonds for the profit-sharing plan, will now be invested in the Covington News and Press.
>
> Denny Hill, news editor since April of 1981, was named editor of the newspaper. Former editor and president of the company, Leo S. Mallard, will remain with the company as a consultant. Leo Mallard and Mary S. Mallard will also remain with the organization.
>
> A Board of Directors was formed to oversee the operation of the company with members being Mike Tatham, president; Larry Nuckols, vice-president of sales; Jeanne Smith, vice-president of advertising; and Lloyd G. (Barney) Barnard, chief executive officer. Herbert Mobley will also serve on the board. The Board of Directors will be elected on a yearly basis with the employees voting their shares of stock.
>
> Barnard said, "On top of being a newspaper, the company has

> always been a well-respected, and primarily, a commercial printer. But until now, we have never had the sales force for that printing." Barnard said that with the addition of Tatham and Nuckols, both proven salesmen, that was expected to change. "Nuckols has a strong graphics background and is well versed in marketing programs and in implementation of those programs," he stated.
>
> Editor Denny Hill said he was enthusiastic about the events of Wednesday, and that he was pleased that the Mallards were staying on.
>
> "While the company could have been sold to a chain newspaper operation or to people with no ties to or concerns about this community, it was not," he continued. "It was sold to the people who work here, to the people who live in this community and who are concerned about this community — and the newspaper will continue to reflect this. And now, not only do we all work here, we all own part of it."

Covington has thus become the only employee-owned newspaper in Georgia, and one of the few in the nation. According to a 1983 article in the ANPA magazine, *Presstime*, there have been only 10 recorded instances in which employees bought daily newspapers. There is little information available on weeklies. Significantly, of the 10 dailies bought by employees, six had been sold, leaving only four still under employee ownership. They are the Milwaukee, Wisconsin *Journal*, *The Milwaukee Sentinel*, the Omaha, Nebraska *World-Herald*, and the Fairbanks, Alaska *News Miner*.

Employee-owned newspapers which have been sold include the Kansas City, Missouri *Star* and *The Kansas City Times*; the Cincinnati, Ohio *Enquirer*; the Redwood City, California *Tribune*, the Palo Alto, California *Times*, and the defunct *New York Sun*.

Most of these were large newspapers with several hundred employees. *The Covington News*, by contrast, is relatively small, with some 60 employees taking part in the purchase. Authority is vested in the board of directors and in Barnard, who is chief executive officer.

Mallard, the former editor and chief operating officer, was not involved in the new ownership as a stockholder or manager. He was given a four-year consulting arrangement and is no longer active in the day-to-day operation of the company.

The ESOP owns slightly more than half the stock and seven individuals — all employees — own the remaining shares.

Henry County, Weekly Battleground

Henry County, which was added to the Atlanta metropolitan area in 1980, has enjoyed less spectacular growth than its neighbors to the north and west. In the 50 years from 1920 to 1970 its population increased by only 3,000 from 20,420 to 23,724. But Henry began to move in the 1970s, rising to 36,309 in the 1980 census, and the prospects are for continuing growth in this large land-area county (420 square miles).

Its potential was enough to attract plenty of newspaper attention during the 1970s, as both a Henry Neighbor and a Henry Sun started publication in 1976, joining the long-time paid weekly, *The Weekly-Advertiser*, which changed its name to *The Henry Herald* in early 1978.

The Sun quit the crowded field in 1979, but by 1983 *The Herald* had begun publishing a paid weekly in Hampton and a free distribution weekly in Stockbridge, giving the county four mastheads a week, *The Henry Herald*, *The Henry Neighbor*, *The Hampton News* and *The Stockbridge News*.

But going back a bit, there were two paid weeklies, *The Henry County Weekly* and *The McDonough Advertiser* being published in Henry County when the Great Depression hit in the early 1930s. Frank J. Linch purchased both papers in 1934 and combined them into *The Weekly-Advertiser*, which he and later his son, Robert C. Linch, published for the next 42 years. In 1975 the newspaper was sold to Quimby Melton Jr. of Griffin and his associates. Publishers under the new ownership have included Robert C. Linch (until 1980), Larry Donald and Norman Wittler. Melton and his son, Quimby Melton III, have also played significant management roles on *The Herald*, and in 1982, the younger Melton spearheaded a remarkable journalistic endeavor for a weekly newspaper (or a daily, for that matter). In 1981, Henry County's sheriff, probate judge and a former county commissioner were all indicted for various drug trafficking offenses.

When the sheriff was tried, *The Herald* bought the transcripts from the court and ran the verbatim testimony in several "extras" which were printed and distributed during the trial. The testimony covered some 30 broadsheet pages, with no advertising.

Shortly afterwards, Melton III was named publisher of *The Griffin Daily News,* succeeding his father. Quimby Jr. took over the supervision of several weekly newspapers he owned in the area, including the Henry papers. *The Griffin Daily News* was sold to the Thomson group on June 30, 1982, with Melton III continuing as publisher.

The Biggest Non-Atlanta Suburb

The only suburban county in Georgia outside of the Atlanta metro area which spawned a new daily newspaper in the past 30 years is Houston County, south of Macon.

Houston and its largest city, Warner Robins, provide a success story as impressive as any of the suburban Atlanta counties. Houston was down to only 11,280 residents in 1930 after Peach County was carved out of its most populous section, around Fort Valley. Perry was the major city and the county seat and Warner Robins did not even exist. But the population doubled during the decade of the 1940s, when the Warner Robins Air Force Base was established and the town of Warner Robins was incorporated in 1943.

Warner Robins had no newspaper, but that kind of growth naturally attracted attention. Ironically, when it did get its own newspaper in 1949, the boom was over, and the air force base and the town were beginning to decline rapidly. But a young would-be publisher named Foy Evans, who didn't know any better, plunged in with a newspaper, *The Warner Robins Sun*, that was to be a trail-blazer in Georgia in several respects. It would become the first suburban daily outside of the Atlanta area. It was one of the first free distribution papers (*The Decatur News* started about the same time), and it was one of the earliest totally cold-type, offset newspapers, converting in 1960. It went from weekly to semi-weekly publication, and then to daily (Monday-Friday) publication in 1969.

The Warner Robins Sun gained another distinction in 1972 when it was the first newspaper purchased by financier Roy Park, who was 62 at the time he bought *The Sun*, and who would own 25 dailies and a large number of weeklies by the time he was 72.

Evans, meanwhile, would be elected mayor of Warner Robins, a post he had held for eight years in 1984. The county's population hit 77,605 in the 1980 census with Warner Robins having 40,000 people in its city limits, making it the state's eighth most populous city.

Evans could hardly have envisioned such a bright future when he published the first issue of *The Sun* on February 24, 1949, and in effect, pioneered the concept of suburban newspapers outside the Metropolitan Atlanta area.

His weekly tabloid got off to an inglorious start, with a total of only four pages and $5 worth of advertising in the first issue.

Warner Robins had boomed during World War II to provide housing and shopping support for Robins Air Force Base, but the city was supposed to dry up following the war and in 1949 it just about had.

When *The Sun* first came out, Warner Robins had shrunk to less than 5,000 people and was still shrinking. "If I had known before I began publishing *The Sun* what I learned soon afterward, I never would have had the courage to start," Evans said later.

But having taken the plunge, he refused to give up and struggled along with four to eight tabloid pages a week until the Korean War brought new life to Robins Air Force Base and a growth that has continued for more than three decades.

For its first seven years, *The Sun* was composed 50 miles away by Southern Printers in Dublin. Until 1953, it was printed on a hand-fed Pony Miehle press two tabloid pages at a time. After four years, *The Sun* had grown enough that the printing was taken on by *The Dublin Courier-Herald* on its web-fed Scott press.

In 1956 Evans was convinced that *The Warner Robins Sun* was large enough to justify its own print shop, so he purchased a used Duplex Press from the weekly newspaper in Gainesville, Georgia, and got some typesetting equipment from the Tuscaloosa, Alabama newspaper.

"That was the last time I bought any used equipment," Evans recalls. "I learned in a hurry that new state-of-the-art equipment is the best investment a newspaper can make."

It turned out that Warner Robins, after the resurgence of the early fifties, became the fastest growing city in Georgia for the next two decades, making it possible for *The Warner Robins Sun* to grow in number of pages and advertising revenue at the same swift pace.

By 1960 Evans was able to make what he considers one of his best moves as owner, editor and publisher of *The Sun*. He purchased a two-unit Thatcher offset press, Justowriters and other offset equipment, making *The Sun* among the first five newspapers in Georgia to convert to the revolutionary (for that period of time) offset process, which soon would change the entire newspaper industry.

Evans credits much of the success of *The Sun* to his willingness to invest in the latest technological advances in the printing industry. "If you do not have the capability of printing a quality newspaper in the numbers you want there is no way to be ready when new advertising opportunities come along," he says. "As chain stores and shopping centers came to Warner Robins I had to prove to the owners that my suburban newspaper had the capability to handle their advertising to keep them from taking it to the Macon newspapers."

The concept upon which *The Warner Robins Sun* was founded and the concept that prevailed throughout Evans' years of ownership was to provide the people of the Warner Robins area with a hometown newspaper, printing news "they could find nowhere else in the world," as he puts it. "People love to read about themselves and see their pictures in the newspapers and we gave them plenty of both every issue."

The city of Warner Robins and *The Sun* had grown enough by 1966 that Evans increased the frequency of his newspaper to twice-a-week with the first semi-weekly issue coming out March 3.

When the twice-a-week *Sun* reached a circulation in excess of 17,000, Evans decided in 1969 that Warner Robins deserved a daily newspaper. "If I didn't meet the challenge I knew someone else would," he says.

By this time the printing facilities of *The Sun* included a new 10,000 square foot building, an eight-unit Goss Community Press with Suburban folder, the latest in phototypesetting equipment — in other words, a printing plant capable of printing a daily newspaper.

So on November 3, 1969, the first issue of the Monday through Friday newspaper — *The Daily Sun* — was printed and distributed.

This called for some difficult financial decisions and a major gamble on Evans' part. The semi-weekly newspaper, with its 17,000 circulation, had an advertising rate commensurate with the number of subscribers. The daily newspaper started out with only about 2,500 subscribers and advertising rates had to be adjusted downward accordingly.

In a sense, Evans remembers, it was almost like starting over again and took a lot of faith to abandon a highly-profitable operation in order to gamble on the success of a daily newspaper.

Public response to the hometown daily newspaper, packed with local news and local pictures with national and state news given limited amounts of space, was very good and circulation climbed steadily, while the volume of advertising also increased.

As a weekly and semi-weekly newspaper, *The Warner Robins Sun* printed only local news. The daily newspaper had to print some wire service news and comics, but at least 75 percent of the news hole was still devoted to local news and pictures. The entire editorial page was local everyday.

"Our editorial policy was a simple one," Evans says. "If you have to make a choice between being popular and being respected, we always opted for respect."

Three years after *The Daily Sun* came into existence, Evans and his wife, Leta, decided to sell *The Daily Sun*. "It was a painful decision," he recalls. "We had worked steadily without a vacation for 24 years and had fought several successful battles against competition. We were tired and believed that we had earned a rest. And we had a tempting offer for *The Daily Sun*. *The Daily Sun* had attained a circulation of 9,400 when we sold to Roy H. Park of Ithaca, New York, on November 1, 1972.

"I am often asked if I had it to do over again, would I sell again," Evans says today. "The answer is no. *The Sun* had been my life for 24 years and, looking back, I can see that, being a workaholic, I did not have the temperament for retirement, which I forced upon myself."

He says that if he had it to do over again he would "step back and try to see and understand myself better and figure a way to give others more responsibility. All of us, perhaps, become too wrapped up in our newspapers, especially when it is something we created, and fail to realize that others can do much of what we do and maybe do it better."

His advice to anyone owning a newspaper who considers selling it is to "think long and hard and be sure you understand yourself and what makes you tick before giving up your newspaper."

He says that retirement — rather, not having a business of his own — has given him the opportunity to do things he never would have done otherwise. He stayed on as editor-publisher of *The Daily Sun* for the new owner for nearly two years, but found it difficult to run the newspaper for someone else and voluntarily stepped down.

He tried retirement for awhile, but a little retirement went a long way with him. Within a few months after building a new home and moving to the small farming town of Marshallville, he realized that he did not want to leave Warner Robins where he had been deeply involved in the growth and development during its formative years.

So in January 1976 he returned to Warner Robins to practice law (He had passed the Georgia bar exam and become a lawyer in 1946 while a student at the University of Georgia.)

Later that year people in Warner Robins began suggesting that Evans should seek the office of mayor, and he decided that was a challenge that appealed to him. In the election that year, he defeated the incumbent mayor, a city councilman and three other candidates without a runoff by polling more than 53 percent of the votes. He became mayor of the City of Warner Robins December 1, 1976, and was elected to a second term four years later without opposition.

"I am not a politician and never will be," he says. "I believe the people elected me mayor because of this. They had read my newspaper for almost a quarter of a century, they had read my personal column for the same period of time and they knew me and my philosophy."

In his role as a public official, Evans believes he has come to understand newspapers better than he did as an owner-publisher. "I believed, for example, when I was an editor and publisher, that all newspapers reported the news accurately, without prejudice, and that we newspaper people had most of the answers to everything," he says. "I now know that this is not so. Too often newspapers set out to get facts to prove a conclusion already reached, editorials often are based on inaccurate information, and corrections of errors seldom, if ever, receive the same play as an original story — all of which disturbs me very much, since I consider myself first, last and always a newspaperman."

He says the old saying "you can't fight city hall" more appropriately should be "never try to win an argument with a newspaper editor. Editors always have the last word and too many apparently do not agree that with the privileges provided by the First Amendment that there should be an equal portion of responsibility."

Public office is much like running a newspaper, according to Evans, but being a newspaper owner and editor is much more satisfying.

As a Park Newspaper, *The Sun* continued to prosper, adding a Sunday edition in 1974. In 1980, Park also acquired the weekly *Houston Home Journal* in Perry, the county seat, and it is now printed at the Warner Robins plant. Jim DeRoy, who was publisher for several years after Evans left the post, started a free-distribution weekly in Warner Robins in 1982.

H. Thomas Reed has been publisher of the *Sun* during the 1980s.

Otis Brumby, Jr. and hierarchy (1984) of The Marietta Daily Journal *and Neighbor Newspapers. L. to R., Jay Whorton, associate publisher; Brumby; Bobby Nesbitt, executive editor; Harris Kettles, general manager. In background is portrait of Otis Brumby, Sr.*

Ground was broken for new plant of Decatur-DeKalb News *building on May 11, 1964. Taking part were Jerry Crane, Laura Rimer (women's editor), Mary Crane, William Crane; (in rear) Robert Miller and architect Howard Stephens.*

Top DeKalb News/Sun *executives are shown in this 1983 photo. L. to R., Mike Traynor, advertising manager; Mary Crane, co-founder; Rick Sauers, vice-president; Jerry Crane, president; William C. Crane, publisher; Linton Broome, executive editor.*

Jimmy and Margo Booth founded This Week *in Peachtree City in 1974 and were co-publishers for eight years (1974-82).*

Quimby Melton III and wife Louisa were operating the competing Fayette County News *most of those years (1975-81).*

Foy Evans, shown with wife Leita, founded Warner Robins Sun *in 1949. It is Georgia's most successful suburban paper outside Metro Atlanta.*

Jim Wood, founder of Clayton News/Daily *and a three-term state legislator, chats with Governor George Busbee (1975-83) at one of Wood's tomato sandwich political rallies.*

The Daily Sun

HOUSTON COUNTY'S FAVORITE NEWSPAPER

th Year, No. 218 | 1553 Watson Blvd., Warner Robins, Ga. 31093 | Wednesday Afternoon, November 1, 1972 | 10c Per Copy

Doctors Label Story Unjust

FOY EVANS (l) AND ROY PARK SIGN AGREEMENT

'Something Left Out'

By JOEL FERGUSON
Staff Writer

"Your story yesterday was an injustice to two fine doctors," Dr. Carl L. Beard said this morning. "I'm talking about Dr. Kennith Raynor and Dr. Carlos H. Barroso. It's not so much what the story said about them, it's what it didn't say."

Dr. Beard's remarks were in response to a story published in The Daily Sun yesterday concerning the findings of the medical staff credentials committee as read ... Hospital Authority at the authority's regular monthly session Monday night.

Dr. Beard, a prominent Warner Robins gynecologist, said the main point that should be emphasized is that Dr. Raynor was granted full privileges in obstetrics and gynecology surgery at the Houston County Hospital here.

... that Dr. Barroso was granted full privileges by the hospital to perform urologic...

Dr. Beard is correct about both doctors. His statement is verified by the findings of the Medical Staff Credentials Committee, which were sent to Hospital Administrator Myron McDonald on Oct. 30, by Chief of Medical Staff Dr. Ronald G. Severs.

Dr. Beard's statement was also verified today by Dr. David N. Harvey, chairman of the credentials committee.

"I want to make it clear," Dr. Harvey declared, "that the credentials committee is not out to get anybody. Doctors apply to perform certain medical procedures, and we must determine if they are properly trained and properly recommended. We even go to the place of their last employment if necessary.

"Dr. Barroso applied to perform additional life-saving procedures in the emergency room in connection with urology," Dr. Harvey continued. "He did not apply to become a gynecologist."

Dr. Harvey was referring to that part of the credentials committee's findings which stated, "Dr. Barroso also requested salpingo-oophorectomy procedures which were denied by the committee, since other physicians with gynecology privileges are constantly available."

Dr. Harvey said the credentials committee approved Dr. Barroso for privileges in 24 life-saving emergency medical procedures, including incision

See DOCTORS....Page 7A

YOU WILL read a most ...gnificant announcement ...sewhere on this page. It is ...ppropriate that this an...nouncement be made today ...hich marks the beginning of ...r fourth year as a daily ...ewspaper, because it is a ...gnificant step forward in our ...ver increasing efforts to ...rovide Warner Robins and ...ouston County with a ...ewspaper worthy of the ...onfidence and en...couragement given to us ...rough the years.

The background on this ...ory may be of interest to the ...eaders who have made The ...aily Sun successful and have ...ken it in as an important ...art of their lives.

Simply put, The Daily Sun ...ined a newspaper group ...eaded by Roy H. Park.

Who, you might ask, is Roy ...ark?

+++

FIRST, he is a good friend of ...ine.

He is one of the country's ...ost successful businessmen ...the communications field. ...e heads the largest broad...cast group in this country ...holly owned by one man.

He is a native of North ...arolina who fell in love with ...eautiful Ithaca, N.Y., more ...an 30 years ago and has ...efused to leave, though his ...ulti-million dollar business ...mpire spreads into 10 states ...nd Puerto Rico.

Roy Park first suggested ...at we join with him in for...ing a newspaper group early ...is year. At first I did not ...ke the idea seriously.

But as time went by . . . as ...e talked with each other ...bout the advantages of such ...n effort . . . as we visualized

Sun Joins New Group

The Daily Sun has been selected as the model for a group of newspapers being put together by one of the country's leaders in the communications field.

Foy Evans, publisher of The Daily Sun, announced this morning that this newspaper has joined the Park Newspapers Inc., a group of newspapers with headquarters in Ithaca, N.Y.

President of Park Newspapers Inc. is Roy H. Park, who has extensive television, radio and billboard holdings, most of them concentrated in the southern states.

A native of North Carolina, Park today revealed that he plans to concentrate his newspaper holdings in the southern states, too.

The Daily Sun, which has received numerous press association awards for excellence, will serve as the key newspaper and model for the group.

Foy Evans, who founded this newspaper 24 years ago and has headed it since, will continue as chief operating officer, editor and publisher of The Daily Sun.

"The changes announced today will, in my opinion, serve to strengthen The Daily Sun and make it possible for us to continue to improve our service to the people of Warner Robins and Houston County," Evans said.

Park pointed out that The Daily Sun will continue to operate autonomously as a "local newspaper" with all business and editorial decisions being made by Evans, as in the past.

At the same time, he said, the new setup will give The Daily Sun access to facilities and personnel presently involved in Park's numerous television and radio stations, ... man.

During the past 10 years Park has invested more than $45 million in television and radio stations.

His broadcast group now includes almost the full complement of stations permitted by the Federal Communications Commission. In addition to 16 stations which were acquired or put on the air in the past 10 years, the Park group earlier this year reached agreements to buy KWJJ-AM in Portland, Ore., and WBMG-TV in Birmingham, Ala., subject to FCC approval.

Other Park stations include: WNCT-TV-AM-FM, Greenville, N.C.; WTVR-TV-AM-FM, Richmond, Va.; WSLS-TV, Roanoke, Va.; WDEF-TV-AM-FM, Chattanooga, Tenn.; WJHL-TV, Johnson City, Tenn.; WUTR-TV, Utica, N.Y.; WEBC-AM, Duluth, Minn.; KRSI-AM-FM, St. Louise Park, Minn., a suburb of Minneapolis-St. Paul; and WNAX-AM, Yankton, S.D.

Park said that his goal is "now to establish a good

See SUN....Page 7A

WEATHER

Partly cloudy and warm this afternoon with a high of 81 is the forecast. The overnight low will be 60 and tomorrow's high will be 82. There is a 40 per cent chance of showers or thundershowers on Thursday.

Yesterday's high was 80 and the low this morning was 52.

At 11:30 a.m. the temperature was 62, relative humidity was 96 per cent and winds were from the east at three miles per hour.

Records for this date are 88 in 1961 and 31 in 1930.

Lake Sinclair is down 5.8 and Lake Jackson is down 3.1

MISS NOVEMBER — Surrounded by colors of Autumn is Miss November Janet George. Janet is the daughter of Mr. and Mrs. J.R. George, Evergreen Street. She is a senior at Northside High School where she is a varsity cheerleader, member of the Pep Club, Junior Civitans and Thespians. Miss November plans to attend Piedmont School of Nursing in Atlanta following graduation. The calendar girl is a monthly feature co-sponsored by Olson's Studio of Photography and The Daily Sun. (Photo by Olson's)

State Opens New Leg Of Highway

By United Press International

The last portion of Interstate 20 from Atlanta to Columbia, S. C., will be opened to traffic next week and highway officials said that 95 miles of Interstate 16 linging Savannah with Macon have been completed.

The leg that completes the Columbia Atlanta superhighway is 22.73 miles between Greensboro, S.C., and Barnett, Ga.

A ribbon cutting ceremony on the Georgia-South Carolina state line at 11:15 a.m. on Nov. 6 officially opens the leg. The opening was delayed two months because of a concrete shortage and Georgia Transportation Director Bert Lance cautioned motorists to drive with care on the newly opened portions because minor finishing details will still be in progress.

With the new leg, there is a total of 265 miles of I-20 open to traffic in Georgia and South Carolina, from Douglasville, Ga., on the west end to Camden, S. C., on the east.

When I-20 is completed west of Atlanta it will connect the city with Birmingham.

Lance told some 200 interested officials at Statesboro Tuesday that 48 miles of I-16 still remain to be let to contract. The highway is to be 165 miles in length.

Lance said that 1977 is the deadline for completion of all interstate projects in Georgia but that it was imperative that I-16 be completed "as soon as possible" because of need arising from the increase in foreign trade coming into the Savannah port. I-16 would link Savannah to Interstate 75 in Macon.

The director said that to hasten the completion of I-16, the state would need to issue $50 million in bonds annually for the next two years.

In a review of other highway developments, Lance said 73 per cent of all interstate highways in Georgia are now complete.

INSIDE STORY

Halloween Is Big Success

By GUY MIDDLETON
Staff Writer

Upwards of 700 costumed youngsters gathered last night at Williams Plaza for a Halloween program, which may well be turned into an annual affair.

"This is much better than having the children out on the streets," declared W.H. "Pip" Rape, Warner Robins Public Safety Department Director.

The idea was a brainchild of the Warner Robins Senior Girl Scout Troop One. Others, including the city's Recreation and Public Safety Departments, pitched in on the program which attracted a more enthusiastic response than had been expected.

Prizes were awarded for the ... McIntyre, Mrs. Walter D. Whiting, and Spencer Doss Jr.

Winners in the pre-school division were Tammy Paulk and Jason Roberts; Ernestine Lane and David Breland took top honors in the first and second grade contest; Mary West and Bryan Cox were winners in the third and fourth grade segment; and Mark Anthony and Dell Barker were winners in the fifth and sixth grade division.

Miss Silengo, special activities recreation supervisor, said this morning that the event very likely will become an annual affair.

She also paid tribute to the merchants, fellow city employees, and civic club members who aided in carrying off the program last

Daily Sun *of Warner Robins was first newspaper bought by Roy H. Park, on November 1, 1972. Park's group would eventually own more than 20 dailies. Foy Evans,* The Sun's *founder, made the sale.*

Robert Fowler started a daily newspaper in Gwinnett County in 1965 which has become one of the fastest-growing in nation.

Elliott Brack became general manager of The Gwinnett Daily News *in 1973 after 12 years with a weekly paper in Jesup. He was also on Grady School faculty for eight years.*

Good To See You, Gwinnett!

WEATHER
Partly cloudy and warm Sunday with widely scattered afternoon and evening thundershowers affecting about 30 per cent of the state. High Sunday, 86; low Sunday night, 70.

GWINNETT SUNDAY NEWS

60 PAGES
10¢

VOL. 1 NO. 1 LAWRENCEVILLE, GA. 30245 SUNDAY, SEPT. 12, 1965 OFFICE PHONES: L'VILLE 963-3441; BUFORD 945-5333

Board Reverse Rezone Ruling

Action Comes On Protest Made By 300 Rockbridge Residents

BY TOM OXNARD

The Gwinnett County Commissioners were overruled Thursday by the County Board of Appeals on a zoning change they had recommended. The man who had requested rezoning indicated late Friday that he was "pursuing another course."

Almost 300 residents from the Rockbridge Road and Norcross-Tucker Road sections showed up for the hearing which was held at night in the courthouse.

The commissioners had okayed, over the objections of the County Planning and Zoning Board, that some land off Rockbridge Road be zoned from R-75 (residential) to C-2 (commercial).

The petitioner for rezoning was Clairmont Development Co. of Chamblee which wanted to construct a shop (retail) office and warehouse across from the new Rockbridge Elementary School and near several subdivisions.

Clairmont never specified exactly what they meant by shop (retail) office and warehouse, according to Grady Holt, secretary of the planning board.

The petition was originally disapproved on July 17 by the planning board on Aug. 17 and the area appealed to the Board of Appeals on Aug. 18.

Reed S. Brill Sr. was the counsel for the petitioning residents.

Officials of the Clairmont Co. never showed up for Thursday's hearing, Holt said. He added that they had been previously notified of the meeting by mail some days ago.

Warren Crider, an official of the company, told the Daily News that he had never been notified about the hearing.

He said he was concerned about the turn of events because "the commissioners had given us a green light."

Crider denied that he had not [illegible] for what he called "a shopping center. He said he had followed "normal procedures" by submitting plans which "even included parking space."

He said he was "concerned" because the commissioners are the county's elected officials and the Board of Appeals should not [illegible]

Crider did not indicate what action he would take, but said something should be decided "by Tuesday."

Arguments by the residents against the planned rezoning move centered on the fact that an area less than a mile away had already been rezoned for a shopping center and that the company had not specifically spelled out its plans for development.

Zoning regulations require a comprehensive site development plan before the planning commission can okay any change in zoning.

The three members of the Board of Appeals are F. L. Kilpatrick, chairman, Edwin Howard and E. E. Hogan.

P & Z Board Sets Hearing On Lilburn

A public hearing will be held Sept. 30 to determine whether or not Lilburn will come under the Gwinnett County Planning and Zoning Commission.

Grady Holt, secretary of the commission, said the meeting would be held at 9 a. m. at the courthouse.

The commission recommended recently that the hearing be held and the county commissioners approved the move late last week.

Earlier, the Lilburn City Council had requested the move.

If the move is approved, Lilburn would become the first county city to come under the commission's jurisdiction.

Lilburn, Duluth and Berkeley Lake have been ex-officio members of the commission since 1963, with honorary members working with commission.

However, Lilburn's planned move would make it official for the first time.

If the public hearing leads to the expected move, the county would

Continued on Page 2-A

Maloney Asks Clarification On Rates Hike

Norcross Mayor W. L. Maloney has written a letter to the firm which recommended raising the county's water rates to get a detailed analysis of their figures.

Maloney said this weekend that the figures the New York firm had given did not "gel" with figures he had.

The Gwinnett County Commissioners hiked the wholesale rates to the county's users on May 15 from 22 cents per thousand gallons to 30 cents per thousand.

Commissioner Ray Morgan said the increase was necessary "because of rising costs."

The wholesale users include several county municipalities and two industrial firms.

Norcross has continued to pay its bill to the county since the increase but has done so

Continued on Page 2-A

AT DULUTH

Hospital Merger Pending Details

Final approval has been given for the inclusion of Duluth's Joan Glancy Hospital into the Gwinnett County hospital system and details are now being worked out.

Jack Whelchel, administrator of the Hospital Authority, said yesterday that the merger will eventually mean an extra 23 beds at the Duluth facility at an estimated cost of $550,000. The hospital now has 27 beds.

Whelchel said it is "conceivable the renovation and additions can be started within a year."

He said there might be a temporary loss of six beds while the hospital is being worked on, but it would definitely have 50 beds once it is completed.

The merger plan, coupled with additions at Button Gwinnett Hospital and construction of a new hospital at Buford, means Gwinnett County may have 169 beds within a year. State figures indicate a county Gwinnett's size should have 200 beds or four for every 1,000 people.

Whelchel said the only conditions to the merger were "small, but important details."

For instance, he said Duluth officials wanted the name, Joan Glancy, retained and wanted to use an architect they had already chosen.

There is also the problem of sewerage, Whelchel said. The present facility's sewerage disposal is inadequate and an oxidation pond may have to be built to be eligible for federal funds under the Hill-Burton Act.

Whelchel noted that his role in the merger plan would be to gather information to present to hospital officials for approval.

He indicated approval is almost assurred and said Dr. R. C. Williams, a director of the medical and health unit of the Atlanta Community Council, had spoken favorably of Gwinnett's hospital program.

In the meantime, the 39-bed addition at Button Gwinnett should be completed within three weeks.

Contingency money of $27,000

Continued on Page 2-A

Turn About Is Fair Play

Just as it appears, this auto has been impaled with a telephone pole. Frederic Daniels hit the pole with his car in Detroit Saturday and cut it off. Then the pole passed over the vehicle and took its jab through the rear window. The driver, who escaped injury, was ticketed for reckless driving. (UPI Telephoto)

Inside The First Issue

Sixty Whopping Pages Of Gwinnett's Daily

For our first issue, we present you with a whopping 60 pages of news, county histories and projects, personalities, comics and editorial comment. We'd like you to read everything, but we are listing below some of the more interesting stories of this issue:

--Page 4-A, Publisher's statement and letters of congratulation from state leaders.

--Page 1-B, Sports coverage, with pictures, of high school football games; also, national sports of interest.

--Page 5-D, A review of the infamous "triple murder" case with courtroom rules which will have to be followed when the trial gets underway on Oct. 4.

--Page 4-E, A little known fact is reported: most of Gwinnett County's schools have vending machines with candy and soft drinks for the kids to buy.

--Page 5-F, An informal portrait of Gwinnett County Sheriff Hoke Huston.

--Page [illegible], The inside story on how this paper, and the ones to follow, is produced; pictures of our staff are included.

--Page 4, Suburban Life, A history of the county fair; this year's fair opens tomorrow.

--Page 5, Suburban Life, A full appraisal of the hospital situation in the county with plans for further growth.

--Page 12, Suburban Life, Aerial photos of the county, shot by our high-flying managing editor, Bev Ballard.

A final word: the theme of this issue is Progress. Gwinnett County is progressing and the stories and pictures say it better than we can here . . .

Betsy Goes North

NEW ORLEANS (UPI) - New floods drove more residents of sodden and wind-devastated New Orleans out of their home Saturday while the remains of Hurricane Betsy brought heavy rains more than 400 miles away.

Betsy, worn to a big area of rain squalls by its journey across cities and countryside, pushed on through Tennessee toward Kentucky. It dropped as much as five inches of rain in

Continued on Page 2-A

EMORY S. WAGES

E. S. Wages, Ex-Ordinary, Is Buried

Funeral services were held Thursday for Emory S. Wages, 80, a lifelong resident of Gwinnett County who served as the county ordinary for 25 years.

The Rev. W. C. Corley conducted the service from the First Baptist Church of Lawrenceville. Interment was in the Shadow Lawn Cemetery.

Mr. Wages died Tuesday following a seven-year illness.

Born April 18, 1885, in the Harbins District, Mr. Wages was graduated from the Perry Rainey

Continued on Page 2-A

Indian Forces Move To Pakistan Border; Fighting Intensifies

Pakistan Drops Paratroopers

United Press International

NEW DELHI (UPI)—Indian troops, counter-attacking after a series of severe reverses, were reported advancing Saturday night on a 30-mile wide front between the Pakistan border town of Kalhara and Kasur, south of Lahore.

A government spokesman announced the advance as both sides reported sharp fighting between armored columns, supported by planes, in a war of attrition along the border between India and West Pakistan. The Pakistani claimed their tank columns had stabbed 10 and 11 miles into Indian territory along two border sectors.

The New Delhi spokesman said two Pakistani commanders—a major general and a brigadier—have been killed in action. He said four colonels, six majors and several other ranks have surrendered.

Attack Bridge

In the air, Pakistani warplanes struck into the far northeastern reaches of India Saturday, attacking a key river bridge in Assam on the invasion route to Red China. Indian government sources said Pakistani planes dropped "several hundred" paratroopers in key areas of Assam State.

A spokesman said the Pakistani planes were driven back after repeated attacks on the Brahamaputra rail and road bridge in Assam. Indian aircraft fire chased the intruders [illegible] damage, the spokesman said.

The bridge was built years ago during the Chinese Communist invasion of India across the Himalayas to the edge of the Assam Plain. Saturday's raid followed a Pakistani air

Continued on Page 2-A

[illegible] ... Miss Gwinnett Contestant [illegible]

MONDAY'S THE DAY

Youngsters Await Fair's Opening

It's funny but a week before it even starts the kids can feel [illegible] somehow they can even smell the candied apples [illegible]

But tommorow they'll be on the rides and can stuff themselves with cotton candy and candied apples to their hearts' content. (But oh, those stomachs.)

The annual Gwinnett County Fair will get underway tomorrow with two beauty contests, crop and livestock contests, rides, sideshows and all the fun and color of a county fair.

First event on the jam-packed calendar of events will be the judging of school exhibits Monday at 9:30, followed by the annual parade in which schools, clubs and businesses will participate.

The parade will probably start in Lawrenceville Elementary on Oak and Perry streets, go south to Perry and [illegible] and then take a right at Clayton. It will then turn right at Lucky street, emerge on Perry at the County Jail and then follow Stone Mountain

Continued on Page 2-A

Expansion Eyed At Loganville

Loganville will attempt to extend its city limits one-half mile in every direction, it was learned recently. The move would affect that part of the city in Gwinnett County as well as in Walton County.

Mayor A. L. Harom said he and the council voted for the expansion after they had had many requests from the residents of the outlying area.

The council's resolution will be sent to the Georgia legislature when it convenes in January and, if approved, a referendum will be held for the affected residents.

If the move is approved, the size of the city will be one and one-half miles in radius from a point in the center of town.

The move is expected to add approximately 300 people to the existing population of 1,200.

First EOA Dollars Set For County

Federal funds for adult education have been allocated to Gwinnett County, it was learned this weekend. This will mark the first local money through President Johnson's poverty program.

Gwinnett will get an initial outlay of $5,808 to set up five teaching center capable of teaching up to 100 adults with less than an eighth grade education.

Mrs. Leslie Jo Bentley, curriculum director for the county school system and J. W. Benefield, assistant superintendent of schools, will direct the program.

Mrs. Bentley said late Friday that the program is being financed through the Economic Opportunity Act. The Georgia Department of Education recieved funds from the federal government and is allocating them to interested counties.

The program will be administered to all people 18-years-old and older who have received less than an eighth grade education. In 1960, there were over 10,000 people in the county who fitted this category.

Hooper-Renwick School is the only center definitely set up so far. The others will be picked according to where the need is

Continued on Page 2-A

Lack Of Water, Sewerage Halts Development

An "urgent need for water and sewerage" is holding up further development of Southern Railway's industrial development acreage west of Norcross.

Allen Douglas, industrial locator for the company, said the 1,500 acre complex will be an "ideal location for new industry" once sewerage and water can be piped in.

Southern's plans, which will be completed in stages, initially call for five or 10 light industries or distributors on a 65-acre area.

So far, 125 acres have been cleared and graded by Southern.

One company, Crown-Zellerbach's Gaylord Container Division, has already started a 250,000 square foot building off Pleasant Dale Road near the DeKalb County line. Douglas said other firms have "shown interest" but have made no definite committments.

The new facility, which is being relocated from downtown Atlanta, will employ around 200 people and will cover 16 acres of land.

Crown-Zellerbach's water for construction purposes come from DeKalb County's supply and its sewerage will be a portable disposal unit.

Douglas said the move for DeKalb water came about because Gwinnett County doesn't have water in that section of the county. Plans are now underway by Gwinnett County Commissioners to install a 16 inch main through the western end of the county, but there are financial matters which have to be ironed out beforehand.

The sewerage disposal at the new plant is "at best, a stop-gap measure," Douglas said.

Gwinnett's commissioners are now in the process of making a full survey of the sewerage situation, particularly in the western end of the county.

Douglas said he has been working closely with the commissioners and the Gwinnett County Chamber of Commerce and "will continue to do so."

He said the problems of water and sewerage can be found "in new developments throughout the Southern system."

"The water problem should be solved sometime after the first of the year," Douglas said.

Douglas has high hopes for the project because the land is "convenient to Atlanta," is close to Interstate 85 and, of course, has rail service from Southern.

CROWN-ZELLERBACK BUILDING THIS MULTI-MILLION DOLLAR PLANT ON INDUSTRIAL TRACT --Other plant construction is being held up because of lack of water and sewerage

Area Deaths

F. N. Franklin, Duluth
Carson L. Green, Lawrenceville
F. M. Watkins, Centerville
Mrs. Frank Summerour, Duluth
Idus Gober, Atlanta
W. Felton Webb, Chamblee
Mrs. J. S. Ethridge, Atlanta
Wilson Baird, Shannon
Lowery Infant, Cocoa, Fla.

Front page of Gwinnett Daily News, *Vol. I, No. I, Sunday, September 12, 1965.*

The "closing" of a sale was a familiar scene for Georgia newspapers during 1970s. Above, Tom Hay (left) is selling The Rockdale Citizen *of Conyers to Millard Grimes. Behind them are Hay's daughter, Elizabeth Staples, who succeeded him as publisher of* The Citizen; *Jewell (Mrs. Tom) Hay, and Charlotte (Mrs. Millard) Grimes. Mrs. Hay and Mrs. Grimes were secretaries of the two corporations.*

Say Hello To A New Rockdale Citizen

Don't Forget To Look For The Rockdale Citizen Every Weekday Afternoon

Here's the first issue of The Rockdale Citizen in its new five-day-a-week schedule of Monday through Friday afternoons.

If you receive your Citizen by carrier it should be delivered between 3 and 5:30 p.m. on those afternoons. Citizens will be on sale in newsracks and at counters by 3 p.m. and should be in Post Office boxes shortly after 3.

With the start of daily publication The Citizen is adding many features usually found in daily newspapers although the emphasis will still be strongly on events in Rockdale County and East Metro Atlanta.

Readers are urged to peruse today's issue carefully, however and see the many new features which include nine of the nation's top comic strips and panels, Joyce Brothers' advice column, an astrology guide, puzzles, and several new editorial page columns which will supplement the best staff - produced editorial page in the metro area.

THE TV SCHEDULE and highlights will now be carried each day instead of just on Thursday and the schedule and highlights for tonight and Wednesday morning are on Page 15.

Local sports and sports news of interest from the UPI wire service will also be carried daily. Today's sports pages, with a special story on Pete Rose and his record efforts in Atlanta, are on pages 6 and 7.

Comics include such popular favorites as Blondie, Snuffy Smith and Beetle Bailey; the new Walt Disney version of Winnie the Pooh, which is for kids of all ages; Hagar the Horrible; Alex In Wonderland, a strip that will grow on you; Archie, the teenage favorite, and two delightful panels, Trudy and Laff-A-Day.

YOU'LL ALSO FIND helpful information in the advice columns of Helen and Sue Boettel.

LETTERS TO THE editor are an important part of any editorial page and we invite readers to send in their comments on The Citizen's new daily format. Just a card will do but we'd like a letter.

The Citizen's name describes its role. It's a Citizen of Rockdale County and now it'll be a daily Citizen, instead of showing up just twice a week.

Each day's issue this week will introduce new features. So be looking for them. And most important, don't forget to look for your Citizen every weekday afternoon.

The ROCKDALE CITIZEN

East Metro Atlanta's Best Read Newspaper

First Daily Edition

26TH YEAR NO. 1 PHONE: 483-7108 CONYERS, GEORGIA, TUESDAY, AUGUST 1, 1978 1 SECTION - 16 PAGES DAILY -- MON. - FRI. 15¢

County Employees Picket While Pay Raise Debated

BY TOM BARRY

A line of county employees carrying picket signs marched in front of the Rockdale County Courthouse Tuesday morning, demanding merit pay increases they said were promised them a year ago.

The activity at the courthouse was in contrast to the lack of activity at the county garage as approximately 40 public works and motor maintenance employees failed to report for work for the second straight day.

County firemen also manned the picket lines, although none were as yet on strike.

MEANWHILE THE COUNTY commission battled to find money for merit increases in the belabored 1978-79 budget, yet to be unveiled, a task made more difficult by the continued divisions and personality conflicts within the commission itself.

Monday's walkout followed an 8 a.m. meeting between an angry throng of county employees and the three county commissioners, one of whom, Chairman Heyward Woodward, Friday issued 45 paychecks containing merit increases.

Because the paychecks did not bear the countersignature of Commissioner Herman Francis, the employees were unable to cash them.

Monday, the county commission ordered "regular" paychecks to be issued to the employees, but indications were that they would not be accepted and the strike would continue.

Statements by Commissioners Herman Francis and Ray Magnusson Monday that the checks were issued in violation of a June 16 board freeze on county salaries and that funds might not be available for merit raises were greeted by jeers from the employees.

The commissioners indicated at the meeting that they would meet with department heads to see if money could be found for the increases.

FRANCIS PROFESSED optimism that it could, but Monday night, Magnusson said, "I have reservations. We won't know until tomorrow afternoon. They'll get whatever we can give them. But I don't want to be optimistic."

"You received checks without a signature because the checks were made out improperly," Magnusson told the employees. "And the chairman knew this when he made them out. He knew (this would happen) for about three weeks and he apparently didn't care. We told him he would be doing you people a disservice."

Supporting the increase all along Woodward was greeted by applause from the employees when he

(See Picket on page 2A)

COULDN'T CASH PAYCHECK. Photo by Harvey Cowan
Fireman Troy Ivey is visibly upset with Commissioner Ray Magnusson.

—Suits Threatened—

Woodward Walks Out

A writ of mandamus ordering Rockdale County Commission Chairman Heyward Woodward to obey the directives of the commission will be sought in the near future, according to a resolution adopted Monday by the board.

In a hot-tempered meeting marked by a walkout by Woodward, the commission directed county attorney Lloyd Hall to obtain "a writ of mandamus or other appropriate legal recourse he may deem necessary" to stop the chairman from "disobeying the lawful resolutions and policies of the Rockdale County Board of Commissioners."

THE RESOLUTION to seek the court order, proposed by Commissioner Ray Magnusson, also directed Woodward to obey specifically actions of the board taken earlier in the meeting.

Those actions, on a resolution by Commissioner Herman Francis, directed Woodward to issue paychecks to county employees in their regular amounts, excluding any merit increases, by 12 noon Tuesday.

Francis said that the chairman "improperly ordered" paychecks including the merit increases to be issued on Friday and that the county was under legal obligation to pay them for services rendered. The checks issued Friday by Woodward were not signed by Francis and could not by cashed.

"This is to give employees checks they're entitled to at the old rate until such time that we can adopt the budget, hopefully with pay increases in it," Francis said.

The Francis resolution stated that if Woodward refused to carry out the directive, it should be executed by Executive Assistant Sandy Jones and that failure by Jones to do so would constitute grounds for immediate dismissal.

The proposed resolution ultimately led to a refusal by Woodward to repeat the resolution for passage an aborted attempt by Woodward to adjourn the meeting and his walkout.

The commission resolutions followed issuance Friday of paychecks containing merit increases by Woodward.

THE PAYCHECKS were not co-signed by Commissioner Herman Francis and resulted in a meeting at 8 a.m. Monday between county employees angry over not being able to cash their checks and Commissioners Francis and Magnusson, intent on adhering to a county pay freeze imposed by the commission June 16. That freeze was lifted Monday by the commission, but only for employees coming off their probationary period with the county.

(See Suits on page 2A)

School Board Adopts $18 Million Budget

Thursday's public hearing on the 1978-79 school budget in excess of $18 million attracted only a handful of concerned citizens.

The meeting was a presentation of School Superintendent Don Joiner's budget recommendations to the Rockdale County Board of Education.

The proposed budget requires a 5.4 percent increase in local funding which will be raised without increasing the milage rate due to the growth in the tax digest.

The current millage rate will remain the same, 22 mils, with maintenance and operations receiving 18.67 mils and the remaining 3.33 mils going for bonds retirement.

SOME SCHOOL board members expressed concern with the budget's ending balance of $8,000.

According to school board member Wayne Doster that is about one-half of one percent of the total school budget.

In an interview Monday Doster said that the state advised the local school systems to maintain a minimum surplus of 10 percent of the budget and they advocate a 20 percent surplus.

"In the past years we have whittled away at our ending budget in order to continue the quality programs we have in our school system without an increase in the millage rates," said Doster.

"If we don't receive financial relief from the state we'll be forced to increase the millage rates next year."

"I don't believe it is in the taxpayers' interest to borrow money and pay interest in order to maintain com-

(See Budget on page 3A)

Storm Wreaks Havoc

BY KAY PINCKNEY

An insurance salesman's car and a fence off I-20 received the most visible damage Monday in Rockdale County's electrical hailstorm which temporarily knocked out more than 1,100 electric meters and 300 telephones.

Scott Foster was sitting in his office at the Gray Realty building, using the telephone, when he saw an old split sweetgum tree turn his Oldsmobile sedan into a convertible.

"I was just sitting here watching it, on the phone, and I said, 'Can I call you back? A tree just hit my

(See Storm on page 2A)

TREE BASHES CAR DURING STORM. Photo by Harvey Cowan
At Gray Realty building near West Avenue – Green Street intersection.

$20,000 Offered For Information In Store Slaying

The brother of a Rockdale County man killed Thursday during a robbery of an adult book store has offered a $20,000 reward for the arrests and convictions of the persons responsible.

R.G. Smith of Atlanta said he put up the $20,000 reward "because he's my brother and that's reason enough."

HIS BROTHER, Ed Hubert Smith of Waterside Drive in Rockdale County, was gunned down in his recently opened Atlanta Newsstand No. 1 on Northside Drive in an apparent robbery.

Smith's death shocked many residents who are active in youth baseball in the county. The 34-year-old father of six children, ranging in age from three to 17, coached a 15-18-year-old division team and a six and seven-year-old team.

Early last week he was coaching the Rockdale County all-star team in the 15-18-year-old state baseball tournament.

(See Murder on page 2A)

Index

First daily edition of Rockdale Citizen, *August 1, 1978, featured a prize-winning photo by Harvey Cowan.*

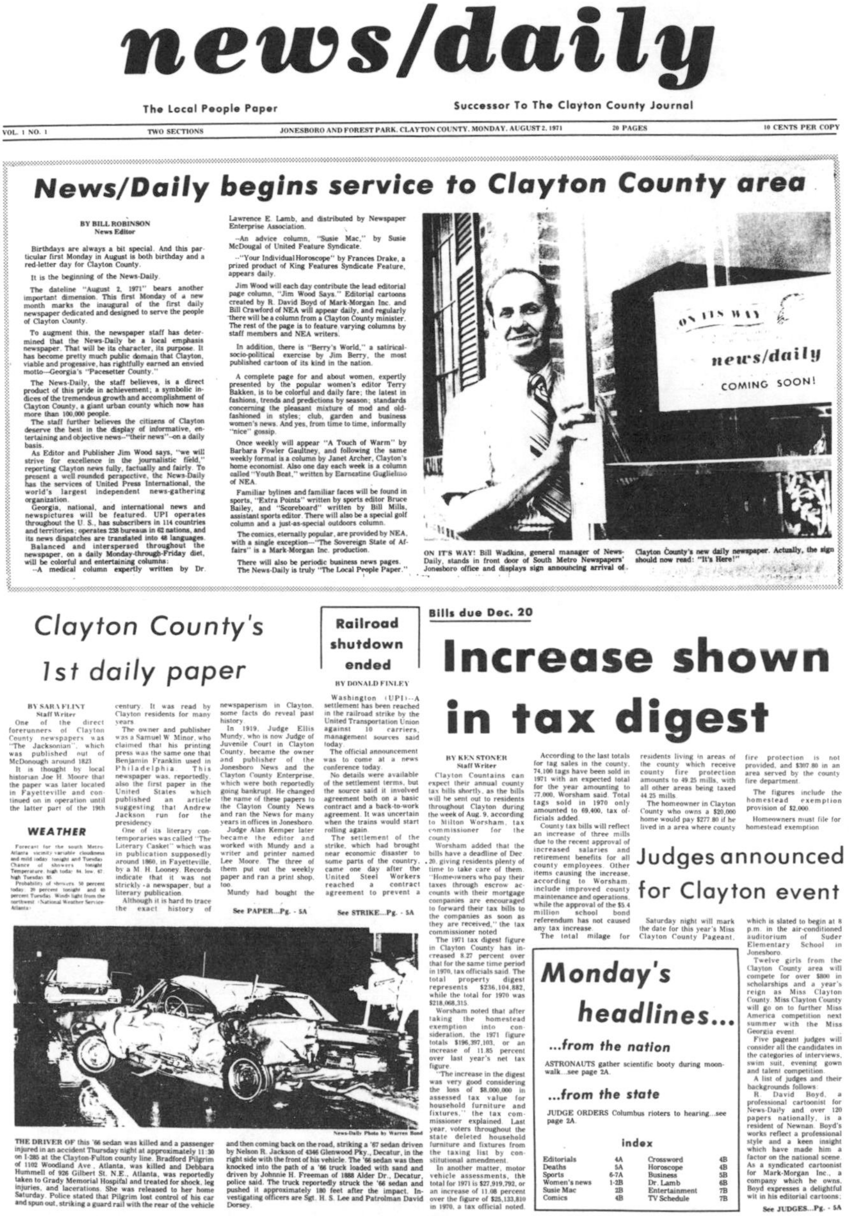

news/daily

The Local People Paper — Successor To The Clayton County Journal

VOL. 1 NO. 1 — TWO SECTIONS — JONESBORO AND FOREST PARK, CLAYTON COUNTY, MONDAY, AUGUST 2, 1971 — 20 PAGES — 10 CENTS PER COPY

News/Daily begins service to Clayton County area

BY BILL ROBINSON
News Editor

Birthdays are always a bit special. And this particular first Monday in August is both birthday and a red-letter day for Clayton County.

It is the beginning of the News-Daily.

The dateline "August 2, 1971" bears another important dimension. This first Monday of a new month marks the inaugural of the first daily newspaper dedicated and designed to serve the people of Clayton County.

To augment this, the newspaper staff has determined that the News-Daily be a local emphasis newspaper. That will be its character, its purpose. It has become pretty much public domain that Clayton, viable and progessive, has rightfully earned an envied motto—Georgia's "Pacesetter County."

The News-Daily, the staff believes, is a direct product of this pride in achievement; a symbolic indices of the tremendous growth and accomplishment of Clayton County, a giant urban county which now has more than 100,000 people.

The staff further believes the citizens of Clayton deserve the best in the display of informative, entertaining and objective news--"their news"--on a daily basis.

As Editor and Publisher Jim Wood says, "we will strive for excellence in the journalistic field," reporting Clayton news fully, factually and fairly. To present a well rounded perspective, the News-Daily has the services of United Press International, the world's largest independent news-gathering organization.

Georgia, national, and international news and newspictures will be featured. UPI operates throughout the U. S., has subscribers in 114 countries and territories; operates 238 bureaus in 62 nations, and its news dispatches are translated into 48 languages.

Balanced and interspersed throughout the newspaper, on a daily Monday-through-Friday diet, will be colorful and entertaining columns:

--A medical column expertly written by Dr. Lawrence E. Lamb, and distributed by Newspaper Enterprise Association.

--An advice column, "Susie Mac," by Susie McDougal of United Feature Syndicate.

--"Your Individual Horoscope" by Frances Drake, a prized product of King Features Syndicate Feature, appears daily.

Jim Wood will each day contribute the lead editorial page column, "Jim Wood Says." Editorial cartoons created by R. David Boyd of Mark-Morgan Inc. and Bill Crawford of NEA will appear daily, and regularly there will be a column from a Clayton County minister. The rest of the page is to feature varying columns by staff members and NEA writers.

In addition, there is "Berry's World," a satirical-socio-political exercise by Jim Berry, the most published cartoon of its kind in the nation.

A complete page for and about women, expertly presented by the popular women's editor Terry Bakken, is to be colorful and daily fare; the latest in fashions, trends and predictions by season; standards concerning the pleasant mixture of mod and old-fashioned in styles; club, garden and business women's news. And yes, from time to time, informally "nice" gossip.

Once weekly will appear "A Touch of Warm" by Barbara Fowler Gaultney, and following the same weekly format is a column by Janet Archer, Clayton's home economist. Also one day each week is a column called "Youth Beat," written by Earnestine Guglielmo of NEA.

Familiar bylines and familiar faces will be found in sports, "Extra Points" written by sports editor Bruce Bailey, and "Scoreboard" written by Bill Mills, assistant sports editor. There will also be a special golf column and a just-as-special outdoors column.

The comics, eternally popular, are provided by NEA, with a single exception—"The Sovereign State of Affairs" is a Mark-Morgan Inc. production.

There will also be periodic business news pages. The News-Daily is truly "The Local People Paper."

ON IT'S WAY! Bill Wadkins, general manager of News-Daily, stands in front door of South Metro Newspapers' Jonesboro office and displays sign announcing arrival of Clayton County's new daily newspaper. Actually, the sign should now read: "It's Here!"

Clayton County's 1st daily paper

BY SARA FLINT
Staff Writer

One of the direct forerunners of Clayton County newspapers was "The Jacksonian", which was published out of McDonough around 1823.

It is thought by local historian Joe H. Moore that the paper was later located in Fayetteville and continued on in operation until the latter part of the 19th century. It was read by Clayton residents for many years.

The owner and publisher was a Samuel W. Minor, who claimed that his printing press was the same one that Benjamin Franklin used in Philadelphia. This newspaper was, reportedly, also the first paper in the United States which published an article suggesting that Andrew Jackson run for the presidency.

One of its literary contemporaries was called "The Literary Casket" which was in publication supposedly around 1860, in Fayetteville, by a M. H. Looney. Records indicate that it was not strickly - a newspaper, but a literary publication.

Although it is hard to trace the exact history of newspaperism in Clayton, some facts do reveal past history.

In 1919, Judge Ellis Mundy, who is now Judge of Juvenile Court in Clayton County, became the owner and publisher of the Jonesboro News and the Clayton County Enterprise, which were both reportedly going bankrupt. He changed the name of these papers to the Clayton County News and ran the News for many years in offices in Jonesboro.

Judge Alan Kemper later became the editor and worked with Mundy and a writer and printer named Lee Moore. The three of them put out the weekly paper and ran a print shop, too.

Mundy had bought the

See PAPER...Pg. - 5A

WEATHER

Forecast for the south Metro Atlanta vicinity: variable cloudiness and mild today, tonight and Tuesday. Chance of showers tonight. Temperature, high today 84, low 67, high Tuesday 85.

Probability of showers 50 percent today, 20 percent tonight and 40 percent Tuesday. Winds light from the northwest. (National Weather Service-Atlanta)

Railroad shutdown ended

BY DONALD FINLEY

Washington (UPI)--A settlement has been reached in the railroad strike by the United Transportation Union against 10 carriers, management sources said today.

The official announcement was to come at a news conference today.

No details were available of the settlement terms, but the source said it involved agreement both on a basic contract and a back-to-work agreement. It was uncertain when the trains would start rolling again.

The settlement of the strike, which had brought near economic disaster to some parts of the country, came one day after the United Steel Workers reached a contract agreement to prevent a

See STRIKE...Pg. - 5A

News-Daily Photo by Warren Bond

THE DRIVER OF this '66 sedan was killed and a passenger injured in an accident Thursday night at approximately 11:30 on I-285 at the Clayton-Fulton county line. Bradford Pilgrim of 1102 Woodland Ave., Atlanta, was killed and Debbara Hummell of 926 Gilbert St. N.E., Atlanta, was reportedly taken to Grady Memorial Hospital and treated for shock, leg injuries, and lacerations. She was released to her home Saturday. Police stated that Pilgrim lost control of his car and spun out, striking a guard rail with the rear of the vehicle and then coming back on the road, striking a '67 sedan driven by Nelson R. Jackson of 4346 Glenwood Pky., Decatur, in the right side with the front of his vehicle. The '66 sedan was then knocked into the path of a '66 truck loaded with sand and driven by Johnnie H. Freeman of 1888 Alder Dr., Decatur, police said. The truck reportedly struck the '66 sedan and pushed it approximately 180 feet after the impact. Investigating officers are Sgt. H. S. Lee and Patrolman David Dorsey.

Bills due Dec. 20

Increase shown in tax digest

BY KEN STONER
Staff Writer

Clayton Countains can expect their annual county tax bills shortly, as the bills will be sent out to residents throughout Clayton during the week of Aug. 9, according to Milton Worsham, tax commissioner for the county.

Worsham added that the bills have a deadline of Dec. 20, giving residents plenty of time to take care of them. "Homeowners who pay their taxes through escrow accounts with their mortgage companies are encouraged to forward their tax bills to the companies as soon as they are received," the tax commissioner noted.

The 1971 tax digest figure in Clayton County has increased 8.27 percent over that for the same time period in 1970, tax officials said. The total property digest represents \$236,104,882, while the total for 1970 was \$218,068,315.

Worsham noted that after taking the homestead exemption into consideration, the 1971 figure totals \$196,397,103, or an increase of 11.85 percent over last year's net tax figure.

"The increase in the digest was very good considering the loss of \$8,000,000 in assessed tax value for household furniture and fixtures," the tax commissioner explained. Last year, voters throughout the state deleted household furniture and fixtures from the taxing list by constitutional amendment.

In another matter, motor vehicle assessments, the total for 1971 is \$27,919,792, or an increase of 11.08 percent over the figure of \$25,133,810 in 1970, a tax official noted.

According to the last totals for tag sales in the county, 74,100 tags have been sold in 1971 with an expected total for the year amounting to 77,000, Worsham said. Total tags sold in 1970 only amounted to 69,400, tax officials added.

County tax bills will reflect an increase of three mills due to the recent approval of increased salaries and retirement benefits for all county employees. Other items causing the increase, according to Worsham, include improved county maintenance and operations, while the approval of the \$5.4 million school bond referendum has not caused any tax increase.

The total milage for residents living in areas of the county which receive county fire protection amounts to 49.25 mills, with all other areas being taxed 44.25 mills.

The homeowner in Clayton County who owns a \$20,000 home would pay \$277.80 if he lived in a area where county fire protection is not provided, and \$307.80 in an area served by the county fire department.

The figures include the homestead exemption provision of \$2,000.

Homeowners must file for homestead exemption.

Judges announced for Clayton event

Saturday night will mark the date for this year's Miss Clayton County Pageant, which is slated to begin at 8 p.m. in the air-conditioned auditorium of Suder Elementary School in Jonesboro.

Twelve girls from the Clayton County area will compete for over \$800 in scholarships and a year's reign as Miss Clayton County. Miss Clayton County will go on to further Miss America competition next summer with the Miss Georgia event.

Five pageant judges will consider all the candidates in the categories of interviews, swim suit, evening gown and talent competition.

A list of judges and their backgrounds follows:

R. David Boyd, a professional cartoonist for News-Daily and over 120 papers nationally, is a resident of Newnan. Boyd's works reflect a professional style and a keen insight which have made him a factor on the national scene. As a syndicated cartoonist for Mark-Morgan Inc., a company which he owns, Boyd expresses a delightful wit in his editorial cartoons;

See JUDGES...Pg. - 5A

Monday's headlines...

...from the nation

ASTRONAUTS gather scientific booty during moonwalk...see page 2A.

...from the state

JUDGE ORDERS Columbus rioters to hearing...see page 2A.

index

News/Daily *of Clayton County was launched as a daily on August 2, 1971. Bill Wadkins, then general manager, is shown on its first front page.*

Chapter VII

Golden Age, Changing Guard: The Smaller Dailies

The Number Grows

Georgia had 29 daily newspapers in 1950. The total had increased to 35 by the beginning of 1984. Only one newspaper on the 1950 list is no longer published in any form. That is *The Macon News*, a casualty of the trend toward the merger of morning and afternoon newspapers in metropolitan areas. One other 1950 daily, *The Cedartown Standard*, became a weekly in 1961, and *The Valley Times News*, which was based in West Point, Georgia, in 1950, moved to a new building across the state line in Lanett, Alabama in 1972 and is no longer listed as a Georgia daily.

Thus nine new dailies have been added in the past 34 years, as all of the other dailies published in 1950 have survived and for the most part have prospered.

This chapter covers medium to smaller dailies in relatively isolated markets — that is at least 30 miles from the nearest large city — and which are in cities that were already well-established and recognized before World War II.

All of the newspapers in these cities have one especially notable characteristic: Without exception, they are better newspapers in the 1980s in content, appearance, number of pages, circulation, advertising layout, and service to readers than they were 35 years ago.

Some have changed more than others but all have changed. A few are in cities and counties which have grown considerably; most however, are in cities and counties which had modest growth. But all have increased their paid circulations. Many of them have survived competition from weeklies, shoppers, or even another daily. Not one of them has lost the dominant position in its community, however, and they all make a great deal of money. The years since World War II were truly a Golden Age for these papers.

The most significant change has come in the type of ownership. In 1950 all 18 newspapers covered in this chapter were owned by corporations or individuals based in the same city as the paper, and the chief executives and decision-makers were persons who lived in the community. By 1985, only five of the 18 still had such an owner. Those five are *The Brunswick News*, owned by the Leavys; *The Dublin Herald-Courier*, owned by the Lovetts; *The Rome News-Tribune*, owned by the Mooneys; *The Albany Herald,* owned by the Grays; and *The Waycross Journal-Herald*, owned by the Williamses.

The other 13 dailies in this chapter are now owned by groups or chains of varying size. The group owning the most Georgia newspapers is Thomson Newspapers, with seven. This should not be surprising since Thomson, based in Toronto, Canada, also owns more U.S. newspapers than any other group. Most of the Thomson papers are small to medium-size, and thus their total circulation does not match the size of Knight-Ridder, Gannett or others, but in number of individual papers, Thomson is No 1. Thomson also owns many newspapers in Canada and Great Britain, and for many years was the owner and publisher of the famous *London Times*, which was one of the few newspapers in the Thomson group that did not make a profit.

Thomson's presence in Georgia began in 1962 when it bought *The Dalton News*. The Dalton paper was only the second newspaper acquisition by Thomson in the United States, the first being in Laurel, Mississippi.

In 1968 Thomson went to the other end of the state to buy *The Valdosta Times*. *The Cordele Dispatch* was added in 1976, and then in the relatively short span of two years from 1980 through 1982, Thomson bought *The Tifton Gazette*, *The Thomasville Times-Enterprise* and *The Griffin Daily News*. In 1984, Thomson added *The Americus Times-Recorder*.

Other national groups represented among Georgia's smaller dailies are Harte-Hanks, with Carrollton's *Daily Times-Georgian;* Knight-Ridder, *The Union-Recorder* of Milledgeville; Multimedia, *The Moultrie Observer;* Gannett, *The Times of Gainesville;* Mid-South Management Company, *The LaGrange News;* Walls Media Inc., *Cartersville Tribune-News;* and Charles Morris Newspapers, *The Statesboro Herald*. Another large national group, Roy Park Newspapers, owns *The Warner Robins Sun*, which is covered in the chapter on suburban newspapers.

The first two smaller Georgia dailies to be bought by a group publisher after World War II were *The Cedartown Standard*, in 1950, and *The Valley Times-News* in 1955, both by Carmage Walls and his associates. Walls, who was born in Cordele and was once publisher of the Macon newspapers, has solid Georgia credentials but his operations are definitely of the group or chain variety. In fact, Walls may have been involved with the ownership and operation of more separate papers, daily and weekly, in the past 30 years than any person in the business.

But as noted, *The Cedartown Standard* reverted to weekly publication in 1961, and *The Valley Times-News* moved its building across the line to Lanett, Alabama, thus becoming basically an Alabama newspaper.

So the distinction of being the first non-metro daily still published as a daily in Georgia in the 1980s that was sold to a bona fide, out-of-state group belongs to *The LaGrange Daily News*, which was bought by Philip Buchheit and his Mid-South Management group in the summer of 1961.

The LaGrange Daily News

The Daily News was owned for about 30 years by Roy Swank and his family, who had purchased it from the old General Newspapers Group, the original chain for small southern dailies. Swank had several financial interests, and although he was listed as the publisher, he actually spent much of his time in Florida and elsewhere, with the operation of the newspaper left (after 1939) to general manager William Coker, and whomever happened to be editor. Among the editors during Swank's ownership were Don Downs, who later went on to a distinguished career in public relations with West Point-Pepperell Mills; Jim Wood, later a suburban publisher and president of the Georgia Press Association, as well as a state legislator; and Phil Harrison, who went into the radio field.

Thousands of travelers know LaGrange for the spectacular fountain in its town square, past which all the major highways passed before the completion of I-85.

Its rolling hillsides and flowers and trees first attracted the eye of a French visitor to the area named LaFayette when he was travelling through the South in 1825. LaFayette was the French general who as a young man had come to the United States to fight on the side of the American Revolution, and who led troops against the British in the decisive battle of Yorktown in 1781.

He came back to America in the 1820s, some 40 years after his role in the Revolution, and traveled extensively in the coastal states of the nation he had helped create. When LaFayette passed through Troup County, he remarked how much the countryside reminded him of LaGrange, which was the name of his country estate in France. So the settlers of the new town decided to honor LaFayette by naming it LaGrange.

General LaFayette's LaGrange connection didn't get much attention for almost 150 years, until Dr. Waights Henry, president of LaGrange College, saw a statue of LaFayette while he was travelling in France, and commissioned a replica to be made and placed in the town square fountain. The statue was completed in 1975 and placed in the fountain to become the city's most notable symbol and landmark.

But the statue in the park might more appropriately be one of Fuller Callaway, who was the most important figure in the development of LaGrange as a textile center. Callaway used funds from a successful dry goods operation, which he started when only 18 years old, to launch Callaway Mills, one of the largest textile mills in Georgia, and the main employer for several generations of LaGrange residents. In addition, the Callaway Foundation helped build schools, libraries and numerous other projects in LaGrange which other cities and counties usually had to finance entirely from tax revenues.

LaGrange, in many ways, was the classic "company town" for most of this century, and both the company and the town benefited.

Callaway's sons carried on the tradition of benevolent stewardship. Cason, who was president of the mills after his father, left the family business in 1935 to devote himself to the development of Callaway Gardens and Blue Springs Farm in Harris County. Callaway Gardens, which was opened to the public in 1953, is known throughout the world for its unique floral beauty, its vegetable garden, and its lakes and recreation areas. The largest lake provides an inland beach for middle West Georgia, 200 miles from the ocean.

Fuller Callaway Jr. became president of the mills in 1935 and presided over their most successful years. But in early 1961, the textile business came upon slow times. On a day still remembered in LaGrange as "Black Friday," more than 100 executives at Callaway Mills were fired, with ominous indications that others might follow, along with many lower-echelon employees.

At the same time, municipal and civic leaders were still protesting the 1960 census figures which showed that both LaGrange and Troup County lost population in the 1950s, a decade when many Georgia counties grew dramatically due to the post-World War II baby boom.

Troup was down from 49,841 in 1950 to 47,189 in 1960, according to the census, evidence of a large out-migration when considering the high birth rate of that period. Despite the protests of a "wrong count," the figures proved correct, and, in fact the decline was continuing. By 1970, Troup's population would drop to 44,466.

Roy Swank decided the time was ripe to sell the newspaper, so he looked around for a prospective buyer, thus starting a trend which would be widely followed, and would affect the state's smaller dailies second only to the technological revolution.

By 1984, the number of dailies outside the five largest cities (Atlanta, Savannah, Columbus, Macon, Augusta) had increased to 26, and 21 of the 26 have different owners than they had in 1961.

LaGrange was the first. The buyer was a company headed by Phil Buchheit, publisher of the Spartanburg, South Carolina newspapers, and one of the many newspaper group owners who sprang from the old General Newspapers organization. Buchheit's group remained small, and LaGrange was — and is — one of its most important properties. The sale was announced in July 1961.

For his money (about $250,000 with long terms), Buchheit got a newspaper of 4,500 circulation, in a declining city with a declining economy. But it turned out to be one of the great bargains among Georgia's newspapers.

Bill Coker, Swank's general manager for many years, continued in that post but primarily concentrated on advertising. Coming in as publisher was Glenn O. Long, who had been managing editor of the Spartanburg newspapers for Buchheit. Long soon brought in another Spartanburg alumnus, Jimmy Crowe, as his managing editor.

At that time *The LaGrange News* enjoyed two distinctions. It was the only Georgia daily with a 9-column page format, and it was the only one with its plant and offices located in a former city jail. The old jail had three levels, with a total of about 9,000 square feet. The editor's office was in a former cell with foot-wide walls, which some editors probably would find helpful on occasion.

Long, primarily a newsman, began editing and putting together the front page as part of his duties when he became publisher, and 22 years later he was still planning the front page and writing the headlines, a rarity for daily publishers.

Long and Buchheit both realized that the success of the newspaper depended on a change in LaGrange's economic direction, and to an extent on a change in its attitude toward new industry and new jobs. Buchheit came to LaGrange and spoke to a joint meeting of civic clubs and business leaders, challenging them to revitalize the Chamber of Commerce and make a real effort to bring in new industry.

An idea was also being promoted in LaGrange in the early 1960s that it could be the site of an international jetport to serve the Atlanta area. Atlanta's Hartsfield airport had not become the facility it would be by the 1980s, and the need for a second large jetport remained a live issue until the new mid-field terminal was completed in 1980. Various counties in the Atlanta metro area were mentioned as possibilities through the years, but LaGrange (Troup) certainly seemed an unlikely prospect, even in 1961, when Atlanta's northward development and population growth was not as definite. LaGrange is about 65 miles southwest of downtown Atlanta, and 80-90 miles from the high growth counties to the north and east.

Interstate 85, connecting LaGrange to the Atlanta area, was not then completed, and in fact, would be one of the last interstates in Georgia to be completed. The final leg between Newnan and LaGrange did not open until November 1977, 16 years after the enthusiasm for a jetport there.

When the jetport idea didn't get off the ground, Long helped organize and became a charter member of the LaGrange Industrial Development Authority, which had as its purpose the buying of land which could be developed into industrial parks.

The accepted rumor in LaGrange for decades was that Callaway Mills didn't want any more industry because new industry would compete for workers and might bring in unions. That was the same talk heard in Columbus and other cities where textiles were the major industry. And there was something to the talk.

Callaway Mills and its Foundation had powerful resources, both in money and influence. In fact, *The Daily News* during Swank's ownership was accused of being virtually a house organ for Callaway Mills.

When an attractive site for a new industry was available for sale in the middle 1960s, the Industrial Authority made an offer for it, with the intention of then selling it to a prospective industry. The rumor was that the owners received a higher offer from Callaway Mills for the same site. The owners, mostly merchants, thought about LaGrange's future and decided to sell to the Authority.

That was a turning point, and LaGrange soon got its first new industry in years, a firm producing polyethylene film.

The Authority then picked up an unexpected ally that would make LaGrange one of the "hottest" cities in Georgia for new industry. That ally was Fuller Callaway Jr. and the Callaway interests.

In 1968 Callaway Mills was sold to Deering-Milliken, a South Carolina-based company which has kept the LaGrange operation remarkably healthy considering the problems of the U.S. textile industry in the past 20 years.

After the sale, Callaway made a large tract of land available to the Authority at a bargain price and that tract became the city's first industrial park. This was at a time when the federal government was providing funds for industrial park improvements and the LaGrange board received $1 million in government help. Some 12 years later, 25 new industries with about 6,000 new jobs had located in the industrial park and there is quality along with the quantity. Among companies now in LaGrange are Westinghouse, *The Wall Street Journal*, Kimberly-Clark, Hanes, Mt. Mills, VisQueen and Duracell Battery. The additional jobs were none too soon or too many, as employment at the city's textile mills dropped in that period from about 8,000 to 3,000.

Long, who played an important role, personally and with the newspaper, believes that the most important advantage LaGrange had in competing for industry was having sites available at reasonable prices when industrial prospects came looking. The Industrial Development Authority scored its most dramatic triumph in 1979 when it borrowed $1.8 million, with the backing of the LaGrange and Troup County governments, bought and prepared a new parcel of land, and sold 130 acres to Kimberly-Clark for $1.2 million.

This Kimberly-Clark operation will not only bring 350 jobs into the community, but will pay $500,000 a month to the city-owned electric power company. Its power usage — and its monthly bill — will be more than the combined usage of the rest of the city's utility customers.

LaGrange aimed for small industries, so that it would not again be dependent on one single employer, and it has worked. The Troup population was up to 50,000 in the 1980 census, from 44,466 in 1970. But it had taken 30 years to get back to its 1950 total.

Long credits the opening of the West Point Lake, which may rival Lake Lanier as a water playground in future years; the attraction of Callaway Gardens; and the continued strength of downtown LaGrange as a shopping area as other reasons for the city's turnaround in the 1970s.

The town square, probably the most attractive in Georgia, combines with Mansour's Department Store, which fills the entire block on the south side of the square, in keeping LaGrange's downtown from fading into the empty storefronts which afflict so many large and small downtowns in the 1980s.

Two significant vacancies did appear in downtown stores when Belk's and Penney's moved to a shopping mall in 1979. But the Penney's location was quickly taken by a furniture store, and after being vacant for four years, the Belk's location has become a mini-mall, with the financing coming from a downtown business organization formed along the lines of the Industrial Authority.

Long moved *The LaGrange News* out of downtown in 1972, going from a former jail to a former bowling alley. In the process, he managed to get a real bargain on building costs.

The company was ready to invest about $500,000 to build a new 12,000 square-foot building when Long noticed an abandoned bowling alley a few blocks from the main business area. He bought the alley for $90,000, spent another $90,000 on remodeling, and came out with an 18,000 square-foot building for $180,000, and its layout is perfectly suited for a newspaper, with ample parking space on the outside premises.

Circulation of *The LaGrange News* has followed advertising volume upward and stood at 14,500 in late 1983. One thing hadn't changed at *The News*, however, it still had the only 9-column format in Georgia, despite having trimmed two inches off the page width in the past 20 years.

"No one ever complains about the 9-column format," Long says, "so we haven't changed it. On a 24-page press, it gives us 27-page capacity." In addition, of course, it provides an extra column of advertising inches for a full-page ad. He is concerned, however, about what will happen if more papers and ads move to the 6-column format. (Editor's Note: *The News* did change to a six-column format in July, 1984, conforming to the standard advertising unit after years of resisting the eight-column format.)

Coker died in November 1977, and was eventually succeeded in the advertising post by Sue A. Long, who happens to be Publisher Glenn Long's wife. She is also a 12-year veteran of the ad staff, and the arrangement has kept the newspaper prospering.

C. Lee West, managing editor, has been with *The News* for 23 years, serving earlier as a photographer and classified ad manager. James Irwin, the circulation manager, is a 37-year employee, who spent many of those years at a linotype machine before the change to cold type in 1967.

LaGrange, the classical southern "mill town" of the early 20th century, has become a model of industrial diversification. *The LaGrange News*, first of the non-metro newspapers to be sold to an out-of-state group, is an example of how group ownership can improve a newspaper, and ironically, it is more of a home-based product today than ever, with a publisher who for more than 20 years sat down each day and put page one together. (Long finally relinquished that task in late 1983.)

The Daily Citizen-News, Dalton

About a year after the LaGrange sale another Georgia daily was acquired by an out-of-state firm. This time the firm wasn't from nearby South Carolina, or even from the United States. It was Lord Roy Thomson's Canadian empire which was to become one of the world's leading newspaper publishers, and eventually, the owner of more Georgia dailies than any other company. The newspaper that was the object of Thomson's first Georgia foray was a three-month old daily in a county whose prosperity was linked to the oft-changing fortunes of the carpet industry.

Dalton had gotten its first daily newspaper since the Civil War on April 2, 1962. Creation of the new daily came 101 years after the first Dalton daily was established in 1861.

At the end of the Civil War the daily publication was halted and the paper, under a new name, *The North Georgia Citizen*, resumed weekly publication.

Another name change came in 1917 when A. J. Showalter Company acquired the newspaper and shortened the name to *The Dalton Citizen*.

This name was retained until late in 1962 when *The Citizen* merged with a previous sister weekly, *The Dalton News*, which had become the new daily on April 2 under the name of *The Dalton Daily News*.

At the time, L. A. Lee was owner of both *The Citizen*, published on Thursdays, and *The News*, published on Tuesdays. Lee, a native of Pembroke, Georgia, purchased the Dalton Printing Company, which owned *The Dalton News*, in 1937, and later changed the name to Lee Office Supply, Inc., which he still operates in the 1980s. In 1941, he bought the A. J. Showalter Company, a famous gospel music publisher, which also published *The Dalton Citizen*.

When *The Citizen* observed its Centennial in 1947, it was the third oldest weekly in Georgia. *The Milledgeville Union-Recorder* was the oldest and *The Warrenton Clipper* was second oldest. In addition, *The Citizen* was the 13th oldest weekly in the Southeast. Those records as a weekly were lost in 1962 when *The Citizen* was combined with *The Daily News* to form *The Daily Citizen-News*.

In the years that preceded the daily, each of the weeklies had a circulation of more than 7,000 which made them the highest paid-circulation weeklies in Georgia.

The newspapers were just one part of a vast printing operation that had become known as L. A. Lee Company, Inc. The firm printed a number of magazines for W. R. C. Smith Publishing Company, Atlanta; city directories for the R. L. Polk Company of Detroit, Michigan and the Rothberger Directory Company of Chattanooga, Tennessee, and a large volume of commercial printing for local chenille bedspread and tufted carpet mills, as well as other businesses and industries. By 1948 the Lee Company had phased out its printing in the gospel-music field.

As the city and the weekly newspapers continued to grow, Lee decided the community and its people needed a local daily. Since the two weeklies were operated by the same staffs and published in the same plant with the same equipment, it was his decision to maintain those facilities as he went into daily production.

Through the years Lee had received but rejected several offers to buy his newspapers. However, in 1962 after he had converted *The News* to a daily while continuing to publish *The Citizen* as a weekly, he received an offer from Thomson Newspapers which he felt compelled to accept. Lee sold the newspapers to Thomson in July and in the fall of that year *The*

Citizen ceased publication as a weekly and became a part of *The Daily News* under the combined nameplate *The Daily Citizen News*.

Mark Pace, who had joined the Lee Newspapers in late October 1945, stayed on as editor, a position he held until March 1982, when he retired at 68 after 50 years of newspaper writing and editing. Only two editorial members of the earlier Lee newspaper era remained in 1984. They are Louise Hackney (1950) the managing editor, and Lloyd Gulledge (1952), associate news editor.

Pace, who served as editor of the Dalton newspapers for 37 years, is a native of Wauchula, Florida. He began writing for his two hometown weeklies, *The Herald* and *The Florida Advocate* in 1931, while still in high school.

He graduated in the years of the Great Depression and went to work at $5.00 a week for *The Herald*. He took the job for two reasons: First, there were no other jobs and no money, and second, he wanted to be a newspaperman and decided this was a way to learn the business.

After Lee sold the newspapers to Thomson, George Lewis III was sent in as interim publisher. Lewis was from a newspaper family in Petersburg, Virginia and was in the business office of *The Progress-Index*, which had earlier been sold to Thomson.

A few months later, Rufus M. Josey was named publisher. Josey assumed duties in Dalton in 1962, from Petersburg, and stayed for seven years before returning to Petersburg in 1969 as publisher of *The Progress-Index*. In 1977 he was named publisher of *The Dothan Eagle* in Dothan, Alabama and was still in that position in 1984.

Josey was born in Darlington, South Carolina and grew up in that state and in south Georgia. After three years with the Air Corps in World War II, he returned to Georgia and entered Henry W. Grady School of Journalism, University of Georgia, from which he graduated in 1947.

He was with the Spartanburg, South Carolina newspaper for nine years, the last four as managing editor. In 1957-58 he was with the news department of *The Washington Star*, and later with *The Winchester* (Virginia) *Star* for four years in various managerial positions. He was managing editor at Petersburg from 1961 until his move to Dalton in 1962.

Following Josey as publisher on March 17, 1969, was Jimmy C. Crowe, who had been publisher of the Troy, Alabama *Messenger*, which was then a Thomson paper.

Crowe, a native of Spartanburg, South Carolina, started his newspaper career with *The Spartanburg Herald-Journal* in 1953. For five years before taking the position in Alabama, he was managing editor of *The LaGrange Daily News*. He left Dalton in 1970 to become associated with Charles Morris in Savannah. He has since established his own business as a newspaper broker-consultant.

It was while Crowe was publisher at Dalton that Thomson began construction of a new, modern building, having occupied the same quarters in the Lee Building since the sale.

Succeeding Crowe as publisher was George N. Clarke, who was publisher when *The Daily Citizen-News* moved into its new plant, 308 S. Thornton Avenue, on Labor Day weekend, 1970.

Clarke was born in Philadelphia, Pennsylvania in 1927, and attended the Old Dominion College, Norfolk, Virginia.

He was publisher of the Dalton paper until August 1977 when he left the newspaper business to form a carpet agency, Clar-Sett. He continues to reside in Dalton.

Clarke was publisher when the newspaper converted from hot metal to the cold-type process in 1976. The final copy of the daily set by hot type and the first copy by the cold-type method were placed, along with other historical data, in a 50-year time capsule on the lawn of Whitfield County Courthouse in Dalton as part of Dalton's Bicentennial observance.

In August 1977 Benjamin Neely Young was named publisher. A native of Cedartown, Young had worked with *The Valdosta Daily Times; The Daily Citizen-News, The Marietta Daily Journal* and *The Cherokee Tribune*.

In 1983 he was president of both the Georgia Press Association and the Associated Press of Georgia.

Even in the years of the weeklies, the Dalton newspapers operated along daily lines in some ways, and at times won AP awards competing against dailies. They published extra newsstand editions on major local issues and late-breaking news stories; they took editorial stands on important local issues, such as a five-man county commission to replace the one-man system; abolition of the old fee system; appointment instead of election of the county school superintendent; expose of a suspected Communist who later left Dalton, and criticism of political candidates for handshaking and distribution of cards too close to election places.

Dalton was later (1976) than most smaller dailies in converting to the cold-type process, which resulted in the layoff of six of about 16 employees in the composing room. In mid-1983, a front-end system and terminals were installed, further modernizing and streamlining the newspaper's production.

The Albany Herald: A Mighty Middleweight

One newspaper in Georgia stands somewhere between the larger dailies and the smaller dailies. It does not quite have the circulation or ad volume that would put it up with the Savannah, Augusta, Columbus and Macon newspapers, but it has more circulation than any of the afternoon papers in those cities, and it is considerably ahead of the circulation and ad volume of the other newspapers covered in this chapter.

The paper is *The Albany Herald*, and it's hard to categorize in more ways than one. It is Georgia's "mighty middleweight" newspaper.

The Herald's 1983 circulation was 35,274 daily, and 40,000 on Sunday, which makes it the second largest afternoon newspaper in Georgia, next only to *The Atlanta Journal*.

Perhaps more important than its circulation total is the fact that *The Herald* is the major daily newspaper for the entire southwest quadrant of Georgia, an area which is difficult for the Atlanta dailies to serve, and where the other large dailies do not circulate at all. *The Herald* has subscribers in 22 counties, and in many of those counties, it is the only daily newspaper available by home delivery.

Location is one reason *The Herald* has grown from 12,000 circulation in 1950 to its present total. Another reason is that Albany and Dougherty County gained metropolitan status in the past 30 years, as Dougherty's population rose from 43,000 in 1950 to 100,978 in 1980. The largest jump was in the 1950s, when the population almost doubled. Neighboring Lee County has gotten some of the overflow, but the rest of the surrounding counties have grown little if any, and several of them (Calhoun, Baker, Terrell, Worth, Clay, Randolph) have fewer people than they did in 1950.

Albany has been an island of growth in southwest Georgia since World War II, surrounded by declining agricultural counties, which have seen many of their black residents, as well as younger whites, move to the metropolitan areas.

The Herald has grown along with Albany, but in most other ways, it has changed very little in the past 33 years. The man who has presided over *The Herald* for all those years, playing a prominent role in the affairs of the city, the area, the state and even the nation is James H. Gray, a quintessential South Georgian. He has built a communications empire rather than an agricultural one, and has grudgingly given way to the economic and social changes of recent decades. He has twice been state chairman of the Democratic party; was the "establishment" candidate for governor in 1966; and has served as Albany's mayor for 10 years.

But James Gray is far from a typical South Georgian. In fact, he is a Yankee from New England, born and raised in Massachusetts, educated at Dartmouth College in New Hampshire, with graduate studies at the University of Heidelberg in Germany before World War II. He developed a friendship with the Kennedy family of Massachusetts in his younger days, and a picture of President John F. Kennedy still hangs in his office.

Gray was in his mid-20s when he first came to Georgia. He had married Dorothy Ellis, daughter of the owner of Ellis Textile Mills in his Massachusetts home town of Springfield, and the Ellises had a plantation home near Albany, which the Grays often visited. Then during World War II, Gray, as a member of the 82nd Airbourne, was stationed at Fort Benning, also close to Albany. Gray liked Georgia and the Albany area enough to stay on after the war. He took a job as a reporter on *The Herald*, which had about 6,000 circulation at the time, and had been owned and edited since its founding in 1891 by only two men, H. M. McIntosh, the founder, and his son, H. T. McIntosh, who took over in 1925.

McIntosh, who was to continue writing a column for *The Herald* for many years, had no heirs and so he sold *The Herald* to Gray in 1946 for a reported $250,000. Gray, then 29, thus became a full-fledged editor, publisher and Georgian, and one who would have great influence on his adopted state.

Gray soon became involved in state politics as an adviser to Herman Talmadge in his first race for governor in 1948. However, Gray never let his involvement in politics keep him from being a vigorous defender of his newspaper's right of criticism.

In 1952 he obtained an injunction that prevented Albany city commission members from conducting business with the city. The city fought back by filing a $150,000 suit against *The Herald* and Gray, alleging malicious libel in its editorials and news stories which led to the injunction against those commissioners doing business with the city. The case went to a jury trial, and the jury returned a verdict in favor of *The Herald*, agreeing with *The Herald*'s defense that it was commenting on "public matters without personal malice."

Because of his early support of Talmadge, Gray became an insider with the political organization which dominated Georgia politics from 1948-1963, and in 1959, Governor Ernest Vandiver appointed him as the state

Democratic chairman. He was the first non-native Georgian to hold the post.

Gray's memorable moment on the national political stage came at the 1960 Democratic convention when he was selected to deliver the minority report on the civil rights plank for the party platform. The speech was carried on nationwide television and was probably the event which made Gray a plausible candidate for governor six years later.

If Gray was an unlikely South Georgia editor or state Democratic chairman, he was an even more unlikely candidate for governor. Besides being a Massachusetts native who still had the clipped accent of his youth, he was a recent divorcee (1963); the head of Democrats for Goldwater in 1964; had never held elective office; had not supported Carl Sanders, the incumbent Democratic governor; and had been ousted from his state Democratic party post. But 1966 produced the strangest gubernatorial election in Georgia history, and Gray emerged as the "moderate alter native" in the field that sought the Democratic nomination.

He got into the race after former Gov. Ernest Vandiver suffered a heart attack and had to withdraw, leaving no strong candidate to carry the flag of the old Talmadge machine. The other candidates included former Gov. Ellis Arnall, who had not run for office in 24 years; Lester Maddox, a restaurant owner in Atlanta, who had gained fame for chasing blacks from his premises with a pistol and axe handles; Jimmy Carter, a little-known state senator who was suspected of being a liberal; and former Lt. Gov. Garland Byrd, who had lost a congressional race to Republican Bo Callaway two years earlier.

Gray, despite his obvious liabilities, was drafted to be the "organization" candidate against the liberal Arnall, the extremist Maddox, the unknown Carter, and Byrd, who was not considered strong enough to defeat Callaway, who would be the Republican candidate for governor in the general election.

In the split vote of the first primary, Gray finished fourth, although he received a sizable vote. The problem was that Gray, Carter — who finished third — and Byrd split the large "centrist" vote, leaving Arnall and Maddox as the leaders with their solid liberal and conservative blocs. Maddox defeated Arnall in the runoff, and then was elected governor by the legislature when neither he nor Callaway received a clear majority in the general election due to a large write-in vote for Arnall.

Maddox surprisingly appointed Gray to a second term as state Democratic chairman, at a time when the Republican party was at its peak in the state. During the campaign, Maddox at one time charged Gray with offering him a large sum of money if he would withdraw.

Carter's ascendancy to the governorship in 1970 brought an end to Gray's prominence outside Albany and he settled in to become a city politician, and a very successful one. He was elected mayor in 1975 and was serving his tenth year in the post in 1985. At the state and national level, he veered sharply to the right, even endorsing Maddox for governor over George Busbee, a fellow Albanian, in 1974. *The Herald* and Gray both supported Republican Gerald Ford over Georgia's Carter for president in 1976, and Ronald Reagan over Carter in 1980.

Gray's company owns the only television station in Albany and southwest Georgia, and also owns stations in other cities. His sons, James and Geoff, came in to help run *The Herald* several years ago although Gray is still listed as editor and publisher.

Because of his political and business activities, Gray has been one of the best-known Georgia newspapermen since World War II. But he is not well-known among his fellow newspapermen in the state. The only Press Association function he has attended in 30 years was the candidates' forum at the summer GPA convention in 1966 when he was running for governor. Few of his fellow editors endorsed him that year.

Although a very personal-style journalist, he has seldom written a personal column, preferring to express his views through unsigned editorials, of which he has turned out thousands on every conceivable subject through the years.

The Herald has prospered and grown but its appearance in 1984 is not markedly different than it was in 1954. The switch to cold type was made in 1973, and an offset press was installed in 1977, but *The Herald* still has many characteristics of hot type days. It is also one of the few Georgia newspapers that still carries ads on page one.

But *The Herald*, perhaps more vigorously than most of its contemporaries, has definitely been a part of its community and has played a major role in the industrial growth which has brought Albany to metropolitan status. Gray has served five terms as president of the Chamber of Commerce, and believes that it was through "the combined efforts of *The Herald* and civic leaders that Albany has become the preeminent metropolitan center and the economic and cultural hub of Southwest Georgia."

The Herald's mottos are "Southwest Georgia's Reading Habit," and "South Georgia's Metropolitan Daily." The most important role of a newspaper, according to Gray, is effective leadership in the progress of the community.

The Americus Times-Recorder

Jimmy Carter not only didn't get James Gray's support for president — although Gray was a former Democratic state chairman — he also didn't get support from a lot of other Georgia newspapers, either in 1976 or 1980. But one newspaper which was with him all the way was *The Americus Times-Recorder*, his home-county daily. Carter's candidacy and subsequent presidential term brought hundreds of visitors from throughout the nation and world to Americus, which is 10 miles from his home in Plains, and had the only public motel-hotel facilities in Sumter County. *The Times-Recorder* office became a frequent stop for well-known reporters. Americus' restaurants became famous — or infamous.

The Times-Recorder was covering the political activities of Jimmy Carter long before the rest of the state, nation and world heard of him. His name was familiar in the school news columns of the 1930s and 1940s, and then in the social news when he married Rosalyn Smith, also of Sumter County. Later, after his service in the Navy, Carter was a frequent news maker as a civic leader, as a church worker, as a member of the county school board, and then as a state senator.

Carter's name was soon written by the most famous reporters in the world, but his first chroniclers were the Plains correspondent of *The Americus Times-Recorder* in the 1930s and 1940s, and Ann Sheffield, the long-time social news editor.

Ironically, near the end of Carter's term as governor, when he was recruiting home-county friends to spearhead his run for the presidency, Sumter County had become one of the most economically-depressed counties in Georgia. Several plants closed in the 1970s, pushing the unemployment rate past 20 percent.

Carter, unlike some governors, did not show favoritism to his home county with roads or industrial prospects, but Sumter residents were still strongly behind him when he ran for president. Later, some of them benefited from the influx of tourists and other visitors who came to Americus and Plains because Jimmy Carter was president of the United States.

During the decade of the 1970s, Sumter's population did increase from 26,931 in 1970 to 29,360 in 1980, modest in comparison with some other Georgia daily newspaper counties, but a great improvement over the 40 years from 1920 to 1960 when Sumter's population dropped from 29,640 to 24,652. Sumter is still the second smallest county in Georgia with a daily newspaper, next to neighboring Crisp (Cordele).

Circulation on *The Times-Recorder* has grown from about 4,280 in 1950 to 7,000 in 1984, and it covers 63 percent of the homes in Sumter County, a high number in a largely rural county with a relatively low per capita income. Among outside dailies, only *The Atlanta Constitution*, with 5 percent coverage, has measurable penetration in Sumter.

The Times-Recorder was once part of the chain called General Newspapers, the prototype of many small newspaper groups in the U.S. today. General Newspapers was formed by Charles C. Marsh and Eugene Pulliam in the early 1930s and it included among other papers, *The Times-Recorder, The LaGrange Daily News,* and a majority interest in *The Macon Telegraph* and *Macon News*. Employees were given a chance to buy into these smaller papers, and often got the opportunity to buy the newspaper altogether.

That was what happened to James R. Blair, who was associated with the Americus newspaper for more than 50 years. Like James H. Gray, his neighboring publisher 30 miles away in Albany, Blair is a southerner to the core, but also like Gray, Blair was born far from south Georgia, in Forest, Indiana, and was in his 30s when he came to Americus to be editor and publisher of *The Times-Recorder* in 1931. By 1936 Blair had purchased all of *The Times-Recorder* stock from General Newspapers and it remained in his family until being sold in April 1984 to Thomson Newspapers.

The newspaper changed to cold type in 1964, and then in 1972 moved into a new building, constructed specifically for a newspaper operation, on the outskirts of Americus.

In 1976, following the death of his wife, Floy, Blair went into semi-retirement, with his son, Billy Blair, becoming editor and publisher. Dana, Billy's wife, is also active on the newspaper. Billy, a former state representative from Sumter County, is also a major owner of a large lighting fixture company in Americus.

For all the years from 1950 to 1982, the key members of the news staff were Rudy Hayes, managing editor, and Ann Sheffield, the society editor. Clarence Graddick was sports editor for 20 years, an important role on *The Times-Recorder* since Americus High is perennially one of the best high school teams in the state.

Being Jimmy Carter's home county newspaper gave *The Times-Recorder* a unique fame, and exposed it to the eyes of the brokers and group buyers who were so active in the 1970s. But the Blairs declined all approaches for possible sales, even during a serious illness Billy suffered in the late 1970s. The most persistent suitor was Thomson, which already owned nearby Cordele, and Americus rejoined the group newspapers in 1984, a half century after leaving General Newspapers.

Sumter County has recovered from its serious economic slump of the middle 1970s but growth projections are not optimistic. Plains' most famous citizens have returned and made it their home again, and in many ways, Sumter County is the same as if they had never gone away.

The Brunswick News

The Brunswick News, published Monday through Saturday afternoons since 1902, is a family-owned and managed newspaper in the truest sense. It was founded by Clarence H. Leavy (pronounced Leh-vy) who was publisher for 44 years until his death in 1946. His brother, L. J. Leavy, and son, Clarence H. Leavy Jr. then became publishers of *The News*. Clarence Jr. was the sole president-publisher after his uncle's death in 1959. In January 1982, Clarence Howard Leavy III became the third generation member of his family to hold the newspaper's top position, following the death of his father.

That *The News* is still family-owned is a tribute to the determination of the Leavy family to maintain *The News* as a newspaper based and controlled in Brunswick. Few dailies in Georgia have been as coveted by the large national chains and other prospective buyers as *The Brunswick News*.

Its daily paid circulation in 1984 is listed as 16,000, more than twice the 1950 circulation of 7,128. Glynn County and Brunswick did not have spectacular growth in the 1970s — in fact, Brunswick (17,605) had a 10 percent population loss — but Glynn County increased in population from 29,000 in 1950 to 54,891 in 1980, and the outlook is good for the rest of the 1980s.

More importantly, Brunswick is a relatively isolated market, 300 miles from Atlanta and its dailies, 75 miles from Savannah, and 50 miles from Jacksonville, Florida. None of the outside dailies have a substantial penetration in Brunswick.

With the Golden Isles of St. Simons, Sea and Jekyll just a few miles off shore, Brunswick is the trade center for an important tourist and resort home area, as well as for the surrounding counties of southeast Georgia.

Its retail sales totals for the early 1980s put it on the same level with Athens, Rome and Gainesville and not far behind Albany. *The Brunswick News*, in 1984, averaged about 176 pages a week, plus many inserts, which makes it a very fat Monday through Saturday newspaper.

In addition, *The News* has shown a commendable propensity for staving off competition, of which it has had plenty in the past 30 years. Mostly the competition came from weeklies and from newspapers seeking to identify with St. Simons Island, which is the fastest growing section of the county.

Homer Rankin, before he bought *The Tifton Gazette* and became a successful publisher, tried his hand at a Brunswick newspaper called *The Banner*, which lasted only a few months. In the 1960s Bill Williams started the weekly *Glynn Reporter* and it was published by various owners for about 15 years. The last editor and publisher was Sparky Newsome, son of Smythe Newsome of *The Washington-Wilkes News-Reporter* in Washington, Georgia. The younger Newsome put out one of the best weekly newspapers in the state, as evidenced by a record number of GPA awards which went to *The Reporter* in its final year. Sadly, the awards were presented posthumously as *The Reporter* had folded several months before the awards ceremony.

An unusual aspect of the operation during the Newsome ownership was that *The Reporter's* pages were flown to Washington from Brunswick each week to be printed on the press in Washington, nearly 200 miles away.

A weekly called *The St. Simons Sun* flared brilliantly but briefly from June, 1975 to January, 1976. Its importance mainly lies in the subsequent success of the young husband-wife team who came to St. Simons from Alabama to publish, edit and compose *The Sun*. Jimmy Johnson, whose cartoons gave *The Sun* part of its unique flavor, later became the chief editorial cartoonist for the Jackson, Mississippi *Clarion-Ledger*, and his cartoons were carried in many Gannett newspapers. Rheta Grimsley Johnson went on to become a columnist and reporter for the Scripps-Howard Newspapers. In 1982 she won the American Society of Newspaper Editors award for best column, and in 1983 she was honored with the coveted Ernie Pyle Award for reporting.

The most persistent and successful "other paper" in Glynn County is *The Islander*, a weekly tabloid on St. Simons, which has been published for about 12 years. Its advertising base is small but it seems to have established a niche among the resident islanders. E. J. Permar and G. L. Bradshaw are its owners and editors.

In 1974 *The Brunswick News* moved from its long-time location in downtown Brunswick, where the press could be seen in operation through a sidewalk window on Main Street, to a modern plant several blocks away. Its exterior wall is made of tabby stone, a material unique to that area of Georgia, which was used for buildings by the earliest colonists. An 8-unit offset press was installed, along with cold type equipment. The change was not as evident in *The News* as in most papers since it retained the same basic appearance. Ten years later it still carries few local photos or art layouts, and its format closely resembles the one used throughout the past 40 years.

But its main eccentricity is that *The Brunswick News* still does not carry local stories or photos on the front page. All front page stories are from the Associated Press wire, and most of them run the full length that AP sends them. Local, or staff-produced stories, whether about Brunswick or the surrounding area, are carried on the back page of the front section, and continued backward into the first section. This policy is even followed on major local stories which are front page news in other parts of the state or even the nation. Occasionally, a teaser headline will be carried across the top of page one, referring to a local story on the back page.

This was a policy also followed for many years by the Savannah newspapers although abandoned back in the 1960s. Brunswick, however, continues the policy.

Howard Leavy, the current publisher, says, "At times we have experimented with changing the policy by putting some local stories on the front page but readers seem to like having all the main local stories on the same page. We do run other local stories on inside pages, of course." The policy started, Leavy believes, when his grandfather ran local stories on the back page and inside pages to attract readers to the ads on those pages.

The Brunswick News carries a heavy amount of international and national news, perhaps more than any newspaper in the state except the Atlanta dailies. Its local report, however, is not as comprehensive as most of Georgia's smaller dailies.

Long time employees include Murray Poole, the sports editor, who has been with the paper for 20 years. The city editor for nine years was Duane Riner, who went on to be Governor George Busbee's press secretary for eight years. Riner later was associated with the World Congress Center in Atlanta, and then became state editor of *The Atlanta Journal-Constitution*.

The Daily Times-Georgian, Carrollton

One of the newest dailies in Georgia is *The Daily Times-Georgian* of Carrollton, and judging by its circulation figures, it is one of the most successful conversions from a weekly the state has ever had.

The Times-Georgian began five-morning-a-week publication in November 1980, increasing its frequency from three editions a week under different names. The groundwork had been carefully laid, and Carrollton is far enough from the center of metro Atlanta (50 miles) to have a definite trade area of its own. The county's population growth has been almost as great as in the counties closer to Atlanta.

In 1983 the Carrollton paper claimed a paid circulation of 12,000 with 55 percent of the homes in Carroll County covered, only a little short of its highest paid circulation as a weekly.

The man most associated with the Carrollton newspapers during the post-World War II era is Stanley Parkman, who has been publisher of one paper or the other in Carrollton for 40 years, and still holds that title in 1985, although his company sold its newspapers and printing operation to Harte-Hanks Communications in 1979.

Parkman, who was born in Cusseta, Georgia, just outside of Columbus, came to Carrollton in 1944 to work for *The Times* and *Free Press*, a venerable newspaper that traced its history back to *The Weekly Times* in 1870. *The Free Press* came into being in 1883, and until 1941 the two were published as separately-owned weeklies. O. W. Passavant brought the two papers under a common ownership that year but continued them as separate newspapers. F. Clyde Tuttle bought them a year before Parkman came.

About a year later, Parkman was approached by several merchants and other businessmen about starting another newspaper in Carrollton, and so in November 1945, *The Carroll County Georgian* was born, in opposition to the long-established *Times* and *Free Press*. *The Georgian* turned out to be one of the rare cases in Georgia of a challenger prevailing over an older, established competitor. (There are no examples in recent years of a new daily having such success.)

The Georgian's beginnings were modest, however, with only $6,800 in capital, and a four-page sheet-fed Babcock press for printing. But Parkman and his partners, who included Roy Richards, the president of Southwire, the county's largest industry, soon gained an edge in the competition.

In 1955 *The Georgian*'s owners bought the competing *Times-Free Press* and made it a Tuesday publication with *The Georgian* continuing to come out on Thursday. This arrangement was followed for 21 years until 1976 when a third weekly publication, called *Saturday*, was added.

In the meantime, the Carroll County Publishing Company was active in acquiring and printing other weekly newspapers. One of its early acquisitions was *The Bremen Gateway*, in 1962, which was bought from H. A. (Hoss) Meeks. Meeks, then 92, had been publisher and editor of *The Gateway* for 50 years. His motto for the paper was "Owned and Edited by a Democrat", no doubt a hold-over from the time when newspapers were very partisan about their party allegiance, and most of them in Georgia were Democratic.

In 1958, the Carroll firm made what was to be its most successful purchase when it bought *The Douglas County Sentinel* from Bowling Brannon. Douglas County was about to become one of those exploding metro Atlanta areas, and its weekly soon became a fat semi-weekly under the leadership of Bruce Thomas.

The Tallapoosa and Buchanan papers were bought from Frances Green in 1973, and *The South Fulton Recorder* of Fairburn from Mrs. W. B. Jones. The only time Parkman and his company strayed very far from their home base was in the purchase of *The Manchester Mercury.* Parkman recalls that a stranger drove up to his house one day in 1968 and asked him if he wanted to buy *The Mercury*. The stranger was Frank Helderman, publisher of the Gadsden, Alabama *Times*, and owner of several newspapers throughout the South. Helderman had bought *The Mercury* from Ralph Rice in the late 1950s, and had a seven-year non-compete with Rice. As soon as the non-compete expired, Rice started an offset weekly printed on a high-grade stock against *The Mercury.* Helderman decided he had better things to do than compete in a small Georgia town. In fact, Helderman had never even been to Manchester during his ownership of the paper. He thought Parkman might be interested since Parkman was a friend of Rice's and thus had a chance to end the competitive situation which was draining both operations.

The editor and publisher of *The Mercury* at that time was Robert (Bob) Tribble, who was to become a formidable figure in Georgia publishing, and he had to make the most important career decision of his life while in the hospital fighting a case of hepatitis. Parkman bought *The Mercury* and also Rice's *Star* and put them together into one newspaper. He went to see Tribble in Manchester and offered him a job as editor of both. Tribble also had an offer from Helderman to come work for him on *The Gadsden Times*. Tribble chose to turn them both down and start his own publishing company in Manchester, which would soon present Parkman with another strong competitor there (see chapter on weeklies).

Parkman expanded his plant to accommodate the increasing printing load of the newspapers which he had acquired, most of which were both composed and printed in Carrollton. He was also looking toward a daily publication as the Carrollton weeklies passed 10,000 in paid circulation, and averaged more than 60 pages a week.

Parkman and his partners began talking to the Harte-Hanks Company in 1979 after Parkman suffered a heart attack. The sale was announced later that year and Bill Martin, who had been publisher of *The Walton Tribune*, a weekly in Monroe, which Harte-Hanks bought from the Camps, came over to be president of the Carroll County operation.

Parkman, recovered from his heart problems, stayed on in the post of publisher, and helped supervise the change to five-day publication in 1980. In April 1982, an eighth unit was added to the press. Commercial printing still accounts for about 28 percent of the company's revenue.

Carroll County has grown steadily since 1960, from 36,451 to 56,346 in the 1980 census, less dramatic than counties nearer Atlanta (Douglas, for example, had 54,000 in 1980, up from only 16,000 in 1960) but the growth came mainly from events in Carroll County itself, most notably a large CBS record and tape company which opened in 1981 and employs more than 2,000 people. Southwire, with about 3,000 employees, is still the county's dominant industry.

West Georgia College is another important factor in the area's progress, and has become one of the largest institutions in the state's university system, with an enrollment in 1983 of 6,300, behind only the University of Georgia, Georgia State and Georgia Tech.

Martin, a native of Texas, is president and general manager of the Carrollton operation, which includes the newspapers and the printing. Parkman's son, Ralph, is general manager of four weeklies connected with *The Times-Georgian*. Andy Bowen is editor of *The Times-Georgian*, a post he had held since it became a daily.

The Daily Tribune-News, Cartersville

The Daily Tribune-News of Cartersville, became a five-day (Monday- Friday) daily in 1946, and for many years it had the smallest circulation of any Georgia daily, staying around 3,500 to 4,000 until the 1970s. By 1983, it had topped the 7,000 mark as its city and county began to feel the growth waves from metropolitan Atlanta when I-75 was finally opened all the way from Atlanta to Chattanooga.

Bartow County jumped from 32,000 population in 1970 to 40,000 in

1980, and the city and county got another shot in the arm when Cartersville's favorite son, Joe Frank Harris, was elected governor in 1982.

The Fleetwood family was associated with the Cartersville newspapers for more than 50 years. Milton L. Fleetwood bought the weekly *Tribune-News* in 1920, and served as its editor and publisher until his son, John, assumed the helm in the 1960s. The elder Fleetwood, while serving as president of the Georgia Press Association in 1935, named a committee to compile a history of Georgia newspapers. Fleetwood then served as chairman of the history committee for 14 years, and was largely responsible for raising the funds from GPA members to underwrite the cost of the history. It was finally published in 1951 — 16 years after the proposal for a history was first made. That history, *Georgia Journalism*, which was written by John Talmadge and Louis Griffith, then both on the University of Georgia journalism faculty, has been an invaluable source of information for this current history, and though copies of *Georgia Journalism* are scarce today, it remains a unique compendium of information on one state's newspapers, and was the inspiration for the GPA resolution in 1975 which led to the current volume. Milton Fleetwood remained active in the GPA and *The Tribune-News* until his death in 1962.

John Fleetwood is one of the several sons of former GPA presidents who have also served in the post. He was GPA president in 1970-71. Shortly after the end of John's term, the Fleetwoods sold the Cartersville newspaper to one of Carmage Walls' companies, and Charles Hurley became publisher, a post he had held since then.

A number of well-known Georgia newspapermen have worked on *The Daily Tribune-News* through the years. Lewis Justus, the associate editor, has been with the paper for more than 25 years; Main Rich, the legendary vagabond editor, who claimed to have worked on 75 different papers in his career, proudly counted *The Tribune-News* in that number; Bill Wadkins, who was publisher of *The Cedartown Standard* when it was the only offset newspaper in the state, and was later to be publisher of *Clayton News/Daily*, was general manager in the 1960s; Paul Miles, later publisher of *The Calhoun Times*, was an assistant to the publisher from 1969 through 1976.

The Cartersville newspaper is also noted for an oddity concerning its long-time society editor, Mrs. George (Sara) Woodrow. She became society editor of *The Tribune News* in 1918, and when she retired fifty years later, she had never set foot in the newspaper's office. She always made her contacts from her home, wrote the copy there, and had the copy picked up by a messenger.

Cartersville continues to publish a paid weekly newspaper, *The Herald-Tribune*, for subscribers — usually former residents who've moved away — who don't want a daily. This was a common practice for new dailies during the post-war period. In 1982 the weekly *Herald-Tribune* listed a circulation of 1,694.

The Cordele Dispatch

Crisp County has the distinction of being the smallest (in population) county in Georgia with a daily newspaper. Crisp is not only small, it also isn't growing. Its population has ranged from 18,653 in 1920 to 19,489 in 1980.

But Cordele, the county seat with about 10,000 population, has been a retail trade center for lower middle Georgia for many years, and it received an economic boost in the 1970s as one of the key intersections for I-75 as that well-traveled thoroughfare wends its way south to Florida. Four major chain motels have outlets at the main Cordele exit. In addition to the usual flow of tourists, those motels were also convenient to Plains, just 40 miles away, during the years of the Carter presidency.

The Cordele Dispatch, like its home county and city, hasn't grown much in the past 35 years. It listed its circulation as 4,341 in 1950, and 33 years later, in 1983, the listed circulation was 5,419. *The Dispatch* covers about 45 percent of the homes in Crisp, and does very well in neighboring Dooly and Wilcox counties, where nearly 30 percent of the homes take *The Dispatch*.

The Dispatch dates back to 1908 as a weekly, and to 1917 as a daily. Crisp County had about as many people when *The Dispatch* went daily as it does today.

In 1950 *The Dispatch* was bought by E. W. (Sassafrass) Mathews, a mid-westerner, who had been hired as general manager by the former owners. Mathews and his son, Jack, owned and operated *The Dispatch* for 22 years, until 1972 when they sold it to Dix Newspapers, a group based in Wooster, Ohio. The Cordele purchase was unusual for Dix since all its other newspapers were in Ohio except for the Frankfort, Kentucky *State-Journal*. Jack Mathews stayed on as publisher during the Dix ownership. Four years later, Dix sold *The Dispatch* to the Thomson group in a three-way transaction which involved the Marianna, Florida daily, plus some weeklies in middle Florida. Jack Mathews has continued as publisher during the years since the Thomson acquisition, thus serving in that post under three ownerships.

In November 1980, the 8,000-square foot *Dispatch* plant, which had been built in 1957, was completely destroyed by fire, along with all equipment and 47,000 pounds of newsprint which was on the floor. The fire occurred on a Friday night and *The Dispatch* printed on schedule the following Monday by using the facilities at *The Tifton Gazette* plant, 50 miles away. *The Dispatch* was printed for 45 days in Tifton until a press and temporary quarters could be arranged in Cordele. In October 1981, less than 11 months after the fire, *The Dispatch* moved into a new 7,500-square foot building with all new equipment.

In addition to Mathews, several other *Dispatch* employees have been with the paper through its three recent ownerships. They include Ralph Drinnon, the editor, since 1970; Harvey Simpson, sports editor, since 1966; and Cecil Geiger, composing supervisor, since 1967.

In 1962 *The Dispatch* won the National Newspaper Association's first place award for community service for a campaign to have city sewer lines extended into sections of Cordele which still had outhouses and no indoor plumbing. Many photos of the slum housing and conditions were carried, even though *The Dispatch* was still letterpress, requiring expensive engravings for its pictures.

In its changeover to the new methods in 1966, *The Dispatch* got an offset press before it got cold type composition equipment. Body type and ads continued to be set on the hot type equipment, and proofs of the entire pages were pulled and made into plates for the offset press. That actually gave *The Dispatch* the best results of both systems, even though it was more expensive. Several other newspapers in the state continued to set body type on linotype machines and pull proofs because the early cold-typesetters did not produce as readable or attractive type as the hot-type machines.

The Dublin Courier-Herald

Dublin has had more newspapers start and stop during this century than just about any place in the state. *The Courier-Herald*, now published Monday through Friday afternoons and on Saturday morning, is a descendant of the weekly *Courier*, established in 1887. It absorbed several newspapers on its way to becoming a daily in 1913, when it merged with the weekly *Herald*.

A prominent editor in the early part of the century was Hal Stanley, who for many years wrote and edited the Editor's Forum for the Georgia Press Association and performed many of the duties that later were taken over by a full-time manager. Stanley served as president of the GPA in 1908 and 1909 and then was corresponding secretary for 22 years and executive secretary until a full-time manager was hired in 1938. The Forum of Stanley's years supplied much of the background information for the book, *Georgia Journalism*, which covered the history of Georgia newspapers and the GPA from 1763 to 1950.

In the 1930s W. Herschell Lovett, one of Laurens County's most active financial and political leaders, became the main stockholder in *The Courier-Herald*. He then bought *The Laurens Citizen*, a competing weekly, and since that time *The Courier-Herald* has been without serious competition in the area. Lovett's grandson, Griffin Lovett, is now the publisher.

But the man most identified with *The Courier-Herald* during the past 40 years is not a Lovett. He is a Champion — W. Harold (Champ) Champion, who purchased an interest in the paper in 1945 and became its editor and publisher. He held both posts for 33 years before relinquishing the editorship to Doug Hall in 1978. He continued as publisher until 1982.

Champion, a native of Danville and a graduate of Mercer, had been a schoolteacher for 15 years when he joined *The Courier-Herald* and started his full-time newspaper career at the age of 35.

The Courier-Herald was one of the state's smallest dailies when Champion took over in 1945, with a circulation of about 3,000. It rose to the 6-7,000 level in the 1950s and 60s, and stayed there for 20 years. That is understandable when looking at Laurens County's population figures from 1930 through 1970. The 1930 total was 32,693; the 1970 total was 32,738. The population was within 1,000 of those figures for 40 years, with the high mark being 33,606 in 1940. But some growth finally occurred in the 1970s, as the 1980 Laurens census total showed 36,990, and *The Courier-Herald*'s paid circulation finally broke the 10,000 mark, helped by nearly a thousand subscribers in neighboring Johnson County, and some penetration into Treutlen.

The Courier-Herald also underwent a format change after Hall took over as editor, dropping "Dublin" from its front page flag, among other things. A six-unit Goss Community press had been installed in 1969, and an expansion into new offices in a restored 100-year-old downtown building occurred in 1981.

In both 1976 and 1980, *The Courier-Herald* endorsed native Georgian Jimmy Carter for president because "Carter offered a choice which best fit the newspaper's expectations in terms of the candidate's personal qualities, leadership and philosophy."

Hall, the editor, a Dublin native, had served for a time as Carter's assistant press secretary during Carter's term as governor.

In the 1982 governor's race, *The Courier-Herald* was faced with a political choice of a different type. One of the major candidates was Billy Lovett, grandson of Herschell Lovett; son of *The Courier-Herald's* major stockholder, and brother of Griffin, who was then assistant to the publisher.

The Courier-Herald endorsed Lovett for governor, and was one of the only newspapers in Georgia to give him support. But Editor Hall says there was no pressure from the family for an endorsement. "Lovett was a favorite son candidate of the county and he had done a fine job when he served as chairman of the Laurens County Commission." Although Lovett ran fifth statewide in the 1982 primary, he led in his home county of Laurens.

The Times of Gainesville

Georgia's northeast lake and mountain country was for many years isolated from the rest of the state, both because of poor roads and culture. It was hard to get there and the welcome wasn't always warm if you did get there.

The welcome has changed considerably in recent years and the roads are getting better. I-85 from Atlanta to the South Carolina border provides a helpful jumping off spot to the state's best mountain region, and Georgia 400 is now four-laned almost to Dahlonega. Fortunately, many of the mountain roads that have been paved are still as twisting and scenic as ever, providing an enchanting access to the mountains and their grandeur.

Lake Lanier is the busiest federal recreational reservoir in the nation, and it was a newspaperman, Sylvan Meyer of Gainesville, who worked hardest to bring Lake Lanier into existence in the 1950s.

There is only one community that could qualify as a "metro" area in the entire quadrant of Georgia north of Athens and east of Atlanta and that is Gainesville, which with a 1980 population of only 15,280, has a slim claim on "metro" or "city" status.

Gainesville's population does not reflect its real importance and size, however. It just hasn't done a good job of annexation in recent years. Hall County's population reached 75,649 in 1980, and Gainesville is THE city for a surrounding area of 12 counties.

Hall County was the hub in that area for transportation, courts, wholesaling, medicine, major retailing and the tourist industry. The 1940 census showed it to be Georgia's 10th most populous county, but at the end of WWII it still did not have a daily newspaper.

Instead, Gainesville had two competing weekly newspapers, each with a circulation of about 2,000, operated by rival clans. The Hardy clan, led by Albert S. Hardy Sr., Georgia's first president of the old National Editorial Association, had *The Gainesville News*. Austin Dean had *The Gainesville Eagle*.

The man who would change the newspaper scene in Gainesville was a radio pioneer, Charles Smithgall, who opened Radio Station WGGA in 1941 while he was still manager of WAGA Radio in Atlanta. After the war, his interest turned to print journalism and he saw the potential in Hall, the largest county in the state without a daily. He moved to Gainesville to manage WGGA and began plans for a daily newspaper.

He got an old Duplex flat-bed press from Sen. Theodore Bilbo in Mississippi, bought a building, made a deal for the weekly *Eagle* with Dean, and capitalized Southland Publishing Company for $65,000. Reversing the usual trend, a radio station became the parent of a newspaper.

Ray Hull was the first editor but lasted only a few months. Sylvan Meyer, fresh out of the Navy, signed on as a reporter three days before the first daily edition on January 26, 1947, and rapidly moved on to managing editor and editor. Lou Fockele, a third-generation newspaperman, came on board shortly thereafter as publisher.

That was the team at the top as the 3,600 circulation daily entered the 1950s.

The community, Fockele recalls, "was somewhat less than electrified by the arrival of a daily newspaper on the scene." The weeklies both were ranked among the state's best. The area generated little fast-breaking, consequential news. Local governments were run by entrenched political figures sympathetic to *The Daily Times*' opposition.

The officials weren't accustomed to having a newspaper closely report their actions, criticizing or editorially commenting on how they conducted the government. "Executive sessions" which barred the press were commonplace. Even the police blotter wasn't available to reporters. Political harassment and advertiser boycotts became routine for *The Times* as it worked to break the barriers to public records.

The difficulty in obtaining information made *The Times* a pioneer in freedom of information efforts. Meyer wrote the resolution creating the Georgia Press Association's Freedom of Information Committee and was its first chairman. Through the years, public records in Gainesville and Hall County were opened one by one.

The Times quickly earned a reputation for newsgathering ethics and journalistic excellence. It was the first newspaper in Georgia history to win the GPA's general excellence and community service awards the same year, at a time when all dailies competed in the same classification.

Smithgall insisted from the start that his newspaper be operated in the public interest. It might not be loved or even liked, but it would be trusted and respected for its integrity. That insistence continued to the day 34 years later when *The Times* was sold to Gannett Newspapers, and Smithgall's desire to see that policy continued was one reason he chose Gannett from among many eager suitors.

"Neither of us are as young as we used to be and neither of us have any hopes for family continuity in the leadership of *The Times*," Smithgall told employees on February 25, 1981, speaking of Fockele and himself. "We had to face the hard reality that we had to pick a successor or we had to leave it up to somebody else . . .

" . . . at least two prospects offered substantially more money but we frowned on their operations. We don't want to hand over what we all have built together to folks that we don't think are in the habit of running a good newspaper. In other words, we didn't want to compromise our reputation . . .

" . . . Gannett people will — in accordance with our creed — publish newspapers here . . . in the balanced best interest of the reader, the advertiser, the community and the employees."

Smithgall had left the day-to-day operation, under those principles, to Meyer and Fockele through the years, and *The Times* fought many battles, eventually winning most.

It was one of the first newspapers in Georgia to take a definite stand for keeping public schools open in the face of integration, editorially opposing legislation which called for closing them. Hall County's legislators were among only eight of a General Assembly of more than 200 to vote against extremist segregation bills.

Sylvan Meyer served as editor for 22 years, until 1969, when he became editor of *The Miami* (Florida) *News*. He was a Nieman Fellow and was the first chairman of the Georgia Civil Rights Commission.

Meyer was succeeded by Robert Campbell, another Nieman Fellow. Both editors, with the full support of Publisher Fockele, measured progress by how much it improved the quality of people's life.

In 1954 *The Times* had 6,233 paid circulation and embarked on a new venture with the publication of *The Georgia Poultry Times*, a weekly trade paper.

Then in 1955 a serious competitor appeared in the form of Georgia's first offset newspaper. (See Chapter II).

Charles Hardy, who had taken over *The Gainesville News* from his father, converted it to *The Gainesville Morning News* in November 1955. The tabloid-size daily, printed in the new photographic process, carried page after page of local pictures reproduced in a quality never before seen in the state. Gainesville already had a daily, two radio stations and a third station on the way. Despite its strong points, the new daily couldn't find enough advertising support in the crowded market, and it folded after eight months.

In 1957, *The Times* abandoned its eight-page Duplex and acquired a 32-page stereo, built in 1919, from Columbia, South Carolina. The following year it became one of the first Georgia papers to carry the *Family Weekly* supplement.

In 1959, James Dunlap, principal owner of WGGA's principal competition, WDUN, John Jacobs Jr., WDUN general manager, and Ted Oglesby, WDUN news director, started a new weekly paper in Gainesville.

The Gainesville Tribune first operated out of a radio station studio and was printed and addressed in Monroe, Georgia. As *The Times* pushed past the 10,000 circulation mark in 1959, *The Tribune* converted to offset printing on a full-size page and quickly gained a paid circulation of more than 3,000. The printing was done in Cedartown, which was a hard three-hour drive, but had a web offset press.

In 1961, *The Times* began a sister publication to *The Georgia Poultry Times* called *The Southeastern Poultry Times* which covered 10 states. *The Times* also adopted a 10-page minimum daily size.

Ted Oglesby purchased *The Tribune* from Dunlap and Jacobs in 1961, for $700 in cash and some prepaid services and rent, and found a partner in Charles Hardy, the former owner of *The News*. The trend was toward one-newspaper towns, particularly towns with dailies, but *The Tribune* owners felt Gainesville could be an exception.

The *Tribune's* progress was interrupted when Publisher Oglesby's Air Force Reserve unit was activated during the Pueblo Crisis in 1968. Before he was discharged in 1969, an agreement to sell had been reached.

The Tribune had competed vigorously against *The Times* editorially, generally taking a conservative approach while *The Times* was considered more liberal. Like *The Times*, it pushed community projects, taking the forefront in such battles as tax equalization, promotion of shopping centers while downtown merchants fought them, legalization of alcoholic beverages, establishment of a two-party system.

The new owners hired part-time workers and changed policy. The part-time staff developed non-controversial features and reprinted stories from other papers. The circulation fell to less than 1,000.

The Tribune, after nearly a quarter-century of competing against a strong daily, was donated to Truett-McConnell College in Cleveland in 1983, to be used as a lab paper. The name was changed to *The Lanier Tribune* but it continued to be headquartered in Gainesville.

Truett-McConnell, finding *The Tribune* to be a financial drain, later sold it, but the venture had been costly. *The Tribune's* future was a definite question mark in early 1985.

Gannett in Georgia

The Times, meanwhile, moved into a new plant and converted to offset in 1970. By then circulation topped 14,000, operating revenues were near $1 million, and a 40-page Goss Urbanite press was on order.

September 12, 1973 is remembered as "Black Wednesday" at *The Times* because that year's newsprint shortage caught the paper short and publication was completed by using every roll end in the warehouse.

In December 1973, the first "extra" since the John Kennedy assassination was printed after a tornado ripped through the county.

Daily circulation topped 20,000 in 1977 and 22,000 in 1980.

On February 25, 1981, the paper was sold to The Gannett Company along with the sister poultry publications. The community held a "Spirit of The Times" appreciation dinner for Smithgall and Fockele. Master of Ceremonies Gordon Sawyer told the large audience, "*The Times* has been a tremendous force for the betterment of this community, and that's why we all got together to pay tribute to a newspaper, our town's version of the American free press at its very best."

Gannett promptly designated Gainesville as one of the printing sites for its new national daily *USA TODAY*. The press had to be upgraded to handle high-quality process color on eight of 40 pages and spot color on most other pages. The accompanying technology spilled over to *The Times* permitting daily process color of the state's highest quality, color on every section front, and increased color in advertising.

Fockele retired as publisher following the sale and Don C. Newton was named to succeed him. Newton had been with *The Times* as general manager since 1977. In 1982, Newton was replaced by W. H. "Dub" Harwell, who moved to Gainesville from Nashville, Tennessee where he had been operations director of the newspaper printing company. He was the only Gannett publisher to have risen from production ranks. In November, 1984 Harwell chose to go back to production as manager of the Gannett newspaper in Willmington, Delaware.

He was succeeded as publisher in Gainesville by Bruce Mackey, who had been circulation and promotions director at Gannett's Shreveport, La. *Times*.

Bob Campbell continued as editor under the Gannett ownership, and Ted Oglesby, who fought *The Times* so long as publisher and editor of the weekly *Tribune*, has been associate editor of *The Times* for more than 13 years. Mike Connell, from Gannett's Huntingdon, West Virginia newspaper, joined the staff in 1984 as editor-in-chief with Campbell becoming editor of the editorial page.

The Griffin Daily News

The name of Quimby Melton (Sr., Jr., and III) was listed as publisher of *The Griffin Daily News* from 1925 through 1983, a span of almost 60 years, covering three generations.

The original Quimby Melton came to Griffin from Atlanta, where he was southern manager for the Scripps Howard Newspaper chain, and bought *The Griffin Daily News* from Judge C.C. Givens, a Kentuckian who owned it briefly. *The News* had several owners during the early 1900s but the Melton family would own and operate it for 57 years, until its sale on June 30, 1982 to Thomson Newspapers.

But the sale did not interrupt the continuity of the Quimby Melton name on the publisher's door. Quimby Jr. had become publisher in 1973, succeeding his father, Quimby Sr. He turned the publisher's post over to his son, Quimby III, just one month before the sale to Thomson.

Quimby III, then 32, previously had been publisher of the weekly *Fayette County News* for five years, and had supervised several other weeklies owned by the family. He was prepared to move on to manage these weeklies after the *Daily News* was sold. But on the day of the sale, St. Clair McCabe, senior vice-president of Thomson, called Quimby Jr. aside and told him he was very impressed with his son. McCabe explained that Thomson's biggest problem in owning and operating more than 70 newspapers in the United States — and many others in Canada and Great Britain — was finding able management people. "Do you think your son would consider staying on as publisher?" McCabe asked. Quimby Jr. advised McCabe to ask Quimby III, and McCabe found the younger Melton agreeable to the idea. He stayed on as publisher and Quimby Jr. moved into an office next door where he assumed a supervisory role over the several weeklies which the Melton family owned in the area.

For Quimby Melton Jr. the sale ended a lifelong association with *The Griffin Daily News*, 37 years of which he served as editor or as both editor and publisher. He was also active politically in his city and state, serving for 14 years (1959-1972) in the Georgia House of Representatives, six of which he was chairman of the powerful Ways and Means Committee. Before his election as state representative, he was a member of the University Board of Regents for five and a half years. Melton also has a law degree and is a member of the Georgia Bar. He was president of the Georgia Press Association in 1955-56.

The Griffin Daily News rose from a circulation of 6,000 in 1950 to 13,500 in 1984 as Spalding County grew from 31,045 in 1950 to 47,899 in 1980. Most of the growth has been in the county's unincorporated areas. The city of Griffin actually declined slightly in population from 22,000 in 1970 to 20,000 in 1980.

Only 40 miles from downtown Atlanta, Griffin has managed to maintain a distinct identity with a strong downtown business district as well as perimeter shopping centers. The Atlanta metro area's growth was slow to affect Spalding, and the metro's future growth to the south seems likely to follow I-75 which is to the east of Griffin, and I-85 to the west, rather than coming directly into the Griffin area, which is not on an interstate.

But more important to the newspaper, and to groups such as Thomson, is the individuality of the community, and its history as a trade center, which Griffin definitely has.

The Daily News moved into a new building in 1949, and changed to cold type in 1969. For several years it had the dubious distinction of virtually having the press in the newsroom, as the news, composing and press operation were all in one large open area. Partitions were erected in the late 1970s and at the same time a front-end system and terminals were installed. Another extensive remodeling was carried out after the sale to Thomson.

For 18 months the Melton tradition continued under a third generation publisher, blending with the new group ownership, a pattern followed to some extent in several other Georgia cities where the Thomson group had acquired newspapers. Then, in December, Melton III resigned as publisher and bought two weekly newspapers owned by his father's company, *The Jackson News-Argus* and *The Monroe County Reporter*.

Bill Knight, the current editor, is another *Daily News* figure of long standing. Knight joined the staff in 1950, just out of college, and has served in various editorial posts ever since.

The Union-Recorder, Milledgeville

The Union-Recorder of Milledgeville is Georgia's newest daily newspaper but is its second oldest newspaper in years of continuous publication, tracing its lineage back to *The Southern Recorder* in 1820. Only *The Augusta Chronicle*, among newspapers still being published, predates *The Recorder*.

About 1825 another weekly, called *The Federal Union*, began publication in Milledgeville. In the Civil War period, that name was obviously a burden, so the owners simply changed it to *The Confederate Union* when Georgia voted to secede in 1861. The name reverted to *The Federal Union* after the War, and in 1872 Jere N. Moore and his partners, who owned *The Union*, bought *The Recorder* and merged the weeklies into *The Union-Recorder*.

Moore was born in Milledgeville in 1835 and went to work as a printer's devil on *The Union* when he was 12 years old. Except for one year when he worked for *The Christian Index*, a statewide Baptist newspaper, Moore was associated with *The Union* for the remainder of his life, a tenure of 54 years. He died in 1902 at the age of 67.

When General Sherman's army passed through Milledgeville on The March to the Sea, Moore and other Union employees hid the printing equipment in the woods and not an edition was missed because of the fighting. In the postwar period Moore led the effort to keep the capital at Milledgeville but a statewide vote in 1877 confirmed Atlanta as the new state capital. Moore was successful a few years later, in 1887, in having the first meeting of the Georgia Press Association held in Milledgeville.

The Moore family was to continue in the leadership of *The Union-Recorder* for 58 more years, as R. Boling Moore became editor and publisher in 1902 on his father's death, and the second Jere N. Moore followed him in 1940.

The second Jere Moore was president of the GPA in 1937-38, and it was during his administration that a full-time executive manager was hired.

While Moore served in the armed forces during World War II, his wife edited *The Union-Recorder*.

In 1959 Moore sold the newspaper to Peyton Anderson, publisher of *The Macon Telegraph* and *News*. Anderson included *The Union-Recorder* in the sale of the Macon newspapers to the Knight chain in 1969. *The Union-Recorder*, in fact, is the smallest daily newspaper owned by Knight-Ridder today, and was one of the company's only weekly properties before its conversion to a daily schedule.

Baldwin County grew very little in population during the 30 years from 1950 to 1980, although the actual census figures were affected to some extent by the dispersion of patients from the huge Mental Health Hospital to locations around the state. At one time there were an estimated 12,000 patients at the Milledgeville hospital. The number had dropped to only 3,000 by 1982, and since patients are counted in the census figures, this naturally lowered Baldwin's population.

New industry came along to bolster the economy, however, and the population of Baldwin rose to 34,686 in 1980, up from 29,000 in 1950, despite the loss of some 10,000 patients at the hospital.

The business community was definitely growing in these years, with the opening of a shopping mall in the late 1970s. *The Union-Recorder* added a second weekly edition in 1979, and then in March 1982, it became a five-day daily, published Tuesday through Saturday mornings.

Roger Coover is the publisher, and supervised the change to five-day frequency.

The Moultrie Observer

The Moultrie Observer, which is now part of the Multimedia group, is believed to have the distinction of bringing the highest price based on its gross income of any of the many Georgia newspapers sold during the past three decades.

A long friendship between former *Observer* President Max E. Nussbaum and J. Kelly Sisk, the late president of Multimedia, was a deciding factor in the newspaper's sale to Multimedia in February 1979, and the price reportedly was nearly five times *The Observer's* gross income. The number of newspaper sales and the prices for them were peaking that year, but three to four times gross income was still regarded as an attractive sum for isolated small dailies. Moultrie broke the mold, apparently because Multimedia was in an expansion mood, having paid a similar multiple in 1978 for the Winter Haven, Florida newspaper. *The Observer* just happened to be available when "the asking was good." For Multimedia, the acquisition fervor subsided after that. It hasn't bought another newspaper since, as of 1985. *The Observer* is also the smallest daily in the group, which owns TV, radio and cable properties, plus syndicated TV programs such as "The Phil Donahue Show".

Moultrie seems an unlikely place for a newspaper that brought such a bountiful price, although *The Observer* has had a distinguished roster of editors and publishers since it was founded in 1894 by W. H. Cooper. At that time, Moultrie had only 700 residents, although Colquitt County was one of the state's leaders in farm production.

By 1920, Colquitt's population was nearly 30,000, which was 10,000 more than neighboring Dougherty, nearly twice as much as neighboring Tift, and about the same as Thomas. Colquitt and Moultrie clearly seemed to be setting the pace for growth in South Middle Georgia. But the shifting tides of population which were to take so many Georgians from the farms to the cities in the next 60 years blunted Colquitt's growth, and Albany, 30 miles to the northwest, became the dominant city of South Georgia. By 1980, Colquitt's population had risen to only 35,376, with almost all of the growth coming in the 1970s.

I-75, that vital artery through South Georgia, runs 20 miles east of Moultrie, boosting such rival cities along the way as Cordele, Tifton and Valdosta. *The Moultrie Observer*, which had 5,000 circulation in 1950, had climbed to about 7,400 by the time of the sale to Multimedia 29 years later, a respectable gain considering that its base area grew very little, and Colquitt is surrounded by counties with their own daily newspapers, offering little opportunity for out-of-county growth.

But nonetheless, *The Moultrie Observer* was — and is — a force in its community. The standard was set by W.D. Allen, who bought *The Observer* in 1896 when he was 20, and served as its editor and publisher for 53 years, until his death in 1949. Allen began the daily *Moultrie Observer* in 1905, mainly to report on happenings at the Georgia Baptist Young People's convention which was held in Moultrie that year. The daily seemed popular so he continued with the daily schedule but also kept publishing a weekly *Observer*. The weekly, in fact, is still being published in 1984, and has a circulation of about 2,000. It goes mainly to former residents who want to keep up with their former home, but don't need the non-local stories and features the daily carries.

After Allen died, William D. Avera was named editor of *The Observer*, and he held the post for 31 years until his retirement in 1981. Dwain Walden, the present editor, is thus only the third editor of *The Observer* in 85 years. A native of Cairo, he joined *The Observer* staff in 1972.

Allen's widow succeeded him as publisher but survived him by only a year. In 1950 Frances Allen Nussbaum, their daughter, became publisher, and her husband, Max Nussbaum, was named president and general manager.

Erle Taylor, the adopted son of the Allens, was vice-president and circulation manager until the sale to Multimedia. At that time he succeeded Nussbaum as publisher and stayed in the post until his retirement in 1982. Gary Boley, a former managing editor of *The Greenville*, South Carolina *News*, another Multimedia paper, succeeded him as publisher.

The slogan of *The Observer* for many years was, "Invest Your Money, Your Time, Your Talent and Your Influence in Moultrie."

The Rome News-Tribune

The Rome News-Tribune calls itself the "patriarch of North Georgia newspapers," and it has a valid claim to the title. *The News-Tribune* traces its history to a weekly founded in 1843, and it has been published continuously since then except for a few months during the Civil War while Union troops occupied the city.

It became a daily shortly after the Civil War, and is thus the oldest daily in the state outside the five major metro areas. During its long history *The News-Tribune* has enjoyed the services of such distinguished journalists and writers as Henry Grady, who worked there for several months before going to Atlanta; Bill Arp, the noted southern humorist of the late 1800s; Frank L. Stanton, a nationally-renowned poet; and John Temple Graves, a distinguished editor whose son was a popular southern editorial columnist on many newspapers in the mid-20th century.

The News-Tribune of today is the survivor of several newspapers published from 1904 to 1924 in Rome. In 1928 the newspaper was purchased by B. H. Mooney and William S. Mudd, both from Alabama.

Mudd died in 1942 and the Mooney family has owned and operated

The News-Tribune since then. B. H. Mooney Jr. is now publisher and chief executive officer, and B. H. Mooney III is general manager.

Rome and Floyd County have enjoyed steady but unspectacular growth during the past 60 years. Located about 90 miles northwest of Atlanta, Rome has long been a center of commerce, industry and education in that quadrant of the state. It is not located on an interstate highway but is connected to Atlanta by a four-lane highway.

Oddly, Floyd County enjoyed its largest 10-year increase in population during the decade of the 1920s, going from 39,800 to 48,000. In the years since, Floyd's population has grown by about 4-5,000 each decade, reaching 79,800 in the 1980 census. That pace has not been enough to hold Floyd's place as one of the state's 10 most populous counties. As recently as 1950 Floyd was the seventh largest county, but it had fallen to 11th in the 1980 census.

The News-Tribune's growth has followed a similar pattern. In 1950 with about 10,000 circulation it was the largest daily outside the five big metro areas (Atlanta, Savannah, Macon, Augusta and Columbus), and while its paid circulation had risen to 22,000 by 1983, it now ranks behind Albany, Marietta, Gwinnett (Lawrenceville) and the combined circulation of the two Athens dailies.

However, in August 1983, *The News-Tribune* launched a program unique in Georgia for papers of its size in isolated locations. It started free-distribution weekly newspapers in several surrounding counties.

The free-distribution weeklies are *The West Polk Press, The Chattooga Press* and *The Gordon-North Bartow Press*. Offices were established for these papers in Cedartown, Summerville and Calhoun. Separate news and ad staffs cover each of the areas. The news emphasis is on features and soft news with full-process color photos carried in most issues. Ads are sold for the circulation of the particular weekly or for the combination. About 12,000 copies of each of the three *Press* papers are distributed by third class mail. In their early months they were running 8-10 broad-sheet pages. *The News-Tribune* also owns and operates *The Rockmart Journal*, a paid-circulation weekly in East Polk County.

The concept of *The Press* papers is based on the Neighbor papers published in the counties of Metro Atlanta by *The Marietta Daily Journal* company. They are just not as large yet, and do not qualify for the second-class, controlled-circulation mailing rate. They differ from the Extras being published for individual counties by *The Atlanta Journal-Constitution* because they are distributed free to homes not taking *The News-Trib-*

une, while the Extras are inserted into the paid circulation of *The Journal* and *Constitution* in the targeted counties and do not go to non-subscribers.

Other Georgia dailies have free distribution newspapers — such as *The Star* in Athens, and *Good Neighbors* in Columbus — but they are not targeted at one specific area or county as *The Press* papers are.

The News-Tribune switched to cold type and an offset press in 1967-68, ahead of the larger dailies, and slightly after the smaller ones.

John L. Perry became editor-in-chief of *The News-Tribune* in 1984, with Don Biggers, a 25-year employee, continuing as the managing editor. Coleman Prophett was chief editor for about 20 years.

The Statesboro Herald

The Statesboro Herald, which changed from weekly to five-day publication in December 1970, has several distinctions among Georgia newspapers. Perhaps the most unusual is that when it was a weekly *The Herald* suspended publication for four years while the three brothers who were its proprietors went off to fight in World War II.

The Herald was founded in 1937 by the Coleman brothers, Leodel, who was editor; Jim, the advertising manager, and G.C. Jr., the associate editor. It started in competition against *The Bulloch Times*, a long-established weekly (1892), which was the survivor of a fierce newspaper war in Bulloch County. At one time, about the turn of the century, five separate newspapers were published there, most of them associated with a particular political party or point of view.

Five years after *The Herald* got started, in May 1942, it became "the paper which went to war," when publication was suspended and Leodel, the oldest brother enlisted in the Marines as a combat correspondent; Jim, second in age, enlisted in the Air Force; and G. C. Jr., the youngest, became a paratrooper. They were gone for four years, but on their return, they resumed publication of *The Herald* in January 1946.

Jim Coleman was killed in an automobile accident in 1948 but Leodel and G. C. continued to operate *The Herald*, and in March 1962, they bought the competing *Bulloch Times*, and merged it with *The Herald*.

Statesboro and Bulloch County enjoyed a spurt of growth in the 1960s — from 24,000 to 31,500 — due in part from the growth of Georgia Southern College. This encouraged the Colemans to change to a daily schedule in December 1970. But the Colemans, after nearly 25 years of operating a weekly, stayed only six months with the daily, before selling it in June 1971, to the new corporation which Charles Morris of Savannah had started after his break with his brother, Billy. *The Herald* was one of Morris' first acquisitions and although his corporate headquarters is in Savannah, the Statesboro paper remains his only Georgia newspaper property.

An interesting sidelight to this sale was that the Colemans had given an option to buy the newspaper to Roy Chalker, the Waynesboro publisher, and Chalker sold the option to Morris who then made the deal.

At the time *The Herald* went daily, it changed its name from "Bulloch" to "Statesboro", thus emphasizing its city of origin rather than the county.

The Herald had a struggle in its early years as a daily. Its weekly circulation had been more than 6,000 and that figure dropped to 4,000 as a daily. To complicate its problems, the weekly *Southern Beacon*, which was started by B. G. Patray in the late 1960s, continued to drain off ad revenue, which *The Herald* now needed more than ever. But two turning points occurred when Joe McGlamery, a native of Statesboro, who had been working with the radio station there, became publisher of *The Herald* in 1975, and *The Herald* bought out *The Beacon* in 1977. Under McGlamery's leadership, *The Herald* switched to morning (Tuesday-Saturday) publication in 1979, giving it a boost that led to the addition of a Monday edition in October 1981, and then a Sunday edition in September 1982. That makes *The Herald*, with seven editions a week, the most frequently published of Georgia's non-metro dailies.

Statesboro's Sunday edition was prompted mainly by the resumption of football at Georgia Southern after an absence of 25 years. Most of Southern's games are on Saturday and are covered in *The Sunday Herald*. After a year, the Sunday edition was running 24-28 pages, and seemed to be justifying its place.

Paid circulation of *The Herald* stood at 6,290 in late 1983, and a total market coverage edition is published on Wednesday. *The Beacon* was still published as a weekly and had a circulation of 2,300.

The Thomasville Times-Enterprise

The Thomasville Times-Enterprise was the fourth South Georgia daily acquired by the Thomson Group. Thomasville and Thomas County, like most of the neighboring area, grew very little in population during the 1920-1980 period. Thomas County showed 33,000 in the 1920 census, and had moved to only 34,500 in the 1970 census 50 years later. There was a spurt in the 1970s to 38,000, and *The Thomasville Times-Enterprise*, which had stayed around 10,000 circulation for many years, finally moved up to nearly 11,000.

Two men have dominated the history of the Thomasville newspaper, both of them serving in an executive position for more than 50 years. The first was E. R. Jerger who became publisher and chief owner of *The Times-Enterprise* in 1907 and was publisher or editor until his death in 1960. The other was Lee E. Kelly Sr., who began as a paper boy on *The Times-Enterprise* in the early part of the century, became a full-time employee in 1911, and continued an association with the newspaper until his death in 1980.

The Times-Enterprise resulted from the merger of two weeklies which had both gone daily in 1888. One of the weeklies, *The Enterprise*, traced its history back to 1855. It didn't take long for the owners to see that two dailies were at least one too many in Thomasville and *The Times* bought out *The Enterprise* in 1889, with John Triplett serving as editor of the combined papers.

Then came the long stewardship of Jerger and Kelly Sr., who were partners in the ownership. They also took in other partners from the community as financial need dictated. In the 1950s, however, Kelly became the controlling owner and his sons, L. Edward Jr., Jack and Dan, all became active in the newspaper's management. Jerger's daughter, Emily, was on the editorial staff.

In 1969, an offer was considered to sell *The Times-Enterprise* to Charles Morris of Savannah. This led to a rather unique twist in the ownership. During the negotiations, the elder Kelly, who had recently recovered from a stroke, changed his mind about selling his majority share of the business, but a commitment had already been made to Ms. Jerger to buy the approximately one-third of the stock she then owned. Morris was only interested in buying a majority of the stock, so the broker who was handling the transaction, Bill Mathew of Clearwater, Florida, bought the Jerger stock at the agreed price.

Then for about 11 years Mathew owned one-third of the stock in the Thomasville paper, while the Kelly brothers owned the rest. Ed Kelly, commenting years later, said that Mathew was "a super guy to have for a partner. He was a silent partner in the truest sense. He never even asked us for a financial statement."

Mathew was helpful in his role as a broker in 1981 when the Kellys decided to sell. He handled the negotiations with Thomson but did not take a broker's fee. He did get to sell his stock, however, and the price had increased considerably in the 11 years since he bought it.

Ed Kelly stayed on as publisher for about a year before leaving to enter the real estate business.

Succeeding him as publisher was Charles L. Blanton, who was from Missouri, but had a background remarkably similar to Kelly's. Blanton and his brother and sister had owned a daily in Sikeston, Missouri, which was about the same size as Thomasville. They sold the paper to Thomson on July 1, 1981, just a month before the Thomasville paper was sold. Blanton remained as publisher for a year, then decided to leave, just as Kelly had done. But the Thomson hierarchy asked Blanton if he'd go to Thomasville as publisher instead of getting out of the newspaper business and he agreed.

Blanton was publisher of *The Sikeston,* Missouri *Standard* for eight years. *The Standard* had been in his family since 1909. The shift to Georgia extended his newspaper career, offering a new set of conditions. "I was burned out in Sikeston," Blanton says, "but feel renewed in Thomasville."

The Tifton Gazette

The Tifton Gazette is another of the smaller Georgia dailies purchased by the Thomson Newspaper Group during the early 1980s. A disaster played a part in bringing about the association of Thomson and *The Gazette*. When the Cordele *Dispatch* building burned in 1980, with the loss of all of its equipment, *The Dispatch* was printed in Tifton, 50 miles away, for 45 days. This led to an acquaintance between Homer Rankin, *The Gazette* publisher and main owner, with the Thomson organization, which already owned *The Dispatch*.

In June 1981, the sale was completed. Rankin retired and Robert F. Morrell, who had been with *The Gazette* as editor for 16 years, was named publisher.

The Gazette is a Monday through Saturday newspaper, with a paid circulation of about 9,700. Its circulation was listed as only 2,975 in 1950, shortly before it was bought by Rankin and the A. C. Tift family in 1952. By 1960 the circulation was listed as 8,728.

Tift County's growth has been steady, if unspectacular, in comparison with counties in North Georgia. It has moved from a population of 14,400 in 1920 to 32,862 in 1980 with the big increase — about 5,000 — in the 1970s. The completion from Atlanta into Florida of I-75, which passes through Tifton, gave the entire area a boost, as the surrounding counties of Worth, Turner, Irwin, Berrien and Cook also enjoyed a spurt of growth in the 1970s.

The origin of *The Gazette* has a peculiar twist in that it began in another county. Established in 1888 as *The Berrien County Pioneer*, the paper was moved from Sparks to Tifton in 1891 at which time the name was changed to *The Tifton Gazette*. At the time the move may not have seemed too wise since Berrien County was larger than Tift. John L. Herring became owner and editor of *The Gazette* in 1896 and he continued in that post until his death in 1923. His son, J. C. Herring, succeeded him, and was editor until 1938. Robert Herring followed him in the position until the Herring family sold *The Gazette* to Rankin and the Tifts in 1952.

Rankin, a native of New Orleans, had married Lutrelle Tift, of the Tift County Tifts, during World War II, and their first newspaper venture was in Glynn County with a weekly on St. Simons and another in Brunswick.

After becoming publisher of *The Gazette*, Rankin was active in civic and school activities, and is credited with writing the plan for consolidating the Tifton and Tift County school systems.

The Gazette had become a Monday through Friday daily in 1914, but it continued to publish a weekly *Gazette* on Thursday until 1974. In that year, Rankin also bought out the stock owned by his brother-in-law, Arthur Tift Jr.

Tift, who owned about 25 percent of the company's stock, had advertised his shares for sale in *Editor* and *Publisher* magazine, and also in *The Gazette*, a rather unusual procedure for a minority stockholder. His ads brought dozens of inquiries, and representatives of large groups came to Tifton to talk to Tift about his stock. He told interested parties that he felt he wasn't getting sufficient dividends from his stock and had no voice in the operation of the newspaper. Despite the interest created by his ads Tift found no outside buyer willing to pay his asking price for a minority block of stock and he eventually sold it to the majority stockholders, Homer and Lutrelle Rankin.

The Rankins thus owned nearly all of *The Gazette* stock when it was sold seven years later to the Thomson group.

The Valdosta Times

The Valdosta Times at one time enjoyed the distinction of having the oldest active employee of any newspaper in the United States. That employee happened to be the publisher, E. L. Turner, who stayed on the job until he was 100 years old. He worked on *The Times* for 74 years, from 1889 to 1963, when he was succeeded by his 73-year-old son, E. M. Turner.

Turner was born in Nashville, Georgia in 1863, at the midpoint of the Civil War. He worked in his father's print shop, and began his remarkable tenure on *The Valdosta Times* as a printer in 1889, when he was already 26 years old. *The Times* was published twice a week at that time. He became business manager in 1897, and it was his decision in 1905 to make *The Times* into a daily newspaper.

He recalled later that he made the decision on the spur of the moment to take advantage of intense interest in a murder trial which was going on in Valdosta. The trial involved the slaying of two children resulting from an old family feud between the Rawlings and Carter clans. J. G. Rawlings, his three sons, and Alf Moore, were on trial for killing two young Carter children during a shoot-out at a Carter farm.

Demand for news of the trial in those days before either radio or television prompted Turner to start putting out *The Times* every day. It was just a four-page paper with a roundup of AP stories in addition to local coverage, but it proved so successful that *The Times* never went back to its semi-weekly schedule. Turner, who was not one of the owners, wrote later that he didn't consult the directors of the company about the advisability of going daily but he "was never raked over the coals about it."

The defendants were all found guilty in the trial, and two of them were hanged by the sheriff at the county jail.

Turner was later elevated to publisher, and through several ownerships, and several periods of economic challenge, he stayed in the post with the exception of three months in 1928.

A chain operation bought *The Times* that year and sent in a man named Edmund Walker to replace Turner as publisher. Turner and editor Charles G. Brantley, who was also displaced, immediately went to work getting together a local group to buy *The Times* back. It took only three months before the group, headed by Dr. Archibald Griffin, was able to buy *The Times* and restore Turner and Brantley to their long-time posts.

The Great Depression was about to hit, and Turner was especially proud that he managed to show a profit on *The Times* in all but one year during the worst of the Depression.

Many reasons were discussed in Valdosta to account for Turner's longevity and keen mind at an advanced age. His regularity of habits some believed, were responsible. He was always in bed by 9 p.m. He spent evenings at home with his family. His lunch periods never varied and he was punctual to the minute in both arriving and leaving the office.

In his 90s he still handled many minor details of the business, and frowning on the wasteful practice of hiring a secretary, he typed his own letters on a L. C. Smith typewriter that was so old it had a separate set of keys for capitals and lower case.

Turner was a writer as well as a businessman and in his final decade he was still contributing bright, thought-provoking articles to *The Times*, plus an occasional letter on some controversial subject.

Turner was honored at a banquet on his 100th birthday, March 6, 1963. Asked how it felt to be 100, he replied: "It feels damn good, else I'd be dead." But when it came to making a speech at that special occasion, Turner said: "I've never made a speech and am not going to start now."

He retired that year as publisher to be succeeded by his son, E. M. (Mann) Turner, an up-and-coming junior executive of 73. The younger Turner served only five years as publisher but he was associated with *The Times* for 45 years in all. He died in 1972 at the age of 83. The elder Turner had died in 1967 at the age of 103.

Another long-time employee of *The Times* was Turner Rockwell who became editor in 1937 and held that post for more than 30 years.

The Times was sold in 1968 to the Thomson group, and Tenney Griffin, grandson of Dr. Archibald Griffin, became publisher. Griffin presided over the installation of cold type equipment and a new offset press in 1968, and then added a Sunday edition in 1972, making Valdosta only the second newspaper (after Albany) in the southern third of Georgia to publish a Sunday paper.

Griffin remained as publisher for 14 years. In 1982 he was named publisher of another Thomson newspaper, the Florence, South Carolina *Herald*.

During his time as publisher, *The Times'* circulation rose from about 11,000 to 18,000, as Lowndes County grew from 49,000 in 1960 to 67,900 in 1980.

Griffin was succeeded by William (Bill) England, a native of Georgia who had been publisher of Thomson's Laurel, Mississippi daily newspaper for several years. Wink DeVane, who had been an editor in Valdosta, succeeded England as publisher in Laurel. In 1984, John Miller was named publisher after England resigned. Miller had been publisher of the Marianna, Florida daily and previously was a circulation manager for several

Thomson papers.

The Waycross Journal-Herald

The Waycross Journal-Herald is another of the shrinking number of family-owned dailies in Georgia. Two third-generation members of the Williams family, Jack Williams III and Roger Williams, are now executives of the newspaper which their grandfather, Jack Williams Sr., put together in 1914 from two competing dailies. Both Jack Williams Sr. and Jack Williams Jr. were presidents of the Georgia Press Association, and Williams Sr. served in both the Georgia House and Senate.

Williams Jr. was one Georgia publisher who had no reservations about supporting Jimmy Carter for president. In fact, he was a member of the "Peanut Brigade" of Georgians who traveled to New Hampshire and other northern states during the 1976 primary campaign to tell other Americans about their former governor and favorite son candidate for president. *The Journal-Herald* endorsed Carter enthusiastically in both 1976 and 1980, one of the few smaller dailies in the state that did not waver in its support.

With a 1983 circulation of 12,500, *The Journal-Herald* is published Monday through Saturday afternoons. It has a Total Market Coverage edition on Wednesday which goes to 9,000 additional homes.

Its editor for 30 years has been James A. (Jim) Pinson, who has also served as mayor of Waycross.

Two veteran newspapermen look at newest equipment in Dalton Citizen-News *plant. L.A. Lee, seated, was owner and publisher of Dalton papers for many years. Mark Pace was editor for 37 years.*

James H. Gray, Sr., editor and publisher of The Albany Herald, has been one of the most politically active newspapermen in Georgia; Albany mayor 12 years, candidate for governor, 1966.

Lou Fockele, at right, longtime publisher of The Times *in Gainesville, talks with Elliott Brack, center, and Don Daniel, publisher of* The Monroe County Reporter.

E. L. Turner, who was still publisher of The Valdosta Times *when he celebrated his 100th birthday, was believed to be the nation's oldest active newspaperman. He was succeeded by his 73-year-old son, and died at 103 in 1967.*

Robert Campbell, editor of The Times *of Gainesville, was among newsmen visiting the White House during the presidential administration of fellow Georgian Jimmy Carter, shown greeting him.*

Quimby Melton, Jr. of The Griffin Daily News *receives plaque honoring him for work on behalf of GPA in 1972 from that year's president, Sam Griffin. May Melton (Mrs. Quimby, Jr.) is at left.*

Robert Marbut, who grew up in Athens and graduated from Georgia Tech, became one of nation's top newspaper executives as president and CEO of Harte-Hanks Communications.

Bill Martin is general manger of Harte-Hanks operations in Georgia, based in Carrollton, and including The Daily Times-Georgian, *several weeklies and a commercial printing plant.*

Lee E. Kelly Sr. was associated with The Thomasville Times-Enterprise *for 50 years, eventually becoming publisher and major owner.*

L. Edward Kelly Jr. succeeded his father as publisher of The Times-Enterprise, *and operated it with his brothers until a sale to Thomson Newspapers in 1981.*

Tenney Griffin, who followed the Turners as publisher of The Valdosta Times, *is one of the few Georgia newspapermen who played varsity football while getting his degree from the University of Georgia.*

Glenn Long, as publisher of The LaGrange Daily News, *helped the city build a new industrial base.*

Roger Coover, as publisher, supervised conversion to daily schedule for Union-Recorder *of Milledgeville, one of state's oldest weeklies.*

Ted Oglesby, publisher of the weekly Gainesville Tribune *for many years, has served as associate editor of* The Daily Times *for even more years.*

Griffin Lovett became publisher of Dublin's Courier-Herald *on January 1, 1983. The Lovett family has owned the newspaper since 1934.*

Charles H. Leavy Jr. was president and editor of The Brunswick News *from 1941 until his death in 1983.*

Brunswick News' *building, completed in 1974, is constructed of tabby stone, glass and steel; has 20,000 square feet.*

The Blairs of Americus owned and operated Times-Recorder *for 50 years (1934-1984). L. to R., James R. Blair, William E. (Billy) Blair and Dana H. (Mrs. W. E.) Blair.*

These portraits of two men long associated with The Courier-Herald *of Dublin hang in conference room of editorial offices. At left is W. Herschel Lovett, chairman of the newspaper company from 1934 until his death in 1978. At right, W. H. Champion, publisher from July 1, 1945 until December 31, 1982.*

LaGrange's City Square features flower park, fountain and statue of Marquis de LaFayette. First Baptist Church steeple is in background. It is one of state's loveliest city squares.

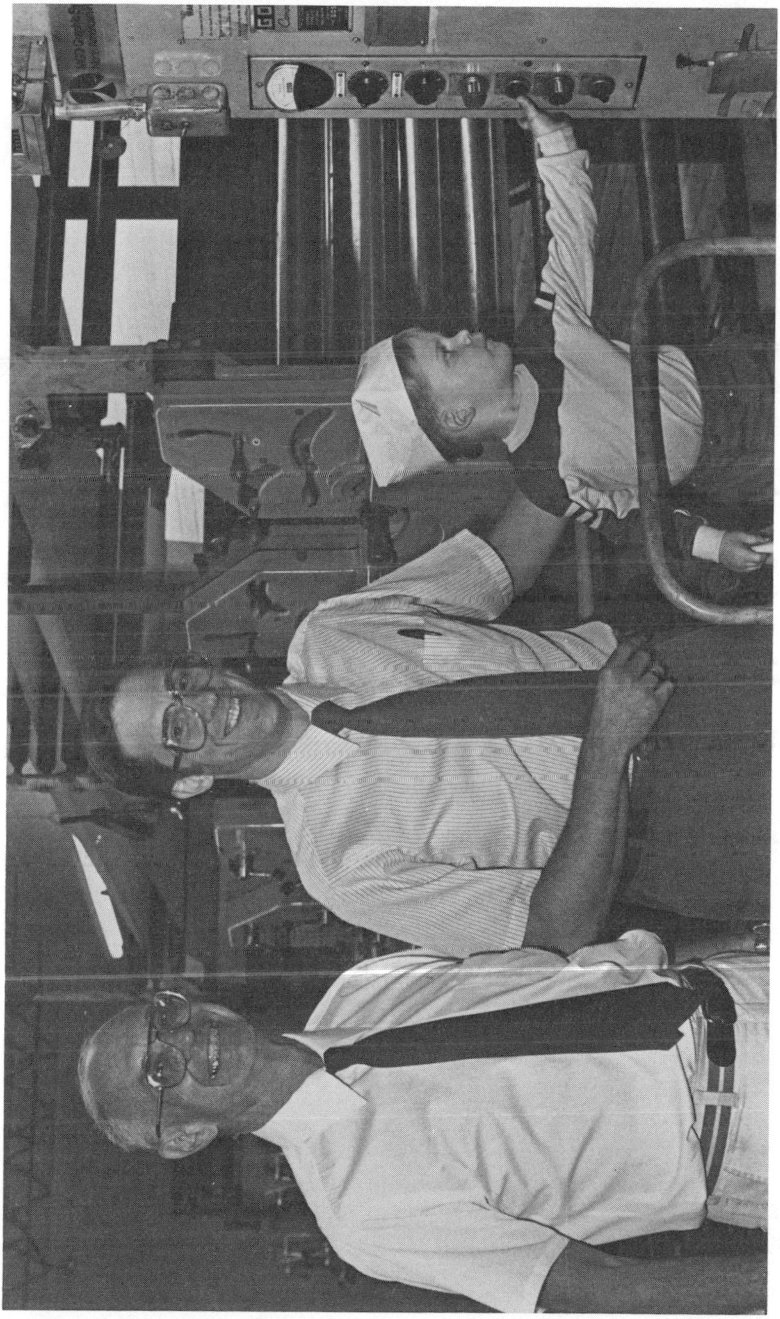

Quimby Melton II, III and IV all help start the new press for their company's weekly newspapers in 1982.

Flames ravaged The Cordele Dispatch *building in November, 1980 despite efforts of firemen.*

Scene shows charred remains of equipment after roof collapsed. Building was rebuilt on same site and was occupied less than year later.

The Weather
Partly Cloudy and Warm.
Details, page 2.

The Statesboro Herald

24 Pages 2 Sections

VOLUME 1 — STATESBORO, GEORGIA 30458, MONDAY, DECEMBER 21, 1970 — NUMBER 1

Rep. Rivers listed in serious condition

BIRMINGHAM, Ala. (UPI) The heart of Rep. L. Mendel Rivers faltered Sunday night but a quick-acting physician restored the heartbeat of the 65 year-old chairman of the House Armed Services Committee.

Rivers, recovering from open heart surgery, was listed in "serious condition" after the incident.

The hospital issued an 8 a.m. report saying "Congressman Rivers remains seriously ill. His circulatory system is sub-optimal. His brain function appears to be normal and his breathing system is functioning well."

Dr. John Kirklin of University Hospital, the South Carolina Democrat's physician, said Rivers' heart stopped beating at 3:55 p.m. EST Sunday but "fortunately, a resident physician was just a few feet away and resuscitative measures were begun promptly."

"These were effective," the physician said in a statement. "All indications are that brain and heart action are again normal. However, this event is a serious one and its occurrence renders the patient seriously ill."

Kirklin said "the sudden cessation of heart action," or ventricular fibrillation, came at the end of "a happy and comfortable day" for Rivers, who underwent surgery Dec. 11. Doctors at that time replaced a leaking mitral valve with a plastic one.

REP. RIVERS
Falters, then recovers

High Court favors 18-year-old vote

State voting laws retain authority

WASHINGTON (UPI) The Supreme Court ruled today that 18-year-olds may vote in federal elections for presidential and congressional candidates but held that state voting age laws will continue to govern state and local contests.

The court divided sharply on the issue with Justice Hugo L. Black delivering the detailing opinion.

The justice were in greater agreement in upholding two other key sections of the law — one striking down state residency rules of beyond 30 days for voting in presidential elections, and the other banning throughout the country literacy tests for voting.

Black said that where Congress attempted to remedy racial discrimination by the states, its authority was enhanced by the 14th Amendment's guarantee of "equal protection of the laws" and other post-Civil War amendments.

But he said Congress had no foundation against Civil War amendments for changing the voting age for the states.

On the other hand, legislation on the voting age in national elections, where Congress has more power, need not be tied to eliminating racial discrimination, he said.

Four justices —William O. Douglas, William J. Brennan Jr., Byron R. White and Thurgood Marshall —said the 18-year-old vote law should have been extended to state and local elections.

Chief Justice Warren E. Burger and Justices John M. Harlan, Potter Stewart and Harry A. Blackmum agreed however with Black that Congress could not interfere with the age set for voters by the states for nonfederal elections.

The new law now becomes operative Jan. 1.

The 18-year-old vote was brought to a direct Supreme Court test because it was enacted in the form of legislation rather than the more drawn out process of a constitutional amendment requiring ratification by the states.

The court decision means that all but three states must revamp their voting procedures in national elections to lower the age eligibility to 18. Georgia, Alaska and Kentucky already allow 18-year-olds to vote.

The court was unanimous on the literacy test section of the law.

The vote on the residency requirements was 8 to 1, with Justice John M. Harlan dissenting.

Oregon and Texas asked the court to declare the law an unconstitutional invasion of the right of states to set voter qualifications.

The Nixon administration opposed passage of the measure on constitutional grounds but was required to defend it under challenge in the high court.

The Justice Department had also asked that sections on residency rules to ban literacy tests be upheld.

PANE BROKEN
Burglar went an in ...

$1,400 taken from bus depot here

More than $1,400 in cash and checks disappeared from the Union Bus station here sometime last night, Mrs. Sandra Burnsed, manager, told the Herald today.

Mrs. Burnsed said that the station attendants closed the station last night about 9:30 p.m. shortly after the Trailways bus destined for New York had departed.

When station attendants reported for work this morning about 7 a.m. they found that the cash register had been robbed and then discovered that receipts left in a desk the day before were missing.

Investigation showed that a pane of glass had been broken from a rear door allowing the burgler or burglars to reach through and unlock the door.

Mrs. Burnsed said that this was the first time money had been left at the station and that due to holiday travel the receipts over the weekend had been heavier than usual. A check of the receipts showed that about $300 of the missing money was in checks with the remainder in currency bills and change.

Loss of the money was not covered by insurance and will mean a personal loss to the station manager, it was reported.

Mrs. Burnsed said that the station would be moved from the present location January 16 and will then occupy the old Volkswagen office and showroom located on U.S. 301 North of Statesboro.

The burglary is under investigation by the Statesboro Police Department.

Five hurt in two-car collision

Five people were injured in a two-car collision Sunday about one mile south of Statesboro on the Cypress Lake Road.

The accident occurred when a 1966 Chevrolet automobile driven by Valerie Millen, 30, apparently failed to grant a right of way to a 69 Buick driven by Clinton [illegible].

Injured in the accident in addition to the drivers of the two cars were R.W. Campbell, 25, Ronald Campbell, 22, and Jackie Clark, 30.

Preliminary reports indicate that all of the persons involved in the accident were Statesboro residents.

The State Patrol Headquarters in Swainsboro stated that complete details of the accident were not available at press time this morning.

The victims of the accident were taken to the Bulloch County Hospital where hospital officials said this morning their condition was satisfactory.

Statesboro Herald photo by Les Witte

Chevrolet heavily damaged in collision

Kosygin promises arms help to Egypt

By United Press International

Soviet Premier Alexei Kosygin told a visiting Egyptian delegation in Moscow today the Soviets will help them curb the ambitions of "Israeli aggressors."

Kosygin guaranteed a steady flow of guns, money and know how to help Egypt thwart the Israelis and pledged that the Israelis will not be allowed to expand their territory.

Kosygin, speaking at Kremlin luncheon where Vice President Aly Sabry of Egypt was guest of honor, attacked Israel and the United States in sharp language and praised the policies of Sabry and other Egyptian leaders.

He spoke as reports from Tel Aviv said Israel on Sunday postponed a decision on whether it will resume the Middle East peace talks. Both Britain and the United States have been pressuring Israe' to do so.

Sabry flew to Moscow Sunday with War Minister Mohammed Fawzi, Foreign Minister Mahmoud Riad and Industry Minister Aziz Sidki.

"Let the Israeli extremists have no illusion that they will be able to get some price for their consent to a peaceful settlement in the Middle East," Kosygin said. "Nobody asks from Israel and its imperialist patrons peace at any price."

"We can state most definitely that th Israeli aggressors and those who back them will never attain the aims of their expansionist policy in the Middle East," Kosygin said.

Kosygin confirmed that the two sides had discussed military matters and said "the Soviet Union will continue to firmly side with the Arab people in their just struggle."

Israel, despite pressures from both the

Continued on page 2

A peek inside . . .

THE NEW LEADER of Polands communist party begins work on an economic revival for his nation to calm uprising that brought him to power. Page 2

THE DEATH TOLL in fires over the weekend soars to 47 with blaze in Tucson, Ariz., claiming 29 lives. Page 3

NFL OFFICIALS pleased with outcome of regular season as it ends with six undisputed champions and two best second-place teams. Page 8

UPI Photo

THESE SOLDIERS READY TO GO HOME
They sit on floor at Tan Son Nhut Airport

U.S. plane fleet arrives for GIs

SAIGON (UPI) —The U.S. Air Force brought in a fleet of its own planes today to fly 376 American GIs home for Christmas after the South Vietnamese government refused to allow a chartered Pan American Airways 747 jumbo jet to land at Tan Son Nhut airbase.

Military sources said the last of the temporarily stranded GIs left late today aboard four Air Force C141 Starlifter jet transport planes. The C141s were rushed to Vietnam after the 747 scheduled to arrive Sunday night failed to arrive.

The Pan Am 747 would have been the first 747 to land in South Vietnam. But the flight was canceled before it left San Francisco after the Saigon government refused permission to land at Tan Son Nhut.

"There are technical problems and the (Tan Son Nhut) landing strip is not available right now for jumbo jets (747s)" a South Vietnamese spokesman said. "The air strip should be modified to be suitable for them."

Pan American officials gave no details on the negotiations with the Saigon government but unofficial sources said Pan Am had tried to get rights for regular commercial 747 jets to stop in Saigon.

The same sources said the South Vietnamese government was trying to get Pan Am to pay fir widening of the runways at Tan Son Nhut before it would grant landing rights for 747s.

The GIS scheduled to board the 747 for the flight home had put on dress uniforms Sunday night and were ready to be taken by bus to Tan Son Nhut from Long Binh, 18 miles north of Saigon.

Crime rate climbs up

WASHINGTON UPI—Serious crime climbed 10 per cent nation-wide during the first nine months of 1970 with the largest increase reported in the suburbs, Attorney General John N. Mitchell announced today.

The rate of increase was the lowest for the 9-month period since 1965 and was 1 per cent lower than for the corresponding period of 1969, according to the FBI's Uniform Crime Reports.

Large cities of over 250,000 reported crime up 8 per cent, compared to a 14 per cent rise in the suburbs and 9 per cent in rural areas.

Violent crimes as a group rose 10 per cent with robbery up 15 per cent, murder 9 per cent, aggravated assaults 7 per cent and forcible rape 2 per cent.

'Statesboro Herald' born today

This issue, Volume 1, Number 1 of The Statesboro Herald, almost 7,000 copies of it, has found its way into the homes and businesses of the people of Statesboro and Bulloch County. With this first copy of the new daily newspaper comes the best wishes of the Publishers, the Editors and all of the members of the Herald staff, along with a pledge of continued service to the people of the region.

This first issue of the Herald is being delivered by paper carriers to all the homes in Statesboro, in the subdivisions, and in other communities in Bulloch County where it has been possible to employ carriers.

Thousands of copies of the new daily are being delivered in the post offices and by rural mail carriers, with an effort being made to deliver at least one copy to every family.

The new Herald will be coming to you each afternoon, Monday through Friday, with the very latest news from the Statesboro area and around the world.

The Herald's publishers have left nothing undone to assure you a hometown newspaper every afternoon carrying the very latest news from home and from around the world.

The wire services to the Herald bring the very latest state, national and international news reports almost as they happen. Along with the news, also by wire, come the latest pictures, allowing you to see the "news in pictures" and to see personalities involved in the news.

Community correspondents, now representing each community in Bulloch County, will continue as correspondents to the daily Herald, allowing quick and accurate reporting of community events to our readers.

News items which are sent to the paper by mail, should be addressed to the editor. Persons using the phone to seek information or to give news should call the main number, 764-6146, and tell the party who answers, the nature of the call. This will allow a routing of the call to the proper person.

The editorial and news departments of the Herald operate independently from the

Continued on page 2A

First edition (Vol. I, No. 1) of The Statesboro Herald *as a daily newspaper came out on Monday, December 21, 1970.*

THE WEATHER
Cloudy, Warmer
Showers Tomorrow

THE BRUNSWICK NEWS

Leased Wire Reports of the Ass^ciated Press and Special NEA Service

TOMORROW'S TIDES
High 12:04 a.m. 12:35 p.m.
Low 6:23 a.m. 7:21 p.m.

VOLUME 63, NUMBER 71 — BRUNSWICK, GA., FRIDAY, NOVEMBER 22, 1963 — PRICE FIVE CENTS

KENNEDY ASSASSINATED

21 CASES; 3 DIE

Jacksonville Battles Polio Case Spiral

JACKSONVILLE, Fla. (AP) — A polio epidemic is threatening Duval County and a mass immunization program is being set up to counter it. Twenty-one cases have been counted by the State Health Board within the past month and three persons have died.

In the rest of Florida only six cases have been reported for the entire year.

A special planeload of 600,000 doses of vaccine arrived in Jacksonville Thursday night.

"There is a clear public indication for the immunization of everyone three months of age and above at the earliest possible practicable date," said Dr. Wilson Sowder, state health officer.

The vaccine will be administered at public schools on Sunday. Officials in three surrounding counties also laid plans for special immunization.

The health board said that the proven cases, chiefly among Negro children, caused a considerable proportion of paralysis of arms and legs.

Sowder said all persons, regardless of age, should take the vaccine whether or not they had previously taken Salk or Sabin vaccines.

We Must Rely On Alliance, Erhard Declares

By HARVEY HUDSON
Associated Press Staff Writer

PARIS (AP)—Chancellor Ludwig Erhard of West Germany declared today: "We can and must rely on the Atlantic Alliance."

. He also said he was "sure the United States would reply with all its force if Europe or any part of Europe was attacked."

Erhard was answering a newsman's question following a luncheon closing an official two-day visit to France.

The question concerned France's independent atomic force. Erhard was asked if he thought it might lead to a European force and eventually replace a multilateral force, such as the United States is proposing. Erhard replied:

"We have the greatest respect for the French effort for atomic power and we understand the reasons why France took the decision. We Germans are convinced that we can and must rely on the Atlantic Alliance. We feel sure that the United States would reply with all its force if Europe or any part of Europe was attacked."

Earlier, he said he considers French - German cooperation and European unity the first steps toward a larger Atlantic union covering political, military, economic and social affairs.

Winding up talks with President Charles de Gaulle and other French leaders, he said in a speech to the French Diplomatic Press Association that French - German cooperation was a driving force in the policies of his government.

"I consider continuance of this work without respite as one of my primary tasks in foreign policy," he said.

His desire for closer ties with the United States clashes with the ideas of De Gaulle, who wants a united Europe as an independent entity rid of American influence. This is one of several points on which De Gaulle and Erhard differ.

Divers Hunt For U-2 Pilot

KEY WEST, Fla. (AP)—Navy divers searched through waters of the Gulf of Mexico today trying to determine the fate of a U2 pilot, Capt. Joe G. Hyde Jr., whose high-flying jet plunged into the ocean northwest of Key West Wednesday.

Other Navy vessels and aircraft checked a wide area with a fading hope of finding him.

The U2's mission was secret. The Defense Department and Strategic Air Command said the reconnaissance plane probably crashed because of mechanical failure. When it went down, it was out of Cuban antiaircraft gun range, and the radar screen on which it was being traced apparently showed no other aircraft.

The Cuban radio commented Thursday that, "the Defense Department does not want to say what the plane was doing when it disappeared."

UG STUDENTS HELD

ATHENS, Ga. (AP) — Two University of Georgia freshmen were bound over to the Clarke County grand jury today under $1,000 bonds on charges of malicious mischief, vandalism and damaging a public burying ground.

* * *

First Lady Shook Hands Despite Agents

By FRANK CORMIER
Associated Press Staff Writer

FORT WORTH, Tex. (AP) — Mrs. Jacqueline Kennedy, perhaps reluctantly, was back in politics and she was a good campaigner.

Her smile charmed thousands in San Antonio, Houston and Fort Worth Thursday as she began a three-day Texas tour with her husband, the President.

She made a speech in Spanish and drew cheers and applause.

She ignored the plans of Secret Service agents and shook hands with hundreds who were forced to stay behind rope barricades.

At every stop the first day, Mrs. Kennedy took a cue from her husband and walked first from the presidential jet. Kennedy sometimes has been criticized for observing presidential protocol and walking a few steps ahead of his wife.

Shortly before midnight Thursday, Mrs. Kennedy still was going through her campaign paces.

When the Kennedys arrived at Carswell Air Force Base outside Fort Worth, the President and First Lady walked several hundred yards along a rope barrier, shaking hands and chatting with the crowd.

When the Kennedys reached the Texas hotel in Fort Worth, where they spent the night, they headed for the nearest throng and went through their handshaking act.

Pamela Turnure, Mrs. Kennedy's press secretary, was asked if the First Lady had enjoyed the experience.

"She loved every minute of it," said Mrs. Turnure.

It was the first day of the first stumping tour Mrs. Kennedy has made with her husband since he became the Democratic nominee for President in 1960.

She appeared to enjoy every minute even though White House aides frankly admit she would prefer to leave political campaigning to the President.

Mrs. Kennedy participated in the 1960 primary campaigns but stayed in the background during the general election when she was expecting John Jr.

Lowndes Solon Hits Tax Hike

WAYCROSS, Ga. (AP) — A Lowndes County legislator says that he is not in favor of a general tax increase until Georgians face up to their responsibility at the local level.

Rep. Fred Walker of Valdosta, who was elected chairman Thursday night of a newly organied 8th District Legislative Association, conceded that the state has pressing needs in education and other areas.

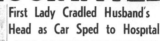

PRESIDENT JOHN F. KENNEDY

Hit Misinformation

President's Final Speech Concerned Country's Security

By JACK BELL
Associated Press Staff Writer

DALLAS (AP) — President Kennedy lashed out today at those he said "confuse rhetoric with reality." Speaking in an area where supporters are booming Sen. Barry Goldwater's chances for the 1964 Republican nomination, Kennedy said that ignorance and misinformation "if allowed to prevail in foreign policy, handicaps this country's security."

In a speech prepared for the Dallas Citiens Council, the Dallas Assembly and the Graduate Research Center of the Southwest, Kennedy did not specifically mention Goldwater by name.

Kennedy said:

"In a world of complex and continuing problems, in a world full of frustrations and irritations, America's leadership must be guided by the lights of learning and reason—or else those who confuse rhetoric with reality and the plausible with the possible will gain the ascendancy with their seemingly swift and simple solutions to every world problem."

Goldwater's recent proposal that American commanders in the field be given authority to use nuclear weapons on their own initiative has drawn bristling criticism from administration leaders.

Kennedy also said:

"There will always be dissident voices heard in the land, expressing opposition without alternatives, finding fault but never favor, perceiving gloom on every side and seeking influence without responsibility," he said.

"Their voices are inevitable," he added.

Kennedy said that these voices were preaching doctrines wholly unrelated to reality and that words will suffice without weapons, that vituperation is as good as victory, and that peace good as vicory, and that peace is a sign of weakness."

Kennedy also took a jibe at Sen. Harry F. Byrd, D-Va., and others who have criticied his economic and financial policies.

"At a time when the national debt is steadily being reduced in terms of its burden on our economy," he said, "they see that debt as the greatest single others who have criticized his threat to our security. At a time when we are steadily reducing the number of federal employes serving every thousand citizens, they fear those hordes of civil servants more than the actual hordes of opposing armies."

Kennedy at Fort Worth, before coming to Dallas, praised the controversial TFX warplane which is being built in Fort Worth. He said Texas ranks fifth in prime military contract spending.

The President scheduled another major speech at Austin tonight. He and his wife will spend tonight at the ranch of Vice President Lyndon B. Johnson near Austin.

Work for It, —No Draft, GOP Warns

ST. LOUIS (AP)—Republican national Chairman William E. Miller warned GOP presidential hopefuls they will have to work for the Republican nomination because there will be no draft candidate.

"I think anyone who wants the nomination in 1964 ought to be about it right now," Rep. Miller of New York said.

"Anyone who just sits by expecting to be drafted will be disappointed."

Thus far, he said, the nomination will go either to Gov. Nelson Rockefeller of New York —who has announced as a candidate—or Sen. Barry Goldwater or Ariona—"who it seems to me will soon announce.

"I believe Nixon (former Vice President Richard M. Nixon) when he says he is not a candidate and does not intend to be a candidate."

Miller called for GOP presidential aspirants to enter state preferential primaries. He said if anyone won all the primaries —as President Kennedy did in 1960—the Republican convnetion could not deny him the nomination.

First Lady Cradled Husband's Head as Car Sped to Hospital

DALLAS (AP) — President John F. Kennedy, thirty-sixth president of the United States, was shot to death today by a hidden assassin armed with a high-powered rifle. Kennedy, 46, lived about an hour after a sniper cut him down as his limousine left downtown Dallas. Automatically, the mantle of the presidency fell to Vice President Lyndon B. Johnson, a native Texan who had been riding two cars behind the chief executive.

Kennedy died at Parkland Hospital where his bullet - pierced body had been taken in a frantic but futile effort to save his life.

Lying wounded at the same hospital was Gov. John Connally of Texas, who was cut down by the same fusillade that ended the life of the youngest man ever elected to the presidency.

Connally and his wife had been riding with the President and Mrs. Kennedy

The First Lady cradled her dying husband's bloodsmeared head in her arms as the presidential limousine raced to the hospital.

"Oh, no," she kept crying.

Connally slumped in his seat beside the President.

Police ordered an unprecedented dragnet of the city, hunting for the assassin.

Soon after President Kennedy was assassinated today in Dallas, a white man in his mid 20s was arrested in the Riverside section of Fort Worth in the shooting of a Dallas policeman.

The man, who has black curly hair and who wore a red shirt, denied that he was connected with the assassination of the President.

His hands were handcuffed and he was taken to the Fort Worth City jail.

They believed the fatal shots were fired by a white man, about 30, slender of build, weighing about 165 pounds, and standing 5 feet 10 inches tall.

The murder weapon was reportedly a 30-30 rifle.

Shortly before Kennedy's death became known, he was administered the last rites of the Roman Catholic Church. He had been the first Roman Catholic president in American history.

Even as two clergymen hovered over the fallen President in the hospital emergency room, doctors and nurses administered blood transfusions.

Kennedy died of a gunshot wound in the brain at approximately 1 p.m. (CST) according to an announcement by acting White House press secretary Malcolm Kilduff.

Kilduff said Johnson was not hit. The new President previously had been reported wounded.

The new President, Lyndon Johnson, and his wife left the hospital a half hour later. Newsmen had no opportunity to question them.

There was no immediate word on when Johnson would take the oath of office.

Kennedy, 46, lived about 30 minutes after a sniper cut him down as his limousine left downtown Dallas. Newsmen said the shot that hit him was fired about 12:30 p.m. (CST). A hospital announcement said he died at approximately 1 p.m. of a bullet wound in the head.

The horror of the assassination was mirrored in an eyewitness account by Sen. Ralph Yarborough, D-Tex., who had been riding three cars behind Kennedy.

"You could tell something awful and tragic had happened," the senator told newsmen before Kennedy's death became known. His voice breaking and his eyes red-rimmed, Yarborough said:

"I could see a Secret Service man in the President's car leaning on the car with his hands in anger, anguish and despair. I knew then something tragic had happened."

Yarborough had counted three rifle shots as the presidential limousine left downtown Dallas through a triple underpass. The shots were fired from above—possibly from one of the bridges or from a nearby building.

One witness, television reporter Mal Couch, said he saw a gun emerge from an upper story of a warehouse commanding an unobstructed view of the presidential car.

Kennedy was the first president to be assassinated since William McKinley was shot in 1901.

It was the first death of a president in office since Franklin D. Roosevelt died of a cerebral hemorrhage at Warm Springs, Ga., in April 1945.

Roosevelt had been enjoying a vacation when he died. McKinley had been shaking hands at a reception at an exposition in Buffalo, N.Y.

Kennedy and his wife had just passed the halfway point in a three-day speaking tour through Texas.

The President already had prepared a luncheon address for a Dallas audience before he died. In his prepared text, he assailed his ultraconservative critics.

Dallas is considered a center of conservative philosophy and finance.

Here, on Oct. 24, Adlai E. Stevenson was spat upon by one heckler and struck by another after making a United Nations Day address.

It was believed that Kenneday's body would be moved shortly to Washington.

Traditionally, funeral services for presidents who die in office are held in the capital city.

Kilduff told newsmen that Gov. Connally, a Democrat, was wounded in the right chest in the same ambush that felled the President.

Connally was rushed into surgery for a two-hour emergency operation.

Connally also was hit in the right wrist.

Though Mrs. Kennedy cried, "Oh, No," in horror and despair after her husband was shot, she did not collapse or give way to hysteria.

When he entered the hospital, her clothing was covered with blood from her husband's wounds.

Lt. Erich Kaminski of the Secret Service said the assassin's weapon appeared to have been a "high-powered Army or Japanese rifle of about .25 caliber." The rifle had a scope on it, he said.

The entire building where the sniper was located was evacuated. People were working in the building at the time of the shooting.

Dallas inspector J. H. Sawyer said, "Police found the remains of fried chicken and paper on the fifth floor. Apparently the persons had been there quite awhile."

After the fatal shots were fired at Kennedy, the stricken President's Secret Service driver raced away from the scene at top speed—heading for the nearest hospital and trying to get the presidential party out of range of further gunfire.

Kennedy, Connally and their wives had been riding together in the President's familiar drak blue, bubbletop convertible. The transparent plastic roof of the vehicle had been removed for the motorcade.

Secret Service agents riding with the President and in a second convertible following close behind, immediately drew pistols and automatic weapons.

But they were unable to get a shot at the gunman.

'Get Fewer; Patients Considerate'

What Happened to MDs' Night Calls?

By WILLIAM J. Conway
Associated Press Staff Writer

CHICAGO (AP) — What has happened to doctors' old-fashioned night calls at homes?

This inquiring reporter made a quick sampling at this week's meeting of the Illinois Academy of General Practice.

Talks with seven family doctors from all parts of the state — all of whom make evening visits — left these impressions:

By and large, family doctors still make night calls. But they get fewer calls because of the patient's consideration for the physicians's health and his own money. One medical man estimated fees are 30 to 50 per cent higher after dark.

"The truth is we don't get as many night calls as we used to," said Dr. John D. McCarthy of Riverside, "largely because the patients have increased concern for the doctor's welfare and have become accustomed to going directly to the emergency room in a hospital, especially in cases of trauma. It gets the patient under treatment quicker, with better results and less expense to everybody concerned."

Some of the doctors asked anonymity.

"When the price goes up, people don't call you as often," commented a physician from a small town in Northern Illinois. "I'm glad to make them (calls) now at the price I charge for them."

"I wish I had a dime for every time I had to dress and go out on a call," said a medic from a community of 15,000 in Southern Illinois.

A gray-haired physician from a sizeable city in the southern half of the state said he makes nocturnal calls.

"It's getting to the point where a lot of them won't do it," he added. "I was brough up in the old school."

"Our county is 600 square miles, and I even make calls outside the county," said Dr. C. J. Jannings of Fairfield. "I have only one rule — if the patient can't tome to me, I go to him."

Required to Pay Georgia Tax, Too

Area Florida Car Buyers Warned

ATLANTA (AP) — State Revenue Commissioner Hiram K. Undercofler said today that Georgians who buy cars in Florida and pay a 2 per cent sales tax still are required to pay a 3 per cent use tax when they bring the vehicles back home.

He charged that dealers in north Florida, principally Jacksonville and Tallahassee, are misleading the customers by telling them that after they pay the Florida tax there will be no charge in Georgia.

"Statements by automobile dealers in Florida or Florida officials to the effect that there is a sales and use tax reciprocity agreement between Georgia and Florida are not correct," Undercofler said.

Ed Olmstead, state sales tax supervisor, said that dozens of complaints have been received in recent months from residents in Bainbridge, Albany, Tifton, Valdosta, Waycross, Thomasville, Moultrie, Brunswick and other south Georgia cities. The complainants paid the Florida sales tax on the cars and became indignant when Georgia officials moved in to collect again.

"The Georgia law will grant credits for payments of like taxes legally imposed and paid to another state provided that state grants credits for taxes paid in Georgia," Undercofler said.

"However, here is no credit for such payments because the Florida Legislature in 1961 struck the reciprocity provisions from their sales and use tax statute."

One complainant, who wrote to the Florida tax authorities, received an answer which said, "This office does not have on file a notice or directive rescinding the reciprocal agreement on vehicles."

This referred to an amendment by the Florida Legislature at the time it revoked the reciprocal agreement law. The amendment allowed reciprocity on motor vehicles to remain on the books.

Dixon Oxford, former Georgia revenue commissioner, however, notified the Florida comptroller's office that Georgia law provides only for reciprocity on an across-the-board basis affecting sales of all commodities.

The Brunswick News *has one of latest afternoon deadlines in Georgia. On November 22, 1963, its regular home-delivered editions carried full account of John F. Kennedy assassination.*

Garfield debuts today in
First daily edition
Comics Page 11

Arp silences Furman bats
Sports, Page 8

The Union-Recorder

Georgia's 'Old Reliable' Newspaper

Vol. 163 No. 17 | 14 Pages | Milledgeville, Georgia | Tuesday, March 2, 1982 | © The Union-Recorder 1982 | 20 Cents

State won't give OK to tick repelling spray

By TOM HINDERLEIDER
Staff Writer

Campers, loggers and everyone who spends time in the woods have a new weapon in the war against ticks, but when we'll have it on the Georgia battlefield, if ever, remains undetermined.

Department of Agriculture researchers in Gainesville, Fla., have developed a synthetic pesticide called permethrin they have found to kill the lone star tick common to Baldwin and Hancock counties.

Entomologist Carl Schreck, who led the research, says permethrin is safe, convenient and effective protection against the tick, and has been developed for personal use as an aerosol to be sprayed on clothing.

"When used as suggested," Schreck said, "permethrin is not harmful if breathed, swallowed or contacts the skin accidently. It kills the tick when it crawls on your clothing, and lasts an unusually long time."

Schreck said that permethrin is being marketed by Fairfield American of Medina, N.Y.

"It should be available in the spring in four states that have granted permission to sell the product: Tennessee, Kentucky, Missouri and Arkansas," he said. "A package has been sent to Georgia, but they haven't approved it yet."

The Environmental Protection Agency and the Georgia Department of Agriculture have the authority to allow pesticides to go on sale in Georgia.

Carlene Durkee, of the EPA chemical division, said that permethrin is currently being used in Georgia as a pesticide on crops, especially cotton. No one else at the EPA was available to comment on the status of permethrin's approval for personal use and Durkee didn't know about the chemical's use as tick protection.

Ron Conolly, head of the Georgia Department of Agriculture Pesticides Division, said that Fairfield American had been denied approval for permethrin by his office.

"Fairfield American applied to us for registration under section 24-C, which provides for temporary approval for a product not yet certified by the EPA if a special, local need for the product can be proven," Conolly said. "They could not give sufficient data to prove their product any better than any of those currently on the market, so we turned them down," he said.

Conolly said the EPA is "primarily responsible for pesticide registration in the state of Georgia." He also said they are studying permethrin and have questions concerning its "neuro toxicity," or long term detrimental effects on the human nervous system.

"The EPA is going very slow on permethrin because of these questions," Conolly said.

He said if there were an emergency need determined by the agriculture department, they would grant special approval for the use of permethrin. They didn't find such a need and Conolly said their decision "protected the integrity of the process."

He thought permethrin had been granted special, local need approval in some nearby states, but he was not sure.

Larry Feller, manager for government regulations at Fairfield American, said that their company had been

See PERMETHRIN, Page 2

Burden trial to hear first witness today

Staff, Wire Reports

SANDERSVILLE, Ga. — Testimony is expected to begin here today as the murder trial continues for a man charged with drowning a woman and her three pre-school children.

Jimmie Burden of Sandersville is charged with murder in the August 1974 drowning deaths of 23-year-old Louise Wynn and her three children: Melinda, 5; Marvin, 3, and James, 2, all of Sandersville.

Middle Judicial Circuit Assistant District Attorney Richard Malone is seeking the death penalty against Burden, who was charged with the deaths after he was arrested last year in Delaware in connection with a Georgia burglary. In a case where two capital felonies occur at the same time the state can ask for the death penalty, Malone explained.

Monday, prosecutors and defense attorneys questioned 60 potential jurors.

"We'll actually strike the jury tomorrow morning," Malone said Monday night. "We'll start seeing witnesses about 11 o'clock."

The first witness to take the stand, Malone said, will be retired Washington County Sheriff J. Euree Curry.

Although the sheriff's testimony will not be lengthy, "it'll be interesting," Malone said.

Another witness that may take the stand late today, Malone said, is Henry Lee Dixon, the nephew of the accused killer.

Dixon is being held in the Washington County jail as a material witness, Malone said. Dixon's testimony is "very important" to the prosecution and there is reason to believe he would not come foward to testify if he were not held under restraint, Malone said. Dixon was jailed after failing to post bond. Dixon was earlier charged in the multiple slayings, but those charges were dropped, Malone said.

Burden, 37, was convicted of burglary in December and faces a 12-year prison term.

A fisherman discovered the body of two-year-old James Wynn on Aug. 15, 1974 in a small pond off state Highway 242. Subsequently, the bodies of Mrs. Wynn and the other children were recovered in the pond. Officials said that although Mrs. Wynn was severely beaten and Melinda Wynn was choked, all four died from drowning.

Judge Walter C. McMillan will preside over the trial.

Photo by Tom Ervin

To catch the Frisbee, you must become one with the Frisbee

...Wade Buendia, a Georgia College freshman, shows his Frisbee prowess during the recent prelude to spring.

Collision kills six, injures two

By JEFFREY DAY
Staff Writer

Six members of the Spiritual Heaven Gospel Singers were killed in an auto accident Sunday night while driving home from a singing engagement at a Gordon church.

Flemming Jones Jr., 42, three of his daughters, a niece and a fellow singer with the group were killed when their brightly-painted van was struck by a pickup truck on the Gordon Highway about 7.5 miles south of Milledgeville near Coopers.

Only one passenger in the van, James Taylor, 31, survived the collision. He was taken to the Baldwin County Hospital where he was treated and released.

The driver of the truck, Bennett "Wayne" Barnes III, of Route 2, Gordon, was reported late Monday afternoon in stable and fair condition in the intensive care unit of the Baldwin County Hospital, according to a hospital spokesperson.

Barnes has been charged with driving under the influence of alcohol, driving on the wrong side of the road and driving without insurance, according to Georgia State Patrol Trooper [illegible].

Jones and his daughters, Annette, 16, Regina, 13 and Gwendolyn, 14, all died at the scene of the accident, according to Mark Godard, Baldwin County Coroner. Patricia Jones, 14, daughter of James Jones, also died in the accident along with Charlie Lester Tucker, 31, of 345 Killings Ave., Milledgeville. All were riding in the van.

According to Flemming Jones' sister, Beatrice Walls, the group had been singing at the New Hope Church on College Street in Gordon, before leaving around 9 p.m. to return to Milledgeville.

Earlier in the day the group sang at a church in [illegible] with the group for about 20 years, Walls said. The girls had been singing with it for five years.

"They were great," said Ailene Butler, of People's Funeral home where Jones worked during the past 20 years.

"He [illegible] smart," she said. "He was a wonderful young person. I was like a mother to him." In addition to working at the funeral home and singing with the gospel group, Jones worked on cars and had worked at the Griffin Pipe Company until it closed several years ago.

He was active in church affairs and was to be ordained as a deacon at St. Paul's Baptist Church in Milledgeville later this month, Butler said.

Annette and Patricia Jones attended Baldwin High School. Gwendolyn and Regina went to Davis Middle School.

Jones and his wife, Eve, have another daughter, Shyvonna. Neither Mrs. Jones nor Shyvonna were in the

See ACCIDENT, Page 14

City beginning repair work on Carrington Woods dam

By PATRICIA O'CONNELL
Staff Writer

Work begins today to repair the Carrington Woods dam, bringing to an end the four-year controversy about what to do about the dam declared unsafe by the state Department of Natural Resources.

"We hope to be going full blast Tuesday," said Albert Sanford, building inspector for the City of Milledgeville.

"Originally we hoped to start Monday, but since it rained over the weekend, it was too wet," Sanford said.

The work on the dam is being done by city and county crews and will cost the city more than $100,000. The repairs will be done in several phases and will continue into the summer or fall, according to Sanford.

The county will have six men working on the dam, according to Wendell Couch, head of the Baldwin County road department.

The county crew will be ripping up soil and hauling it to fill in the back side of the dam, Couch said.

He said he did not think having six employees involved in working on the dam would create a hardship on his department.

"I think we'll be able to handle everything all right," Couch said.

See DAM, Page 14

New health center needed, commissioners say

By JEFFREY DAY
Staff Writer

After several years of bad reviews for the 30-year-old Marion Ennis Health Center, the Baldwin County Commission may have to seriously consider replacing the building, admit commissioners.

Near the begining of each year a Baldwin County Grand Jury inspects county facilities and procedures. This year the grand jury recommended the center be replaced — the same recommendation that has been made by the grand jury in 1979, 1980 and 1981.

The difference this time is that the county commission is already thinking about replacing the center rather than spending money to repair the obsolete building.

"It's just a matter of time before we have to build a new health center," said Buddy Johnson, the commissioner in charge of the center. "It's something we'll have to look at real hard the next year or so."

The grand jury committe responsible for inspecting the center at 130 S. Elbert St. had a long list of problems found at the center.

Among the problems, there is inadequate insulation which results in large heating bills. Several walls in the building need replastering and office space is inadequate, according to the committee report. The floors in the center are uneven and the roof leaks in several places, the report continues. Parking at the facility is also inadequate, with 14 of the 16 spaces reserved for the staff.

The committee recommended that a new center be constructed in a more central location.

According to the report, only one improvement recommended by the grand jury last year was made — the installation of a door on the venereal disease examining room.

"In the last couple of years we have spent quite a bit of money (on the center)," said Sammy Hall, commission chairman. In 1980 the county spent about $30,000 making repairs at the center. The county also increased the center's budget from $97,000 last year to about $123,000 for the 1981-1982 fiscal year.

"We realize there are problems with the center," Hall said. "The economics of it is the real problem."

Now, commissioners are at a point where they must decide to fix the facility or replace it, he added.

See CENTER, Page 14

good morning

NINE PERSONS were injured in a rash of automobile accidents in the city. See Page 2.

STUDY, PRAYER and group support helps some inmates at the Women's Unit of the Middle Georgia Correctional Institution cope with life behind bars. See Page 5.

OLD SOUTH week is coming soon and plans are being made. See Today's Living, Page 6.

INDEX

The Union-Recorder *of Milledgeville made its debut as a daily with this front page on Tuesday, March 2, 1982.*

Carter Wins

Americus Times-Recorder

VOLUME 98 – NUMBER 279 AMERICUS, GEORGIA 31709, WEDNESDAY, NOVEMBER 3, 1976 2 SECTIONS-20 PAGES-PRICE 15c

Unseats President Ford in Close Race

Sumter Countian Fulfills Goal To Hold Nation's Highest Office

Bright New Day Dawns in Sumter

By RUDY HAYES
Managing Editor

Thousands of Sumter Countians and millions of others over the land will long remember election day 1976, the day that Jimmy Carter won the presidency.

For along with his victory came true the promises and predictions that the native son had been making for 22 months, ever since he announced he would be a candidate for president.

He began as "Jimmy Who?" on the national scene and for more than a year never figured in any of the polls, instead being included in the "All Other Candidates, 1 per cent" category.

Jimmy never waivered in his confidence and those who doubted his beliefs were made believers when he won a string of primary victories over the most formidable candidates the Democratic party could muster.

There were some, however, who still were not convinced even after he had won the Democratic nomination last July.

But today, November 3rd, 1976 there are no longer any doubters. Jimmy Carter is President-elect.

And with his victory came a swelling of pride among all Sumter Countians — indeed America also — that a home community figure will move into the White House next January 20th.

Election day dawned bright and clear, making it perfect for record numbers of voters to go to the polls over the country. It was the same in Sumter County for some 65 per cent of the 12,000 registered voters cast ballots. The lines were long from the time the polls opened at 7 a.m. until they closed. A long line of voters in line at 7 p.m. were allowed to vote at the Americus precinct even though it was past closing time.

The president-elect won eight of nine precincts in his Sumter County, losing narrowly in Concord Community (New 26th District) by a margin of 109 to 92.

Carter won the county by a 72 per cent margin, his overall figure being 5,008 votes to President Ford's 1,920.

A further breakdown by precinct shows the following:

Carter won over Ford in the 15th District (Leslie) 483 to 170; 172 to 29 in the New 16th (Sumter City); 44 to 16 in the Old 16th (Huntington); 127 to 35 in the 17th (Thompson); 481 to 99 in the Old 26th (Plains); 3,399 to 1,393 in the 27th (Americus); 110 to 50 in the 28th (Chambliss); and 100 to 19 in the 29th (Andersonville).

In neighboring Schley County Carter was victorious 783 to 268.

In the race for U.S. Representative, incumbent Jack

(See BRIGHT Page 3)

President-elect Jimmy Carter Of Plains

Plains Center Of World's Attention

By DONALD M. ROTHBERG
AP Political Writer

WASHINGTON (AP) — President-elect Jimmy Carter's long, once-solitary journey from Plains, Ga., will carry him to the White House in January with a victory forged from the traditional Democratic party coalition of the Old South and industrial North.

Carter was declared the victor over President Gerald Ford early today when his electoral vote total reached 272, two more than the 270 needed for election. Wisconsin and Mississippi were the states that established the

Bulletin

WASHINGTON (AP)—President Ford conceded defeat today to Jimmy Carter in the 1976 presidential race.

In a "Dear Jimmy" telegram to the Democratic victor, read for the hoarse President by his wife, Betty, Ford pledged a smooth and effective transition. Mrs. Ford said her husband had also telephoned his message to Carter.

Democratic candidate's majority in The Associated Press tabulation.

Three states — Oregon and Maine, where Ford held a slim lead, and Ohio, where Carter was ahead — remained too close to call. If Ford were to carry all three, Carter's victory margin would remain just two electoral votes.

The lead in California passed back and forth through the night with Ford finally declared the winner near daybreak.

Returning to Plains from his election headquarters in Atlanta, Carter received a tumultuous, emotional welcome from a crowd that included most of the town's 683 residents.

Beaming his now-famous smile, Carter told the crowd, "I told you I didn't intend to lose."

But when he tried to continue speaking, his voice choked, he turned his head and then embraced his wife, Rosalynn, who was sobbing.

"It was a long night," he said when he regained his composure. "But I guarantee you, it's going to be worth it to all of us."

The latest returns showed Carter carrying 22 states and the District of Columbia with 272 electoral votes. Ford had

(See CARTER Page 3)

Jimmy Carter Star

Plains Becomes 'Movie Set'

By LEILA BARRETT
Staff Writer

PLAINS, Ga.—This tiny Southwest Georgia hamlet had taken on the aura of a Hollywood movie set with the star attraction their favorite son, Jimmy Carter.

Crowds began gathering as early as mid-afternoon awaiting the 5 o'clock appearance of Carter who spoke to the thousands of his supporters from a platform erected on Main Street before leaving for Atlanta to wait out the election returns.

And the throngs continued to wait all through the long night until the candidate returned home the victor, President-elect of these United States of America.

In a "battle of the bands" type of competition three local high school bands heralded Carter's Tuesday afternoon arrival with the strains of "Happy Days Are Here Again," as the candidate made his way to the platform. People lined the streets, leaned out of store front windows as Carter addressed the placard waving crowd.

As he stood there looking into the familiar faces of his hometown folks he said, "this is the last day of a long effort, on my part and on your part. I think win or lose we've made political history, coming this far from a town the size of Plains."

Television cameras rolled and the nation and world was watching as the hometown boy who made good spoke to his neighbors and friends with a message especially for them, "I think because of your help and what we stand for I'll come back as President-elect."

(See PLAINS Page 3)

WEATHER REPORT

State Forecast

GEORGIA: Cloudy with widely scattered showers extreme southeast and mostly fair elswhere today. Fair and turning colder over the state tonight. Fair and cooler statewide Thursday. Highs today mostly 60s. Lows tonight mid 20s mountains to low 40s southeast. Highs Thursday low 50s mountains to mid 60s south.

LOCAL: The high temperature recorded here Tuesday was 66 degrees; the low last night, 40; and noon today, 64.

2 to 1 Edge

Democrats Hold To House Control

By JIM ADAMS
Associated Press Writer

WASHINGTON (AP) — Democrats held on to their 2 to 1 House control, a domination that could give President-elect Jimmy Carter solid backing for his programs.

With returns from Tuesday's election almost complete, Democrats were staying dead even with the previous 290 to 145 House margin that put them in constant veto battles with defeated President Ford.

Despite polls showing public disenchantment with Washington and Congress, few sitting congressmen — either Republicans or Democrats — were thrown out.

Women appeared to be losing one of the 19 seats they had. The 17 black House members won re-election.

Two Democrats lost their seats in sex and bribery

(See DEMOS Page 3)

Here's how Jimmy Carter's home-town newspaper — The Americus Times-Recorder *— played the story on the day after he was elected U.S. president.*

Chapter VIII

Newspaper Laboratory: Athens And The University

The Red And Black

Most newspaper people find several hometowns during their career, as they wander through the industry looking for experience, a pay raise, the right person or the right place.

For perhaps a majority of Georgia journalists in the years since World War II, one of the hometowns has been Athens, where the University of Georgia is located. Some 6,000 aspiring journalists have graduated from the Henry Grady School of Journalism during the past 50 years, and about a fourth of those worked on Georgia newspapers.

Athens is also the annual site of the Georgia Press Institute, held each year since 1928, and the second most important function of the year for Georgia Press Association members, next only to the annual summer convention.

And if you had to select the newspaper which gave more Georgia journalists their first byline, their first chance to write a headline and lay out a page, their first frustration, their first idea of what awaited them in their chosen profession, it would have to be *The Red and Black*, Georgia's student newspaper. It was the classroom where a lot of the state's reporters, editors, ad salespeople and publishers learned the nuts and bolts of the business.

The Red and Black was more demanding in its way than the regular classrooms and more demanding even than the newspapers on which they would work after college days.

Especially in its weekly years, few headlines appeared in *The Red and Black* that had not been rewritten five or six times. Stories also got frequent rewritings, from editors who seldom left *The Red and Black* offices before 5 to 6 a.m. on Tuesday and Wednesday mornings.

In the early 1970s *The Red and Black* went from once-a-week publication to five times a week publication, later cutting back to only four times a week. That provided more students an opportunity to work, and more chance for long hours — and often poor grades — by the editors.

Immediately following World War II, most of the editors of *The Red and Black* were armed services veterans, who were older and often already experienced at working on newspapers. During this time there was very little supervision from the journalism school faculty or from the publications board which each quarter would select the main editors and a business manager. Students were allowed to hold key positions for only one quarter because of the large influx of students brought into the university by the GI Bill. Before World War II the university enrollment had never surpassed 4,000. After World War II it reached a peak of more than 8,000 in 1948 before dropping back during the 1950s. Then in the 1960s enrollment began the surge which would reach 24,000 by 1985.

There was no lack of candidates for the editors' jobs in the post-WWII years, despite the quarterly change of editors, and perhaps at no other time in *The Red and Black's* history did its staff include so many young men and women who would go on to play prominent roles in the communications field.

Staffers and editors in the 1947 to 1956 period included George MacArthur, Spier Collins, Charles Skinner, Marvin Wall, Raleigh Bryans, Rex Edmondson, J. David Cook, Alan Patareau, Millard Grimes, John Pennington, Jim Minter, Dewey Benefield, Mike Edwards, Glenn Vaughn,

Marilyn Johnson Pennington, Chuck Martin, Bill Shipp, Dan Kitchens, Billy Morris, Carroll Dadisman, Walker Lundy and many others.

A dispute between *The Red and Black* and the Georgia Board of Regents over an editorial attacking one of the regents, Roy Harris, led to closer scrutiny by an advisor after 1953 when the entire staff was ousted and new guidelines instituted.

An uneasy relationship existed between *The Red and Black* and its "publisher," who officially was the University president, during the hectic 1960s and 1970s when the Georgia campus, like others, had its days of turmoil. The more liberal and outspoken students gravitated to the editorial positions on *The Red and Black*.

Dr. Fred Davison, University president since 1967, always had a wary attitude toward *The Red and Black*, and not without good reason, since its editors were almost without exception severe critics of Davison and his administration.

Finally, in 1978, Davison became convinced he no longer wanted to be associated with *The Red and Black* in the nominal role of publisher, which exposed him and the University to responsibility for what was printed in the paper. Noting that at many universities of Georgia's size the student newspapers were independent of the University, Davison appointed a committee in 1978 to study the feasibility of placing *The Red and Black* in an independent status, removed from the University's supervision completely, and also from its financial assistance. By that time, although some money still came from student fees, *The Red and Black* was mainly supported by the advertising revenue which it generated. Nevertheless, the newspaper was definitely dependent in many ways on its ties to the University. The university paid its general manager and provided the benefits of a tax-exempt institution.

The committee met off and on for a year-and-a-half, studying the route to independence at other universities. Finally, it issued a report on "how" independence could be achieved but with no recommendation on whether it was the wisest course. That actually was a question for The Board of Regents, on advice from President Davison.

Momentum for independence was obvious, however, when *The Red and Black* offices moved out of the Journalism building into an old bank building on North Jackson Street, across from the campus in a declining downtown Athens.

In September 1980 the Board of Regents approved independence for *The Red and Black* by one vote, 8-7. Nine founding directors were selected as incorporators and formed a non-profit corporation to oversee the independent operation. The Regents stipulated that if the corporation should ever cease to publish *The Red and Black*, the name and assets would revert to the university.

On September 4, the organizational meeting was held of the original directors. They were Bill Fields, formerly of the Atlanta newspapers; Bill Hartman, Athens insurance executive; Millard Grimes, a suburban newspaper publisher who lived in Opelika, Alabama; Frank Hawkins, former Pittsburgh, Pennsylvania, newspaper executive, and at that time a School of Journalism faculty member; Dan Kitchens, School of Journalism; John Ginn, Anderson, South Carolina, newspaper publisher; Ed Stamper, Atlanta newspapers advertising department; Elliott Brack, *Gwinnett Daily News*; and Steve Crabill, general manager of *The Red and Black*.

At the initial meeting, Brack was elected president; Hartman, vice president; and Kitchens, secretary. The initial meeting also authorized a search for a general manager to replace Crabill, who had resigned.

The search led to Charles Russell, a former student advertising manager of *The Red and Black*, who came to the new post from the advertising staff of the *Orlando Star-Sentinel*.

On May 29, 1981, three more persons were added to thc board of directors of the corporation. They were Dewey Benefield of Sea Island; Adelaide Ponder, editor of *The Madisonian* in Madison; and Helen Strickland, Abraham Baldwin Junior College faculty advisor for the student newspaper. In 1983, Bill Krueger and Kathy Davis-Tucker, two recent graduates of the University, became board members.

In a letter to President Davison in 1981, the corporation cited the overall progress of independence of the newspaper. In the fiscal year before independence, the newspaper's gross income had been less than $200,000. In 1980-81, revenues rose to $265,000; then to $336,000 for 1981-82; and reached $363,400 for 1982-83.

The increase in revenue was fortunate because expenses kept pace. Operating profits were very small each year. Additional expenses after independence included the paying of the minimum wage to every student who worked on *The Red and Black*, a change from the status while linked to the University when only a few staff members were paid.

A full-time general manager also had to be paid, and later full-time paid positions were added for an advertising manager and a bookkeeper. The University had previously paid the general manager, who was part of the administration.

Bill Krueger was the editor during the year 1979-80, and supervised the move from the journalism building and the beginning stages of independence. Brian O'Shea was editor for the year 1980-81, the first full year of independence, and Linda Spikes was advertising director.

Russell and the board felt that a full year was too much of a load on a student editor, and beginning in the fall of 1981, editors were elected for the fall quarter, the winter-spring quarters, and then one for the summer. Justin Gillis served as editor in fall, 1981; Mack Browning was editor for winter-spring, 1982; and David Nelson was editor in fall, 1982. Chuck Reece, who had been summer editor twice, made it a full four quarters in that position by serving as editor in winter-spring, 1983.

Krueger, now a member of *The Red and Black* board, became a reporter on the *Raleigh, North Carolina Times* and *Observer*; O'Shea went with Associated Press; Ms. Spikes is an advertising accountant with the *Atlanta Journal-Constitution*; Gillis is a reporter with the *Miami Herald*; Browning is with the Columbus, Georgia, *Ledger-Enquirer*. They were the students who were most involved with the change to independence, and in the process, they had to become concerned with more aspects of *The Red and Black* than any previous student executives.

All composing and page paste-up was done at the Athens office, requiring a large production staff and upgrading of equipment. The printing is awarded by bid every other year and has been done at Walton Press in Monroe, some 25 miles from Athens, since 1981. Pages are carried to the plant about midnight, and the paper is printed between six and seven the following morning for distribution on campus by 9 a.m.

The student editor and advertising manager are selected by *The Red and Black* Board of Directors, and the editor and ad manager in turn select the other student managers and editors. In years past, the publications board had named all sub-editors as well, although usually on the recommendation of the previous and incoming editor.

An annual banquet for *The Red and Black* was reinstated in May 1981, a throwback to the long-time tradition of a quarterly beer party at Charlie Williams' Lodge at which awards were given and new editors announced.

The latest banquets, usually held in motel banquet rooms, are more formal — but not much. Cash awards were added in 1982 to reward staff members whose work is judged most outstanding in selected categories. Speakers at these banquets have included Bill Shipp, associate editor of *The Atlanta Constitution*; Reg Murphy, publisher of *The Baltimore Sun* papers; and Carroll Dadisman, publisher of *The Tallahassee Democrat*.

As an independent paper, *The Red and Black* has definitely grown in advertising volume, and by most accounts has improved in quality. Its relations with President Davison have not improved much, however, and its relations with the University in general remain strained. The Administration, with some cause, feels *The Red and Black* does not adequately report on the positive side of the University, especially its academic progress. *The Red and Black*, on the other hand, is proud of its expose of asbestos in many campus buildings which is now being removed as a possible health hazard and several of its recent editors have concentrated on the University's failure to attract enough black students and black faculty members. *The Red and Black*, however, has had only one black staff member — an ad sales person — in recent years and no black news staffers.

In the fall of 1983, Russell resigned as general manager after serving for three years to accept a job as retail advertising manager of *The Pensacola Journal-News* in Florida. Russell told the board that his goal had been to put *The Red and Black* on sound financial ground and he felt that was accomplished. "I've never thought I could make *The Red and Black* a career for Charles Russell," he added.

Russell, a 1979 graduate of the University, played a unique role in Georgia journalism, being the general manager — or publisher — who led *The Red and Black* through three crucial years in which it had to prove that it could indeed provide its own financial support without the anchor of the University. In addition, Russell had the task of convincing the students of their additional responsibility in working for a newspaper "on its own," fully responsible for its content. Russell was succeeded by Harry Montevideo, a University of Florida graduate, who had been business manager of Florida's independent student paper.

The Red and Black is now roughly equivalent to a competitive daily newspaper in the Athens market, and the Athens market is a crowded one for people who must sell advertising to stay in business.

The Banner-Herald, 150 Years Plus

Legend had it that Athens, then just a village, was selected as the site of the University of Georgia in 1801 because there was a tavern in nearby Watkinsville, the first choice, and the trustees did not want students too close to such an establishment. So Athens got the University and Watkinsville got an historic structure in the Eagle Tavern.

The many grand old homes still standing in Athens are evidence that it was a substantial community throughout the nineteenth century, but it still remained a relatively small city as late as World War II. The 1920 census showed a population of 26,000 for Clarke County, which at 125 square miles, is the state's smallest county in area. By 1980 the population (which includes students) had grown to 74,498, an impressive jump in comparison with other non-metro counties, although not in the same league with its neighbors to the west in the Atlanta suburbs. Industries moved into Clarke county after World War II, providing some impetus for growth, but the main growth, of course, resulted from the rise in enrollment and personnel at the university. Even Watkinsville, after 184 years, is finally benefiting from the university as population spills over into Oconee County, boosting its population from 7,900 in 1970 to 12,424 in 1980.

The most striking evidence of how highly retail businesses regard Athens and its potential is Georgia Square Shopping Mall on the Atlanta Highway, about seven miles from downtown. It is the largest mall in Georgia outside of metropolitan Atlanta, even though Clarke County has less than half the population of such counties as Bibb, Chatham, Muscogee and Richmond.

As the state's cultural center, Athens would be expected to have good newspapers throughout its history, since the audience is more highly-educated and literate. Its oldest newspaper — and one of the state's oldest — is the *Athens Banner-Herald*, which traces its origins to the *Southern Banner*, founded in 1832. The *Banner-Herald* published an impressive and informative 150th anniversary edition on February 28, 1982, which contained reproductions of many front pages and stories from throughout those years, as well as giving information on the several newspapers which have been published in Athens.

The *Banner* withstood several challenges from other newspapers and then merged with the afternoon *Herald* in 1921. Earl B. Braswell became publisher of the *Athens Banner-Herald* and held that position for forty-four years, until the sale of the *Banner-Herald* in 1965 to Billy and Charles Morris.

Braswell was a native of Lithonia and his first newspaper job was on the *Fitzgerald Leader* at $3 a week. He eventually became managing editor of the *Augusta Herald*, then owned by Bowdre Phinizy, who also owned the *Athens Banner*. When the *Herald* and *Banner* merged in 1922, Phinizy asked his young managing editor to go to Athens and become the publisher.

During Braswell's long tenure, the *Banner-Herald* was a solid but undistinguished newspaper for the state's leading cultural city. Its circulation reached about 7,000 in its best years, which was low for a county of Clarke's population and reader potential. It had little readership among students and made no strong effort to circulate in the counties to the north which were served on a daily basis mainly by the Anderson, South Carolina, *Independent*.

Braswell served one term on the Board of Regents and was instrumental in preventing the relocation of some university schools, notably the pharmacy school, from Athens to Atlanta.

A number of notable journalists worked on *The Banner-Herald*. Ed Pope became sports editor when he was only sixteen, and received nationwide publicity for being the youngest sports editor of a daily newspaper in the nation. Later he was a sports writer for *The Journal-Constitution* and then sports editor of *The Miami Herald*. Other sports editors included Dan McGill and Loran Smith, later both with The University of Georgia in several capacities; F. M. Williams, who became a newspaper legend in Tennessee; John Bradberry, a future sports editor of *The Atlanta Constitution*, and Guy Tiller, a top writer on *The Atlanta Journal* for many years.

Ed Thilenius, the radio voice of The Bulldogs in the 1950s and 1960s, was a *Banner-Herald* city editor, as were George Abney and Ernie Hynds, both later on the faculty of the Grady School. Hynds is also the author of a book on American newspapers.

The *Banner-Herald* relied heavily on its wire service in those days and ran few photos, which was not unusual for small dailies in pre-cold type years. It was not a bad newspaper but it did little out of the ordinary, and Athens seemed to deserve something better. The *Banner-Herald*, in its 150th anniversary edition, described the paper of that time as playing the role of "a newspaper of record."

But something out of the ordinary was definitely coming to Athens. Beginning in 1965, it became one of the liveliest newspaper battlegrounds in the South, and the newspapers which emerged would be among the finest in the state, in both content, technology, advertising endeavor, and perhaps most important of all, in discovering better ways to use the cold type and offset methods which were just beginning to make an impact throughout the state, a full ten years after Charles Hardy printed the first cold type paper in Gainesville.

The *Athens Daily News*, Offset Pioneer

The changes started when Claude Williams, a newspaper and radio ad salesman in Athens and Gainesville for many years, converted a shopper into a weekly newspaper in 1963. He called it *The Athens Advertiser*, and it was livelier in nearly every way than the staid, virtually unchanging *Banner-Herald*. Mainly, it had lots of photos, sharply reproduced, printed on an offset press. By 1965, *The Advertiser* was running 12 to 16 pages a week and was well-received in the community but had not made a big breakthrough in advertising.

It was generally known in newspaper circles that Bowdre Phinizy's will stated that *The Banner-Herald* could not be sold until at least five years after his widow's death. Mrs. Phinizy had died in 1960 which meant that *The Banner-Herald* might be for sale in 1965. Braswell by now was in his mid-70s, and there were many potential suitors for *The Banner-Herald*, which was in an attractive market, from both a business and news standpoint, and was regarded as not having fully developed its place in that market.

Williams, already having a toehold in the market with *The Athens Advertiser*, felt that he should make a serious move toward challenging *The Banner-Herald* before it was sold, and perhaps put his company in a position to be the buyer. Others had similar thoughts. One of them was Millard Grimes, then editor of *The Columbus Enquirer*, who happened to see a copy of *The Advertiser* at the Center for Continuing Education while attending the Georgia Press Institute in February 1965. He contacted Williams and they met to discuss the possibility of turning *The Advertiser* into a daily.

In 1961, Grimes had explored a similar possibility and talked to several Columbus businessmen about financing the venture. Now, four years later, the venture seemed to make more sense. He and Williams quickly found a financial backer — and, in fact, the only one in the first years of the new paper's existence — in Charles McClure, who owned several radio stations, including one in Columbus. McClure and Williams had once been in the radio business together in Athens. In March, with an initial investment of $75,000, most of it borrowed on McClure's credit, Williams ordered a 12-page Goss offset press, and rented a building at 233 West Hancock, near Athens First Baptist Church. The wheels were finally in motion for a new daily newspaper in Athens — and the first real challenge to *The Banner-Herald* since 1922. Grimes was planning to resign as editor in Columbus and move to Athens to be editor and publisher and help Williams run the paper. But in April, Grimes had a change of heart — or perhaps feet is the more precise term. His heart was still warm for the venture but his feet got cold. (See Chapter V.)

Fortunately, an able substitute was available in Glenn Vaughn, then managing editor of *The Columbus Ledger*, who also had long relished the chance to launch a new paper, especially in Athens, where he had attended college, met his wife, and where he felt there was a serious need for a more imaginative and progressive newspaper.

As it turned out, Vaughn and Williams were an ideal team for the difficult years ahead in which they would produce a newspaper that was the first in Georgia to take full advantage of offset's potential.

Williams and Grimes had already decided to call the new paper *The Athens Daily News* and to put the University of Georgia arch in the middle of the page one flag. They planned it first as an afternoon publication which would compete head on with *The Banner-Herald* in a battle for circulation which would produce one clear winner. They did not feel Athens was a market which could long support two separately-owned daily newspapers (and they had the Gainesville example of 1955 to guide them). Grimes, in particular, felt that a morning paper would be much more difficult to produce because of the night schedule, and also, that it would not be as effective in reducing *The Banner-Herald's* circulation, which he felt was necessary for *The Daily News* to prevail.

But Williams and Vaughn later decided to take the more judicious route of a morning newspaper, hoping that there were enough potential readers for a local morning paper to gain a large circulation without having to depend on taking afternoon readers away from *The Banner-Herald*.

The all caps banner headline in the June 2, 1965, edition of *The Athens Advertiser* read: "Advertiser To Begin Daily Morning Paper." Williams and Vaughn's pictures accompanied the story which reported that the first daily issue would be on June 14 and that a 12 page Goss press was being installed. The new *Athens Daily News* would be published Tuesday through Sunday mornings. That edition of *The Advertiser* had its usual 16 pages, and Williams and Vaughn felt they would have to publish a minimum of 80 pages a week to be a legitimate daily. Perhaps more ominous was the fact that *The Advertiser* had only 400 bona fide paid subscribers.

The venture was starting on a financial shoestring. McClure had actually put up only $17,000 in cash to match what was ascertained to be the value of *The Advertiser*, which was Williams' contribution. Vaughn was granted 12 percent of the stock in the form of bonuses and commissions, with McClure and Williams having 44 percent each.

The first person Vaughn hired for the news staff was Gerald Rutberg, an Auburn student he had interviewed for a summer internship while still at *The Columbus Ledger*. Next, he approached Wade Saye, *The Banner-Herald's* sports editor. Saye had returned to his native Athens after a stint as an United States Air Force officer and was earning $50 per week at *The Banner-Herald*. Vaughn offered him $100 per week, which persuaded him to defect. That not only got the attention of *The Banner-Herald* management, but it also demonstrated to the community that the new paper was serious. The final edition of *The Advertiser* bannered the defection of Saye to *The Daily News*.

To fill out the sports staff, Vaughn hired an 18-year-old University of Georgia freshman named Lewis Grizzard, who apologized for needing a shave. He started at $1 per hour.

Next to be hired was Larry Young, who had been a reporter for *The Augusta Chronicle*, but was down on his luck at the time and in need of a job. He had a reputation for moving around, but he would eventually be the only member of the original staff left on *The Daily News*. Young provided a perpetual air of excitement which the young staff, mostly students, quickly were caught up in and which was a good fit for Vaughn's "let's-do-it" philosophy. Young was a prolific writer, with a special talent for developing news sources.

The Athens Daily News was launched in an agonizingly slow fashion. The first issue of the morning paper did not come off the press until 1 p.m. on Thursday, June 17, some ten hours late. But it started with a scoop. Banner lines across the front proclaimed that President Lyndon Johnson was flying to nearby Winder that day to attend the funeral of Judge Robert Russell, nephew of Johnson's good friend, U.S. Senator Richard B. Russell.

The Daily News' masthead contained a line in small type, "formerly *The Athens Advertiser*." This was to prove very important in the struggle ahead.

That first issue of *The Daily News* had 14 pages. Larry Young wrote the lead story on President Johnson's visit, and also took the ten photos carried of the event. (In one of the photos is the Rev. Claude McBride, who later became a columnist for *The Daily News*, and in 1983 joined the staff of the University Alumni Office.)

A Georgia Datelines column ran down the first two columns of the front page and an "Around the World" roundup column of news was on page two. Sports started on page three. The editorial page carried UPI columns and Sydney Harris, the syndicated columnist, a favorite of Grimes who signed him up in the early planning.

On the editorial page, Vaughn wrote: "Our goal is to produce a daily newspaper that will be equal to this magnificent community . . . I have full confidence in the business success of *The Daily News*, but I would be less than honest if I didn't admit to being a bit frightened by the unusually knowledgeable Athens audience."

There were four supermarket ads, offering hope that support would be coming from that important source. Harold Powers was ad manager, with Williams providing help in that department. Williams was listed in the masthead as president and general manager, with Vaughn listed as editor and publisher. After a shaky start with two others, Cecil Dill came as head pressman. Julian Maddox was circulation manager, later succeeded by Roy Holliday.

Vaughn kept *The Athens Daily News* mostly local with national and international news from United Press International pretty much confined to briefs on pages one and two. On one occasion then-*Gainesville Times* Editor Sylvan Meyer dropped by to comment: "Gee, you fellows sure carry a lot of local news; how many reporters do you have?" To which Claude Williams replied: "One." Larry Young was, in fact, the only full-time news reporter.

The Daily News covered things that *The Banner-Herald* probably didn't even consider newsworthy, such as a story on the front page for several days running about reports that a black bear had been sighted in East Athens; the front page treatment given the death of Athens' legendary madam, Effie Matthews ("Prominent Businesswoman Dies," the headline said); the story which squelched the widespread rumor that seeress Jean Dixon had predicted the University Coliseum would collapse on that year's graduating class ("Let's Stop That Rumor," the banner line read).

Williams, like Vaughn, welcomed new ideas, and was a major stabilizing influence in the newspaper's success. Although he left editorial and news policies strictly to Vaughn, he managed financial affairs with a cool-headedness which totally belied *The Daily News*' fragile position. The company never missed a payroll.

Another individual who played a major role in *The Daily News* operation was Vaughn's wife, Nancy. Her first job was the organization of the classified section. Then she took over the women's section, producing up to six pages on some days, more than many newspapers with larger staffs. She, almost as much as her husband Glenn, was responsible for creating the special flair which *The Daily News* achieved.

In its thirty-first issue, on Wednesday, July 21, *The Daily News* had the biggest story of its short history. At least it ran the biggest headline to that time on the story. It read: "Augusta-Savannah Syndicate Buys Athens Banner-Herald."

The subhead was: "Evening Paper Brings Whopping $1.7 million in Augusta Sale." Obviously, *The Daily News* editors wanted to bear down on the fact that people from Augusta and Savannah would now control the other daily in Athens.

Williams, Vaughn and McClure had known that *The Banner-Herald* would be sold within the year and had even feared that there might be a hurry-up sale earlier in the spring when word got out that a competitive daily was being planned. Safely past that danger, they had hoped to have at least several months to establish *The Daily News* as a legitimate force in the Athens market so that it would have to be considered by either the sellers of *The Banner-Herald* or the buyers. But the sale came just 32 days after the first issue of *The Daily News* and before it had become a proven commodity, either in circulation or as an advertising competitor.

According to the story in *The Daily News*, bids had been taken on *The Banner-Herald* by the trustees of the Phinizy estate. The high bidders were William (Billy) S. Morris III and Charles Morris, who bought the paper as individuals. Their bid amounted to $1,708,217, the story said, although the assets of *The Banner-Herald* included several hundred thousand dollars cash on hand which reduced the actual sales price.

Under terms of the Phinizy will, the proceeds were to be used to establish trust funds to benefit the Medical College of Georgia at Augusta and University Hospital in Augusta.

Others who either bid or expressed interest in bidding on the paper included Peyton Anderson, publisher of the Macon newspapers; Charles Smithgall, chairman of *The Gainesville Times*; and an Athens group headed by H. Randolph Holder, an Athens radio station executive.

An interesting sidelight to the sale of *The Banner-Herald* was a tentative attempt to bid on the paper by the Georgia Press Association. At its summer meeting a few weeks earlier, the press association approved a resolution for a committee to make a feasibility study on the possible purchase of *The Banner-Herald* by the GPA.

Glenn McCullough, executive manager of the GPA at the time, felt that *The Banner-Herald* could be operated by the GPA as a money-making project and also as a training ground for university students. Included in this plan was moving the GPA offices from Atlanta to Athens. The GPA was located at that time in offices at Georgia State University.

One of the first moves the Morris brothers made after closing the deal for *The Banner-Herald* was to contact Williams and Vaughn with an offer to buy *The Daily News*. The offer (a modest one, Vaughn recalls) was turned down, and the real battle of newspapers in Athens was about to begin.

Several months later *The Daily News* got word that Braswell was unhappy with the treatment he was getting at *The Banner-Herald* in his new role as publisher emeritus. Braswell was asked to pay for the car the company customarily provided him and had been shunted away in a tiny office in the back.

Vaughn and Williams decided to offer Braswell a position as executive editor of *The Daily News*, pay him $50 per week, give him access to a secretary and allow him to do a Sunday column. Delighted with the attention, Braswell, who had done very well financially with the sale of his shares of stock in *The Banner-Herald*, accepted.

The Braswell move extracted an important and deep local root from *The Banner-Herald*. In the eyes of many Athenians, *The Daily News* then became the real local paper. Also, it was locally-owned, with Williams and Vaughn having the majority of stock.

It turned out that among Earl Braswell's close friends were the sheriff, the Clerk of Court and the Judge of Ordinary. Those were the three individuals who had the responsibility of determining the legal organ for Clarke County.

At the time The Daily News started, The Athens Advertiser had about 400 paid subscribers. The *Daily News* was considered to be a continuation of *The Advertiser* and, therefore, met the two-year qualification period for becoming a legal organ. In rather short order, *The Daily News* became the legal organ, further strengthening its status as *the* local paper.

The Daily News brought a fresh new approach to newspaper journalism in Georgia. It was filled with local pictures, many of them in the earliest days provided at cost by the late John Renka, who was associated with Bridges Funeral Home. Later Browny Stephens, whom Vaughn thought was the best newspaper photographer in the South, joined *The Daily News* staff, and the paper's outstanding photo coverage drew plaudits far and wide.

Sports coverage was thorough, right down to the Little League level. It also helped that first year that both the University of Georgia and Athens High School had exciting football seasons. Athens High, led by quarterback Paul Gilbert, who would later be a starter for Georgia, won the North Georgia championship and played perennial powerhouse Valdosta High for the state championship.

The Daily News' headline before the game read: "Okay, Valdosta, You're Next."

Unfortunately, the Valdosta coaches saw a copy of that paper and pasted the headline all over the Valdosta dressing room in an attempt to fire up the players against Athens.

Grizzard covered the championship game for *The Daily News*. Years later he not only remembered the score and the disappointing defeat — 14-13 in favor of Valdosta — but remembered that Chuck Perry, a mail room employee of *The Daily News* who was still in high school, missed the extra point that would have tied the game. Perry later was a news executive for *The Atlanta Journal* and then chief editor and vice-president of Peachtree Publishers in Atlanta which has produced all of Grizzard's books as well as other national and regional best sellers.

Soon *The Athens Daily News* dubbed itself "The People Paper" and Athens artist Don Smith developed an outstanding promotion on the "people paper" theme. So popular was a radio jingle that school children were singing, "the people paper is the paper people pick."

Other Georgia newspaper professionals liked *The Daily News*, also. The first year it was eligible to compete in the Georgia Press Association's Better Newspaper Contest, *The Daily News* received more awards than any other newspaper, large or small, including the coveted Community Service First Place Award for its efforts in getting a new state park developed at Watson's Mill Bridge near Comer, Georgia.

After the awards sweep, Don Smith developed a full page promotion ad which read: "Even Paper People Pick the People Paper."

Aggressive, yet friendly and accommodating, *The Daily News* in its relatively short life as an independent newspaper (a little more than 30 months) chalked up an impressive string of editorial victories. These included saving the Brumby House, Athens' oldest residence, from being torn down; expanding the school board (a measure *The Banner-Herald* opposed), and helping pass a sweeping local bond issue.

In the 1966 Democratic primary, *The Daily News* was the first of only two dailies in the state that endorsed Jimmy Carter for governor, the other being the Cartersville *Tribune News*. Carter came in third but was first in Clarke County. *The Daily News* supported Ellis Arnall in the runoff, which Lester Maddox won, but Arnall easily carried Clarke County. In the general election, *The Daily News* supported Howard (Bo) Callaway, who ended up losing the election (in the legislature) but carried Clarke County.

The Daily News also took on a heavy-handed Civil Service Board which controlled the Athens Police and Fire Departments and forced the board to reverse a decision it made on appointing an unpopular fire chief.

But *The Daily News* became best known for its coverage of football with its emphasis on the color, excitement and exceptional photos. As it was with any big story, the entire staff turned to the task supporting the efforts of Wade Saye, Lewis Grizzard, Johnny Futch and Browny Stephens. Streamer lines, in 96 point type, captured the prevailing spirit. This Larry Young headline is an example: "Hot Diggity Dog, Mr. Dooley, You Have Wrecked Ole Tech Again."

By the time *The Daily News* had been operating 18 months, it passed *The Banner-Herald* in ad linage, and after its second year of operation, it squeaked into the black. However, by this time both McClure and Williams had extended their personal debt positions to the limit. The shoestring start-up meant they both had to borrow a good deal just to meet payrolls in those first two years.

Besides owing for the press and other equipment on which monthly payments were being made, the *Daily News* owed the Fourth National Bank of Columbus $135,000 and the C and S Bank of Athens $35,000. While the *Daily News* had a small operating profit, it could not begin to remove the debt pressure from Williams and McClure.

About this time, William T. Heard, operator of Bill Heard Chevrolet in Columbus, the state's largest dealership, assumed responsibility for most of the debts in exchange for 44 percent of the *Daily News* stock with Williams and McClure each relinquishing 22 percent.

With Heard's infusion of staying power, the *Daily News*' bargaining position was considerably strengthened at a time when the Morrises were again making an effort to buy the increasingly competitive morning newspaper.

During one marathon negotiating session at Athens' old Georgia Hotel, the *Daily News* group offered to buy the *Banner-Herald* for $2 million or sell the new morning paper for $1 million. The session ended in a stalemate.

Representing the *Daily News* at the marathon session, which Vaughn recalls as being punctuated by periods of fishing stories, tensions and long silences, were Heard, Williams, McClure and Vaughn. On the *Banner-Herald* side were Billy and Charlie Morris, Beverly Carter, then *Augusta Chronicle-Herald* general manager and now president and general manager of the *Miami Herald*, plus a stockbroker member of the Morris board.

When negotiations broke down, Bill Heard, who had the financial resources to do so, seemed ready to continue the newspaper battle indefinitely. However, some time after that, and for reasons which were never made public, Heard became disenchanted with his *Daily News* involvement and asked "to be restored to his former position." McClure arranged through Columbus connections to assume responsibility for the accumulated *Daily News* debts and in the process wound up controlling 66 percent of the stock.

McClure then struck a deal with the Morrises at an airport meeting in Macon. It is not clear whether the Morrises were aware that Heard was no longer a part of *The Daily News* ownership.

Before final action could come about on the proposed acquisition of *The Daily News*, the U.S. Justice Department's anti-trust division had to be satisfied that the two competing dailies could not continue on their own. A University of Georgia professor had gotten wind of the proposed merger and had alerted the Feds, who finally approved the sale after an investigative visit to Athens.

The Morrises agreed to pay $443,000 for *The Daily News* plus assume its considerable debts. Billy Morris later commented that *The Daily News* purchase was "the best bargain he ever got."

The sale was announced in the 1967 Christmas Eve issue of *The Daily News*. It was a sad day for a valiant staff who did what couldn't be done, which was starting a competing daily newspaper on a financial shoestring and making it work for nearly three years. An incredible team spirit consumed every *Daily News* employee, Vaughn recalled. There was understandable disappointment among some of the staffers because they did not share in proceeds from the sale.

Whatever the task, everybody had pitched in to make *The Daily News* go. For example, Robert C. (Bob) Fort, now with Norfolk-Southern Railroad, recalls being assigned by *The Banner-Herald* to cover a school board meeting and being shocked to see Publisher Vaughn there covering the meeting for *The Daily News*. It was also quite common for everyone to pitch in to insert papers, which with limited press capacity became a daily affair.

A legendary Georgia journalist who became involved in the Athens newspaper wars was Billy Dilworth. Dilworth has worked for the Anderson, South Carolina, *Independent*, the short-lived *Atlanta Times* and the Athens newspapers, but has always lived at his rural home at Red Hill, near Carnesville, Georgia.

In 1965, Dilworth became the featured columnist for *The Atlanta Times*. When the *Times* folded in August 1965, competition between *The Daily News* and *Banner-Herald* was just heating up, and Vaughn offered Dilworth a position. He said he would think it over.

The next time Vaughn saw Dilworth was at an evening civic club meeting at which Athens Congressman Robert Stephens was to speak. It was a relatively small group and Vaughn noticed that soon after they greeted each other, Dilworth disappeared.

When the meeting was over, Dilworth suddenly appeared at the walkway outside and told Vaughn he had accepted a position with *The Banner-Herald* and therefore didn't want Vaughn to see that he was covering Stephens' speech for the competition before he could announce it face-to-face. Dilworth had taken notes on the speech from the kitchen, listening through a cracked door into the dining room.

When the two Athens newspapers were merged, Dilworth was switched to the morning *Daily News* to take better advantage of his popularity throughout northeast Georgia. For many years, Dilworth has hosted a country music program each Saturday from 9 a.m. to 5 p.m. in Toccoa. He probably knows more country music personalities than anyone else in the South.

After the sale, Vaughn remained as editor of *The Daily News* for a little more than a year. He then returned to Columbus to become editor of *The Enquirer*, succeeding Millard Grimes who had put together a group to purchase the Opelika, Alabama, *Daily News*. Eventually Vaughn would become president and publisher of the Columbus newspapers.

Some of the young newspaper talents who got a start on *The Athens Daily News* included Chuck Perry, Jim Wooten, Colleen Kelly Teasley, Johnny Futch, Sharon Bailey and Lewis Grizzard, all later with Atlanta Newspapers, Inc.

Wade Saye was later editor of *The Columbus Enquirer* and an associate editor of the Knoxville, Tenn. newspaper. Larry Young retired after 17 years on *The Daily News*, most of them as associate editor. Browny Stephens had a variety of positions, including editor of *The Poultry Times* in Gainesville. Claude Williams operates a vastly expanded Georgia Outdoor Advertising Company based in Athens. Charles A. McClure, owner of several radio stations, still is based in Columbus. Among other notable *Daily News* staffers were Harold Powers, now with Georgia Outdoor in Athens and Mark Smith, now advertising director for *The Daily News* and *Banner-Herald*. Gerald Rutberg graduated from the University of Georgia Law School and is a practicing attorney in Casselberry, Florida, outside Orlando.

Years later, when he had become one of the nation's most popular newspaper columnists, Grizzard immortalized Rutberg, whom he met while working on *The Daily News*, as "a man who can do anything." The column mainly referred to Rutberg's ability to get tickets to the Sugar Bowl game between Georgia and Penn State the day before the game. Grizzard's 1983 best-selling book, *If Love Were Oil, I'd Be About a Quart Low*, is in part about his first wife, who was a receptionist for *The Daily News*, and includes his own experiences on *The Daily News*.

The Banner-Herald, of course, was not standing still during its three-year struggle against *The Daily News*. As soon as the Morrises bought the paper, they began upgrading it in people, plant and promotion.

Braswell was replaced as publisher by another former *Augusta Herald* managing editor, William C. (Bill) Bailes. Bailes, 35 at the time, had the task of revamping *The Banner-Herald*, while warding off the aggressive morning competitor.

He also had to oversee the conversion of *The Banner-Herald* to cold type and offset printing, and the moving of the operation from the 46-year-old building at Thomas and Hancock to One/Press Place, another old building which had been completely remodeled for a newspaper plant.

Bailes strengthened and expanded *The Banner-Herald* staff with such people as Dilworth, a popular writer in northeast Georgia; Steve Mitchell, who became managing editor; Steve Teasley, who replaced Saye as sports editor and would move on to become editor of the Sun papers in DeKalb County; and young talents such as Coke Ellington, Bob Fort and most importantly, Robert W. Chambers.

In early 1967, N. S. (Buddy) Hayden was brought in as associate editor. Hayden, originally from Miami, had been publisher of the weekly *Hartwell Sun*. He was at the start of one of the nation's most adventurous newspaper careers.

When Bailes tragically and unexpectedly died a few months later of a heart attack at the age of 37, Hayden was named publisher of *The Banner-Herald*. This happened about the time the Morrises were in the process of buying *The Daily News*. As noted earlier, that deal was consummated and announced on Christmas Eve, 1967, and Hayden was named publisher of both Athens daily newspapers.

The decision was made to continue publishing both a morning and evening newspaper although Athens was relatively small for two newspapers under the same ownership. The combined circulation of *The Banner-Herald* and *Daily News* was only about 14,000. But there was a strong feeling that folding the popular *Daily News* would be a mistake and could even open the way for another competitor.

There was plenty of room for growth by the newspapers, especially in the surrounding northeast Georgia counties where the Anderson, South Carolina, *Independent* had long been the most widely circulated daily. The morning *Daily News* was considered the best means for the Athens newspapers to extend circulation into those counties.

The Sunday editions of the two newspapers were combined on March 3, 1968, and a Saturday morning edition for both papers was added in 1975. In 1985, *The Banner-Herald* and *Daily News* were still being published as separate morning and afternoon papers, with a 1984 combined circulation of 22,000. Athens is the smallest metropolitan area in the South and among the smallest in the nation that still has a morning-afternoon combination.

Hayden led the Athens newspapers through four eventful and successful years. Both advertising and circulation increased, and the two newspapers continued to be trail-blazers in the use of process color and cold type photography, especially for sports.

In early 1972, Hayden left the Athens newspapers to become publisher of the Gannett-owned newspapers in Huntington, West Virginia, which had a combined circulation of 60,000. Hayden later was publisher of *The Oregonian* in Portland, Oregon, and *The Philadelphia Bulletin* in the final months of its struggle to survive as an afternoon daily. Hayden won industry-wide attention for his rescue efforts at *The Bulletin*, particularly in gaining agreement for wage restraints by employees, but the forces long in motion against *The Bulletin* proved too strong and *The Bulletin* finally went under. Afternoon competition from suburban newspapers and television, plus the strength of the morning competition were blamed.

After *The Bulletin* folded, Hayden was named president of *The Los Angeles Herald-Examiner*, another afternoon newspaper in a competitive major market.

When Hayden left the Athens newspapers, his successor was Robert W. Chambers, who had been the executive editor. Chambers, only 31 at the time he became publisher, had little experience on the business side of newspapers, but he was widely credited with transforming *The Banner-Herald* into a formidable competitor for *The Daily News*.

Chambers, an Emory graduate, came to Athens in 1966 from the Augusta newspapers at a time when the outcome of the battle was still uncertain. As managing editor, he changed the format to reflect the new cold type technology and also shifted front page emphasis from wire stories to local to local stories. After the two newspapers came under common ownership, Chambers had the responsibility of maintaining the new product at the level attained under the spur of competition. By the end of the 1960s, Athens had two of the brightest, most innovative newspapers of any city its size, and a large number of Press Association and AP awards attested to that fact each year.

In 1982, Chambers marked his tenth year as publisher in Athens by commissioning an impressive 150th anniversary edition of *The Banner-Herald*, complete with many reproductions of front pages from throughout those years, starting with a page from an 1832 *Southern Banner*, the original forerunner of *The Banner-Herald*. Chambers also sponsored a hardback edition called a *Pictorial History of Athens*, which was made available to readers and contained hundreds of photos of Athens and its people from the past 125 years. It was compiled and written by James Reap.

But despite having morning and afternoon newspapers that were considered among the best of their size in the South, plus a four-day campus newspaper, Athens spawned another weekly newspaper in 1974 which found an audience and enough advertising support to survive. It soon set a standard for weeklies as impressive as the standards *The Banner-Herald* and *Daily News* were setting for dailies.

The Athens Observer

The Athens Observer began as what was popularly known in the 1960s and 1970s as an "alternative newspaper," implying it was an alternative to the established daily or weekly in the community and usually meaning that it stressed an anti-establishment viewpoint. Georgia did not harbor many such publications. Atlanta's *Great Speckled Bird* was perhaps the best known, but it soon flew away along with the large hippie community that once sprawled along a stretch of Peachtree Street.

The Observer's founders, two of whom had once been arrested during a sit-in in the office of University President Fred Davison, didn't really think their newspaper was a protest or part of a mission. They just wanted to start a newspaper, and to prove they didn't know much about it, they launched the paper in the first week of January, which anyone familiar with the business could have told them is the start of the worst eight weeks of the year for newspapers.

The first issue of *The Athens Observer* came off the press January 3, 1974, financed by a $900 loan co-signed by Charles M. (Chuck) Searcy and Rollin M. (Pete) McCommons. "From that modest beginning, the loans have grown larger and more numerous through the years," McCommons recalls.

Originally housed in a second-floor one-room art studio, *The Observer* began as an eight-page free-circulation tabloid with a press run of 10,000. The first few issues were printed at *The Hartwell Sun*, but the paper soon moved its printing to Greater Georgia Printers in Crawford, where it has been printed ever since.

Aside from the borrowed capital, there were only a few other assets. Searcy knew how to type fast, and he owned an electric typewriter. McCommons owned a truck.

The first week's ad sales almost matched the printing cost. Salaries could not be afforded.

Wayne Nail, head of production for *The Red and Black* campus newspaper, took one look at the first edition of *The Observer* and came by to share some pointers about layout. Nail ended up becoming a regular production worker. Other friends pitched in and helped with production chores and delivery.

A college student named Don Nelson was a friend of Chuck's. Don broke his ankle in a construction job accident and while recuperating began helping at the office. During this period, he began calling advertisers, learning production techniques and teaching himself photography. By the time his ankle had healed, Nelson had made himself indispensable. Soon a financial crunch came along and Nelson, having some money, became a 24 percent owner in the business.

In the same way, Chatham McCommons, a local artist who lent her studio for the paper to use as offices, also bailed it out at a critical juncture and became a five-percent stockholder. Chatham's cartoons and illustrations have graced *The Observer's* pages since the beginning, contributing to the paper's distinctive graphic style.

The Observer thus caught hold because it was able to attract people who were willing to work for very little remuneration. Since Athens is a college town, talent was abundant and the freely-contributed services were in most cases better than money could buy in many towns.

With little advance planning and no market research, *The Observer* slipped into a niche in the crowded Athens media market. *The Observer* became a truly popular newspaper, widely read on the campus and in the town. Lacking money to pay editorial writers, the paper from the beginning solicited articles of opinion from readers and soon had several who wrote well and regularly.

There was a feeling of openness about the paper, a sense that anyone with something to say could find a forum in *The Observer*. The editors made a concerted effort to avoid any appearance of trying to manipulate public opinion through the newspaper. Thus, although the paper regularly took stands on public issues, it did not endorse political candidates.

After four months of free distribution at restaurants, newsstands, supermarkets, bars, dormitories and classroom buildings, *The Observer* owners decided to move into "total market coverage."

Two men had started a delivery service, and they convinced *The Observer* editors to pay them to distribute the *Observer* to virtually every household in Athens. The two men could not sustain it and quickly went out of business, leaving *The Observer* to follow through on its home delivery commitment. Through the heroic efforts of Anne Brightwell, who oversaw the delivery system involving eight supervisors and around 60 carriers, *The Observer* went on with home delivery, while circulation peaked at around 24,000.

It did not work. *The Observer* was ahead of its time. The large advertisers were not impressed. The costs of printing and delivery took their toll.

"When we finally sat down and did a little cost accounting," Searcy recalled, "we realized we were broke."

The home delivery experiment ended, but during the six months it lasted, *The Observer* introduced itself to everybody in Athens.

"We threw it into every front yard in town," Nelson said, "and it's hard to throw a rolled-up 12-page tab. On windy days it just blew right back at us."

By the time the home-delivery experiment ended, *The Observer* had attained a personality, but it was hard to define. One discount-store advertising manager said he couldn't advertise in a "leftist-rightist" paper.

To some extent that observation was correct, because *The Observer* eschewed political labels and welcomed any well-expressed point of view. Balancing the liberal and radical writings that flowed out of the college atmosphere and from such resident radicals as writer Ed Tant, were early *Observer* stalwarts John Talmadge, retired writer and English professor. Robert West, the retired head of the University's English Department, contributed carefully-reasoned conservative views. If West and Talmadge didn't provide enough ballast for the starboard side, Jack Thomas, a local plumber, gave his own outspoken views every week until he was later hired away by the opposition. Buck Pennington, an erstwhile graduate student, became house gadfly to the arts.

Neither Searcy nor McCommons had any journalism training, though Searcy had some radio news background and a feel for building reader interest. Nelson had taken some introductory journalism courses. When they launched the enterprise, Searcy and McCommons wondered what they would do if the paper's content offended advertisers. They finally decided that if they produced a paper that people read, the advertisers would want to be in it regardless of its content. *The Observer* has pretty much followed that stratagem ever since and has had very little pressure from advertisers.

From the paper's inception, a long period of severe financial uncertainty followed. For most of the first year, the editors could never be sure that the next week's paper would come out. After four months of operation, they borrowed from a private lender enough money to buy a Compuwriter Junior and a 7200 headliner but, of course, had spent half the money just to keep going by the time the equipment arrived.

McCommons recalls the day the machines came. He went out to the sidewalk to see if he could help the driver unload.

"Do you deliver a lot of these?" he asked the driver.

"Yep," the driver replied. "Pick up a lot of them, too."

A popular feature of the early *Observer* was free classified ads, which started slowly and then took off like kudzu, aided by the period of home-delivered market saturation. Before the year was out, *The Observer* started charging $1.00 for the ads, but still their number increased.

The "Closeup" interview also drew readers. Each week a local person was interviewed, and the result was run as a verbatim conversation with the interviewer, edited for length and repetitiveness, but containing only the dialogue spoken. What was sometimes lost through the artlessness of the spoken word was more than returned by the freshness and directness of the interviewee's thoughts unfiltered through a writer's brain.

Each week the paper also did a "Street Poll," in which the editors interviewed four or five people, printing their pictures and their responses to a question about some current issue.

A weekly calendar of events, started by Ron Kilgore, also proved popular.

Typical of *The Observer's* good fortune in being able to attract writers were two who came along in 1975. Jimmy Cornelison was a young local man who, after going broke in the dry cleaning business, had decided that his real ambition was to be a writer. Cornelison liked sports and he agreed to write sports for *The Observer* in return for being allowed to bring in his own desk and electric typewriter. *The Observer* got an instant sports department and a writer whose prose was original and unsullied by any teaching save his own. Cornelison proved so popular *The Observer* finally had to pay him.

Michael Booth, Randy Travis and Ted Smith successively carried on the difficult job of weekly sports-writing in a sports-hungry town.

Also in 1975 William Tate, Dean of Men Emeritus at the University of Georgia, huffed up the steps leading to *The Observer's* second-floor offices and announced that he proposed to write a four-part reminiscence of Athens as it was from 1920 to 1924 when he was a student. Tate said his method of composition would be to take several strolls along primary streets, recalling as he went the houses, people and businesses there during the early 1920s.

The Dean proved a faster talker than walker, and his proposed four episodes grew to 17 weekly installments that were later published by *The Observer* in book form as *Strolls Around Athens*. Thus warmed up, Dean Tate continued to write a weekly column on various subjects for *The Observer* almost literally until the day he died, composing his last submission from the intensive care unit of Athens General Hospital a few days before his death.

Phil Sanderlin was the first paid writer at *The Observer*, and in December 1983 he had been on the staff for nine years. In addition to his general assignment, reporting and feature writing, Sanderlin also writes a highly popular and award-winning weekly humor column and draws a cartoon for the television pages every week.

John Toon was the second reporter hired, and he helped make *The Observer's* reputation for investigative reporting and scrupulously fair attention to factual detail. Toon was with the paper five years before leaving to join the staff of the Advanced Technology Development Center at Georgia Tech.

Toon and Sanderlin held down the reporting until they were finally joined briefly by Lee Shearer, who had for a long time contributed occasional pieces to *The Observer*. Lee was succeeded by Merrill Morris, the first woman reporter on the paper and one who is adept at everything from investigative reporting to light features.

Wayne Nail, who returned to the paper as head of production for several years, was a perfectionist in the habit of biting anyone who, in his presence, made an assumption.

One of Nail's victims was *The Observer's* first professional editor, Phil Williams, whom Nail bit the day Williams came to work. Williams still looks over his shoulder anytime he hazards an assumption.

Williams is typical of the direction *The Observer* has taken as it has evolved from a one-room, everybody-do-everything effort to an urban weekly with a rather highly differentiated staff.

Williams had eight years experience in newspaper work when he came to *The Observer*, and he quickly set about trying to bring organization to what had been an intuitive, hip-pocket operation.

His task was not an easy one, especially because the owners, those same hip-pocket operators, were still around.

The original two Compugraphic machines have been augmented by a two-terminal Compugraphic 8400 multiple component system with interface and modem for off-site feed. No front-end terminal system for reporters is in place as yet, but the capacity is there.

The Observer advertising representatives are more or less in the front trenches, competing as they do against two daily newspapers, a four-day daily on the University campus, numerous radio stations and a plethora of billboards. Because *The Observer* has neither the frequency nor the reach of the shopper-augmented dailies, *The Observer* ad reps have to resell their product every week.

In 1981 *The Observer* bought controlling interest in *The Oconee Enterprise*, a weekly in a neighboring county.

Another *Observer* venture is Observer Television. This is a cable-cast station that began operating on the local cable system March 1, 1983, beginning with cable-text printed messages, including some paid advertising. Observer Television plans to upgrade its offerings gradually to include live and taped local events, news, entertainment and advertising, probably including classified advertising from *The Observer*.

The Athens Observer has through the years been forced to substitute hustle for capital and has had to fight for its gains. In 1977, for instance, the weekly was named county legal organ and had to withstand a legal challenge by the dailies that went all the way to a unanimous Georgia Supreme Court decision in favor of *The Observer*. A change in county officials took the legals back to the dailies in 1983, meaning a loss of some $40,000 a year in revenue for *The Observer.*

The Observer also challenged a University of Georgia decision to withhold a report on personnel difficulties in its mathematics department.

The Observer's attorney, David Griffeth, also took that case to a successful landmark decision in the Georgia Supreme Court.

In its eleventh year of publication, *The Observer* still faces the uncertainty of any weekly published in a city with daily competition. Searcy, who spent two years (1979-1981) in Washington during the Carter Administration as an official of the Small Business Administration, has been mainly involved since 1983 with the television operation, while McCommons and Nelson have carried on at *The Observer*.

The Observer, now broad sheet size, has maintained a steady 10,000 circulation for several years, but the loss of the legal advertising definitely made a dent in the number of pages and the cash flow. About half of its circulation is through the mail and about half is on racks and over the counter; at 35 cents per copy, it is priced higher than any of the dailies circulating in Athens.

Other alternative newspapers, along the lines of *The Observer*, have generally not been successful in Georgia, although comparisons are difficult from city to city and market to market, and there are now several varieties of "second" or alternative papers, such as shoppers and free distribution newspapers, as well as the traditional paid weekly.

Athens, because of its unique characteristics, became virtually a newspaper laboratory during the 20 years from 1965 to 1985, and there is certainly no other city in Georgia which supports morning and afternoon dailies, a four-day independent daily for University students, and a weekly of 10,000 paid circulation which averages 24 to 36 pages. There may not even be another city in the nation that is so well-endowed with newspapers, and when you add the many other magazines, TV and entertainment guides, the *Leonard's Losers* weekly report during football season, *USA Today*, and the strong penetration of the Atlanta dailies, Athens indeed offers a bountiful feast for the inveterate newspaper reader.

In addition, the Athens dailies have a Total Market Coverage (TMC) paper called *The Athens Star* which is distributed to 30,000 homes throughout the northeast Georgia area each Wednesday.

The dailies, *The Red and Black* and *The Observer* all publish special football editions on Saturdays when Georgia has home games, which are distributed free to those attending the game.

The Man Called "Dean"

For most Georgia journalists, memories of the University of Georgia and the Grady School summon to mind one remarkable and unforgettable personality: Dean John Eldridge Drewry.

When he was born in Griffin on June 4, 1902, his parents no doubt named him only "John Eldridge" without the "Dean," but "Dean" became the name by which he was called by virtually all who knew him or studied under him.

He came to the University and its fledgling journalism school as a student, and was the second person to receive its bachelor of journalism degree. He immediately joined the faculty as an instructor in 1922, rising to the rank of professor in 1930 and being named director of the school in 1932 when he was only 29.

As director, and then dean after 1940, he guided the Henry Grady School of Journalism for 37 years, retiring in 1969.

His contributions to state and national journalism, and to education, were numerous, but it was as the droll lecturer and facile coiner of phrases that Dean Drewry became a legend to three generations of students.

Dan Kitchens, a faculty member at the Grady School, wrote of Drewry: "His natural habitat, the place for which he was created, was the lecture hall. It was there that all his talents fused into virtuoso performances that illuminated, inspired, delighted and captivated his audiences.

"One of his favorite truisms was, 'Nothing is work unless you had rather be doing something else.' In that case Dean Drewry never worked a day in his life because his 'work' was a labor of love."

When Drewry died February 11, 1983, an *Atlanta Journal-Constitution* editorial called him "the most important figure in Georgia journalism since Henry Grady."

The editorial continued: "For almost half a century Dean Drewry held court in the journalism school. Showman, stump orator and educator, he entertained and educated thousands. Not uncommonly at the end of the quarter his students gave him standing ovations."

The Red and Black, not noted for lavishing praise on university officials, wrote of Drewry: "The death of Dean John Drewry leaves the J-School without a familiar presence. Let it not leave the school without an inspiration. Drewry, practically alone, built the school into a nationally prominent place to learn journalism. He did that with intense demonstrations of care and concern for students and their fortunes. That legacy should live on in the J-School, and all across the campus Drewry loved."

Drewry was the author of four books, two of them on book reviewing. He was the editor of 26 other books. He began writing a book review column in 1921 which he continued for 61 years, until shortly before his death. He helped found the Georgia Press Institute, the Georgia Scholastic Press Association, the Georgia Collegiate Press Association, the Georgia Radio and Television Institute and the George Foster Peabody Awards.

But it was his unique voice — a voice that gave each word and syllable a full measure of respect and wrung from each rolling phrase the full impact of its meaning — that truly made Dean Drewry unforgettable. His golden tones recalled the orators of an earlier time and might have served him well in politics had he not sounded so erudite, so intellectual, so gently sure of himself, always leavening his lectures with dry humor.

He exuded a poise that seldom wavered. He was, in fact, like a skilled actor, expertly performing his assigned role as the impeccable college dean, but seldom exposing the real personality behind the performance.

This was all the more remarkable since his personal life was not free of tribulation and contained one traumatic episode which threatened his career, and in fact, his life.

During Christmas holidays in 1949, Dean Drewry's former wife of 23 years, whom he had divorced the previous July, entered a private home where Drewry was sitting in the living room with his wife-to-be and fired five shots at them. Three bullets struck Drewry and two struck his fiancée. Fortunately none of their wounds proved fatal although both Drewry and the future Mrs. Drewry were hospitalized; she was in critical condition for several days. Doctors were unable to immediately remove two of the bullets which had lodged in Drewry, but he was released from the hospital within a few days.

Students in Dean Drewry's quarterly class speculated on whether he would be at the lectern when winter quarter began. The shooting had received heavy news play around the state because of Drewry's prominence. But Drewry was on the job the first day of January classes — still with bullets in him — and his wit and smile were as poised and effective as ever, giving no clue of what the person behind the smile had experienced during the past two weeks.

The worst of the publicity was still to come. During Mrs. Drewry's trial she was allowed to give an unsworn statement in which she made lurid accusations against Drewry. In fact, sensational testimony occurred throughout the trial, and *The Atlanta Journal*'s editions delivered in Athens carried eight column, two-line, all capital, banner headlines about the case for several days. That quarter's *Red and Black* editors, seeking to cover some of the fading paint, clipped the huge headlines and pasted them on the walls of the editor's office in the basement of the Commerce-Journalism building. They felt secure since Dean Drewry had seldom been seen in *The Red and Black* offices. They also may have been frustrated by a decision that *The Red and Black* would not run a story on the shooting or the subsequent trial. The decision was made voluntarily by the student editors and there was no official pressure. An editorial in the first *Red and Black* after the shooting stated:

> We realize that students expect *The Red and Black* to mention what has been built into the University's biggest news story of the year — the shooting of Dean Drewry.
>
> For this reason, as well as to get the matter off our chest and have some defense to the inevitable charge that "*The Red and Black* is afraid to touch it," we hereby voice the following sentiments.
>
> We feel that what happens in a man's private life is primarily his own concern as long as it does not affect his public duties. The affair is in the past; President Rogers has quite properly announced that it will not affect the Dean's standing, and we feel that the subject should be dismissed from the wagging tongues of campus gossip mongers.
>
> Interest motivated by morbid curiosity is interest better done without.

The reasoning seemed a bit strained since the shooting of a governor or the University's president would obviously have been of news interest, and at that time Dean Drewry was a more prominent figure in Georgia education than the University president.

In fact, the president, Joseph Rogers, had already announced his retirement for the following summer and Drewry was considered a leading candidate to succeed him in the presidency. The shooting effectively ended that possibility, and thus did influence the course of higher education in the state.

The headlines about the trial and shooting were still on the walls of *The Red and Black* office the following summer when Dean Drewry suddenly appeared at the editor's door one day. *The Red and Black* staffers were horror-struck as the Dean coolly surveyed the room and its wall adornments. He chatted with them briefly about the matter for which he had come, and then as he turned to leave, he smiled and said: "These walls really do need repainting. I'll send the painters down in a few days."

As usual, his performance was flawless.

R. W. (Bill) Bailes Jr. came to Athens as Banner Herald *publisher in 1965. He died two years later at age 37.*

N. S. (Buddy) Hayden succeeded Bailes and later was publisher of both Banner-Herald *and* Daily News *before leaving in 1972.*

Claude Williams Jr. got competition started in Athens with his Athens Advertiser *then founded and was president of* The Athens Daily News.

Wade Saye was subject of a page one banner headline when he defected from Athens Banner-Herald *to* Athens Daily News *to be sports editor.*

Robert W. Chambers was named publisher of The Banner-Herald *and* Daily News *in 1972 at the age of 31. He came up through the news ranks.*

Larry Young was only fulltime reporter on The Daily News *in its early months. He later became associate editor and retired in 1983 after 18 years on Athens newspapers.*

Earl B. Braswell was publisher of Athens Banner-Herald *for 44 years (1921-65). In 1966 he joined the competing* Daily News *in a ceremonial position for $50 a week.*

Deans of Henry Grady School of Journalism

Dean John E. Drewry (1940-69).

Dean Warren Agee (1969-75).

Dean Scott Cutlip (1975-83).

Dean Tom Russell (1983-).

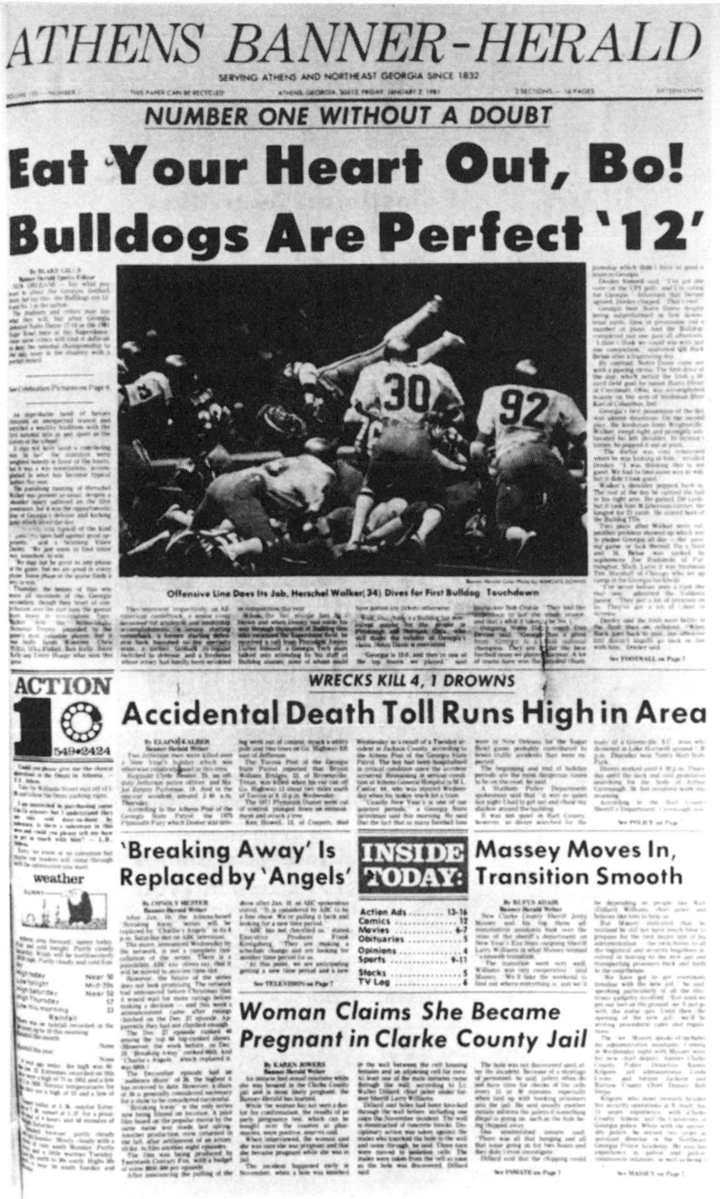

ATHENS BANNER-HERALD

SERVING ATHENS AND NORTHEAST GEORGIA SINCE 1832

NUMBER ONE WITHOUT A DOUBT

Eat Your Heart Out, Bo! Bulldogs Are Perfect '12'

Offensive Line Does Its Job, Herschel Walker(34) Dives for First Bulldog Touchdown

ACTION 10 549•2424

weather

WRECKS KILL 4, 1 DROWNS

Accidental Death Toll Runs High in Area

'Breaking Away' Is Replaced by 'Angels'

INSIDE TODAY:

Action Ads	13-16
Comics	12
Movies	6-7
Obituaries	5
Opinions	4
Sports	9-11
Stocks	3
TV Log	6

Massey Moves In, Transition Smooth

Woman Claims She Became Pregnant in Clarke County Jail

A memorable Banner-Herald *front page, Friday, January 2, 1981, proclaiming Georgia Bulldogs No. 1 in nation after Sugar Bowl victory over Notre Dame.*

THE
ATHENS DAILY NEWS

Formerly The Athens Advertiser — Northeast Georgia's Morning Newspaper

Volume 1, Number 1 — Athens, Ga., June 16, 1965 — 5c

LBJ Flying to Winder Today For Funeral of Judge Russell

Georgia DATELINES

(By United Press International)

Macon: Baby Killed in Auto Crash

Madison: Child Labor Court Order

Augusta: FBI Nabs Holdup Suspect

Atlanta: Matron Found Dead

Macon: Bootle Enjoins Contractor

Decatur: Youth Drowns in Pool

NEW $600,000 CONVALESCENT AND NURSING CENTER ANNOUNCED FOR ATHENS

'Copters Collide; 18 Die In Fiery Georgia Crash

Light Showers Forecast Today

$600,000 Home Set In Athens

Senate Lops Off $4.7 Billion Tax

An Editorial

Strictly A Positive Move

You hold in your hands a newborn daily newspaper. The birth of a new daily is not a common event in these times. A large investment of money, time and effort is necessary. But most important, an opportunity and a need must exist -- a need that is not being filled by another newspaper.

The publishers of The Athens Daily News believe that such a need exists in Athens.

Athens deserves a daily newspaper that is equal in every way to the city itself. Athens is no longer the quiet, college community of two decades ago. It is a city. It is a cultural center of the state. Next to Atlanta, there is not another community in Georgia which exerts such an influence on the affairs and the future of the state.

Athens is the hub of an expanding trade area. Its merchants deserve an appropriate and economical instrument for sending their message to homes in the [illegible] Clarke County for that matter.

The daily newspaper is the best instrument yet discovered for that job.

Athens today is a classical city that looks both to the past and to the future. Its skyscraping dormitories and ultra-modern architecture do not detract from the lovely old homes. The blend merely makes Athens a more delightful and interesting place to live and visit.

A daily newspaper in Athens must be equal in brightness, in quality, in completeness to the city itself. The people of Athens should no more depend on newspapers from other cities than they depend on grocery stores or radio stations in other cities.

Yet, 57 per cent of the homes in Clarke County do not receive a local newspaper. The Athens Daily News hopes to fill that vacuum -- and also to reach into thousands of homes in the Athens trade area.

The News is not AGAINST the existing daily. It is FOR Athens; FOR the University of Georgia, and FOR Northeast Georgia.

Its objectives are simple:

1. To present a complete, accurate, informative and entertaining daily newspaper for the people of Athens and Northeast Georgia.

2. To provide merchants with an effective daily newspaper that carries their message to a majority of the families of Clarke County, to good circulation among the 12,000 students at the University and in the surrounding counties.

Newspapers from Atlanta, Gainesville, and Anderson, S. C. go into many homes of this area, carrying the merchants' advertising from those cities. The Athens merchants need a medium to effectively tell their story.

The Athens Daily News proposes to be that medium -- to fill the need.

Athens' total income per year shows that retail sales should be much greater than they are. We believe that the answer lies in attracting more area trade to Athens stores. That can best be done through a strong daily newspaper.

We ask only that each person receiving a copy of The News give it a fair consideration. If you believe that it provides a nickel's worth of information, stimulation or entertainment that you are not getting in another medium -- then subscribe.

If you believe it is the best newspaper medium you are receiving, and you can afford only one, then please consider subscribing The Daily News for your present newspaper.

Give it a chance.

Page one of the first issue of The Athens Daily News, *June 16, 1965. It was 12 hours late off the press.*

The Athens Observer's *management trio of Don Nelson, Chuck Searcy and Pete McCommons*

The Red and Black, *a newspaper for UGA students, became independent of the University in 1980 under leadership of general manager Steve Crabill (left) and Editor Bill Krueger.*

Chapter IX

Life Beyond the Print Shop: The Non-Metro Weeklies

Feudalism's Last Stronghold

Georgia was feudalism's last stronghold in the United States. The feudal lords of the Middle Ages had fiefdoms and serfs. In Georgia the fiefdoms were called counties. When a Georgia feudal lord became powerful enough he asked the legislature to create a county to be his fiefdom. One result was that Georgia ended up with 159 counties — more than any state except vast Texas. Another result was that every county wanted its own newspaper — or a newspaper owner wanted county legals — and so Georgia also ended up with an unusually large number of small rural weekly newspapers, many of which existed on the thin edge of survival.

To get an idea of how Georgia compares in number of counties, consider these comparisons: Georgia, with 58,000 square miles of territory, has 159 counties; Alabama, slightly smaller at 50,000 square miles, has only 67; Arkansas, at 53,000 square miles, has 75; Florida, at 54,000 square miles, has 67; Mississippi, 47,000 square miles, has 82; North Carolina, slightly smaller in area but more populous, has an even 100; Tennessee, at 41,000 square miles, has 95.

Outside the South, the difference is even greater. Arizona is twice the land area of Georgia, but has only 14 counties; California has 58; Michigan, with almost the identical land area as Georgia, has 83 counties; most of the large western states have fewer than 50 counties; and several of the small geographic eastern states, with similar populations to Georgia, have less than 20 counties.

Only a handful of states have more than 100 counties. Texas, as noted, is high with 254 counties, but its land area is 260,000 square miles — almost five times the size of Georgia. After Georgia's 159, there is a sharp drop to the 120 counties in Kentucky, a state of 40,000 square miles, and the only state that even approaches Georgia in counties per capita and per square miles.

Two long-time peculiarities in Georgia's voting laws and legislative apportionment helped produce its unusual number of counties. Most important was the legislative factor. Until the U.S. Supreme Court decisions of the 1960s, every county in Georgia, no matter how small, got one seat in the state House of Representatives. There was also a gentleman's arrangement under which the State Senate seat for a district was rotated among the counties in a district, no matter how small or large the counties were.

Thus there was a great temptation and incentive to carve out new counties when some political aspirant wanted a seat in the General Assembly.

What made this arrangement even more attractive for new and smaller counties and the residents who would live in them, was that the maximum number of representatives for a county was three. So the smallest, newest county automatically gained at least one third as much voting power in the Assembly as the largest county in the state.

In addition, when the county unit system of voting for state primaries was in use, the smallest counties got two units each in the final count, and the largest counties had just six units, again giving disproportionate weight and importance to a vote in the smaller counties, and more incentive to form and maintain them.

But everything has a limit, and Georgia's total number of counties topped out in 1924 when Peach County was created out of Houston and Macon, so that Fort Valley wouldn't have to be in the same county with Perry. Perry was happy to see Fort Valley go, blissfully unaware that a few miles up the road a far more powerful competitor to its dominance in the county would arise 20 years later in the form of Warner Robins.

Peach's creation brought the number of Georgia counties to 161, but two were subtracted when Campbell and Milton merged with Fulton in 1933, the only merger of Georgia counties on record.

In the 1980 census, Georgia had 47 counties with less than 10,000 population and nine counties with less than 5,000 population. By comparison, neighboring Alabama has just one county with less than 10,000 people.

The effect which this phenomenon has had on Georgia is difficult to gauge because it is seldom discussed by politicians, even those pledging to "reduce government and reduce taxes." For certain, however, it has complicated the task of providing government services in those counties which have such small population and economic bases. This is especially true for education and law enforcement.

In the past 35 years, many of Georgia's smaller counties have gotten smaller. They have also lost the political advantages for which most of them were created. The county unit system was abolished in 1962, and General Assembly representation is now based strictly on population, not geography.

During the twentieth century, the number of weekly newspapers in Georgia has ranged from about 150 to 200, depending on the precise definition of what a weekly newspaper is. For the purposes of this chapter, a weekly is defined as a paid circulation newspaper, eligible for legals and full second-class mail classification.

The 1953 Georgia Press Association Directory listed 202 weekly newspapers, and that was the high water mark in the post World War II years, and probably in the state's history. The 1984 Directory, 31 years later, listed 150 weekly newspapers, the low point in number since World War II.

There are several reasons for this drop and the net result has been better and stronger newspapers among the survivors, and no real loss to the public.

In 1953 there were a number of counties with competing paid weeklies, most of which soon faded away or were merged. There were also more paid weeklies in the suburban counties. The advent of free distribution papers and shoppers reduced their ranks. Weeklies in at least 10 counties have converted to daily schedules in the past 30 years, and in several counties semi-weeklies operating under different names now publish under the same name.

Only five of the 159 counties did not list a paid circulation weekly in 1953. Those counties and their 1950 populations were Baker, 5,952; Chattahoochee, 12,149; Echols, 2,494; Quitman, 3,015; and Webster, 4,081.

In 1984, there were nine counties without a home-based newspaper, that is, a newspaper in which the county or a major town's name was dominant in the masthead. Several of these counties do share a masthead with a neighboring paper, such as *The Stewart-Webster Journal* and *The Coastal Courier,* which serves Liberty and Bryan counties.

Those nine counties and their 1980 populations are: Baker, 3,808; Bryan, 10,175; Calhoun, 5,717; Chattahoochee, 21,723; Clay, 3,553; Echols, 2,297; Quitman, 2,357; Schley, 3,433; and Wilcox, 7,682.

Five of the nine are the same five from 1953 — Baker, Chattahoochee, Echols, Quitman and Webster, and except for Chattahoochee, which is in large part the Fort Benning military reservation, they have all lost population since 1950.

Interestingly, six of the nine counties without home-based newspapers are in a narrow stretch between Columbus and Albany, in the southwestern corner of the state. (See maps.) There are no counties in the northern two-thirds of the states that do not have a paid weekly or daily paper. **(Editor's Note: County-based weeklies were started in Wilcox and Bryan Counties in late 1984.)**

Dramatic Growth in Circulation

When the paid circulations of Georgia's weeklies in 1953 are compared with circulations in 1983, a dramatic improvement is evident.

In 1953 no less than 150 of the 202 weeklies in the directory listed circulations of less than 2,000, and some of the counts of those with more than 2,000 were certainly open to question. But even accepting the publisher's own figures, nearly three-fourths of the state's dailies had less than 2,000, and more than half of those, 76, reported less than 1,000 circulation.

A number of well-known and influential weeklies of 1953 were in the sub-2,000 circulation group, including *The Alma Times; The Wiregrass Farmer* of Ashburn; *The Baxley News-Banner; The Camilla Enterprise; The Commerce News; The Dahlonega Nugget; The Dawson News; The*

Jesup Sentinel; The Houston Home Journal; The Vidalia Advance; The Lowndes County News of Valdosta; and *The Waynesboro True Citizen*.

An indication that circulation size had no effect on the publisher's influence in the Georgia Press Association can be seen in the fact that from 1947 through 1957, seven of the 10 GPA presidents represented one of those below-2,000 weeklies mentioned above, and an eighth was from a weekly just barely over 2,000 circulation.

The figures in 1983 were vastly different. Of the 150 weeklies listed in the 1983 Directory, only 38 reported less than 2,000 paid circulation, and of these 38, only four reported less than 1,000—four compared to 76 in 1953. In 1983, as in 1953, the GPA directory figures are being accepted as reasonably accurate. They are based on each newspaper's postal statement.

Improvement was also evident at the higher levels of circulation. In 1953, only eight weeklies claimed circulations of more than 3,000. Only one, *The Metropolitan Herald* of Atlanta, claimed a circulation above 5,000.

Significantly, among the eight weeklies with more than 3,000 in 1953, only *The Elberton Star* and the jointly-owned Dalton weeklies, were outside of the Atlanta metropolitan area, which meant that virtually all of Georgia's non-metro weeklies had circulations below 3,000, and the vast majority had circulations of less than 2,000.

Thirty years later the improvement in paid circulation can be seen in the fact that there were 55 weeklies in the 3,000 to 5,000 range, and 19 weeklies with circulations of more than 5,000. Virtually all of these are in non-metro areas, and are true representatives of the smaller community or rural press.

What this means is that in those 30 years, the average circulation of Georgia weekly newspapers more than doubled, and that simple fact is evidence not only of the revolution in newspaper production and procedures at the weekly level, but also in the reading habits of Georgians in the counties primarily served by the weekly press. The number of pages carried in most of these weeklies has also gone up sharply, an indication of the expanded business and shopping facilities in most Georgia counties, and their inclination to use weekly newspaper ads.

These increases in paid circulation, advertising and general acceptance occurred during a period when many of Georgia's non-metro counties were growing slowly if at all, and when paid newspapers were facing the challenges of television, shoppers, circulars and a perceived trend away from the printed word. It was also in a period when most of the large dailies in the state either lost circulation or grew very little.

Several reasons suggest themselves for the remarkable circulation advances of the weeklies. First is the definite improvement in education in Georgia during the past 30 years compared to the first 50 years of the 20th Century. Secondly, the readership pie is being divided by 150 weeklies instead of 202. And most importantly, the weekly newspapers of 1985 are superior products in almost every respect. The technological changes had an impact far beyond simply how newspapers are composed and printed. They also changed the allotment of money and effort involved in a newspaper operation.

The effect of the new technology was much greater for weeklies than for dailies, especially larger dailies. On the dailies the news personnel were usually not directly involved with the production of the newspaper. In hot type days, as in cold type days, they covered their beats, wrote their stories, dummied up the pages and let the printers take it from there. There have been some changes, of course, especially when technology moved into the newsroom with terminals to replace typewriters. But for the average newsroom employee on dailies, cold type and offset did not change their work pattern significantly from what it was in 1950.

Not so for the employees of weeklies, for which the coming of cold type and offset meant a whole new way of life, and allowed them to become journalists more than printers. For many smaller weeklies — those that in 1953 had less than 1,000 circulation — cold type and its cheaper, simpler operation meant survival itself.

In the following article, Robert Tribble, who took a few of those small weeklies when they were about to go bankrupt, and used them to start a group that grew to include 14½ newspapers, relates what he feels cold type meant to the small weekly publisher:

BY ROBERT TRIBBLE

Twenty-five years ago the role of the small town newspaper editor and publisher was very different from what it is today. And thank goodness for that. Many of us might not be in the publishing business today if changes for the better had not come about.

In 1960 when I first entered the weekly newspaper field as advertising manager for *The Manchester Mercury, The Mercury* averaged 12-14 pages a week, composed by hot type, and printed on an old flatbed duplex press. It was not uncommon to be reading along and have the type completely fade out.

In order to produce this newspaper and have it ready for mailing on Thursday morning, the publisher, editor, ad salesman, and many times the bookkeeper, had to spend long hours in the back shop around the hot metal. What you really had in those days was not a newspaper editor, but a printer. His time had to be spent in production, rather than news writing and sales.

I know of several old-time editors and publishers who never wrote a story or called on an advertiser. The stories and advertisements that ran in each edition of the weekly press "walked" in the front door. Editors and publishers were too busy in hot metal composition and job printing to bother with news stories or ads.

During the early 1960s, offset — a sometimes 'washed out' product — began to pop up at scattered newspapers across the state. By the middle 1960s the offset product had improved, and small-town publisher/printers began to look at its feasibility. The product was clean and the pictures were beautiful. It proved to be the salvation of the small-town publisher/printer.

Our operation in Manchester today is the publishing house for eight weekly newspapers, all printed for counties adjoining each other in the West Central Georgia area. I believe that if it had not been for the coming of offset, it would not be economical for at least four of these newspapers to be published.

Another factor which has contributed to the continuance of these small town newspapers is central composition and printing. Our weekly in Stewart County is 62 miles from our home base in Manchester. We operate it without a full-time staff member there, and without an office in the county, but the people get a good newspaper with news and ads about their communities.

In today's economy, it is nearly impossible to earn a living of any sort on an 8-page weekly, with no commercial printing income. But put three small-town, 8-page weeklies together in the same production shop and you have a 24-pager which will pay its way if you are any sort of a manager at all.

To be able to do this, the weeklies almost have to be in adjoining counties to establish an advertising base for stores in nearby cities, and to offer pickup rates from one publication to the other. A paid circulation of 1,400 doesn't sound like much, but 3 x 1,400 (4,200) doesn't sound too bad.

The coming of offset has, without a doubt, made our small-town Georgia newspapers much better products. Now the editor doesn't have to spend his entire time in the back shop in production, and can get out, write news, take pictures, and solicit advertising.

I began my publishing career with four small-town weekly newspapers in 1968. One of them folded at the outset. Our largest town was 1,400, and the largest circulation newspaper supposedly had 1,500 paid. At this writing (1984), our publishing company has 12 weekly newspapers, with a combined paid circulation of over 32,000, the largest being 4,200 and the smallest 975. There are 65 employees on the newspaper staffs, and an average week produces about 220 pages. (Tribble added *The Vienna News* to his group in July, 1984, and *The Phenix Citizen* of Phenix City, Alabama, in November, 1984.)

My philosophy of running a small-town weekly newspaper is to let your number one goal be to make a profit, and then you will be able to do the things that need to be done in order to serve your community.

Of course, nothing beats hard work and patience to see the job through. Those, along with versatility, are entirely necessary to be successful in the small-town weekly newspaper field.

Bo McLeod Remembers

How tough was it for weekly publishers and printers to get their newspapers out in the old hot type days? It was plenty tough. In Chapter II, "The Last Linotype," some of the problems are explored, such as the cost and inconvenience of running even one local picture, which had to be engraved in a nearby city, the uncertainty of the machinery and the scarcity of repair service, and trying to make ads look attractive when every illustration was a piece of lead cast from a mat.

And of course, that didn't even include the vagaries of the press, and the usual chore of hand-folding and inserting the paper.

Waldo (Bo) McLeod, the sage of Seminole County, has been editor of *The Donalsonville News* since 1949 and he's seen the bad and the good, and most of the changes in production through those years. He recalls when he didn't have time to sit down and try to think up an amusing line or thoughtful homily.

In the following article written especially for this history, McLeod recalls how a lot of newspapers got started in the small towns, and tells of life for the small town printer when the printing was done with hot lead instead of ecktomatic paper, and with a flatbed press in your own shop, instead of the rotary in a central shop that has regular pressmen to keep them running instead of having to depend on the publisher or editor.

BY BO MCLEOD

First of all, let it be placed on the record that I do not claim to remember all of the history of newspapers in Georgia, and admitted that memory cited in this chapter is subject to the errors of passing years, misunderstandings at the time and facts set straight and sustained by other sources.

Nor is it true that I was here when they unloaded the presses from the ark, and I was not in the building when Johann Gutenburg turned around to shout, 'By golly, you can move this type around. . . .'

Details of dates, names and places are being handled in other pages of this history book. If there are instances when simple, unaided memory clashes with more reasonable dates and places, the smart thing for the reader to do is to go with the facts presented by the more reliable pages.

I do remember when newspapers were planned and established and nurtured into being by committees of local citizens who wanted their towns to have a voice too, since so many other communities had one or were trying to get one.

Mayhaw has a paper, we ought to have one too. Let's all chip in and raise some cash and find a printer and he can publish for us a Briarpatch Dispatch . . .

Folks all over the world (!) can read our paper and learn how nice and progressive we are, and they'll want to move down and become part of us. Unless we find us an editor and get a paper printed with regularity, Briarpatch is going to dry up to nothing . . .

Not the soundest business or journalistic reasoning, maybe, but it explains how many of the publications of olden days came into being.

One example is *The Donalsonville News,* established in February 1916. A group of citizens got together and raised some money and started searching for an editor and a press and some type.

The organizers were not looking for a prize-winning, pace-and-trend-setting journalist. And it was not easy to find any kind of a printer because the trade was young and struggling all over the country at that time.

Many times there was community-wide disappointment when a new man would come in, fresh and sassy with promises and dreams of greatness and progress, only to fall quickly by the wayside as the facts of life having to do with income and outgo came home to him.

And in honesty, it might be noted that the situation was ripe for con artists. The locals did not know anything about how a newspaper was produced, and this left them with no guidelines as they inspected and examined the candidates for the helm. They were reduced to using intuition, instinct and guesses and this was as unreliable then as it is today.

In those a'borning days of many of the publications in Georgia, no journalism degrees were necessary in the smaller communities. No degree in anything was required, but it did help to have a gift of flattery and the good sense to know that the smart way to succeed in the task was to use much space to praise and boost the community and the members of the sponsoring committee. This had the benefit of building images for the home county, and it usually resulted in gifts and support for the newspaper from the citizenry. These started coming in the form of paid advertising and led to today's pattern by which advertising dollars provide the support for the newspaper, apart from the few cents collected by the sale of copies.

The columns in earlier days were various widths, with 13 picas or so being a popular size. In passing years the widths of columns shrank to as narrow as seven picas when somebody realized that the narrower the columns, the more advertising inches you could get per page.

In early days as now, the newspaper had to have enough income to pay its bills and salaries. Then as now, the newspaper could not be free and independent as long as it had to scuffle and scrape for income. This is a simple explanation of why the days of the committee sponsorship were doomed to failure because of the obligation and dependency factor.

One basic reason for wide columns in the older days was because many of the newspapers, especially smaller ones, were set into type by hand. The printer simply sat for long hours at a type case with a job stick in hand. He formed words and sentences and eventually paragraphs and complete stories in the job stick, each line separated by a thin piece of metal called a rule or slug. Each line had to be justified by the adding of thin and thinner pieces of material which tightened the lines so they could be locked into a page chase and placed on the press. And remember, too, those little letters and spaces and lines had to be put back into the cases after the paper was printed.

It would be appropriate to pause for a moment to marvel at how the pioneers were able to produce a paper with hand type. The work was delicate, and accuracy in following the copy (We follow the copy if it goes out of the window!) was an absolute necessity. Printers worked from daylight and into the night, six days a week. Some of the setters were very good at what they did, too, and they could always manage to fill up the columns by the deadlines which came too early then, even as they rush in today.

After the type was set into the lines and carefully placed in columns to make a page, then came the time for more justifying and packing until the page was ready to be locked by the use of pieces of metal called quoins. This was done by squeezing two pieces of metal with a "key" until all of the thousands of letters and spaces were wedged tightly enough to remain in position through the press run. (Our definition of "justified" means ready to face pressure and hard knocks along the way to a finished product. As Ben Franklin mentioned, it was and is to feel corrected, set right and made into a perfected final edition.)

But the press was not ready to run.

After the page of type was moved carefully from the building table, or stone, it had to be planed or made level on the bed of the press. This was done by loosening the quoins a little and moving over the type with a smooth, hard piece of wood, then striking the wood with a hammer or mallet so all letters would be of the same height. After this step, the quoins could again be locked and if the page form had been locked on to the press, the printing could begin.

The "if" about the page being locked on the press is important. If the printer forgot to lock the page on, it would quickly sail out of the back end and hit the wall or floor and break into those thousands of original pieces again. Many new curse words and obscene phrases were invented at times like this.

There were many different sizes and styles of printing presses, depending on the amount of money the organizers had been able to collect. Some presses could print only one page at a time, and others could print an entire edition in one run.

The News had a two-revolution press, made by the Lee Company, Serial No. 981, which could print two "regular" (if there was such a thing) size pages at once.

Another set of pages would be inserted after that first run, and the blank "other side" of the first run was printed, the result finally being pages ready for folding and forming into a handy size for the reader. Some shops had folding machines, but many of them, including *The News*, had to fold the finished product by hand, another time-consuming labor which was usually shared by young boys of the community who would do the folding for a few pennies a week, and they were glad to get those few pennies.

Most of the smaller newspapers addressed copies to be mailed by handwriting, so it was just as well that mailing lists were small in those days, despite the low price of subscriptions. The formation of newspapers was encouraged in the early years of the Republic to be spreaders of information to the people, so they received very generous rates from the Post Office and the cost of postage was very small, especially when compared to today's rates.

Pages from earlier newspapers now are recognizable for at

least a couple of characteristics. Most of the pages were simply columns of type, with headlines, if any at all, being the same size and width as the news they led, because of the physical and mechanical difficulties of making attractive layouts to catch the eye of the reader. Illustrations were rare because of the time and cost involved. And, as much as it hurts to admit it, much of the printing is not, and was never, crystal clear because of the lack of knowledge about the trade, and the weaknesses caused by using machinery and equipment that simply could not do the job.

The work of the printers was helped greatly by the coming of a magical, miraculous machine called a linotype, because it set a line of type at a time (usually at a speed of about six lines a minute, if the operator was skilled), which freed the printers from having to spend so much time setting type by hand. At the time of its coming, this machine was hailed as the final, ultimate weapon in the pursuit of producing a good newspaper, quickly and regularly.

The linotype machine did have a great impact on newspapers, even in small communities, and it did result in the publications being able to improve and better serve. But it brought problems, too.

The bigger, wealthier publications were able to purchase and operate more than one new linotype machine, and they were able to attract the more qualified operators, leaving the smaller papers the option of picking up a used machine from one of those bigger papers, and finding and/or training their own operators, by hit-and-miss efforts.

The man who could operate the linotype was the number one man in the plant, usually the editor and publisher, because he was the heart of it all. He could not be replaced easily and he knew it. The question of whether he was a printer who also edited, or was an editor who was also a printer was never fully answered.

And the public suffered for it. Many of the linotype operators were not trained in writing, ethics, theory or anything other than what they could produce at the keyboard.

The publications suffered also because human endurance would simply not allow time for experimenting, for departures from the way it had always been done. The level of quality of the papers being published remained much the same until fairly recent years.

Ambition and enthusiasm were present, of course, then as it is now, but noble motives were quickly dampened as the passing of weeks taught that just to be able to set enough type into lines and pages to fill the minimum space required was about as much as an editor or publisher could hope for. To hear those old machines slam and bang and bump and crunch along until they finally brought forth one more completed paper (and it hardly matters whether the bump and spits were coming from the linotype machine or those old presses) is a continuing nightmare for survivors of that period.

Looking back at it all now, it can be seen that many newspapers were born and grew despite the handicaps of being formed by strangers to the task, continued and managed by other strangers, all the while depending on equipment that was unreliable and inadequate. But survive and grow they did.

Today, type is set on electronic and automatic machines by fingers directed by young minds which have been educated and trained to do the job at hand. Type can be set faster today than the copy can be prepared for it.

Today's editors and reporters come out of college or trade school and when they hit the ground they can move so much quicker, and do the work so much better than the old timers that it completely undermines the old saying that experience is the better teacher.

They have learned to spread stories on a page in a way to make it draw the eye and attention of the reader. The stories are well-organized and headed, and the use of pictures and drawings is now so common nobody even notices them.

But what today's generation of journalists can never know is the sense of satisfaction and excitement of accomplishment we used to feel when we finally were able to "get a paper out" no matter what the content or quality.

Sufficient to their day were the methods and systems of newspapering in Georgia in years past. And sufficient to tomorrow will be the methods yet to come and the papers yet to be written and published.

I have said nothing about the job printing or commercial printing factor that was an important part of the early weekly press. Newspapers felt they had to also serve the public by printing circulars, flyers or handbills, letterheads, envelopes, posters, anything that required ink on paper or cardboard. This practice enabled small papers to afford a competent printer by giving him something profitable to do during times when there was no newspaper type to set or newspaper press to feed.

Without this commercial printing business, the small publications could not afford full-time people as printers. Checking some of the price lists for this type of printing of earlier days (would you believe 100 letterheads for $5.25?) makes one wonder how they could have considered this printing service a worthy business venture or fringe extra, but they did, and they made it, somehow.

The result was often one in which there was a constant battle between the need for income for advertising and commercial printing, and the newspaper itself, and the newspapers usually suffered from neglect. This is another aspect of early newspapers that can be checked out by any casual examination of them.

While in earlier days an important portion of the newspaper plant's income was from selling printing to the public, today most of the successful newspapers have stopped doing printing for the public, or have set up a separate company to handle it.

Before you scoff and make fun of the idea of a newspaper doing something as distasteful and foreign to journalism as commercial printing, recall the point of a first law of the free press: The newspaper must be self-supporting and have sufficient monies to remain independent, and to be the free press of which we like to boast, and about which we can feel so smug and warm when we enjoy our position in the community. Commercial printing helped to make it that way in our formative, struggling years, during which we were so hungry and eager to become an establishment. So, dear young journalist, please be kind about a situation our calling has outgrown — at last — maybe.

Nothing in these recollections should be considered anything other than admiration and appreciation for the pioneers and creators of what has become a successful, vibrant business which always strives to serve the people of its community. That so many of the early publications became lively and strong and are still active today, still seeking better and newer ways of doing the job, is a daily or weekly reminder of this.

There have been innovations and improvements from the time the first page came off the first press. Those engaged in the business of printing newspapers have never been and will never be satisfied to remain static and in a set pattern or format.

The earlier newspapers had no standards to guide them, apart from the newspapers of large cities and counties, and they were content to realize a country newspaper is different from a metropolitan daily and it ought to be. The readers want it to be this way, too.

The editors and publishers were mostly people of high ideals and noble ambitions for themselves, their community and its people. Many of the reforms in government, society, education, and even religious practices and beliefs can be traced to aggressive reporting and editorializing over the years. The wonder is how they could make so many historic accomplishments with the equipment they had to work with. Lesser men and women would have become discouraged and frustrated over

> the pressures and problems and would have thrown in the cap and apron.
>
> Many of the pioneers seemed to enjoy nothing more than calling a spade a spade, and they often took delight in jumping on the mayor, commissioner, governor, anybody who violated the paper's creed of what should have been done or left undone. They used plain words and simple phrases and everybody could understand where they stood.
>
> Some of their stands cost the editors injury to their bodies and some of them were shot at and hit, many were cussed at and subjected to angry responses now and then. But mostly, they were respected and admired for having the courage to place themselves on the line for principles and truth.
>
> As former Governor Marvin Griffin used to proclaim in his *Bainbridge Post-Searchlight* which he published and edited before and after he served as governor: "The spoken word is on the air . . . the printed word is always there."
>
> It can be a comforting or disturbing thought for journalists of today to know that a hundred years into the future, somebody might pull out a story they wrote and pass judgement on it. Having your work inspected by people yet to be born is a sobering consideration, just another blessing and curse of a newspaper life. It ought to make us ponder and hesitate to strive for anything less than excellence, a quest that has been going on since the newspaper you read this morning was first brought off the press. May it always be the same.

McLeod, when last heard from, was complaining that it's harder to get service on a Compugraphic machine than it was to get a linotype running again. But he wouldn't swap, of course, and his account of the tribulations of printing and publishing a newspaper in times past provides a useful point of reference for recent journalists, as well as a reminder to the older generation that the "good old days" are better remembered than repeated.

Beckerman's Battle With the Klan

The mechanical problems were only part of the ordeal which weekly publishers sometimes suffered, of course. There was also the consequences of what they put in their papers, a problem with which any generation of journalists is familiar. But when it came to trouble in big doses, former Georgia publisher Milton Beckerman may have had the most unique, harrowing and enduring experience of any Georgia weekly editor since World War II.

Beckerman, who moved on to the daily field and then became a newspaper broker, was publisher of *The Swainsboro Forest-Blade* from 1945 to 1950, and then publisher of *The Claxton Enterprise* from 1950 to 1954. Those were years when Georgia newspapers did not carry news about the colored residents of their community, and when it was not exactly healthy for the editor of a small weekly to campaign for what would later become known as "civil rights."

But even before *The Atlanta Constitution*'s Ralph McGill began advocating equal treatment of the races, Milt Beckerman was carrying stories in his weeklies about colored citizens, and even referring to them as "Mr." and "Mrs."

Beckerman has written an account of his experiences as a weekly editor and publisher in Georgia during the 1940s and 1950s for this book. Some of the details have never been published before.

He now lives in Fort Lauderdale, Florida, and specializes in the marketing of shoppers and suburban publications. His story follows:

BY MILTON BECKERMAN

The Civil Rights volcano that erupted in the '60s had earlier rumblings and movements in the '40s and '50s.

Before the late '40s, it was rare for black people to be referred to as "Mr. and Mrs." in weekly or daily newspapers, in Georgia or elsewhere in the South. Rarer yet was the picture of any black person in a newspaper except in connection with a serious crime.

And how many Negro "country" correspondents were there in the more than 200 Georgia weeklies? Where were the Negro reporters or columnists? There were none, except in the few "colored editions". Almost a third of the population was ignored, unreported non-people as far as the Georgia press and its readers were concerned. They were relegated to whatever coverage they could get in the few, poorly-supported and badly-edited black newspapers. Those publications weren't statewide. There were a handful in the major cities. Ignoring the non-people was a tradition honored by city dailies and country weeklies alike.

This was a setting into which the Ku Klux Klan could easily move. After a long period in which the KKK was more or less an underground organization, it began to operate more openly in the late 1940s.

A major event was planned in August 1948, by the state and national Klan leaders. It was to be a "media event". They wanted coverage, and not just in Swainsboro, Georgia, where the activity was to take place. Their ambition was to see the news on the front page of every paper in the U.S. and other parts of the world. They succeeded.

But the Klan members in Swainsboro thought this meeting, like other meetings, was to be a secret gathering. They weren't told of the leaders' plans for wide publicity.

UPI, AP, editors in Atlanta, Savannah, Macon, and perhaps other major state newspapers were informed by KKK leaders well in advance so they could give full photo and news coverage of the Klan in full regalia. Thanks to staged and posed group shots, there was plenty of headline news and photos for the state papers and wire subscribers everywhere. Rooms had been reserved at Swainsboro's Coleman Hotel by state and national press representatives. Photo assistants were on hand to develop and process pictures so they could be transmitted direct from Swainsboro.

The following day the state and national press representatives all left. But *The Swainsboro Forest-Blade* was still there — a venerable paper that had been there 90 years at that time. It still had an editor-publisher who had to deal with the aftermath. Local Klansmen weren't pleased that *The Forest-Blade* had reported on the historic event in the community, and were even less pleased . . . even incensed . . . by the editorials that condemned them for what they were.

It was the beginning of the Klan's battle against this editor and it didn't even stop when he sold his interest in *The Forest-Blade* two years later and became publisher-owner of the weekly in Claxton. The Klan dogged him and his family for the six years they were in Claxton and for three more years in Louisiana where word was passed along to "brothers" in that state that he was an editor they needed to "get".

The Claxton Enterprise may have been the first newspaper in Georgia to call black people "Mr." and "Mrs." in its regular news. The black country correspondents wrote it that way. And the paper also carried pictures of black people in other than crime scenes. There were the usual sports, weddings, and mug shots . . . few, indeed, but there were some. And, of all things, a black columnist. He was a school teacher. He wasn't paid for his column, but whatever he wrote was printed.

White citizens in Evans County generally accepted this change. There was *some* negative comment by advertisers and regular subscribers, but nothing dramatic. There was *some* favorable comment. But there was *plenty* of rumbling from the KKK and its sympathizers.

It culminated one night in March 1950, when Kluxers around the state were notified to come to a rally in Claxton. The main purpose of the rally was to burn a cross in the editor's yard, and intimidate him as an example to other Georgia journalists.

The meeting was called in response to a strong anti-Klan editorial in *The Claxton Enterprise* citing five acts of Klan violence, recently committed in Evans County. The editorial was a call to "Throw Out The Klan!"

Unfortunately for the Klan, some of those who knew of the rally were also friends of the editor and his family. They warned the editor.

Our decision was to make a stand at our home, but this time, due to several previous incidents, there was good communications with the Savannah FBI office.

There was no federal law (or Georgia law) at the time that could prevent the Klan from holding its rally. City and County officials not only didn't object, but wouldn't object, for fear of personal or political repercussions. The Evans County sheriff had his own bone to pick with the editor who had exposed him in a speed-trap rip-off of out-of-state drivers coming through town on U.S. 301.

So, as out-of-town and local Klan members started the parade from the assembly grounds, the sheriff led them to the editor's home. His deputies helped keep traffic moving in the right direction.

What the sheriff and Klansmen didn't know was that the FBI was seeking documented cases of law enforcement officers taking part in lawless incidents in order that Congress would have sufficient proof to pass a law against such action in the future. The FBI thought this was a perfect opportunity. But the agents couldn't act until there was an overt violation.

There was. First came the cross-burning on the lawn of the editor's home. Then a group got out of their cars intent on "getting the editor". They were discouraged by a sudden rifle shot by their intended victim through the front window.

The sheriff and Klansmen probably thought that the editor didn't own any firearms since he wasn't a hunter. They didn't know that his attorney and friends in the community had loaned him the necessary arms and ammunition. They didn't know that the editor had been a marksman in the Army nor that his wife had been brought up on a South Dakota farm and wasn't afraid or unable to handle a gun. They may not have known that the editor had gone through a similar incident about three years earlier in Swainsboro and had observed then that a well-aimed shot could turn a hooded mob.

Also, as soon as a phone call to Savannah notified the FBI that the sheriff was actively leading and supporting the mob action with his deputies, two car loads of agents were on their way across the 55 miles to Claxton. The FBI arrived in time to disperse the crowd and get their evidence.

One Evans County resident drove his pick-up around for weeks proudly showing the hole in his pick-up where the editor's bullet had hit.

What were the repercussions of the Claxon incident in some other parts of the Georgia press? Very interesting.

The Claxton editor, prior to the cross-burning incident, was local correspondent for *The Savannah Morning News* and *Evening Press*. They chose to give this story almost no coverage. They then notified the editor that his services as a correspondent were terminated. A new "stringer" had been appointed.

Ralph McGill and *The Atlanta Constitution* played up the case. McGill put his very erudite and astute focus on the Klan action in his column, news and editorial pages. That turned the tide. Previously, little was ever said in the Georgia press or by politicians, especially in rural areas, about Klan violence or its hate-mongering activities. But now other editors began writing and speaking out against the Klan.

One lady in particular led an effort by religious groups to win passage by The General Assemby of Georgia's anti-mask (anti-Klan) law. Mrs. Possie Daniel of Claxton was head of the Women's Society for Christian Service in Georgia, and the WSCS worked with lobbyists and friends in the B'nai Brith. The law was passed in 1951, and never again would the Klan hold sway over politicians and other citizens of the state. Unmasking them was their undoing.

The Georgia press, through reporting and editorializing against violent incidents perpetrated by the Klan, helped shape the changes in public opinion from acquiescence to the Klan's actions to condemnation of them . . .

But being a Georgia editor in the '40s and '50s wasn't all drama, violence, and dealing with nefarious characters. In fact, that played a small role.

A classic incident was the faux pas on the "society" page shortly after the Beckermans acquired *The Blade*.

It was customary then, and may still be, to give the new Methodist minister and his family a welcoming party. It wasn't unusual for it to be the lead story and have the largest headline on the Society page.

When setting "hot type", letters were sometimes dropped or lost. It was a minor disaster for a new publisher to feature the minister's "PANTRY PARTY" with the "R" missing from the first word, thus producing a "PANTY PARTY".

And it took some adjusting to local customs, after we became Claxton publishers, for my wife — the only professional photographer in town — to be called to many homes and funeral parlors to take pictures of the deceased in their coffins. We kept a small ladder in the back shop for these occasions. The photos weren't published but were bought by the family of the deceased.

It's a tradition in rural communities to publicize the biggest and best of every fruit and vegetable. The proof is in the showing. We still have negatives of dozens of pictures of giant watermelons, tomatoes, corn, eggs and a wide variety of other edibles.

Perhaps the most interesting food story was the time in Swainsboro, when we wrote about eating eggs with green yolks. It was to prove the county agent's point that your chickens are only the product of their feed. If you add that color to their feed, you'll get green egg yolks. Not very appetizing to look at, but the taste was okay.

We first came to Swainsboro in 1939 as editor for Bobo Hobby, the publisher. He introduced us to his system of barter. There was a big refrigerator in the print shop, which held the eggs, vegetables and sometimes meat that farmers gave him for their annual subscriptions.

Our newspapers also played a role in helping the community and state recognize the devastation of one of its major crops, forestry. Emanuel County Agricultural Agent Earl Varner, like many other county agents, had talked for years against farmers burning off the forests. It was customary, especially in spring, for farmers to "burn the fields". New grass would quickly spring up for cattle to feed. This was especially advantageous to the share cropper or farmer with a lot of cattle and limited pasture. It would allow him to burn his neighbor's fields, so his cattle could roam extensively and find good forage. (Fires were set at night. No one ever knew by whom.)

A major problem with the system was that fire didn't stay in the pastures. In fact, the forests were the main victims. Not only did the underbrush burn, but so did the trees. The odor of acrid smoke from forests burning was as familiar to anyone driving Georgia's highways and back roads years ago, as the sight of laborers in the field picking cotton or tobacco. The more progressive farmers were aware of the damage to their forests and that of their neighbors. But to a great extent there was tenant-farming in Georgia and those who didn't own the land didn't have the same respect for its value. Their few scrawny cattle were far more important to them. So they burned.

Early in 1945, County Agent Varner had the bright idea to try to convince the next generation — the 4-H'ers — and through them, their parents, of the problems being created by this indiscriminate burning. He developed an idea that caught the enthusiasm of Emanuel County 4-H'ers. Why not have a forestry festival and celebrate with an annual parade the benefits that come from trees and their by-products? Once Varner got the attention of his young friends, he needed publicity to put the plan across.

The 4-H'ers and Varner came to *The Forest-Blade* office and we devised and publicized the first Pine Tree Festival parade. Only other weekly newspaper editors and those who participate in community events know how many hours of planning and preparation go into developing a full-fledged parade, especially the first of its type.

Floats illustrated the many aspects of well-managed forest resources. There were stories in the paper to tell of every attribute of the forest. Merchants gave the idea enthusiastic support with advertisements. It became a major Swainsboro event, and it also got the attention of the state press.

Awareness of forest resources was greatly advanced in Georgia by The Pine Tree Festival, which sprang from the agricultural agent and 4-H'ers idea combined with the local newspaper's publicity. The 38th Pine Tree Festival was held May 7, 1983 . . .

Typical of so many "Mom and Pop" owned weekly newspapers, ours were joint ventures of Milton and Bernice Beckerman. We were, in fact, co-publishers and editors.

I specialized in selling ads, writing editorials and news stories, and for most of the nine years of ownership and two years of management I wrote a weekly column. My spouse did the same except for the column, did most of the ad layouts, did the photography (in Claxton we were the only professional photographers) and generally ran the office. Feature stories were her specialty for which we earned many state awards. She also often wound up with the "social news" chore and was the bookkeeper and office supply buyer. In a pinch, I operated or repaired the Linotype, presses, folder and other equipment.

Every editor and his wife can attest to the many hours a week attending meetings as either reporter or participant (most of us have forgotten for how many organizations we served in committee and office posts) and the hours we put in attending or giving social functions.

But most of us had kids so we had an ulterior motive. We wanted a better community in which they could grow up and enjoy and have good memories. For instance, that's why Bernice worked so hard, through the Women's Club, to have fluoride added to the drinking water and why she organized the Claxton Band and we editorialized on its need and attributes and helped raise the funds to find a band leader and raise money for uniforms and instruments.

There are never-ending opportunities for service to those whose ambition is to be a country editor. Georgia, for 11 years, gave us that chance to enrich our lives and those around us.

'We're Only Human'

As Milt Beckerman's colorful recollections show, the life of a weekly publisher-editor is a mixture of the dramatic and the trivial. What a newspaper person has to learn is that nothing is trivial to the individuals involved. Dealing with a misplaced Garden Club report can create as much grief sometimes as taking on the County Commission over its most cherished boondoggle.

The following 1984 column by Cal Beverly, then-editor of *The Fayetteville News,* written 30-40 years after Beckerman's experiences in Swainsboro and Claxton, shows that many things remain the same for newspaper folks, despite all the changes in equipment, circulation and Georgia customs.

Beverly wrote:

> I used to pass newspaper offices and wonder what strange things took place behind those doors. Now I know.
>
> Behind those doors are folks who are generally about three hours behind where they are supposed to be by that time of day, who have one telephone line on hold, and are trying to placate a caller on the other line about not getting the paper on Wednesday, like it's supposed to be, instead of on Thursday.
>
> I received a call Monday, a few hours before our absolute deadline, wanting to know what happened to the photo of a toddler who won a beauty contest in a large city in another state. That person was calling long distance and said the photo was sent sometime just after Christmas. I assured the caller we will look through the photos in the composition room to see what happened to that one.
>
> I go back to the composition room and there are at least 50 to 60 photos all received in just the past week. Did you hear my groan?
>
> We had a lady call up on Tuesday afternoon at 4 p.m. several months ago to attack our insensitivity to a particular scout troop. She was sure there was some conspiracy afoot to keep the scouts out of our paper. Tuesday is the day we send the paper to the printers, and we were at that time one hour away from the deadline for the paper to leave for its printing that evening. The

lady was irate, and it was several minutes before we could assure her we loved scouting in general and her troop in particular. We set up a photo session the next afternoon and the lady was one hour late showing up for the appointed photo. But the paper got out that week and we still love scouts.

I know how personally important each person's child, parent, or special project is to that person and his immediate family. And that is what keeps a family weekly newspaper in business. You want to read about the goings on of people you know. And Lord knows, we try to deliver as much of that as we have column inches for each week.

We would dearly love to have enough warm bodies to send to every school assembly play, every garden club white elephant sale, every church bazaar, every troop meeting, every groundbreaking for a new office addition, every financial seminar in every bank meeting room in the county — but we don't.

And neither do the Atlanta newspapers or any paper, regardless of size. But we know those things are important, especially to the ones involved. And so we need some help: your help.

Help us out by writing down information about these kinds of events. If you have a camera handy, help us out with that, too.

We need your constant, steady input to us — not only your legibly written items and carefully focused photos — but also your constructive criticism and an occasional thanks.

I'm just being honest — and human — with you about this business. We have our limitations and we try to stretch those limits every week to excel and provide you with a superior product.

We are grateful for the opportunities to serve you, and hope you will be tolerant when we turn out to be — every now and then — just human.

The Worst Problem of All

Unreliable machinery, unreasonable subscribers and even the Ku Klux Klan might be agitating problems to a weekly newspaper publisher, but with fortitude they can be surmounted. There is one problem, however, that every publisher fears more than any other.

That problem is — competition. Now competition comes in all forms, from posters to billboards, from high school yearbooks to intrusions by papers from nearby cities, from the electronic media to the printed shopper.

But the type of competition that publishers fear most is direct competition in a small isolated city from another separately-owned, paid-circulation newspaper covering virtually the same news, and soliciting the same advertisers. If history is any judge, it is a competition with only one survivor.

In 1953 there were a number of smaller communities in Georgia which had head-on competition between two weekly newspapers. They included Carrollton, Cartersville, Douglas, Fitzgerald, Irwinton, Madison, Ringgold, Statesboro, Sylvania and Thomaston.

Through the ensuing 30 years a number of other non-metro communities saw competing papers arise and struggle for supremacy.

Of all the places which had competing paid weeklies in 1953, plus all those that had competitors in the years since, only three Georgia cities or towns still had two separately-owned paid weeklies in 1984. They are Douglas, Hiawassee and McRae, and McRae's competition is less than a year old. Of the three, only Douglas had two paid weeklies in 1953, and Douglas enjoys the distinction of being the one community in Georgia to support two separately-owned weeklies for all of the years since World War II. In fact, *The Douglas Enterprise* and *The Coffee County Progress* have fought it out since 1913 and somehow both have survived. But they are the lonely exception to the obvious rule, which is that in a battle between paid circulation weeklies in non-metro communities there is only one survivor.

Unlikely Battlegrounds

Hiawassee, in Towns County which ranks 147th among Georgia's counties in population (5,638) has had two weekly newspapers for almost 10 years although it would seem hard-pressed to support one. Each of the weeklies has sister papers which help out. The older paper is *The Towns County Herald* which was established before World War II (exact year unknown). It is owned by Wanda West, who also owns *The North Georgia News* in Blairsville. Mrs. West's husband, Harold, bought *The Towns County Herald* in the mid-60s, and had owned the Blairsville paper since 1953. Mrs. West assumed the management of the papers at his death in 1975. Most of the ads in the 12-16 page *Herald* are sold in combination with the 20-24 page *North Georgia News*, and news coverage and ad soliciting are handled out of the Blairsville office.

The competing weekly is *The Mountain News*. It was started in 1976 and is owned by Jerue Babb, whose company owns all of the paid weekly newspapers in a seven-county area of north Georgia which includes Fannin,

Union, Towns, Rabun, Lumpkin, White and Habersham, except for Mrs. West's two weeklies. **(Editors' Note: Babb died on December 31, 1984, and these papers are now owned by his heirs.)**

A minority stockholder in *The Mountain News* is Ernestine Youngblood, its founder, who is no longer actively involved in the management.

Both of the Hiawassee weeklies and the Blairsville paper are printed at a plant in Murphy, North Carolina, which is also owned by Babb.

Despite the small advertising and population base, neither side has shown any sign of giving up or selling out. Mrs. West has rejected overtures to sell her papers, and Babb has resources from his other holdings to maintain *The Mountain News*.

Circulation is high relative to county population on *The North Georgia News* and the two Hiawassee papers, mainly due to readers from out of state, who spend the summers in the North Georgia mountains, and live elsewhere. *The News* has close to 5,000 subscribers; *The Towns County Herald* has about 2,000, and *The Mountain News* about 2,500.

McRae, in Telfair County, also seems an unlikely spot for competitors. Telfair, famed as the home county of the Talmadges, has 11,394 people, and ranks exactly 100th among the 159 counties in population. The population held its own during the 1970s but the trend has been generally downward since a peak of 15,291 in 1920.

The newspaper scene in Telfair took a new turn in October 1983 when *The Lumber City Log* was sold by Murphy McRae to Mark and Julie Joiner, a young husband-wife team. The Joiners moved *The Log* to the county seat of McRae, renamed it *The Telfair Times*, and set it up in direct competition with the long-standing McRae weekly, *The Telfair Enterprise*.

Actually, *The Log* and *The Enterprise* had been nominal competitors for 30 years, but they were not in the same town, and theoretically, at least, they were serving different constituencies and advertisers. Lumber City had a 1980 population of 1,426, and is located about 10 miles east of McRae. McRae's population is 3,409, and its census district has 6,604, almost three times the population of Lumber City's district. In addition most of the advertising for both newspapers was from McRae. Thus, a long time competitive situation in the same county just moved to the same city.

The Telfair Enterprise, published by Edwin Bowen, dates back to 1887, when it was founded by A. L. Ryals. Ryals was later the U.S. minister to Vancouver in the second Grover Cleveland administration. Bowen and his father, W. L. Bowen, have been owners and publishers of *The Enterprise* since before World War II.

The Lumber City Log had an unusual origin. In 1954 Georgia Power Company was sponsoring the Better Hometowns Contest, which honored Georgia communities for making certain civic improvements. One of the requirements was that the town have a newspaper or some sort of regular publication. Joe Prescott was mayor of Lumber City and he wanted Lumber City to enter the contest but at the time Lumber City didn't have a newspaper. So in March 1954, Prescott, his wife Jane, and Tommy Brewer, the first editor, launched *The Lumber City Log*, which was given its distinctive name by Jane Prescott. Lumber City won second place in its division that year in the Better Hometown Contest, and *The Log* continued in publication under several subsequent owners, including Byron Thompson, Jimmy Ryals and Sambo Burkett.

In 1960, Burkett sold *The Log* to Murphy McRae, who would be its owner and editor for the next 23 years. In *The Log's* final edition, McRae wrote: "I started in the newspaper business out of sheer desperation. I had been looking for a job for two months in Atlanta and was still out of work . . . My love for the newspaper business has been exceeded only by the lack of profit associated with it. When I purchased *The Montgomery Monitor* in 1970 I enjoyed being called a magnate. With this addition I had one of the youngest newspapers (*The Log*) and one of the oldest in Georgia and that pleased me. I actually began to make a little money with both papers but the recessions of 1973-75 etc. were hard to live with. The first thing a merchant cuts out in bad times is advertising, and if times are good, he feels that he doesn't need it, and if times are real good he'll say he can't handle any more business . . . A newspaper is a lot of fun but it needs a little profit to continue operating. . . . "

So McRae sold *The Log* and *The Monitor* to Mark and Julie Joiner, both in their early 20s, both natives of Telfair County and graduates of Georgia Southern. The following week the masthead flag was changed to *The Telfair Times*, and underneath was a smaller line reading, "Combined with *The Lumber City Log*."

Julie Joiner, in her first column, explained the change. "We want people to view our paper as a county paper. We plan to cover news and events in McRae, Helena, Lumber City, Scotland, Milan and Jacksonville, yet we don't want the paper to lose its identity and origin in Lumber City . . . We plan to open an office in McRae soon since McRae is the county seat and the most central point in the county."

Bill Ricks of *The Soperton News*, which was printed in the same plant as *The Log,* wrote a column about the departing McRae. Ricks observed:

"Perhaps the most significant of McRae's many accomplishments was to survive to adulthood in turbulent Telfair County. Some of his lesser achievements include: attaining a law degree from the University of Georgia; working in New York City; military service in Panama, and traveling around the world as steward for a ship's captain. In 1960 he left all that to become editor of *The Lumber City Log* . . . It seems wise to me to let *The Lumber City Log* retire with Mr. McRae. He's been identified with it for most of its 29 years and it's for certain the paper could never have another editor quite like him, because there isn't another person in the world quite like him."

McRae went into the insurance business after selling his newspapers.

The 70-Year Battle in Douglas

Only the Douglas example offers any evidence that two paid weeklies can survive for a long period in Hiawassee and McRae, or in any future competitive situation. Douglas, a city of 10,000, in Coffee County, which had a 1980 population of 26,894, has had competing paid weeklies since 1913, easily the longest period that any Georgia city has supported such a competition. What made Douglas unique in this respect? Apparently it is a combination of pride and determination on both sides, and a desire among some important businessmen to maintain a competitive situation

The Douglas Enterprise dates back to 1888 and calls itself "the oldest institution in Coffee County." W. R. Frier Sr. bought *The Enterprise* in 1909 and was publisher until his death in 1939, at which time his son, Thomas Frier Sr. succeeded him. Frier Sr. remains publisher in 1984, and his two sons, Thomas Jr. and David, are editor and advertising manager, continuing the family tradition into a third generation.

This stability of leadership and the overall quality of *The Enterprise* through the years — as recognized by many awards, especially for editorials — would seem to have assured its dominance in the community. But the competing *Coffee County Progress*, established in 1913 by 100 "leading citizens and merchants", has also had some strong leadership. From 1916 to 1947 it was owned and edited by Fred Ricketson, and then from 1947 to 1972 by Melvin C. Waters. It was not unusual — although certainly not common — for competing weeklies to survive before World War II. But in the past 35 years most of these competitions have been short-lived. Waters, a retired military man, kept *The Progress* going by plowing any profits back into the operation and by using commercial printing income to bolster the newspaper. In May 1972, poor health prompted Waters to sell *The Progress* to Steve Chapin, a newspaperman from Chattanooga, Tennessee. Six months later, Chapin sold *The Progress* to Waters' employee of 20 years, Carl Al Hulsey. Hulsey had gone to work for *The Progress* in 1953 and had worked in all departments, primarily composition and commercial printing. At the time he took over *The Progress,* it was publishing two editions a week, compared to *The Enterprise's* one, although ad volume was about the same.

The two competitors were both hurt by the recession of the mid-1970s when some advertisers who had been running with both began to alternate their ads. Also new competition for commercial printing had come on the scene, causing *The Enterprise* to abandon its printing business. One advantage for *The Progress* was that it owned its own press, a four-unit Fairchild, installed in 1967 when Waters changed over to cold type. Commercial web work helped foot the overall costs.

A shopper began publishing in Douglas in 1981, adding a third print competitor. Hulsey, who had bought the neighboring *Atkinson County Citizen* and *Pearson Tribune* in 1974, decided to sell *The Progress* and devote his full time to the Atkinson operation. In May 1982, after discussions with the Friers about a sale to *The Enterprise,* he sold *The Progress*, its building, press and other equipment to L. W. (Woody) Beville, who had previously operated a shopper in Ocala, Florida. The Friers decided there was more debt on the operation than they wanted to assume.

In July, 1984, *The Progress* was sold again, this time by Beville to Robert H. Snow of Corinth, Miss., an accountant who once worked with the Richard Hamill newspaper group in Florence, Alabama. Snow later relinquished his ownership with Beville returning. In early 1985, *The Progress* was on an irregular schedule, and there were signs that the long competition between *The Progress* and *The Enterprise*, which has survived since 1913 through economic depressions, technological revolutions and the introduction of other competition for the ad dollar, may be near an end.

Its kind is unlikely to ever be seen in Georgia again.

Victorious Challengers

There are examples too numerous to mention of challengers that soon folded or were bought out after being launched against long-established weeklies. More interesting — and more common than often realized — are the examples of challengers that managed to supplant long-established weeklies and become the surviving paid newspaper.

The circumstances vary widely from case to case, and usually the challenging weekly had to buy out the older weekly.

In Barnesville, a competing weekly was started in 1978 by Frank Heflin against the long-established *Barnesville News-Gazette*, published by Bill Dennis, son of Belmont Dennis, who bought *The News-Gazette* shortly after World War II. The competitor, called *The Herald*, was soon sold by Heflin to Quimby Melton Jr. of Griffin, whose daughter and son-in-law, Laura and Walter Geiger, came in to operate it.

Dennis, nearing retirement age, then sold *The News-Gazette* to Robert Tribble of Manchester, who owned several other weeklies in the area. That put strong multi-paper organizations behind both *The Herald* and *The News-Gazette*.

After about a year of competition, the two owners recognized that neither one could prevail, nor was it likely that enough advertising support was available in Barnesville to make two weeklies profitable.

Tribble and Melton got together and Melton bought *The News-Gazette* and merged it with *The Herald*. Thus the challenger became the survivor — but only by buying out the established paper.

In Eastman, *The Times-Journal* was the long-established paper and had been published since 1902 by two former Georgia Press Association presidents, C. M. Methvin, and his son, E. T. (Ed) Methvin. Competition came in 1972 when *The Dodge County Spotlight* was started by veteran newspaperman F. A. (Bulldog) Jones and his son, F. A. Jones Jr.

The elder Jones had retired earlier that year for health reasons, from *The Daily Sun* in Warner Robins, where he worked at everything from linotype operator to sports editor and makeup man. The younger Jones was an Eastman banker.

The Joneses, like most newspaper challengers, felt the established paper was deteriorating, and that the people of Eastman and Dodge County deserved better.

But Bulldog Jones died on October 1, 1972, just a couple of months after the paper was started, leaving the fledgling *Spotlight* without an experienced hand to guide it.

In December of that year, Joe and Julia Jones Roberts took over the newspaper which had been started by Julia's father and brother. Julia had worked for a number of years with Foy Evans at *The Warner Robins Sun* before and after her marriage to Joe. Joe left a position as press secretary to a Georgia congressman to join the newspaper.

Joe's background in Army public information and on Capitol Hill and Julia's newspaper experience gave *The Spotlight* an immediate edge in its competition with *The Times-Journal*.

The *Spotlight* was hand-delivered free for a year, throughout Dodge County. The Robertses decided to have a subscription drive in the late fall of 1973 and the Dodge County 4-H Club sold almost 1,000 subscriptions in return for a percentage of the sales revenue. The owners felt they needed to have a second class mailing permit to give the paper status and eliminate the expense of the hand-delivered give-away. They also wanted a chance to become the legal organ of the county and the city of Eastman, thus gaining more credibility.

The subscription drive was successful, and *The Spotlight* was no longer thought of as a shopper. It also lost its 'underdog' image.

The Spotlight by then was averaging 12 pages or so a week, including two full-page independent grocery store ads. But the chains stayed with *The Times-Journal*, which improved noticeably in the face of competition. It was averaging two more pages per week than *The Spotlight*. But in 1974 Methvin was 65 years old and Mrs. Methvin was in declining health. For those reasons and the prospect of a long struggle against an aggressive competitor, Methvin accepted an offer by the Robertses to sell *The Times-Journal*.

In August 1974, the new combined *Times Journal-Spotlight* was published for the first time. *The Spotlight* had overcome the old established newspaper.

In 1984, *The Times Journal-Spotlight* averages 22 to 24 pages per week, with a paid circulation of 4,250. In 1978, it joined with three other newspaper companies to build a central printing plant in nearby Soperton.

Julia Jones Roberts is publisher and editor of the paper, carrying on what her father and brother started, and her husband helped nourish to success.

A Challenger Spawns An Empire

The battles in Barnesville and Eastman were fairly short, two years or less. But a prolonged struggle developed between a challenger and the established paper in Jesup. It would go on for 17 years, second in length since World War II only to the head-to-head competition of *The Enterprise* and *Progress* in Douglas.

The Jesup situation involved several unusual factors, not present in other weekly wars around the state. For many years, the challenging paper was a tabloid. Later it was owned by a large out-of-state group. Then, it became the first newspaper in the state to lease and operate a TV channel, with local programming. And finally, it became the principal paper in one of the largest paid weekly groups in the state.

But it all began because a young doctor in Jesup didn't like the way *The Jesup Sentinel* was covering a controversy concerning the handling of public funds by the Wayne County sheriff. That was in 1960. The doctor was Lanier Harrell. Dr. Harrell got in touch with a real estate man turned printer named Norris B. Strickland, who was introducing offset printing to Southeast Georgia and the result was *The Wayne County Press*. Its first edition, 16 tab pages, was published on November 3, 1960, in the final week of the Kennedy-Nixon campaign for president. Mershon Aspinwall, a veteran newspaperman, was the first editor.

As the area's first offset paper, *The Press* carried many more photos than the readers had ever seen, along with hard-hitting news and even harder-hitting editorials. Merchants were eager to see what was "in *The Press*," but what usually wasn't in there were their advertisements.

Aspinwall was soon succeeded by Strickland's wife as the editor. Also about that time a young Macon native named Elliott Brack, who was doing research for his master's thesis in journalism at Iowa State University, came to Jesup to interview the two Jesup publishers.

A friendship developed between Brack and the Stricklands, and in 1962, Brack and his wife, Barbara, moved to Jesup. He became publisher of the upstart weekly and soon thereafter acquired Strickland's 50 percent of the company making him a co-owner with Harrell.

The newspaper that many observers predicted "won't make it six months" had gotten a publisher who for 10 years would give around-the-clock devotion to make it a product of credibility and excellence. With "A Few Words" column, editorials signed by EEB and replies to "Presstalk" letters, Brack became the spark of the community.

Officials knew their actions were being watched, reported and often questioned. For years, the sheriff, clerk of court and ordinary withheld the legal organ status as a means of punishing what they felt was an adversary. Rotation of the legal organ status was an issue *The Press* pursued and finally won after years of insistence. Despite the opposition from some public officials and a lack of major advertising accounts, *The Press* continued to grow under Brack's leadership.

In the summer of 1971, Brack and Harrell made a bid to buy *The*

Jesup Sentinel from W. B. Rhoden who had owned it since the early 1950s. While a California broker negotiated between the two newspapers, discussion with a recent college graduate also began. W. H. (Dink) NeSmith Jr., a native of Jesup, was having second thoughts about entering law school at the University of Georgia. He had become acquainted with Brack during his high school and college days when *The Press* printed many of his campus political materials. Harrell was his family's doctor. NeSmith respected both men and shared their enthusiasm about the opportunities ahead in his hometown.

Within a couple of weeks, the three sealed an agreement with a handshake and NeSmith joined the 11-year-old publication as advertising manager. Despite a journalism degree in public relations, NeSmith's last job before joining *The Wayne County Press* was as a training director at a chicken processing plant in Athens. Before that, he sold used cars for a Ford dealership while waiting to report to Army basic training.

By Christmas of 1971, Brack, Harrell and NeSmith could see that their hopes of buying *The Sentinel*, its modern 20,000-square-foot building and web-printing operation were fading. In June of 1972, Brack and Harrell sold NeSmith a third interest in the corporation and elected him president.

Reflecting after a dozen years of heading the company, NeSmith commented, "If I had known how to read a balance sheet in those early days, I would have probably jumped ship. Instead, I just looked to my partners for encouragement and kept on selling so that we could meet the payroll."

Shortly after forming the new partnership, the company bought the building it was renting and started planning for expansion. A three-unit King press was ordered. The battle for advertising and circulation superiority continued to escalate. Convincing out-of-town chain food stores to switch or split their budgets seemed impossible. *The Sentinel* had seven pages of grocery advertising, *The Press* had none.

In late summer, 1973, Brack got a phone call from Athens. A department head was leaving the University of Georgia's School of Journalism, creating a vacancy on the faculty. The University wanted Brack to be a guest professor for nine months. Turning to his young partner, Brack asked, "Do you think you could hold things down while I am in Athens? It will only be nine months." NeSmith replied, "Sure."

But the following summer, Brack made another surprising announcement. "Besides teaching college, the other thing in life that I really want to do is to run a daily newspaper," he said. Brack had been asked to take the job of general manager of *The Gwinnett Daily News* in Lawrenceville, a position which would also let him continue teaching at the University. He accepted, and NeSmith became the full time publisher of *The Press*.

By this time, *The Press* had begun to gain ground on *The Sentinel*. Major advertisers were beginning to spend some of their dollars with the growing newspaper. An audit by the Bureau of Circulation showed *The Press* had taken the lead in paid circulation. A fourth unit to the web press was added.

In the mid-1970s, N. J. (Jerue) Babb, who operated a group of weeklies in the Southeast, including several in Georgia, contacted the owners of *The Press*, and also Rhoden of *The Sentinel*.

After several years of negotiating, the 16-year newspaper war was finally coming to an end. On December 28, 1976, NeSmith, Babb and James E. Hickey of Atlanta formed Press-Sentinel Newspapers, Incorporated, and bought the two Jesup newspapers. They were combined into *The Press-Sentinel* in February of 1977, as a twice-weekly with 6,000 circulation.

Rhoden, one of the state's pioneers of centralized offset web printing, retired and later moved with his wife Dorothy to her hometown of Cobbtown. Brack continues as general manager of *The Gwinnett Daily News* and Dr. Harrell practices radiology at Wayne Memorial Hospital in Jesup.

The new Jesup company soon became active in acquisitions. Within four months, *The Baxley News-Banner* was acquired. Nine months later, *The Camden County Tribune* in St. Marys was added. In 1979, Babb and NeSmith purchased Hickey's interest. In two more years, *The Alma Times*, *The Camilla Enterprise* and WOFF-FM in Camilla were bought.

In 1981, Press-Sentinel Newspapers, Incorporated became the first newspaper in Georgia to lease a cable television channel and provide videotaped local programming.

"Ted Turner said newspapers would be gone in the near future. We had too much invested and we figured it was time to take a look at this thing that was supposed to do us in," NeSmith said concerning the plunge into cable television.

"After three years of study and a pile of money spent on experimenting, I am not convinced cable is any real threat to the strong community newspaper. I am not ashamed of our pioneering effort, but I don't plan to capitalize any future expansion with our cable profits either."

On December 31, 1983, the company closed its video operation but continued a news and advertising read-out to cable subscribers.

NeSmith acquired Babb's interest during 1983 and became sole owner of the Jesup operation as well as the Camilla newspaper and radio station.

On July 1, 1983, seven years of off-and-on negotiations ended when NeSmith and Manchester publisher Robert E. Tribble formed a partnership to buy *The Adel News* from Grover C. Patten. They subsequently traded *The Lanier County News*, which had also been obtained in the transaction, for *The Cook County Tribune* in Adel.

NeSmith explained his company's aggressive growth theory: "It is actually easier to operate several newspaper properties than just one. Jerue Babb is a perfect example of that. He taught me some very valuable lessons. Besides, it also offers greater economic stability to your organization by relying on several local economies rather than just one."

In 1984, *The Press-Sentinel* is published on Wednesday and Friday with a circulation of 7,200. Its walls are filled with more than 200 state and national awards for excellence. In addition to publishing *The Ludowici News*, *The Patriot* (the civilian enterprise newspaper for Fort Stewart in Hinesville and Hunter Army Airfield in Savannah), and a non-duplicating shopper, the company operates an extensive web printing division on a six-unit King press.

From its meager beginnings in 1960, *The Press* not only prevailed and became the surviving weekly newspaper in Jesup, but has also provided the base for one of the largest weekly communications groups in Georgia. Among Georgia's non-metro communities, it is the best example of how tall oaks from small acorns grow.

KOs by the Challengers

The three most decisive and relatively quick victories by a new paid weekly over a long-established weekly occurred in Forsyth, Nashville and Metter. In these cases, the older paper just expired, rather than being bought out, although in Metter, the surviving paper did buy the mailing list. In Forsyth, the challenger scored a clean knock-out, although the fight was longer. Nashville has the distinction of being the earliest example in the post-war period of a new weekly winning out over a long-established competitor. Its battle was won in the 1960s while the others were in the 1970s.

Forsyth, in Monroe County (1980 pop. 14,610) is 25 miles north of Macon on I-75. It is perhaps best known as the home of Tift College, a small Baptist school, and for a high school named Mary Persons which is a perennial football powerhouse. The coming of I-75 brought many travelers and some motels but the town and county had changed little for 40 years when Don Daniel stopped there in 1972 to ask the owner of the weekly newspaper if he'd like to sell it.

Daniel at the time was publicity director for Six Flags Over Georgia, but he had a newspaper background. A native of Dublin, he grew up in Swainsboro and worked for *The Forest-Blade* as advertising manager. He later was editor and publisher of the weekly *Clayton County Journal* in Jonesboro before going to Six Flags in 1968.

Laurice Cox, who was also an active member of the U.S. Merchant Marine, owned the venerable *Monroe Advertiser*, which dated back to 1854, and for many years was published by the Reverend J. H. Clarke and his son, Harold Clarke. *The Advertiser*'s greatest claim to fame, however, was that from 1867 to 1870 it was edited by Joel Chandler Harris, later the author of the Uncle Remus stories. The type stand at which Harris worked was preserved and on display with a bronze marker in *The Advertiser* office for many years.

But as one Forsyth editor wrote some years later, "*The Advertiser* had become little more than a historic relic."

Cox was not adverse to selling but he wanted a price higher than Daniel could pay. Daniel, who was ready to get into the weekly business and thought Forsyth had one of the brightest futures of any small Georgia town, decided he could start a new weekly newspaper for a lot less money, and he considered *The Advertiser* vulnerable.

So in November 1972, Daniel founded *The Monroe County Reporter*. Its motto was "Monroe County's First Total News Newspaper." For a year *The Reporter* was mailed third class to all homes in the county. Then Daniel began building a paid circulation. He ran a lot of photos and covered governmental meetings which had never been done regularly by *The Advertiser*. In 1974 he hired Wendall Ramage as his assistant and Ramage became one of the best weekly editors in the state.

Soon after *The Reporter* was started, Cox sold *The Advertiser* to Garner Childres who operated it until a fire destroyed the building. Childres sold it to Walter Preswood, who sold it to Gainer Bryan, a former editor of *The Gwinnett County News*. Bryan was a solid newsman but he got into the battle late and *The Reporter* by then had gained the upper hand. In 1975 Bryan left *The Advertiser* and it disappeared from the Georgia newspaper scene, leaving *The Reporter* alone as the surviving paid weekly in Forsyth and Monroe County. Daniel bought nothing, not even a mailing list or a masthead. *The Advertiser* was 121 years old at its death, the oldest Georgia newspaper in this century to be discontinued.

Ramage, writing of Don Daniel's impact on Forsyth in a column several years later, said, "There were a few antediluvians (in Forsyth) who never forgave Don for 'killing *The Advertiser*.' There were others who could not accept a Monroe County newspaper that refused to be a mouthpiece for a self-appointed 'select' few. But the majority of people understood what Don was doing and appreciated it. *The Reporter* grew in circulation and number of pages . . . County historians are going to remember that Don Daniel gave Monroe County a real newspaper, one they could be proud of. And in giving them that newspaper he exerted more than passing influence on the development of Monroe County and Forsyth."

Daniel had won the war of newspapers in Monroe County but the victory exacted a toll. For more than three years he had the expense of competition and of start-up costs, such as free circulation for a year. There was also the emotional cost, which comes high in competitive situations.

Daniel began thinking of selling *The Reporter* in the late 1970s, but it was not until April 1983 that he made a deal with Quimby Melton Jr.'s Hometown Newspapers, which owned several other weeklies in the area. Walter Geiger became the new publisher with Ramage staying on as editor. Daniel announced that he was going "to sit on my porch and rock for awhile." Actually he opened up a commercial print shop and a small public relations business in Forsyth.

But in Georgia newspaper annals Daniel accomplished what no one else exactly duplicated in the post World War II years: a complete victory by a new paid weekly over a long-established weekly, without any buy-out provision. And perhaps most uniquely, Daniel was an "outsider", always a handicap in small counties.

Almost the same feat was accomplished in Metter, the main difference being that the challenger was a home-town girl.

Like *The Monroe Advertiser, The Metter Advertiser* (same name by an odd coincidence) had an interesting although not as lengthy past. What made *The Metter Advertiser* unique among Georgia newspapers was that its first owner was the city of Metter.

This came about in 1912 when F. H. Sills, a veteran newspaperman and preacher, persuaded the mayor and city council of Metter to finance and publish a weekly newspaper with the main purpose of promoting Metter as the county seat of a yet-to-be-formed county. (As mentioned early in this chapter, getting counties formed was a popular political pastime in Georgia for many years.) The city launched the newspaper in October 1912, with Sills as editor. He sent all the copy and ads to Atlanta for printing, with the papers then expressed back to Metter for distribution. Also a copy of the paper was sent to all members of the Georgia legislature, all state house officials, and to every daily and weekly newspaper in the state.

Each issue contained editorial pleas and reasons why a new county should be formed with Metter as the county seat. Because of the targeted distribution, all of the influential people in Georgia were aware of Metter's ambitions. The name Candler, for Gov. Allen Candler (1898-1902), was chosen for the county. The effort achieved success in July 1914, with an amendment passed by both state houses, signed by Gov. John Slaton, and ratified by the state's voters in November.

The city of Metter then bowed out of the newspaper business, presenting *The Advertiser* to Publisher Sills as a gift. Sills is the only publisher in Georgia history who ever got a city government to finance a newspaper for him, or got a county established through its influence.

Later *The Advertiser* was bought by R. G. Daniell, who published it for more than 40 years, and was the publisher in 1977 when competition came to Candler County, population 7,518, which was less people than it had when *The Advertiser* won its establishment in 1914.

Virginia Snell was curriculum director for the county school system when she decided to go into the newspaper business. By her own admission, she didn't even know if a press would run 14 pages, which was what she ended up with the first week. She was a lifelong resident of Candler County, however, and felt that her home town and county needed a better newspaper. She got encouragement from several merchants and the largest bank in Metter. So with her son, Carvey, as managing editor, Ms. Snell launched Metter's *Town and County News* on December 1, 1977. It was printed in Swainsboro at the plant of *The Swainsboro Blade* where she got sage advice from Bill Rogers Sr., one of the best weekly publishers in the state.

From the beginning, one of *The T&C News'* advantages over the older *Advertiser* was a sharper print job. Nine months after *The News* started, Daniell sold *The Advertiser* to Elliott Brack and Doug Joiner. This was the same Elliott Brack, of course, who himself had been involved with a challenging paper for years in Jesup. Brack, at this time was in Lawrenceville as general manager of *The Gwinnett Daily News*, and Joiner came to Metter as editor and publisher of the beleagured *Advertiser*.

But in small Georgia counties there is a big advantage to being a "born and bred" publisher, which Ms. Snell was and Joiner wasn't. On October 10, 1980, less than three years after the competition started, *The Advertiser* sold its mailing list and masthead to *The Town and Country News* and gave up the fight. Ms. Snell chose to combine the names, and because *The Advertiser* was older, she took its volume number. The combined paper is known as *The Metter News and Advertiser,* and had about 2,500 paid circulation in 1984.

Nashville is another small town that had a big newspaper war. Berrien County had more people (15,573) in 1920 than it had (13,525) in 1980, although it did show some growth in the 1970s.

The Nashville Herald was founded in 1905 by Albert Sweat and for many years was owned by Joe Lawrence of Ashburn, father of Nora Lawrence Smith. When Lawrence died in 1939 *The Herald* was taken over by his long time associate, A. W. Starling, who operated it until 1958 when he sold it to Belmont Dennis, publisher of *The Covington News*.

The sale prompted S. T. Hamilton, who had worked for *The Herald* since 1939, to start a competitor, *The Berrien Press*. His partner in the venture was Jamie Connell, who also worked at the Air Force base in nearby Valdosta.

When Dennis died in 1961 *The Herald* passed into the hands of Elsie and Geunie Griner, a sister and brother who were a talented musical and comedy team as well as would-be journalists. Their entry into the newspaper business was timely for the Georgia Press Association, if not ultimately successful for them. Elsie and Geunie were valuable performers at the early Cracker Crumble shows, and also provided impromptu entertainment at many late night gatherings during summer conventions on Jekyll Island.

But Nashville and Berrien County could not support two paid weeklies, and Hamilton, with his 20 years experience on *The Herald,* and Connell, gave the challenging *Berrien Press* more roots and experience than *The Herald* could claim.

In 1966 *The Herald* simply folded with no sell-out or merging of names with *The Press*. At the time both *The Herald* and *The Press* claimed about 2,000 paid subscribers.

Despite their brief time in the business, the Griners were among the most colorful Georgia journalists of the past 35 years. Their mother, Elsie Griner Sr., as she was known, was an attorney in Nashville. She handled the estates which owned *The Herald* and finally took it over to save it, which was how Elsie Jr. and Geunie, neither with newspaper backgrounds, came to be its editor and publisher.

Geunie died in the 1970s and Elsie Jr. still lives in Nashville.

Sandersville produced a unique example of triumphant competition. It more closely resembled a straight buy-out, and although the owners of the newer weekly became the owners of the surviving weekly they folded their own paper and kept the long-established one as the on-going publication.

David Wickersham and Robert Garrett were young school teachers in the Atlanta area when they got a notion they'd like to operate a weekly newspaper. Although both were originally from Washington, Georgia, their wives were from Sandersville (Washington County) and were friends of the daughter of the publisher of *The Sandersville Progress,* Jesse D. Mize.

Wickersham and Garrett approached Mize about buying *The Progress* but he turned them down. So they decided to start their own weekly in Sandersville. It was launched in May 1971, as *The Sandersville Georgian*. The first issue had 40 pages but the number dropped sharply after that. Just three months later, Mize agreed to sell them *The Progress*, and *The Georgian* was folded in favor of the 84-year old *Progress*. Wickersham recalled later that he and Garrett were near the point of having to fold *The Georgian* when Mize agreed to sell. "We survived, but it wasn't a case of defeating the older paper," he said. "We just bought it out."

It proved a fortunate development for Sandersville and the newspaper business in Georgia. Wickersham and Garrett not only published a strong newspaper for Washington County but soon expanded their operation with the purchase of *The Wrightsville Headlight* from Charles McMichael in 1975, and the purchase of *The Cochran Journal* from Jewell NeSmith in December 1983.

A Mountain Feud

Another challenger that scored a knockout over the long-established paper was *The White County News* in Cleveland, but its founders and publisher of longest tenure weren't around to celebrate.

The White County News was started in May 1968, with a name revived from a newspaper which had operated in Cleveland from 1941 to 1945. The long-established paper in White County (population 7,000 at that time) was *The Cleveland Courier,* dating back to 1896. It was published for many years by J. P. Davidson. His slogan under the masthead of *The Courier* claimed: "Covers The Mountains Like Moonshine."

Henry and Linda McMillan were the first publishers of *The White County News* but they sold it to Alton C. Brown in 1970 who became its best-known editor. Brown was a crusader who got people's attention.

The News was offset while *The Courier* was still letterpress, which was an advantage for *The News*. The Alpine village of Helen, just north of Cleveland, was giving White County an economic boost about that time, and population was beginning to increase after 50 years of stagnation.

Then tragedy intervened when Brown was found dead at his home in 1974. It was reported that he had suffocated after a plastic garbage can liner was wrapped around his face. His death was ruled a suicide.

Davidson also died about that time, leaving *The Courier* to his son, Richard. Brown's wife sold *The News* to Robert Yates, then publisher of *The Northeast Georgian* in Cornelia, and Yates managed to bolster *The News* by selling combination ads with *The Georgian*. Several offers were made to Davidson to buy *The Courier* but he declined them, saying his father had stipulated in his will that he not sell *The Courier.*

The Courier folded about 1976, after a fire forced it to abandon its hot-type, letterpress equipment. *The White County News* became part of the group of newspapers in central and northeast Georgia owned and operated by Jerue Babb of Spartanburg, South Carolina.

Ironically, and tragically, Babb became the second owner of *The White County News* to die under unusual circumstances. Babb, whose chain of 42 weeklies included virtually all of the paid circulation papers in Northeast Georgia, was found dead in a Spartanburg, South Carolina motel on New Year's Eve, 1984. He apparently had taken his life by slitting his wrists.

When police sought his wife to notify her of the death they found her body near the Babbs' home in Asheville, North Carolina. Police ruled the deaths a murder and suicide.

Mrs. Babb, the former Mary Christine Cogburn, had been elected president of Community Newspapers in May, 1984, with Babb becoming chairman. She was 31 at the time of her death.

Babb, 49, had earlier been married to the daughter of Phil Buchheit, who for many years was publisher of the Spartanburg newspapers, and also head of the company which owns *The LaGrange Daily News*. Following a divorce from his first wife, Babb formed Community Newspapers, Inc. in the early 1970s, and began to acquire weeklies at a fast pace. In addition to his North Georgia holdings he also owned a number of South Georgia newspapers at one time in partnership with Dink NeSmith and Jim Hickey.

Ownership and management of Babb's newspapers was assumed by his three children from his first marriage, Phillip Babb of Spartanburg; Laurie Babb Barnett of Hilliard, Florida, and Andrew Babb of Greenville, South Carolina.

Other Fierce Competitors

There were other fierce competitors through the years among paid weeklies in the smaller Georgia counties and cities. One of the longest and most closely-contested was in Fitzgerald between *The Leader, Enterprise and Press*, and *The Herald*. In fact, Fitzgerald and Ben Hill County (1980 pop. 16,000) have had 22 different newspapers at one time or the other in the past 100 years.

The Leader, Enterprise and *Press* (one paper) traced its origins to *The Enterprise*, founded in 1896. For a half century this newspaper was owned and published by Isidor Gelders, a founding father of Fitzgerald who wrote its city charter in 1896. Gelders also was an early advocate of free textbooks in public schools and municipal ownership of water and power plants.

In 1912, *The Enterprise* absorbed *The Leader*, which had been started in the same year, 1896. But it soon found itself competing again, as *The Press* was founded in 1915, and *The Herald* in 1916. *The Enterprise-Leader* bought out *The Press* — accounting for its elongated name — and then began the long competition between *The L-E-P* and *The Herald* which lasted for 47 years.

The Herald had been established by the Pryor Brothers Printing Company and was owned and operated by S. G. Pryor Jr. and J. J. Pryor until 1956 when J. J.'s son, Gerald (Jerry) W. Pryor, became editor and publisher. It was published twice weekly for most of those years, on Tuesday and Friday.

Isidore Gelders sold the other Fitzgerald weekly to his son, Albert, in 1950, and members of the Gelders family continued to operate it until 1962 when it was sold to E. W. Mathews, publisher of *The Cordele Dispatch*. The Gelders family and the Pryor family were Fitzgerald pioneers and the new ownership found that local roots were important in keeping a competitive weekly going. In 1964 *The Herald* finally bought its long time competitor from Mathews and merged the two papers into *The Fitzgerald*

Herald and *Leader*. The name was simplified in 1980 to *The Herald-Leader*.

Pryor joined with several other South Georgia publishers in establishing a central printing plant at Ocilla in 1971, at which time *The Herald* and *Leader* switched to cold type and offset printing. Pryor thinks he may have been the last Georgia weekly publisher to buy a brand new linotype machine, which he purchased in 1962 for $35,000. "It was the latest model," he says, "and probably the last model."

In 1981, *The Herald-Leader* became the second Georgia weekly newspaper to own and operate a local television channel, following *The Jesup Press-Sentinel* by just a few days. The Fitzgerald TV operation was more ambitious than Jesup's, or any others started by newspapers in Georgia. It had a staff of eight and presented a 30-minute newscast each day, a local talk show, a call-in show, and televised tours of area places and homes.

Delayed telecasts of local sports events were also carried on the newspaper's channel. News from the AP wire was shown on the screen during the non-live broadcast hours.

A connection with a local TV channel was one which many Georgia newspapers considered during the early 1980s and Fitzgerald provides the most extensive case study because Pryor put both the people and the equipment into his effort to give it a chance for success.

After three years he decided to close down the TV operation in March 1984. A major problem he cited was the difficulty of filming effective and professional-looking commercials. He also found that it was hard to win viewers away from the regular, full-time channels for the short period during the day when there was live programming on the local channel.

Pryor is selling his equipment and channel rights to a company that hopes to revive local programming in Fitzgerald. *The Jesup Press-Sentinel* discontinued its live channel TV operation late in 1983. Still in operation in mid-1984 was a local channel owned and operated by the weekly *Athens Observer* in Athens.

Liberty County's Free-for-All

One of the most unusual competitive battles among Georgia weeklies in recent years occurred in Liberty County, home of Fort Stewart, and the state's third fastest growing county in the 1970s. Liberty County is one of the oldest in the state, having been among the original counties created by the first state constitution in 1777. It took its name from the independence movement which was proclaimed in the Declaration a few months earlier. It is a large county (for Georgia) in land area, with 510 square miles, but the population was only 17,500 in the 1970 census. The revival of Fort Stewart at Hinesville sent the population soaring, however, and by 1980 the census showed 37,583, a 118 percent rise during the decade.

Till the 1970s the weekly newspaper at Hinesville had languished along with the county. It dated back to 1871 and had been in the Gill and Clark families for many years. In late 1977 Lottie Clark, widow of the long-time publisher, M. F. Clark, and her son, Nicky, decided to sell *The Herald* and among the prospective buyers was a veteran Georgia newspaperman named Jim Wynn, who had organized a group of local merchants and businessmen to make a bid.

The twisting career and personal path that led Wynn to Hinesville was as strange as the subsequent newspaper war which would rage there during the next four years. He was born in Thomaston but spent most of his younger years in Canton. He attended Mercer and the University of Georgia where among other things he was a roommate of Reg Murphy, a future newspaper great. After graduation he worked at *The Waycross Journal-Herald* and *The Macon News*, was Atlanta Bureau chief for the Macon papers, and then did a two-and-a-half year stint as press secretary for Lt. Gov. Garland Byrd.

Byrd was the favorite for governor in 1962 before he suffered a heart attack and had to withdraw from the race. That sent Wynn back to the newspaper business with *The Columbus Ledger-Enquirer* for a couple of years, then to *The Marietta Daily Journal* as editor during Otis Brumby Jr.'s early years as publisher.

He returned to the Columbus newspapers in 1965 as their Atlanta bureau chief, later becoming associate editor. Among his assignments in those years was the turbulent 1968 Democratic National Convention in Chicago. Wynn went to Bradenton, Florida in 1971 as editor of *The Herald*, which was owned by the Columbus papers, and held that post until 1975 when he resigned to return to Georgia.

Till that time he had never worked on a weekly newspaper and only briefly on small dailies, but he decided to give a small daily a try and accepted a job as managing editor of *The Opelika-Auburn News* in Opelika, Alabama, whose publisher, Millard Grimes, was an old associate from his Columbus days. Nine months later when Grimes bought the two weekly newspapers in Thomaston, Georgia he asked Wynn to go there as publisher and editor, thinking that Wynn's Thomaston roots and his overall ability and experience would help the operation get past the "new ownership" stage. Also Wynn was in the process of getting a divorce and a change of locations seemed desirable.

Wynn later recalled that he "ran into a wall of resentment" in Thomaston. "Even though I was a native Thomastonian, my family had moved away when I was still a child and I had been gone for some 35 years. There were few personal ties, and besides, I wasn't the owner. The newspapers were owned by 'out-of-towners,' as far as the people there were concerned."

There were also other problems, including a divisive political battle going on in the county over school consolidation, and some resistance to Wynn from long-time employees of the Thomaston weeklies. Although owned by the same company and published from the same office, the early week Thomaston paper was called *The Free Press* and the middle-of-the-week paper was called *The Thomaston Times*. The two papers were combined under one name while Wynn was publisher, a move which met surprisingly little opposition from either readers or employees.

In 1977 Grimes sold *The Thomaston Times* to Ben Smith of Ft. Payne, Alabama, a protege of Carmage Walls. As part of the deal, Grimes' company acquired the daily *Enterprise Ledger* of Enterprise, Alabama from Smith in one of the more interesting newspaper transactions during the 1970s. Smith still owned *The Thomaston Times* in 1984 and under publishers Perry Sherrer and Cy Wood, it has prospered.

While at Thomaston Wynn married Linda Fletcher, the composing room supervisor, who was from Hinesville. It was through Linda and her relatives that he heard that *The Liberty County Herald* was for sale. His experience in Thomaston had taught Wynn the value of local support so he set about persuading several Hinesville businessmen to put up money to buy *The Herald*, thus avoiding the "out-of-towner" barrier. The group, when completed, included three local realtors, two insurers and the owner of Coastal Utilities, the local telephone company, and his son. Four of Wynn's brothers-in-law and one of his brothers wanted in, too, making a final total of 12 stockholders. The group paid $350,000 for *The Herald* and assumed management in mid-1978, with Wynn as editor and publisher.

Instead of meeting complaints of "out-of-town" ownership, Wynn was confronted with the accusation that *The Herald* had been the victim of a "political takeover." Telephone company owner Glenn Bryant, a 10 percent stockholder, was chairman of the County Commission. He later was elected to the State Senate. Realtor Clay Sikes, also a 10 percent stockholder, was the son of Sheriff Robert V. Sikes.

Protests of a "political takeover" quickly subsided, however, when readers saw that the newspaper had not become political. Aside from the cancellation of a major automobile dealership's advertising account within hours after the purchase had been announced, there was no notable adverse economic impact.

The Herald, serving a community going through an unprecedented boom as the result of a massive military buildup at Ft. Stewart, had grossed $150,000 during the year before the sale. That figure doubled during the first year of ownership by the new group. The newspaper was converted from weekly to twice-weekly publication and the following year bought and merged with *The Bryan County News* in neighboring Pembroke under a new name, *The Coastal Courier*. In the three years under Wynn's management, the newspaper quadrupled its gross to more than $600,000.

But, then came trouble.

In April of 1981 *The Courier* published a story quoting the mayor of nearby Richmond Hill as saying Liberty Cable TV, owned by Bryant, was dragging its feet in fulfilling a franchise contract to provide cable service for his city. Bryant, angered by the story, bought up controlling interest in the newspaper and then dismissed Wynn as editor and publisher. Bobby Branch, another veteran Georgia newspaperman, who had grown up in Hinesville, was hired to replace Wynn.

Three months later, backed by a group made up mostly of local advertisers, Wynn began publication of a new, free-circulation newspaper — *The Hinesville Star*. *The Star* was circulated by mail and eventually by carriers to every home in Liberty and adjoining Long County, a total distribution of 13,000, which was considerably more than *The Courier*'s paid total of about 7,000.

The Star succeeded in taking away much of *The Courier*'s locally-placed advertising, but it could not penetrate the big corporate accounts — K-Mart, Winn Dixie, Piggly Wiggly, TG&Y and the like — which were placed by out-of-town decision-makers and who, according to Wynn, "had no concern about who controlled the local newspaper." The result was a split of newspaper advertising by the two competitors.

After six months of competition and deficit bottom-line figures by both newspapers, Bryant's group approached Morris Newspapers Corporation, headed by Charles Morris of Savannah, with an offer to sell. Morris already had begun operation of a shopper, *The Penny Saver*, in Hinesville.

With *The Courier* offer in hand, Morris contacted Wynn and also offered to buy *The Star*. The sales were completed in February of 1982 and publication of *The Star* was immediately discontinued by the new owner — an "out-of-towner." Wynn benefited financially from both sales since he still owned 20 percent of *The Courier*, which he was competing against.

Wynn, who later became executive editor of The Meridian (Mississippi) *Star,* one of that state's largest newspapers, believes the trend away from local ownership of weeklies will continue, just as it has with dailies. "The reader often looks on his weekly newspaper as he does an old pipe or a comfortable pair of shoes. He is wary of change, particularly when an 'out-of-towner' replaces an owner-editor who lived down the street and had been a lifelong friend, and often of a family in the community for several generations," Wynn says. "But most new owners improve the newspaper product and often are more independent of the kind of old-line pressure which hurts a newspaper."

Actually the record indicates that "out-of-town" ownership is not a serious liability in many cases. Other factors are usually more important. Looking back through this chapter at the competitions among paid weeklies in Georgia counties, it can be seen that in several cases — Forsyth, Barnesville and Sandersville to name the most notable — the "out-of-towners" were the victors. In all of these cases, however, the new owners did move to the community.

Several other competitions should be mentioned. Frances Greene, a school teacher, started *The Tallapoosa Beacon* against *The Journal* in that small West Georgia town in 1958, and eventually *The Beacon* bought out *The Journal*. Later the paper was owned by Stanley Parkman's Carroll County Publishing Company and then by Harte-Hanks.

Zebulon had competitive weeklies for about three years, and the battle was resolved when their sister papers in Barnesville were merged.

The Pike County Journal was founded in 1889 and was owned at various times by A. W. Quattlebaum, J. W. Preston and Col. Frank Adams. It was also operated for a time by Mrs. Quattlebaum's sister, Onnie Smith. By 1976 when *The Pike County Reporter* was launched by Frank Heflin, *The Journal* was down to four pages. In 1979 the papers were sold to the owners of the two papers in Barnesville, the Meltons and Bob Tribble. The Meltons then got both Zebulon papers in 1980 and merged them into *The Pike County Journal and Reporter*. Rachel Norris McClellan, who started as a typesetter on *The Reporter* in 1976, is the editor-publisher.

Another interesting newspaper competition developed in Franklin

County up in northeast Georgia, near the South Carolina line. In 1965, Franklin County with a population of only 13,000 was supporting three in-county newspapers, *The Carnesville Herald and Advance* in Carnesville, *The Lavonia Times* in Lavonia, and *The Royston Record* in Royston. These were small papers but they had distinguished histories, dating back to the turn of the century. Dewey Holland, who also operated a furniture store, acquired all three of the Franklin weeklies by 1965, and on May 1 of that year he combined them into *The Franklin County Citizen*, with headquarters in Lavonia.

Holland was editor and publisher of this countywide weekly until 1973 when he sold it to Jerue Babb, who was then starting his weekly group. Holland died January 2, 1975.

Competition came to Franklin County again when Bob Williford of Elberton and his associates started *The Royston News-Leader* in Royston in May 1978, exactly 13 years after Holland merged the county's three weeklies. *The News-Leader* was sold along with Williford's other properties to Morris Communications in 1979. "Royston" was dropped from the masthead in 1980 and *The News-Leader* became a countywide competitor to Babb's *Franklin County Citizen*. Linton Johnson was editor of *The News-Leader* in 1985.

Women as Publishers

There are few fields of business and professional endeavor in which women have played such a vital and increasing role since World War II as newspapers and communications in general.

Although women had traditionally handled the "women's news," and been the county correspondents for weekly newspapers, only a few had broken into the harder news side of the business or into the executive ranks before World War II. Nor were many seen in the composing room or on ad staffs.

A sea-change has occurred. In departments where women were seldom seen 30 years ago, a man is seldom seen in 1985. The change has been more sweeping on weekly newspapers than on dailies. Women were the instigators of several new weeklies and are the publishers or owners of about 20 Georgia weeklies. Women also have taken over most of the composition and makeup duties on weeklies, and in many cases are the editors, reporters and the ad sales persons. Wives of publishers have often played integral roles as bookkeepers, office managers, and whatever else was needed for the success of the family newspaper.

Even before getting the right to vote, a few women were already running newspapers and telling the men how to vote. One of the pioneer women publishers in Georgia — and in the nation — was Zula Brown Toole of Colquitt. She not only was one of the earliest woman publishers, but she was the founder of *The Miller County Liberal* in Colquitt in 1897. Born in Decatur County, Georgia in 1863, Zula Brown attended Andrew College at Cuthbert and graduated from Troy State Teachers College in Troy, Alabama. She was a postmistress in rural Miller County in 1893-98 and also began her teaching career of 40 years during that time. She felt Miller County needed a newspaper and she traveled around the county on a bicycle to obtain 500 signatures of residents saying they would subscribe. She bought a flat-bed press and other necessary equipment and started *The Miller County Liberal* in 1897.

While also teaching, Mrs. Toole remained editor and publisher of *The Liberal* for 36 years, until 1933, when other family members took over management. Her grandson, Terry Toole, is the publisher in 1984. Mrs. Toole, who married twice, had two sons and two daughters. She died in 1947.

According to a history of Miller County "Zula B. Toole wrote in the same vein as all publishers of her day — the unvarnished truth with her ideas and beliefs paramount."

Although little known outside Miller County, Zula Brown Cook Toole was truly the pioneer in Georgia among women newspaper publishers, editors and owners.

Another pioneer for women was Virginia Saxon, who also owned and edited a very small Georgia weekly, *The News and Farmer* of Louisville. A forerunner of *The News and Farmer* was *The State Gazette*, founded in 1779 when Louisville was the first capital of Georgia after independence was declared.

Shortly before Ms. Saxon came along, 40 men in Louisville had put up $10 apiece to buy *The News and Farmer*. In 1920 Ms. Saxon bought them out. She then acquired the building, printing equipment and the nearby *Wadley Herald*. She combined the two papers to serve all of Jefferson County, which then had a population of about 22,000.

Ms. Saxon, later known as Virginia Polhill Price, owned and edited the Louisville weekly for 46 years, until selling it in 1966 to an editorial writer from St. Petersburg, Florida. Although she often claimed to be the first woman editor-owner of a Georgia newspaper — and certainly she was deserving of notice as a pioneer — she was 23 years behind Zula Brown Toole. Mrs. Toole did continue teaching for most of the time she ran *The Miller County Liberal*, so Ms. Saxon-Polhill-Price may have been the first full-time woman editor-owner.

Jim Horton bought *The News and Farmer*, *Wadley Herald* in 1969 for $65,000, even though it had declined to about four pages at that time. He switched to offset printing and has brought the paper back to financial health.

Other early women publishers and editors included Emily Woodward, of *The Vienna News*, founder of the Georgia Press Institute, and the only woman president of the GPA as of 1984; and Rosalia Adkins, who took over *The Calhoun County News* of Edison, at her father's death in the early 1930s, and operated it for 40 years. Ms. Adkins, for most of those years was a one-person staff, who could operate a linotype machine, make up pages, write the news and take photos. Like many publishers in small-town Georgia she accepted ads when merchants brought them in. She sold *The News* to R. Taylor Harris of Cuthbert in the late 1960s, and continued as editor under Harris, and then Mrs. Harris, after Harris died. Millard Grimes, who bought *The News* in 1971, combined Ms. Adkins' paper with the *Tri-County Courier* of nearby Arlington during his three-year ownership. It was later owned by Billy Fleming of Blakely.

Rosalia Adkins was a lady but she would have been the first to admit she didn't look the part. She had a hard life and it was written in the lines of her face. She usually dressed in jeans or slacks and was a chain smoker. In the 1970s the offices of *The Calhoun News* still looked like the classic 1930s version of a small-town newspaper office. In fact, as late as 1972 there was still a 1937 calendar hanging crookedly on one peeling wall.

But Ms. Adkins was a surprisingly able reporter, even in her declining years, and she devoted her life to the newspaper which her father left her, never questioning her fate as editor and publisher of a newspaper that struggled to serve a county losing population and had four separate municipalities and two newspapers for most of her years. She died in 1975.

Legendary 'Miss Nora'

Probably the best-known of Georgia's pre-World War II women publishers was the legendary Nora Lawrence Smith of Ashburn. Her portrait now graces the conference room of the Georgia Press Association office to which she donated generously.

Austin Saxon, who worked for Ms. Nora for 20 years, has written the following portrait for this book:

Born as an heir to Irish charm and courage and reared on the grits and gallantry of South Georgia, Nora Lawrence Smith was a pioneer among women publishers.

Her father, Joe Lawrence, an Irish immigrant who made his way from New York to Dodge County and then to a pine wilderness which was to become Ashburn, founded *The Wiregrass Farmer* in 1899 in the village which grew up around a sawmill in timber-rich territory that was designated Turner County in 1906.

The Bible-pounding merchant intended for his weekly publication to be a messenger for the Wesleyan Methodist Church but the suddenly-flourishing community demanded a regular newspaper, so Joe Lawrence responded.

Miss Nora — even those who did not know her personally called her by that affectionate name — claimed she came to Ashburn in a covered wagon, holding a lantern to guide the way.

That lantern which illuminated the pages of *The Wiregrass Farmer* burned brightly for 72 years in which Miss Nora became a close confidante of Georgia governors, among the first to demand women's rights, an unwavering Democrat who played a key role in nominations of presidential candidates and an eloquent if arrogant reporter and editorialist whose only family was an entire community.

Born at Dempsey on Christmas Day, 1885, Miss Nora learned to set type by hand in her father's back shop, preferred writing in a florid script — she never learned to use a typewriter — but reluctantly agreed to a college education at church-related Houghton College in upstate New York.

When her short-lived marriage ended in divorce, she returned to Ashburn to work with her father. Their leadership in promoting diversified farming through a project called "The Cow, Hog and Hen Program" won *The Wiregrass Farmer* national attention in the 1920s and the GPA's first community service award in 1924. She was honored again by the GPA in 1929 for her efforts to get U.S. Highway 41 paved. She continued through the years to promote the highway until Governor Ernest Vandiver asked her to dedicate the first link of Interstate 75 more than 30 years later.

Devoted to Governors Ed Rivers, Ellis Arnall, M. E. Thompson, Herman Talmadge and particularly Carl Sanders, Miss Nora thrived on the complexities of politics and was a vocal, influential delegate at Democratic Conventions in New York in 1924, Houston in 1928, and Chicago in 1932 when she informed the Georgia delegation, "You'll never get back in the damned White House until you nominate that man in the wheel chair (Franklin D. Roosevelt)."

At her father's death in 1939 Miss Nora became editor-publisher of *The Farmer* in a partnership with F. M. Tison Sr. and later with F. M. Tison Jr.

One of Georgia's most zealous promoters, she once won a jaw-to-jaw confrontation with the president of Southern Railway in her battle to keep passenger train service in her hometown. She was the old Henry Grady Hotel's most cherished guest, spending Christmas holidays there for many years. She thought little of attacks on congressmen, socialites or bishops by letter, phone or editorial columns if they stood in her way of reaching what she considered a worthy goal. She was often tender-hearted, immensely fond of children, prayed every day although she seldom darkened the door of a church, admired John F. Kennedy, would not tolerate television, and for all her swearing and bravado, lived a genteel life.

Following a changeless regimen, she arose each day at 6:30 a.m., telephoned a dozen persons within an hour, invited herself to a hearty noon lunch with friends, left her office at 5:20 p.m., spent two hours on the telephone each evening and retired promptly at 9:50 p.m.

Miss Nora was honored for outstanding journalistic achievements by a woman with the NNA Emma McKinney Award in 1969. For more than 30 years, she never missed a GPA Convention. Hampered by arthritis, she spent two weeks each year at Hot Springs, Arkansas.

She sold *The Wiregrass Farmer* to Grover C. Patten, a long-time friend, in 1969. She was in the care of three devoted friends, F. M. Tison, Jr., Beaulah Little and Austin Saxon, her managing editor, when she died July 17, 1971, at the age of 85.

Since World War II women publishers have become more common in the Georgia weekly field. The first of the post-war group was Marian A. Sumner, publisher of *The Sylvester Local* since 1959 and sole owner since 1963. Ms. Sumner first became associated with the newspaper when she and several other Sylvester citizens bought *The Local* from Dr. Gerald Sanders, a retired English professor, in April 1955. She became editor in 1956, then formed a partnership with W. A. Banks to buy out the other owners in 1959, at which time she also assumed the publisher's duties. On January 1, 1963, Ms. Sumner became the sole owner of *The Local* and has operated it for 22 years through 1984.

Sylvester is the county seat of Worth County, which reversed a population decline in the 1980 census, rising to 18,064, after dropping to 14,770 in 1970. *The Local*'s circulation has also increased, rising from below 2,000 in the late 1960s to a 1984 circulation of 3,600. Its name was changed in early 1985 to *The Sylvester Local News*, because Ms. Sumner said she got tired of people asking "The Local What?"

Ms. Sumner has been very active in the Georgia Press Association, and was the only woman member of its Board of Managers for several years.

Another veteran woman publisher in Georgia is Julie Graham Weddle of *The Springfield Herald* in Effingham County. She bought *The Herald* in 1970 when she was 28. Although she had no formal training or background in journalism, Julie learned in a hurry. In a 1978 magazine interview, she recalled, "I sold all the advertising, did all the writing, did the management, learned to run the machinery. I can remember weeks when I put in 18-hour days consistently. I cried a lot the first year, I'll admit, when that machinery would break down and I wouldn't know what to do."

But she persevered and *The Herald* has grown in the 14 years of her ownership from 1,500 to 3,800 circulation and Effingham County spurted from 13,000 population in 1970 to 19,357 in 1980.

Jewell NeSmith was publisher of *The Cochran Journal* for many years before selling it to David Wickersham and Robert Garrett in 1983; Wanda West succeeded her late husband as publisher of *The North Georgia News* and *Towns County Herald*; Adelaide Ponder has for nearly 30 years been closely involved with her husband, Graham, as editor of *The Madisonian* and other wives such as Cathy Lipsett in Kingsland, Marianne Thomasson in Newnan, and Julie Joiner in McRae are virtually co-publishers and editors with their husbands.

The total number of women weekly publishers in Georgia is still less than 20, and through 1984 only one woman — Elizabeth H. Staples of *The Rockdale Citizen* — has been publisher of a Georgia community daily. Frances Beck is publisher of *The Fulton County Daily Report*, which is the official legal organ for Fulton County and Atlanta, and is now issued daily.

The Largest Weekly

Georgia's largest weekly in paid circulation and number of pages is *The* Newnan *Times-Herald*, which in 1984 is the only newspaper of any kind published in Coweta County. *The Times-Herald* listed a paid circulation of 11,505 in 1983, more than many of the state's smaller dailies. It averages 60 pages in its one edition a week, plus several pre-printed inserts.

The city of Newnan, about 40 miles south of Atlanta, had 11,000 population in 1980, and Coweta County had a population of 39,268, up from 32,310 in 1970. Slightly beyond the growth circle of metropolitan Atlanta, Coweta's population did not change much from 1920 (29,047) to 1970, but completion of I-85 all the way from Atlanta to the west Georgia border helped spark growth in the 1970s. For nearly a decade, I-85 stopped at the city limits of Newnan and did not resume again for 30 miles, on the west side of LaGrange.

Newnan and Coweta have been important in the state's history, Coweta having been established as a county in 1825. Two prominent governors were from Newnan. The first was William Y. Atkinson (1894-1898), a progressive for his time, who supported many Populist issues, such as election of the state school superintendent and Supreme Court justices, and anti-trust laws. Atkinson failed, however, in efforts to pass anti-lynching laws and to establish the office of lieutenant governor.

The second governor from Newnan, Ellis Arnall (1943-47), was one of the most progressive governors in the South and the nation, rewriting Georgia's constitution, lowering the voting age to 18, battling discriminatory laws against southern railroads and industry, and eliminating the White Primary.

Newnan was once known as the "richest city per capita" in Georgia and one of the richest in the nation.

Its newspapers have also been outstanding. *The* Newnan *Herald* was founded in September 1865, shortly after the end of the Civil War, by J. S. Bigby and J. C. Wootten. *The Herald*'s most noted editor was James Evans Brown, who held the post for 40 years, from 1887 until 1928.

The Newnan *Times* was founded in March 1936 by Evan W. Thomasson and his son, James. The Thomassons were the son and grandson respectively of J. J. Thomasson, publisher of *The Carroll County Times*, on which they had worked before coming to Newnan.

For a short time during World War II, George N. McNabb published a daily tabloid *Herald* along with the weekly, the only time that Newnan has had a daily newspaper. For health reasons, McNabb sold *The Herald* to the Thomassons in 1946 and they soon merged *The Times* and *Herald* into *The* Newnan *Times-Herald*, with the first issue of the combined weekly being published on Christmas Eve, 1947.

In 1985, William (Billy) Thomasson is a fourth generation publisher and the third generation publisher of *The Times-Herald*. His father, James, died in 1979, and his mother, who was news editor of *The Times-Herald*, died in 1981. Evan W. Thomasson lived to be 95, dying in 1983.

In addition to its circulation and size, *The Times-Herald* also leads Georgia weeklies in number of awards from state and national press associations. Its mechanical excellence and sharp reproduction have long been recognized and admired throughout the newspaper industry. Through the years, its management has concentrated solely on the weekly *Times-Herald*, accepting no outside printing jobs, and buying no other papers.

The Thomassons have also resisted the temptation to increase frequency to twice weekly or daily, as many other newspapers in similar markets have done. "We take a poll of merchants every year on whether we should go daily," Billy Thomasson says, "and they've always voted that we should stay weekly." **(Editor's note: *The Times-Herald* did increase to twice-a-week publication in June, 1985.)**

The Last Handset Newspaper

Oddly, Georgia still had a completely handset newspaper after the last weekly linotype machine was retired in 1978. That relic was *The Doerun Courier*, located in the small town of Doerun, between Albany and Moultrie. It managed to stay in business from 1916 to 1979 even though Doerun never had more than 1,000 people, and *The Courier* mainly served a small area of north Colquitt County.

What kept *The Courier* going was a man named Homer W. Garrett, who took over *The Courier* in 1920 and operated it for 59 years until a few months before his death at the age of 94 in 1979. Sometimes in those later years *The Courier* didn't make an appearance every week, and the feistiness which once characterized its stories and commentaries was less evident. But one thing stayed the same. Garrett still composed the whole newspaper when it did come out, by hand setting all of the type, and then printing it on a hand-fed press.

"Everybody's got a linotype machine," he once said in answer to why he kept hand setting his newspaper. "This is what makes me different." Garrett made that comment long after most newspapers in Georgia had already abandoned their linotypes for cold type composition.

In an article by Charles Postell in the magazine, *Georgia Monthly*, Garrett's son-in-law, "Bub" Lang, described Garrett as a man "who didn't care who he made mad. He never hesitated one bit. At one time or another everybody in Doerun has been mad with Garrett."

In that same article, Garrett admitted he wanted a paper that said what he wanted it to say and he didn't care who liked it. That was one reason he set all the type himself and clung to outdated equipment. He also kept cans of food stored at his shop to "keep from starving," when the advertisers boycotted him. "They once quit advertising with me," he told Postell, "because I caused a ruckus about the way the town was operated. The city fathers didn't even publish a financial statement. I bored too deep and talked too plain." Garrett said he even reported that a candidate for office was getting too thick with another man's wife. "I didn't just call a spade a spade, I called it a goddamn shovel."

Appropriately, Garrett's hero was Benjamin Franklin, who he considered the father of American printing and journalism. He kept printing just like Ben Franklin did until a day in 1979 when he was so feeble that he had to be placed in a nursing home. "I'd planned to go back," he told Postell, "but my fingers are getting too slow. Life is too damn quick. I don't know where all the time went."

Well, for Homer Garrett, a lot of his 94 years were spent hunched over a type case, plucking out letters to be placed in a type stick, locked in a page and then transferred to paper on a Country Campbell press. A tornado blew the side off his building in the early 1970s. He never got around to replacing it, and so had an open-air building in his later years.

Garrett was married twice, the second time to Maude Howard who was editor of *The Dawsonville News* in Dawson County, north of Atlanta. Garrett died in July 1979, a few months after closing down *The Courier*.

The Courier was not only Georgia's last handset newspaper, but is believed to have been the last handset paper in the entire United States.

Bull Chism and His Sons

When J. B. (Bull) Chism, long-time publisher of *The Pelham Journal*, died on December 27, 1982 at the age of 68, he received a unique tribute which any man or woman would cherish. Both of his sons wrote eloquent and touching columns about him in the following week's *Journal*.

Neal Chism, who had succeeded him as publisher, said: "J. B. did not come to work this morning. But that was not unusual. He had been in the habit since retirement to remain at home with Francine, his invalid wife. He did not send in 'The Trail' either, and that was unusual. He always wrote 'The Trail.' He had written 'Down the Chism Trail,' which appeared on the front page of this newspaper, every week since Christmas of 1955.

"But he would not be bringing in the trail. As the week began it was

'30' in the life of J. B. Chism, Jr., a newspaperman since early childhood days . . . we shared an office together. I look over at his desk, the chair now empty. Though his chair is empty the memories of an exceptional man will always remain. He was not only my Daddy, but also my best friend."

His younger son, Billy Chism, a public relations man in Toccoa, wrote of when his seventh grade teacher assigned the class to write a paper on "My Most Unforgettable Character."

"I didn't blink an eye," Billy wrote. "I knew right away my most unforgettable character was J. B. . . . I can remember him sitting at the linotype machine, setting his column, and about every other story in the paper. And who else but Daddy would carry me along to all the Hornet football games, in town and away, from the time I was in the third grade. (Bull Chism was the radio announcer for the Pelham High football games for many years.) I was the only seventh grader in town who could take pictures with a Speed Graphic camera, develop those big pieces of film and print a photo . . .

"Mrs. Scruggs (his teacher) knew an unforgettable character when she saw one. She put an "A" at the top of the page. Daddy, you framed it, hung it up on the wall, and I loved you for it."

Interesting Facts, Some Fiction

Following are some interesting facts — and maybe a little fiction — collected from responses to a survey of Georgia weekly editors:

The publisher of the *Wilkinson County News*, Irwinton, wrote: "This newspaper has one staff member, publisher Joe Boone. On October 20, 1978 a Compugraphic Jr. was added to the equipment of the paper. The circulation has increased due to coverage of Swampland Opera House, a popular community spot that has been covered with both news stories and photos."

The Winder News started a policy in 1964 of taking an entire week of July for all staff vacations, with no paper published that week . . . Col. Harry O. Smith, publisher of *The Winder News* for many years, was appointed State Director of Selective Service by Governor Carl Sanders in 1963, and served in that post until 1968.

The Danielsville Monitor has been owned by the Ayers family since 1915, and has had only two publishers from 1915 to 1984, Mrs. C. B. Ayers (1915-1945) and Jere Ayers (1945-1984) who continues as publisher.

The Eatonton Messenger was owned in part for nine years

(1941-1948) by Louis Griffith, co-author of *Georgia Journalism*, the first history of Georgia newspapers, who later was a faculty member and administrator at the University of Georgia for 35 years.

The Clinch County News, Homerville, was owned and published by Iverson Huxford for more than 40 years . . .

The Tribune of Gainesville, founded in 1959, is the only newspaper in Georgia once owned by a college. It was donated in 1983 to Truett-McConnell College in Cleveland. The name was changed to *The Lanier Tribune*, to associate it more with the entire Lake Lanier recreation area.

Danielsville, with a 1980 population of 354, is the smallest town in Georgia with a weekly newspaper, but Hiawassee, with a 1980 population of only 491, has two weekly newspapers.

Carl Rountree of *The Dawson News* says the "best thing that happened to *The News* was when my son, Tommy, joined me in publishing the newspaper. He graduated from Georgia and came straight home and began working. Next best thing, maybe conversion to offset. It's easier, but still tough."

The Swainsboro Forest-Blade won first place for general excellence in the National Newspaper Association contest in both 1971 and 1972. That meant it was judged the best weekly newspaper in the country — two consecutive years.

The Southern Miscellany, a forerunner of *The Madisonian* of Madison, had as its first editor, William Tappan Thompson, a noted southern humorist of the pre-Civil War period. He wrote under the pseudonym of Major Jones, and much of the material in his most popular collection, "Letters From Major Jones," was first published in *The Miscellany*. *The Madisonian* was also owned and edited by William T. Bacon, first editor of the University of Georgia campus newspaper, *The Red and Black*. Bacon was associated with *The Madisonian* for nearly 50 years from 1894 to 1943.

The Decatur-DeKalb News/Era seldom endorses candidates in state and national races but almost always makes endorsements in local and county races, which are the ones that really get a newspaper in hot water.

Legend has it that *The Monticello News* was started after a tramp printer left a press at a boarding house operated by the Penn family. The Penns decided that since they had a press they might as well start a newspaper. That was in 1881 and members of the Penn family owned and operated *The News* for more than 70 years.

The Camilla Enterprise said that it endorsed Jimmy Carter for president in 1976 and 1980 because "he was a Georgian and from our part of the state, and we thought he would look favorably on the farmers of our area and give them the help they so desperately needed."

Two paragraphs from Jack Parks' page one column in the April 20, 1951 issue of *The Dahlonega Nugget*, were reprinted in newspapers throughout the country. Parks wrote, concerning the firing of General Douglas MacArthur: "We had planned to write a thunderous editorial this week on the firing of General MacArthur, but we regret to report that news from Yaahoola and Frogtown, plus other disturbances in and around Dahlonega have crowded the General off the front page of *The Nugget*.

"If anyone is interested in getting our views on the MacArthur issue they may secure same by calling on us at our offices in The Nugget Tower."

The Claxton Enterprise changed to a six-column format in 1975, one of the first weeklies in the state to make the switch.

The Soperton News was the first newspaper ever printed on paper made from southern slash pine. That was in March 1933, and *The News*' publishers say "there is plenty of documentation to prove it, despite some claims by Texas newspapers to have been first." Soperton also claims the highest circulation per person for its county population of any Georgia weekly.

The Wheeler County Eagle of Alamo won the Herschell Lovett Award for reporting on governmental affairs for three consecutive years.

The Vidalia Advance, explaining why it didn't endorse Jimmy Carter for president, minced no words. "Democrats, then as now, were taking the country to hell in a handbasket with their irresponsible entitlement and sundry giveaway programs."

The Southern Israelite began publication as a small bulletin, then changed to a magazine format and moved to Atlanta in the 1920s. For awhile it was strictly a magazine. In the 1930s a tabloid weekly newspaper was added and the magazine became a quarterly publication. The magazine was discontinued in 1973 and full emphasis was placed on the newspaper.

The Southeast Georgian of Kingsland has been located in all three of Camden County's incorporated cities, having started in Kingsland in 1894, moved to Woodbine in 1900, then to St. Mary's in 1907, and back to Kingsland in 1926. The editor writes that no endorsements for presidents were made in 1976 or 1980 because "you can vote Republican around here but you sure don't endorse them."

Max Gardner, publisher of *The Baxley News-Banner*, is also a cartoonist, and received the George Washington medal from the Freedom

Foundation at Valley Forge in 1978 for a cartoon on voting rights.

The Oglethorpe Echo began operation in Crawford in 1874 but moved to Lexington three years later because the city council would not let the editor keep three goats near the office. W. A. Shackelford bought *The Echo* in 1880 when he was only 19 and was its editor and publisher for 63 years.

Explaining why *The Echo* did not support Jimmy Carter for president, the editor wrote: "Carter was not a good governor of Georgia. He lied to all Georgia editors when he told them at a meeting at the governor's mansion that any state department head could veto any part of the government reorganization bill he didn't agree with. Carter didn't say he would override their veto."

The Sylvania Telephone had a different view of the only Georgian to become U.S. president. Its editors wrote: "Carter was a Georgian who made the South look good!!"

The Telephone was founded in 1879 and was named for Alexander Graham Bell's invention which had recently been announced. Since the telephone was at that time the latest thing in communication, Charles Medlock, *The Telephone*'s founder, thought the name was appropriate. Ironically, the newspaper was the only *Telephone* in Screven County for 20 years. The first real telephone was not installed until 1899.

The Blackshear Times, although a small weekly in a small town, scooped most large dailies on one of the biggest stories of World War II, the Allied invasion of France. "Europe Is Invaded," read the lead headline on the copy of *The Times* which was on the streets at 7 a.m. June 6, 1944. In anticipation of the pending event, Editor Sherwood Broome and his brother Lee had already prepared a front page and had a headline and some type set for this special edition. When radio reports of the invasion began coming in shortly after midnight they rushed to the office and hurriedly completed the single-page edition. They took it to Waycross for printing and had the news on the streets before any other weekly newspaper in Georgia, or possibly the nation, and before most dailies.

The Miller County Liberal, commenting on its endorsement of Jimmy Carter for president, said: "He was a Georgia boy, a friend and the best candidate. Wish we had him back."

The Coastal Courier of Hinesville also offered a sympathetic view of Carter's presidency: "As time goes by it is evident that Carter's unpopular decisions during his administration are being viewed differently today. Carter, each day, is looking better and better by political history analysts."

A former editor of *The Jackson Herald* in Jefferson, Floyd Hoard, was murdered in 1967 while serving as solicitor general of the judicial circuit. As solicitor, Hoard had cracked down on bootlegging operations in Jackson County. An alleged bootlegging kingpin and four other men were subsequently convicted of Hoard's murder.

The News and Farmer of Wrens is proud of the fact that the Georgia Press Association office, and other newspaper offices around the state, were once wallpapered with replicas of front pages of *The Louisville Gazette*, a forerunner of *The News and Farmer* when Louisville was Georgia's capital city.

Newspapers Merged or Discontinued in Georgia 1960-1983

The Fannin County Times, Blue Ridge — Ceased publication, 1970
The Royston Record, Royston — Ceased publication, 1971
The Herald and Advance, Carnesville — Ceased publication, 1970
The Metropolitan Herald, Atlanta — Ceased publication, 1968
The Weekly Star, Atlanta — Ceased publication, 1967
The Atlanta Suburban Reporter, East Point — Ceased publication, 1975
The South Fulton Recorder, Fairburn — Ceased publication, 1980
The Herald and Sun, Roswell — Merged with Neighbor Newspapers, Inc., 1969
The Enterprise, Sandy Springs — Merged with Neighbor Newspapers, Inc., 1969
Buford Advertiser and News, Gwinnett — Ceased publications, 1967
The Weekly Herald, Lawrenceville — Ceased publication, 1970
The News and Farmer, Louisville and
The Herald, Wadley — Two newspapers merged, 1967
The Lee County Journal, Leesburg — Ceased publication, 1971
The Baldwin Free Press, Milledgeville — Ceased publication, 1973
The Baldwin News, Milledgeville — Ceased publication, 1966
The Nashville Herald, Nashville — Ceased publication, 1966
The Bartow Herald, Cartersville — Merged with *Cartersville Weekly Tribune,* 1969
The Bryan Countian, Pembroke — Ceased publication, 1969
Tri-County Courier, Arlington and
Calhoun County News, Edison — Merged in 1972; discontinued in 1983
The News-Record, Fort Gaines — Merged with *Cuthbert Times-News,* 1971
The Observer, Unadilla — Merged with *Vienna News*, 1976

The Monroe County Advertiser, Forsyth — Ceased publication, 1977
The Sun, Ellaville — Merged with *Marion Patriot-Citizen,* 1970
The Screven County News, Sylvania — Purchased by *Sylvania Telephone,* 1979
The News-Examiner, Tifton — Ceased publication, 1977
The Thomaston Times and
The Thomaston Free Press, Thomaston — Two newspapers merged, 1978
The Tallapoosa Journal was bought by *The Beacon* in 1960
The DeKalb New Era, Decatur — Purchased by News-Sun Publications, 1979
The Jesup Sentinel and
Wayne County Press, Jesup — Press bought Sentinel, 1978
The Courier, Cleveland — Ceased publication, 1976
The Wilcox County Chronicle, Abbeville — Ceased publication, 1967
The Glynn Reporter, Brunswick — Ceased publication, 1979
The News and
Martinez-Evans Times, Columbia — *News* bought *Times,* 1971
The Times-Journal and
The Spotlight, Eastman — *Spotlight* bought *Times Journal,* 1975
The Fitzgerald Leader, Fitzgerald — Merged with *The Fitzgerald Herald,* 1964

The following newspapers were purchased by James Wood in 1968 to form News/Daily, Jonesboro: *Forest Park Free Press, Clayton County News, Forest Park News, Clayton County Journal.*

The following newspapers were purchased by Otis A. Brumby Jr. in 1968 to form Neighbor Newspapers, Incorporated: *Mableton Mail, North Cobb News, Smyrna Herald.*

Bo McLeod, the Sage of Seminole County, writes in this chapter about what it took to be a small weekly publisher in "hot-type" days — and what it still takes.

Nora Lawrence Smith, long-time publisher of The Wiregrass Farmer *in Ashburn, is shown with portrait of her father, Joe Lawrence.*

Photo taken in 1928 in Fitzgerald building still occupied by The Herald-Leader *shows J. J. Pryor, (father of Gerald Pryor) seated at left; S. G. Pryor, standing at counter; and Florence Henderson, bookkeeper.*

Scene in Sandersville Progress *office in 1920s. Man seated by heater is C. B. Chapman, longtime editor. Much of equipment shown is still in* Progress *building.*

A familiar scene during 1960s and 1970s at Georgia weeklies was the hauling away of the old letterpress. Dixon Hollingsworth, publisher of The Sylvania Telephone *says goodbye to his Whitlock Flatbed Cylinder as it goes to junkyard in 1970.*

B. T. (Tom) Burson of The Camilla Enterprise *wasn't hauled away; he retired happily in 1982 and had a special front page to mark the occasion.*

Happy award winners are a familiar sight at GPA conventions. James Windsor, Carolyn Jordan and Murphy McRae are showing off awards for one of state's smallest weeklies, The Wheeler County Eagle.

The Oglethorpe Echo *is a Maxwell family affair and the whole family got together to celebrate the* Echo's *102nd birthday in 1975. L. to R., Scott, Ralph Jr., Ralph Sr., (Mrs.) Clyde Maxwell and William.*

Billy Fleming admires 50-year medallion presented to his father, W. H. Fleming. Both were (and are) publishers of The Early County News *in Blakely. Billy has also served as Blakely's mayor.*

Marianne and Billy Thomasson (shown in early 1970s) are husband-wife team that helped Newnan Times-Herald *become state's largest weekly. Billy is a fourth-generation publisher.*

Homer Garrett . . . he kept setting The Doerun Courier *by hand even after the last linotype was abandoned.*

Jack Parks continued W. B. Townsend's tradition of personal journalism on Dahlonega Nuggett. *He was publisher-editor for 34 years.*

Leodel Coleman, with beloved pipe, studies copy of Bullock Herald *which he and his brothers founded.*

Paul Miles was a former big-city city editor on The Columbus Enquirer *who became a weekly publisher on* The Calhoun Times *in 1976.*

Max and Helen Gardner are husband-wife team who operate The Baxley News-Leader. *Max is also a prize-winning cartoonist.*

Isidor Gelders was publisher of The Fitzgerald Leader, Enterprise *and* Press *for 50 years and a founding father of Fitzgerald itself.*

Robert (Bob) Williford, publisher of The Elberton Star *for 16 years, is the very picture of the weekly publisher of the 1970s who donned printer's apron on publishing day to help "get the paper out." Linotype machine in background was still used for commercial jobs.*

Marian A. Sumner has been associated with The Sylvester Local *since 1956 and its sole owner since 1963. She was one of the first women publishers who had no previous family connection with the company.*

Julia Jones Roberts is another South Georgia woman publisher, following in footsteps of her father, F. A. (Bulldog) Jones and husband, Joe Roberts, as publisher of The Times-Journal-Spotlight *in Eastman.*

W. T. (Bill) Hughes was once business editor of the state's largest newspaper, The Atlanta Journal. *He forsook the big city (and paper) to become publisher and editor of* The Monticello News, *one of the state's smaller weeklies, which he and wife Chris have operated since 1976.*

Col. Harry O. Smith was publisher of The Winder News *from 1939 to 1963 when he was appointed state director of Selective Service by Gov. Carl Sanders. Smith sold* The News *to Bob Fowler's company in 1972.*

Marvin Griffin, publisher of The Post-Searchlight *of Bainbridge, is the only full-time Georgia newspaperman to become governor in 20th century. He was elected in 1954 and served until January, 1959. He earlier was Lt. Governor and State Adjutant General.*

Carl Rountree, center, publisher of The Dawson News, *holds portrait of his father, C. D. Rountree, at time of C. D.'s induction into Hall of Fame. With Rountree are sons, Tommy, left, and Don.*

Georgia's last hand-set newspaper was The Doerun Courier, *owned, operated and personally set by Homer A. Garrett, shown here at his type case.* The Courier *ceased publication in 1979 shortly before Garrett died at the age of 93.*

Three generations of Friers are shown here as Tom Frier and Tom Frier Jr. stand beneath portrait of W. D. Frier. All three worked with The Douglas Enterprise.

W. B. Townsend, in printer's apron, was nationally-known editor of Dahlonega Nugget *in years before World War II, because of his witty "paragraphs."*

The Telfair Times

Combined with The Lumber City Log

VOLUME 30 NUMBER 41 — PRICE: 15 CENTS — MARK & JULIE JOINER, CO-EDITORS — OCTOBER 5, 1983

Julie's Corner

Over the past several months, many of you may have heard rumors that Murphy McRae was going to sell the Lumber City Log and the Montgomery Monitor to Mark and Julie Joiner. Well, that rumor is now a reality, and this week we printed our first editions of each paper.

Mark and I are already acquainted with a large number of our readers, but for those who are unfamiliar with us:

We are lifelong residents of McRae. Mark's parents are Mr. and Mrs. Clyde Joiner, and my parents are Mr. and Mrs. Arthur Wilkes.

Mark graduated last spring from Georgia Southern College with a Bachelor of Business Administration. He will direct the business end of the papers and will work with selling ads. He will also periodically write his own column.

I graduated from Georgia Southern in August with a Bachelor of Science in journalism. I worked on the school newspaper at Southern, and did my internship at the Statesboro Herald. I hope to be able to cover the news and features in and around our counties.

Mark and I were married September 3, and we feel that we have a wonderful opportunity to be able to start right to work on these papers.

We realize that we are taking on a heavy load by graduating from college, getting married, building a house and going into business all in a matter of months. We know we will make some mistakes before we get used to working full-time on the newspapers. We just want everyone to know that we are trying, and we ask everyone to please bear with us these first few weeks, as we adapt to our new jobs.

Although we are new at this, we hope that in a short time we will be able to build both papers into larger and better publications, which will reach a greater number of people. We are excited about this new venture, and look forward to working with everyone in these communities.

As for changing the name of the Lumber City Log to The Telfair Times combined with The Lumber City Log, we want people to view our paper as a county paper. We plan to cover news and events in McRae, Helena, Lumber City, Scotland, Milan and Jacksonville, yet we don't want the paper to lose its identity and origin in Lumber City.

We plan to open an office in McRae soon. Since McRae is the county seat and the most central area in the county, we feel that a McRae office will make the paper more accessible to the citizens who want to submit news and information. Our McRae address for now is Post Office Box 429.

We would like to add many new features and sections to our papers, and are open to any suggestions from any of our readers on how we can better serve our circulation area. To submit an idea, simply send a Letter to the Editor to either paper. We will be glad to consider any ideas for improvement.

McRae Receives Block Grant

The city of McRae has been selected to receive a Community Development Block Grant of $425,682, according to Mayor Chester Ryals. Mayor Ryals was officially notified by the governor's office Monday, that the City of McRae will receive the funds for use in community development and upgrading projects.

Ryals said that a portion of the grant will be used to build a 4,000-square-foot building to house a new mental health center. The present center is located in Workmore.

The grant will also include rehabilitation of about 18 houses located in the vicinity of 6th Avenue, Grant Street and Magnolia Street. It will also include the construction of sewer lines in this area, Ryals said. He added that Sixth Avenue will be paved, part of Magnolia and Grant Streets will be paved, and Bowen Street will be paved between Third and Fourth Avenues. Curbs, gutters and sidewalks will also be constructed on these streets.

Ryals said that this is the third CDBG grant approved for McRae since 1981.

More Pot

A raid was executed about 10:30 Wednesday night of last week, September 28th in Telfair County about one mile from the home of James Julian Bland, age 40. Bland and another Jacksonville person, Gary Lowe, arrived and began to load a pickup with marijuana that had already been cut and stacked earlier.

The agents moved in after the truck was loaded and arrested Bland, but Lowe fled on foot through the woods and is still a fugitive.

Another truck was also seized in the raid, a Chevrolet pickup with a small amount of marijuana in it.

The crop weighed over 400 lbs. and had a street value of over $200,000. This is the third raid in three weeks in Telfair County.

Several weeks ago when three people were arrested in the China Hill Area, a Hugh Hulett fled and is still at large, and there is believed to be a close relationship between Lowe and Hulett, according to the authorities.

Bland is still in the Laurens County Jail under $50,000 bond.

Honors Night At Telfair High School

Telfair County High School held its 1982-83 Honors Night Program September 15. Students with a cumultive average of 90.0 were recognized and presented awards. Sudents at Honors Night were: Front Row: Stephanie Knight, Julie Dopson, Amy Culpepper, Peggy Butler, Kim Beachamp, Janel Ashley. Second Row: Leslie McLean, Miriam Lowe, Vickie Johnson, Teresa Henderson, Tammie Gunn and Sajuana Wilson. Third Row: Sheritha Caldwell, Tammie Boone, Linda Yawn, JoAnn Williams, Sherri Rogers, Sara Elizabeth Pope, Christie Smith and Kathy Floyd. Back Row: Brian Neal, Sherry Pitts, Michelle Jones, Mary McRae, Susan Barber, Cathy Quinn, Lisa McVey, Linda Gail Cliett, Molly Neal, Samantha McGowan and Leanne Clark.

Suzanne Stanley Is Queen of Fair

Suzanne Stanley of McRae was crowned queen of The Heart of Georgia Fair during the pageant held Saturday, October 1, at the Veterans Administration Medical Center auditorium in Dublin. Suzanne is the daughter of Mr. and Mrs. Mark Stanley.

The pageant was open to young ladies living within the Heart of Georgia area, and was sponsored by the Dublin Civitan Club and directed by Elaine Owens. Proceeds will go to Renee Etheridge, a kidney transplant patient.

First runner-up was Betty Hanson, daughter of Mrs. Ed Hanson of Dublin. Second runner-up was Jodi Harville, daughter of Mr. and Mrs. Randell Meeks of Glenwood. Third runner-up was Michelle Jones, daughter of Mr. and Mrs. Charles Jones of Jacksonville. Fourth runner-up was Michelle Warren, daughter of Mr. and Mrs. Johnny Warren of Dublin.

One of Suzanne's duties as queen was to officially open the Fair by assisting in the ribbon cutting Monday, October 3, at 5 p.m., in Dublin.

Jaycettes Raise $1,000 for Shannon

The McRae Jaycettes raised over $1,000 last weekend for the Shannon Melvin Hospital Fund, according to Ann Burress of the Jaycettes. They held a roadblock at the intersection of Oak Street and Third Avenue.

The Jaycettes have also placed cannisters throughout the county to collect additional funds. Burress said the cannisters have been out for two weeks and have collected about $300. These cannisters will be out through October.

Shannon Melvin, 10, of Helena had a swimming accident July 4, and is paralyzed from the neck down. She is the daughter of Linda Melvin of Helena.

Anyone wishing to make a contribution to the fund should contact Ann Burress at 868-2427, Rosemary Hester or any McRae Jaycette. Contributions can also be sent to The Shannon Melvin Hospital Fund at the Security State Bank in McRae.

We're Going To Miss Murphy

By Bill Ricks

Back in 1954 the Georgia Power Company, being "a citizen wherever we serve", sponsored some competition to honor communities. It was called the Better Hometowns Contest or something like that.

One of the requirements of the contest was that the town have a newspaper or some sort of regular publication, and that presented a problem to the community of Lumber City, because it did not have a newspaper. There was a county paper named the Telfair Enterprise, but it was up the road in McRae.

So Mayor Joe Prescott decided that Lumber City would have its own newspaper. Tommy Brewer was named editor, and Joe Prescott's wife, Jane, gave the paper a name. And that's how the Lumber City Log came into being in March 1954.

The above story was told to me by Editor and Publisher Murphy McRae about three years ago, and I suppose that all the statements are true, although Mr. McRae has been known to over-embellish some stories. For example, his account of the Bible story of David and Goliath has young David standing and staring at the Giant for so long that Goliath, in the heat and annoyance, lifts the visor of his helmet, permitting David to hit him with the fatal stone.

When confronted with the literal version from the Bible (which has no mention of a helmet, visor, heat or annoyance) Mr. McRae's only comment was "There's no point in telling a story if you can't make it better than the way you heard it told."

Mr. McRae left a life of many pursuits to become a newspaper editor. Perhaps the most significant of his many accomplishments was to survive to adulthood in turbulent Telfair County. Some of his lesser achievements include: attaining a law degree from the University of Georgia, employment in New York City, military service in Panama, and traveling around the world as steward for a ship's captain. In 1960 he left it all to become Editor of the Lumber City Log.

In taking over the newspaper, he was not settling down to such a peaceful existence. His editorials brought attacks, both verbal and physical, from the prevailing powers in politics at that time. Although some of the county's highest officials are presently being investigated on various charges of drug trafficking, the situation in Telfair today may be considered mild to what it was a couple of decades ago.

Mr. McRae has been at the forefront of reporting the recent investigations. So good is his information that some of the investigating officials have demanded to know how he has learned so much about their progress. That which he hasn't mentioned in news accounts he has attacked in his personal editorial, a column read by journalists from all over the state. He is on a first name basis with editors of the largest papers in the state, and he doesn't hesitate to call on them when a local story merits state coverage.

One newspaper was plenty to maintain the single lifestyle of the Editor his first few years, but marriage and three children sent him looking for other sources of income, so about 1970 he bought the Montgomery Monitor.

In December 1972 Mr. McRae and James Windsor, who had become owner of the Soperton News a year earlier, together launched a new enterprise, Suburban Printing Corporation at Higgston. It was a pioneering venture, being one of the first operations in the state where two or more papers went together to do their composition work. A few years later the two publishers added the Wheeler County Eagle to their family of newspapers.

Ten years and eight months ago Murphy McRae became my boss, and he has gotten along very well with me. My other boss, James Windsor, could tell you that it is a remarkable accomplishment to get along with me, but Mr. McRae has done just that. I've gotten along with him, too, but it hasn't been without frustration.

For example, there was the time that I got a new trailer to haul newspapers. The trunk of my car was always so full of junk that the newspapers I hauled back to Soperton on Wednesday nights would fill the rest of the car, so I got a nice trailer with a steel cover that would protect the papers from the rain. The first time I used it, I brought the Eagle back from Lyons from being printed and backed the trailer to the back door at Suburban.

Mr. McRae, being anxious to help me unload, grabbed the lid of the trailer, before I could even stop, and threw it into the air. It pivoted on its hinges and fell on the trunk of my car, leaving two creases which are there to this day. Mr. McRae couldn't understand why any company would make such a lid; he thought it should be like the trunk lid of a car that would only go so far and stop.

Another time we asked Mr. McRae to deliver a load of lumber to the Soperton News office. It seemed a simple request. We needed the lumber for shelves; he had a pick-up truck; and Soperton wasn't so very far out of his way. But weeks and months dragged on without any lumber. I finally had to meet him at Thompson's in Ailey to order the lumber and see it loaded. Then I went back to Soperton and waited for his arrival. In typical Murphy McRae style, he made a grand entrance, dropping half the load under the redlight in the middle of town.

Those are two examples of my exasperating experiences with Murphy McRae, but he causes frustration for just about everybody who comes into contact with him, yet it's about impossible not to like him. There may be a few people in the world who dislike him, but they just haven't had a chance to get to know him.

As of midnight last Friday, the long and illustrious career of the fabled editor came to an end. He had been threatening to sell out for months, and he finally did. It's certainly going to be different. Murphy may help us with the papers for a while, but how much and for how long I can't say. It's going to be hard to imagine a Wednesday at Suburban without him.

Mr. Windsor introduced the buyers of Mr. McRae's papers to you in his column a few weeks ago. It's going to be exciting having some new blood and young blood connected with the papers. Mark and Julie Joiner have a rare opportunity and a tremendous challenge as they enter the world of country journalism. With lots of long hours and hard work, success is sure to come their way. They've chosen a new name, The Telfair Times, for their newspaper, and it seems wise to me to let The Lumber City Log retire with Mr. McRae. After all, he has been identified with it for most of its 29 years, and it's for certain that the

paper could never have another Editor quite like him, because there isn't any other person in the world quite like him.

First front page of The Telfair Times, *successor to* The Lumber City Log. *Julie Joiner, one of new owners introduces new name, etc. in her column while Bill Ricks' column pays tribute to former publisher Murphy McRae.*

Wayne County Press

Vol. 1, No. 1 --- Jesup, Ga., Thursday, November 3, 1960 --- Ten Centc

National & Local Races Set Tuesday

Next Tuesday is another voting day.

Wayne countians will be going to the polls to help decide who will occupy the White House for the next four years, and who will officially be named the local justices of the peace.

They will also be called upon to vote for a number of amendments, including a proposed amendment to change the method of electing the county Board of Education. The proposal, Constitutional Amendment No. 84, would have five members elected only by their districts, and the sixth by the county at large.

Voters interested in seeing Kennedy and Nixon's names on the ballot will be disappointed. Instead they will find the names of the presidential electors who traditionally vote later in the year for the man who has been nominated by their party.

The only contested local race is between Sheriff J. Clarence Reddish, who was nominated in the Democratic primary, and N. J. Green who is opposing him for re-election and is listed on the ballot as an independent candidate.

The Wayne County Mental Health Association has expressed interest in the passage of Constitutional Amendments No. 13 and 14. Both have to do with long-range improvement of the mental health program in Georgia.

Recently organized, the officers are: Mrs. Jack Taylor, president; Mrs. Ronald Adams, vice-president; Mrs. W. O. Pope, secretary; Dean Strickland, treasurer, and Mrs. J. P. Harris, publicity chairman.

In addition to the local race interest, many have expressed more than the usual interest in the presidential outcome. Both the county Democrat and Republican committees have been active during recent weeks.

Mrs. D. C. Hodge, Screven, is chairman of the county's Nixon-Lodge committee. G. L. Madray heads the Democrat group.

Mass Immunization in Wayne Stops Spread of Diphtheria

SHOTS ARE NOT THE MOST FUN -- Holding her nose takes Cathrine Brooker's attention off the diphtheria shot being given by Mrs. Bessie Brannen, county health nurse. Cathrine lives on Rochelle street in Jesup and is in the second grade at T. G. Ritch School. Mrs. Brannen is being assisted by Nurses Aid Pearly Morgan. Mrs. Alice Latham, district nursing director, looks on at left while classmates await their turn. (Photo by Broadhurst)

Fast action on the part of the Wayne County Health Center, local physicians, and the State and U. S. Public Health Service has apparently stopped the possible spread of diphtheria in Wayne county.

No cases of diphtheria have been reported in the county since October 17. Some 4,317 shots have been given by the county health center. "It is estimated that more than a thousand shots have been given by private physicians during the diphtheria "scare" period.

The giving of shots is continuing with the schools in Odum and Piney Grove being covered this week.

Wayne countians became acutely aware of the pending danger when a 2-year old negro child died in Wayne County Memorial Hospital on October 7. The child had not been immunized.

An earlier case had been reported in September. This was a 6-year old negro child from the Screven area.

On October 10, a third case, that of a 17-year old negro boy from Screven, was reported by the attending physician.

By this time the county health center and local physicians had begun to take action, and on October 11 a mass immunization drive got underway. Additional vaccine was sent from the branch laboratory at Waycross and upon call from the local authorities, the U. S. Public Health Service

(See page 8, col. 3)

STUDENTS CHECK PROGRAM -- Guidance Department assistants and student guides for "College Night" look over the program in Guidance Director Miss Helen Bruce's office. They are, left to right, Dana Brannen, Miss Bruce, Sandra Downing, Chip Baker, Charles Abner, Jo Ann Tootle, Fred Bishop and David Madray. For more pictures and story about the big night at Wayne County High School, turn to page 5. (Photo by Tim Cockfield)

Jesup - Waycross Clash Friday

OUCH! IT HURTS --Hershell Tyre isn't too sure that he likes diphtheria shots even if the nurse is smiling. He was one of over 4,000 who took the shot during the mass immunization program carried out in Wayne county. The nurse is Mrs. Jane Thompson. Assisting is Pearly Morgan, nurses aid. (Photo by G. M. Broadhurst)

The Jesup Yellow Jackets, resting on a 7-0-1 season record and 16 consecutive games without a loss will tangle with the Bulldogs of Waycross here in Jaycee Stadium Friday night.

The Waycross Eleven will be one of the toughest teams Jesup will play, judging by past performances of the Waycross team. The Bulldogs will come into the game sporting a team-scoring a team-scoring record of 311 points. The season's total surpassed the old team record of 286 points scored by the 1955 Waycross Eleven.

Jesup and Waycross are tied at this point for the 1-AA North leadership with only Appling County still in the race for the title; they are trailing third.

As the tension mounts and the big one approaches, the emphasis seems to be on "Jacket sting Dog" or "Dog eat Jacket."

The Waycross and Wayne County fans will witness the traditional crowning of the Homecoming Queen, a highlight that will add to the excitement of the game. The Homecoming parade is being planned for Friday afternoon with floats expected to be among the loveliest ever.

The Yellow Jackets, two-time State Champions, will be defending the title they won last year when they defeated Waycross in the 2-AA sub-region playoff, 13-6. That game in Waycross was sweet revenge for a 20-0 regular season win by Waycross.

Convict Escapes, Borrows Pants From Clothesline

Mrs. Davis looked out of her window just in time to see her husband's pants and jacket disappear off the clothes line and into an outbuilding, accompanied by an escaped convict.

Mr. H. B. Davis, Screven, would like to see the quick moving convict who jumped in front of a train to elude his guards... He doesn't care for the stripes

Oscar The Lady Otter Enjoys Domestic Living

OSCAR ENJOYS CHILDREN -- Best of all, besides fishing and swimming, Jesup's most unusual pet, enjoys people, particularly children. Shown with his owner, G. L. Lastinger, are some neighboring child-

Jesup's most unusual pet resides at the home of the G. L. Lastingers on the Brunswick highway.

They call her Oscar because she is an otter. It was sometime after naming her that it was discovered she was a lady.

Oscar is about nine months old now. She has been enjoying civilization for about seven months. She was caught in the Altamaha river swamp by Roy Mansfield of Gardi who let Lamar Barwick of Jesup have the animal.

Perhaps to the surprise of her owners she quickly began to adopt the ways of domesticated animals and, though otters seldom do so, she soon became as friendly as a dog and as playful as a kitten.

Mr. Lastinger bought the animal a few months ago and found her quick to learn and ready to obey.

Asked if he knew of any other otter which had been tamed, Mr. Lastinger said that he did not. It is generally believed that they are a wild-type animal and difficult to handle, etc.

Not so Oscar. She goes about

Page one of the first issue of The Wayne County Press, *Jesup, November 3, 1960.* The Press *was a weekly tabloid.*

The Dahlonega Nugget

"THE GOLD OF THE NEWS"

Volume 61 — No. 8 DAHLONEGA GEORGIA, FRIDAY, APRIL 20, 1951

The Editor's VIEWPOINT

BY JACK PARKS

We had planned to write a thunderous editorial this week on the firing of General McArthur, but we regret to report that news from Yahoola and Frogtown, plus other disturbances in and around Dahlonega, have crowded the General off the front page of the Nugget.

If anyone is interested in getting our views on the McArthur issue, they may secure same by calling on us at our offices in the Nugget Tower.

We were lying abed last Sunday morning, quietly turning over in our mind the outline of an editorial on world peace, when suddenly the wild clamor of a civil disturbance on the public square, one block away, reached our ears.

It developed that Sam Davis and two of his womenfolk had arrived in town and were under'aking to carry out their announced mission of whipping Police Chief Z. L. Davenport.

The fracas seems to have had its beginning Saturday night, when, according to police charges, Davis sped out of town in a reckless manner while under the influence of grain spirits. Davenport gave chase, overtook Davis and made a case against him.

Then, on Sunday morning, the angry Davis, along with his wife, Mrs. Bonnell Collins Davis, and his niece, Mrs. Fannie Marie Calhoun Burt, came back to town for a "settlement."

Davis alighted, approached Davenport and announced that he fain would chastise the law. According to charges, Davis also puctuated his announcement with boisterous and profane language.

With a large group of prominent citizens seated on the wall of the courthouse square observing, the two men hitched, and both soon were rolling on the ground. Then the women entered the fray. While Davenport was preoccupied with Davis, Mrs. Davis pounced upon the policeman and seized his blackjack, while Mrs. Burt attempted to remove his gun from the holster. Davenport says that he called for assitance from the crowd of observers, but only a College student offered a helping hand.

Davenport then struck Davis with the only weapon he could reach—his handcuffs—and at this point, Deputy Sheriff Robert Ragan happened to peer from the door of his nearby restaurant and see the disturbance. He quickly arrived on the scene, as did Sheriff J. R. Gibson, who was sitting in his car on the opposite side of the courthouse. The three officers soon reestablished law and order, and Davis was taken to county jail.

This, however, did not close the matter, for along toward noon Sheriff Gibson was again parked on the square observing the passing scene when Davis, who was supposed to have been securely locked up, drove up on the square and waved a good-bye greeting to the Sheriff.

It developed that Davis had knocked the door off his jail cell and had made his departure without leave.

When Gibson attempted to restrain him, Davis announced that he had a stone in the car, with which he intended to strike the Sheriff. Gibson then attempted to reach for the switch key, but Davis had his car motor running and drove off from under the protesting Sheriff. So many people were standing around that he hesitated to fire his pistol at the departing auto.

The services of all the law officers in Lumpkin county, plus two state highway patrol cars, were pressed into service and the county was honeycombed in search of the missing Davis.

Two hours later, Policeman A. L. Christian and Deputy Sheriff Robert Ragan found Davis at the home of Lonnie Martin. As the officers approached, Davis departed from the back of the house, and as Ragan rounded the corner, he saw Sam running toward the woods at terrific rate of speed.

The young Deputy gave chase, and the race was on for a distance of almost a mile, through hill and dale, forest and swamp.

Seeing the two men depart for tall timbers, Policeman Christian reports that the young Deputy was "running like a greyhound, and anyone who doubts that he's fleet of foot should have seen him chasing Davis."

Davis ran until completely exhausted, and when he sat down to catch a breath, Ragan laid hands upon him and escorted him back to Martin's house.

At this point, Wayne Martin entered the picture. He emerged from the Martin house and urged Sam not to go with the officers, since, according to his legal reasoning, they did not have proper credentials.

This put new life into Sam, who again began resisting the officers. After a brief scuffle, Ragan and Christian were able to stuff him into the car, head foremost.

The exhausted officers returned to town and again lodged the likewise exhausted Davis in county jail, where he was held without bond until tried in City Court Monday night.

The women were charged with interfering with an officer and were lodged in city jail for a few hours Sunday before they were bailed out.

After Sam was safely back in jail, officers Ragan, Christian and Davenport went out in search of Martin, and they met him in an auto at Clay Creek Falls.

When Wayne spied the officers, he hustled out of the car. He paused a moment to secure a quart of moonshine under his overalls, but the liquor fell to the ground as he started to run. The delay permitted Ragan to grab Martin without much of a chase. He was charged with possessing illegal liquor, intoxication and resisting officers, and was placed in county jail, from which place he was released later in the day under $500 bond.

Thinking that he would end the day on a quiet note, Sheriff Gibson motored out to the Garnet Bridge neighborhood, where he found "Wild Bill" Anderson soundly asleep by the roadside, with a half gallon of moonshine nestled beside him. The hapless Anderson ended his quiet Sunday siesta in jail.

We often have heard of people talking their way OUT of jail, but Cobb "Key of G" Tolbert is one of the few we've ever known who talked themselves INTO the hoosegow.

After a minor squabble at the school house last Thursday involving Tolbert's daughter, Cobb, upon returning home from work, decided to visit Sheriff J. R. Gibson and straighten out the matter, when in fact the dispute already had been settled to everyone's satisfaction.

Spotting the Sheriff on the public square, Tolbert walked up and began expounding his views about the incident.

"Now get this clear," Cobb kept insisting.

"The matter is already closed and settled, and I know all about it," the Sheriff replied.

"But I want you to get this clear," Tolbert continued to demand in a MacArthur-like tone of voice.

Sheriff Gibson, getting the point, instructed Tolbert to get into his car, whereupon the Sheriff took him to the county hotel as an overnight guest, and charges of public intoxication were lodged against the protesting citizen.

The next day, Tolbert declared that he positively was not intoxicated the night before, and that he merely was suffering from a blow on the head from a falling limb sustained while working at a sawmill.

Cobb bandaged up his head to protect the supposed wound, but by Saturday the sackcloth had been removed and he apparently had completely recovered from his injuries.

New Drug Store Opening Sale Begins Friday

The Dahlonega Pharmacy, this city's new Walgreen Agencey drug store, will hold its grand opening sale Friday and Saturday, April 20 and 21.

Robert A. Ledbetter, owner and operator, announced that many unusual bargains will be available during the two days, and that everyone will have an opportunity to buy top-quality merchandise at greatly reduced prices during the sale.

A beautiful Mixmaster will be given away at 4 o'clock Saturday, and other door prizes will be distributed throughout the day on both Friday and Saturday.

Ledbetter is a native of Tallulah Falls, a licensed pharmacist and a graduate of Southern School of Pharmacy, in Atlanta. His wife, the former Miss Doris Hill, of Gainesville, assists him in the business.

Bloodmobile To Be Here Wednesday

The Red Cross Bloodmobile will be in Dahlonega at the Community House from 9 a.m. to 4 p.m. on April 25 for the purpose of receiving blood from donors.

A recent request from the Defense Dept. has doubled the quota which the Red Cross has set up. That means that Lumpkin County will have to double its efforts if we give as much as is needed.

The Rev. Charles Williams is county chairman of the blood program this year. He urges that everyone take the time to give a pint of blood for in so doing it will save the lives of our service men.

The giving of blood is a simple job. It does not take a great deal of time.

RED CROSS DRIVE GOES ABOVE GOAL, WITH $502 COLLECTED

Lumpkin county oversubscribed its goal for this year in the recent Red Cross funds drive, according to Mrs. Orby Southard, who reports that $502 was subscribed.

The goal was $480, and Mrs. Southard issued a statement thanking those who assisted in the canvass, especially the colored workers, who accomplished so much among their people.

CORN CONTEST PRIZE WINNERS ARE ANNOUNCED

Clyde Calhoun has been announced Lumpkin County first prize winner in a five-acre corn contest sponsored during 1950 by J. D. Jewell, Inc., of Gainesville. Calhoun's yield was 101 bushels per acre. He won $50 cash prize.

Second prize winner was Ted Copeland, with an average yield of 96 bushels per acre. He received $15.

J. G. Seabolt was third, with a yield of 72 bushels per acre. His prize was $10.

Francis Smith had a yield of 66 busheld, and Y. D. Anderson, 57 bushels.

A similar contest will be sponsored this year, and the rules are as follows:

1. There must be 3 acres in not more than 2 corn fields. May be bottom or upland.
2. The seed must be yellow corn. No restrictions as to variety.
3. Should not top corn or pull fodder. Both these practices reduce yields.
4. You must estimate yield according to formula No. 3, suggested by E. D. Alexander, agronomist for State Extension Service.
5. Yield and measurement must be certified to by disinterested parties.
6. Corn should be planted by May 20.
7. Counties includeed in contest are: Hall, White, Lumpkin, Dawson, Forsyth, Gwinnett, Banks, and Jackson.
8. Decision of the judges will be final.

Anyone interested in the contest should sign up with the County Agent.

FOR RENT: Four-room house, with bath, gas heat and hot water $25 per month. W. B. FRY, Smith House, Dahlonega. A-27

CITY SHOE SHOP . . . In J. W. Nix building is open for shoe repairs, also shines given. VERNON HOOD.

FROM THE NUGGET FILES

FROM 1915 VOLUME

Alice Howell was in jail at this place for four months before she was sentenced to six months at the state farm, and if a single preacher or lady, except Mrs. Fry, or any other Christian, or others claiming to be such, ever visited the jail and talked with her we never heard of it.

Yet, these good people will go to a heavy expense in sending men off to foreign lands to hunt up sinners. Isn't it strange? This woman has done wrong, but so have thousands of others, some in high society even.

If we understand it correctly, one soul is just as valuable as another in heaven, yet a much bigger effort is made to save the soul of a rich person than that of a poor one, and a woman who does wrong has less sympathy, if any at all, than a man, even if their wrongdoing is equal.

When those bank robbers, and the old man Miner and his two associates who held up the conductor and other employees of a Southern train at the point of a pistol and robbed its safe, were in jail here, people flocked to the jail to see them.

Although the bank robbers shot and tried to kill the Sheriff and others, they got the sympathy of a lot of people, some of whom now are signing a petition asking the governor to set one of them free.

The woman referred to had two children. The eldest was taken away from her and bound out. No one would take the youngest child, and the authorities would not take the defendant at the state farm, because there is no law to cover imprisonment of an innocent child. Being unable to get rid of either child or mother, she was released from prison here the other day and told to leave.

But where can she go? She has no money and no friends—nothing but an innocent baby. Nevertheless, the far-away heathen must be cared for, when we have a needy subject right here at our doors who is talked about by some who are just as guilty as this poor, unfortunate woman, who is cast out into the world with no work, nothing to eat and no shelter for herself and a little child.

If only persons without sin would cast stones at her, she wouldn't be undergoing so many hardships.

Uncle Isaac Woody came into town Monday for the first time in six months, and while here he called down and made ye editor smile by placing a dollar bill in his hand for the Nugget, which has been going to his home for many years.

Before doing this he jumped up and clicked his heels gether, showing how active he is at the age of 80. During the Civil War, he had many close calls, with the enemy shooting 12 different holes through his clothing. The old man shrunk enough during the time that none of the lead even so much as scorched the skin.

Franklin Owen To Conduct Baptist Revival

The Rev. Franklin Owen, pastor of the First Baptist Church of Gainesville, will conduct a revival at the Dahlonega Baptist Church beginning April 29 and continuing through May 6, it was announced this week by the pastor, the Rev. A. C. Johnson.

M. K. Slinger, minister of music at the Central Baptist church, also of Gainesville, will be in charge of music.

Rev. Johnson stated that "everyone, both in Dahlonega, and throughout the rural section of Lumpkin, is cordially invited to attend."

FROGTOWN

By Mrs. Sarah Grindle

Mr. and Mrs. Roy Grindle and mother went to Marietta Sunday to see her brother, John Dockery, who was very ill at that time in the hospital there.

Mr. and Mrs. Benson Cantrell announce the birth of a baby girl last Friday.

Baby chicks seem to be scarce now as several houses around here are empty

Leon Sullens sold his milk cow last week, but bought another one Monday.

Oscar Helton has a new son-in-law. His last daughter has married.

We were surprised one Christy, from Hermon, Tenday last week to see Tom nessee, in these parts. I hadn't seen him in years. He looked as natural as cornbread.

Ruth Hurd and Nannie Snoffeitt visited Mrs. Sarah Hester Sunday.

Wesley Dockery and his family visited in these parts Sunday.

Oliver Winkler visited Charlie Nix Sunday.

JOHN A. DOCKERY FUNERAL RITES HELD THURSDAY

Funeral services for John A. Dockery, retired rural mail carrier who died in an Atlanta hospital Tuesday night, were held Thursday afteroon at Cavender's Creek church. Mr. Dockery was a widely known and highly respected citizen of Lumpkin county.

UPPER WAHOO

By Mary Abercrombie

Every year we think our case of Spring fever will be fatal. However, after eating a few messes of poke salad we are able to go through the usual routine of the year's work. This vegetable is a good spring tonic that knocks out that lazy feeling.

The Rev. Guy Lee preached at Holly Springs Sunday night.

It was like a revival at Wahoo last Sunday. The Rev. Marvin Wheeler preached. Six went to the altar and two were saved.

Due to illness the Bethel writer was not able to attend church Sunday. Rev. Morris is a good singer and an active church worker, and was missed in the worship service.

The Rev. Ted Anderson preached at Zion last Sunday.

Jack Ledford was the first of our near neighbors to get a television set.

Mr. and Mrs. Art Stanley and children, from Des Moines, Iowa, are visiting their parents, Mr. and Mrs. Henry Hoppers.

Friends and neighbors met Tuesday at Theodore Thomas' for a working — building a 5,000 capacity chicken house.

A very odd thing is a rabbit that lost its tail. A boy put a rabbit in his chicken house. The rabbit tried to scratch out. A plank fell on its tail, holding it fast. As the rabbit jumped it jerked its tail completely off.

We heard a whip-o-will Sunday night.

One night Henry Davis heard something after his chickens. He found a possum trying to get in the chicken house. While he was getting the possum, he heard a fox barking.

The other night a squalling hen set off the burglar alarm. Brother Ernest and our dog Dan found a thief pulling feathers out of a big red hen. Dan grabbed the possum and shook him before he did much damage to the hen. Possum is his favorite game, as he likes to show his superiority over the grinning, blowing, animal.

Last week Dan kept gnawing on an old car tire. Ernest shook out a big wharf rat which Dan caught and killed it.

PVT. SAVAGE ASSIGNED TO FT. BRAGG UNIT

Private Cleaborn D. Savage, Dawsonville, Rt. 3, at Fort Bragg, N. C., has been assigned to Battery C, 449 Field Artillery Observation Battalion for basic training.

Private Savage lived with his father, Mr. N. M. Savage, before he entered the service this past March. He attended Lumpkin County High School.

FOR SALE: Kelvinator refrigerator, in excellent condition, for sale cheap. Six-foot capacity. See Mrs. W. T. King, Dahlonega, Ga.

Rufe T. Davis, of Cartersville, states that he expects to open a new ladies' ready-to-wear shop in Dahlonega within the next month. It will be located in the old theatre-automatic laundry building on the square.

Davis Fined $200 Monday Night In City Court

Sam Davis was fined $200 by Mayor [illegible] Baker in City Court Monday night on charges of disorderly conduct and resisting arrest in Dahlonega last Sunday morning.

Mrs. Davis was fined $33 for disorderly conduct in removing a blackjack from the person of Police Chief Z. L. Davenport while he was engaged in a scuffle with Davis.

Mrs. Fannie Marie Calhoun Burt, a niece of Davis, also was fined $33 on a charge growing out of her attempt to take Davenport's gun while the fracas was in progress.

All three pled guilty to the charges.

BETHEL

By The Rev. D. F. Morris

The Mt Olive writer mentioned the Wahoo writer's nice suit, but he didn't say a word about our pretty striped overalls.

We don't have much news at this time, since we've been on the sick list. The Rev. Clifton Wheeler carried us to the doctor in Gainesville Thursday. While there, we met our good friend, The Rev. Tunnie Lawson, and had a friendly conversation with him. Tunnie always has pleasant words to say.

G. D. Adams visited our home one day last week and had prayer with us, for which we are thankful.

Several preachers and deacons and other members from my home church visited the home of Mr and Mrs. Claud Clark in Gainesville one night last week. We feel that much good was accomplished. Mrs Clark has been in bad health for some time.

Little Jimmy Lee, form Bethel community, visited our home last Sunday. We were glad to have him. I think neighbors should visit each other more.

I'm always glad to hear of a distillery being destroyed, as that stuff is very harmful.

Ottis Carroll and little sister, Marie, visited us last Sunday. We always appreciate company, especially if we are sick.

We wanted to go to the singing at New Bridge last Sunday night, but had to postpone it owing to our physical condition. We do not get every thing we want but we do get what we need.

HERE & THERE

By W. H. White

We are enjoying this sales tax. We haven't found but three men who admit voting for Talmadge.

A merchant is looking for more business (cash business). A traveling salesman is looking for more sales (bigger sales). An undertaker is looking for more folks (dead folks). A doctor is looking for more sick folks. A dentist is looking for more teeth (decayed teeth).

Our son, Travis, who went to Indiana, was telling us when he got back about how they used napkins.

When eating, they just touch their lips with one. Around here, we Walka Mt. folks just wipe our mouth with our coat sleeve

Aunt Sarah Anderson, and daughter, Zora, aren't doing well at this writing.

The writer is kind of knocked out again. We had to go to the hospital last Sunday for more shots and medicine.

The first two paragraphs of Jack Parks's column in this April 20, 1951 edition of The Dahlonega Nugget *were printed by newspapers throughout the country. Actually the rest of the column was even more interesting, recounting in detail an attack on the police chief. The makeup of this page was typical of many Georgia weeklies in hot-type days. Looks sort of like the* Wall Street Journal *in 1984. ''From the Nugget Files 1915'' contains writing by W. B. Townsend.*

Devoted to the Progress of Jackson County

The Jackson Herald

Vol. 92 No. 9 — 10¢ PER COPY — Wednesday, August 9, 1967

LEADS 'THAT SOUND GOOD' BEING FOLLOWED UP IN GANGLAND-STYLE KILLING OF FLOYD HOARD

Sol. Gen. Floyd Hoard — a crusading officer who had struck hard at auto thievery and bootlegging — was killed gangland-style Monday morning when a bomb ripped his automobile.

The 40-year-old Jeffersonian was about to leave his home on the Brockton Road at 7:25 a.m. when a blast went off that was heard in downtown Jefferson, three miles away. He died a few seconds later.

Mr. Hoard was thrown into the back seat of his sedan, the steering section atop his body. Various other parts of the car littered the yard. Windows in the front of his home, some 50 feet away, were broken by the blast.

The solicitor general's oldest child, 16-year-old Peggy Jean, jumped out of bed when she heard the blast. Running out, she tried to save her father by applying mouth to mouth resuscitation.

"He mumbled and he breathed a few times," she said. "I tried to bring him back."

It was only by chance that Peggy Jean herself, and some other members of the family, [illegible] planned to go to town Monday for her driving test and she and her mother had discussed [illegible] the sedan rather than their other car, a station wagon. However, Mrs. Hoard had pointed out that the sedan contained the police radio and that Mr. Hoard might need it. They could swap cars in town, she had said.

The two younger children, Vivian and Claudine, ages 9 and 7, were not home at the time, having gone to visit relatives in Macon. Dickie, the 14-year-old son, was home.

Peggy Jean said later she was not surprised that this happened to her father.

"He couldn't live," she said. "I hadn't thought of their getting him this way . . . I had thought they'd shoot him. But [illegible]"

Peggy Jean said her father had made no particular statements that gave her this feeling but said she "just knew it."

The solicitor general began carrying a gun about a year ago and had urged other court officials to do the same. He also had reportedly received threats but he didn't talk much about them.

Sheriff L. G. Perry said six to 12 sticks of dynamite were [illegible] the solicitor's car. They had been placed between the motor and dash of the dark green Ford sedan. The hood had to be raised in order for the dynamite to have been put there, he said. No more than five minutes would have been required to do the task, the sheriff continued. One could have seen the dynamite had he been looking for it, said the sheriff.

[illegible] the dead man's brother, said the solicitor had mentioned to him several months ago the possibility that his car could be bombed.

The Hoards have several dogs and there was some barking during the night, members of the family said, but this was not unusual. After the blast, one of the dogs, the "most fierce one," disappeared for a time. However, all dogs were back as of late Tuesday, the sheriff said.

Mr. Hoard was on his way to the opening of the August term of Jackson Superior Court when the explosion occurred. The grand jury was to have convened simultaneously.

So far as is known, Mr. Hoard had only rather routine matters to bring before the grand jury. However, [illegible] perhaps he was onto "something hot." Others speculate that it was his previous activities in crime-busting which brought about his death.

Some officers have been quoted as saying it was probably a "revenge" killing.

SOL. GEN. FLOYD HOARD

Officers have some leads "that sound good to us," Capt. J. E. Carnes, who is directing the investigation, told The Herald about noon today (Wednesday).

Earlier Col. R. H. Burson, State Public Safety Director, told The Herald by telephone from his office in Atlanta that there have been two interesting leads, "one of which may prove helpful."

One lead is reportedly taking officers out of the state. Every lead is being followed it is noted, including the possibility that the killing was [illegible] crime syndicate. One officer said the killing was apparently done by a professional and there has been much speculation that it was done by a hired killer. Another officer said the pay for killing a solicitor general may run as high as $15,000.

Anyone having any information which might be helpful in the investigation of the Hoard death is asked to call [illegible], Sheriff L. G. Perry has announced.

Col. Burson was in Jefferson Tuesday helping organize the probe into Sol. Hoard's death. A team of eight state officers, in addition to Sheriff L. G. Perry and his force, is working on the case. Headquarters is at the Crawford W. Long Inn.

Capt. Carnes told The Herald today that nothing new of significance has been uncovered since Tuesday.

Sheriff Perry had high [illegible] operation by all the officers concerned.

"I feel that at the present everything is being done that possibly can be done. There is full cooperation by the law enforcement agencies and we are concentrating on it. No one who has been asked to help has turned us down," the sheriff said.

Reward Fund Totals At Least $3,500

Rewards totaling at least $3,500 have already been announced in connection with the murder Monday of Sol. Gen. Floyd Hoard.

Gov. Lester Maddox offered [illegible] $1,000 from the state and in addition provided $1,000 of his personal funds.

The Board of Commissioners of Roads and Revenues of Jackson County has offered $1,000 "to any one producing evidence resulting in the arrest, indictment and conviction of the person responsible" for Mr. Hoard's death.

In addition, the Georgia Sheriff's Assn. has offered $500 and it is understood that some other groups such as the Solicitors' Assn. may add to the fund.

A grassroots plan by interested citizens of the community to raise a reward fund was stymied at the last moment by the possibility that anyone who contributed to such a fund could be disqualified as a juror in the event someone is brought to trial in the case.

Legal opinions from several court officers and attorneys in the Piedmont Judicial Circuit were that there would likely [illegible] successful one, to disqualify anyone who had contributed.

Ord. Griffeth Said Improving

[illegible] H. Griffeth entered the hospital Monday but was reported "improved" Wednesday.

He is at the Banks-Jackson Commerce Hospital.

Mrs. Tom Daniel is working at the office during his absence.

DEATH CAR
. . . solicitor turned key to set off bomb

DEBRIS LITTERED YARD
. . . roped off for investigative purposes

An Editorial

They killed Floyd Hoard.

Or was it "they"?

Did we in Jackson County by our apathy, our ignorance, our fear, our failure to lend law enforcement and the courts our full-hearted support help create a climate which led to this heinous crime?

If Mr. Hoard had had staunch, unrelenting support from the public, if we had let it be known, time and time again, that we were not going to tolerate these hoodlums in our midst, would Floyd Hoard be alive today? Would they have decided the cost too great in Jackson County and moved on to some softer spot?

It is almost a certainty.

But the past is behind us.

When they put the dynamite under Floyd Hoard's car, they put a dynamite under Jackson County. In this tragedy, we as a community were jarred to an anger, an awareness, a determination, a unity which we had not before known.

This resolution [illegible] in the heat of emotion this week—must not waver. It's time to get tough with hoodlums and gangsters and stay tough. We can no longer be a soft spot where such can find a solace. We can no longer be intimidated.

We have an enemy in Vietnam. But we in Jackson County have another enemy, under our doorstep, and we must not rest until he is routed and put to flight.

We must serve on juries when called, never shirking for some puny excuse this sacred duty. We must think in terms of maximum penalties, not minimum. We must constantly assure our law enforcement officers of our support and let them know that only the best is expected from them as well.

We must, in short, vigorously seize any opportunity that comes our way to make this a better place in which to live and rear our children . . .

. . . To make it a place where a child will not have to run out in the wake of an earth-shattering blast and see the mangled body of a father who had tried, too much alone, to make this a decent place in which to live.

County Reels From Shock

"You hear about things like this happening in Chicago or New York. I never thought it could happen here."

"It's unbelievable."

"What a dreadful thing to have happen right in a man's yard . . . his children and wife nearby."

These were a few of the comments one heard in Jackson County Monday as word spread of the tragedy which befell Floyd Hoard.

Countians reeled from the shock, as did the state. Most people here said the crime situation was worse than they had thought.

Leading men and women from throughout the county had gathered in Jefferson Monday morning for the opening of the August term of Jackson Superior Court.

They assembled at the courtroom at 9:30 a.m. as scheduled. But everyone knew no court would be held.

Judge Mark Dunahoo, Sheriff L. G. Perry, Clerk of Court Billy Elder and other court officials took their places

(Continued on Page 8)

No Successor To Mr. Hoard Appointed Yet

No one has yet been named to succeed Floyd Hoard as solicitor general of the Piedmont Judicial Circuit.

It is understood that Gov. Lester Maddox will appoint a successor who would serve until an election could be held. Mr. Hoard's term ends Dec. 31, 1968.

The governor's office told The Herald today (Wednesday) that no one had been named and that it was not known just when an appointment would be made.

In the meantime, the August term of Jackson Superior Court—which was to have begun the day Sol. Hoard was murdered—has been recessed indefinitely. It cannot proceed until a solicitor general is named.

JHS Grid Season To Open Aug. 25

The Jefferson High School football season will open Aug. 25 with a home game. White County will be calling.

[illegible] the schedule:

Sept. 1, North Habersham, Away; Sept. 8, Toccoa, Home; Sept. 15, Green Co., Away; Sept. 15, Green Co., Away; Oct. 6, Morgan Co., Away; Oct. 13, Lovett, Away; Oct. 20, [illegible] Wilkes, Home; Nov. 3, Oglethorpe Co., Away.

Maddox Sends In More State Officers

Gov. Lester Maddox announced today he is sending "a large number" of state alcoholic tax agents into the Jackson County area.

"The purpose for sending the agents into the circuit is, of course, to investigate violations of the state's liquor laws," he said. "They have been instructed to remain there until the district is dried up or those guilty of the brutal murder of Sol. Gen. Floyd Hoard are brought to Justice."

Gov. Maddox continued: Sol. Hoard fought a good fight against crime and criminals in his circuit and we do not intend to permit it to end. In fact, I have instructed both the GBI and the Department of Revenue agents to intensify the war on crime. On yesterday, I offered a $1,000 reward from the state of Georgia [illegible] the arrest and the conviction of the person or persons responsible for his death. To that I added $1,000 from my own personal funds. I expect the full cooperation of all law enforcement officers and officials as we carry on Sol. Hoard's fight.

"I urge all citizens to help us solve this heinous murder and to come forth with any information they might have in connection with this gangland type killing."

'...He Had Counted The Cost'

". . . he made his decision, he had counted the cost and yesterday he paid the full price . . ."

These were the words of the Rev. Robert Ramsey, pastor of the Jefferson Methodist Church, as he delivered the eulogy to Floyd Hoard Tuesday afternoon at the little stone church where Mr. Hoard had been a Church School teacher and official board member.

The Rev. Mr. Ramsey continued:

"As long as there is one shred of decency, as long as truth, honor and love prevail, this state, community and area and each of us shall always owe an immeasurable debt to Fuzzy Hoard.

"Like a sword piercing our heart, the question that hangs over our heads is: 'Did Floyd Hoard die in vain?' The answer shifts to you and me and will be found in whether all of us see to act responsibly and courageously that crimes such as these shall never again be committed.

It was announced only last week that Mr. Hoard had been selected to appear in the 1967 edition of "Outstanding Personalities of the South."

Other recipients of this honor include governors, U.S. senators and Congressmen of the southern states. Persons are selected because of "past achievements and service to their community, state and/or nation."

Members of Mr. Hoard's family said he may never have known of the honor. The announcement was made in a release to The Herald.

"Fuzzy Hoard lit a torch and we pray God that it has not fallen but that we shall take it and hold the light high in word and deed."

The young minister called Mr. Hoard "a rare individual," noting his wide spectrum "of interests, gifts and concerns."

"Those who have seen him on the gridiron or baseball diamond say he could have achieved fame in athletics. He was a man's man. A teacher, a coach and developer of boys and youth. Such a warm sense of humor yet a man of seriousness who could express deep thoughts about life, death and God. He had the gift of poetry to express his thoughts, sometimes humorously and sometimes seriously, in rhyme.

"But he turned his back upon teaching or athletics and chose through diligent study a career in the legal profession. It was here in his chosen field that God worked in his life and we pray in his death . . ."

Mr. Hoard was 40 years of age, a native of Fayette County. He attended the Spaulding County schools, Georgia Military College and was a graduate of Mercer University. Mr. Hoard taught at Georgia Military College and was football and basketball coach at Soperton High School.

He completed the LaSalle Extension Course in Law and passed his bar exam in 1955. Mr. Hoard was associated with the late George Westmoreland in law practice in Jefferson. He served as temporary editor of The Jackson Herald in the late 1950's.

Mr. Hoard was elected solicitor general of the Piedmont Judicial Circuit in 1964 and took office on Dec. 1, 1964. He was a past president of the Piedmont Bar Assn.

The solicitor general was a U.S. Navy veteran of World War II, a member of the Jefferson Lions Club, Unity Lodge No. 33, F and AM, and the Jefferson Methodist Church where he had taught the Men's Bible Class and served on the official board.

Surviving his wife, the former Miss Imogene Westmoreland; one son, Dicky Hoard; three daughters, Peggy Jean, Claudine and Vivian, all of Jefferson; the parents, Mr. and Mrs. Richard G. Hoard of Griffin; two sisters, Mrs. James Helms and Mrs. Mary Goodman, both of Griffin; and six brothers, Joe of Jefferson, Troy, Bob, Lewis, Edward and Tom, all of Griffin.

Funeral services were held at 4 p.m. Tuesday at the Jefferson Methodist Church with the Revs. Mr. Ramsey, Phillip Fair and Marvin Brewer officiating. Interment was in Woodbine Cemetery, Jefferson.

Pallbearers were: Tifton Greer, Billy Elder, Henry Robinson, Judge Mark Dunahoo, Sheriff L. G. Perry and Judge Jim Barrow. Jackson Funeral Home had charge.

Mrs. Hoard had asked that in lieu of flowers, contributions be made in her husband's memory toward the Jefferson Methodist Church's property purchase project now underway. The church is trying to raise $13,000 for the purchase of adjacent property to be used for youth activities.

Among those attending the funeral were the president, vice president and secretary-treasurer of the state solicitors general association.

Murder of Jackson County Solicitor General Floyd Hoard is reported on this Wednesday, August 9, 1967 front page of The Jackson Herald. *Hoard had been editor of* The Herald *for a short time in the late 1950s.*

ADOLPH ROSENBERG
Dedicated Journalist

the SOUTHERN ISRAELITE

A Weekly Newspaper for Southern Jewry.

Established 1925

VOL. LIII One Section, 20 Pages Atlanta, Georgia, Friday, January 21, 1977 25¢ NO. 3

TSI Editor & Publisher Adolph Rosenberg Dies

Adolph Rosenberg lost a four year battle with cancer Monday afternoon. He was 65 years old.

For over 35 years, Rosenberg had been editor of The Southern Israelite. Since 1951, he had been its publisher as well.

Born August 14, 1911, in Albany, Ga., Rosenberg was the son of Aaron and Anna Rosenberg. He graduated from Albany High School, where he began his journalistic career on the high school newspaper. He also began at that time a tradition of service when he was elected president of the Georgia Scholastic Press Assn. Many journalism organizations have benefitted from his leadership since.

While a student at the Henry W. Grady School of Journalism at the University of Georgia, from which he graduated in three years, Adolph Rosenberg was one of two nominees for the prestigious Rhodes Scholarship.

Before affiliating with The Southern Israelite, Rosenberg worked for the Albany Herald, the United States Daily in Washington, the Carroll Country Free Press and was a reporter for both the *Atlanta Constitution* and the *Atlanta Journal.*

Over the 37-year-span of his identification with The Southern Israelite, Rosenberg was known for his total and uncompromising dedication to maintaining the integrity and ethical standards of Jewish journalism.

Active in the American Jewish Press Assn. almost since its inception, Adolph Rosenberg filled every office of that national organization of English-Jewish newspapers. In 1966, he was elected the AJPA president. It was during that first term of office, that Rosenberg determined to broaden the direction of the AJPA. He devoted his first year in office to expressing tangible personal support of the troubled Jewish State by arranging for and leading an unprecedented convention in Israel.

As he wrote later, "As time for the convention departure came, history was to take an unexpected part, catapulting the AJPA event into astounding proportions. First came the withdrawal of the UN forces and the blockading of the Gulf of Aqaba.

"These two 1967 occurrences pressed a panic button among the 20,000 tourists then in the State of Israel and they began to stampede literally into getting out of this potentially dangerous place."

As the time of decision drew near, Adolph Rosenberg grew more determined to go, since he felt that "the times called for a group to come in confidence and in solidarity, to stand beside the Israelis during this time of crisis . . ."

With full intent to carry out the trip, even if he went alone, Rosenberg found that a great many of those who had signed up were willing to accompany him.

The group's presence drew the admiration and gratitude of both Israeli officials and the "man in the street."

At convention's end, though the rest of his colleagues left for

—TURN TO PAGE 14

I Remember. . . . .

by VIDA GOLDGAR

I remember my first meeting with the man who was to so completely change my life.

A missed deadline . . . a Hadassah publicity story hand-delivered instead of mailed . . . an offer: "I've been meaning to call you," Adolph Rosenberg said. "I like your style — I like the way you write. Would you like a job?"

"No" was my answer. "I've got a job."

Nonetheless, he was persuasive and a part-time arrangement was worked out. A week later I sat down at an ancient Underwood and stared at blank paper. It's only temporary, I thought.

• • •

I remember our final meeting. Last Friday, with that week's Southern Israelite off the press, I approached the hospital bed: "When you get back to the office," Adolph instructed, "I want you to write my obituary . . . to hold until the proper time."

I promised — making no attempt to hide my tears — and we talked of other things.

Just as I prepared to leave, Adolph — a newspaperman right to the end — said, "Your lead might be 'Adolph Rosenberg lost a four year battle with cancer today.'" Seventy-two hours later, he did lose that battle. His words are the lead for this issue's page one story.

• • •

And *I remember* the 13 years between the first meeting and the last. Thirteen years during which Adolph Rosenberg hand-walked me through the occasionally intricate paths of Jewish journalism — sharing both his *naches* and his disappointments. Sharing, too, his occasionally flaring temper and his more frequent spoken "That's a good story."

I remember, a year or so after I joined The Southern Israelite, Adolph's decision to finally make that long-postponed first trip to Israel. How thrilled he was to finally see this land for which he, like so many, had worked and dreamed. That was not to be his only trip.

None, however, was as momentous as the second visit, which began in May 1967 as a convention of his beloved colleagues in the American Jewish press, and ended with Adolph remaining in Israel as the only accredited Jewish journalist throughout the Six-Day War.

He returned to talk of bunkers and the Suez, of children in shelters and of aging adults volunteering for service, of bullet holes in his hotel room and of camouflaged Israeli soldiers resting at the ready under JNF trees.

I remember Adolph reaching for the candy jar kept ready when mothers visiting his office brought their youngsters. His patience and affection for children was a delight to watch. Never married, he had no children of his own. But he must have been at least nominal "godfather" to dozens. His sisters' children were close to his heart. His sense of family was unexcelled.

Somewhere in that 13 years *I remember* quitting in something of a huff. And *I remember* being fired . . . neither of which survived the day. Others of his staff, from whom he received an intense loyalty, had that experience. Hardly anyone who ever worked for Adolph Rosenberg was a short-termer.

Adolph's sadness on that dreary March day in 1973 — that day when the last issue of The Southern Israelite to be produced in his own printing plant roll-

—TURN TO PAGE 14

Lipshutz: Carter Committed To Aid Soviet Jewry

WASHINGTON, Jan. 17 (JTA) — Native Atlantain Robert Lipshutz, President-elect Jimmy Carter's designated White House Counsel, told a B'nai B'rith Board of Governors lucheon here Monday that the incoming President was committed to "remove the log jam on emigration" of Jews and others from the Soviet Union, but "how that will be done will be determined at a later date." He also cited Carter's long stated opposition to the Arab boycott of Israel but could not be specific as to what action the new President will take on that issue.

Lipshutz received a warm welcome from 200 B'nai B'rith officials and guests attending the closing luncheon of the Board of Governor's three-day meeting. It was his first public appearance since his appointment was announced. B'nai B'rith president David M. Blumberg introduced the Georgian as a former president of the Atlanta Lodge of B'nai B'rith, a member of the Reform Temple in Atlanta and active in Atlanta's Jewish Federation.

In his remarks, Lipshutz recalled that his grandparents came to the U.S. almost 90 years ago to escape oppression in Czarist Russia. He said that his involvement in public life always had been essentially on Jewish religious teachings and U.S. democratic system

Carter Inaugural Has "Jewish Flavor"

Jimmy Carter's inaugural as 39th President of the United States had a definite religious flavor on Thursday. He chose to add the words, "so help me God," to the oath of office and quoted a famous passage from Micah in the Old Testament in his acceptance speech.

There was also a Jewish flavor to the ceremony as Cantor Isaac Goodfriend, a yarmulke firmly in place, concluded the formal inauguration by singing the National Anthem in a deep, strong baritone. Cantor Goodfriend's part in the ceremony was perhaps symbolic of Carter's avowed sensitivity to the problems of the Jewish people. The Cantor represented not only the Jews of the world, but as a survivor of the Holocaust is living testament that Jews can struggle against seeming insurmountable odds and continue to dream of freedom.

Carter, a "born again Christian," has surrounded himself with several key Jewish advisors. Atlantans Robert Lipshutz and Stuart Eisenstat will occupy offices in the White House and are expected to have considerable input to the Oval Office. Secretary of Defense Harold Brown is an active Jewish leader from California and although Secretary of Treasury Blumenthal no longer practices the Jewish faith, he can be expected to have a sensitivity in Jewish matters.

Carter's liberal choice of minorities for key positions and the role of Cantor Goodfriend at the inaugural seem to contradict the protest earlier in the week by a national Jewish organization that a rabbi should have been among those delivering prayers at the inaugural.

The Southern Israelite *is a weekly published in Atlanta, and serving the entire southeast. Page shown here tells of death of Adolph Rosenberg,* The Israelite's *editor for 35 years. Date is Friday, January 21, 1977, the week of Jimmy Carter's inauguration as U.S. president.*

Chapter X

The Georgia Press Association: Century of Struggle, Success

An Unlikely Founder

Georgia was relatively late getting started on an association of newspaper publishers and editors, perhaps because its publishers were of such fiercely independent nature. Louis Griffith, writing in *Georgia Journalism*, which covers the history of the Georgia Press Association from its founding in 1887 through 1950, describes southern rural newspapers in the period following the Civil War as "a group of highly individual enterprises . . . Their attitude was not resistant to the flow of affairs, but rather a determined affirmation of individuality."

Thomas D. Clarke, a historian of the period, said that "the country press has been one of the most vigorous institutions in the New South. It has functioned alongside the country store, the church and school as a common man's institution."

An attempt to form a weekly association had been made during the Civil War, with one meeting being held in Milledgeville in 1863. A name — Weekly Press Association of Georgia — was adopted but no further meetings were held. Neighboring Alabama got a press association going as early as 1871, and it was well-established by the time Georgia newspapermen finally put together a formal organization in the summer of 1887.

The Atlanta Constitution, which was founded in 1868 and quickly became the state's leading daily newspaper, had editorially suggested several times that Georgia's weekly publishers should form an organization for social and business purposes.

Then in the spring of 1887 a weekly newspaper editor picked up the campaign and was successful in bringing about the first convention of what was to become the Georgia Press Association.

The Constitution reported on June 21, 1887: "Weekly Editors Propose to Have a Press Association of Their Own." The story was datelined "Conyers, Ga.," and it read: "The movement for a convention of the weekly press magnates has taken definite form. Mr. M. D. Irwin, editor of *The Solid South*, has just issued the following call: The question of a weekly press convention having been suggested by *The Solid South* some two months ago, has been very thoroughly discussed, and with possibly a few dissenters, the demand is general for such a convention . . . "

The Conyers Solid South and its editor, Mark D. Irwin, were unlikely instigators of a state press association. Conyers at the time was little more than a village. *The Solid South* was a small weekly which would not survive into the 20th century. Irwin was not a prominent journalist in his own day, nor is much still known about him. Despite his role in starting the GPA, he is not even a member of Georgia's Newspaper Hall of Fame.

But for one year, 1887, Irwin and *The Solid South* were at the right time in the right place and making the right appeal. Irwin not only rallied the state's editors and publishers for a convention, but he also set forth the objectives and purposes for the association.

Other press associations in those days were mainly concerned with social activities and excursions. Irwin wanted the Georgia group to be of value to its members from a business standpoint, especially advertising, and his ideas on those lines were probably the decisive factor in finally getting the fiercely independent weekly newspapermen of the state to band together.

Irwin proposed that the group "establish uniform rates for foreign advertisements, based upon circulation; establish a bureau of information to protect the weekly press against fraudulent advertisers and advertising agents; demand cash contracts of all agencies and otherwise free the press of many impositions put upon it."

Irwin thus deserves credit not only for getting the GPA started, but also for recognizing and pinpointing needs of the rural press at that time. Small newspapers were dependent on "foreign advertising," or ready-print ads, sent in by companies from throughout the country, and often no payments were forthcoming. Irwin felt that as a combined force the weeklies would be in better position to identify and avoid the worst of these advertisers.

This was the identical premise on which the Georgia Newspaper Service and the national advertising service for small papers were formed some 50 years after Irwin's proposal.

Irwin was asked by several other publishers to set a date and select a site for the convention, and he designated August 5, 1887, with the site being either Conyers or Milledgeville. Both the date and the site caused some dissension. Editors in Milledgeville, which had recently lost the state Capitol to Atlanta, were particularly sensitive about their city's threatened decline (which, as it turned out, was a justified concern).

The editor of *The Sparta Ishmaelite* made the case for Milledgeville most convincingly, however, when he wrote: "Aside from all other advantages, Milledgeville has the Lunatic Asylum, the grandest institution in the state . . . "

Milledgeville was thus agreed on as the site, with Conyers losing out, not just for that year, but in the years since. Even in the period when the convention was held in a different town — usually small — each year, Conyers was never chosen. Irwin's date proved too early to make arrangements, and it was August 30 before about 20 of the state's weekly publishers and editors gathered in the Hall of Representatives of the old State Capitol for the first convention. Irwin was recognized for his determined efforts in bringing the meeting about by being elected the first president. The Georgia Weekly Press Association was adopted as the group's name and annual dues were set at $1 per newspaper.

According to GPA records the newspapers represented at the organizational convention were: *The Athens Chronicle, The Atlanta Sunny South, The Blackshear Georgian, The Canton Advance, The Cartersville Courant-American, The Conyers Solid South, The Conyers Weekly, The Crawfordville Democrat, The Cumming Clarion, The Cuthbert Liberal,*

The Dublin Post, The Fairburn News, The Franklin News, The Greensboro Herald, The Irwinton Southerner and Appeal, The Jasper County News, The Milledgeville Chronicle, The Milledgeville Recorder, The Monroe Advertiser, The Perry Home Journal, The Sandersville Progress, The Savannah Local, The Sparta Ishmaelite, The Swainsboro Pine Forest and *The Warrenton Clipper*.

What is remarkable about that group of newspapers which sent the GPA's founders to the first convention is that only three of them will send a representative to the 100th convention. All the others have either gone out of business, merged with competitors, or changed their names in some particular.

The three still having the exact same name are *The Warrenton Clipper, The Sparta Ishmaelite* and *The Sandersville Progress*, all of them in adjoining counties in east central Georgia and all by coincidence very near to Milledgeville.

Although Irwin had cited business reasons as the main basis for forming the association, it was conventions and annual "jaunts" that quickly became the main attraction, and helped attract more members.

The very first convention sent a request to organizers of the Piedmont Exposition in Atlanta asking that time be set aside for the group of newspapermen to meet President Grover Cleveland who was scheduled to attend the Exposition.

The request was granted and six weeks after the first convention, the GPA founding members met with President Cleveland at the Kimball House in Atlanta, "enjoyed a handshake and a few words with the first and last Democratic president of the United States in the last half century," according to an account by John H. Hodges of the Perry *Home Journal*.

Undoubtedly the audience with a U.S. president gave the Press Association early credibility. Most newspapermen of that period seldom ever saw a U.S. president, much less met him, and since Georgia and the South were solidly Democratic in those years, Cleveland was the only man most of the GPA founders ever voted for who actually became president. (In the 52 years from 1860 to 1912 Cleveland was the only Democrat elected to the presidency).

During its first 60 years the Press Association moved from city to city in Georgia for its annual summer convention, meeting at Gainesville in 1888 and Cartersville in 1889. Other convention sites included Brunswick, Elberton, Newnan, Cuthbert, Dublin, Commerce, Wrightsville, Cedartown, Toccoa and Adel.

According to Carl Rountree of *The Dawson News,* there was only one city that did not invite the GPA to return another year. That was Toccoa, following a convention in 1941 at Latournea Retreat on Lake Louise. Rountree says there was a party one night that "terminated" the GPA's welcome in Toccoa. He recalls that it was also at that convention that Gordon Chapman of *The Sandersville Progress* lost the presidency by one vote to Otis Brumby Sr.

In the year the Weekly Press Association was formed, there were about 200 weeklies in the state, up from only 60 at the end of the Civil War. Many of them were nothing more than political pamphlets to satisfy the editor's ego, but a change of emphasis was taking place in journalism. The news pages were becoming more important than the editorial page.

Irwin served one year as president and was succeeded by Ben F. Perry of *The Canton Advance*. Irwin was elected to another year's term in 1891. Then in 1894, W. S. Coleman of *The Cedartown Standard* was elected president. Like Irwin, Coleman is not well known in journalism annals, but he holds the distinction of serving as GPA president for 10 consecutive years, 1894-1904, by far the longest tenure in the association's history. At the time of his presidency the association's membership had grown to 132 papers.

Coleman's years witnessed the peak of "jaunting," including trips to New York, Kansas City (for a Democratic National Convention), Washington, D.C., and often into Tennessee and Florida, all by train, of course, which was the only means of lengthy travel in those years.

The Association also began having seminars and discussions on relevant subjects. One subject discussed at the 1896 convention was: "Should Women Journalists Marry?"

Dailies Join Association

In its first 30 years the Press Association did not have daily newspaper members although representatives of dailies often attended conventions as guests or speakers. Then in 1918, virtually without debate, the constitution and bylaws were changed to admit daily members, "weekly" was dropped from the name and the modern Georgia Press Association was born. That 1918 convention was held in Wrightsville, one of the smallest towns ever to host the GPA.

Three years later W. G. Sutlive of *The Savannah Evening Press* became the first daily executive to be elected president. Sutlive served for two years, as was the custom in the period between the world wars. The only exception to the two-year presidency was a three-year term by Jack Williams of *The Waycross Journal-Herald* in 1931, 1932 and 1933. Williams was the only daily executive other than Sutlive to serve as president until 1956 when Quimby Melton Jr. of *The Griffin Daily News* became president, and daily executives began serving on a regular basis, usually every third year, but sometimes more often.

Sutlive's son, Kirk, known to later members of the GPA as the master of ceremonies for many years at awards night, was president of the Association in 1936-1937, serving only one year. He was publisher of *The Blackshear Times* and later worked for Union Bag in Savannah, which sponsored the Awards Night banquets in the 1960s and 1970s.

The GPA elected its first and only (as of 1984) woman president in 1927. She was Emily Woodward of *The Vienna News*. It was during Miss Woodward's presidency that the Georgia Press Institute was begun, with the first Institute held at Mercer University in 1928. John Pascall of *The Atlanta Journal* was chairman of the first Institute, and also served as chairman of four more Institutes — in 1934, 1935, 1936 and 1937.

Although the Institute was the brainchild of Miss Woodward, she never served as Institute chairman. In its early years the Institute moved from college to college, just as the summer convention moved from city to city. It was held at Mercer in Macon in 1928; then at the University in Athens in 1929; and at Emory in Decatur in 1930 and 1933. But in 1934 the Institute found a permanent home in Athens, mainly due to the efforts of John E. Drewry, head of the Henry Grady School of Journalism which became a co-sponsor of the Institute.

In 1936 the Association held its 50th convention, returning to Milledgeville, site of the first convention, and the Senate chamber of the old Capitol, which was then a part of the Georgia Military College campus. Hal Stanley, the long-time editor of *The Forum*, told the convention that all but 50 newspapers in Georgia were now members of the GPA. Its annual dues had by then increased to $15 a year, which included an initiation fee. Five charter members of the Association were present for the 50th convention. They were P. T. McCutcheon, R. B. Moore, Clem Moore, Douglas Wickle and R. J. Guinn. Of these, McCutcheon, publisher of *The News and Banner* of Franklin, had the most remarkable attendance record, being present at every GPA convention from 1887 until 1945. He died in 1947 at the age of 81, the oldest surviving GPA charter member. One of the speakers at the 50th convention was Peggy Marsh, a former *Atlanta Journal* reporter who had just published the year's biggest best-seller novel, *Gone With The Wind*, under her maiden name, Margaret Mitchell.

Manager's Position Established

Several important changes took place in the Association, its programs and its procedures during the late 1930s.

At the 1937 convention, held in Adel, Gov. E. D. (Ed) Rivers addressed the opening session, which was apparently the first time a convention had invited a Georgia governor to be the speaker. Several members protested that Gov. Rivers' appearance violated the constitutional provisions against politics and political discussions. The objections were overridden however, and the governor's state of the state address became a traditional part of the GPA summer conventions.

Jere N. Moore of Milledgeville, a grandson of one of the charter members, was elected president, and he declared that his main goal would be to establish a full-time field manager for the GPA. Previously, members of the Association had handled the secretarial duties, and written and put out *The Forum*. Conventions and Institutes were handled by committees of members and their wives. There was no "office staff," nor indeed any office.

With the aid of Emory University the GPA hired J. C. Seymour, a native of Minnesota, and assistant manager of the Minnesota Press Association, to be the first field manager. Emory agreed to carry Seymour on its payroll as a member of the teaching staff, during which time he would also be available to the GPA for as much time as was necessary. Emory also made available offices and equipment. The GPA was to compensate Emory for the time and materials used on GPA duties.

The manager's duties were to include helping newspapers sell more national advertising, publicity control, legislative efforts (lobbying for additional legal ads and protection against libel suits), and publication of weekly and monthly bulletins.

During this period the GPA affiliated with the National Editorial Association, and has maintained a close relationship ever since. Albert S. Hardy of Gainesville was the first Georgia representative on the NEA board and became NEA president in 1943.

Georgia was the first southern state to hire a full-time manager for its press association but neighboring states soon followed the example. Jim Seymour and other state managers began to discuss a national advertising service which would provide ads to smaller papers for one order, one bill and one check. Eventually their ideas led to the creation of an advertising arm of NEA, which for 40 years was the main agency handling national ads for weeklies and many small dailies.

In 1941 the GPA moved its offices from Emory to the Atlanta National Bank Building, although Manager Seymour still spent time on the Emory faculty. The summer convention, (mentioned earlier) was held at Lake Louise near Toccoa, with speeches by Gov. Eugene Talmadge and Attorney General Ellis Arnall, who would be bitter opponents for governor the following year.

In September 1942, a second full-time person was added to the office staff. She was Frances P. Haley, who was to be Seymour's assistant.

World War II was raging by then and had its impact on the GPA and Georgia newspapers. The GPA president during the first two years of the war was Otis Brumby Sr. of Marietta. When Seymour, the first GPA manager, resigned in February 1943 to take a job with Agricultural Marketing Administration, Brumby and the board named Miss Haley as his replacement. It was at a time when women were moving into many newspaper positions previously held only by men. In fact, some newspapers that had never employed women were now hiring them as the male employees were called to military service.

During the war years of 1942, 1943, 1944 and 1945, the summer conventions were all held in Atlanta, which was easier to get to under wartime travel limitations. These were the first summer conventions held in Atlanta since 1904, and only two have been held there since.

The GPA fell on hard times in early 1945 when Miss Haley became ill and the office could not keep up clipping and publicity services on which it depended for operating funds. For several months Mrs. Martha McIver was in charge of the office. The Institute was not held that year for the only time since 1928.

Outgoing President R. E. L. Majors outlined the Association's financial problems at the convention, held in September at the Biltmore Hotel, and suggested that a decision be made on whether to hire "a halftime manager" or "continue on our own."

New President Belmont Dennis and the board voted to hire a full-time manager, and a suite of offices was rented in the building of Georgia Evening College, which became Georgia State, and would be GPA headquarters for the next 24 years. Sid Williams of Atlanta was hired as the new executive manager.

Postwar economic recovery was helping the Association and its members, and Williams was able to report that the 1946 convention in Savannah "was the largest and (in the opinion of many) the best convention ever." Dennis had been reelected president by 22 votes over a challenge from Ed Methvin. New bylaws were adopted which limited the president to a one-year term, and which restricted the executive manager from work not related to the GPA.

For the 1947 convention the board approved a cruise to Cuba, reminiscent of the Association's early "jaunting" years. But shortly before the convention and cruise, *The Statesman,* which was the Talmadge family's weekly political newspaper, ran a story saying that Executive Manager Sid Williams was on the state payroll, and had been since 1944. *The Atlanta Journal* investigated and confirmed the information, causing President Dennis to notify Williams that he was suspended for violation of the Association rule that the executive manager not be engaged in outside activity.

Williams had been given 90 days following the adoption of the new regulation to sever his outside business connections, including those with the state.

At the 1947 convention members were so upset at the turn of events that they voted to abolish the office of executive manager, on a motion by Jere Moore, under whose administration the office had been established 10 years earlier.

Like other conventions of that period, the 1947 convention had a lively business session, in which strong feelings were vented. One resolution was adopted to prohibit any closed meetings of the GPA Board of Managers, and another stated that "no publicity of any kind would be released through the central office, paid or otherwise."

Ed Methvin was elected president in a close race against June Norwood, who had been vice-president. One of Methvin's first actions was to ask for the resignation of all members of the board of managers and to name new ones in their place.

Williams officially resigned as manager and went on to a career as a publisher of weekly newspapers in the Atlanta area. He also wrote a column on state politics, "Politics on Parade," which was carried in many weekly newspapers. He died in 1972 at the age of 57.

In another reorganization of the central office, Methvin and the new board made an arrangement with the Grady School of Journalism at the University of Georgia, and with the Georgia Evening College, under which a general manager would be selected by the Grady Dean, and made available to the Press Association while also serving on the faculty of the journalism school. This was similar to the plan arranged with Emory when Seymour had been hired. The Board unanimously approved this plan and Stanford Smith was selected as the new executive manager. Smith, 28, was a graduate of the University of Georgia who had worked for *The Augusta Chronicle*, and spent five years in the infantry during World War II.

His tenure as executive manager would be relatively tranquil after the turbulent previous 10 years when the Association was seeking to expand its role and satisfy members both on financial and professional grounds. In fact it would be almost a quarter of a century before the GPA would again face a crisis as serious as those which plagued it almost constantly during its first 60 years, from 1887 to 1947. In the following four decades its nature and its role would change as drastically as the newspapers which it served, with the long-time divisiveness greatly reduced,and the degree of service to newspapers and the general public greatly increased.

Smith reported to the 1949 convention that the Association now had 246 members, which included 27 dailies, 188 weeklies and 31 associate members. The amount of advertising handled through the central office rose from $16,000 in 1947 to $28,000 in 1949. An annual directory of Georgia newspapers was published for the first time; a weekly bulletin was being sent to all members, punched for binding in covers, and indexed periodically; and *The Forum* resumed a monthly schedule.

In 1949 Stiles Martin of *The Atlanta Constitution* and Milton Fleetwood of *The Cartersville Tribune-News* announced that the historical project of the Association launched in 1935, when Fleetwood was president, was finally being completed and that a book, *Georgia Journalism*, written primarily by John Talmadge and Louis Griffith, faculty members of the Henry Grady School, would be published in 1950. The book would cover the history of Georgia newspapers from 1763, when *The Gazette* was founded in Savannah, through the present, and would include a section on the Georgia Press Association.

First Jekyll Convention

In June 1948, the GPA held its first convention on Jekyll Island, which had been purchased the previous year by the state of Georgia from the so-called Millionaires' Club which owned it for nearly 60 years. The state planned to make Jekyll into a resort and convention center but at that time there was no bridge connecting Jekyll with the mainland, and the conventioneers had to take ferries across the famed Marshes of Glynn to the island. The convention was held in the partially-restored Crane House, and the old Jekyll Hotel. *The Forum* reported: "Business sessions were punctuated with sightseeing tours around the island, softball games on the broad green lawn at the dockside, midnight tours of the 500-foot beach to watch great sea turtles come in and deposit their eggs, and wee-hour singing sessions on the brink of the beautiful pool in front of the hotel." The conventioneers ferried to the mainland for the main dinners, since food service was not available for large groups on the island.

Descriptions of that first summer convention on Jekyll are interesting, of course, to many later GPA members and their families who would never know any summer convention site except Jekyll, which has hosted the GPA for 22 of the 24 years from 1962 through 1985.

The First History (1763-1950)

During the administration of Carl Rountree, *Georgia Journalism* was published by the University of Georgia Press. Copies of this 400-page account of Georgia's newspaper history are relatively scarce. The GPA central office has only one copy, and many members have never seen or read this relatively unique book about a state's newspapers and its press association.

Georgia Journalism is divided into three sections. The first section, written by John E. Talmadge, then a journalism professor at the Grady School, is entitled "A History of Georgia Newspapers." It tells of the state's newspapers from 1763, when the first newspaper, *The Gazette*, was founded in Savannah, through 1950 (which is roughly when this current volume picks up). Titles of the chapters in Talmadge's section provide an idea of the content: I — The 18th Century Printer; II — A Developing Press: 1800-1836; III — The Press Debates Secession: 1837-1860; IV — A War and a Free Press: 1861-1865; V — A New South and a New Journalism: 1866-1890; VI — The Press in a Troubled World: 1890-1900; VII — The Modern Georgia Press: 1900-1950.

The second part of the book was written by Louis Griffith, also a professor at the Grady School, and later the assistant to the University of Georgia president. It was called "The Georgia Press Association: A Chronological History," and had been started by Griffith as part of his master's thesis more than 10 years earlier. Chapters in this section included: I —

Birth of the Weekly Press Association; II — Expanding Interests; III — Progress in Current Affairs; IV — The Association Grows Stronger; V — The Association Approaches Maturity; VI — During World War II; VII — Reconversion; VIII — Georgia Press Association Today.

The third section of the book is "Georgia Newspapers, 1950: An Annotated Listing." Griffith also compiled this section which contained a short sketch of each newspaper in the GPA as furnished by the newspapers. As Griffith explained in a preface: "The material is based on data furnished by the newspapers themselves. Under the direction of the Georgia Press Association historical committee a questionnaire was prepared and three separate mailings were dispatched over an interval of nine months. Response from busy editors was gratifying although it was not 100 percent. Supplementary material was provided from the thesis of Mildred Lois Miscally, who in 1946 wrote 'An Historical and Annotated Compilation of Current Georgia Newspapers with a Tracing of Trends in the Modern Press.' The newspaper picture in Georgia is constantly changing, but what follows does give essential information about the Georgia press at mid-century."

A similar process was followed in compiling this updated history of Georgia newspapers, and as Griffith noted, the picture is constantly changing. The current volume reflects the situation in the mid-1980s, or about 35 years after *Georgia Journalism*.

Carl Rountree, as GPA president at the time of publication, expressed the Association's appreciation in a foreword. "Publication of this book has been made possible," Rountree wrote, "by members of the Georgia Press Association who have underwritten the costs of publication . . . Guiding genius of this project has been Dean John E. Drewry of the Henry W. Grady School of Journalism. Special appreciation is due the authors of this book — Louis Griffith and John Talmadge. Their long hours spent in research and writing will always be remembered by the Association. Every president of the GPA since the project was begun in 1935 has cooperated to the extent of the Association's ability. They deserve fully as much credit for this book as the present officers." (See Introduction to this book).

New Generation of Leaders

A new generation of leaders was emerging on the newspapers themselves in the 1950s and assuming official posts in the Association. The summer convention no longer moved around from city to city, as had been the custom before World War II. Eight of the conventions from 1950-60 were held in Savannah, usually at the General Oglethorpe Hotel; one was held at the Bon Air in Augusta (1957) and two were held in Atlanta.

Awards became a more important part of the convention during the 1950s although a few awards had been presented as early as 1924. The number of awards grew slowly through the years, usually when a publisher or editor donated a trophy in his name. There were about 10 separate awards by 1940, including awards for "Largest Percentage of Local News," and "Best Job Printing." Most of the awards honored editorials. It was not until the 1950s that the award for General Excellence was introduced. Even later came the award for Best Column, which now attracts the largest number of entries each year. General Excellence, of course, became the most coveted award. (See listing later in this chapter).

In 1953 Executive Manager Smith resigned. He later became executive manager of the American Newspaper Publishers Association, a tribute both to him and to the GPA. Selected to replace him was Harvey Walters, 32, who had organized the public relations department of the Southern Presbyterian church, and would later become a Presbyterian minister. Walters proved a worthy successor to Smith. He encouraged the GPA board to expand seminars or clinics on specific aspects of newspapering such as advertising, news writing and circulation. He was instrumental in producing a booklet on "Newspaper Law," which outlined the various laws and regulations affecting newspapers.

Perhaps the GPA's most significant achievement during Walters' term as manager was Georgia's first "Sunshine Law," which was approved by the legislature and signed into law by Gov. Ernest Vandiver in 1959. Before passage of this law public officials at the state and local levels could refuse to open certain public records to the press. Walters, with the help of the GPA legislative committee, managed to get this law through the legislature with scarcely a dissenting vote once it made the Senate and House floors.

Walters was also involved with arranging two very special summer conventions of the GPA. In 1960, May 4-7, the National Editorial Association held its 75th anniversary convention at the Dinkler Plaza Hotel in Atlanta, with the GPA as host. The GPA's annual summer convention was held in conjunction with this event. Carl Rountree headed the convention committee and had issued the invitation on behalf of the Georgia Association.

Following the convention, GPA members took many of the visiting publishers on a tour of Georgia, with Savannah and Jekyll Island being the final stops.

The following year was the GPA's 75th anniversary, and the board decided to hold the convention at Milledgeville, site of the first and 50th conventions. Charles N. Martin of *The Atlanta Surburban Reporter* was president for the Diamond Jubilee convention.

A problem with Milledgeville in 1961 was that it didn't have the facilities to accommodate the number of people that now attended GPA conventions. As a result, the convention events were rather scattered, with a past presidents reception held at the Milledgeville Country Club; programs at the old Capitol Building; one luncheon on Lake Sinclair, five miles from Milledgeville; dinner at the country club; a breakfast at Ray's Restaurant; the GPA business session at Baldwin County High; the awards night banquet at the Carl Vinson National Guard Armory; then back to the Country Club for a dance.

Past President Jere N. Moore was chairman of the convention. Speakers included Pierre Salinger, press secretary for President John F. Kennedy; General Harold Maddux, vice commander of the Continental Army Command; and Gov. Ernest Vandiver. One of the famed "big bands", Claude Thornhill and Orchestra, played for the Friday night dance following the awards dinner.

The GPA made it three landmark conventions in a row in 1962 when the site was Jekyll Island, and the convention setting was the newly-completed Aquarama, a modernistic meeting facility which the state had erected on the beaches of the Atlantic Ocean. Its glass walls provided a panoramic view of pounding waves, expansive beach and often gathering clouds.

Unlike 14 years earlier, the conventioneers did not have to take a ferry, but could cross the marshes on a five-mile bridge and causeway which had been opened eight years earlier. Development of motels on the island had just started, but three were open in the summer of 1962, plus the old Jekyll Island Hotel, built by the millionaires when they owned the island. It was now operated as a regular hotel for the public.

The GPA convention had found what would prove to be its most popular and enduring site. Only twice — 1968 and 1969 — in the next 25 years would the convention be held away from Jekyll and the Aquarama.

The 1962 convention was also Harvey Walters' final official event as executive manager. He had resigned to become business manager of the California Newspaper Publishers Association. Later Walters would go on to the Seminary and become a Presbyterian minister, which had long been his ambition.

McCullough's Decade

At the 1962 convention the board hired Glenn McCullough, a native of Rome, as Walters' successor. McCullough would hold the post of executive manager for 10 years, the longest tenure of any manager as of 1984, and the GPA would reach new dimensions of service, attendance and general activity during this time. It would also buy its own building and start an Educational Foundation to give financial assistance to journalism students in the state.

McCullough, like Walters, was a graduate of the University of Missouri journalism school. He had been a reporter for *The Rome News-Tribune* and the weekly *Dade County Sentinel* in Trenton. From 1953-57 he was a reporter in the Associated Press bureau at Charlotte, North Carolina. He then became special events coordinator for the Petroleum Institute, based in New York City, and it was from that position that he came to the GPA.

Several definite trends were now established in the Association. Attendance at the summer conventions was increasing. Traditionally the conventions had been mainly for publishers and their wives, and sometimes the editors or top executives, but now more and more staff members were attending, mainly for the expanding awards night program. When the conventions settled on Jekyll more children began coming, further swelling the overall attendance. And at the conventions, the Institute and the seminars, more representatives from daily newspapers were now attending and taking part in the Association's activities.

When Homer Rankin, publisher of *The Tifton Daily Gazette*, became president in 1959, he was only the fourth daily executive to be president of the GPA in its 72 years. But in the next nine years, five of the nine presidents would be from dailies.

McCullough was a flamboyant manager with plenty of ideas. He planned festive conventions and even festive board meetings. One of his innovations at conventions was to have the officers and board members march into the Friday night banquet after everyone else was seated and be announced with a flair from the podium. Executive Manager McCullough and his wife, Shirley, would be the last to enter and be announced.

Rather than a tie, McCullough often wore a colorful scarf around his neck at dress occasions.

He was an enthusiastic lobbyist at the State Capitol for Press Association interests, and he also expanded the number of seminars and clinics sponsored by the GPA.

But McCullough's most important legacy to the GPA is the Cracker Crumble, an annual satirical show and dinner which is the main source of funds for the Georgia Press Educational Foundation.

The Cracker Crumble started as an idea of McCullough's and some Atlanta ad agency executives, who have, through the years, provided support, material and performers for the shows. A committee of GPA members met in the fall of 1963 to write the first Cracker Crumble, which was conceived as a satire on Georgia, Atlanta and national politicians. A variety of performers, including newspaper people, politicians, and night club comedians were recruited. To assure a large crowd for the first Crumble, Art Buchwald, the nationally-syndicated humor columnist, was paid $5,000 to be the main speaker.

Finally the script was ready, with much of the material centering on the popular president of the United States, John F. Kennedy. The first Crumble was scheduled for December 6, 1963. But the assassination of Kennedy on November 22, 1963, caused a postponement, since much of the program had to be scrapped and new segments written.

The Crumble was finally held on March 21, at the Biltmore Hotel, with GPA President Jim Hobgood presiding. Buchwald came as the speaker and was a great hit, but he told the GPA members they didn't need a speaker, that they could put on the show on their own and use all of the money for the scholarship fund — and that's the way it has been in the 20 years since. Master of Ceremonies for the first Crumble was Ernie Rogers, *The Atlanta Journal*'s popular columnist who was crippled by polio as a child. Norman Shavin was the director, and Shavin and Bruce Galphin did much of the final writing. Gov. Carl Sanders was a star performer, setting a precedent which future governors and other politicians have followed, even when the skits they perform are at their expense. Gov. George Busbee, in his eight years as governor, appeared frequently as a performer in the Crumble.

After six consecutive years at Jekyll, the summer convention moved across the state to West Georgia in 1968 for a one-year stand at Callaway Gardens, the lake-beach resort and floral area developed by Cason Callaway between Columbus and LaGrange. Louis Harris, editor of *The Augusta Chronicle*, was president at this convention, which featured addresses by U.S. Sen. Herman Talmadge and Gov. Lester Maddox.

The following year the convention returned to Savannah, its favorite site of the 1950s. Then it was back to Jekyll in 1970 and that has been the site in all the years through 1985. Lodging facilities on Jekyll improved dramatically in the 1970s with the addition of a Holiday Inn with a tropical decor and the conversion of the Sand Dollar condominium complex into the Jekyll Hilton Hotel, which became the regular headquarters for the convention in the 1980s.

In almost every respect the decade of the 1960s had been the GPA's most successful. It was also a time of important change in Georgia's newspapers, as most of the weeklies and small dailies switched from hot type to cold type composition, and from letter presses to offset. The central office staff had been expanded to meet the growing services and activity of the GPA. National advertising and political advertising, which were usually handled through the Georgia Newspaper Service, the GPA's advertising arm, reached a peak in the 1960s.

But relations between the board of managers and Executive Manager McCullough had become increasingly strained. The Association was also again experiencing financial problems. Matters came to a head after McCullough was embroiled in an argument with state legislative leaders at a reception in February 1972. Sam Griffin, GPA president at the time, heard of the incident and after consulting with the other board members, flew to Atlanta from his home in Bainbridge to discuss the on-going problems with McCullough.

McCullough resigned February 11, 1972, after the talk with Griffin. The board appointed Julia Dyar, who had been assistant manager since 1958, as acting manager.

Griffin and the other officers also recognized that dues were going to have to be raised sharply in order for the Association to have adequate financing, and that the members needed a better idea of what the Association meant to them.

This concern led to a series of meetings and clinics throughout the state, hosted by past presidents and members of the board. Lou Fockele, publisher of *The Times* in Gainesville, coordinated the meetings.

Alva Haywood, publisher of *The Warrenton Clipper*, and members of the central office staff, usually attended the meetings and told publishers how they could use ideas from other newspapers to promote and sell advertising for their own newspapers. A promotional brochure was prepared which outlined how individual publishers could put on a dinner or barbecue for advertisers or prospective advertisers in their home community.

The idea of the meetings, as Griffin explained, was to "carry the Association to the membership in the state," and reaffirm the value of the Association in building advertising and circulation for its members. The seminars undoubtedly helped many newspapers become more effective in delivering their advertising message but the most important result was the stronger unity and interest the seminars and meetings brought to the Association. These meetings, or clinics, were held at Elberton, Carrollton, Waynesboro, Jesup and Camilla.

At the 1972 summer convention Julia Dyar was named executive manager. Dues for member newspapers, which had been traditionally low after starting at $1 a year in 1887, were increased, especially for larger newspapers which were asked to pay dues more in line with their circulation.

A $10,000 loan to the GPA from *The Dublin Courier-Herald* helped it pay off an outstanding note. The tax-exempt status of GPA and GPEF was also clarified and fully reinstated. Financial solvency came from the additional dues revenue, and attendance at conventions and seminars increased, with no loss of members because of the dues increase.

Julia Dyar: First Lady of the GPA

Julia Traylor Dyar was a veteran of GPA activities, having attended her first convention in 1944 while a student at LaGrange College. She remembers that first one quite well because she met a young publisher from Royston named Hubert Dyar, who would become her husband. Julia and Hubert were married in 1948 and for the next 10 years she was associate editor of *The Royston Record*.

They moved to Atlanta in 1958 when Hubert was named executive director of the Georgia Literature Commission. Julia was soon hired by Harvey Walters as assistant manager of the GPA.

A native of LaGrange, Julia was a graduate of LaGrange College. While working with *The Royston Record* she was a Sunday columnist for the Anderson, South Carolina *Independent* and a correspondent for *The Atlanta Constitution*. In conjunction with her duties at the GPA office she became editor of *The Editor's Forum* in 1962 and continued as its chief editor until 1978.

Looking back at her 30 years of close involvement with the GPA —

20 years as a full-time employee and 10 years as part of a husband-wife team on a small weekly — Julia recalls most fondly the strong friendships among publishers who were brought together by the GPA.

"The annual summer convention was the family vacation for many GPA members," she wrote in a special recollection for this volume. "As a result, life-long friendships were established among the members which strengthened the organization. Visiting publishers from out of Georgia, and judges for the better newspapers contests, commented to me many times about the bond of friendship that exists between our weekly and daily members, a friendship that overshadowed any political or competitive business interests.

"Many happy memories stand out for me personally . . . meeting my husband-to-be, Hubert, at my very first convention at Atlanta in 1944; dancing with GPA President Belmont Dennis during a storm at sea on the GPA's post-convention trip to Havana, Cuba in 1947; laughing and crying during many of the Cracker Crumbles but loving every minute of them; burning the mortgage of the 1075 Spring Street building; relaxing at the RORAR Afterglows following conventions at Jekyll Island; feeling the love and support of my GPA family during Hubert's illness and death; seeing some of our part-time student-employees become publishers and staffers on our Georgia newspapers; seeing the Newspaper-In-Education program grow and prosper; hearing the Board of Managers vote me a life membership following my resignation to move back to my home in LaGrange; and seeing Kathy Chaffin become executive manager of the GPA.

"When I joined the Press Association Central Office staff in June of 1958 there were very few offset newspapers in the state. One of the greatest changes that I saw during my tenure was the conversion from letterpress to offset production by almost all of our members. At that time in 1958 we offered more services to our weekly newspapers than to our dailies because we were placing ads in the weeklies but in very few of the dailies. As the years went by more and more of the dailies allowed the advertising service to represent them, especially on political advertising. The Central Office made a determined effort to offer more information for all newspapers through the weekly Confidential Bulletin and the addition of staff-training seminars in advertising, mechanical, editorial and management. We wanted our dailies to look to us as well as to SNPA and ANPA for services that were meaningful. I hope that our daily newspaper members would agree that we made some improvement in this area.

"Something else that stands out to me in my years at GPA was the dedication of members of the Board of Managers. Officers and board members gave of their time and paid their own expenses to attend board meetings. They directed the affairs of the Association and made the decisions that have made it into one of the leading press associations in our country. We have also offered leadership on the national level through our members who have served in offices in ANPA, SNPA, NNA and ANR.

"I am especially proud to have been a part of the creation of the Georgia Press Educational Foundation, our scholarship arm; the purchase and retirement of the debt on our association's headquarters building; the expansion of our programs of editorial, mechanical, management and advertising seminars; and the beginnings of the Newspaper in Education program."

A Building of Its Own

During the early 1960s a feeling grew among several members of the Georgia Press Association that the organization should own its headquarters building. Some publishers had visited buildings owned by other press associations while attending NNA conventions, and they thought Georgia could do as well.

The need for a building suddenly became urgent when Georgia State University notified the GPA that it needed the rooms being leased to the organization.

In one of his first acts as GPA president in 1962, Jack Williams of Waycross appointed a building committee with James R. Blair of Americus as chairman.

Plans for a building were drawn up and estimates on construction obtained. Then the committee began looking for a site in Atlanta suitable for the building. Many were inspected but the good ones were all too expensive in the opinion of the committee. So the publishers began looking at existing buildings for sale. They finally settled on a building at 1075 Spring Street, which was owned by the Chuck Shields Advertising Agency. The price was $85,000, an amount the committee felt the association could handle.

The building was purchased in early 1969 and was occupied by the GPA staff soon after. An open house was held on March 28. Constructed in 1966, the building was only three years old when the GPA occupied it. Its second floor was not in a finished condition, and in fact, would not be used by the GPA for nearly nine years.

Donations to help pay for the building were solicited from members and several thousand dollars were collected. A donation of $10,000 was made by Nora Lawrence Smith of Ashburn's *Wiregrass Farmer* and the board voted to name the conference room the "Nora Lawrence Smith Conference Room" in her honor.

The GPA convention in July 1977, on the recommendation of immediate past President W. H. Champion of Dublin, voted to purchase additional property at the rear of the building for parking and a rear entrance to the building. The board authorized the sale of 20-year debentures to members and member newspapers and the solicitation of gifts to finance the $30,000 purchase price. A total of $34,750 was raised from the sale of debentures and $4,205 from gifts.

The land was cleared, a rear entrance and fire escape were constructed and other improvements were made from time to time. When the sale of debentures brought in the amount paid for the building, the board felt it could start remodeling the inside and utilize the second floor space for an attractive and convenient conference room for the Board of Managers and other committee meetings held in the Central Office.

Frank Traylor of LaGrange, an architect and brother of Executive Manager Julia Dyar, studied the building and suggested changes and future use — all at no cost to the Association.

After remodeling the second floor, and constructing the new board room, then-GPA President Otis Brumby saw a further need to improve the appearance of the inside of the building. He launched weekly paint parties, when members and staff of the GPA would meet on Saturdays and paint the inside of the building. Members of GPA who helped with the painting project included Brumby, Bob Williford, Jimmy Bennett and W. H. Champion. Helping the painter-publishers were members of the GPA staff: Kathy T. Chaffin, Edna Waits, Kay Kent, Donna Espy and Thomas A. Chaffin.

All the paint used on the interior of the building was paid for by President Brumby. The crew completed most of the painting in just three Saturdays. West Point Pepperell gave the Georgia Press Association enough carpet to re-carpet the building.

In appreciation of President Brumby's interest and contributions of time, money and inspiration, the GPA presented him a plaque, naming him to the "Order of the Golden Paint Brush."

The final payment on the building was made January 5, 1976, when Executive Secretary Dyar sent a check to the National Bank of Georgia for $546.59.

The sale of debentures to members, both active and associate, enabled the association to complete the renovations. The debentures are being paid off every year on a lottery basis of the dates of redemptions, and should be completely paid off by 1989.

Growth and New Challenges

After overcoming the financial and morale problems of the early 1970s, the GPA enjoyed a remarkable period of growth and activity for the rest of the decade. In addition to the dues increase and the selection of Julia Dyar as new executive manager, the administration of Albert Jenkins witnessed another significant change with the merger of the GPA and GNS boards. For several years there had been separate boards for what was basically one operation, and this occasionally caused problems of communications and duplication. The merger created one board with the same officers and members for both GPA and GNS.

Attendance at the summer conventions in the 1975-1979 period ranged from 700 to 800 at the Friday night awards banquet, as newspapers sent more staff members to the awards ceremonies, and more families brought children. The meals and receptions at conventions were sponsored and paid for by associate members, holding down costs to the newspaper members.

Sponsorship of meals by associate members — usually large corporations — had been a sore subject with some members for years, and those who felt most strongly against it were given the option of paying for their meals.

An Atlanta magazine article in 1979 explored the issue in an unflattering light which further disturbed those publishers and editors already against having large utility companies or banks pick up the $8,000 tab for a big banquet at the convention.

"The GPA convention, as almost anyone who goes will tell you, is basically a way for newspaper people to take their families to Jekyll for a few days vacation and then write it all off on their taxes," the article, by Robert Coram, stated. "The most diligent exegesis of a convention program reveals little taking place that advances the cause of journalism. The program instead shows numerous parties, luncheons, brunches, family activities, tennis tournaments, golf tournaments and dances."

At the next annual business meeting the matter of sponsored meals at both the convention and Press Institute was a topic of long and heated debate. The majority of members at the meeting opposed doing away with sponsorships, pointing out that they could not be "bought" with a meal if they could not be bought with an advertising schedule. It was also mentioned that the sponsored meals and receptions for the entire convention had replaced numerous small parties once given by associate members for selected GPA participants.

A committee was appointed to study the matter further and report to the Board of Managers. On a 3-2 vote, the Committee recommended that sponsored events be discontinued except for the All-Georgia Products dinner, and the board endorsed the recommendation in December 1981.

Jim Minter of *The Journal-Constitution*, chairman of the study committee, made a simple but compelling case. "Sponsorships don't compromise us as individuals," he said, "but they may compromise us as an organization."

The main result has been fewer children at meals, but the subsequent conventions have been well-attended and the 1984 Press Institute had the highest participation in years by GPA members.

In August 1978, Julia Dyar submitted her resignation as executive manager, ending 20 years as either the assistant manager or manager, the longest tenure thus far by a paid staff member. Ms. Dyar, whose husband Hubert died in October 1973, told the board she had accepted a job as head of public relations at LaGrange College, and "would be going home," after 30 years.

Otis Brumby Jr., who had just taken over as president, appointed a committee to begin looking for a replacement. In the interim, Kathy Chaffin, the assistant manager, was named acting manager.

Several applicants were interviewed but in May 1979 the board asked Ms. Chaffin to take the job on a permanent basis and she accepted. Ms. Chaffin, a native of Savannah, was 28 when she became GPA executive manager, the same age as Stanford Smith when he took the post 31 years earlier. A 1972 graduate of Georgia State, with an AB in journalism, she had begun working for the GPA in April 1973. She later worked one year as the southeast sales manager for American Newspaper Representatives Inc., before returning as assistant manager of GPA.

Under Ms. Chaffin's managership, the GPA continued to function smoothly, and in 1985 she marked her seventh year as manager, surpassing Julia Dyar's tenure in that post. Edna Waits served as assistant manager during this period.

The GPA's role was changing in the 1980s, however, as its advertising arm, GNS, and its national affiliate, ANR, handled fewer advertisements for smaller newspapers. This reduced the income to GNS, which previously had helped pay some of the GPA's expenses.

For about a year the GPA also lost the revenue from a clipping service agency while it considered starting a clipping service of its own. But advertising for the Cracker Crumble program and *The Editor's Forum* both increased, and a new statewide classified service, started during Neely Young's presidency, has helped replace some of the lost revenue.

A Newspaper-in-Education program is also conducted from the central office, financed in its first three years by a generous donation from Lou Fockele, former publisher of *The Times* of Gainesville.

Pattern of Leadership

As the Georgia Press Association nears its 100th birthday, it has become a respected trade association, providing both service and social activity to its members, as well as representing them at the General Assembly on legislative matters of interest. One of the most valuable services is a weekly newsletter which contains information from throughout the industry, often providing tips on improving business, news presentation and circulation, as well as personal information on members, and a classified section of items for sales, jobs wanted and positions open.

Although started as the Georgia Weekly Press Association, the GPA today enjoys strong support and participation from dailies, large and small, and there is little of the friction which once existed between the daily and weekly press. Presidents from daily newspapers were rare until the mid-1950s but all three GPA officers for 1983-1984 represented daily newspapers. The four immediate past presidents were all from weeklies.

If that pattern seems haphazard and unplanned, it may be because the method of selecting GPA officers remains quaintly unstructured and uncertain after nearly 100 years. There is no nominating committee nor any recognized path to becoming a candidate for treasurer, which is the first step up the ladder to president. For the past 30 years the only contests at conventions have been for the treasurer's post, with the treasurer then succeeding to vice-president the following year, and to president the next year. But in earlier years there were close and bitter battles for the presidency at annual meetings, with wounds often slow in healing.

Official minutes of the conventions held immediately after World War II tell of regular contests for president, with close votes, and an apparent conflict between two strong factions in the association. In 1946, Belmont Dennis, in his bid for a second year as president, which was then customary, had to turn back a strong challenge from Ed Methvin. The following year Methvin defeated the incumbent vice-president, June Norwood, 51-45. This was at the convention when the executive manager's post was abolished and Sid Williams was dismissed as manager. Following his election Methvin named an entire new GPA board, claiming that the appointments of most of the current members were indefinite or not in keeping with the bylaws. An amendment was also adopted limiting presidents to one-year terms. Among the ousted board members were Jack Tarver of *The Constitution* and W. H. Champion of Dublin.

In 1948 Norwood defeated Vice-President Albert Hardy Jr. by only four votes, 56-52, but Hardy was reelected to the vice-president's post. The next year Hardy was elected president without opposition, and this set a precedent for vice-presidents to automatically move up to the presidency. In the 1950s most of the contests at conventions were for the vice-presidency, and sometimes three candidates would be nominated. The treasurer's post was not considered a stepping stone until the early 1960s. Since then all floor contests for officer positions have been for the treasurer slot.

The path to the treasurer's post is still a mystery however, even to some men who have taken it. Usually the word is passed before the summer convention that a certain member would like to run. That member then must muster support, sometimes by his own efforts, and other times with the help of friends who are promoting him. Several members then nominate the candidate during the annual business meeting and tell of his or her accomplishments. Nominations for officers are opened promptly at 11 a.m. the day of the conventions by stipulation of the constitution. This rule was made so that all members know when elections are to be held and can be on hand if they desire. It is also to prevent officers from calling for the election when certain members are absent.

The system has produced capable officers, and in the past 25 years has led to only an occasional contest at the convention over the treasurer's job. In 1964, a contest developed between Bob Fowler of *The Gwinnett News* and Charles McMichael of *The Wrightsville Headlight*, with Fowler winning. McMichael, a board member at the time, never came back to another convention and eventually sold *The Headlight*.

A campaign was mounted for Otis Brumby Jr. at the 1968 convention against John Fleetwood, the apparent "establishment" choice. Fleetwood won over Brumby, who was then only 28 years old. Brumby remained very active in the Association but disavowed any further interest in campaigns for GPA office. Eight years later, in 1976, after Brumby had departed the convention he was nominated from the floor by Carroll Dadisman of *The Columbus Ledger-Enquirer*, and was elected without opposition, even though he had made no effort to win support, and had even told several friends not to nominate him.

The first contest since 1968 came in 1977 when Robert Williford of *The Elberton Star* and Billy Blair of *The Americus Times-Recorder* were both nominated. Williford, an incumbent board member, won the contest. At the time, both the already-elected president and vice-president (Jim Wood and Otis Brumby Jr.) were from dailies, and Blair would have been a third daily publisher among the three officers.

Bob Tribble of Tri-County Newspapers won the treasurer's post in 1980 in a contest with Bob Chambers of *The Athens Banner-Herald* and *Daily News*, although Tribble had not been a declared candidate before the convention. Two years later Chambers was nominated again and elected without opposition.

The method of election has been debated by several boards, and in 1977 an amendment to the bylaws was adopted by the board and submitted to the convention for approval. It would have established a nominating committee, composed of former presidents, to make nominations for the three major offices each summer.

After a lengthy debate the amendment was tabled, with the board advised to bring back another proposal the following year. A perspiring Bobby Branch presided over the proceedings at which Ralph Parkman, a board member, made the motion for adoption of the amendment, while his father, past-president Stanley Parkman, was one of the most vocal opponents.

Fortunately, the contests of recent years have left few scars and a general feeling of cooperation and good will characterizes the Association's activities, publicly and for the most part privately.

At the summer convention in 1985 an amendment to the constitution was adopted which sets up a nominating committee composed of five past presidents.

Father-Son Presidents

In its first hundred years, the GPA has had nine presidents who were sons of former presidents, an indication of the family orientation of the newspaper business during this period.

Kirk Sutlive, in 1937, was the first son of a former president to be elected. His father, W. G. Sutlive, had been president in 1921, just 15 years earlier, which is the shortest span between any of the father-son presidents. By contrast, Albert Hardy Jr., third son of a former president to hold the post, was elected in 1949, 40 years after his father in 1909.

Listed below are the father-son presidents and the year they were first elected:

Albert S. Hardy Sr., 1909 *Gainesville News*	Albert S. Hardy Jr., 1949 *Commerce News*
C. M. Methvin, 1911 *Eastman Times-Journal*	Edwin T. Methvin, 1947 *Eastman Times-Journal*
W. G. Sutlive, 1921 *Savannah Evening Press*	Kirk Sutlive, 1936 *Blackshear Times*
C. D. Rountree, 1923 *Wrightville Headlight*	Carl Rountree, 1950 *The Dawson News*
Ernest Camp, 1925 *The Walton Tribune*	Sanders Camp, 1964 *The Walton Tribune*
Jack Williams Sr., 1931 *Waycross Journal-Herald*	Jack Williams Jr., 1962 *Waycross Journal-Herald*
M. L. Fleetwood, 1934 *Cartersville Tribune-News*	John Fleetwood, 1970 *Cartersville Tribune-News*
Otis A. Brumby, 1941 *Cobb County Times*	Otis A. Brumby Jr., 1978 *Marietta Daily Journal*
Quimby Melton Jr., 1955	Quimby Melton, III, 1986 (in line).

100 YEARS OF GPA PRESIDENTS, 1887-1986

1887—Mark D. Irwin, *Conyers Solid South*
1888—Ben F. Perry, *Canton Advance*
1889—Elam Christian, *Cartersville Courant-American*
1890—J. L. Underwood, *Dawson News*
1891—Mark D. Irwin, *Conyers Solid South*
1892—S. W. Roberts, *Sparta Ishmaelite*
1893—S. T. Black, *Fayetteville News*
1894—W. S. Coleman, *Cedartown Standard*

1895—W. S. Coleman, *Cedartown Standard*
1896—W. S. Coleman, *Cedartown Standard*
1897—W. S. Coleman, *Cedartown Standard*
1898—W. S. Coleman, *Cedartown Standard*
1899—W. S. Coleman, *Cedartown Standard*
1900—W. S. Coleman, *Cedartown Standard*
1901—W. S. Coleman, *Cedartown Standard*
1902—W. S. Coleman, *Cedartown Standard*
1903—W. S. Coleman, *Cedartown Standard*
1904—W. S. Coleman, *Cedartown Standard*
1905—C. M. McKenzie, *Cordele Sentinel*
1906—C. M. McKenzie, *Cordele Sentinel*
1907—Hal M. Stanley, *Dublin Courier-Dispatch*
1908—Albert S. Hardy, *Gainesville News*
1909—Albert S. Hardy, *Gainesville News*
1910—L. A. Morgan, *Americus News*
1911—C. M. Methvin, *Eastman Times-Journal*
1912—C. M. Methvin, *Eastman Times-Journal*
1913—P. T. McCutchen, *Franklin News and Banner*
1914—P. T. McCutchen, *Franklin News and Banner*
1915—J. C. McAuliffe, *Milledgeville News*
1916—J. C. McAuliffe, *Milledgeville News*
1917—Paul T. Harber, *Commerce News*
1918—Paul T. Harber, *Commerce News*
1919—J. K. Simmons, *Telfair Enterprise*
1920—J. K. Simmons, *Telfair Enterprise*
1921—W. G. Sutlive, *Savannah Press*
1922—W. G. Sutlive, *Savannah Press*
1923—C. D. Rountree, *Wrightsville Headlight*
1924—C. D. Rountree, *Wrightsville Headlight*
1925—Ernest Camp, *Walton Tribune*
1926—Ernest Camp, *Walton Tribune*
1927—Emily Woodward, *Vienna News*
1928—Emily Woodward, *Vienna News*
1929—Louie L. Morris, *Hartwell Sun*
1930—Louie L. Morris, *Hartwell Sun*
1931—Jack Williams, *Waycross Journal-Herald*
1932—Jack Williams, *Waycross Journal-Herald*
1933—Jack Williams, *Waycross Journal-Herald*
1934—M. L. Fleetwood, *Cartersville Tribune-News*
1935—M. L. Fleetwood, *Cartersville Tribune-News*
1936—W. Kirk Sutlive, *Blackshear Times*
1937—Jere N. Moore, *Milledgeville Union-Recorder*
1938—Jere N. Moore, *Milledgeville Union-Recorder*
1939—J. Roy McGinty, *Calhoun Times*
1940—J. Roy McGinty, *Calhoun Times*
1941—Otis A. Brumby Sr., *Cobb County Times*

1942 — Otis A. Brumby Sr., *Cobb County Times*
1943 — R. E. L. Majors, *Claxton Enterprise*
1944 — R. E. L. Majors, *Claxton Enterprise*
1945 — A. Belmont Dennis, *Covington News*
1946 — A. Belmont Dennis, *Covington News*
1947 — Edwin T. Methvin, *Eastman Times-Journal*
1948 — J. W. Norwood, *Lowndes County News*
1949 — Albert S. Hardy Jr., *Commerce News*
1950 — Carl Rountree, *Dawson News*
1951 — W. H. McWhorter, *DeKalb New Era*
1952 — Cooper Etheridge, *Houston Home Journal*
1953 — Roy Chalker, *Waynesboro True Citizen*
1954 — Stanley Parkman, *Carroll County Georgian*
1955 — Quimby Melton Jr., *Griffin Daily News*
1956 — C. J. Broome, *Alma Times*
1957 — Roscoe Ledford, *Vidalia Advance*
1958 — M. A. Perry, *Metropolitan Herald*
1959 — Homer Rankin, *Tifton Gazette*
1960 — Charles Martin, *Atlanta Suburban Reporter*
1961 — James R. Blair, *Americus Times-Recorder*
1962 — Jack Williams Jr., *Waycross Journal-Herald*
1963 — James Hobgood, *Calhoun Times*
1964 — Sanders Camp, *Walton Tribune*
1965 — Graham Ponder, *The Madisonian*
1966 — Robert Fowler, *Gwinnett Daily News*
1967 — Louis C. Harris, *Augusta Chronicle*
1968 — Thomas Frier, *Douglas Enterprise*
1969 — William Rogers, *Swainsboro Blade*
1970 — John Fleetwood, *Cartersville Tribune-News*
1971 — Sam Griffin, *Bainbridge News-Searchlight*
1972 — Albert Jenkins, *Baxley News-Banner*
1973 — Foy Evans, *Warner Robins Sun*
1974 — Alva Haywood, *Warrenton Clipper*
1975 — W. H. Champion, *Dublin Courier-Herald*
1976 — Bobby Branch, *Houston Home Journal*
1977 — Jim Wood, *Clayton News/Daily*
1978 — Otis Brumby Jr., *Marietta Daily Journal*
1979 — Robert Williford, *Elberton Star*
1980 — Robert Williams, *Blackshear Times*
1981 — W. H. "Dink" NeSmith, *Jesup Press-Sentinel*
1982 — Robert Tribble, *Manchester Star-Mercury*
1983 — Neely Young, *Dalton Citizen-News*
1984 — Robert Chambers, *Athens Banner-Herald/News*
1985 — Millard Grimes, *Rockdale Citizen*
1986 (in line) — Quimby Melton III, *Jackson Progress/Argus*

GEORGIA PRESS INSTITUTE CHAIRMEN

FOUNDER OF THE INSTITUTE — Miss Emily Woodward, Vienna News

1928, 1934-37 — John Pascall, *Atlanta Journal*
1930-33 — Mark Etheridge, *Macon Telegraph*
1938-41 — Albert S. Hardy Sr., *Gainesville News*
1942 — Wright Bryan, *Atlanta Journal*
1943 — Louie L. Morris, *Hartwell Sun*
Maynard Ashworth, *Columbus Ledger-Enquirer*
1944 — Robert L. M. Parks, *Augusta Chronicle*
1945 — L. L. Patten, *Lanier County News*
1946 — Jack Tarver, *Atlanta Constitution*
1947 — Maynard Ashworth, *Columbus Ledger-Enquirer*
Louie Morris, *Hartwell Sun*
1948 — J. Roy McGinty, *Calhoun Times*
1949 — Jack Williams, *Waycross Journal-Herald*
1950 — Jere N. Moore, *Milledgeville Union-Recorder*
1951 — Leo Aikman, *Atlanta Constitution*
1952 — Stanley Parkman, *Carroll County Georgian*
1953 — John T. Fleetwood, *Cartersville Tribune-News*
1954 — Leon Smith, *Thomaston Times-Free Press*
1955 — Homer Rankin, *Tifton Gazette*
1956 — Albert Hardy, *Commerce News*
1957 — James R. Blair, *Americus Times-Recorder*
1958 — Alva A. Haywood, *Warrenton Clipper*
1959 — Frank Hash, *McDuffie Progress*
1960 — Bill Ott, *Macon Telegraph*
1961 — Jack Williams Jr., *Waycross Journal-Herald*
1962 — Jim Hobgood, *Calhoun Times*
1963 — Edge Reid, *Columbus Ledger-Enquirer*
1964 — Bob Fowler, *Marietta Daily Journal*
1965 — Henry Schulte, *Savannah News-Press*
1966 — Tom Frier, *Douglas Enterprise*
1967 — Bill Rogers, *Swainsboro Forest-Blade*
1968 — Carroll Dadisman, *Marietta Daily Journal*
1969 — Millard Grimes, *Columbus Enquirer*
1970 — N.S. Hayden, *Athens Banner-Herald & News*
1971 — Tom Burson, *Camilla Enterprise*
1972 — Bo McLeod, *Donalsonville News*
Billy Blair, *Americus Times-Recorder*
1973 — Lou Fockele, *The Times,* Gainesville
1974 — Bob Chambers, *Athens Banner-Herald & News*
1975 — Billy Thomasson, *Newnan Times-Herald*
1976 — Robert M. Williams Jr., *Blackshear Times*

1977 — Neely Young, *Dalton Citizen-News*
1978 — Adelaide Ponder, *Madison Madisonian*
1979 — W. H. "Dink" NeSmith, *Jesup Press-Sentinel*
1980 — Smythe Newsome, *Washington News-Reporter*
1981 — Durwood McAlister, *Atlanta Journal-Constitution*
1982 — Jimmy Bennett, *Cherokee Tribune*
1983 — Quimby Melton III, *Griffin Daily News*
1984 — Jim Minter, *Atlanta Journal-Constitution*
1985 — Glenn Vaughn, *Columbus Ledger-Enquirer*

Brief Biographies of GPA Presidents, 1945-1985

Belmont Dennis

Ed Methvin

J. W. Norwood

A. BELMONT DENNIS, 1945-47

Belmont Dennis, publisher of *The Covington News* for 30 years, was the first post-World War II president of the Georgia Press Association, and also the last president to serve for two years. Before and during the war, the customary term for president was two years, and in the early years of the association presidents often served for several years, the record being held by W. S. Coleman of Cedartown, who was GPA president for 10 years, from 1894 to 1904.

Dennis was born in 1891 in Columbia, Tennessee. He joined the U.S. Navy when he was only 15, serving a four-year enlistment from 1906-1910. He also was in the Navy from 1917-1921, during which he fought in World War I. His Navy experience was the beginning of a lifelong love of the sea.

Dennis began his newspaper career on the Memphis, Tennessee *Commercial Appeal*, and later worked on *The Chattanooga Times, The New York Times, The Charleston,* South Carolina *Post, The Nashville Tennessean, The Nashville Banner, The Atlanta Constitution* and *The Atlanta Georgian*.

In 1931 Dennis and his wife, Mabel Sessions Dennis, and Mrs. Dennis' sister, Mary Sessions, pooled their resources and bought *The Covington News*. From then until his death in 1961, he was editor and publisher of *The News*, as well as owner and publisher of several other Georgia weeklies. These included *The Eatonton Messenger, The Conyers News, The Madisonian, The Walton County News, The Barnesville Gazette* and *The Nashville Herald*. Dennis pioneered commercial web press printing in weekly newspaper shops, and for many years *The News* had one of the largest web presses of any weekly in Georgia. He also established radio station WMOC in Covington.

Dennis was active in the First Baptist Church serving as Sunday School superintendent, deacon, teacher of the Adult Bible Class, and member of the building committee.

During his two years as GPA president, Dennis initiated the movement that resulted in the formation of the Georgia State Chamber of Commerce, but his tenure was not without dissension. He ran for state lieutenant governor in 1946 while serving as GPA president, losing to M. E. Thompson and Marvin Griffin, another publisher. Sid Williams, the GPA executive secretary was also accused during this time of engaging in outside political activities. At the 1946 summer convention, Dennis was reelected president by a 22-vote margin over E. T. Methvin, and Williams got a unanimous vote of confidence from the board of managers to continue as executive secretary.

During his second year as president Dennis had the unpleasant duty of suspending Executive Secretary Williams, after a story in *The Atlanta Journal* charged that Williams had been on the state payroll since 1944.

At a busy summer convention in 1947, Dennis presented his proposal for a state Chamber of Commerce and this project was enthusiastically supported, alleviating some of the unrest created by problems with the executive secretary.

Belmont and Mabel Dennis had three children. Their son, William, was publisher of *The Barnesville Gazette* for many years.

Dennis died on Christmas morning, 1961 at the age of 70.

EDWIN T. METHVIN, 1947-48

Edwin T. (Ed) Methvin was elected GPA president on his second try. He lost in 1946 to Belmont Dennis but then won over the incumbent vice-president, J. W. Norwood, by six votes at the 1947 summer convention. Methvin was described by one of his board members as "aggressive and unintimidated. He turned the GPA around."

During Methvin's presidency, a new executive manager, Stanford Smith, was hired and a plan for financing the GPA office and staff was worked out with the University of Georgia and Georgia State. Methvin presided over the first GPA convention on Jekyll Island in the summer of 1948. Those attending had to be ferried back and forth from the island.

Methvin was the second son of a former GPA president to succeed to the post, his father, C. W. Methvin, having served in 1911 and 1912. He was a lifelong resident of Eastman, in Dodge County, where the elder Methvin was publisher of *The Eastman Times-Journal*, which he bought in 1902.

He succeeded his father as publisher of the Eastman paper in 1941 and held the post for 33 years. In 1974 he sold *The Times-Journal* to a competing weekly, *The Spotlight,* which had started in 1972. Methvin was a veteran of World War II and a member of First Presbyterian in Eastman. He died in February 1977, at the age of 68, in an unusual accident when his car caught fire in the driveway of his home and exploded before he could get out.

JUNE WEST NORWOOD, 1948-49

June (J. W.) Norwood was born July 13, 1897 in Nashville, Georgia, and started as a printer's devil on *The Nashville Herald* when he was 13. He graduated from Nashville High School and attended Valdosta Business College.

Norwood enlisted in the U.S. Navy in 1915 and served during World War I.

In 1921 he returned to *The Nashville Banner*, and later worked on *The Albany Herald, Valdosta Times* and *Pensacola*, Florida *Journal* as an advertising salesman.

Norwood joined with John Connell and Dewitt Roberts in June 1935, to start the weekly *Lowndes County Tribune* in Valdosta, but two years later he started another weekly in Valdosta, *The Lowndes County News,* the newspaper with which he was associated for the next two decades. His wife, Daisy, was society editor and a columnist. The Norwoods also owned and operated *The Hahira Gold Leaf* during most of these years.

Norwood was an old-fashioned crusading editor, endorsing political candidates at the local, state and national level. He also opposed segregation, the county unit system and the poll tax, when all of those were cherished convictions in South Georgia.

Norwood lost his first bid for GPA president by five votes, 51-46, to Ed Methvin in the turbulent summer convention of 1947. He then won a four-vote victory over Albert Hardy Jr. in 1948.

Norwood sold his printing business and closed down *The Lowndes County News* in the 1950s. Later he opened an office supply business in Valdosta which he sold in 1971. It still operates today as Norwood's Office Supply.

Norwood died in November 1977, at the age of 80.

Albert Hardy Jr.

Carl Rountree

W. H. McWhorter

ALBERT HARDY JR., 1949-1950

Albert Sidney Hardy Jr. was born December 5, 1902 in Gainesville, Georgia, son of a newspaper publisher. Both Hardy Sr. and Hardy Jr. were destined to be GPA presidents.

He graduated from Gainesville schools and the University of Georgia, and started his journalism career as a reporter for his father's weekly *Gainesville News*. He later spent eight years as a reporter on *The Atlanta Constitution*, and also worked for *The Thomaston Times*. He was married in 1939 to Estelle Erwin.

In 1943 Hardy bought *The Commerce News* from Mrs. P. B. Trawick, and operated it until the 1960s when his nephew, Charles Hardy, succeeded him as publisher.

Hardy was active in both the GPA and the National Editorial Association. His father was the first NEA president from Georgia. He was elected GPA president in the summer of 1949, without opposition, after serving two years as vice-president.

His father had been elected president exactly 39 years earlier in 1909.

In 1959 Hardy founded Commerce's first radio station, WJJC.

He was a deacon of First Baptist Church, president of the Commerce Chamber of Commerce and Kiwanis Club and served as chairman of the Commerce Board of Education.

He died at his home December 5, 1977, on his 75th birthday.

CARL ROUNTREE, 1950-51

Carl Rountree was another second generation GPA president. His father, C. D. Rountree, had been president in 1923-24.

Rountree was born in Wrightsville, Georgia, in 1904, where the elder Rountree was publisher of *The Wrightsville Headlight*. He began working at *The Headlight* as a child, graduated from Wrightsville schools and attended Mercer University at Macon.

Rountree worked for two years with *The Macon Telegraph*, nine years with the Montgomery, Alabama newspapers; two years as a correspondent for *The Miami Herald* in Fort Lauderdale, and also did stints as a reporter in Los Angeles and New York.

When his father retired, he returned to Wrightsville to publish *The Headlight*.

Then in 1946 Rountree bought *The Dawson News* from Clem E. Rainey and has been associated with that newspaper for nearly 40 years. He relinquished the day-to-day operation to his son, Tommy, in 1981, and he and his wife, Clara, traveled extensivcly.

All three of the Rountrees' children are graduates of the Henry Grady School of Journalism at the University of Georgia.

Rountree was elected GPA president in the summer of 1950 and was president when *Georgia Journalism*, the first history of Georgia newspapers and the GPA, was published. It covered the years from 1763 to 1950.

As president, Rountree also started the movement for a printing school at the University.

Rountree served four years as mayor of Dawson, and was a councilman for two years. He was president of the Dawson Rotary Club; Georgia chairman for the National Newspaper Association; chairman of the NEA's government affairs committee in 1965; a charter member and second chairman of the Terrell County Hospital Authority.

Rountree says his proudest moment was when his son, Tommy, joined him in publishing *The Dawson News*.

He died April 24, 1985, at the age of 81.

W. H. MCWHORTER, 1951-52

W. H. McWhorter, publisher for many years of *The DeKalb New Era*, was born in July 1894, in Watkinsville, Georgia. He began setting type at the age of 15 for his father, J. W. McWhorter, who was editor and publisher of *The Oconee Enterprise*.

Like two other recent GPA presidents, Dennis and Norwood, he served in the U.S. Navy from 1911 to 1914. He worked for a time on *The Vidalia Advance* and then went to *The DeKalb New Era* in 1922 as a one-man management and mechanical department. *The New Era* had 400 paid subscribers at the time, was printed on a hand-operated press and hand-folded. McWhorter was publisher of *The New Era* for more than 40 years.

He was also active in politics, serving in the Georgia House of Representatives from 1945 to 1960, and then for two terms in the State Senate.

He was married to Edna Fenwick, and they had two daughters.

McWhorter sold *The New Era* in the 1960s when it listed a paid circulation of more than 20,000, and was the state's largest paid weekly.

He died on August 15, 1979, at the age of 85.

Cooper Etheridge

Roy Chalker

Stanley Parkman

COOPER ETHERIDGE, 1952-53

Charles Cooper Etheridge was born in Jackson, Georgia, in 1914, but his family moved to Perry when he was five years old, and Perry was to be the place he lived and worked for most of his life. He graduated from Perry High in 1931 and studied law and journalism at Mercer, graduating in 1933.

Etheridge worked briefly at *The Milledgeville Times*, then from 1936-40 at *The Macon Telegraph*, and from 1940 to 1941 at the Richmond, Virginia *Times-Dispatch*. During World War II he was with the FBI in Texas, Ohio, Pennsylvania and Georgia.

In March 1946, Etheridge came "home" to Perry and bought *The Houston Home Journal*, which he published and edited for the rest of his life.

He was married to Carolyn Scharff and they had three children.

An active member of the First Baptist Church, he served as chairman of deacons, Sunday School superintendent and chairman of the building committee. He was president of the Perry Kiwanis Club, and was named Man of the Year by the club.

In 1952, Etheridge was the first in a succession of younger publishers — all in their 30s — who rose to power in the GPA.

On December 5, 1972, Etheridge died unexpectedly at the age of 58, just a few hours after covering a controversial hospital board meeting in Warner Robins. His wife wrote that on the day of his death "he was still doing the work he had capably and lovingly done for most of his adult life."

ROY F. CHALKER, 1953-54

Roy F. Chalker, second in the line of "young turks" who were president of the GPA in the mid-50s, was born in Swainsboro, Georgia in September, 1915. He graduated from Vidalia High, and began working on *The Vidalia Advance* in 1933.

When he was just 21 years, he founded *The Georgia Guide*, a weekly newspaper in Gibson, Georgia.

He was another GPA president who joined the Navy, serving from 1941-44 during World War II. After the war he purchased *The Waynesboro True Citizen* in 1945, and was associated with that paper until his retirement in 1979.

Chalker also was co-founder of radio station WBRO in Waynesboro; and started a Press Ready News Service which serves Georgia and other southeastern states.

He was active in politics, serving as mayor of Waynesboro in 1954-55, and then holding several important positions at the state level during the Marvin Griffin administration. He was director of State Parks in 1955-56, and was promoted to chairman of the State Highway Department in 1957-58, one of the most powerful positions in Georgia. In that post he was also chairman of the Rural Roads Authority and of the State Bridge Building Authority.

He married Mae Evelyn Glisson in 1944 and they have two sons. Roy Chalker Jr. is now owner of *The True Citizen* and its related operations.

Chalker published a collection of his writings in 1982, entitled "All-Day Hanging and Dinner on the Grounds."

STANLEY PARKMAN, 1954-55

David Stanley Parkman was born in Columbus on July 15, 1915, and spent his early years in nearby Cusseta, Georgia. In his teens, his family moved to north Florida and he got his first newspaper job in the print shop of *The Chattahoochee News*.

Parkman was a printer and ad manager of newspapers in Marianna and Quincy, Florida, and then became general manager of *The Gadsden County Times*. He moved to Carrollton, Georgia in 1943 to be advertising manager of *The Times-Free Press*, and Carrollton was to become his permanent home.

In 1945, he and a group of Carrollton citizens started *The Carroll County Georgian*. By 1955 *The Georgian* had become the dominant paper in the county, and was able to buy out *The Times-Free Press*. Other newspapers later acquired by Parkman's company included *The Bremen Gateway, Douglas County Sentinel, Tallapoosa Journal-Beacon, South Fulton Recorder, Manchester Star-Mercury* and *The Haralson County Tribune*.

Parkman and his partners sold the newspapers and a large printing operation to Harte-Hanks Communications in 1980. Parkman remained as publisher and in November 1980, *The Times-Georgia* began five-day-a-week publication.

He was married in 1937 to Frances Middlebrooks and they had four children. Frances died in 1971, and Parkman married Mary Pass a few years later.

In addition to having been GPA president, Parkman was chairman of the Press Institute, state chairman of the National Newspaper Association, and the first chairman of the GPA Past-Presidents Club.

An active member of First Baptist church, he has been chairman of deacons, Sunday School superintendent, and teaches a Men's Bible Class.

Quimby Melton Jr.

C. J. Broome

Rosco Ledford

QUIMBY MELTON JR., 1955-56

Quimby Melton Jr., the second of the three Quimby Meltons to be publisher of *The Griffin Daily News*, has also been a lawyer, a military officer, a university regent, and a 16-year member of the state House of Representatives.

Melton was born in 1922 in Americus, Georgia, but his family soon moved to Griffin when his father bought *The Daily News* in 1925. He graduated from Griffin High, Baylor School in Chattanooga, and the University of Georgia, where he was editor of *The Red and Black*. His wife-to-be, May Wingfield, a native of Athens, was the first woman editor of *The Red and Black*. They were married in 1943 at Fort Riley, Kansas, and have a son and three daughters.

Melton served in the Pacific theater during World War II as a cavalry officer. Returning to Griffin after the war he became editor of *The News*, while his father continued as publisher. He was a member of the University Board of Regents for seven years, and then served in the state legislature from 1959 to 1972. For six of those years he was chairman of the powerful House Ways and Means Committee. He received a law degree from the Woodrow Wilson School of Law.

Melton was elected GPA president in 1955 at the age of 33, one of the youngest presidents to that time. He was also the first daily newspaperman to be GPA president since Jack Williams Sr. of Waycross in 1933.

He was Griffin's "Man of the Year" in 1958, and wrote and published a "History of Griffin, 1840 to 1900," in 1959.

He became publisher of *The Daily News* after leaving the legislature in 1972, and held that post until his son, Quimby III, succeeded him in June 1982. A month later *The Daily News* was sold to the Thomson Newspaper Company. Melton formed a management and investment company which owns and operates weekly newspapers in Henry, Butts, Monroe, Pike and Lamar counties, with a central plant in Barnesville.

C. J. BROOME, 1956-57

C. J. (Cunnard) Broome became editor of *The Alma Times* when he was 18, and publisher and owner on his 21st birthday in December 1944. He bought *The Times* from his father, Carl J. Broome, who owned several South Georgia newspapers including *The Brantley Enterprise, The Pearson Tribune, The Cuthbert Times* and *Blackshear Times*.

Broome was elected GPA president in 1956 at the age of 32, slightly younger than his immediate predecessor, Quimby Melton. He was also elected to the state legislature from Bacon County that year. He served one term in the Georgia House of Representatives.

Broome took his political ambitions a step further in 1958 when he was a candidate for lieutenant governor in the Democratic primary, finishing second in a five-man race won by Garland Byrd. Broome got a sizable popular vote but Byrd led in 156 of the 159 counties, and thus was an overwhelming winner in those county-unit system days.

Broome received a business and commerce degree from what is now Georgia State University in Atlanta, and he has been very active in economic and community development programs throughout Georgia.

He sold *The Alma Times* in the 1960s and became executive director of the Heart of Georgia Planning Association, headquartered in Eastman, Georgia. He is a past president of the Georgia Planning Commission.

In 1984 Broome was in the real estate business in Waycross, where he and his wife now live.

Broome had four brothers who were also active in newspapers or publishing. Linton Broome is executive editor of *The Sun/News* papers in Decatur; Sherwood Broome was once editor of a statewide magazine called *Atlanta*; Dean and Lee Broome operated *The Blackshear Times*, which is now owned by Lee's son-in-law, Robert Williams.

Broome's father, Carl J. Broome, in addition to owning and operating several weekly newspapers, was a missionary Baptist minister for 35 years.

ROSCOE E. LEDFORD, 1957-58

Roscoe Ernest Ledford was publisher of *The Vidalia Advance* for 50 years, assuming ownership in 1926, and holding that post until his death in October 1976.

He was born in Gainesville, Georgia on December 10, 1899, and began his newspaper career on the weekly *Gainesville News* under Albert S. Hardy Sr., another past GPA president. He also worked on the Anniston, Alabama *Star*, and a newspaper in Canton, Georgia before coming to Vidalia to take over *The Advance*. He married Frances Hanna in 1923, and she was also active on the newspaper and in press association activities.

Ledford had 28 years perfect attendance in the Vidalia Kiwanis Club, a streak which was interrupted during his years as vice-president and president of the GPA, which required him to be out of Vidalia more often. Following his service as GPA president Ledford was the southern representative on the National Editorial Association for nine years. He was a district governor of both the Kiwanis Club of Georgia and the Lions Clubs.

He was selected as Vidalia's Citizen of the Year in 1970.

Ledford was succeeded as publisher of *The Advance* by his son,

William F. Ledford, who previously had been managing editor. The Ledfords also owned and operated *The Soperton News*. Frances Ledford has remained faithful in attendance at GPA conventions in the years since her husband's death.

Ledford, who was 57 when elected GPA president, reversed the five-year reign of under-40 presidents, and ushered in a period of somewhat older leaders.

M. A. Perry

Homer Rankin

Charles Martin

M. A. PERRY, 1958-59

McKenzie A. (Mac) Perry was born in 1911 in Oglethorpe, Georgia, one of the state's smallest towns, but he would find his greatest fame in the state's largest city, Atlanta, and would become the first Atlanta newspaperman to serve as president of the GPA.

Perry became a reporter for his home county weekly, *The Montezuma Georgian*, while still in high school, and was also a correspondent for *The Macon Telegraph*. He attended Mercer University, majoring in journalism, and was editor of *The Mercer Cluster*. In 1933 he became co-owner of *The Lineville,* Alabama *Tribune*, and then in 1935 returned to Montezuma as editor and co-owner of *The Citizen-Georgian*.

He attended his first GPA convention in 1936 to receive the first place award for best weekly newspaper column. He was the first chairman of the Macon County Welfare Board, and a member of the citizens committee that supervised building the high school gym, solely from private contributions, with no tax money used.

During World War II Perry was on active duty with the U.S. Navy as Lt. Junior Grade, serving in the South Pacific on the USS Tryon. He later was with the occupation forces in Japan.

In 1946 while associated with a printing plant, Perry made plans for an Atlanta suburban weekly which would concentrate on the Northside-Buckhead area. *The Metropolitan Herald* was started in 1947 by Perry and Harry R. Maugans. It became eligible for GPA membership in 1951 and won many state Better Newspaper Contest awards.

Perry served two terms on the GPA Board of Managers before becoming president in 1958. His term was a busy one, a highlight being the passage by the state legislature of the first Georgia Open Records law. Before this law it was possible for officials to refuse to allow the press or members of the public to see records of the public's business as enacted by governmental bodies.

Perry gave credit for passage of the law to that year's GPA legislative committee — W. H. McWhorter, Quimby Melton and Frank Kempton; to Harvey Walters, then the executive secretary of the GPA; and to the help of Lt. Gov. Garland Byrd, State Sen. Carl Sanders, the Senate floor leader, and Gov. Ernest Vandiver.

The 1958-59 officers were also involved with planning for the National Editorial Association convention which was to be held in Atlanta the following year at the invitation of GPA Past President Carl Rountree, the state's NEA representative, who headed the convention committee.

Perry is married to Margaret Lowery and they have two sons and two grandchildren. He left the newspaper business in the 1960s and *The Herald* was absorbed by the wave of free suburban weeklies for which *The Herald* in great measure had been the model.

HOMER M. RANKIN, 1959-60

Homer Meade Rankin was a native of New Orleans, Louisiana, and attended schools in Louisiana and California, getting a bachelor's and doctor's degree from Tulane University.

From 1941 to 1945 he was a special agent for the Federal Bureau of Investigation, serving in Texas, California, Washington and New York City, and as an undercover agent outside the U.S. during World War II.

He and other investors purchased *The Tifton Gazette* in 1952 and he was editor and publisher of *The Gazette* for the next 29 years, until it was sold in 1981 to the Thomson Newspaper group.

In 1944 he married Lutrelle "Weetie" Tift, a graduate of the Henry Grady School of Journalism, who was editor and publisher of a weekly newspaper on St. Simons Island while she served as a WAVE officer during World War II.

Rankin was president of the Tifton Rotary Club, Chamber of Commerce, United Givers and the Tift Booster Club. He was Sunday School superintendent and senior warden of Saint Anne's Episcopal Church.

While a member of the Tift County Board of Education, he wrote the legislation which consolidated the Tifton city and Tift county school systems. He was also on the famed Sibley Committee, appointed by the state legislature in 1960 to draw up a plan for keeping Georgia's public schools open in the face of racial integration.

Rankin was GPA president for the joint convention of the GPA and National Newspaper Association which was held at the Dinkler-Plaza Hotel in Atlanta, May 4-7, 1960, one of the few times the GPA's annual convention was not held in the summer months.

Homer and "Weetie" Rankin have eight children and 10 grandchildren, and after selling *The Gazette* they divide their time between Tifton and a beach-front home in Daytona Beach, Florida.

CHARLES N. MARTIN, 1960-61

Another Fulton County resident who was a pioneer in suburban newspapers followed Rankin as GPA president. He was Charles N. Martin, editor of *The Atlanta Suburban Reporter* in East Point, and a partner in the Martin-Johnson Printing Company.

Martin was born in Atlanta, November 16, 1918, and graduated from Russell High School, East Point, and Georgia Tech. His degree was in industrial management. He entered the U.S. Navy in 1943 as an Ensign and served as a communications officer in the Pacific Theater during World War II. He was released from active duty in 1946, and eventually discharged in 1952 as a Lt. Commander. Martin was another of several naval veterans of World War I and II who have served as GPA president in the past 40 years.

He became a partner in the Martin-Johnson Printing Company of East Point when just out of high school, and this connection led him to the newspaper business when the company started a weekly newspaper aimed mainly at the East Point, College Park and Hapeville area.

Martin was an officer of the GPA for five years, serving one year as secretary, when that was an elective post, one year as treasurer, two years as vice-president and then a year as president. He presided at the GPA's 75th anniversary convention held in Milledgeville, site of the first convention in 1887.

He was a member of the Fulton County Board of Education for eight years, chairman of the suburban newspaper committee of the National Editorial Association, member of the vestry of Saint John's Episcopal Church in College Park, and was selected by *Time* magazine in 1955 as one of the 100 Metro Atlanta Young Businessmen Most Likely to Succeed.

After selling his printing business and *The Suburban Reporter* in 1971, Martin moved to Longboat Key, Florida, near Sarasota. He is president of the board of directors of Sutton Place, the island condominium in which he lives.

James Blair

Jack Williams Jr.

James Hobgood

JAMES R. BLAIR, 1961-62

James R. (Jim) Blair was elected GPA president at the association's 75th anniversary convention. Blair himself was 63 at the time, making him one of the oldest presidents in the GPA's history. He was also the first president who was not a native of a southern state.

Blair was born in Forest, Indiana, November 1, 1897, and lived there through high school. His years at Indiana University were interrupted by a stint in the army during World War I. He graduated from Indiana U. in 1920 and began his newspaper career on *The Peru* Indiana *Daily Tribune*. He eventually became associated with Eugene Pulliam, who owned a number of small newspapers throughout the country.

In 1931 when Pulliam and Charles Marsh formed the General Newspapers group, forerunner of many such groups in later years, Blair was sent to Americus, Georgia, to be editor and publisher of *The Times-Recorder*, one of three Georgia dailies in the group.

In 1934 Blair purchased a third of the newspaper and by 1936 had become sole owner. He eventually served as editor and publisher of *The*

Times-Recorder for more than 40 years before relinquishing the reins to his son, William E. (Billy) Blair.

Blair was married to Floy L. Crocker, who died in 1976.

In addition to being GPA president, Blair was chairman of the Press Institute, and chairman of the building committee which acquired the present GPA building on Spring Street, Atlanta.

JACK WILLIAMS JR., 1962-63

Jack Williams Jr. was another son of a GPA president who also attained the office. He was born in Waycross, Georgia, May 2, 1913, about the time his father was putting together the newspapers which would become the daily *Waycross Journal-Herald*. He graduated from Davidson College, North Carolina, with a B.S. degree, and attended the Pulitzer School of Journalism at Columbia University in 1935.

During World War II Williams served in the 4th Infantry Division in Europe.

He married Margaret Annette Rogers in 1940, and they have two children, Jack Williams III and Roger Lee Williams, who are both active in the management of *The Journal-Herald*.

Williams succeeded his father as publisher of *The Journal-Herald* in 1957, and still held that post in 1984. He has been an elder in the Presbyterian church for 45 years, was president of the Sons of the American Revolution in Georgia, president of the Waycross Red Cross, and has the reputation of attending more Southern Newspaper Publisher workshops and seminars than any other SNPA member. His election as GPA president came at the first convention held on Jekyll Island after the building of the bridge from the mainland and completion of the Aquarama.

He and his wife divide their time between Waycross and a home in Fernandina Beach, Florida.

JAMES H. HOBGOOD, 1963-64

James H. (Jim) Hobgood is a native of the county of Calhoun in southwest Georgia, but his years as a publisher were spent in the city of Calhoun in northwest Georgia.

Born in 1914, Hobgood lived in Calhoun County, near Edison, through his high school years. He earned a journalism degree at the University of Georgia, where he was president of Sigma Chi fraternity, and secretary of Sigma Delta Chi honorary journalism fraternity. He was with the advertising department of *The Atlanta Journal* until joining the army in

1940. A year later he enlisted in the Navy (an old GPA president's tradition) and was a Navy pilot in the Caribbean and the Pacific during World War II.

After the war he worked on *The Dalton News and Citizen* and *The Columbus Ledger-Enquirer*. In 1950 he purchased *The Gordon County News* in Calhoun (city), and then bought *The Calhoun Times* in 1951. He was editor and publisher of the two weekly newspapers (issued under their own names once a week on separate days) for 25 years until selling them to the Walls group in 1976.

Hobgood is one of three *Calhoun Times* editors to be president of the GPA, the other two being J. Roy McGinty (1939-40) and Elam Chrisian (1891-92). Hobgood was also a chairman of the Press Institute, and was president of the 7th District Press Association. The first Cracker Crumble was held during Hobgood's year as president.

In civic activities he was the first chairman of the Calhoun Recreation Commission, on the Calhoun-Gordon Planning Commission, and a member of the Gordon County Courthouse Building Committee.

He is married to Mary Lou Nevin and they have two daughters and a son. Mary Lou is the daughter of an editor of *The Dalton News* and granddaughter of an editor and publisher of the old *Atlanta Georgian*.

The Hobgoods still reside in Calhoun after his retirement.

Sanders Camp

Graham Ponder

Robert Fowler

SANDERS CAMP, 1964-65

Sanders Camp was the son of Ernest Camp Sr., who was GPA president in 1925-26, 39 years before his son held the post. Camp was born in Monroe, Georgia, and took an early interest in *The Walton Tribune* which was owned and edited by the elder Camp.

During World War II, Camp served for five years as a captain and major in the U.S. Army. He later attained the rank of colonel in the reserves. After the war he returned to Monroe where he directed the operation of *The Tribune* and its printing facilities for 30 years. *The Tribune* was one of the earlier plants in Georgia to switch to cold-type composition and offset printing. Camp also moved his company into applications of computers and developed a full range of corporate accounting services, creating a sizable business as a computer center for that area of Georgia.

The Tribune became a semi-weekly newspaper in 1973, and with its printing operations it employed 55 people and occupied half a dozen downtown Monroe buildings.

In 1975 Camp and his family sold *The Tribune* to Harte-Hanks, one of the major communications companies in the country. Camp continued to manage the printing operation, Walton Press Inc., which was later taken over by his son, Randolph W. Camp.

Camp died in July 1980.

W. GRAHAM PONDER, 1965-66

William Graham Ponder was born in Rutledge, Georgia, November 5, 1923, and is a graduate of Clemson University. He married Adelaide Douglas Wallace in 1948 and they have been a team in the newspaper business as well as marriage.

Ponder was a cotton broker until he and Adelaide bought the weekly *Madisonian* in Madison in 1957. Graham became publisher and Adelaide the editor. He also headed the Madisonian Printing Company, and is secretary-treasurer of the Greater Georgia Printers, a central printing plant for several Georgia weeklies in the vicinity of Athens.

Ponder was a Madison city councilman from 1958-62, president of the Madison Kiwanis Club; a charter member of the Atlanta Press Club, and has been a senior warden of the Episcopal church for 20 years. In 1984, Ponder was also in his 27th year as a rural postal carrier, delivering a full route each day.

Under the Ponders' leadership *The Madisonian* has been one of the leading award-winning newspapers among Georgia's smaller weeklies.

The Ponders have four children, one of whom, Anne Ponder Tamplin, is active in *The Madisonian*.

ROBERT D. FOWLER, 1966-67

Robert D. (Bob) Fowler was a weekly newspaper publisher when he was elected treasurer of the GPA, the first step toward president, but he had become a daily publisher by the year he was president, the only time that has happened in GPA history.

It also illustrated the changing nature of the business in the 1960s as suburbia reached into rural counties and made them metropolitan areas.

Fowler was born in Marietta on September 1, 1930, and graduated from the University of the South at Sewanee, Tennessee. After four years as a lieutenant in the Air Force he returned to Marietta in 1956 and became editor of the weekly *Cobb County Times*. In 1958 he moved over to be editor of *The Marietta Daily Journal* and held that post for six years. In 1964, the year he was elected GPA treasurer, he bought the weekly *Lawrenceville News-Herald* in Gwinnett County. He was also chairman of the Press Institute in February of that year.

Fowler converted the newspaper into a six day daily, *The Gwinnett Daily News*, in 1965, and it became one of the fastest growing newspapers in the country in the 1970s. Both Gwinnett County and *The Daily News* continued to surge in the 1980s, and Fowler by then had installed one of the most modern printing operations in the state.

Fowler is also involved with a radio station in Dalton and several cable TV systems. He is a warden in the Episcopal church, and has served as a board member of the Georgia Division of Children and Youth, and the Atlanta Crime Commission.

Fowler married Judith Knox Lidstone in 1956 and they have two daughters.

Louis Harris

Thomas Frier

William Rogers

LOUIS C. HARRIS, 1967-68

Louis Carl (Lou) Harris was only the second executive of one of Georgia's larger dailies to become president of the GPA. He also presided over the western-most GPA convention to be held in the association's first 100 years. The site was Callaway Gardens in Harris County, near the Alabama line.

That was appropriate since Harris was an Alabama native, born in 1912 in Montgomery, and began his newspaper career as a carrier for *The Montgomery Advertiser*. He went to *The Augusta Chronicle* for the first time in 1932 as an assistant circulation manager. Later he was named state editor, then telegraph editor before leaving Augusta in 1938 to become a reporter for *The Pontiac,* Michigan *Daily Press*.

He served in the army during World War II, and then returned to Michigan for a year. He was lured back south to be executive editor of *The Columbus Ledger* but found that there was some confusion over what he was supposed to be doing. After a few weeks in Columbus he accepted an offer to return to Augusta as managing editor of *The Chronicle*.

When *The Chronicle* and *Herald* became part of the same organization in 1955, Harris was named executive editor of both newspapers. Three years later he became editor of *The Chronicle*.

Harris was a popular figure throughout the state, but especially in Augusta. He was president of the United Way, president of the Greater Augusta chapter of the Association of the U.S. Army, and president of the Kiwanis Club.

In March 1978 he was honored at a dinner attended by "500 friends, dignitaries, colleagues and government officials." Three months later, he died of cancer after a two-year battle. He was 66.

THOMAS H. FRIER SR., 1968-69

Thomas H. (Tom) Frier was born into the newspaper business and has spent his entire career as publisher and editor of *The Douglas Enterprise*.

Frier was born June 23, 1918, son of Mr. and Mrs. W. R. Frier. His father was then publisher of *The Enterprise*. When Tom graduated from the University of Georgia in 1939 he took over *The Enterprise*, succeeding his father who had died earlier in the year. He has held the post for 46 years.

In addition to his service with the GPA, Frier is very active in religious and education circles. He was chairman of the board of *The Christian Index*, the statewide Baptist weekly newspaper, president of the Baptist Village at Waycross, and a long time deacon in the Douglas First

Baptist Church.

In 1978, Gov. George Busbee named Frier to a seven-year term on the Board of Regents. Frier and Quimby Melton are the only GPA presidents since World War II to serve on this powerful and prestigious board. He was reappointed to another term by Gov. Joe Frank Harris in 1985.

Frier is married to the former Ruth Crumley of Cornelia, and their two sons, Tom Jr. and David, are executives on the paper. His brother, Ryan Frier, was publisher of *The Bartow Herald* for a number of years.

As GPA president, Frier presided over the 1969 convention which was the only one held in Savannah during the past 25 years, an oddity since Savannah was the site for 11 of the 14 conventions in the years immediately following World War II.

WILLIAM C. ROGERS, 1969-1970

William C. (Bill) Rogers was the second Georgia publisher to become president of the National Newspaper Association (formerly the National Editorial Association). During his term (1980) he was given a major share of credit for leading the NNA out of near bankruptcy and to a position of greater service for its members.

Rogers was born in Commerce, the son of Dr. and Mrs. A. A. Rogers Sr. He was a star athlete in high school, a rarity among journalists-to-be, captaining the football and track team at Commerce High, and winning the state 100-yard dash championship in 1944.

He graduated from Emory University in 1949 with a major in psychology, and then obtained a masters degree in journalism at the University of Georgia in 1950.

Rogers began his newspaper career as news editor and advertising manager on *The Calhoun Times* where he worked from August 1950 to December 1954. For a brief time he entered the public relations field with the Central of Georgia Railway, but soon returned to newspapers as editor of *The Waynesboro True Citizen* during the years 1954-59 when Publisher Roy Chalker was holding high state office in the Griffin Administration.

In 1959 Rogers bought *The Swainsboro Forest Blade* in Swainsboro and has served as its editor and publisher for 25 years. The name was changed to *The Blade* in the 1970s, but by any name it has won more GPA Better Newspaper Contest awards and NNA awards than any weekly in the state, including first place for general excellence among all U.S. weekly newspapers.

Rogers has served for many years on the Emanuel County Board of

Education; is a former chairman of the board of First Methodist Church, Swainsboro; and a director of the Georgia School Board Association.

After serving as GPA president he was selected as the regional representative to NNA in 1974, and also was president that year of American Newspaper Representatives, the advertising arm of the NNA. After four years on the NNA board he was named president-elect in 1979 and then president in 1980. Hiring of a new executive manager and a restructuring of NNA took place during his presidency.

Rogers is married to the former Virginia Kesler of Jefferson, Georgia, and they have four children.

John Fleetwood

Sam Griffin

Albert Jenkins

JOHN FLEETWOOD, 1970-71

John Trafton Fleetwood was another second-generation GPA president, being the son of Milton L. Fleetwood, president, 1935-36. The elder Fleetwood set the wheels in motion for the first history of Georgia newspapers, and was chairman of the History Committee for 14 years.

Fleetwood was born on July 6, 1921 in Cartersville and attended schools there. He graduated from the University of Georgia, helping pay his way by working as a photographer for the Atlanta newspapers, the University and *The Athens Banner-Herald*.

During World War II he served as an intelligence and public relations officer for the Calvary School at Fort Riley, Kansas. As a captain he commanded the last T/O troop in the U.S. Army.

Fleetwood returned to Cartersville in 1945 and helped his father convert *The Tribune-News* from weekly to daily publication in 1946. The company also began a series of acquisitions which included *The Bartow Herald, The North Bartow News* in Adairsville, and *The Chatsworth Times*.

Fleetwood retired after selling the newspapers and an office supply company to Walls Media in early 1973.

In addition to being GPA president, he was chairman of the Press Institute in 1953, president of the Georgia AP Association and the Georgia-Alabama Daily Advertising Executives Association. In Cartersville he was president of the Rotary Club, Chamber of Commerce, Jaycees and the country club. He was named by Gov. Jimmy Carter to a seven-year term on the World Congress Center Authority, and is also on the board of Reinhardt College. He married Jane Ackert in 1943 at Fort Riley and they have seven children.

SAMUEL M. GRIFFIN, JR., 1971-72

Samuel Marvin (Sam) Griffin Jr., son of a Georgia governor and a third-generation newspaperman, served as GPA president in one of its most hectic years. He had to ask for the resignation of the general manager of 10 years, and get the organization back on an even keel financially.

Griffin was born in Bainbridge, Georgia, son of S. Marvin Griffin Sr. and Lib Griffin. He graduated from Decatur County public schools and attended Georgia Tech on a navy scholarship, graduating in 1958 with a degree in industrial management. After five years as a naval aviator he returned to Bainbridge in 1963 to become editor of *The Bainbridge Post-Searchlight* which had been founded by his grandfather, E. H. "Pat" Griffin. He became publisher in 1973.

He is married to Mary Ann Hill of Cordele and they have one son and one daughter.

In February 1972, midway of Griffin's term as GPA president, differences between Glenn McCullough, the executive secretary, and the board of managers reached the breaking point, and McCullough's resignation was accepted. (See earlier section on GPA history in this chapter). Griffin then led a series of rallies around the state to promote unity and activity among all the association's members.

Griffin has continued his interest in the GPA and served a term on the board of managers in the late 1970s, as well as taking part in many seminars and programs throughout the state.

ALBERT S. JENKINS, 1972-73

Few GPA presidents have had as varied a career as Albert Jenkins of Baxley. A native of Sardis, Georgia, Jenkins was editor of *The Briar Creek Bulletin* which was published in Sardis from 1923 to 1924 while he was still in high school. He enrolled in Mercer University in 1924 and taught school for five years while also attending Mercer. He graduated with honors from North Carolina State in 1931 and accepted a teaching fellowship at the University of Tennessee in the Department of Agricultural Economics.

While teaching marketing at UT Jenkins compiled "An Economic Inventory of Tennessee," a report which was used extensively by the TVA during those years when TVA was revitalizing the economy of southern Tennessee and northern Alabama.

From 1932 to 1936 Jenkins held administrative positions with the Federal Emergency Relief Administration, and supervised a Social Security Survey of Georgia. In 1936 he joined the Department of Public Welfare as editor of the monthly publication, *Public Welfare*. From 1939 to 1941 he was director of the Memphis, Tennessee Social Planning Council.

Then, in 1941, Jenkins ended his career in government service and bought a small weekly newspaper in Baxley, Georgia, *The News-Banner*, which he edited and published for 36 years except for time in the armed services during World War II. While he was away, his wife, Dorothy, took over management of *The News-Banner*.

A highlight of his newspaper career was a model urban renewal project which Jenkins initiated in Baxley and which made a show place of the downtown business area.

Jenkins sold *The News-Banner* in 1977 and he and Dorothy now travel a great deal, including to GPA functions. In his term as president, Julia Dyar was named executive manager, and dues were increased to give the GPA a greater degree of financial stability. Also, the GPA and GNS boards were combined after several years as separate entities with different members.

Foy Evans

Alva Haywood

W. H. Champion

FOY EVANS, 1973-74

Foy Evans was born in Americus, Georgia, November 7, 1919. He is another GPA president and newspaper publisher who is also a lawyer and has been a successful political leader.

He graduated from Americus High and Georgia Southwestern College in 1938. He began his career on *The Macon News* as assistant sports editor and soon became its sports editor. He went to *The Fort Lauderdale*, Florida *News* as city editor when he was only 22. Military duty called soon after and he spent four years on active duty with the Navy during and after World War II.

Evans got his law degree from the University of Georgia in 1947, and was an active member of the Georgia Bar throughout his newspaper career.

That career got under way in earnest when he founded *The Warner Robins Sun* in February 1947 (see Chapter VI). *The Sun* went through several transitions, from free to paid circulation, hot to cold type (one of the earliest), weekly to semi-weekly, semi-weekly to daily, and then from Evans' individual ownership to become the first link in the large newspaper chain built by Roy M. Park over the past 12 years. Evans sold *The Sun* to Park in November 1972, and remained as publisher through his year as GPA president.

Evans left *The Sun* in 1974 and practiced law for two years. In 1976 he offered as a candidate for mayor of Warner Robins and was elected without a runoff against four opponents including the incumbent mayor. He was reelected without opposition in 1980.

Evans and his wife Leta have one son.

ALVA A. HAYWOOD, 1974-75

A native of Greensboro, Georgia, Alva Haywood's first job was delivering Hearst's *Atlanta Georgian* to its 11 subscribers in Greensboro.

As a junior in high school, Haywood started a statewide high school newspaper in which he selected all-district and all-state athletic teams. At 15 he was the youngest sports editor in the state.

He served with an airborne company of the Signal Corps in the South Pacific during World War II, and was editor of the troop newspaper.

Following the war Haywood bought an interest in *The Warrenton Clipper*, and in 1950 became its sole owner. Later he also became the owner and publisher of *The Gibson Record & Guide*, *The Richmond County Times* and *The Sparta Ishmaelite*.

Active in the GPA and the NNA, he was awarded the Gen. James O.

Amos award by the NNA in 1974, the year he was elected president of the GPA. He also served for many years as the GPA parliamentarian, was Press Institute chairman in 1958, and published GPA reports in booklet form during his years as an officer.

Haywood is married to the former Julia Ann Norris and they have two sons.

W. H. CHAMPION, 1975-76

W. H. (Champ) Champion's active participation in GPA and NNA stretches over nearly 40 years, and there are few, if any, newspapermen in the state who have had a hand in so many GPA projects for such a sustained period.

He was born December 10, 1910 in Danville, Georgia, attended public schools in Macon and got his AB degree from Mercer University in 1931. He earned a masters degree from Mercer in 1934, and began a high school teaching career which lasted for 14 years. He taught at schools in Monticello, Moultrie and Macon.

During World War II, Champion taught aircraft instrument repair at Warner Robins and later did chemical work at the Macon Naval Ordinance Plant at night while teaching physics and aeronautics at Lanier High School in Macon during the day.

For several years he was a correspondent for *The Macon Telegraph*, but his real newspaper career began in 1945 when he purchased an interest in *The Dublin Courier-Herald* and became its editor and publisher.

Champion has served four terms on the board of managers of the GPA, in addition to his years as an officer. He was also chairman of the National Newspaper Association Governmental Relations Workshop in 1977, and a member of the NNA 100th anniversary committee.

In the 1950s and 60s Champion bred and showed Tennessee Walking horses, and was president of the Georgia Walking Horses Association in 1961-62.

He was elected GPA president when he was 64.

He retired as publisher of *The Courier-Herald* in 1982, but still contributes two columns a week, a general interest column, and a column about Dublin and Laurens County 99 years ago. In addition he has taught journalism classes at Georgia Southern, and classes at Brewton Parker College. He is compiling a history of libel cases against newspapers in Georgia.

Champion married Edna Hendrix of Columbus in 1937 and they have one daughter and three grandsons. They reside on a farm near Dublin, and travel extensively.

Bobby Branch

Jim Wood

Otis Brumby Jr.

ALLEN R. BRANCH, 1976-77

Allen Robert (Bobby) Branch was born in Savannah in 1941 and grew up in Hinesville where he was a star football player at Bradwell Institute. He attended South Georgia College and Georgia Southern and began his newspaper career on a weekly which started in competition to *The Liberty County Herald* in Hinesville.

In 1965 Branch moved to Perry and became part-owner of *The Houston Home Journal*. Following the death of GPA past-president Cooper Etheridge in 1972, Branch became editor and publisher of *The Home Journal*.

After his year as GPA president Branch sold *The Home Journal* to Grimes Publications but continued as publisher and editor until 1980 when he took a position with the Ports Authority in central Florida.

He returned to the newspaper business as editor and publisher of *The Coastal Courier* (formerly *The Liberty County Herald)* in his old home town of Hinesville in April 1981. Two years later Branch joined Coastal Utilities, a telephone company in Hinesville, as marketing director.

He is married to the former Becky Yawn of Jesup and they have three sons. The Branches make their home on St. Simons Island.

JAMES M. WOOD, 1977-78

Although several pre-World War II GPA presidents also served as state legislators, James M. (Jim) Wood is the only president since World War II who was a legislator during his entire year as president. C. J. Broome served in the legislature for part of his term as president, and

Quimby Melton was elected to the legislature several years after his term.

Wood was born in Dade City, Florida, November 7, 1926, but his family soon moved to Lanett, Alabama, where he graduated from high school. He served with the Army of Occupation in Germany after World War II, and got a journalism degree from the University of Alabama. Wood began his newspaper career on *The Chattahoochee Valley Times* and *West Point News*, weeklies in his home town, and then moved to *The Columbus Ledger* for two years. He was named editor of *The LaGrange News* in 1951 and held that post until 1956 when he went into public relations for several years. While editor of *The News* he was president of the LaGrange Chamber of Commerce.

He came back to the newspaper business in 1963 when he bought *The Fayetteville News* and The Bowen Press, a printing company in Grantville, Georgia. His holdings expanded to *The Hogansville Herald* and *Clayton County Journal* soon after, and in 1969 he moved his operations to Jonesboro and bought the other two weeklies in Clayton County. They were combined and converted into *Clayton News/Daily* in August 1971. Wood was named Citizen of the Year in Business for Clayton County in 1970 and 1972 by the Chamber of Commerce.

Wood's company launched a daily newspaper in South Fulton county in 1975, and soon merged it with *The South Fulton Recorder*, a weekly in Fairburn. He also originated and developed the idea for *ATL*, a newspaper for employees of Hartsfield International Airport.

He was elected to the Georgia House of Representatives from the Clayton-Fayette district in 1976, and was reelected in 1978 and 1980, serving six years in all. In 1982 Wood left his legislative seat to run for Georgia's 6th District seat in the U.S. House of Representatives. He won the Democratic nomination but lost to incumbent Republican Rep. Newt Gingrich in the 1982 general election.

In 1981 Wood had sold his newspaper and commercial printing business to Grimes Publications.

He is married to the former Martha Maxwell of Memphis, Tennessee. They have four sons and are active members in the Jones Memorial Methodist Church of Forest Park.

OTIS A. BRUMBY, 1978-79

Otis A. Brumby Jr. has been one of the great newspaper innovators in Georgia during the past 20 years. Rather than buying newspapers he simply created new ones. He took the concept of free distribution and used it to establish his Neighbor Newspapers in most of Georgia's fastest growing communities.

Brumby was born April 9, 1940 in Atlanta, the son of Otis and Elisabeth Brumby. Brumby Sr., publisher of the weekly *Cobb County Times*, was GPA president in 1941-43. Elisabeth Brumby has been chairman of the board of the newspaper company which her son runs since the death of the elder Brumby in 1954.

Brumby Jr. is a graduate of the Capitol Page School, Washington, D.C., the University of the South at Sewanee, Tennessee, and the University of Georgia Law school. He joined the family newspaper, *The Marietta Daily Journal*, in 1965, and has been president and publisher since shortly thereafter. In 1969 he launched the Neighbor newspapers, which now include 27 weekly mastheads, patterning them on a similar group of newspapers in the Chicago area.

Brumby became president of the GPA in the summer of 1978 just as Julia Dyar, executive manager for the past six years, and a GPA staffer for 20 years, was resigning. During most of Brumby's year as president, the GPA operated with Kathy Chaffin as acting manager while a search was made for Ms. Dyar's successor. Because of his proximity to Atlanta, Brumby spent many hours at the central office helping direct the association's activities. He also led and participated in the remodeling and painting of the upstairs. Shortly before his term ended, the GPA board named Ms. Chaffin as executive manager.

Brumby is married to the former Martha Lee Pratt of West Hartford, Connecticut, and they have four daughters and a son. They are active members of the First Methodist Church in Marietta, where he is on the administrative board.

Brumby has also been president of Atlanta's Sigma Delta Chi chapter, a director of Southern Newspapers Publishers Association, member of the board of visitors of the University of Georgia, board of trustees of Kennesaw College Foundation, and state chairman of the National Newspaper Association.

Robert Williford

Robert Williams

Dink NeSmith

ROBERT L. WILLIFORD, 1979-80

Robert Lamar (Bob) Williford was relatively late in becoming a newspaperman but he soon made his presence felt, especially in the Georgia Press Association.

He was born in August 1920, in Madison County, Georgia, and his family moved to Elberton when he was 10. He graduated from Elberton High and attended Brewton-Parker College and the University of Tennessee, completing several business and management courses.

During World War II Williford was an aviation cadet on a B-29. After the war he was in sales and marketing with W. B. Reilly Company, a large coffee distributor in New Orleans, for 18 years.

In 1963, at 42, he came back to Elberton and bought *The Elberton Star* from his uncle, G. T. Christian, and became its publisher. Later he also bought *The Star* office supply and printing company, and a controlling interest in *The Hartwell Sun*. He helped organize *The News-Leader* in Royston.

As a GPA board member, Williford spearheaded the idea of selling debentures to retire the debt on the GPA building.

During his year as president the GPA began its Newspaper-in-Education program.

Williford sold his newspaper interests to Morris Communications in 1979. He and his wife, Betty, were married in 1948, and they have two daughters. Since his retirement they travel extensively and are involved with the Golden Age Club and senior activities at Elberton First Baptist Church.

ROBERT M. WILLIAMS JR., 1980-81

Robert M. (Bob) Williams Jr. is the youngest person ever to serve as president of the GPA. He took office when only 30 years old, breaking the age mark set by his wife's uncle, C. J. Broome, who was elected GPA president in 1956 at the age of 32.

Williams was born in Springfield, Georgia in 1950, graduated from Effingham High and attended Georgia Southern and the University of Georgia. He was in the first group of recipients of a Georgia Press Educational Foundation scholarship. He began his journalism career with *The Springfield Herald* at age 16, and later worked for *The Savannah Morning News* and was sports information director for Georgia Southern College.

He bought an interest in *The Blackshear Times* in 1971 and became the youngest editor-publisher in Georgia. He later bought out his partners and became sole owner of *The Times*. He is also a co-owner of *The Nassau Record* in Callahan, Florida.

Williams served two terms on the Blackshear City Council; was secretary-treasurer of the Blackshear-Pierce County Industrial Authority; and a member of the First Methodist church administrative board.

He was appointed to two terms on the GPA board of managers, and was active as a chairman and participant in many committees and seminars. He began his first term on the board at 23.

Williams is married to the former Joy Broome of Blackshear, who is principal of an elementary school there. They have a son, born the week Williams became GPA president, and a daughter, who was born on Christmas Day, 1983.

Following his year as GPA president, Williams was chairman of a committee that rewrote the GPA constitution and bylaws.

W. H. NESMITH JR., 1981-82

The youth movement continued for GPA presidents when the youngest president was succeeded by 32-year-old W. H. (Dink) NeSmith Jr., publisher of *The Press-Sentinel* of Jesup.

Born in Jesup in 1948, NeSmith showed an early aptitude for business when at the age of 10 he began buying *Jesup Sentinels* for a nickel and selling them for a dime to workers leaving the shirt factory. He graduated from Jesup public schools and the University of Georgia and originally planned to attend law school. But after service in the army he returned to Jesup and became advertising director of *The Wayne County Press*. He later bought a one-third interest in the newspaper and printing operation.

The 17-year-old *Press* and the 112-year-old *Sentinel* were combined under a single ownership in 1976 and NeSmith became publisher of the resulting semi-weekly. NeSmith became sole owner in 1983, and is also owner of *The Camilla Enterprise, The Ludowici News*, and a Camilla radio station. He and Bob Tribble are co-owners of *The Adel News-Tribune*.

The Press-Sentinel has won 125 state and national awards during the 10 years of NeSmith's leadership.

NeSmith has been president of the Jesup Rotary Club, president of University of Georgia Journalism Alumni, member of University Board of Visitors and district vice-president of the University Alumni Society. In 1981 he received the John E. Drewry Award for Distinguished Achievement in Journalism.

He is married to Pam Shirah, a former educator who has been statewide chairman of the Newspaper in Education program, and also serves as secretary-treasurer of the NeSmiths' publishing company. They have three children and are members of Jesup First Baptist Church.

Robert Tribble

Neely Young

Robert Chambers

ROBERT E. TRIBBLE, 1982-83

Robert E. (Bob) Tribble started his newspaper company with several weekly newspapers that no one else wanted, and now owns and operates more paid weekly newspapers than any other publisher in Georgia. The purchase in 1984 of *The Ft. Valley News-Leader* and *The Vienna News-Observer* brought Tribble's total to 14 newspapers in 14 separate counties. His newspapers are the legal organ in 12 of those counties, also the most of any single publisher in Georgia. All of the newspapers are weeklies, and several of them are very small weeklies. Two of them serve two counties each — *The Patriot* for Marion and Schley, and *The Journal* for Stewart and Webster.

Although his newspapers are concentrated in central Georgia, Tribble was born in the northeast Georgia county of Franklin on September 15, 1935. He attended schools in Lavonia through 10th grade, and finished high school at Manchester, which would become his home and the headquarters of his newspaper operations.

He attended South Georgia College at Douglas, Georgia State in Atlanta and Columbus College before serving in the U.S. army for two years, most of his tour being spent in Germany.

Tribble entered the newspaper business as ad manager of *The Manchester Mercury* in 1960, and was named editor and publisher in 1964. He started his Tri-County newspaper company in 1968 with four small weeklies, *The Meriwether Vindicator, The Harris County Journal, The Talbot New Era* and *The Marion County Patriot*, all of which had less than 1,000 circulation.

In 1975 he acquired *The Manchester Star-Mercury* which gave him both of the weeklies in Meriwether County, and a newspaper in the city which was the main source of advertising for several of his other weeklies.

He added two larger weeklies, *The Fayette County News* and *This Week in Peachtree City*, in 1981.

Tribble served on the GPA board continuously from 1974, when first appointed, through 1984, as immediate past president. During his years as an officer he visited more than 100 newspaper offices in the state. The board approved hiring a full-time ad solicitor for the GPA office during Tribble's year as president.

He and his wife, Frances, were married in 1956 and have one son. Frances is also active in the management of the newspapers. They are members of First Baptist Church in Manchester where Tribble has been a deacon, president of the brotherhood and Sunday School superintendent.

B. NEELY YOUNG, 1983-84

Benjamin Neely Young became publisher of *The Daily Citizen-News* of Dalton in 1977 at the age of 35 and in 1984 he is the senior publisher on the seven Thomson newspapers in Georgia.

Young was born in Cedartown, July 3, 1942, and graduated from

Cedartown High and the University of Georgia with a business degree. He began working on *The Valdosta Times*, a newspaper which was owned by his mother's family, while he was still in high school. At various times he was a printer's devil, a reporter and an ad salesman. When *The Times* was sold to the Thomson organization in 1969 Young was transferred to Dalton for his first stint there. In 1972 he joined *The Marietta Daily Journal*'s advertising department, and went from there to be editor and publisher of *The Cherokee Tribune* in Canton, another Brumby newspaper.

In August, 1977, Young moved back to Dalton to become publisher of *The Daily Citizen-News*, the position he held while serving as GPA president.

In Canton he was selected Young Man of the Year by the Jaycees and served as chairman of the Bicentennial Festival in 1976. Since moving to Dalton he has been president of the Whitfield County Heart Fund, and a trustee of Dalton Junior College.

Young helped start the SHARE Fund in Dalton, which offers electric power customers an opportunity to donate part of their monthly utility bill to a fund which helps needy residents pay their utility bills. The SHARE program has since been adopted statewide by the Georgia Power Company.

Young is married to the former Kathy Thomas of Marietta and they have two sons. They attend Dalton Methodist Church.

As GPA president, Young initiated the Statewide Classified Ad program and took the lead in other efforts to bolster the GPA's revenue base.

ROBERT W. CHAMBERS, 1984-1985

Robert W. (Bob) Chambers Jr. was born in Quitman in 1942, and is a graduate of the Quitman public schools and Emory University. He demonstrated an early interest in newspapers, serving as editor of his high school newspaper and as a correspondent for his hometown weekly newspaper.

He was a copy boy for *The Atlanta Constitution* while at Emory, and interned as a reporter at *The Augusta Herald*, which led to an association with Morris Communications which has continued throughout his career.

Following college he went to work for *The Herald* as a copy editor and later as state editor. He moved to *The Athens Banner-Herald* as managing editor in March 1966, and held that post until becoming executive editor of *The Banner-Herald* and *Athens Daily News* in November 1969.

He was named publisher of the Athens newspapers in February 1972, when he was only 29 years old, making him one of the youngest (if not the youngest) non-family members ever to become publisher of a major Georgia newspaper. Chambers has continued in that post through 1985.

In addition to his leadership role in the GPA, Chambers has been president of the Athens Area Chamber of Commerce, is the advisor for Sigma Nu Fraternity at the University of Georgia, is on the advisory boards of the Athens Salvation Army and Athens Tech, is a member of Kiwanis, Gridiron Secret Society and First Methodist Church. He was selected as one of the five outstanding young men in Georgia by the Jaycees in 1974.

Chambers was appointed to the GPA board in 1979 and was elected treasurer in 1982, succeeding to the presidency at the summer convention in 1984. For his first board meeting as president, Chambers brought board members, committee chairpersons and the office staff together for a three-day session in Dillard, a North Georgia mountain resort. The meeting was highlighted by a "brain-storming" session which produced a number of ideas for further improvements in the Association's programs, conventions and bylaws.

Writing to participants following the meeting, Chambers said: "I feel our Dillard meeting was a milestone gathering . . . one that could shape the future of the GPA for years to come . . ."

BETTER NEWSPAPER CONTEST WINNERS IN TOP CATEGORIES, 1960-1982

GENERAL EXCELLENCE

1960 *The Tucker Tribune* and
The Blackshear Times (W)
Dalton News-Citizen (W)
Cedartown Standard (D)
The Columbus Ledger (D)

1961 *The Sylvania Telephone* (W)
The Bulloch Herald, Statesboro (W)
The Daily Times, Gainesville (D)
The Atlanta Constitution (D)

1962 *Camden County Tribune* (W)
Cobb County Times (W)
Waycross Journal-Herald (D)
The Atlanta Journal (D)

1963 *The Bremen Gateway* (W)
Newnan Times-Herald (W)
Rome News-Tribune (D)
The Atlanta Constitution (D)

1964 *The Hartwell Sun* (W)
The Covington News (W)
The Marietta Daily Journal (D)
The Atlanta Journal (D)

1965 *Wayne County Press* (W)
The News Herald, Lawrenceville (W)
The Daily Times, Gainesville (D)
The Augusta Chronicle (D)

1966 *The Douglas County Sentinel,*
Douglasville (W)
Newnan Times-Herald (W)
The Daily Times, Gainesville (D)
The Atlanta Constitution (D)

1967 *The Hartwell Sun* (W)
The Walton Tribune, Monroe (W)
Rome News-Tribune (D)
The Atlanta Journal (D)

1968 *The Hartwell Sun* (W)
The Newnan Times Herald (W)
The Athens Banner-Herald (D)
The Atlanta Journal (D)

1969 *Fayette County News,* Fayetteville (W)
The Newnan Times-Herald (W)
The Marietta Daily Journal (D)
The Atlanta Journal (D)

1970 *The Commerce News* (W)
The Newnan Times-Herald (W)
The Sandy Springs Neighbor (W)
The Athens Banner-Herald (D)
The Marietta Daily Journal (D)

1971 *The Columbia News,* Martinez (W)
Swainsboro Forest-Blade (W)
The Daily Sun, Warner Robins (D)
Marietta Daily Journal (D)

1972 *The Madisonian,* Madison (W)
The Swainsboro Forest-Blade (W)
Athens Daily News (D)
The Atlanta Journal (D)

1973 *The Swainsboro Forest-Blade* (W)
The Madisonian, Madison (W)
The Gwinnett Daily News,
Lawrenceville (D)
The Macon News (D)

1974 *The Blackshear Times* (W)
The Swainsboro Forest-Blade (W)
The Daily Sun, Warner Robins (D)
The Marietta Daily Journal (D)

1975 *The Madisonian* (W)
The Post-Searchlight, Bainbridge (W)
Swainsboro Forest-Blade (W)
Athens Banner-Herald (D)
Marietta Daily Journal (D)O

1976 *The Madisonian* (W)
The Newnan Times-Herald (W)
The Times, Gainesville (D)
The Columbus Enquirer (D)

1977 *Monroe County Reporter,* Forsyth (W)
Houston Home Journal, Perry (W)
Athens Banner-Herald, Athens (D)
The Marietta Daily Journal (D)

1978 *Hawkinsville Dispatch & News* (W)
Newnan Times-Herald (W)
News/Daily, Jonesboro (D)
The Marietta Daily Journal (D)

1979 *The New Glynn Reporter,* Brunswick (W)
Decatur-DeKalb News (W)
Gwinnett Daily News, Lawrenceville (D)
The Atlanta Journal (D)

1980 *The Cuthbert Times and News-Record* (W)
Hawkinsville Dispatch & News (W)
The Blade, Swainsboro (W)
Gwinnett Daily News (D)
The Atlanta Journal (D)

1981 *The Herald Tribune,* Cartersville (W)
The Georgia Gazette, Savannah (W)
The Athens Observer (W)
Gwinnett Daily News, Lawrenceville (D)
The Atlanta Journal (D)

1982 *Metter News & Advertiser* (W)
The Hartwell Sun (W)
The Athens Observer (W)
The Courier-Herald, Dublin (D)
Athens Banner-Herald (D)
The Marietta Daily Journal (D)

COMMUNITY SERVICE

1960 *The Columbus Enquirer* (D)
The Walton Tribune, Monroe (W)

1961 *Jeff Davis County Ledger* (W)
The Macon News (D)

1962 *North DeKalb Record*, Chamblee (W)
Waycross Journal-Herald (D)

1963 *The Summerville News* (W)
The Atlanta Journal (D)

1964 *Carroll County Georgian*, Carrollton (W)
Columbus Ledger (D)

1965 *The DeKalb Tribune*, Tucker (W)
The Augusta Chronicle (D)

1966 *Quitman Free Press* (W)
The Augusta Chronicle (D)

1967 *Fayette County News*, Fayetteville (W)
The Atlanta Constitution (D)

1968 *The True Citizen*, Waynesboro (W)
The Atlanta Journal (D)

1969 *The Jackson Herald*, Jefferson (W)
The Atlanta Journal (D)

1970 *The True Citizen*, Waynesboro (W)
The Athens Banner-Herald (D)

1971 *The Bainbridge Post-Searchlight*
The Columbus Enquirer

1972 *The Douglas County Sentinel*, Douglasville (W)
The Columbus Ledger (D)

1973 *The Hartwell Sun* (W)
The Atlanta Constitution (D)

1974 *The Carroll County Georgian*, Carrollton (W)
The Atlanta Journal (D)
The Gwinnett Daily News, Lawrenceville (D)

1975 *The Madisonian* (W)
The Commerce News (W)
The Augusta Herald (D)
The Augusta Chronicle (D)

1976

1977 *The Progress-Argus*, Jackson (W)
Forest Blade, Swainsboro (W)
Athens Banner-Herald (D)
The Columbus Ledger (D)

1978 *Monroe County Reporter*, Forsyth (W)
The Jackson Herald, Jefferson (W)
Athens Banner-Herald (D)
The Columbus Enquirer (D)

1979 *The Soperton News* (W)
Hartwell Sun (W)
Athens Banner-Herald (D)
The Columbus Enquirer (D)

1980 *The Monticello News* (W)
Hawkinsville Dispatch and News (W)
The Cherokee Tribune, Canton (W)
Augusta Herald (D)
The Atlanta Constitution (D)

1981 *The Blade*, Swainsboro (W)
The Augusta Herald (D)
The Atlanta Constitution (D)

1982 *The Islander*, St. Simons (W)
The Courier-Herald, Dublin (D)
Savannah *Morning News* (D)

BEST EDITORIAL PAGE

1960 *The Baldwin News*, Milledgeville (W)

1961 *The Bulloch Herald*, Statesboro (W)

1962 Swainsboro *Forest Blade* (W)

1963 *The Bulloch Herald*, Statesboro (W)

1964 *Wayne County Press*, Jesup (W)

1965 *The DeKalb Tribune*, Tucker (W)

1967

1968

1969 *The Houston Home Journal*, Perry (W)
The Columbus Ledger (D)

1970 *The Jeff Davis County Ledger*, Hazlehurst (W)
The Atlanta Constitution (D)

1971 *Clayton County Journal*, Jonesboro
Augusta Chronicle

1972 *The Jeff Davis County Ledger*, Hazlehurst (W)
The Atlanta Constitution (D)

1973 *The Bainbridge Post-Searchlight* (W)
The Gwinnett Daily News, Lawrenceville (D)

1974 *The Times-Journal*, Eastman (W)
The Columbus Ledger (D)

1975 *The Cuthbert Times & News Record* (W)
Houston Home Journal, Perry (W)
Gwinnett Daily News, Lawrenceville (D)
The Macon News, Macon (D)

1976 *The Madisonian* (W)
Wayne County Press, Jesup (W)
The Times, Gainesville (D)
The Marietta Daily Journal (D)

1977 *The Blackshear Times* (W)
Swainsboro Forest-Blade (W)
The Times, Gainesville (D)
The Columbus Enquirer (D)

1978 *The Cuthbert Times & News Record* (W)
Houston Home Journal, Perry (W)
Gwinnett Daily News, Lawrenceville (D)
Marietta Daily Journal (D)

1979 *Camden County Tribune*, St. Marys (W)
The Union-Recorder, Milledgeville (W)
Augusta Herald (D)
Columbus Ledger (D)

1980 *The Cuthbert Times & News Record* (W)
The Commerce News (W)
The Athens Observer (W)
Gwinnett Daily News, Hawkinsville (D)
The Atlanta Journal (D)

1981 *Herald Tribune*, Cartersville (W)
The Walton Tribune, Monroe (W)
The Press-Sentinel, Jesup (W)
Gwinnett Daily News (D)
The Atlanta Constitution (D)

1982 *The Oconee Enterprise*, Watkinsville(W)
Monroe County Reporter, Forsyth (W)
The Winder News (W)
News/Daily, Jonesboro (D)
Augusta Herald (D)
The Atlanta Journal (D)

BEST PERSONAL COLUMN

1960 *Quitman Free Press* (W) Dorothy Daniel
The Atlanta Constitution (D) Ralph McGill

1961 *Gordon County News,* Calhoun (W) James W. Hobgood
The Times, Gainesville (D) Sylvan Meyer

1962 *The Gainesville Tribune* (W) Charles Hardy
Columbus Ledger-Enquirer (D) Millard Grimes

1963 *The Warner Robins Sun* (W) Foy Evans
Cartersville Daily Tribune News (W) Lewis C. Justus

1964 *The Nashville Herald* (W) Elsie Griner Jr.
Columbus Ledger-Enquirer (D) Millard Grimes

1965 *Quitman Free Press* (W) Dorothy Daniel
The Columbus Ledger (D) Carlton Johnson

1966 *The Nashville Herald* (W) Elsie Griner Jr.
Augusta Chronicle-Herald (D) Louis C. Harris

1967 *Fayette County News,* Fayetteville (W) James Wood Jr.
The Atlanta Constitution (D) Eugene Patterson

1968 *Weekly Tribune-News,* Cartersville (W) Lewis C. Justus
The Athens Banner-Herald (D) N. S. Hayden

1969 *Swainsboro Forest-Blade* (W) William C. Rogers
Cartersville Daily Tribune News (D) Lewis C. Justus

1970 *The Bremen Gateway* (W) Noel Brown
The Athens Banner-Herald (D) N. S. Hayden

1971 *The Herald-Tribune,* Cartersville (W) Lewis C. Justus
Macon Telegraph & News (D) Joseph B. Parham

1972 *Swainsboro Forest-Blade* (W) William C. Rogers
The Macon News (D) Joseph B. Parham

1973 *Carroll County Georgian,* Carrollton (W) Stanley Parkman
The Macon News (D) Joseph B. Parham

1974 *Wayne County Press,* Jesup (W) Jamie Denty
The Macon News (D) Joseph B. Parham

1975 *Hawkinsville Dispatch & News* (W) Skippy Lawson
Forsyth County News, Cumming (W) Jim Cosey
Athens Banner-Herald (D) Hank Johnson
Augusta Chronicle-Herald (D) Louis C. Harris

1976 *Hawkinsville Dispatch News* (W) Skippy Lawson
Douglas Enterprise (W) Thomas Frier Jr.
News/Daily, Jonesboro (D) Jim Wood Jr.
The Columbus Ledger (D) Jack E. Swift

1977 *Hawkinsville Dispatch & News* (W) Skippy Lawson
Swainsboro Forest-Blade (W) Bill Rogers Jr.
The Augusta Herald (D) John Barnes
The Marietta Daily Journal (D) Mike Waldron

1978 *The Darien News* (W) Jingle Davis
The Cherokee Tribune (W) Jimmy Townsend
Americus Times Recorder (D) Ann Sheffield
The Macon News (D) Joe Parham

1979 *The Darien News* (W) Jingle Davis
Walker Co. Messenger, LaFayette (W) Alvin Benn
Thomasville Times-Enterprise (D) Tara Wright
The Atlanta Journal (D) Ron Hudspeth

1980 *The Soperton News* (W) Jeanna C. McHendry
This Week In Peachtree City (W) Keith Graham
Walker County Messenger, LaFayette (W) Ed Fowler
LaGrange Daily News (D) Andrea Lovejoy
Savannah Evening Press (D) Thomas F. Coffey Jr.

1981 *The Oconee Enterprise,* Watkinsville (W) Peggy Lowery
Monroe County Reporter, Forsyth (W) Wendell Rammage
The Jackson Herald (W) Virgil Adams
Athens Banner-Herald (D) Robert W. Chambers
The Atlanta Constitution (D) Lewis Grizzard

1982 *The Oconee Enterprise,* Watkinsville (W) Vinnie Williams
The Blackshear Times (W) Robert Williams
The Thomaston Times (W) Barbara Boyler
The Times-Enterprise, Thomasville (D) Coke Ellington
The Times, Gainesville (D) Ted Oglesby
Macon Telegraph (D) Ed Corson

GPA SUMMER CONVENTION SITES

1950 — August 10-11 Ansley Hotel, Atlanta
1951 — July 26-28, DeSoto Hotel, Savannah
1952 — July 10-12, General Oglethorpe Hotel, Savannah
1953 — June 25-27, General Oglethorpe Hotel, Savannah
1954 — June 24-26, General Oglethorpe Hotel, Savannah
1955 — June 2-4, DeSoto Hotel, Savannah
1956 — June 14-16, General Oglethorpe Hotel, Savannah
1957 — June 13-15, Bon Air Hotel, Augusta
1958 — June 12-14, General Oglethorpe Hotel, Savannah
1959 — June 12-14, General Oglethorpe Hotel, Savannah
1960 — May 4-7, Dinkler Plaza, Atlanta* *
1961 — June 16-19, Milledgeville
1962 — June 14-16, The Corsair, Jekyll Island
1963 — June 13-15, The Corsair, Jekyll Island
1964 — June 11-13, Carriage Inn, Jekyll Island
1965 — July 8-10, The Corsair, Jekyll Island
1966 — June 15-18, The Corsair, Jekyll Island
1967 — July 5-8, The Corsair, Jekyll Island

* *Joint meeting with the National Editorial Association

1968 — June 19-22, Holiday Inn, Callaway Gardens
1969 — July 2-5, Savannah Inn & Country Club, Savannah
1970 — June 24-27, Carriage Inn, Jekyll Island
1971 — June 16-19, The Buccaneer, Jekyll Island
1972 — June 21-24, Carriage Inn, Jekyll Island
1973 — June 20-23, The Buccaneer, Jekyll Island
1974 — July 11-13, The Buccaneer, Jekyll Island
1975 — June 25-28, The Buccaneer, Jekyll Island
1976 — July 21-24, The Buccaneer, Jekyll Island
1977 — July 20-23, The Buccaneer, Jekyll Island
1978 — June 14-17, The Buccaneer, Jekyll Island
1979 — June 13-17, The Buccaneer, Jekyll Island
1980 — June 18-21, The Buccaneer, Jekyll Island
1981 — June 17-20, Jekyll Island Hilton, Jekyll Island
1982 — June 16-19, Jekyll Island Hilton, Jekyll Island
1983 — June 15-18, Jekyll Island Hilton, Jekyll Island
1984 — June 13-16, Jekyll Island Hilton, Jekyll Island

First meeting of Georgia Press Association, August, 1887, in Milledgeville

GPA past presidents posed for a photo in 1972. Back row, Homer Rankin, Sanders Camp, Graham Ponder, Stanley Parkman, James Blair, Louis Harris. Seated, Carl Rountree, Albert Hardy Jr., Cooper Etheridge, Sam Griffin, Jere Moore, R. E. Ledford, Jack Williams Jr.

Executive Manager (1962-72) Glenn McCullough always put on a good show at conventions. This year it was a luau.

Julia Dyar, executive manager (1972-1978), and a GPA employee for 20 years, got a silver loving cup in 1972 for duty beyond the normal call. Sam Griffin, 1972 president, made the presentation.

As Georgia's governor (1971-75), future U.S. president Jimmy Carter was an annual speaker at four GPA conventions. Above, he chats with Jane Fleetwood and Albert Jenkins.

Emily Woodward, founder of The Georgia Press Institute, is shown with Dean John E. Drewry and Bill Hartman, chairman of the Georgia Athletic Fund. Ms. Woodward was also the only woman president (1928) of the GPA through 1985.

Hall of Fame inductions and presentations of 50-year medallions are made at Press Institutes. Above, 1964 GPA President Jim Hobgood places medallion on past President Roy McGinty. Hobgood and McGinty were both publishers of The Calhoun Times.

Kathy Chaffin, who had just become executive manager, found one of her first jobs was helping paint the GPA building in 1978.

Otis Brumby Jr., as 1978-79 president, spearheaded the painting and was presented this special award at the 1979 convention.

Bo McLeod of Donalsonville has been frequent MC at GPA's Cracker Crumble in Atlanta.

Art Buchwald, popular syndicated columnist, highlighted first Cracker Crumble in 1964 but he was expensive.

Glenn McCullough, GPA general manager (1962-72), is credited with launching the Cracker Crumble as major fund raiser for the Georgia Press Foundation. Above, McCullough thanks Betty Sanders for participating while her husband, Gov. Carl Sanders, looks on.

Georgia politicians are the most common target of Cracker Crumble's satire. Atlanta Journal *Editor Durwood McAlister (at right) has done brilliant impersonations of former U.S. Senator Herman Talmadge. Above he distributes dollars from Talmadge's famous overcoat.*

Jimmy Carter, then a state senator and candidate for governor, had a role in the 1966 Crumble.

Julie Harrellson Weddle of The Springfield Herald *and Doug Hall of* Dublin Courier-Herald *take part in Crumble skit of early 1980s.*

These three newspapermen posed as Georgia state troopers for Crumble skit. L. to R., Bob Chambers, Athens; Bob Williams, Blackshear; Carroll Dadisman, Columbus.

1984-85 officers of GPA are (L. to R.) Millard B. Grimes, Rockdale Citizen, *vice-president; Robert W. Chambers,* Athens Banner-Herald *and* Daily News, *president; and Quimby Melton III,* Jackson Argus-Progress, *treasurer. Grimes is scheduled to become president in 1985-86, and Melton in 1986-87.*

Tombstone of Marcus D. Irwin, founder and first president of GPA, is in a cemetery at Conyers, but oddly it contains no information about him.

ANNOTATED LISTING OF GEORGIA WEEKLY NEWSPAPERS

The following information on Georgia weeklies with paid circulation includes location, owners, chief executives, circulation, previous owners, year newspaper was established, year it switched to offset printing and average number of pages run each week. This information and the newspapers listed are based on the 1984 Georgia Newspaper Directory and on additional data provided by the individual newspapers for this book.

*In the case of ownership, the chief stockholder or corporation president is listed when corporation is relatively small. When there are two chief stockholders or partners both are listed.

* *Not all of previous owners since World War II are listed for some newspapers.

City or Town County	Newspaper	Paid Circ.	*Owner	Publisher/ Chief Exec.	* *Previous Owners Since WWII	Year Est.	Off-Set	Avg. No. Pgs.
Adairsville (1,734) Bartow (40,760)	*North Bartow News*	1,127	Chas. Hurley	Chas. Hurley	J. Fleetwood			
Adel (5,570) Cook (13,490)	*Adel News-Tribune*	3,310	Dink Nesmith, R. Tribble	J. H. Sanders	G. Patten	1886	1968	16
Alamo (984) Wheeler (5,000)	*Wheeler* Co. *Eagle*	1,700	J. T. Windsor	J. T. Windsor	W. Adams	1916	1975	8
Albany (74,471) Dougherty (95,400)	*The Journal*	4,590	W. O. Davis	W. O. Davis	None			
Alma (3,494) Bacon (10,000)	*Alma Times-Statesman*	2,482	M. Gardner	F. Gardner	C. J. Broome	1912		
Ashburn (4,788) Turner (8,800)	*Wiregrass Farmer*	2,800	R. Tribble	Austin Saxon	Nora Smith, G. Patten	1899	1969	16

City or Town County	Newspaper	Paid Circ.	*Owner	Publisher/ Chief Exec.	* *Previous Owners Since WWII	Year Est.	Off-Set	Avg. No. Pgs.
Athens (41,432) Clarke (71,200)	*Athens Observer*	10,000	Don Nelson, Pete McCommons	Don Nelson, Pete McCommons	C. Searcy	1974	1974	32
Atlanta (422,293) Fulton (1,906,700)	*Atlanta Business Chronicle*	8,000	Cordovan Corp.	Dick Gentry	Same	1978	1978	28 Tab
Atlanta (422,293) Fulton (1,906,700)	*Southern Israelite*	6,000	V. Goldgar	V. Goldgar	A. Rosenberg, G. Geldbart	1925	1973	28
Augusta (46,732) Richmond (294,300)	*Richmond Co. Times*	1,087	A. Haywood	A. Haywood	Bernard Myers	1954	1967	8
Bainbridge (10,513) Decatur (26,700)	*Post-Searchlight* (Wed.-Sat.)	6,188	Sam Griffin	Sam Griffin	Marvin Griffin, Pat Griffin	1907	1964	44
Barnesville (4,872) Lamar (11,900)	*Herald-Gazette*	3,750	Walter and Laura Geiger	W. Geiger	Q. Melton, Jr., W. Dennis, R. Tribble	1871	1974	22
Baxley (3,578) Appling (15,600)	*Baxley News-Banner*	4,800	M. Gardner	Max Gardner	A. Jenkins	1884	1967	24
Blackshear (3,168) Pierce (11,500)	*Blackshear Times*	3,423	R. Williams	R. Williams	Lee Broome, Dean Broome	1869	1969	20
Blairsville (522) Union (9,100)	*North Georgia News*	4,758	Wanda West	Wanda West	Harold West	1923	1973	20
Blakely (5,840) Early (13,600)	*Early Co. News*	3,800	Bill Fleming	Bill Fleming	A. Fleming, W. Fleming	1859	1963	18
Blue Ridge (1,391) Fannin (15,500)	*Summit-Post*	1,657	Phil Babb	L. Britt				

City or Town County	Newspaper	Paid Circ.	*Owner	Publisher/ Chief Exec.	**Previous Owners Since WWII	Year Est.	Off-Set	Avg. No. Pgs.
Bowdon (1,753) Carroll (53,300)	*Bowdon Bulletin*	2,433	Harte-Hanks	Stan Parkman	Stan Parkman, Kate Smith	1890		
Bremen (3,961) Haralson (18,000)	*Haralson Gateway-Beacon*	5,958	Harte-Hanks	R. Parkman	Stan Parkman, H. Meeks	1902		
Buchanan Haralson (18,000)	*Haralson Co. Tribune*	Merged in 1984 with *Bremen Gateway*				1898		8
Buena Vista (1,409) Marion (6,600)	*Patriot-Citizen*	975	R. Tribble	R. Tribble	H. Taylor, A. McCarter	1879	1966	8
Butler (1,861) Taylor (8,300)	*Taylor Co. News*	2,350	Jim Cosey	Jim Cosey	Chas. Genns, Verna Griggs	1876		12
Cairo (8,761) Grady (19,600)	*Cairo Messenger*	5,169	R. H. Wind Jr.	R. H. Wind Jr.	H. H. Wind, F. J. Wind	1904		
Calhoun (5,318) Gordon (29,800)	*Calhoun Times* (Wed. + Sat.)	7,800	Walls Group	Paul Miles	J. McGinty, J. Hobgood	1870	1972	80
Camilla (5,449) Mitchell (20,100)	*Camilla Enterprise* (Wed. & Sat.)	4,000	W. NeSmith	L. Shirah	B. T. Burson	1908		30
Canton (3,589) Cherokee (44,400)	*Cherokee Tribune* (Sun. + Wed.)	7,996	Otis Brumby	B. Hefner	R. D., C. E. Owens	1934	1968	32
Cartersville (9,483) Bartow (37,800)	*Herald Tribune*	1,242	Walls Group	C. Hurley	John Fleetwood, M. Fleetwood	1896	1964	
Cedartown (8,540) Polk (31,100)	*Cedartown Standard* (Tues. + Thurs.)	3,618	Walls Group	J. Williams	Roy Emmet	1889	1958	
Chatsworth (2,486) Murray (17,800)	*Chatsworth Times*	3,757	Walls Group	A. Edwards	John Fleetwood, Roy McGinty	1879		26

City or Town County	Newspaper	Paid Circ.	*Owner	Publisher/ Chief Exec.	* *Previous Owners Since WWII	Year Est.	Off-Set	Avg. No. Pgs.
Clarkesville (1,354) Habersham (26,600)	*Tri-County Advertiser*	6,000	Phil Babb	B. Williams	Amalee Graves, Chas. Graves	1879	1960	10
Claxton (2,699) Evans (9,100)	*Claxton Enterprise*	3,533	M. Peace	M. Peace	R. Majors, M. Beckerman	1912	1965	16
Clayton (1,812) Rabun (10,100)	*Clayton Tribune*	3,975	Phil Babb	J. Wallace	L. + E. Cross, E. Barker	1924	1971	24
Cleveland (1576) White (1,722)	*White Co. News*	2,750	Phil Babb	B. Williams	H. McMillian, A. Brown	1968	1968	14
Cochran (5,096) Bleckley (11,000)	*Cochran Journal*	3,100	David Wickersham, Robert Garrett	D. Wickersham	J. NeSmith, W. R. Smith	1918		16
Colquitt (2,046) Miller (7,200)	*Miller Co. Liberal*	2,668	T. Toole	T. Toole	B. Priest	1897	1970	8
Comer (914) Madison (16,600)	*Comer News*	1,284	Jere Ayers	Jere Ayers	C. B. Ayers	1909	1969	20 (Tab)
Commerce (3,751) Jackson (24,300)	*Commerce News*	3,800	C. Hardy	C. Hardy	Albert Hardy	1875	1962	24
Cornelia (3,161) Habersham (26,600)	*Northeast Georgian*	6,850	Phil Babb	B. Williams	R. Yates	1892	1956	22
Covington (10,431) Newton (36,300)	*Covington News*	3,500	Employees	B. Barnard	Leo Mallard, Belmont Dennis	1865	1964	24
Crawfordville (588) Taliaferro (2,400)	*Advocate-Democrat*	660	C. Williams Sr.	C. Williams Sr.	None	1876		8

City or Town County	Newspaper	Paid Circ.	*Owner	Publisher/ Chief Exec.	* *Previous Owners Since WWII	Year Est.	Off-Set	Avg. No. Pgs.
Cumming (2,062) Forsyth (24,100)	*Forsyth Co. News* (Wed. + Sun.)	6,050	Bob Fowler	Eddie Stowe	R. Otwell, T. Maddox	1908	1972	24
Cuthbert (4,335) Randolph (8,800)	*Cuthbert Times/ News-Record*	2,065	Joel Smith	J. Smith	R. Taylor Harris, Carl Broome	1873		10
Dahlonega (2,799) Lumpkin (10,000)	*Dahlonega Nugget*	2,900	Phil Babb	C. Pendleton	Jack Parks	1890	1970	12
Dallas (2,433) Paulding (23,800)	*Dallas New Era*	5,700	T. Parker	J. S. & J. T. Parker	Same	1882	1973	22
Danielsville (349) Madison (16,600)	*Danielsville Monitor*	1,500	Jere Ayers	Jere Ayers	C. B. Ayers	1882	1969	20 (Tab)
Darien (1,744) McIntosh (9,300)	*Darien News*	2,437	C. Williamson	C. Williamson	W. Lunsford	1951	1957	1
Dawson (5,746) Terrell (10,900)	*Dawson News*	2,652	T. Rountree	T. Rountree	C. Rountree	1856	1970	18
Dawsonville (342) Dawson (4,800)	*Advertiser/News*	1,246	Don Waldrip	Cathy Puckett	M. Howard	1887		8
Decatur (18,404) DeKalb (497,100)	*DeKalb News/Era*	8,500	Bill Crane	Jerry Crane	W. H. McWhorter, Britt Fayssoux	1869	1963	40
Donalsonville (3,312) Seminole (8,500)	*Donalsonville News*	3,000	Bo McLeod	Bo McLeod	Julian Webb	1916	1965	12
Douglas (10,600) Coffee (25,900)	*Coffee Co. Progress*	3,850	L. Beville	L. Beville	M. Waters, C. Hulsey	1913	1967	26
Douglas (10,600) Coffee (25,900)	*Douglas Enterprise*	4,000	Tom Frier Sr.	Tom Frier Sr.	Same	1888	1970	28

City or Town County	Newspaper	Paid Circ.	*Owner	Publisher/ Chief Exec.	* *Previous Owners Since WWII	Year Est.	Off- Set	Avg. No. Pgs.
Douglasville (7,274) Douglas (53,900)	*Douglas Co. Sentinel* (Tues. - Thurs.)	7,060	Harte-Hanks	Bruce Thomas	S. Parkman, B. Branham	1902	1965	50
Eastman (5,259) Dodge (17,500)	*Times Journal-Spotlight*	4,250	Julia Roberts	Julia Roberts	E. Methvin	1871	1973	22
Eatonton (4,676) Putnam (9,700)	*Eatonton Messenger*	2,730	B. & M. Smith	B. Smith	T. Gregory	1878	1969	12
Elberton (5,645) Elbert (19,000)	*The Elberton Star* (Tues. + Thurs.)	4,735	Morris Com- munications	Jon Hunt	G. Christian, R. Williford	1888	1973	36
Ellijay (1,510) Gilmer (11,500)	*Times-Courier*	4,274	G. Bunch	G. Bunch	C. Owen, R. Cook	1875	1967	20
Fayetteville (2,713) Fayette (25,000)	*Fayette County News*	3,800	R. Tribble	G. Cornwell	Jim Wood, Quimby Melton III	1886	1963	26
Fitzgerald (10,088) Ben Hill (16,000)	*Herald-Leader*	5,005	G. Pryor	G. Pryor	J. J. & S. G. Pryor, I. & A. Gelders	1896	1971	32
Folkston (2,183) Charlton (7,400)	*Charlton Co. Herald*	1,900	D. Lewis	D. Lewis	R. Harrison	1898	1969	12
Forsyth (4,424) Monroe (14,610)	*Monroe Co. Reporter*	3,486	Q. Melton III	Q. Melton III	D. Daniel	1972	1972	16
Fort Valley (8,900) Peach (19,100)	*Leader-Tribune*	4,500	R. Tribble	R. Tribble	W. Walton, Dan Grahl	1888	1965	22
Franklin (709) Heard (6,200)	*News & Banner*	1,150	B. McCutchen	B. McCutchen	P. McCutchen	1876	1964	6

City or Town County	Newspaper	Paid Circ.	*Owner	Publisher/ Chief Exec.	* *Previous Owners Since WWII	Year Est.	Off-Set	Avg. No. Pgs.
Gainesville (15,280) Hall (75,649)	*Lanier Tribune*	4,353	Truett-McConnell College	D. Smith	Ted Oglesby	1959	1960	
Gibson (717) Glascock (2,600)	*Gibson Record and Guide*	774	A. Haywood	A. Haywood	C. Thigpen, R. Chalker	1893	1967	6
Glennville (4,112) Tattnall (17,600)	*Glennville Sentinel*	2,448	H. Rhoden, P. Waters	P. Waters	F. E. Phillips	1925	1973	16
Gray (2,085) Jones (17,400)	*Jones County News*	1,835	G. Moore III	G. Moore III	W. C. Davis, Jere Moore	1895		12
Greensboro (2,945) Greene (11,000)	*Herald-Journal*	3,570	C. Williams	C. Williams	None	1864		
Greenville (1,222) Meriwether (21,400)	*Meriwether Vindicator*	2,465	R. Tribble	R. Tribble	Nell Stovall	1874	1968	18
Hamilton (495) Harris (13,100)	*Harris County Journal*	1,715	R. Tribble	R. Tribble	J. Woodall	1871	1968	20
Hampton (2,036) Henry (31,900)	*Hampton News*	747	Q. Melton	N. Wittler	None	1976	1976	12
Hartwell (4,879) Hart (17,000)	*Hartwell Sun*	4,370	Morris Communications	S. Carswell	N. S. Hayden, L. Morris	1876	1965	24
Hawkinsville (4,390) Pulaski (8,100)	*Dispatch and News*	2,650	Hawkinsville Publ. Co.	C. Southerland	E. Methvin, J. McCune	1867	1969	20
Hazlehurst (4,233) Jeff Davis (10,800)	*Jeff Davis Co. Ledger*	3,098	T. Purser, Roy Chalker Sr.	T. Purser	John Rogers	1906	1969	20

City or Town County	Newspaper	Paid Circ.	*Owner	Publisher/ Chief Exec.	* *Previous Owners Since WWII	Year Est.	Off-Set	Avg. No. Pgs.
Hiawassee (494) Towns (5,000)	*Towns Co. Herald*	1,998	Wanda West	Wanda West	Harold West, Zell Miller	1928	1973	12
Hiawassee (494) Towns (5,000)	*Mountain News*	2,700	Phil Babb	J. Wallace	E. Youngblood	1975	1975	10
Hinesville (11,152) Liberty (32,400)	*Coastal Courier*	7,500	Chas. Morris	R. Morton	Lottie Clark, Jim Wynn	1871	1972	50
Hogansville (3,000) Troup (45,000)	*Hogansville Herald*	1,275	R. Tribble	R. Tribble	C. Hamby, J. Wood	1944	1964	8
Homerville (3,079) Clinch (6,800)	*Clinch Co. News*	1,710	I. Huxford	I. Huxford	None	1890	1974	8
Irwinton (843) Wilkinson (10,200)	*Wilkinson Co. News*	1,939	J. Boone	J. Boone	None	1922		
Jackson (4,068) Butts (12,700)	*Progress-Argus*	3,780	Q. Melton III	W. Cawthon	Doyle Jones, Vincent Jones	1873	1974	22
Jasper (1,573) Pickens (12,100)	*Pickens Co. Progress*	4,200	J. R. Pool	J. R. Pool	John W. Pool R. M. Edge	1887	1976	22
Jefferson (1,770) Jackson (24,300)	*Jackson Herald*	6,650	H. & H. Buffington	H. Buffington	J. Holder J. Davidson	1875	1967	32
Jeffersonville (1,474) Twiggs (8,400)	*Twiggs Co. New Era*	1,540	C. Fountain	C. Fountain				
Jesup (9,222) Wayne (20,200)	*Press-Sentinel* (Wed.-Sat.)	6,780	W. NeSmith	W. NeSmith	Elliott Brack, W. B. Rhoden	1865	1960	56

City or Town County	Newspaper	Paid Circ.	*Owner	Publisher/ Chief Exec.	**Previous Owners Since WWII	Year Est.	Off-Set	Avg. No. Pgs.
Kingsland (2,111) Camden (13,371)	*Southeast Georgian*	2,800	Alan Lipsett	Alan Lipsett	W. King, N. Inlow	1894	1960	13
LaFayette (6,546) Walker (55,500)	*Walker Co. Messenger* (Wed.-Fri.)	4,579	Jim Boone	J. Murchison	E. P. Hall, Joe Hall	1877		24
Lakeland (2,603) Lanier (5,500)	*Lanier Co. News*	1,050	D. Hamlin	D. Hamlin				
Lavonia (2,044) Franklin (14,300)	*Franklin Co. Citizen*	3,640	Phil Babb	Fred Lee	J. Little, D. Holland	1971		16
Lawrenceville (8,891) Gwinnett (150,500)	*Home Weekly*	7,206	Bruce Still	Bruce Still	None	1971	1971	12
Leesburg (1,200) Lee (14,500)	*Lee Co. Ledger*	1,335	D. Quinn	D. Quinn	Winston Skinner, Ed McMinn	1978	1978	10
Lexington (283) Oglethorpe (8,400)	*Oglethorpe Echo*	2,350	R. Maxwell	R. Maxwell Jr.	H. Arnason	1874	1969	12
Lincolnton (1,404) Lincoln (5,900)	*Lincoln Journal*	1,625	J. T. Drinkard	J. T. Drinkard	J. P. Drinkard	1893		
Lithonia (2,604) DeKalb (466,000)	*Lithonia Observer*	1,800	Bill Crane	Jerry Crane	Britt Fayssoux, Harry Murphy	1915	1965	12
Louisville (2,812) Jefferson (17,600)	*News and Farmer Wadley Herald*	2,820	J. Horton	J. Horton	V. Saxon	1867	1970	18
Ludowici (1,313) Long (3,500)	*Ludowici News*	1,177	W. H. NeSmith	W. H. NeSmith	W. Rhoden	1921	1973	10
Lyons (4,035) Toombs (22,300)	*Lyons Progress*	3,218	H. Rhoden	H. Rhoden	None	1903	1972	16

City or Town County	Newspaper	Paid Circ.	*Owner	Publisher/ Chief Exec.	* *Previous Owners Since WWII	Year Est.	Off-Set	Avg. No. Pgs.
McDonough (2,722) Henry (31,900)	*Henry Herald*	4,476	M. B. Grimes	N. Wittler	F. Linch, Bob Linch	1894	1967	28
McRae (3,059) Telfair (12,100)	*Telfair Enterprise*	3,100	Ed Bowen	Ed Bowen	W. Bowen	1888	1969	16
McRae (3,059) Telfair (12,100)	*Telfair Times* (formerly *Lumber City Log*)	2,700	Mark and Julie Joiner	Mark and Julie Joiner	Murphy McRae	1954	1971	8
Madison (2,880) Morgan (10,700)	*Madisonian*	3,569	Adelaide & Graham Ponder	Adelaide & Graham Ponder	Earl Leonard, Belmont Dennis	1841	1965	20
Manchester (4,781) Meriwether (21,400)	*Manchester Star-Mercury*	4,054	R. Tribble	R. Tribble	Ralph Rice, Stan Parkman	1911	1966	26
Martinez (15,866) Columbia (36,400)	*Columbia News*	4,050	P. Blanchard	P. Blanchard	Carey Williams	1919		
Metter (3,519) Candler (7,400)	*Metter News and Advertiser*	2,523	Virginia Snell	V. Snell	E. Brack, R. Daniell	1912		14
Millen (3,974) Jenkins (8,200)	*Millen News*	2,080	F. Edenfield	F. Edenfield	W. Harrison	1903		
Monroe (8,802) Walton (31,300)	*Walton Tribune* (Tues.-Thurs.)	5,398	Larry Nash	Larry Nash	Harte-Hanks, Sanders Camp	1900	1960	48
Montezuma (4,598) Macon (12,200)	*Citizen & Georgian*	2,500	Julian C. Cox	J. E. Medlin	John C. Cox	1879	1976	14
Monticello (2,374) Jasper (7,553)	*Monticello News*	1,950	Bill Hughes	Bill Hughes	Penn, Key Estate, J. Haney	1881	1974	10

City or Town County	Newspaper	Paid Circ.	*Owner	Publisher/ Chief Exec.	* *Previous Owners Since WWII	Year Est.	Off-Set	Avg. No. Pgs.
Mt. Vernon (1,713) Montgomery (6,500)	*Montgomery Monitor* (Discontinued in 1984)	1,392	M. Joiner, J. Joiner	M. Joiner, J. Joiner	Murphy McRae, Hugh Peterson	1886	1967	6
Nahunta (946) Brantley (8,500)	*Brantley Enterprise*	1,680	John Ellis	John Ellis	Geo. Stewart, Carl Broome	1920		
Nashville (4,718) Berrien (13,200)	*Berrien Press*	3,500	S. Hamilton	S. Hamilton	Jamie Connell	1959		16
Newnan (11,446) Coweta (38,700)	*Newnan Times-Herald*	11,000	W. Thomasson	W. Thomasson	J. Thomasson, E. Thomasson	1865	1964	60
Ocilla (3,385 Irwin (9,000)	*Ocilla Star*	2,190	W. Bradford	W. Bradford	B. Maxwell, A. Lewis	1903	1971	14
Peachtree City (6,411) Fayette (25,000)	*This Week*	3,350	R. Tribble	R. Tribble	J. Booth, M. Grimes	1974	1974	24
Pearson (1,777) Atkinson (5,900)	*Atkinson Co. Citizen &* *Pearson Tribune*	703	Carl Hulsey	C. Hulsey	Carl Broome	1914		6
Pelham (4,303) Mitchell (20,100)	*The Pelham Journal*	3,100	Neal Chism	Neal Chism	J. B. Chism Jr.	1902	1976	18
Perry (9,392) Houston (77,300)	*Houston Home Journal*	4,300	Roy Park	J. Kerce	Bobby Branch, C. Etheridge	1870	1970	24
Quitman (5,187) Brooks (15,255)	*Quitman Free Press*	3,200	M. & R. Mason	M. & R. Mason	G. Patten, R. Daniel	1876	1968	16
Reidsville (2,278) Tattnall (17,600)	*Tattnall Journal*	3,200	R. Rhoden	R. Rhoden	None	1879		18
Richland (1,790) Stewart (5,400)	*Stewart-Webster Journal*	1,475	R. Tribble	R. Tribble	J. Anglin, M. Grimes	1873	1970	10

City or Town County	Newspaper	Paid Circ.	*Owner	Publisher/ Chief Exec.	* *Previous Owners Since WWII	Year Est.	Off-Set	Avg. No. Pgs.
Ringgold (1,843) Catoosa (36,700)	*Catoosa Co. News*	3,813	J. Caldwell	J. Caldwell	J. Brewster	1949	1970	16
Roberta (855) Crawford (7,100)	*Georgia Post*	1,303	R. A. O'Neal	V. Dennis	J. C. Cox, Mrs. C. Moncrief	1921		8
Rockmart (3,646) Polk (31,100)	*Rockmart Journal*	2,800	B. H. Mooney	B. Mooney III	E. Sanders	1929	1967	20
Royston (2,633) Franklin (12,784)	*News-Leader*	2,000	W. S. Morris	L. Johnston	R. Williford, B. Bridges	1978	1978	16
St. Marys (3,565) Camden (12,600)	*Camden Co. Tribune*	3,200	Babb Estate	Liz Brown	K. Harrison	1950	1965	18
St. Simons Isl. (6,486) Glynn (50,900)	*The Islander*	2,400	E. Permar, G. Bradshaw	E. Permar, G. Bradshaw	None	1972	1972	16 (Tab)
Sandersville (6,148) Washington (16,600)	*Sandersville Progress*	4,600	D. Wickersham, R. Garrett	D. Wickersham, R. Garrett	J. Mize, C. McMichael	1887	1971	24
Savannah (133,672) Chatham (194,400)	*The Georgia Gazette* (Discontinued, March 1985)	3,500	A. Scardino	M. Scardino	None	1978	1978	16
Soperton (2,930) Treutlen (6,400)	*Soperton News*	2,450	J. Windsor	J. Windsor	M/M Lawton, R. Ledford	1914	1970	12
Sparta (1,718) Hancock (9,900)	*Sparta Ishmaelite*	1,511	A. Haywood	A. Haywood	Geo. Moore Sr.	1878	1978	8
Springfield (1,056) Effingham (18,800)	*Springfield Herald*	3,850	Julie Weddle	Julie Weddle	P. &. F. Sheaouse, M. Stephens	1908	1964	14

City or Town County	Newspaper	Paid Circ.	*Owner	Publisher/ Chief Exec.	**Previous Owners Since WWII	Year Est.	Off-Set	Avg. No. Pgs.
Statesboro (14,776) Bulloch (36,500)	*Southern Beacon*	2,365	Chas. Morris	J. McGlamery	B. Patray	1970	1970	22
Summerville (4,866) Chattooga (22,500)	*Summerville News*	6,442	W. E. Espy	W. E. Espy	D. T. Espy	1886		
Swainsboro (7,511) Emanuel (22,100)	*The Blade*	5,900	W. Rogers Sr.	W. Rogers Jr.	W. Gray Sr.	1859	1968	40
Sylvania (3,323) Screven (13,800)	*Sylvania Telephone*	3,750	C. Hollingsworth	C. Hollingsworth	N. Chalker	1879	1970	20
Sylvester (5,858) Worth (17,500)	*Sylvester Local News*	3,550	Marion Sumner	Marion Sumner	D. Hollingsworth, A. McGill	1884	1970	20
Talbotton (1,138) Talbot (6,600)	*Talbotton New Era*	915	R. Tribble	R. Tribble	Bill Watts, H. Taylor	1880	1966	18
Tallapoosa Haralson (18,000)	*Tallapoosa Journal Beacon*	2,700	Harte-Hanks	Frances Greene	F. Greene, H. Meeks	1880	1969	12
Thomaston (9,589) Upson (25,900)	*Thomaston Times* (Mon.-Wed.)	6,300	Ben Smith	Cy Wood	S. Carswell, Leon Smith	1869	1969	40
Thomson (6,971) McDuffie (20,000)	*McDuffie Progress*	4,000	Walls Media	J. Whittle	Claude McEver	1899		24
Toccoa (8,995) Stephens (23,300)	*Toccoa Record*	6,814	C. Hamilton	C. Hamilton	R. W. Graves	1891		40
Trenton (1,639) Dade (11,800)	*Dade Co. Sentinel*	2,489	Jim Boone	E. Gifford	Elbert Foster	1965		10

City or Town County	Newspaper	Paid Circ.	*Owner	Publisher/ Chief Exec.	* *Previous Owners Since WWII	Year Est.	Off-Set	Avg. No. Pgs.
Vidalia (10,317) Toombs (22,300)	*Vidalia Advance*	4,300	W. Ledford	W. Ledford	R. E. Ledford	1903	1969	36
Vienna (2,884) Dooly (10,800)	*Vienna News-Observer*	2,568	R. Tribble	R. Tribble	C. M. Methvin, Emily Woodward	1875	1967	14
Warrenton (2,138) Warren (6,200)	*Warrenton Clipper*	1,599	A. Haywood	A. Haywood	Ruby Felts	1843	1967	12
Washington (4,444) Wilkes (10,200)	*News-Reporter*	4,650	P. S. Newsome	P. S. Newsome	H. Zumbro, J. Stoddard	1921	1971	32
Watkinsville (1,194) Oconee (13,200)	*Oconee Enterprise*	2,400	C. Searcy, Don Nelson	V. Williams	Sanders Camp, M. Johnson	1884	1960	8
Waynesboro (5,760) Burke (19,349)	*The True Citizen*	4,495	R. Chalker Jr.	J. Bennett	R. Chalker Sr.	1882		
Winder (6,640) Barrow (21,000)	*Winder News*	6,300	Bob Fowler	Miles Godfrey	H. O. Smith	1893	1965	36
Wrens (2,427) Jefferson (17,600)	*Jefferson Reporter*	1,885	R. Chalker Jr.	R. Chalker Jr.	C. W. Stephens	1905		
Wrightsville (2,498) Johnson (7,700)	*Wrightsville Headlight*	1,645	D. Wickersham, R. Garrett	D. Wickersham, R. Garrett	G. Pryor, C. McMichael	1880		10
Zebulon (1,007) Pike (9,100)	*Pike Co. Journal-Reporter*	2,200	Q. Melton Jr.	Rachel McClelland	A. Quattlebaum, J. Preston	1889		

POPULATION OF GEORGIA COUNTIES

1920 - 1980

	1980	1970	1960	1950	1940	1930	1920
Appling	15,565	12,726	13,246	14,003	14,497	13,314	10,594
Atkinson	6,141	5,879	6,188	7,362	7,093	6,894	7,656
Bacon	9,379	8,233	8,359	8,940	8,095	7,055	6,460
Baker	3,808	3,875	4,543	5,952	7,344	7,818	8,298
Baldwin	34,686	34,240	34,064	29,706	24,190	22,878	19,791
Banks	8,702	6,833	6,497	6,935	8,733	9,703	11,814
Barrow	21,293	16,859	14,485	13,115	13,064	12,401	13,188
Bartow	40,760	32,911	28,267	27,370	25,283	25,364	24,527
Ben Hill	16,000	13,171	13,633	14,879	14,523	13,047	14,599
Berrien	13,525	11,556	12,038	13,966	15,370	14,646	15,573
Bibb	151,085	143,366	141,249	114,079	83,783	77,042	71,304
Bleckley	10,767	10,291	9,642	9,218	9,655	9,133	10,532
Brantley	8,701	5,940	5,891	6,387	6,871	6,895	....
Brooks	15,255	13,743	15,292	18,169	20,497	21,330	24,538
Bryan	10,175	6,539	6,225	5,965	6,288	5,952	6,343

	1980	1970	1960	1950	1940	1930	1920
Bulloch	35,785	31,585	24,263	24,740	26,010	26,509	26,133
Burke	19,349	18,255	20,596	23,458	26,520	29,224	30,836
Butts	13,665	10,560	8,976	9,079	9,182	9,345	12,327
Calhoun	5,717	6,606	7,341	8,578	10,438	10,576	10,225
Camden	13,371	11,334	9,975	7,322	5,910	6,338	6,969
Campbell	....	....	....	....	....	9,903	11,709
Candler	7,518	6412	6,672	8,063	9,103	8,991	9,228
Carroll	56,346	45,404	36,451	34,112	34,156	34,272	34,752
Catoosa	36,991	28,271	21,101	15,146	12,199	9,421	6,677
Charlton	7,343	5,680	5,313	4,821	5,256	4,381	4,536
Chatham	202,226	187,816	188,299	151,481	117,970	105,431	100,032
Chattahoochee	21,732	25,813	13,011	12,149	15,138	8,894	5,266
Chattooga	21,856	20,541	19,954	21,197	18,532	15,407	14,312
Cherokee	51,699	31,059	23,001	20,750	20,126	20,003	18,569
Clarke	74,498	65,177	45,363	36,550	28,398	25,613	26,111
Clay	3,553	3,636	4,551	5,844	7,064	6,943	5,557
Clayton	150,357	98,126	46,365	22,872	11,655	10,260	11,159
Clinch	6,660	6,405	6,545	6,007	6,437	7,015	7,984
Cobb	297,694	196,793	114,174	61,830	38,272	35,408	30,437
Coffee	26,894	22,828	21,953	23,961	21,541	19,739	18,653

Colquitt	35,376	32,298	34,048	33,999	33,012	30,622	29,332
Columbia	40,118	22,327	13,423	9,525	9,433	8,793	11,718
Cook	13,490	12,129	11,822	12,201	11,919	11,311	11,180
Coweta	39,268	32,310	28,893	27,786	26,972	25,127	29,047
Crawford	7,684	5,748	5,816	6,080	7,128	7,020	8,893
Crisp	19,489	18,087	17,768	17,663	17,540	17,343	18,914
Dade	12,318	9,910	8,666	7,364	5,894	4,146	3,918
Dawson	4,774	3,639	3,590	3,712	4,479	3,502	4,204
Decatur	25,495	22,310	25,203	23,620	22,234	23,622	31,785
DeKalb	483,024	415,387	256,782	136,395	86,942	70,278	44,051
Dodge	16,955	15,658	16,483	17,865	21,022	21,599	22,540
Dooly	10,826	10,404	11,474	14,159	16,886	18,025	20,522
Dougherty	100,978	89,639	75,680	43,617	28,565	22,306	20,063
Douglas	54,573	28,659	16,741	12,173	10,053	9,461	10,477
Early	13,158	12,682	13,151	17,413	18,679	18,273	18,983
Echols	2,297	1,924	1,876	2,494	2,964	2,744	3,313
Effingham	18,327	13,632	10,144	9,133	9,646	10,164	9,985
Elbert	18,758	17,262	17,835	18,585	19,618	18,485	23,905
Emanuel	20,795	18,357	17,815	19,789	23,517	24,101	25,862
Evans	8,428	7,290	6,952	6,653	7,401	7,102	6,594

	1980	1970	1960	1950	1940	1930	1920
Fannin	14,748	13,357	13,620	15,192	14,752	12,969	12,103
Fayette	29,043	11,364	8,199	7,978	8,170	8,665	11,396
Floyd	79,800	73,742	69,130	62,899	56,141	48,677	39,841
Forsyth	27,958	16,928	12,170	11,005	11,322	10,624	11,755
Franklin	15,185	12,784	13,274	14,446	15,612	15,902	19,957
Fulton	589,904	605,210	556,326	473,572	392,886	318,587	232,606
Gilmer	11,110	8,956	8,922	9,963	9,001	7,344	8,406
Glascock	2,382	2,280	2,672	3,579	4,547	4,388	4,192
Glynn	54,981	50,528	41,954	29,046	21,920	19,400	19,370
Gordon	30,070	23,570	19,228	18,922	18,445	16,846	17,736
Grady	19,845	17,826	18,015	18,928	19,654	19,200	20,306
Greene	11,391	10,212	11,193	12,843	13,709	12,616	18,972
Gwinnett	166,903	72,349	43,541	32,320	29,087	27,853	30,327
Habersham	25,020	20,691	18,116	16,553	14,771	12,748	10,730
Hall	75,649	59,405	49,739	40,113	34,822	30,313	26,822
Hancock	9,466	9,019	9,979	11,052	12,764	13,070	18,357
Haralson	18,422	15,927	14,543	14,663	14,377	13,263	14,440
Harris	15,464	11,520	11,167	11,265	11,428	11,140	15,775
Hart	18,585	15,814	15,229	14,495	15,512	15,174	17,944
Heard	6,520	5,354	5,333	6,975	8,610	9,102	11,126

Henry	36,309	23,724	17,619	15,857	15,119	15,924	20,420
Houston	77,605	62,924	39,154	20,964	11,303	11,280	21,964
Irwin	8,988	8,036	9,211	11,973	12,936	12,199	12,670
Jackson	25,343	21,093	18,499	18,997	20,089	21,609	24,654
Jasper	7,553	5,760	6,135	7,473	8,772	8,594	16,362
Jeff Davis	11,473	9,425	8,914	9,299	8,841	8,118	7,322
Jefferson	18,403	17,174	17,468	18,855	20,040	20,272	22,602
Jenkins	8,841	8,332	9,148	10,246	11,843	12,908	14,328
Johnson	8,660	7,727	8,048	9,893	12,953	12,681	13,546
Jones	16,579	12,270	8,468	7,538	8,331	8,992	13,269
Lamar	12,215	10,688	10,240	10,242	10,091	9,745	....
Lanier	5,654	5,031	5,097	5,151	5,632	5,190	....
Laurens	36,990	32,738	32,313	33,123	33,606	32,693	39,605
Lee	11,684	7,044	6,204	6,674	7,837	8,328	10,904
Liberty	37,583	17,569	14,487	8,444	8,595	8,153	12,707
Lincoln	6,949	5,895	5,906	6,462	7,042	7,847	9,739
Long	4,524	3,746	3,874	3,598	4,086	4,180	....
Lowndes	67,972	55,112	49,270	35,211	31,860	29,994	....
Lumpkin	10,762	8,728	7,241	6,574	6,223	4,927	5,240
McDuffie	18,546	15,276	16,627	11,443	10,878	9,014	11,509

	1980	1970	1960	1950	1940	1930	1920
McIntosh	8,046	7,371	6,364	6,008	5,292	5,763	5,119
Macon	14,003	12,933	13,170	14,213	15,947	16,643	17,667
Madison	17,747	13,517	11,246	12,238	13,431	14,921	18,803
Marion	5,297	5,099	5,477	6,521	6,954	6,968	7,604
Meriwether	21,229	19,461	19,756	21,055	22,055	22,437	26,168
Miller	7,038	6,424	6,908	9,023	9,998	9,076	9,565
Milton	....	....	....	....	....	6,730	6,885
Mitchell	21,114	18,956	19,652	22,528	23,261	23,620	25,588
Monroe	14,610	10,991	10,495	10,523	10,749	11,606	20,138
Montgomery	7,011	6,099	6,284	7,901	9,668	10,020	9,167
Morgan	11,572	9,904	10,280	11,899	12,713	12,488	20,143
Murray	19,685	12,986	10,477	10,676	11,137	9,215	9,490
Muscogee	170,108	167,377	158,623	118,028	75,494	57,558	44,195
Newton	34,489	26,282	20,999	20,185	18,576	17,290	21,680
Oconee	12,427	7,915	6,304	7,009	7,576	8,082	11,067
Oglethorpe	8,929	7,598	7,926	9,958	12,430	12,927	20,287
Paulding	26,042	17,520	13,101	11,752	12,832	12,327	14,025
Peach	19,151	15,990	13,846	11,705	10,378	10,268	....
Pickens	11,652	9,620	8,903	8,855	9,136	9,687	8,222
Pierce	11,897	9,281	9,678	11,112	11,800	12,522	11,934

Pike	8,937	7,316	7,138	8,459	10,375	10,853	21,212
Polk	32,386	29,656	28,015	30,976	28,467	25,141	20,357
Pulaski	8,950	8,066	8,204	8,808	9,829	9,005	11,587
Putnam	10,295	8,394	7,798	7,731	8,514	8,367	15,151
Quitman	2,357	2,180	2,432	3,015	3,435	3,820	3,417
Rabun	10,466	8,327	7,456	7,424	7,821	6,331	5,746
Randolph	9,599	8,734	11,078	13,804	16,609	17,174	16,721
Richmond	181,629	162,437	135,601	108,876	81,863	72,990	63,692
Rockdale	36,747	18,152	10,572	8,464	7,724	7,247	9,528
Schley	3,433	3,097	3,256	4,036	5,033	5,347	5,243
Screven	14,043	12,591	14,919	18,000	20,353	20,503	23,552
Seminole	9,057	7,059	6,802	7,904	8,492	7,389	....
Spalding	47,899	39,514	25,404	31,045	28,427	23,495	21,908
Stephens	21,763	20,331	18,391	16,647	12,972	11,740	11,215
Stewart	5,896	6,511	7,371	9,194	10,603	11,114	12,089
Sumter	29,360	26,931	24,652	24,208	24,502	26,800	29,640
Talbot	6,536	6,625	9,127	7,687	8,141	8,458	11,158
Taliaferro	2,032	2,423	3,370	4,515	6,278	6,172	8,841
Tattnall	18,134	16,557	15,839	15,939	16,243	15,411	14,502
Taylor	7,902	7,865	8,311	9,113	10,768	10,617	11,473

	1980	1970	1960	1950	1940	1930	1920
Telfair	11,445	11,394	11,715	13,221	15,145	14,997	15,291
Terrell	12,017	11,416	12,742	14,314	16,675	18,290	19,601
Thomas	38,098	34,562	34,319	33,923	31,289	32,612	33,044
Tift	32,862	27,288	23,587	22,645	18,599	16,068	14,493
Toombs	22,592	19,151	16,837	17,382	16,952	17,165	13,897
Towns	5,638	4,565	4,538	4,803	4,925	4,346	3,937
Treutlen	6,087	5,647	5,874	6,522	7,632	7,488	7,664
Troup	50,,003	44,466	47,189	49,841	43,879	36,752	36,097
Turner	9,510	8,790	8,439	10,479	10,846	11,196	12,466
Twiggs	9,354	8,222	7,935	8,308	9,117	8,372	10,407
Union	9,390	6,811	6,510	7,318	7,680	6,340	6,455
Upson	25,998	23,505	23,800	25,078	25,064	19,509	14,786
Walker	56,470	50,691	45,264	38,198	31,024	26,206	23,370
Walton	31,211	23,404	20,481	20,230	20,777	21,118	24,216
Ware	37,180	33,525	34,219	30,289	27,929	26,558	28,361
Warren	6,583	6,669	7,360	8,779	10,236	11,181	11,828
Washington	18,842	17,480	18,903	21,012	24,230	25,030	28,147
Wayne	20,750	17,858	17,921	14,248	13,122	12,647	14,381
Webster	2,341	2,362	3,247	4,081	4,726	5,032	5,342
Wheeler	5,155	4,596	5,342	6,712	8,535	9,149	9,817

White	10,120	7,742	6,935	5,951	6,417	6,056	6,105
Whitfield	65,780	55,108	42,109	34,432	26,105	20,808	16,897
Wilcox	7,682	6,998	7,905	10,167	12,755	13,439	15,511
Wilkes	10,951	10,184	10,961	12,388	15,084	15,944	24,210
Wilkinson	10,368	9,393	9,250	9,781	11,025	10,844	11,376
Worth	18,064	14,770	16,682	19,357	21,374	21,094	23,863
Georgia	5,464,265	4,587,930	3,943,116	3,444,578	3,123,723	2,908,506	2,895,832

COUNTIES OF GEORGIA
with 1980 Census Population

Bibliography and Sources

An indication of how much an updated history of Georgia newspapers was needed can be found in the scarcity of books which pertain to Georgia's newspapers and the people who work for them or own them.

Research for this book had to rely mainly on interviews with the people involved or written recollections submitted by them especially for this project. Also helpful were copies of the newspapers themselves; articles in magazines and trade publications; press association news releases; and memoranda and information which the chief editor had saved during the period.

One book was invaluable in preparing this volume, however, and that was the earlier history of Georgia newspapers, *Georgia Journalism*, compiled and written by Louis Griffith and John Talmadge. Published in 1951 by the University of Georgia Press, it covered the period from 1763 to 1950. Copies are difficult to find in 1985, as it has been out of print for many years. At this writing there is discussion about reissuing *Georgia Journalism* as a companion book to this one during the Georgia Press Association's centennial year, 1986-87.

Although the present volume mainly covers the years since 1950, *Georgia Journalism* provided essential information on the earlier background of the state's newspapers and was especially relied on for the chapter on the Georgia Press Association, in which the entire 100-year history of the GPA is covered. Readers of this volume will find *Georgia Journalism* a rewarding reading experience if they can find a copy. The most likely places are public libraries in the state's larger cities, at the University of Georgia library, and in the personal libraries of older Georgia newspapermen or their descendants.

Louis Griffith, the co-author, still lives in Athens where he retired in 1984 after nearly four decades with the University, serving for many years as assistant to the president and in the Alumni office. He is now associated with *Georgia Journal*, a statewide magazine published in Athens. The book which he co-authored was not only a frequent source of information but also the inspiration for this current volume.

Only two Georgia newspapers had true books published about them during the period from 1950-1984. One of these was *The Augusta Chronicle*, the oldest continuing newspaper in the state, having been established in 1785. A volume written by Kenneth Crabbe and Earl Bell, entitled *The Augusta Chronicle, Indomitable Voice of Dixie*, came out in 1960, commemorating *The Chronicle's* 175th birthday. An updated volume is scheduled for 1985 to commemorate the 200th birthday.

Portions of the earlier book are reprinted in the section about the Augusta newspapers (Chapter IV). Crabbe and Bell, both staff members of the *Chronicle-Herald* at the time, produced a book that was both informative and entertaining, with the kind of details usually missing in authorized or commissioned biographies.

Oddly, the only other Georgia newspaper to be the subject of a book was one which existed for only 14 months — the ill-fated *Atlanta Times*, circa June, 1964-August, 1965. In fact two books were published about *The Times*, both by former employees. Frank Veale, who was associate editor, told the story of his tribulations on *The Times* in a book of limited distribution, which was read by the editor of this volume in the 1960s. It may be best-remembered for the rather succinct review which appeared in *The Journal-Constitution* book section, reading in full: "A newspaper such as *The Atlanta Times* deserves a biography such as this."

Veale's book, in fact, deserved a fairer evaluation, but it was overshadowed soon by the second book on *The Times*, written by Robert Carney, who served as its advertising manager. Carney's book, *"What Happened at The Atlanta Times"*, was published in 1969, and it provided a classic story of money, ambition and management gone astray, on a venture in which thousands of individual Georgians invested their money to bring a "conservative newspaper" to the capital city.

Carney's book is quoted several times in Chapter III, and was the source for several of the anecdotes and much of the financial information about *The Times*. It was published by the Economics Press, Decatur, Ga. Carney was later the southeastern representative of *Family Weekly* magazine for many years.

On the other newspapers of the state, including Atlanta's *Journal* and *Constitution*, there have been only booklets, special sections, promotional pamphlets and magazine articles published since World War II. Many of these were utilized in obtaining information for this volume. A special mention must be made of the magazines and the articles on newspapers which they produced, most of them in the years since 1975.

Often the articles seemed intent on presenting a less-than-flattering picture of their subjects. Some of the articles could only be described as "hatchet-jobs", especially one in *Brown's Guide*, Mar-April 1977, concerning the Atlanta dailies. The author, Farnum Gray, had been fired by *The Constitution*, which partially explains his antipathy. The article, *"Battle at the Atlanta Constitution*", was compellingly written, however, and provided some insight into events on the Atlanta papers during the 1960s when many of journalism's prominent names worked there. The article is quoted in Chapter III.

Brown's Guide, during its decade on the Georgia scene, carried a number of articles on newspapers and newspaper people, and the two others quoted for this volume are "James Gray, Albany's Mr. Power", by Sharon Thomason, Mar-April, 1978, and a short piece on *The Athens Observer*, Jan-Feb., 1977.

Other journalists profiled extensively in *Brown's* articles about their home counties were Julie Graham Weddle of Springfield and Robert Williams of Blackshear. Both articles were written by Bill Cutler.

Especially in the middle and late 1970s *Brown's Guide to Georgia* was a vibrant and valuable addition to the state's literary scene. During that period it possessed a distinct style, somewhere between amateurism and professionalism, which imbued each issue with a peculiar charm. Perhaps no other publication was so instrumental in making Georgians aware of the tourist possibilities in their own state; of the historic homes, the unusual restaurants, the mountain trails, the wandering streams, as *Brown's Guide*, and its brilliant editor and founder, Fred Brown.

It awakened many Georgians to the state's geographical variety and also to an extent to the great Atlanta metropolis which was rising to new heights in the 1970s.

Certainly *Brown's* restaurant rating section was a journalistic phenomenon, and raised Georgians' awareness about "eating out" and finding different places and dishes.

The *Guide's* demise in 1982 was regrettable, although it already had lost some of the raw appeal of its earlier years, and had become a bit too slick and predictable.

Despite the advent of many other magazines in Georgia, nothing has really replaced *Brown's Guide*, nor did anything approximate it during its existence.

Atlanta Magazine, *Atlanta Business Chronicle* and *Georgia Monthly* are other magazines which publish occasional articles on Georgia newspapers, and which are quoted in several chapters. *Georgia Monthly* editor Charles Postell also provided the intriguing photograph of Homer Garrett in Chapter IX, which shows Garrett in his old printing office, still handsetting his newspaper in the 1970s.

A Master's Thesis by Dan Kitchens of the University of Georgia journalism school faculty also provided essential data in tracing the shift from hot to cold type among Georgia's weekly newspapers. Kitchens' thesis, *"A Profile of Georgia Weekly Newspapers, 1957-1977"*, was based on his study of Georgia Press Association annual directories for those years, and many of his findings were relied on in the chapters on weekly and suburban newspapers.

Other directories on which information in this volume is based included *Editor and Publisher Yearbooks* from 1957 through 1985, and the annual *Circulation Yearbooks* by American Newspaper Markets Inc.

Chapter by Chapter Sources and Bibliography

Chapter I, The Great Newspaper Era — *Georgia Journalism* (see above); *Lost Legacy of Georgia's Golden Isles; Once Upon an Island*, Tallu Fish, 1959; *Cason Callaway of Blue Springs*, Paul Schubert, 1964; *The Story of Helen*; *Why Not the Best?* Jimmy Carter, 1975; *Georgia Historical Markers*, Bay Tree Grove Publishers, 1976.

Chapter II, The Last Linotype — *The Newspaper Industry in the 1980s*, B.M. Companie, 1980; *Ottmar Mergenthaler*, a pamphlet issued on the occasion of the presentation of a bust of Mergenthaler to the American Newspaper Publishers Association in June, 1973; *Profile of Georgia Weekly Newspapers* (see above); interviews with Charles Hardy Sr., Robert Yates, Bill Wadkins, Shelton Prince, Joe Rivais, Ted Oglesby.

Chapter III, The Heavyweights — Calvin Cox, a 30-year employee of the *Atlanta Journal-Constitution*, submitted the information on those newspapers; Richard Hyatt, a member of *The Atlanta Times*' staff in 1964-65, submitted information on *The Times*; *What Happened at The Atlanta Times* (see above); *Brown's Guide* (see above).

Chapter IV, The Lightheavyweights — *The Augusta Chronicle*, Crabbe and Bell, 1960; *Forbes Magazine*, February, 1983; *Editor and Publisher*, 1969, 1970; *Sojourn in Savannah*, Rauters and Taub, 1968; information on Augusta supplied by David Playford; information on Savannah supplied by Tom Coffey; information on Macon supplied by Ed Corson.

Chapter V, A City and Its Newspapers — *Governors of Georgia*, James F. Cook, Strode Publishers, 1979; *The Wynnton Stocking Strangler*, T. W. Moody Jr., 1980 (undistributed); *Soldier of Fortune* Magazine, April 1983, written information submitted by Tom Sellers, Carroll Dadisman, Millard Grimes; interviews with Maynard R. Ashworth, Glenn Vaughn, William Brown and Ray Jenkins.

Chapter VI, Rise of the Suburban Press — Written information submitted by Robert Fowler, Bobby Nesbitt, Foy Evans, Linton Broome, Jim Wood, Jimmy Booth, Tom Hay, Libby Staples, Millard Grimes; statistics and data from U.S. censuses, 1920-1980, Atlanta Regional Council projections and publications.

Chapter VII, Golden Era, Changing Guard — Written information submitted by Ted Oglesby, Lou Fockele, Mark Pace, Gary Boley. Interviews with Glenn Long, Jack Matthews, Robert Morrell, W. H. Champion, C. Howard Leavy, Stanley Parkman, Neely Young, B. H. Mooney III, Joe McGlamery, C. L. Blanton; information on E. L. Turner from pamphlet marking his 100th birthday; *Brown's Guide*, Jan.-Feb. 1977 (article on James Gray).

Chapter VIII, Newspaper Laboratory — Written information submitted by Elliott Brack, Glenn Vaughn, Pete McCommons, Millard Grimes; interviews with Bob Chambers, Claude Williams, Charles McClure, Charles Russell; tribute to John Drewry by Dan Kitchens.

Chapter IX, Life Beyond the Print Shop — Written material submitted by Waldo (Bo) McLeod, W. H. (Dink) NeSmith, Milton Beckerman, Robert Tribble, Austin Saxon; article by Charles Postell, *Georgia Monthly Magazine; Georgia's County Unit System*, book by Louis Rigdon, 1961. A large number of interviews were conducted for this chapter due to the many newspapers covered.

Chapter X, The Georgia Press Association — Written material submitted by W. H. Champion for profiles of presidents since World War II; James R. Blair (concerning purchase of building); Julia Dyar (recollections), Editor's Forum publications provided many details on GPA activities, also minutes of annual meetings. *Georgia Journalism* by Griffith and Talmadge was source for most of information on GPA's first 63 years. Lists of presidents, institute chairmen, meeting sites and Better Newspaper contest winners from GPA office files.

The Chief Editor and Writer

Millard B. Grimes, chief editor and writer of *The Last Linotype,* was born in Newnan, Georgia, on March 8, 1930, and grew up in LaGrange and Columbus. He began working for *The Columbus Ledger-Enquirer* newspapers as a copy boy, proofreader, and sports correspondent while still in high school.

Following graduation from the University of Georgia he worked for the Columbus newspapers in various news and editorial positions for nearly 20 years. During this period he twice left those papers, once to found and edit a weekly newspaper in nearby Phenix City, Alabama, and another time to be editor of *The Valley Times-News* in West Point, Georgia.

He was named editor of *The Columbus Enquirer* in 1963 and served in that post for more than six years.

In 1968 Grimes organized a group of investors to buy *The Opelika Daily News* in Opelika, Alabama, and became its editor and publisher. He soon changed the name to *The Opelika-Auburn News,* added a Sunday edition, and saw its paid circulation increase from 7,000 to 20,000 in the next nine years.

Following the sale of *The Opelika-Auburn News* in 1977, Grimes formed a new company which owns and operates several daily and weekly newspapers in Georgia, including *The Rockdale Citizen* of Conyers, and *The Clayton News/Daily* of Jonesboro.

Grimes was named chairman of the Georgia Press Association's history committee in 1978, which launched him on the project that resulted in *The Last Linotype*. He was elected treasurer of the Georgia Press Association in 1983, vice-president in 1984, and president for the 1985-1986 year.

He and his wife, Charlotte, live in Opelika, Alabama. They have three children, James, Kathy, and Laura.

Index of Names

Index of Newspapers